Second Edition

THE COMMUNIST REVOLUTION IN ASIA

TACTICS, GOALS, AND ACHIEVEMENTS

Edited by

ROBERT A. SCALAPINO

University of California, Berkeley

PRENTICE-HALL, INC.

Englewood Cliffs, New Jersey

13-153049-6
Library of Congress Catalog Card Number 77-76307
Printed in the United States of America
Current printing (last digit):
10 9 8 7 6 5 4 3 2 1

PRENTICE-HALL INTERNATIONAL, INC., London
PRENTICE-HALL OF AUSTRALIA, PTY. LTD., Sydney
PRENTICE-HALL OF CANADA, LTD., Toronto
PRENTICE-HALL OF INDIA PRIVATE LIMITED, New Delhi
PRENTICE-HALL OF JAPAN, INC., Tokyo

CONTENTS

CONTRIBUTORS

Robert A. Scalapino is professor of political science at the University of California, Berkeley. He is also editor of *Asian Survey*. He has written a number of books and articles on Asian politics and American far eastern policy, among them *Democracy and the Party Movement in Pre-War Japan* (1953), "Neutralism in Asia," *The American Political Science Review* (1954), "The United States and Japan," in *The United States and the Far East* (1962), Section 4 of the *United States Foreign Policy—Asia*, a study for the Senate Foreign Relations Committee (1959), *Parties and Politics in Contemporary Japan* (with Junnosuke Masumi; 1962), and *The Japanese Communist Movement: 1920–1966* (1967). He has undertaken a number of field studies in Asia and has served as guest lecturer at Asian universities. He has served as consultant to the Ford Foundation and to the Rockefeller Foundation. He has been the recipient of grants from the Carnegie Foundation, the Social Science Research Council, the Rockefeller Foundation, and the Guggenheim Foundation.

John H. Badgley is associate professor in the School of Advanced International Studies of The Johns Hopkins University. The holder of a joint appointment at the Washington Center for Foreign Policy Research, an SAIS affiliate, he is the author of *Burma's Revolutionary Process* and of many articles in *Asian Survey, Pacific Affairs,* and *Problems of Communism.*

Hans H. Baerwald is associate professor of political science at the University of California, Los Angeles. He is the author of *The Purge of Japanese Leaders Under the Occupation, Chinese Communism: Selected Documents* (with Dan Jacobs), and *The American Republic: Its Government and Politics* (with Peter H. Odegard), and of articles on Japanese politics in *Asian Survey.*

John C. Donnell is professor of political science at Temple University. He has taught at Dartmouth and served the State Department and the U.S. Information Agency in several Asian countries, including North and South Vietnam. His publications include articles on Vietnamese politics in *Asian Survey, Journal of Asian Studies, Journal of the Asia Society, Pacific Affairs,* and *Problems of Communism.* He is the author of a forthcoming book, *The Ngos' Vietnam: The Politics of Manipulation.*

The late **Bernard B. Fall** was professor of government at Howard University and author of *Street Without Joy: Indochina at War, The Two Viet-Nams, Hell in a Very Small Place: The Siege of Dien Bien Phu,* and *Last Reflections on a War,* and of many articles dealing with Southeast Asia and revolutionary warfare operations. His death in 1967 removed one of our most perceptive observers in Southeast Asia.

Melvin Gurtov is a staff member in the social science department of The RAND Corporation and specializes in Communist China and Southeast Asia. He is the author of *The First Vietnam Crisis: Chinese Communist Strategy and American Involvement, 1953–1954,* and a contributor to several books and journals.

M. T. Haggard is head of the Asia-Africa section of the Foreign Affairs Division, Legislative Reference Service (Library of Congress), the research analysis arm of the U.S. Congress. He is the author of several articles on political developments in Asia.

Chalmers Johnson is professor of political science and chairman of the Center for Chinese Studies at the University of California, Berkeley.

He is the author of *Peasant Nationalism and Communist Power: The Emergence of Revolutionary China, 1937–45* (1962), *An Instance of Treason: Ozaki Hotsumi and the Sorge Spy Ring* (1964), and *Revolutionary Change* (1966).

Robert N. Kearney is associate professor political science at Syracuse University. He has taught at Duke University and conducted research in Ceylon. He is the author of *Communalism and Language in the Politics of Ceylon* (1967) and of many articles on the politics of Ceylon.

Chong-Sik Lee is associate professor of political science at the University of Pennsylvania and the author of *The Politics of Korean Nationalism*. He has contributed many articles to scholarly journals on Korean Communism and various aspects of Korean politics.

Guy J. Pauker is senior staff member in the social science department of The RAND Corporation. He has taught at Harvard and the University of California, Berkeley, where he was chairman of the Center for Southeast Asia Studies. His research has taken him to Southeast Asia annually over the last fifteen years. He is the author of many articles and studies on Southeast Asian affairs.

Ralph H. Retzlaff is associate professor of political science at the University of California, Berkeley. He is the author of *Village Government in India: A Case Study* and various other articles on Indian politics.

Leo E. Rose is a member of the research staff of the Institute of International Studies at the University of California, Berkeley, and is director of the Himalayan Border Countries Project and associate editor of *Asian Survey*. He is the author of *Democratic Innovations in Nepal: A Case Study of Political Acculturation* (with Bhuwan Lal Joshi), and several other studies of political developments in the Himalayan area.

Frances L. Starner is associate professor of political science at the University of North Carolina, Charlotte. As a free-lance journalist and as a scholar he has spent much time in Southeast Asia and contributed extensively to scholarly books and journals on Southeast Asia. He is the author of *Magsaysay and the Philippine Peasantry: The Agrarian Impact on Philippine Politics*.

COMMUNISM IN ASIA

TOWARD
A COMPARATIVE ANALYSIS

ROBERT A. SCALAPINO

Communism in Asia is not a new phenomenon. Its earliest beginnings extend back into the late nineteenth century, when a handful of young Asian intellectuals first came into contact with Marxism. The initial Communist Parties were established much later, but even this development took place nearly a half century ago. Many of the veteran Asian Communists still alive are now in their mid-seventies and, as we shall note, are presently giving way to a new generation of leaders. Despite this rather extensive history, however, the great Communist gains in Asia are products of the last two decades, and centrally connected with the events surrounding World War II. Undoubtedly this is one reason why most Asian Communists, of whatever generation, tend to be of a different type than the contemporary Russian leaders, and espouse different policies.

MARXISM AND THE ASIAN INTELLECTUAL

Asian Communism began as an intellectual movement and, while it has become vastly more complex, the intellectual element is still an important one. As we shall presently observe, ideologues continue to play a significant leadership role in most Asian Communist Parties. Moreover, the good Communist, of whatever station, is expected to study and learn. He is supposed to master the Marxist classics, search his mind in order to root out error, supplant it with truth, and then apply this truth "creatively" to the circumstances of his own society.

It might not be amiss, therefore, to commence this analysis with some attempt to understand the appeal of Marxism-Leninism to the Asian intellectual. At the outset, however, it should be emphasized that at no point has Communism represented the dominant political trend among the modern Asian intelligentsia, except when Marxian doctrines have been imposed by state fiat. Even then, the degree and nature of intellectual adherence to Communism is debatable. One must appreciate both sides of the coin: The great majority of Asian intellectuals have never espoused Communism; and a small but significant minority have either supported Communism or been strongly influenced by Marxist-Leninist doctrines. This latter group, moreover, has included some individuals who have occupied commanding heights in the intellectual firmament of their societies.

The Marxist-Leninist appeal has been intimately connected with the massive problems of confrontation with and independence from the "advanced" West. It has also been a part of the quest for political, economic, and social modernization. Thus the Asian Marxist, in certain critical respects, has not seen or interpreted his creed in the manner of Marx. Revisionism, of course, is implicit in the journey of any doctrine from theory to practice, but few doctrines in human history have undergone more extensive revisions than Marxism in Asia. Let us then explore the wellsprings of Marxist appeal to the Asian intellectual, noting both the themes that Marx would have appreciated and those he would have regarded as strange or unacceptable.

Marxism as a Progressive, Avant-Garde Theory

The modern Asian intellectual has accepted drastic change as essential for his society, and he has tended to accept also the Western model of change. Indeed, his goals have been governed to a major extent by the teleological insights derived from Western experience. The Asian intellectual has seen—or thinks he has seen—the future of his own society mirrored in the advanced Western world. (In this, he may well be partly mistaken, but that is beside the point.)

To understand the burdens imposed by being thus able "to see the future" is to appreciate the enormous intellectual and psychological gap separating the intelligentsia of those societies which pioneered in modernization from the intelligentsia of Asia and Africa. The Asians and Africans were placed in a position of being perpetual followers, a position tending to frustrate creativity and abet resentments against Westernism even as it bound at least two generations to the Western model. The great nationalist upsurge in the Afro-Asian intellectual world today, including the attack by Asian Marxists upon Western Marxists, is in some measure connected with this problem.

In an earlier period, however, intellectual independence was even more difficult for the modern Asian to attain than national freedom. For him, to be progressive was imperative, and to be progressive was, in essence, to be "Western." Hence, the goal became to grasp the latest developments, the furthermost reaches of Western thought. At the end of the nineteenth century, the latest developments were reflected in liberalism and the parliamentary system; by the early twentieth century, to be *avant-garde*, one had to espouse socialism. The most radical Asian intellectuals had discovered anarcho-syndicalism, an extreme expression of Western dissidence currently in vogue. It was natural that, as anarchism declined and Marxism-Leninism rose in Western radical circles, the Asian intellectual vanguard would be swept toward a new "wave of the future." The successful Bolshevik Revolution redefined for the Asian radical the essence of futurism.

Marxism-Leninism as the "New Democracy"

The West implanted in the modern Asian intellectual a profound commitment to the concept of democracy—the ideas of freedom, equality, representation, and above all, the central importance of "the people." Most Asian intellectuals have retained those commitments, but their philosophic and practical expression of the concepts has taken drastically different forms. At first the dominant, almost sole, model was that of Western parliamentarism. In one Asian society after another, however, disillusionment with parliamentary democracy arose. It was already strong in Japanese and Chinese intellectual circles shortly after World War I. To many, parliamentarism had become synonymous with corruption, special privilege, factionalism, and continuous political crisis.

Wherever and whenever such disillusionment occurs, the "new democracy" of Marxism-Leninism is likely to have a certain appeal. It enables the Asian intellectual to retain his commitment to the broad, theoretical values of democracy—to invoke the sacred words—while freeing him from the traditional democratic forms and practices. The "new democracy" is based upon a tutelage of the masses by a highly organized elite drawn partly from the intellectual class itself. Theoretically, the people continue to be the objects of worship, the source of supreme authority. the fountainhead of truth. In practice, however, they become the subjects of intensive indoctrination, mass mobilization, and total commitment to the purposes of state as defined by their "vanguard."

Two powerful and exceedingly important myths underwrite principle and practice in these respects, "the mass line" and "democratic centralism." The mass line, in its essence, is the doctrine that all power and all ideas must derive from the people, with the Party's task that of discerning and then carrying out those ideas, thereby wielding power in the people's name. On the other hand, democratic centralism connotes the fact that while policies and leaders are to be created through democratic means, once created, both must be universally and uniformly obeyed. Legitimacy flows from the bottom up; authority flows from the top down—and in Communist theory, both take on an absolute quality.

Thus, the "new democracy" is not hobbled by attempts to practice freedom, equality, or popular sovereignty. Without abandoning claim to these principles, the Communists build an elitist-controlled, fully mobilized state geared to execute rapid and drastic changes. The central paraphernalia of democracy are retained: supreme people's congresses, parties, and elections. Indeed, the people are caused to participate in politics on a more intensive scale than at any time in the past. But this is organized participation, under the supervision of the vanguard Party. Hence, representation is scientific; participation is positive; elections are ceremonies of support. The confusion, uncertainty, and chaos surrounding the "old democracy" are avoided.

With this organizational structure goes a program of revolutionary socioeconomic changes intended to make democracy total and complete. Can man be politically free if he is permanently bound by caste or class lines, or if he is the victim of continuous economic exploitation? Utilizing these powerful themes, the Marxist-Leninists promise to unite social, economic, and political democracy, producing true equality and total liberation.

This is the blueprint of the "new democracy." It is not surprising that it has attracted a number of Asian intellectuals, particularly during the period when it is still a blueprint, not yet a reality.

Marxism-Leninism as a Technique of Nation Building

Despite the fact that it is probably the most important single political force in Asia, nationalism remains today an essentially elitist phenomena throughout most of the area. Its import to the intellectual, however, is substantial. Nationalism is the property of no single political leader or movement. Almost every segment of the Asian political elite can be described as nationalist. There can be no doubt, however, that Asian Communists have made a special effort to harness Marxism-Leninism to the climactic stages of the Asian nationalist revolution, seeking to make of it an instrument for the swift, thorough, and purposeful creation of a nation-state where none previously existed.

Highly developed organizational techniques are combined with in-

tensive ideological training, both having the purpose of creating a powerful, unified society. Disparate peoples, divided by ethnic, class, and regional ties, are given a common Party, a common set of political values,
common hatreds, and common tasks in an effort to remove past sources
of separateness and identity. The old loyalties to family, tribe, and
region are put under sustained and heavy assault. Every attempt is made
to forge new loyalties to the Party and to the fatherland. There is no
hesitation in playing upon xenophobia, chauvinism, and other classical
forms of ultra-nationalism when this appears to suit Communist purposes.

The results are not unimpressive. China, North Korea, and North
Vietnam have rapidly acquired a high level of state power, military
and political. In considerable measure, this power derives from the
state's capacity to commit its people to whatever tasks it chooses. And,
as has been shown both in the Korean and Vietnamese Wars, that capacity is substantial. Penalties for noncompliance, rewards for outstanding performance, and individual conviction resulting from the new edu-
cational-indoctrination program each form a part of the Communist
system conducive to nationalist ends. The three Communist states in
East Asia, moreover, are each viewed by their leaders as merely a
part of a divided state. (Some day, this may also be true of Mongolia.)
Communist determination to carry out unification under their sole control thus shapes the strongly military character of the nationalist movements in these states at present.

At this point, however, it is still unclear what shape the ultimate political and economic structure of the largest of these societies, China,
will take. Recent developments make it clear that we have overestimated
the degree to which centralization prevailed and the extent to which
nation building had been accomplished. Unquestionably, massive changes,
political and economic, have taken place under the People's Republic
of China, including the emergence of a new generation potentially more
nationalist and more unified than its predecessors. The problems remain
vast, however, and a China weak and divided in certain respects is not
beyond the range of possibility. Indeed, it is permissible today to wonder
whether societies as populous and complex as China and India can easily
or quickly be modernized by any of the techniques currently known
to man, irrespective of their ideological content.

Marxism-Leninism as the Science of Rapid Modernization

For the Asian Marxist, Communism represents not the culmination of
the modernization process but its potential means. Now it is Hegel who
has been righted, and Marx turned on his head. The latter-day Asian
Communist has as his goal a one-generation industrial revolution, a

concentrated thrust toward modernity. He sees in Communism a method of mobilizing manpower, allocating resources, providing the power and organization for this purpose. Many intellectuals at least inwardly acknowledge that great sacrifices will be involved in such a rapid pace, but they have rationalized these sacrifices as temporarily necessary to provide prosperity and equality with the advanced world.

Once again, it is permissible to question whether Communism has proven itself more effective as an instrument of economic development in Asia than mixed economic-political systems involving both state and private sectors. The Western observer seeking to make an objective judgment on this question faces serious problems: the paucity of reliable statistical data, the problems of comparative measurement, and the differences likely to be present in developmental sequence as between Communist and non-Communist societies.

At this point, however, the available evidence suggests doubts that Communism—at least in the forms thus far advanced in Asia—has proven itself the clearly superior instrument of economic development. Its forte has lain in the industrial sector, and particularly in the field of heavy industry, as was the case with the Soviet Union. Similarly, agricultural productivity has been the major problem. Nor have productive increases generally been translated into proportionate rises in living standards. The gap between Gross National Product and living standards, indeed, has increased, alleviated to some extent perhaps by the enforcement of shared poverty. Once again, it must be remembered that the Communist societies of Asia were historically among the poorest of Asia, insofar as the masses were concerned. But it is equally important to remember that they still are.

Marxism-Leninism as an Ideology in Harmony with Selected Aspects of Asian Traditionalism

The pattern of personal and group behavior in any society is intimately connected with cultural traditions not easily nor quickly overturned. In Asia, political behavior has often clashed sharply with the institutional and ideological requirements of Western-style democracy. For most Asians, including many within the intellectual class, Western parliamentarism is based upon types of behavior contrary to custom and extremely difficult to acquire.

The ideological-organizational structure of Communism, however, provides a certain comfort and sense of familiarity. The Communist premium is upon elitist tutelage and the educative state, two concepts deeply implanted in Asian tradition. There is a certain sense in which Marxism-Leninism represents a continuation of the classical traditions of Asian scholarship, notably in its appeal to authority. Moreover, Communism emphasizes collectivism and group responsibility, striking out against the "selfishness" of individualism. It provides for decision making on the basis of consensus rather than majoritarianism. Its final goal is a unified, harmonious, classless society instead of a state tolerating differences, espousing minority rights, and placing its greatest stress upon the dignity of the individual. Consciously or unconsciously, many modern Asian intellectuals have found in Communism certain revitalized elements of a tradition with which they retain very strong ties.

Communism in power, however, has generally used tradition *against* the modern Asian intellectual, rather than on his behalf. Few elements within the society have faced more complicated problems of adjustment, as events in each of the Asian Communist states make abundantly clear. In the final analysis, a profound gulf between men like Mao Tse-tung and Kim Il-sŏng on the one hand, and the scholars of Peking University or Keijo Imperial University on the other, was likely to exist. Mao and Kim have wanted *their* intellectuals cast in the mold of the new socialist man. Their ruralist, guerrilla traditions, moreover, have made them profoundly suspicious of the urban intelligentsia—in some degree, of urbanism in general.

Marxism-Leninism as a Universalist Creed and a Philosophy of Optimism

In his contact with the West, the Asian intellectual has often suffered from an acute sense of separateness; a despair of overcoming his intellectual isolation. In this context, Marxism appears as a philosophy of hope. It asserts that all societies are united by the same basic truths, the same fundamental social laws. It guarantees that all societies will go through the same broad stages of development and reach the same ultimate position with respect to values and institutions. In an era when the Asian intellectual has desperately wanted to "belong," Marxism poses as a universal creed and a doctrine of certainty in the midst of a very troubled, uncertain world. Not even the strong nationalist tides have obliterated this desire for some broader identity and affiliation.

Marxism-Leninism as an Advanced, Scientific Methodology

In Asia, political Marxism cannot really be separated from academic Marxism. The forerunners of most Asian Communist Parties were Marxist study societies, and where the Communist movement has been truly powerful, it has often been underwritten by a favorable academic atmosphere—"progressive scientific" journals, Marxist professors, left-oriented student movements, and similar assistance.

Most classical scholarship in Asia took the form of the baldly factual chronicle, the textual exegesis, or the legalistic tome. Suddenly—and in the context of an overpowering faith in "science"—a new "scientific" approach to human society was revealed, one that presented a grand, cosmic theory of human behavior and social evolution, a theory "documented" by a vast array of socioeconomic data. Marxism was essentially simple, easy to comprehend and apply. Moreover, it had the greatest validity for societies in the initial stages of modernization. It is not surprising that it took many progressive Asian intellectuals by storm, particularly since the West offered no formidable methodological competition prior to World War II.

A TYPOLOGY OF ASIAN COMMUNIST LEADERS

The intellectual has been only one element in the Asian Communist movement. While he has generally been very important at the leadership level, even here he has usually not remained at the helm as the Party approaches power. To appreciate the full range of Communist leadership, therefore, one must go beyond the intellectual class. Additional motivations and appeals to those outlined above must also be set forth. To be sure, the appeals of Marxism-Leninism already suggested were certainly not applicable to the Asian intelligentsia alone. Many of these appeals were felt, and felt deeply, by the supporters of Communism who came from other social classes. But it is necessary now to cast a wider net, one that will encompass a broader range of human motivation in connection with politics, and suggest the three basic types of leadership that have emerged within Asian Communism.

The Ideologue

This type is overwhelmingly intellectual, but its representatives do not necessarily all come from the recognized intellectual class. Whatever their socioeconomic background, they tend to combine, in equal proportions, frustration and resentment over the *status quo*, desire for rapid change, conviction of the scientific truth of Marxism, and the desire to play the role of philosopher-king. Theirs is essentially an ideological commitment to the cause, and they are most comfortable in the roles of pamphleteers, philosophers, and intellectual tutors.

These are deeply sincere, deadly serious men in whom burns an inner fire. They have, generally, a high level of integrity, dedication, and purpose. They are prepared to sacrifice and to demand sacrifice. On occasion, their commitment is broader than Marxism-Leninism—or narrower, depending upon one's interpretation. Within this group are nationalist Communists who seem as much motivated by national patriotism as by fervor for the international proletariat. Indeed, in the process of intertwining nationalism and Communism, some ideologues take on the qualities of Tom Paine as much as those of Nicolai Lenin. At this stage of Asian Communism, we cannot be certain of the precise quotient of nationalism that will ultimately remain in Communist ideology. We can only know that it will be high.

Not infrequently, the personality of the ideologue is very different from that generally associated with the radical leader. Many ideologues are introverts, soft-spoken, moderate in personal actions, and with no particular mass appeal. Indeed, they often are men who cannot operate effectively in the open arena and who seem extremely ill at ease when confronted directly with a common man. Their support comes from the hard core of inner workers. Both their words and their personality carry respect at this level because they have demonstrated devotion to the cause, skill in tactics, sensitivity to issues, and personal integrity. They are particularly prone to factionalism, however, perhaps their most basic weakness in terms of the movement.

The Activist

Another prominent type of Communist leader is the activist. The activist is attracted to Communism because it provides an outlet for his organizational skills, his leadership capacities, and his penchant for purposeful action—or possibly, for action in any form. Doctrinal niceties may be of little concern to him. He may find theory boring and intellectual discussions tedious, but association with fellow human beings in a common endeavor that combines drama, movement, and the challenge implicit in revolution is fundamentally satisfying.

Activists can come from any socioeconomic group. Often they emerge from the ranks of the common man, but more frequently they come from the lower middle class. Most of them are natural leaders: They are strongly extroverted, possessed of a commanding personality that attracts and holds the absolute loyalty of their followers, shrewd judges of men and clever tacticians. If they were not Communists, such men might well be leaders of industry or heads of democratic labor or farmer movements. Indeed, in societies where there is sufficient economic development and social mobility, the Communist movement undoubtedly loses a significant number of such individuals.

The Careerist

A third type of Communist leader has been drawn into the movement because of the opportunities for personal advancement which it offers. There are various kinds of careerists: the peasant lad for whom the Party means an education and the chance to escape the monotonous drudgery of farm life; the worker who hopes to gain status as a member of the proletariat, the favored class; the student who sees the possibility of gaining both intellectual and political authority in a disciplined organization; the man with military inclinations who may have the chance to lead a dedicated, powerful army.

Opportunities will vary, of course, with the given Party and with its size, importance, and stage of development. No matter how weak and unpromising the Party, however, it offers career possibilities or hopes to certain individuals. Life as a Communist may be difficult and dangerous, but if it brings some sense of career or of personal advancement, it can produce a continuing commitment even under the most trying circumstances. If the Party comes to power, careerists in new forms emerge: the opportunists who recognize the movement as the only route to prestige and success, and the technocrat-administrators who at every level of Party and government perform the crucial operational services.

The three kinds of Communist leaders presented here have been depicted as pure types. In reality, most Communist leaders have been drawn into the movement for a variety of reasons and are mixed types. It may still be useful, however, to attempt a portrait of the leadership of the various Communist Parties of Asia, using these three types as categories, indicating both dominant and subordinate types where these are present, and suggesting current trends where a change seems to be in process. In doing so, I am acutely aware of the fragmentary nature of the evidence upon which this portrait and others soon to be presented are based. Over the past ten years, I have conducted a number of interviews with Asian Communist leaders, and my hypotheses are based partially upon these interviews. Various primary and secondary sources relating to Asian Communism have also been utilized. Nevertheless, the generalizations advanced here must be treated only as preliminary explorations, based upon scattered data and subject to correction and refinement as our knowledge becomes more extensive.

The three charts that follow summarize the author's present knowledge and will serve as a basis for a short general discussion of Communist leadership in Asia.

Types of Leadership

What generalizations can be drawn about Asian Communist Party leadership from these three charts, assuming their basic accuracy?

Ideologue leadership has predominated in the initial phases of a Party's emergence and development. In weak Parties this has frequently continued. As most Parties have developed strength, however, and be-

Chart 1

*DOMINANT AND SUBORDINATE TYPES OF LEADERSHIP WITHIN THE ASIAN
COMMUNIST MOVEMENT, AND CURRENT TRENDS*

Ideologue	*Activist*	*Careerist*
	Chinese Communist Party[a] ⟶	
		Mongolian People's Revolutionary Party
	Korean Workers' Party ⇒	
	Vietnamese Workers' Party ⇒	
	National Liberation Front of South Vietnam ⟶	
	Pathet Lao — — — — — — — — — — ⟶	
Japanese Communist Party(ies)[b] — — — — — — ⟶		
	Philippine Communist Party	
⟵ — — — — — — — Malaysian Communist Parties[c]		
	Indonesian Communist Party	
Cambodian Communist Party ⇒		
	Thai Communist Party	
⟵——————— Burmese Communist Parties[d]		
Indian Communist Parties		
	CPI (Right)	
	CPI (M) (Left)	
	Naxalites	
Nepal Communist Party — — — — — ⟶		
Pakistan Communist Party — — — — ⟶		
Ceylon Communist Parties ——————⟶		
⟵ — — — — (pro-Peking faction)		
(pro-Moscow faction) — — — — ⟶		

Note: The position of the Party or group in the columns above indicates the dominant type of leadership, a dotted line indicates a subordinate type of importance, and a straight line indicates a significant trend.

[a] The Chinese Communist Party has been placed midway between the two columns because it is led by men who must be considered to represent combined ideologue-activist types more fully than other Asian Communist leaders.

[b] Today, the mainstream of the Japanese Communist Party has become increasingly activist in a parliamentary sense: recruiting members, augmenting finances, and competing for elected office in local as well as national contests. Its principal leaders, however, must still be considered essentially ideologues. The small, pro-Peking faction, now outside the main Party, is strongly activist in orientation but so small as to be impotent at this point.

[c] The various Malaysian Communist groups, seemingly in a state of imperfect coordination at present, are not identical in this or other respects. Naturally, the Sarawak and Chen Ping Communists are led essentially by activists, whereas the Singapore Communist movement contains a certain number of ideologues, although their number has declined in recent years.

[d] In earlier years, the formerly legal Communists of Burma, connected with the National Democratic United Front, had a higher percentage of ideologues than either the White Flags or the Red Flags, as would have been expected. In a man like Red Flag leader Thakin Soe, however, one finds a perfect ideologue-activist combination. The White Flags, incidentally, are the Communists recognized internationally as the Communist Party of Burma.

Chart 2

CURRENT SOCIOECONOMIC CLASS REPRESENTATION WITHIN THE TOP LEADERSHIP OF THE ASIAN COMMUNIST PARTIES AND COMMUNIST-CONTROLLED MOVEMENTS

	Worker	Farmer	Intellectual petit bourgeois	Other bourgeoisie	Military
Chinese Communist Party	Weak	Medium	Strong	Very weak	Very strong
Mongolian People's Revolutionary Party	Weak	Medium	Strong-Medium	Very weak	Strong-Medium
Korean Workers' Party	Weak	Weak-Medium	Strong-Medium	Very weak	Very strong
Vietnamese Workers' Party	Weak	Weak-Medium	Strong	Medium	Very strong
National Liberation Front of South Vietnam	Weak	Medium	Very strong	Medium	Very strong
Pathet Lao	Very weak	Weak	Medium	Medium	Very strong[a]
Japanese Communist Party(ies)	Medium-Strong	Very weak	Very strong	Medium	Very weak
Philippine Communist Party	Weak	Medium-Strong	Very strong	Weak	Strong[a]
Malaysian Communist Parties	Medium	Very weak	Strong	Strong	Strong
Indonesian Communist Party	Medium-Strong	Medium	Strong	Medium	Weak
Cambodian Communist Party	Very weak	Very weak	Very strong	Strong	Weak
Thai Communist Party	Very weak	Medium	Strong	Strong	Medium
Burmese Communist Parties:					
National Democratic United Front	Strong	Very weak	Very strong	Medium	Very weak
Red Flags	Very weak	Weak	Very strong	Weak	Strong[a]
White Flags (Burmese Communist Party)[b]	Weak	Medium	Very strong	Weak	Strong[a]
Indian Communist Parties					
Communist Party of India (Right)	Medium	Weak	Very strong	Strong	Very weak
Communist Party of India (Marxist)	Medium	Medium	Strong	Medium	Very weak
Naxalites	Weak	Medium	Very strong	Weak	Very weak
Nepal Communist Party	Very weak	Weak	Very strong	Strong	Weak
Pakistan Communist Party	Weak	Weak	Very strong	Strong	Very weak
Ceylon Communist Parties	Medium	Weak	Very strong	Strong	Very weak

gun to vie seriously for political and military power, the trend has generally been toward activist control. Finally, among Parties firmly ensconced in power, or of sufficient significance to offer major opportunities, careerist leadership has become increasingly important. Thus, the typical progression of leadership in a Party, moving from its earliest development through the struggle for power and thence to control of the whole or a part of its society, is from ideologue to activist, and finally, careerist dominance. At every crucial stage in this progression, the probability of internal conflict is high, as current events in China make abundantly clear.

Most Asian Communist Parties are moving toward activist dominance if they are not already in that category. Today, Communist leaders give primary attention to party organization, cadre training, and revolutionary tactics. Indeed, it is crucial to recognize that in contemporary Asian Communism, concern over organization often takes precedence over all other considerations, including those of program and policy. The present generation of Communist leaders has discovered that the route to power lies more in superior organization than in appealing issues, a fact difficult for Western liberals to perceive. Making use of the

---

Note: Top Leadership, as used here, refers to members and alternate members of the politburos and central committees and to those occupying positions of comparable importance. Strength is assigned on the basis of a five-term scale: Very weak, Weak, Medium, Strong, and Very strong. Strength relates to numbers and importance within the Party, not to whether the representation is greater or less than the numerical proportion of the class in the society at large.

It is recognized that the separate designation, Military, may be challenged in terms of the other categories employed, and that some of these categories may appear vague. Worker covers manual workers, lower clerical workers, and those labor leaders who can truly be considered a part of the working class as distinct from the intellectuals who have taken up labor leadership. Farmer includes all individuals whose primary income is derived from agriculture, irrespective of status. Intellectual Petit Bourgeois encompasses academicians, literati, journalists, students, and other brainworkers, including the very important category of professional bureaucracy. Other Bourgeoisie includes entrepreneurs, merchants, and such professional men as doctors, lawyers, and engineers. Military covers not only professionally trained military men, but also individuals who in the course of revolutionary careers have devoted primary or substantial energy to military pursuits, men who consider themselves, by occupation or knowledge, at least partially military specialists. It is this latter group, of course, which comprises the great bulk of the Military category within the Asian Communist movement.

Needless to say, these categories are not mutually exclusive. And if the full background of the current leaders were added, an even more mixed profile of many leaders would emerge. To take one example, Mao Tse-tung is of peasant origin and has continued throughout most of his active life to work with the rural masses. By virtue of his education and career, he also must be considered an intellectual. But much of his life was spent in military pursuits, and he prides himself on being the father of modern guerrilla warfare. He must thus be accorded full recognition under both the Intellectual and Military categories, and be given half-status under the Farmer category.

[a] These are parties in which the Military (almost all the nonprofessionals described in the Note to this Chart) are strong only in relation to internal Party composition. In some cases, however, Chinese or North Vietnamese training programs have greatly facilitated the emergence of guerrilla leadership and, in nearly all cases, the classics on guerrilla warfare written by Mao, Giap, and others have been available for study.

[b] Now legally defunct.

Chart 3

DATE OF ESTABLISHMENT OF COMMUNIST PARTY, CURRENT GENERATION OF LEADERSHIP, AND GENERAL AGE SPAN OF TOP LEADERS IN 1969 (Transitional Cases Indicated by Arrow)

Date party established	First-generation leadership[a]	(Age)	Second- and third-generation leadership	(Age)
1921 (1920)[b]	Chinese Communist Party	(65–80)		
1921			Mongolian People's Revolutionary Party	(50–60)[b] → (40–50)
1925 (1919)[c]	Vietnamese Workers' Party	(60–80)		(50–60)
1930 (1925)[d]	People's Revolutionary Party (National Liberation Front of South Vietnam)	(30–50)	Korean Workers' Party	(45–60) → (45–60)
1962 (1961)[e]		(40–60)		(30–50)
1946[f]	Laotian People's Party			
1922	Japanese Communist Parties	(65–75)	Philippines Communist Party	(30–55)
1930			Malaysian Communist Party	(35–60)
1931[g]			Indonesian Communist Party	(30–55)
1920				(25–60)
1951 (1945)[h]	Cambodian People's Revolutionary Party	(25–50)		
1942 (c. 1925)[i]	Burmese Communist Parties	(45–60)	Thai Communist Party	(25–45)
1943 (1938–39)[j]	Indian Communist Parties	(60–75)		(25–40) →
1928 (1925)[k]				(40–60) →
1949	Nepal Communist Party	(35–55)		
1948 (1928)[l]			Pakistan Communist Party	(40–60)
1940 (1935)[m]	Ceylon Communist Party (Moscow faction)	(50–70)	Ceylon Communist Party (Peking faction)	(35–60)

ᵃ The designation *First Generation Leadership* does not necessarily refer to the first leaders of the Party, but to the continued prominence of men who were a part of the Party's formative period.
ᵇ A Communist study group was organized in Shanghai in 1920, after the arrival of Gregory Voitinsky, by Ch'en Tu-hsiu. The second generation group (50–60) has been especially hard hit by the Great Proletarian Cultural Revolution.
ᶜ Prior to the establishment of the first Korean Communist Party in Seoul in 1925, various *emigré* groups had founded Communist organizations. One, founded in Irkutsk in 1919, was named the All-Russian Korean Communist Party, and several others emerged during this period.
ᵈ In 1925, Nguyen Ai Quoc (Ho Chi Minh), already a Communist with five years experience in Paris, Moscow, and China, founded the Vietnam Revolutionary Youth League, a predecessor to the Vietnam Communist Party which was created in 1930. The present Vietnamese Workers' Party was launched in 1951.
ᵉ The National Liberation Front of South Vietnam was created in 1961, and its hard-core Party, the People's Revolutionary Party, was established in 1962. Unquestionably, this Party takes its ultimate instructions from the Vietnam Workers' Party, of which it is a subordinate unit.
ᶠ In 1945 *Lao Issara* was organized. The following year the Communist *Pasachone Lao* (Laotian People's Party) was founded, although it was not openly proclaimed until 1955. It now operates through the *Neo Lao Hak Xat*, founded in 1956. This latter replaced the *Neo Lao Issara* and was legalized in 1957 via the Vietiane Agreement. It has the Pathet Lao as its armed force.
ᵍ Chinese Communists were in Malaya as early as 1924, and Communist activity was significant in Singapore by 1927–1928. Many authorities date the founding of the Malayan Communist Party as 1930, but one official document specifies 1931. The early Party was almost completely wiped out by the Japanese during World War II, and a new Party emerged. The Clandestine Communist Organization in Sarawak, of course, is of much more recent vintage, its predecessor being the Sarawak Overseas Chinese Democratic Youth League, established in 1951.
ʰ Cambodian Communism got its first start with the Khmer Issara movement at the close of World War II. It is reported, however, that a Cambodian Communist Party was established in 1951, although there is little evidence of it as an active organization. The Pracheachon Party, formed in 1955, is the Party through which Cambodian Communists probably have operated. According to Sihnouk it had 100–200 active members in 1967.
ⁱ Communist activity among the Thai Chinese goes back to the era of Chinese Communist Party–Kuomintang collaboration, and for many years, a Chinese Communist Party of Thailand existed. Even now, there may be some separatism in the Thai Communist movement. The Communist Party of Thailand dates its founding from 1942, but this was probably the date of the First Party Congress. A Communist Party was formed in Thailand as early as 1929 by the Siam Special Committee of the South Seas Communist Party.
ʲ While the Burmese Communist Party was officially founded in 1943, proto-Communist groups, springing out of the Thakin movement and various contacts with Indian and British radicals, date back to 1938–1939.
ᵏ An *emigré* Indian Communist Party was organized in the Soviet Union in 1921, and there were even reports of one such Party established in Tashkent in 1920.
ˡ It is manifestly impossible to separate the early history of the Pakistan Communist Party from that of the Indian party, although, in a strict sense, the Pakistan party dates only from the partition, and was founded in 1948.
ᵐ The Ceylonese *Lanka Sama Samaja* Party, which encompassed a wide range of socialists, including Communists, was founded in 1935. In 1940, the Communists were expelled and founded the United Socialist Party, which was Communist in all but name. The United Socialist Party officially became the Ceylon Communist Party in 1943.

many techniques now available for mobilization and commitment, they concentrate upon creating a disciplined, tightly structured, efficient machine in an otherwise loosely jointed society. Activist dominance and organizational priority are two key symbols of Asian Communism today.

Class Origins of Leaders

In socioeconomic terms, Asian Communist Party leadership has come predominantly from what might be termed the middle class, or, as the Marxists term it, from the *bourgeoisie* and especially from the *petite bourgeoisie*. In occupational terms, a majority can be described as intellectuals, military men, or a combination of the two. Most have had some higher education, the central fact that distinguishes them from so many of their compatriots. Asian Communist leaders, in short, are far closer to both traditional and other modern Asian leaders in their socioeconomic attributes than they are to the proletarian leadership projected in Marxian theory. The Communist leaders share many traits with the other elements of the modernizing elite with whom they are in competition—education, status, and even a common core of values.[2] Some Communist leaders, indeed, are closely related in certain respects to the more traditional segment of the modernizing elite: They come from the upper classes, and a portion of their appeal is based upon status, ethnic, or regional considerations.

This is not to deny certain significant differences nor to negate the features that make these men Communists. They are individuals distinguishable, among other things, by their particular ideological convictions, by their customary political tactics and techniques, and by their very special domestic and foreign ties. In broad terms, however, contemporary Asian Communist leaders have, from the beginning, been more a part of than apart from the elite of their society.

Special emphasis should be given to the importance of the military in the Asian Communist movement. There has been a tendency to minimize or ignore this fact because of a partly justified belief that, since the Party controls the army, political considerations are therefore paramount—and because many Communist leaders can be called "military" only if that term is used somewhat loosely. In my opinion, Communist leaders should be classified as military or quasi-military if they function wholly or in an important sense as military men, irrespective of their formal training and self-identification. If this view is accepted, the military component within Asian Communist Party leadership is, without exception, seen to be strong or very strong in those parties holding power. Indeed, both China and North Korea are military regimes in certain respects. Even in Parties not in power, wherever the tactic of guerrilla warfare is being pursued the military have naturally assumed a crucial role. Perhaps the most dominant single form of leadership for successful Communist Parties is the hyphenated intellectual-military (or military-intellectual) type. Men like Mao Tse-tung, Kim Il-sŏng, and even Ho Chi Minh can be included in this category. These men—and many others who have come to power—are old guerrilla fighters, wedded to an intellectual (or, more accurately, a quasi- or semi-intellectual) tradition. Whether they will be succeeded by "civilians" or more orthodox military men remains an intriguing and critical question.

Those Asian Communist leaders who come from outside the orthodox elite classes tend to have agrarian antecedents, reflecting the fact that they emerge from overwhelmingly agrarian societies. In such cases, the normal background is that of middle or rich farmer, not that of tenant. Only the former two categories generally afford the opportunities for education, mobility, and the other attributes essential for political leadership. But such a background can produce the type of hostility or ambivalence toward the urban intelligentsia exemplified by Mao and Kim Il-sŏng.

Very few Communist leaders currently come from the urban working class. Even leaders who are so labeled are often intellectuals who became professional labor organizers, not true members of the proletariat. Leaders from the working class are almost entirely second-generation men, younger men not yet at the top rungs of the hierarchy. Even these are relatively few in number in most Parties.

Age of Communist Leadership

Asian Communist leaders in key positions, or moving into those positions, are generally second or third-generation leaders in the age bracket from 40 to 55. This makes them somewhat younger than their competitors for power in most Asian societies. First-generation Communist leaders are fading away, becoming Communists emeriti, if indeed they are still alive. There are some exceptions—mainly in the newer Parties —but for the most part, the veterans of the Asian Communist movement are now passing from the scene. Thus, in terms of leadership, a great transitional era is currently under way.

The older generation, tending to be more strongly ideologue in type, was also generally conditioned to an international Communist organization dominated by Moscow. They emerged and spent most of their active political lives in the era of monolithic world Communism, when orthodoxy and heresy were pronounced in final tones from the Kremlin. Not all the older-generation leaders were totally submissive, but the strong tendency was for the more creative and independent thinkers to leave the Party or be ordered out. Those who remained were either conditioned to an acceptance of Moscow directives or survived because in some fashion they had created an indigenous base of power, one not heavily dependent upon the Soviet base.

These days, and among the second generation, the activist type is more prominent. Interest in organizational work, both political and military, is high even at the grass-roots level. The international Communist movement is no longer monolithic, and the new generation tends to regard Moscow with suspicion, if not hostility. After 1950, Peking developed substantial influence over many young Asian Communists, serving as a newer, more applicable model than Moscow—and one with which they could feel greater cultural affinity. The quotient of nationalism, however, tends to be uniformly high among the current group of Asian Communist leaders, much higher than in most of their predecessors. Even if the Peking model were to prove more attractive in the future than it does at the moment, therefore, it is doubtful that a Peking-directed Asian Comintern, possessed of the same monolithic qualities as the old Moscow model, can emerge, *unless*, of course, the Chinese are prepared to use a full range of coercive as well as persuasive techniques.

This is not to minimize Chinese influence upon the Asian Communist movement, particularly with respect to revolutionary tactics and strategy. That influence, as we shall see, has been very great. Moreover, in the absence of any broader political equilibrium in Asia, and providing it was able to keep its own political system in order, China might seek to exert the type of influence via force upon smaller Asian Communist Parties and states that the Soviet Union has attempted recently in East Europe. Nevertheless, the swing of the pendulum is currently toward adaptation rather than mechanical borrowing, toward pragmatism (i.e., doing what will work) rather than ideological purity, toward national Communism rather than full-fledged internationalism. Throughout Asia, Marxism-Leninism is being consciously and unconsciously revised in accordance with these trends. Thus, the world struggle over who are the revisionists becomes all the more ironic.

REVOLUTIONARY TACTICS, PARTY ORGANIZATION, AND MEMBERSHIP

Lenin first established the basic tactical and organizational principles that have governed Communist revolutions in "late developing" societies, but it remained for the Communist leaders of China to carry Leninist principles forward on the most successful and dramatic scale in Asia. Unlike the establishment of Communist power in Mongolia and North Korea, which was primarily a product of external power, the victory of the Chinese Communists was essentially the result of indigenous developments.³ Consequently, the Chinese revolutionary model has had a major impact upon other Asian Communist Parties. It is a model involving not only a series of revolutionary tactics but also corresponding organizational techniques, and these two must be viewed as interactive, inseparable elements. Briefly, then, let us set forth the essentials of the Chinese model, following its development stages from Party beginnings to the aftermath of total victory. (It will be noted that I frequently use Chinese Communist language in presenting the model, so as to convey more vividly its essence. Only the parenthetical remarks, therefore, should be considered as a full effort at objectivity.)

Stage 1: Party Emergence

A premium must be placed upon the earliest possible creation of a Communist Party as the only legitimate organ of the proletariat. This Party must be organized by the vanguard of the proletariat (i.e., intellectuals) and protected against all liquidationists, whatever travails have to be faced.

Simultaneously, the permanent Party structure should be created in miniature. The Party Congress meets once a year or less frequently. The supreme Party organ is composed of delegates chosen by Party members. (In reality, Congress delegates must be carefully selected, with due regard to regional, ethnic, and functional representation.) The Congress has as its primary purpose the debate over alternative courses of action and the determination of basic Party policy. (In fact, the Congress serves as a sounding board and primary communications outlet for leadership, ratifying, but never making or even altering, policy.)

The Central Committee is established as the working committee of the Congress, and generally has from 60 to 100 members chosen for their service to the Party, experience, and ability. (They are chosen, also, for their absolute loyalty to the Party and are often protégés of the top leaders.) The Central Committee usually meets several times a year to hear reports, discuss, and on occasion debate concrete policies. (In the initial stages of the Party—or in the event of a serious struggle for power or basic policy differences among top leaders—true debate may take place in the Central Committee, and its final decisions may have a critical influence. More usual, however, is the gradual subordination of the Central Committee to the primary leaders, and its loss of any independent decision-making powers.)

In the committees appointed by the Central Committee, and particularly in the Political Committee, or Politburo, resides the real power to direct the party—and, in the event of victory, the nation. The Politburo normally numbers some eight to twelve men, carefully ranked and, almost without exception, the most powerful men in the Party. (The Politburo makes all basic decisions for the Party, unless these decisions are made by one man—the Party Secretary-General or Chairman—or a small inner clique.) A number of other executive-administrative committees are created, including a secretariat or organization committee handling organizational work, and a control committee in charge of security matters. (The key positions in all of these bodies are held by an interlocking directorate of a dozen men or less.)

This Party structure, established at the outset and modeled almost precisely after the Soviet Party, is permanent. Significant changes occur, however, in the actual distribution of power within this structure, particularly among the top leadership. As a general tendency, the Party commences its existence with a reasonable amount of freedom of internal discussion, a freedom which extends to the Central Committee and may on occasion reach even as far as the Party Congress. Decisions have a collective quality, and criticism—at least "constructive" criticism —is permitted. The majority position, to be sure, is binding upon the minority, and the rules of democratic centralism always prevail: There is rank-and-file representation from the grass roots by means of successively elected bodies, and the leadership, thus legitimized, exercises its absolute authority from the top down. Nevertheless, in the formative stages, power within the Party is often held more loosely and by a wider circle of men.

In time, the power circle tends to become more narrow, the decision-making process more rigid. The very structure of the Communist Party— and the ideology that underlies that structure—are conducive to a struggle for supremacy that must culminate in the victory of one man. The absence of any tradition of minority rights, and of any mechanism for a peaceful alternation in power, makes every contest for power a final one. Hence the struggle must be ruthless, with no holds barred. Rivals are castigated in absolute terms: "false Marxist-Leninists," "opportunists," and "traitors." When the battle is decided, purges almost inevitably follow. In the end, one man tends to emerge as supreme leader, without a serious competitor. (Rarely, this same process can take place as a natural product of Party evolution.)

The formal Party structure then becomes the instrument of the supreme leader and the followers whom he groups around him. It is not uncommon, however, for an element of oligarchy to persist, with the supreme leader sharing his power more or less voluntarily with two or three trusted colleagues who will never challenge his final authority. As the supreme leader ages, the pattern of power distribution may become more perfectly oligarchic, with the small group around him acquiring even greater authority. At this point, the Party power structure may be similar to that before the struggle for supremacy had been decided.

When the supreme leader has been seriously weakened by massive errors or by age and ill health, or when he dies, a new struggle generally occurs, making possible a temporary widening of the power circle.[4]

Stage 2: Broadening the Base of the Party

With the Party launched and its permanent organizational structure established, the initial task is to develop it from a small conspiratorial coterie composed largely of intellectuals to a mass-based political organization of depth and authority.

What are the primary techniques of growth? First, it is essential to divide the society into two broad categories: the "people" and the "enemies of the people." The people are the workers, peasants, intelligentsia, and other "patriotic, national *bourgeoisie*." They represent 90 per cent of the society—and they must be wooed and won. Contradictions will exist among the people, and between the people and the Party, but these can be resolved by discussion. They are not fundamental.

The enemies of the people include the feudal gentry, the big capitalists, and the reactionary political leaders—that 10 per cent of the society that must be fought and destroyed. Contradictions between enemies and the Party can only be resolved by a struggle unto death. They are fundamental. (One can, moreover, slip from being "people" to "enemy of the people" by willfully opposing the Party.)

Having defined the basic target, it is equally essential to define the issues that will make possible mass mobilization and commitment to the Party. The basic issues are twofold: internal reforms, all of which are basically bourgeois-democratic in nature; and an appeal to nationalism, another bourgeois concept. In sum, the Communist Party at this stage must begin its effort to capture the bourgeois-democratic revolution by seeking to capture the very issues that are intrinsically bourgeois in character.

No element of the people is more important than the peasantry, comprising 80 per cent of the masses. To them are attuned the promises of land reform, elimination of corrupt officials and rapacious warlords, lower taxes, and a host of other benefits; to the workers, new freedoms and dramatic rises in status and living conditions; to the intellectuals and other bourgeois elements, participation in a new, noble experiment in nation building and social justice. And to all groups, the promise of first-class citizenship in a first-class nation, rid of foreign imperialists. Indeed, the struggle to lead the nationalist movement becomes paramount—and sometimes decisive—in the fortunes of the Party. Both the successful utilization of united front tactics and the favorable development of mass associations as front organizations are heavily dependent on the Party's capacity to play upon nationalist themes.

Throughout this and the succeeding stages, however, an emphasis upon organization remains of supreme importance. Those whom the Party cannot woo, it coerces. And by means of both coercion and persuasion, it seeks to build a powerful, integrated structure capable of committing members to execute orders with unquestioning obedience, and liquidating or silencing those who would interfere.

Stage 3: Mounting the Challenge to the Ruling Party (Class)

As the Party base is extended, political and economic activities can be intensified. To the extent that bourgeois democracy does not exist, heavy pressures must be exerted upon its behalf: agitation for freedom of speech, press, and association; demands for freedom of unionization, rights for tillers, and other socioeconomic reforms. To the extent that bourgeois democracy does exist, the central tactic must be the use (and abuse) of the democratic system.

In concrete terms, this latter tactic takes two forms: (1) the simultaneous appeal for unity with, and the sustained trenchant attack upon the dominant national-bourgeois Party; and (2) the coupling of legal activities with semilegal and illegal ones. At this point, it is vital to extend the Party reach by joining in a united front with the more powerful primary nationalist party, in order to combat imperialism and feudal reactionaries. At the same time, however, Party integrity and independence of action must be fully protected: A constant vigil must be maintained against the threat of absorption or destruction by a superior force.

An important aspect of this tactic is the struggle to share with the national *bourgeoisie* the prestige of the central charismatic figure of the nationalist movement, the Father of the Country. To utilize and, if possible, to capture this figure is to add great impetus to the party's legitimization. Success in this effort enables the Party, as the rightful successor to the great leader, to inherit the nationalist revolution upon his demise. The act of uniting with the dominant nationalist party and cultivating its leader, however, must not prejudice the task of attacking and undermining this same party and leader. Bourgeois weaknesses and crimes must constantly be drawn to the attention of the masses, and bourgeois forces must be divided, the more progressive elements being subordinated to the Party and the reactionary elements being isolated and destroyed.

At this stage, it is essential that the leadership of the national democratic revolution be captured by the proletariat (i.e., the Communist Party) so that a continuous, uninterrupted march toward socialism can be achieved. Under no circumstances can the *bourgeoisie* be allowed to retain control of the bourgeois-democratic revolution until its comple-tion. If that should occur, a second revolution would be necessary to complete the transition to socialism. The final stages of the bourgeois-democratic revolution must be managed by the proletariat.

To capture the bourgeois-democratic revolution, the Party cannot and must not depend upon parliamentary tactics alone. No ruling class voluntarily relinquishes power. Thus, in this stage, it is essential to couple legal and illegal actions, to pursue different routes to power simultane-ously, the exact admixture depending upon conditions. As the Party's political and economic power develops, its potential for a truly revolu-tionary challenge to the ruling party grows, and it must prepare to take advantage of this fact.

Stage 4: The People's War

When conditions are ripe, or when circumstances necessitate it, the Party must be prepared to shift its primary emphasis from political to military action. This does not mean the abandonment of politics, but an advance to the final, climactic stage where the decision will be deter-mined by the outcome of military struggle, a struggle to which all political and economic resources must be directed.

Military action must follow the principles of guerrilla warfare. The red army must be built largely with peasant recruits and must find its natural habitat in the rural areas. Here it is protected against its nu-mercial weakness, provided it is careful to cultivate the people and win them as allies. In the initial stages, it must be prepared for highly mo-bile warfare, striking at the enemy when and where he least expects it, making certain that it strikes in superior numbers and then fades away when the enemy musters a major force.

As these tactics succeed, it will be possible to establish a secure territorial base and create a shadow government. Party officials will now perform the necessary tasks of administration, acquiring experience in preparation for governing the entire country. Party activities also ex-pand. There is no relaxation of politics. The cadres, greatly increased in numbers, educate and guide the people in the liberated areas. In enemy territory they operate in covert fashion, and a steady flow of recruits files out of such territory as a result of their efforts.

If the military phase goes well, the Party gradually acquires a sizable portion of the country in which it reigns supreme, and it infiltrates much of the enemy's territory, operating a government-by-night, a dual administration. From its relatively self-sufficient rural bases, the Party watches—and abets—increasing unrest in the urban centers and govern-ment enclaves, the product of economic chaos, administrative disorder, defeatism and low morale, and massive social dislocations. Ultimately, the cities fall like overripe fruit when the process of disintegration has run its course.

Stage 5: The Establishment of People's Democracy

With military victory comes the transition from bourgeois democracy to people's democracy, and thence ultimately to Communism. First, the final stages of the bourgeois-democratic revolution must be completed under proletarian management. Land redistribution—based upon a tri-partite classification of the rural classes into poor, middle, and rich—is carried out. Full freedom is announced for the people, and swift ret-ribution for their enemies. A series of purges against "traitors and ex-ploiters" gets under way.

The united front tactic, however, is preserved. A number of small "progressive" parties are encouraged—indeed, forced—to continue, so that the nonproletarian classes can be represented and properly prepared for their own demise. But policy determination rests solely with the vanguard Party. And its first great goal is the elimination of all forms of dissidence and division, a rapid movement toward political centraliza-tion, the creation of a monolithic nation—perhaps the first nation that its society has known.

The transition to socialism is quickly under way. Land reform is fol-lowed in rapid succession by cooperatives and full collectivization. Business and industry are transformed into joint government-private ven-tures, thereby making the transition to full nationalization possible. Eco-nomic planning, its emphasis upon rapid industrialization, is totally di-rected by the Party.

At this stage, Party organization takes a giant leap forward, at least in numerical terms and in depth of penetration into the society. Millions of persons join the Party, anxious to ride on the crest of the new wave. Party cells are established in every rural district, urban factory, and institution of higher learning. Vast numbers of new cadres are trained so that the basic tasks of indoctrination and administration can be carried out at the local level. All citizens, whether Party members or not, are forced into political participation. In this stage, man does in-deed become a political animal. Self-criticisms, drills on Party ideology and goals, discussion meetings on how best to effectuate national pol-icies—all are essential elements of mass education. By means of the block, commune, and factory associations, the Party extends its power to the very perimeters of the society, standing guard over the thoughts of all its people. But the supreme Communist myth, the mass line, is rigorously retained: All ideas come from the people, and the Party has as its pri-mary function only the transformation of those ideas into policy.

CHINESE COMMUNISM AS THE PROTOTYPE OF
ASIAN COMMUNISM

In basic outline, these five stages represent the Chinese revolutionary model. To what extent is this model, and its accompanying organizational pattern, applicable to the Communist movement in the rest of Asia? Charts 4 and 5 suggest some correlations. Bear in mind, however, that a close adherence to the model does not necessarily mean that a given Communist Party is "pro-Chinese" or currently dominated by the Chinese Communist Party.

What general themes can be drawn from the above charts?

There are no significant organizational differences among the Communist Parties of Asia. In each case, the Party structure, established in the initial stage of Party emergence, has remained basically intact and similar to the early Soviet model. As can readily be discovered, however, there is a substantial difference among current Parties in the location and distribution of decision-making authority.

Among the Asian Communist Parties in power, two—those of North Korea and Mongolia—have in the past undergone extensive struggles for supreme power, attended by numerous purges. Kim Il-sŏng having eliminated his last major rivals in 1958, now appears to rule his country with an iron hand, controlling all major appointments and policies. Tsedenbal's position and present role are less clear, although he appears to be dominant, powerful enough to determine all basic policy. His status, however, seems inseparably connected with Russian support.

The other two dominant Parties—those of China and North Vietnam—are Parties in which a supreme leader has long existed. But these supreme leaders are now aging and nearing the end of their active political careers. In both instances, a succession crisis is under way, or at hand. As we noted earlier, the situation in China is highly confused, and there can be little doubt that a lengthy period of struggle is likely before a single leader with Mao's authority reemerges after his death. In North Vietnam also, senior leaders appear to be far from united, although the war prevents disunity from reaching unmanageable bounds. In both of these settings, meaningful discussions and decisions undoubtedly go beyond the top man, possibly even beyond the top inner circle, although the latter group sets policy in the most basic sense. Collective leadership, in these terms, is on the rise. Moreover, younger cadres are now pushing their way up into the power structure, many of them serving as protégés —and stalking horses—for the senior men who are engaged in sharp contests for power. In both China and North Vietnam, therefore, and particularly China, the political situation is fluid, subject to rapid change, possibly of major proportions.

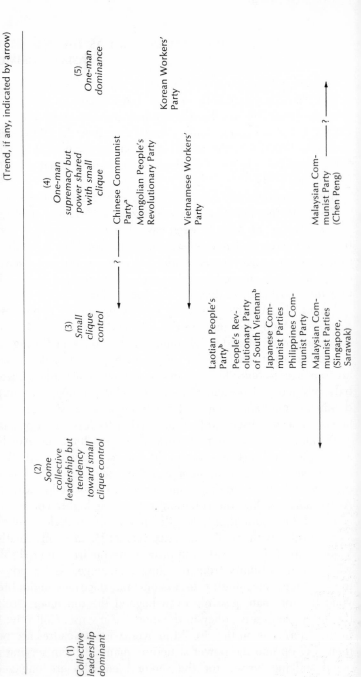

Chart 4

TRUE DISTRIBUTION OF POWER WITHIN THE ORGANIZATIONAL STRUCTURE OF VARIOUS ASIAN COMMUNIST PARTIES AS OF MID-1968

(Trend, if any, indicated by arrow)

(1) Collective leadership dominant	(2) Some collective leadership but tendency toward small clique control	(3) Small clique control	(4) One-man supremacy but power shared with small clique	(5) One-man dominance
			Chinese Communist Party[a]	Korean Workers' Party
		——— ? ———→	Mongolian People's Revolutionary Party	
			Vietnamese Workers' Party	
		Laotian People's Party[b]		
		People's Revolutionary Party of South Vietnam[b]		
		Japanese Communist Parties		
		Philippines Communist Party		
		Malaysian Communist Parties (Singapore, Sarawak)	Malaysian Communist Party (Chen Peng) ——— ? ———→	

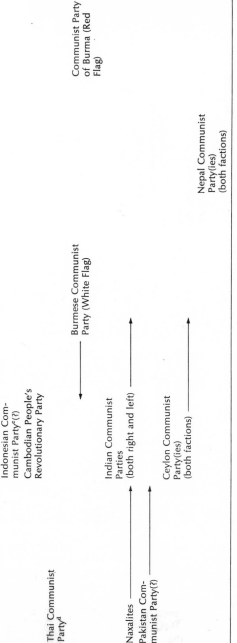

Thai Communist Party[d]

Indonesian Communist Party[c](?)

Cambodian People's Revolutionary Party

Burmese Communist Party (White Flag)

Communist Party of Burma (Red Flag)

Indian Communist Parties (both right and left)

Naxalites

Pakistan Communist Party(?)

Ceylon Communist Party(ies) (both factions)

Nepal Communist Party(ies) (both factions)

NOTE: This categorization warrants some explanation. In a highly organized Party fitting Category 1 (*Collective Leadership Dominant*), Party Congress or at least Central Committee decisions would be of critical importance, and a maximum amount of policy initiation would take place at this level as well as via the local or regional Party units. In less structured Parties (probably the only Parties which have ever come under this category), the entire membership has access to the decision-making process.

Category 2 is a mixed type. Membership, Party Congress, or Central Committee decisions are of significance, either consistently or sporadically, but Politburo or other forms of small group control are important to the decision-making process.

In Category 3 Parties, the Politburo, or the dominant clique within it, plays the key role and no individual holds sustained paramount power.

Category 4 is again a mixed type. One leader is clearly *primus inter pares,* but a small group working with him plays a significant role in fashioning basic decisions.

In Category 5 Parties, one leader has acquired sufficient power to make the Politburo, and all other Party organs, his creatures and can readily translate this will into Party policy.

[a] The damage done to the Chinese Communist Party as a result of the Cultural Revolution has made the effectiveness of the central Party—even under Mao and his Cultural Revolutionary Advisory Group—open to serious question. Thus, local and provisional authority—much of it military—has currently supplanted or supplemented that of the Party headquarters, and the future is extremely unclear.

[b] The degree to which the Laotian People's Party and the People's Revolutionary Party of South Vietnam are independent entities capable of making basic decisions, and the degree to which they are creatures of the Vietnamese Workers' Party, is debatable. In our view, the latter Party has no independent authority, and is merely an appendage of the Hanoi Politburo, albeit with individuals holding different opinions on occasion, due to regional and situational differences.

[c] The disrupted state of the Indonesian Communist Party makes any firm opinion on the distribution of power impossible. There is some evidence that no single leadership or group currently is acceptable to all elements of the underground and exiled (Peking) Party.

[d] The unity and the degree of external direction of the Thai Communist Party are also debatable. Clearly, Hanoi once trained the bulk of the northeast guerrilla leaders, but Peking has also played a significant role in establishing the Thai Patriotic Liberation Front and in abetting unrest among tribal elements in the north. (The Pathet Lao is also involved in training Mao dissidents in the north.)

Chart 5

STAGES OF DEVELOPMENT OF THE VARIOUS ASIAN COMMUNIST PARTIES BASED ROUGHLY UPON THE CHINESE MODEL, AND DEGREE OF APPLICABILITY OF THAT MODEL, USING A SCALE OF 0–5 (NOT APPLICABLE TO TOTALLY APPLICABLE)

(Dual stages or transitions indicated by arrow)

Stage 1	Stage 2	Stage 3	Stage 4	Stage 5	Degrees of applicability
				Mongolian People's Revolutionary Party	0
				Korean Workers' Party	0 (3)
				Vietnam Workers' Party	4
			Laotian People's Revolutionary Party[b]		3–4
			People's Revolutionary Party (National Liberation Front of South Vietnam)		4
South Korean Communist Party[a] ↑					1
	Japanese Communist Party(ies) ↑				3
	Philippine Communist Party ↑				
		Malaysian Communist Parties ↑			3–4
Indonesian Communist Party[c]					3–4?
Cambodian People's Revolutionary Party ↑					3–4?

Thai Communist Party   3–4

Burmese Communist Parties   4

Indian Communist Parties ⟶   2–3

   3

⟶ Nepal Communist Party   3–4

Pakistan Communist Party

⟶ Ceylon Communist Parties ⟶   2–3

---

[a] The emergence of the Korean Workers' Party into power bore no relation to the model, since Korean Communism was ensconced in authority via the Soviet Red Army. Now, however, Kim Il-sŏng has clearly outlined a program for the South Korean revolutionary movement closely parallel to this model—except that he is seeking to telescope developments somewhat, moving into acts of sabotage, attempted assassination and other forms of violence before the Party has a mass foundation in the South, possibly before it truly exists as an organization that can function. As in the case of Hanoi, P'yongyang expects to direct Southern operations.

[b] In the case of the Laotian People's Revolutionary Party also, the most limited mass base exists, but guerrilla warfare is sustained via external (North Vietnamese) power, thus diverging from the ideal model. The Philippine, Malaysian (Ch'en Ping), Cambodian, and Burmese Communist Parties also are engaged, with varying intensity, in guerrilla warfare without having successfully completed stages 2 or 3.

[c] The Indonesian Communist Party, having failed in the abortive coup, must now rebuild the Party from the ground up. Its position is roughly similar to that of the CCP after 1927, although the future may be different.

Among the other Asian Communist Parties, the most pronounced tendency is domination by a small clique, an inner group that may include an acknowledged leader but that in any case exercises some degree of collective power. This clique may number three or four members, it may number five or six, but it is generally smaller than the Politburo, constituting merely the majority or the powerful figures therein. Small clique domination occurs under a variety of circumstances. It is most likely to exist when a final power struggle has not yet taken place and when leaders roughly equal in prestige are willing and able to work together. And even when a supreme leader has emerged or is in the process of emerging, political exigencies, personality factors, or other conditions may encourage oligarchy rather than one-man rule. A subtle combination of the two is, of course, often the most logical development at one stage.

A few cases of one-man dominance can be found among the weaker Asian Communist Parties, but they are unusual. One-man dominance exists currently among the Red Flags of Burma, and possibly in the jungle forces of Chen Ping in Malaysia, but not elsewhere. More common is some degree of collective leadership, which may exist as the natural product of a young Party in which power relationships have not yet solidified or in Parties in which there is a substantial degree of factionalism, preventing the acknowledgement of a supreme leader and causing the distribution of power on a wider scale. Under these conditions, a considerable degree of inner Party democracy can exist as long as the key leaders wish to avert a major power struggle and open split.

In exploring these organizational differences, one certainly should not ignore the political culture of the society. Modes of political behavior and styles of political organization traditional in the broader cultural patterns of the society clearly help to determine the character of a party's leadership and organizational structure. The consensual, groupistic orientation of most Asian societies undoubtedly moderates monolithism in some parties. But "objective conditions"—the character of the colonial heritage, the stage of economic development, the nature of the opposition—also affect party tactics and structure. Our basic thesis, however, appears to be valid: The nature of Communist ideology and organizational theory lends itself to the movement from collective to individual leadership, with the strong possibility of cyclical trends over longer periods of time.

It is clear that most Communist Parties of Asia have patterned their revolutionary tactics after aspects of the Chinese experience. Even where the idea was that of Lenin or some other non-Asian Marxist, it was Chinese practice which gave the idea relevance and vitality. While the Bolshevik Revolution remains a great historical event for the Asian

Communists, the Chinese Revolution has represented current revolutionary tactics most likely to work, and current desires with respect to economic and political modernization. In light of the current crisis in China, will this continue to be true?

Only one Asian Communist Party, the Mongolian People's Revolutionary Party (MPRP), has paid scant attention to the Chinese model. Its revolution predates the Chinese Communist Revolution by a full generation, and it continues to reflect extensive Soviet guidance. The Russians brought Mongolian Communist leaders to power, and they keep them there. But in the timing of their revolution and in the external source of their power, the Mongolian Communists are unique among their Asian comrades.

No doubt Mongolian nationalism, which must be directed primarily against China, is a major factor in limiting Chinese influence, a factor now beginning to influence other Asian Communists in their attitude toward China. It should be noted, however, that there is nothing in the present stage of Mongolian development that precludes the applicability of advanced (Stage 5) Chinese Party techniques, and it is always conceivable that a pro-Chinese leader might, with Chinese assistance, topple a pro-Soviet ruler.[5]

Where does the Chinese model of revolution tend to be most useful? In general, it has greatest applicability in those societies where economic development is least advanced, where political control by "bourgeois-democratic" forces is most precarious, and where conditions are most suitable for the exploitation of the nationalist issue, preferably in the form of a "national liberation" movement. Some or all of these circumstances currently exist in the highest degree in Burma, Cambodia, Laos, Thailand, and Vietnam. There are also close ethnic and cultural bonds to China within the Communist movements of Malaysia and Thailand, as a result of the strong Chinese composition of the Communist Parties of these two countries.[6] Thus, in these seven countries Chinese revolutionary tactics have special meaning. And it is worthy of note that, in five of these nations, the Communist Party has already entered Stage 4. Only in Cambodia, where special circumstances prevail, is the Communist Party at a more rudimentary level of development, and even there, violence has now erupted.

There are two other societies—Nepal and Pakistan—where, at least potentially, conditions are only slightly less propitious for the application of this model. Some of the same economic and political circumstances characteristic of the seven countries noted above exist. There is a wider cultural gap, certain facets of which may make the Chinese model more difficult to apply. At the moment, moreover, as in Cambodia the circumstances and stage of emergence give the Communist Parties of these two countries somewhat less room for maneuvering. In all three countries, for example, relatively strong leaders have followed policies of conciliation, repression, or a combination of both, in such a fashion as to prevent the Communist Party from moving far beyond Stage 2. This situation, however, may easily prove only temporary, and we must assume that, for all of these societies, the Chinese model has potentially a relatively high level of applicability.

The Chinese model may be somewhat less relevant in India and Ceylon. The colonial histories of these societies, the circumstances of their liberation, the trends since their independence, and general cultural factors combine to render Chinese Communist Party (CCP) tactics less meaningful. Parliamentarism has a stronger hold upon the elite, a fact reflected even within the Communist movements of these two societies. Utilization of the nationalist movement by the Communists, moreover, will clearly be more difficult, especially in India. In addition, the political and economic intrastructure of these countries is somewhat more highly developed, requiring different political techniques.

Nevertheless, at the grossest level, the socioeconomic character and problems of India and Ceylon are sufficiently similar to those of other underdeveloped societies to give the Chinese revolutionary model a certain appeal and validity. With the proper adaptations, it might become a serviceable instrument for the Indian and Ceylon Communist Parties, as Naxalbari indicates.

North Korea is a special case. The Korean Communists came to power because of Russian support, not on the basis of their own indigenous development.[7] The early stages of Chinese experience, therefore, had little meaning to North Korea. Post-revolutionary Chinese Communist practices, however, have had an influence upon Pyongyang, although Party-to-Party relations are distinctly cool at present and Chinese influence currently is low. Unquestionably, however, this model—with modifications—is being applied in Korean Communist strategy in the South.

In Japan and the Philippines, the Chinese model appears to have distinctly limited applications. Both societies, and particularly Japan, have gone beyond that stage of economic and political development for which the Chinese model was fashioned. In relative terms, they are "advanced" societies. Parliamentarianism functions with considerable effectiveness; the nationalist issue is more difficult (although not impossible) to exploit; and economic modernization is well advanced.

In summary, the Chinese revolutionary model has had a tremendous influence upon the thinking and activity of the great majority of Asian Communist leaders. Most Asian Communist Parties are now seeking to follow the five basic stages that characterized the Chinese Communist Revolution. They are seeking to shape their basic tactics after those laid down by Mao Tse-tung and his associates, while at the same time firmly asserting that their fundamental task is that of adapting Marxism-Leninism creatively to the realities of their own society, not the blind copying of any other revolutionary experience. However, Chinese Communist chauvinism and the great upheaval of the recent past are likely to alter attitudes toward the CCP, even if interest in the model remains high. Indeed, that has already occurred in some instances.

STRENGTH AND COMPOSITION OF ASIAN COMMUNIST PARTIES

Having established the basic tactical and organizational lines of the Asian Communist Parties, let us now assess their relative strength and the socioeconomic composition of their membership (Charts 6 and 7). Once again, extreme caution must be used in reading the following charts. In many cases, the data are incomplete and uncertain; thus, the charts should be regarded as approximations, not precise tabulations.

Accepting these charts as roughly accurate, what conclusions can we draw from them?

Almost all Asian Communist Parties must be regarded as highly elitist. This generalization holds for Parties in power as well as for those in initial stages of development. The Korean Workers' Party alone deserves the label "mass Party" on the basis of its membership and the relation of that membership to the total population of North Korea. The only other Parties approaching mass status in terms of membership are those of China and North Vietnam, but, in both cases, particularly China, Party members constitute only a tiny fraction of the total adult population. Thus, even in societies where the Party is dominant or strong, its members rarely constitute more than 5 per cent of the adult population, and usually much less.

Membership alone does not necessarily provide a good index of Party power. The formal membership of the Communist Parties of India and Laos, for example, is scarcely indicative of the true political or military strength of these parties.

What Factors Make for the Strength or Weakness of a Communist Party in Asia?

A detailed answer to this question involves the type of country-by-country analysis undertaken in the succeeding sections of this volume. In general terms, the most critical factors would appear to be these: Is the Party able to utilize effectively—and if possible, to capture—the nationalist movement? Is it able to develop mass foundations, particularly among the peasantry, so that it can have a broad base for military and political activities? Can it neutralize, capture, or discredit the prevailing national leader and his party? And the answers to these ques-

Chart 6
RELATIVE STRENGTH OF THE ASIAN COMMUNIST PARTIES AND GROUPS

Dominant Communist parties	Population of nation	Party membership	Electoral strength (where relevant)	Geographic distribution of strength
Chinese Communist Party	750,000,000 (est.)	No official figures since July 1, 1961: at that time, 17,000,000; (80% joined after 1949; 70% during First Five-Year Plan). 20,000,000 cadres reported in 1963; some non-Party current estimates range from 17–22 million.		National.
Mongolian People's Revolutionary Party	1,200,000	"Almost 50,000" as of March 1, 1968.		National.
Korean Workers' Party	13,000,000	Over 1,600,000 members and candidate members in 1969; only 366,000 members in 1946.		National in North Korea, but influence in Republic of Korea negligible as of early 1969.
Vietnamese Workers' Party	18,500,000	760,000 in April 1966; possibly higher now; in 1946, only 5,000–20,000 members.		National in N. Vietnam, influence via NLF in S. Vietnam.
Strong Communist Parties				
Pathet Lao	2,500,000	The hard-core Party is the Lao People's Party, with an estimated 750 members. However, Neo Lao Hak Xat, a "patriotic front" which is the primary Communist instrument at present has a membership estimated at 1,500–		Regional; more than one-half of Laos, in 1969.

Party				
People's Revolutionary Party (National Liberation Front of South Vietnam)	15,000,000	had between 15,000–30,000 troops and possibly 3,000 cadres in 1969. (The movement, however, gets major military and political support from the presence of 45,000 N. Vietnamese troops in Laos.) The People's Revolutionary Party has a small hard-core membership, but the general Communist movement in South Vietnam may command as many as 150,000 full and part-time guerrillas, 30,000 cadres, and has the support of possibly 15–25% of the populace.		With N. Vietnamese forces, 30–40% of total area of S. Vietnam, involving 17–20% of population in early 1969. Regional: mainly Java.
Indonesian Communist Party	110,000,000	Current Party membership impossible to estimate since Party now exists in underground fragments. In 1965, PKI claimed 3,000,000 members and 10–15 million in front organizations, although hard-core elements were undoubtedly much smaller.		
Indian Communist	525,000,000	Split into Left and Right factions in 1964, and split further subsequently. The CPI (Right) had 104,000 members in 1969, half of them active. The CPI(M) had 80,000 members, the majority active. The Naxalites had 10–20,000, almost all active. The number of Party members, of course, is less important in some respects that the votes which the Party can garner.	From 40 percent in Kerala to negligible strength in Gujarat and Mysore, Madhya Pradesh. Overall national strength in 1967: CPI (Right), 4.8%: CPI (Marxist), 4.3%.	Regional: strongest in Kerala, West Bengal, and Andhra Pradesh.
Weak Communist Parties				
Japanese Communist Party(ies)	100,000,000	Party claimed close to 300,000 in 1969, but only 200,000 "fully committed"; outside estimates—250–260,000	3–5%	Regional: primarily metropolitan areas, especially

Chart 6 (cont.)

Dominant Communist parties	Population of nation	Party membership	Electoral strength (where relevant)	Geographic distribution of strength
Weak Communist Parties (cont.)				
		members. 30,000 members in July 1947; 200,000 in December 1949; 83,000 in June 1951. Pro-CCP and pro-CPSU splinter groups outside the JCP number a few thousand at most.		Kyoto, Osaka, and Tokyo.
Burmese Communist Parties	24,000,000	CPB (White Flag): Possible 3–4,000 in 1969 but numbers and territory controlled very fluid. BCP (Red Flag): not more than a few hundred. Burma Workers' and Peasant Party (and other National Democratic United Front proto-Communists): 5,000–10,000 in 1963; outlawed in 1964.		White Flags now seek to "liberate" territory on Burma-China border with Chinese aid; Red Flags confined to tiny area in Arakan.
Cambodian People's Revolutionary Party	6,500,000	100–200 hard-core members and 1,000–2,000 sympathizers in proto-Communist Pracheachon Party in 1968. (not including NLF and N. Vietnamese forces in Cambodia).		Regional: Phnom Penh and Battambang Province.
Malaysian Communist Parties	11,500,000 (including Singapore, now independent, and Sabah)	800–1,000 guerrilla fighters in North Malaya, and 1,500 sympathizers. Possibly 1,000–2,000 hard-core Communist Party members in Singapore. 100–300 hard-core Communist Party members in Sarawak, plus small number of guerrilla fighters in 1969.	Barisan Socialis (united front party): 20% of Singapore vote	Regional: Thai-Malaysia Border, Singapore, and Sarawak - Indonesian border.
Nepal Communist Party(ies)	10,500,000	Estimates vary; possibly no more than 500 active workers in all factions in 1969. Some 300–500 exiles in India		Regional: Kathmandu valley and Terai

Party	Population	Membership	%	Regional
Ceylon Communist Parties	11,000,000	Pro-Moscow factions, approximately 1,100–2,000; pro-Peking faction, 200–800 in 1968. Each faction has possibly 1,000 close supporters.	3–4%	Regional: mainly Colombo and Southwest Ceylon.
Philippine Communist Party	35,000,000	Less than 500 guerrilla fighters in the People's Liberation Army, but possibly as many as 25,000–30,000 sympathizers and 1,000–12,000 hard-core political workers in the Huk movement. An additional 1,500–2,000 members, mainly in Manila, with perhaps 12,000–15,000 sympathizers. A Philippine branch of the Chinese Communist Party also reportedly exists, working with the Chinese community, with some 300–500 people actively involved.		Regional: Manila and scattered areas of central Luzon.
Thai Communist Parties	33,000,000	Formal Party membership unknown. As of early 1969, 3,500–4,000 hard-core guerrillas, presumed party members: Northeast, 1,500; North, 900 (mainly Neo); middle South, several hundred; far South, 1,000 (Thai Moslems numerous and Chinese-dominated); plus a Bangkok underground of unknown size, probably not large.		Regional: Bangkok and scattered parts of northeast, north and Malaysia border.
Pakistan Communist Party	108,000,000	Figures very uncertain; reportedly 2,700 in East Pakistan, 750 in West Pakistan in 1968. However, although the Party is illegal, having been banned in July 1954, evidence is that recent political upheavals plus developments in West Bengal have strengthened Party considerably.		Regional: East Pakistan, particularly Dacca.

Chart 7

SOCIOECONOMIC DISTRIBUTION OF THE ASIAN COMMUNIST PARTIES AND COMMUNIST-DOMINATED GROUPS

Dominant Communist parties	Worker	Farmer	Intellectual	Other bourgeois	Military
Chinese Communist Party	Strong	Strong	Weak	Very weak	Strong
Mongolian People's Revolutionary Party	Medium–strong	Medium–strong	Medium	Very weak	Medium–Strong
Korean Workers' Party	Strong	Strong	Weak	Very weak	Strong
Vietnam Workers' Party	Medium	Strong	Medium	Weak	Very strong[a]
Strong Communist Parties					
Laotian People's Party	Very weak	Strong	Weak	Weak	Very strong[a]
People's Revolutionary Party (National Liberation Front of South Vietnam)	Weak	Very strong	Medium	Medium	Very Strong[a]
Indian Communist Parties					
Communist Party of India (Right)	Strong	Medium	Medium–Strong	Medium	Very weak
Communist Party of India (Marxist)	Strong	Very strong	Medium–Strong	Medium–weak	Very weak
Naxalites	Weak	Strong	Strong	Very weak	Very weak

Weak Communist Parties					
Japanese Communist Parties	Strong	Very weak	Strong	Weak	Very weak
Burmese Communist Parties	Weak	Strong	Strong	Weak	Strong[a]
Cambodian People's Revolutionary Party (Pracheachon Party)	Very weak	Very weak	Very strong	Medium	Medium[a]
Malaysian Communist Parties	Strong	Very weak	Very strong	Weak	Very strong[a]
Nepal Communist Party	Very weak	Very weak	Very strong	Medium	Very weak
Thai Communist Party	Weak	Strong	Strong	Weak	Very strong[a]
Ceylon Communist Parties	Medium–strong	Weak	Very strong	Medium	Very weak
Indonesian Communist Party	Weak	Strong (?)	Medium–strong (?)	Weak	Weak–Medium (?)[a]
Philippine Communist Party	Very weak	Strong	Strong	Very weak	Very strong[a]
Negligible Communist Parties					
Pakistan Communist Party	Very weak	Very weak	Very strong	Very weak	Very weak

[a] Included in this category are guerrilla fighters, whatever their previous occupations.

tions in turn may lie in even broader issues: At what stage of socio-economic development is the particular society in this, the late twentieth century? What are the cultural legacies and ethnic divisions, and who can best utilize them? How united and how skillful are the opponents of the Party? Do the Party leaders exhibit organizational skills? Upon what external aid can the Party count and how much external resistance must it face?

At this point, it will be sufficient to present a general profile of the strong and the weak Communist Party. First, the strong Party almost always has a military component of significance. Among the dominant and strong Communist Parties of Asia, only those of India lack this element. The Indian Communist Parties appear to be experimenting with the peaceful route to power, but it is uncertain as to how long that experimentation will continue. Formerly, of course, that was the case with the Indonesia Communist Party (PKI), until the abortive coup—but that Party is unlikely to return to the parliamentary route.

Almost all of the important Communist Parties of Asia also have a substantial *petit bourgeois* intellectual element in their membership, indicating the vital significance of capturing as many of the educated elite as possible. This element, to a large extent, constitutes the middle-level leadership of the society, a group commanding the respect of the masses.

Perhaps the most distinguishing feature between strong and weak Communist Parties in Asia, however, is the presence or absence of some mass base. And at this stage, that mass base, if existent, is likely to be peasant. Among the dominant or strong Parties, all have medium to strong worker or peasant representation. These are the classes that compose the guerrilla forces or the red army; these are the classes that provide the potential for meaningful economic or political action.

The weak or negligible Communist Parties are generally characterized by very strong intellectual dominance, practically no mass base, and minimal military potential. As might be expected, these Parties are largely divorced from reality, operating more in the fashion of intellectual debating societies and lacking any capacity for significant political, economic, or military action. And, as is usual among small, intellectual-type groups, factionalism tends to be high.

Except for those holding power, the Asian Communist Parties must be considered regional, not national, parties. Their primary strength, with few exceptions, is in the key metropolitan areas and selected rural districts, generally those most involved in the modernization process. The exceptions are cases where the Party has been able to cultivate a remote rural area because its terrain makes it easy to defend against hostile forces or because the Party has been able to exploit grievances indigenous to the area. The most notable of such exceptions are in Burma, Laos, Malaysia, and Thailand.

In a number of cases, however, the Communist Parties of Asia derive their greatest opportunities from modernization and have their primary bases in urban centers. Whatever their hopes for large-scale peasant participation, most Asian Parties are strongly dependent upon Tokyo, Osaka, Manila, Singapore, Bangkok, Phnom Penh, Calcutta, Dacca, Kathmandu, and Colombo.[8] Perhaps the rapid urbanization of Asia and the concomitant increase in the numbers of industrial workers will reduce the need for peasant support. There is a double-edged problem, however, which Chinese Communist experience does not necessarily answer for other societies. If the cities increasingly provide a potent source of manpower for the Communist Party, Communist urban bases will remain exceedingly vulnerable in the event of serious conflict with the government. Indeed, they will grow more vulnerable as various Asian governments achieve some measure of authority and power. In part, the Indonesian crisis proved this point.

On the other hand, the difficulty of committing the peasantry to long-range, militant political action is great, especially if tight organization is important. Chinese experience notwithstanding (and the assistance provided the CCP by the circumstances of the anti-Japanese war was tremendous), most attempts to organize the peasants on behalf of Communism in Asia have thus far been unsuccessful. Thus far, at least, the Chinese model has proved a failure in Japan, the Philippines, Malaysia, and Burma. Only when a strong nationalist quotient could be added, as in Vietnam, has that model shown its potential strength.

Undoubtedly, Asian Communism will continue to be characterized by dual tactics: the establishment of urban bases from which the political and economic tactics suitable to parliamentarism can be mounted and through which the proletariat can be recruited; and the establishment of rural bases which in normal times serve as auxiliary outposts but which, in time of emergency, become crucial to the Party's survival—wellsprings of guerrilla warfare, centers of mass recruitment, and the beginnings of a territorial base.

CURRENT POLICIES OF THE ASIAN COMMUNIST PARTIES

It remains for us to analyze the current line of Asian Communist policy, searching out the dominant themes. While the various Parties are at radically different stages of development and while there are a few notable exceptions to the major trends, these policies, in general, follow a consistent pattern. Here are the key policies being pursued and the basic theses that underlie them, some distinction being made between those Parties which are in power and those which are struggling for control. (Again, Communist terminology is used.)

The Enemy

The primary enemies of the Party are two: (1) world imperialism, led by the United States; and (2) the reactionary feudalist and capitalist elements at home. The most immediate and serious threat, however, comes from American imperialism; hence, this must be made the central target. If American imperialism is defeated, the domestic reactionaries will have lost their ally and source of support. They will automatically become weak and ripe for destruction.

Among the Communist Parties in power, this thesis is strongly espoused by all except the Mongolian People's Revolutionary Party, and even its policy has recently hardened. The parties of China, North Korea, and North Vietnam are currently following the hard line on the United States and insisting that all true Marxist-Leninists must do likewise. The attack upon American policies and motives is everywhere shrill; no interest is evidenced in any accommodation with America except on Communist terms, and policy toward the United States is a test of a Party's revolutionary sincerity. At the same time, none of these Parties is interested in becoming involved in a direct confrontation with a nation vastly superior in military power. Consequently, militancy is confined mainly to words—and assistance to guerrilla fighters who cannot be fully identified with the existing Communist states.[9]

Among the Parties not in power, the hard line toward the United States, and priority to the struggle against world imperialism is the dominant theme. In some cases, this position was reached only after an inner Party struggle, but it is now the official line with very few exceptions.

The Use of Force

Whether the socialist revolution can be conducted by peaceful means or only by the ultimate use of force depends upon the attitude of the enemy. It should be assumed, however, that force will probably be necessary; consequently, the Party should not be bound either ideologically or practically to a concept of peaceful revolution only.

The Communist Parties in power, all of whom attained their position via civil or international war, generally take a very hard position on the question of revolutionary tactics, insisting that the probabilities that force will be necessary are overwhelming, outlining the principles of guerrilla warfare as an essential revolutionary tactic, and strongly condemning the "soft" position—of the Soviet Union and various European parties—which suggests that socialism may be attained through peaceful coexistence, gradual evolution, or the structural reform of capitalism. Once again, the Mongolian Party is an exception, siding with the Soviet Union on this matter, as on others.

A *strong majority of the Asian Communist Parties not in power* are currently committed to the assumption that they will probably have to resort to force in order to come to power. While not interested in abandoning legal tactics, they are not prepared to be bound by them. With few exceptions, their faith in the parliamentary route to socialism is very limited. Consequently, they accept guerrilla warfare as a likelihood at some stage, and they are studying closely the Chinese and Vietnamese experience.[10] Militancy and a penchant for action are rising in most Parties. The Party organization is increasingly a tightly disciplined one which is yet sufficiently flexible to operate at different tactical levels at the same time.

The United Front

The united front tactic is essential in order to develop a mass base and to harness both the nationalist and the reform issues to the Communist cause. Even should guerrilla warfare prove necessary or desirable, there should be no abandonment of political action or the united front technique.

The Chinese, North Korean, and North Vietnamese Parties continue to regard the united front technique as a valuable one, and consequently, they plan to retain it for the indefinite future. Thus, in Communist China, North Korea, and North Vietnam, a multiparty facade is maintained. The multiparty system is defended theoretically on the score that all classes deserve representation and that internal contradictions between and among classes will be long-lasting. In practical terms, this policy enables the Communists to have diverse channels for mass mobilization and indoctrination, to continue a broad nationalist appeal in the period of "people's democracy," and to maintain a high degree of continuity with the past—all without jeopardizing Party control in the slightest.

The central myth of Communism in power is summed up in the concept of the mass line: All ideas and ultimate authority derive from the people; all power to enforce those ideas and that authority lies within the Party. Meanwhile, a process of experimentation continues with respect to a number of vital political issues: What is the appropriate combination of centralization and decentralization? What is the best size and character of administrative units? How many cadres can best be utilized and how can the people be caused to participate? None of these questions has been determined with finality in the present stage of Asian Communist development. The broad outlines of political organization and control, however, are clear, and these will not be altered in the foreseeable future, unless the Party proves unable to function.

For the Parties not in power, this is generally a period of seeking to challenge the ruling party, primarily through political action. A number of Parties, however, have added military activities to political ones or are contemplating such action. Indeed, the simultaneous development of legal and illegal action—the union of parliamentary and extraparliamentary tactics—summarizes the main trend among those Parties struggling for dominance in their societies.

The success of both tactics depends upon the effective creation of a mass base, the meaningful development of a united front. This in turn revolves upon the ability of the Party to interact positively with all available nationalist and reformist issues. The central tactic is to connect the struggle for "national liberation" from imperialism with the struggle for the overthrow of "feudalism" and reaction at home, and then to establish a national democratic government composed of all "progressive" classes. At this point, the "bourgeois-democratic" stage of the revolution must be completed, and its proper completion requires ultimate management by the vanguard Party. The Asian *bourgeoisie*, in short, cannot be trusted to effect their own revolution, particularly if the final transition to socialism is to be a peaceful one.

Thus, the parliamentary tactic requires the Party to emphasize the menace of imperialism, colonialism, and neocolonialism, while at the same time espousing the full range of bourgeois-democratic internal reforms. Meanwhile, the extraparliamentary tactic requires the development of a strongly disciplined organization, capable of sustaining major sacrifices and able to count upon the masses sufficiently to operate a successful guerrilla struggle which initially will be against heavy numerical odds.

How to merge with the broad progressive forces of the society and yet maintain a totally independent, militant organization deeply committed to its own unchallenged authority is, and always has been, a central problem for the Communists. United front tactics—the tactics of parliamentarism—are not proving effective for most Asian Communist Parties at present. The Communists indeed have reason to lose faith in the ballot. In most open societies, the rate of growth of their voting strength is too slow to be comforting and, in those few societies where their gains offer some hope, parliamentarism itself often proves ephemeral. Communists could not win more than a minority of votes in any Asian society where they are not now in power, including South Vietnam and Laos. Hence, they are forced to maneuver for power on a different basis.

Despite the emphasis upon united front tactics, moreover, the Asian Communist Parties have never been so isolated as they are today. Only in a few countries, such as South Vietnam and possibly Laos, where the "national liberation" movement is nearing its full crest, do the Communists have close liaison with other groups, and the independent status of these groups is highly suspect. Even where the united front tactic has had some success, new problems develop that often prove difficult to resolve. How strongly should the national-bourgeois forces be supported, and the national leader? Can military preparations be safely postponed, or does this jeopardize the Party's future in case of a rupture? Again, the lesson of Indonesia is sharply etched into the Communist minds at present. In short, the united front tactic, while useful and necessary, is not a panacea, as the whole history of the Asian Communist movement so clearly indicates. At this point, however, the problem confronting the Communists is generally how to achieve a united front, not how to control it.

The Two-stage Revolution

In specific terms, the political and economic programs of the Asian Communist movement must be geared to the concept of a two-stage but uninterrupted revolution. In the first stage, the emphasis must be upon constitutional rights, free political participation, full civil liberties, broad social welfare measures, land reform, protection for the rights of the working class, and a mixed economy. In theoretical terms, the Communist Party in this stage must aid in the completion of bourgeois democracy. In practical terms, it must seek to weaken state power, extend the libertarian aspects of the society, and mobilize the dissident elements of the community. There is a strong conflict between the progressive and the destructive elements of this program, but this can be a paradox beneficial to the Party.

The second stage of the revolution, that of the transition to socialism, requires radically different policies. Now, the emphasis must be upon the sharp demarcation between the people and their enemies. Under a people's dictatorship, "the people" are to have full freedom, their "enemies" no freedom. All the political policies of "people's republics" must be understood in this light. Economic policies are now geared less to social welfare and more to the total mobilization of manpower and resources for productive purposes. In theoretical terms, the Communist Party must act as vanguard and undisputed leader, so that an uninterrupted peaceful transition can take place from managed bourgeois democracy to socialism. In practical terms, the new stress is upon the establishment of undisputed Party supremacy, the creation of a powerful, monolithic state, and the conduct of a sustained drive for economic modernization.

The Communist states of Asia have established Party supremacy and until recently at least, we believed that they had gone far toward achieving formal unity. The situation in China at the moment permits of substantial doubt. It seems unlikely that even the Chinese Communists fear a mass uprising at this point, but it is much less certain that a monolithic unity can be imposed upon this huge society. Indeed, it is probable that we overestimated the degree to which the unity was achieved in the earlier period of Communist rule. The evidence now available suggests that a considerable amount of authority was retained at provincial levels, with fairly lengthy tenures of office both for military and political personnel. Moreover, we know that substantial experimentation with respect to administrative units and allocation of power took place.

Nevertheless, the nationalist quotient in the political programs of all Asian states, including China, is likely to remain high, reflecting the fact that the nationalist and the Communist revolutions are reaching their peak in these societies at approximately the same time. In the final analysis, however, as noted earlier, nationalism is still an elitist phenomena, and the voluntary element is probably less than the coercive in these first-generation Communist states, although coercion has many gradations and it is a primary purpose of the Party to move from coercion to voluntarism by means of organization and education.

Even in the economic sphere, the nationalist emphasis is currently strong. Stimulated by the Sino-Soviet dispute, the Asian Communist states have all enunciated a policy of developing an independent and self-sustaining economy, one not primarily dependent upon external aid —and control. Moreover, at least in China the earlier, romantic notion of walking on two legs—that is, of a simultaneous emphasis upon rapid industrial and agrarian modernization—has been modified. As is well known, agriculture has been recognized as the key to modernization and given a clear priority. The pace of the drive, moreover, has been relaxed, at least temporarily. In general, however, the primary appeal of the Communist regimes is one calling for sacrifice, for Spartanism, so that the catching-up process can be completed in the shortest possible time. It would be unwise to deprecate the economic gains, particularly in the industrial sector, that have been attained under Communist rule, and it would be equally unwise to minimize the costs— human and material. Once again, however, the final balance sheet remains in doubt, particularly since agriculture has proven to be an Achille's heel for all of the Asian Communist states.

The Parties of the non-Communist states, almost without exception, are seeking to pursue bourgeois-democratic policies while, at the same time, preparing for their future tasks under a people's dictatorship. Today, the fundamental tactic is to insist on a united front against American imperialism, on the struggle for social reform measures, and on the realization of full democratic rights. Some of the leading Parties, to be sure, have difficulty in assigning priorities: The Japanese Communist Party assigned prior emphasis to the struggle against American imperialism, rather than against monopoly capitalism, only after a fierce internal fight. The question of political versus military tactics has long plagued the Parties of the Philippines, Burma, and Malaysia. The Parties of India, Nepal, and Ceylon are constantly debating specific policies in terms of the degree of support or opposition that should be given to the national government. The broad formula outlined above, however, has now been officially accepted by almost every Asian Communist Party.

Stated Principles of the International Communist Movement

The international Communist movement is based upon the principles outlined in the Moscow Declaration of 1957 and the Moscow Statement of 1960. The essential themes of these two documents (particularly as interpreted by Peking) can be outlined as follows:

1. All Parties are independent, equal, and sovereign entities, and no external decisions can be forced upon them against their will.
2. All decisions pertaining to the international Communist movement shall be reached on the basis of consultation, consensus, and unanimity.
3. The primary threat from within the Communist movement is modern revisionism, a deviation which manifests itself primarily in the reluctance to support revolutionary movements, in the search for accommodation with the capitalist and imperialist forces of the world, and in the abandonment of true Marxist-Leninist principles of internal socialist development.
4. Comradely aid and assistance from one Party to another, and from one Communist State to another, are essential to the health of the Communist movement, but such assistance should fully respect the integrity of the recipient. Big-power chauvinism and the use of aid as a means of political pressure are anti-Marxist actions.

THE SINO-SOVIET DISPUTE

As is well known, escalation of the Sino-Soviet dispute has now reached the stage where reconciliation between the present ruling elites of the two states seems virtually impossible, and every Communist Party in the world has been affected. The primary issues between Russia and China have been threefold: (1) the struggle over issues of organization; (2) Communist revolutionary tactics in the late twentieth-century world; and (3) the terms and conditions of comradely assistance.

Each of these issues reflects the different cultural legacy, historical background, timing of revolution, and current world status of the two major Communist states. Thus, the basic differences are fundamentally expressions of differing national interests. The Chinese, from a minority

position, naturally emphasize equal decision-making rights and total independence for weak and small Communist Parties within any supra-
national organization; the Russians, from a different position, emphasize
the necessity for those having primary responsibility also to have certain
primary rights. The Chinese, from a position of military weakness,
stress the importance of unfolding the world revolution as the basic
method of competing with the imperialist forces which are led by the
United States; the Russians, from a position of power, emphasize the
importance of nation-to-nation competition based upon peaceful coexistence and the avoidance of nuclear war. The Chinese want maximum
comradely aid under conditions of full sovereignty and complete noninterference in their internal affairs; the Russians believe that they must
give priority to their own internal development, and that aid produces
reciprocal rights and duties. No doubt, the personality of Nikita Khrushchev exacerbated the quarrel and helped to account for some of the
bitter polemics. There is no indication, however, that a mere change in
leadership has solved the fundamental issues that separate the two Communist giants. On the contrary, the evidence strongly suggests that despite Khrushchev's ouster, the cleavage remains a deep one.

Two of the three small Communist states in Asia—North Korea and
North Vietnam—are now "neutral," seeking to establish an independent
position between the giants, although currently, the North Koreans tend
to be gravitating back toward the Russian orbit, having once been
extremely close to Peking, and Hanoi also has probably become unhappy
over developments in China since 1965.

During the Khrushchevian era, the Chinese enjoyed increasing support
from the Communist Parties of non-Communist Asia, largely because
of the militancy of their line. Only in South Asia (in the dominant
Parties of India, Pakistan, Nepal, and Ceylon) was the Soviet line accepted
by a majority of Party leaders. Other Asian Parties'—those of Japan,
the Philippines, Indonesia, Malaysia, Cambodia, Laos, Thailand, and
Burma—views on basic tactics and policies tended to parallel those of
Peking.

As we have noted, many of these Parties initially tried desperately to
establish and maintain a neutral position, thereby avoiding the internal
repercussions of partisanship, and some Asian leaders sought to serve
as mediators in the quarrel. But that tactic failed, and increasingly
the Parties were forced to speak out on such burning issues as Albania,
Yugoslavia, Cuba, the Sino-Indian border dispute, the Treaty banning
above-ground tests of nuclear weapons, and certain broader issues such
as modern revisionism.

As was feared, debate over these issues, and the broader external
pressures involved, created splits in the Parties or widened splits that
were already existent. The result is that most of the Asian Communist

Parties have been factionalized. Some—such as those of India and Ceylon—have been split asunder. In others, notably those of Japan and Burma, earlier cleavages have been aggravated. Even within the dominant Communist Parties, the reverberations have been serious. Indeed, this fact has constituted the most basic pressure upon the Russians and Chinese to mend their breach.

Since 1965, however, the influence and prestige of China has slipped, even within the Asian Communist movement. The disasters of the Great Leap, coupled with the excesses of the Cultural Revolution and especially Red Guard activities, have damaged the prestige of the CCP. Some Parties—notably those of Japan and North Korea—have shifted from friendship to enmity. Others—such as Indonesia's—must feel that Chinese advice was exceedingly bad. The Chinese Communists are still influential in such Parties as those of Thailand, Burma, and Malaysia, and the Chinese model of revolution—apart from the CCP itself—is still extremely important for Asian Communism, as we have emphasized. Mao's star, however, has waned in recent years.

In the long run, one may suspect that China's influence over Asian Communism—assuming the continuance of a unified, Communist China —will be substantial. No small Asian Communist state or party can ignore the presence and the power of this major state. Moreover, in forging a modern revolution in a backward society and in finding its primary opponent the United States, the CCP has much in common with other Asian Communist Parties. There are also cultural and ethnic affinities, although these can work in different directions.

FUTURE POLICIES

Whatever China's future influence, however, it would be wrong to assume that other Asian Communist Parties intend to become satellites of Peking. That may in fact occur, but undoubtedly the primary objective of the Asian Communist leaders is to establish the maximum independence, power, and maneuverability for their own Parties and movements. The nationalist tide, as we have already observed, is running strong, not only in the CCP but in most other Asian Communist Parties as well. In the short run, a number of Asian Communist Parties will probably continue to pursue a political line similar to that of China, out of self-interest. But it is doubtful that Peking, even if it wishes to do so, can ever effect the type of control that Moscow once exercised via the Comintern. Chinese influence and controls will be more subtle, although not necessarily less effective, reflecting the new age of polycentrism and of separate Communist nation-states.

Meanwhile, within each Asian Communist Party, in the future as in the past, it is likely that one fundamental difference will be that between men who are basically nationalist Communists and men who are primarily internationalist Communists. At present, the nationalist Communists are generally dominant, but it is possible that, at some future point, the internationalists may again emerge to challenge the prevailing nationalist tides. No point in the evolution of the Communist movement is a more interesting one to follow.

The future of Communism in Asia remains in doubt. In the past, it has taken a massive war to bring the Communists to power. The first Asian Communist state, Mongolia, was born in the aftermath of World War I. The Communist states of China, North Korea, and North Vietnam were produced as a result of World War II. Now, some Communists are seeking to expand their power on the basis of a different type of war: the national liberation movement. Their greatest chance of success appears to be in South Vietnam and Laos, with the possibility of a later chance, in Cambodia, Thailand, Malaysia, and South Korea. Less promising, at least immediately, are the prospects in the Philippines and Indonesia although the general balance of political and military power in Southeast Asia will ultimately affect basic trends in all of these nations. If a general political equilibrium is not established in Eastern Asia, Chinese influence over, or control of both Communist and non-Communist states is more likely.

Where the tactic of national liberation is premature or unsuitable, other Communists are now seeking to advance via the united front. In such cases, the immediate prospects are not promising. Some states, notably Japan, are in reality post-Marxist societies, nations in which economic and political evolution has moved beyond the range of massive communist appeal. Certain other states have nationalist leaders capable of engaging in successful political competition with the Communists.

But the two central issues, of course, remain to be answered. What major power configuration will ultimately dominate Asia? Have those backward societies which are forced by their circumstances to undergo rapid modernization a suitable alternative to Communism? The future of Asian Communism will be determined by the answers to these questions.

NOTES

1. Japan and the Philippines have attained a high level of national unification. The military strength of Taiwan, the Republic of Korea and Indonesia is appreciable. In general, however, the non-Communist states of Asia currently lack the unity, discipline, or power of their Communist counterparts.
2. For example, they would pay homage to the four major concepts bequeathed by the West to the world—progress, science, industrialization, and democracy—insisting only that these concepts be defined and executed in a particular fashion.
3. This statement should be modified, since the Japanese invasion provided the

springboard for Communist victory; nevertheless, internal developments were critical to Chinese Communist success.

4. It should be noted here that the most basic long-range struggle within a Communist state may well be the struggle to establish some orderly means of leadership succession and to achieve the continued primacy of collective rather than individual leadership. It is yet too early to determine whether in their further evolution, such Parties as the Communist Party of the Soviet Union and the Chinese Communist Party can attain these conditions. One can only assert that, to date, the cycle noted above has prevailed, and that current Communist Party structure and ideology continue for the most part to support such cycles.

5. It is impossible at present to know whether pro-Peking elements exist in the MPRP and whether recent purges were connected with the issue. It would not be surprising if such were the case.

6. As noted, there were formerly two Communist Parties in Thailand: a small Party composed of Thais, and a more significant Chinese Communist Party in Thailand, composed of Chinese. There is also a substantial commitment to Hanoi among the Vietnamese refugees in the northeast, and a certain number of adherents to the Malaysian Communist Party among elements in the extremity of south Thailand where Chen Ping and his guerrillas operate.

7. At a more elementary level, this point would also apply to the Pathet Lao, whose position to date has been heavily dependent upon North Vietnamese support.

8. The National Liberation Front of South Vietnam (NLFSV) and the Pathet Lao, of course, are exceptions, but even for them—and particularly for the NLFSV (or its hard core, the People's Revolutionary Party)—Saigon may prove to be a decisive factor.

9. Although the facts are somewhat unclear, North Vietnamese attacks upon American ships in the Gulf of Tonkin would appear to be a mysterious exception to general Communist policies. More recently, the North Koreans have twice provoked incidents, presumably confident that the United States would not retaliate.

10. Japanese Party leaders have spent much time studying Peking's approach, as have the leaders of Burma, Malaysia, Thailand, the Philippines, and Indonesia. The Indonesian leaders have also observed Hanoi's methods, as have comrades from the National Liberation Front of South Vietnam, the Pathet Lao, and the Cambodian Communist Party.

SELECTED BIBLIOGRAPHY

Barnett, A. Doak, *Communist Strategies in Asia: A Comparative Analysis of Governments and Parties.* New York: Frederick A. Praeger, Inc., 1963.

Brimmell, J. H., *Communism in Southeast Asia: A Political Analysis.* London: Oxford University Press, 1959.

Brzezinski, Zbigniew K., *The Soviet Bloc.* Cambridge, Mass.: Harvard University Press, 1960. Revised paperback ed., New York: Frederick A. Praeger, Inc., 1961.

Hoover Institution on War, Revolution, and Peace, *Yearbook on International Communist Affairs.* Stanford, Calif.: Stanford University Press, 1967, 1968.

Hudson, G. F., Richard Lowenthal, and Roderick MacFarquhar, eds., *The Sino-Soviet Dispute.* New York: Frederick A. Praeger, Inc., 1960.

Problems of Communism (Washington, D.C.). Monthly journal.

Rose, Saul, *Socialism in Southern Asia.* London: Oxford University Press, 1959.

Trager, Frank N., ed., *Marxism in Southeast Asia: A Study of Four Countries.* Stanford, Calif.: Stanford University Press, 1959.

World Strength of the Communist Party Organizations. Washington, D.C.: Annual Publication of the Department of State.

BUILDING A COMMUNIST NATION IN CHINA

CHALMERS JOHNSON

No method of operation is more characteristic of the Maoist era of Chinese Communist Party history than the "mass line," according to which the Party derives its policies from the ideas of the people themselves and then leads the people on the basis of these policies. The Chinese Communists have used the mass line as both a long-term strategy and a short-term tactic. The greatest guarantee of eventual success in any enterprise is believed to be the support of the masses, and the day-to-day *modus operandi* for every type of chore is: "Learn from the masses, unite with the masses."

The mass line is the basic line of the Party and this line must be followed at all times, by all departments, and for all types of work. During the period of the revolutionary wars, the Party in all its work used the method of integrating the efforts of the leadership and the masses.[1]

The last sentence of the above quotation suggests that the revolutionary period is an important key to understanding Chinese Communist organizational methods. The so-called mass line was developed at that time, and it lies at the heart of Mao Tse-tung's theories of revolutionary war. Western scholars have devoted much attention to the mass line as it exists in the thought of Mao Tse-tung;[2] however, they have done little toward evaluating the relative significance of various pronouncements by Mao and relating these to their concrete historical context. I believe that in order to understand the viability and the logic of the mass line one must explore the influence of military victory on the leadership of the Party. The persistence of the mass line reveals the continuity of Mao's methods as leader of the Revolutionary War and as leader of the struggle for economic growth.

The experiences of the revolutionary period between 1927 and 1949 have served as an endless source of precedents and examples for the Communist leadership since their coming to power. In devising methods for reaching its goals for economic growth and political development, the Party has turned again and again for inspiration to the policies used in Yenan and earlier. Let us begin, therefore, by looking at the Party's pre-1949 revolutionary strategy. There are three overriding aspects of this strategy that have made it so influential: (1) the same leadership that guided the revolutionary struggle for power has guided the revolutionary struggle in power; (2) the revolutionary strategy of the Chinese Communist Party (CCP) is a domestic product, not a Russian import; and (3) this strategy produced a stupendous military victory against overwhelming odds.

THE GUERRILLA HERITAGE

After the Kuomintang-Communist Party rupture of 1927, the few Communists who remained began to reexamine the history of their movement, to evaluate their mistakes, and to develop a strategy that might lead them to victory. It was Mao Tse-tung and the group of mutinous military officers who joined him in 1927 and 1928 who ultimately perfected a winning strategy. Their theory of revolution did not come fully into being as early as 1928, but neither is it entirely a modern, retrospective rationalization. The period between 1927 and 1936 was one of experimentation and development. By the time the Sino-Japanese War began, the Party thought it understood the techniques of making a revolution in China; and, from 1937 on, it drove to eventual success in accordance with its wartime conception. The victory of 1949 served to lend an unimpeachable authority to the ideas and techniques that Mao had developed in the early Yenan period.

What were the problems connected with making a revolution in

China, as Mao and his associates gradually began to perceive them after 1927? First, the Comintern-dictated policy of placing major reliance on a united front with bourgeois forces was clearly wrong. After 1927, the Chinese Communists used the united front as a *tactic* but never again as a fundamental strategy. In a more profound sense, Mao's Party redefined the idea of united front to mean union with the masses, but it never again placed basic trust in the original idea of joint operations with a rival elite group.

The rejection of the Comintern's united front strategy was implicitly a rejection of Leninism, since it was Lenin's *Left Wing Communism: An Infantile Disorder*, presented as a guide to the Second Congress of the Comintern in 1920, that had laid down the united front as international Communist policy for making revolutions. Mao and his associates did not reject Lenin, however; they incorporated and transcended his ideas. What they did reject was Soviet leadership of the Chinese Revolution. One lesson of 1927 was that China's revolution would have to be made by *Chinese* leadership; no revolution was ever likely to succeed so long as the Chinese Communist Party was merely the agent of Russian foreign policy. The new Chinese attitude did not necessarily imply hostility to Stalin, but it did imply independence.

The second major conclusion that Mao and his group drew from their experiences in 1927 was that military force would play a central role in China. Chiang had temporarily managed to crush the Communists because he had an army; Mao eventually won by forging a better army. In Shanghai in April 1927, in Canton in December 1927, and in Ch'angsha in July 1930, the Chinese Communists learned that unarmed masses or weak armies cannot stand up to professional armies. The choice the Party faced was to wait in preparation for a windfall that might destroy Chiang's forces or to devise methods that would overcome them frontally. Mao chose the latter course.

Strategy of the People's War

The Maoist strategy of revolution is basically one that supplies an answer to the question: How does an objectively weaker military force vanquish an objectively superior, professionally trained military force at the command of the *status quo* power? Mao's answer—probably his most lasting contribution to Communist theory—is what he calls "people's war." This doctrine of revolution via people's war can be divided into five main principles.

Mobilization of a Sustaining Population. On January 27, 1934, Mao stated, "Revolutionary war is a war of the masses; it can be carried out only by means of mass mobilization and by relying on the masses."[3] On May 4, 1939, he reiterated, "What is the lesson of the revolution in the last fifty or more years? Fundamentally it is a lesson of 'arousing the masses of the people.' . . . All must know that only by mobilizing the broad masses of workers and peasants, who constitute 90 per cent of the country's population, can we defeat imperialism and feudalism."[4] In a directly military context, he asserted, "Because guerrilla warfare basically derives from the masses and is supported by them, it can neither exist nor flourish if it separates itself from their sympathies and cooperation."[5] Even his enemy, the army of the Kuomintang, conceded, "Mao believes that the true source of strength to sustain a war lies with the people; war can be won only with the support of the mass of the population."[6] Thus, Mao Tse-tung's answer to the technical superiority of the Kuomintang armies was the mobilization of a totally hostile population against them.

It is easy to speak of mobilizing an entire population, but it is a difficult thing to carry out in practice. What is needed is a broad ideological appeal that will gain the revolutionary party the support of the masses without alienating any significant segment of those masses. The Chinese Communists tried two such appeals during the Maoist period of their Revolution: First, during the Kiangsi Soviet period, they promised land reform to the poor peasants of south-central China; then, after 1937, they appealed to Chinese nationalism in launching resistance to the Japanese invasion.

The first appeal met with a favorable response, but it encountered several major difficulties. It was attractive only to the poorer segments of rural society and therefore did not produce the overwhelming mass support required for guerrilla operations. Nor was the appeal to land reform exclusive with the Communists. Probably most important, reformed areas could not be consolidated over an area sufficiently wide to prevent their encirclement by Kuomintang troops. As Benjamin Schwartz has observed, "the fragmentized nature of the Chinese countryside did not make for the spread of political contagion beyond the area immediately affected."[7] In 1934, despite several brilliant military victories by Mao's forces, the Kuomintang armies overwhelmed the Communist-controlled areas. The Communists retreated to the northwest where, after 1937, they successfully made their second appeal: to the nationalism of the rural population, awakened by the Japanese invasion.

Organization of the Mobilized Population. After discovering the key to the support of the people, the Party had to organize them. In Mao's strategy, organization complements mobilization. The Party and its military cadre organized the people into mass associations, which then provided military support as well as giving the masses a sense of political participation. One of the major functions of Party organization was to provide the people with political and practical education; mass associations also served to isolate persons who did not support the mass movement. The final stage of organization was the creation of territorial bases. As the bases expanded and were consolidated, they became a regular guerrilla infrastructure, supplying the Communist troops with food, refuge, training centers, and sources of manpower. These Communist rural enclaves also weakened the *status quo* power by removing land from its control.

Creation of a large, Party-led Revolutionary Army. Having organized a mass movement and set up a rebel infrastructure, the Party began to recruit a revolutionary army. This army was built around and trained by the nucleus of Red Army veterans from the Kiangsi Soviet. It was characterized by an extreme emphasis on discipline and on maintaining friendly relations with the local population. Good civil-military relations were not so much a sign of the Party's humanitarianism as they were an integral part of its revolutionary strategy. Since the Party's army was pitted against an objectively more powerful force, it had to employ guerrilla tactics, and it had to have the support of the population militarily (i.e., actively) as well as logistically (i.e., passively). The people provided the troops with intelligence, labor, guides, recruits, and material supplies, and they served as a defending militia when the formal army was fighting outside the bases.

In order to guarantee the closest cooperation between the guerrilla army and the sustaining population, Mao devised his "three disciplinary rules" and "eight points of attention." The Red Army first enforced them in 1928, and the People's Liberation Army (PLA) reissued them on October 10, 1947. Today the PLA and the militia still teach and demand from their troops "good three–eight style." Although some professional military officers would like to eliminate the guerrilla quality from China's armed forces, the persistence of such ideology into the present is a sign of Mao's faith in his earlier methods.

The three disciplinary rules were: (1) Obey orders in all your actions; (2) Don't take a single needle or a piece of thread from the masses; and (3) Turn in everything captured. The eight points of attention were: (1) Speak politely; (2) Pay fairly for what you buy; (3) Return everything you borrow; (4) Pay for anything you damage; (5) Don't hit or swear at people; (6) Don't damage crops; (7) Don't take liberties with women; and (8) Don't ill-treat captives.[8]

Since May 1960, the three disciplinary rules have been redefined as follows: (1) Correctly grasp the trend of politics; (2) Endure difficulties and practice thrift; and (3) Respect shrewd and positive strategies. The eight points of attention have been reduced to an eight-character phrase calling for unity, dedication, austerity, and activity (*t'uan chieh, chin-chang, yen-su, huo-fa*).[9]

Guerrilla Tactics. Mao Tse-tung's writings on military subjects reveal his basic belief that in China (and, today, elsewhere) there was no path to revolution other than armed struggle. He advocated waging guerrilla warfare against the army of the enemy in order to wear it down to the level at which it could be defeated. His tactics all display two characteristics: (1) They are intended to create battle situations in which a weaker force may defeat a stronger force; and (2) the implementation of these tactics depends upon the existence and functioning of a mass guerrilla infrastructure. With the support of the population, the relatively weaker Communist forces could have prior knowledge of the enemy's strength, could set ambushes, could fight only at times and places of their own choosing, and could avoid enemy mop-ups.

Mao's basic military proposition is simple: to concentrate a temporarily superior force in order to guarantee the success of every pitched battle and to avoid all evenly matched or unfavorable contests. "Our strategy is to pit one against ten, while our tactic is to pit ten against one—this is one of the fundamental principles on which we beat the enemy."[10] From this slogan, endlessly repeated and elaborated from 1936 to the present, have come the famous beliefs that all enemies are "paper tigers," that all popularly supported revolutions are invincible, and even a good deal of the Chinese theory of "contradictions."

The Stages of Protracted War. In order to make his strategy of revolution work, Mao insisted that the revolutionaries commit themselves to a long struggle. Guerrilla fighting, as seen by Mao, had one specific purpose: to weaken the enemy via a protracted war of attrition. In 1948, as parity between the rebel and defending armies approached, the guerrilla armies went over to larger and larger mobile campaigns of encirclement and destruction. Finally, in the last stages of the war, the Chinese Communist forces reverted to positional warfare in order to complete their revolutionary conquest. In an authoritative exegesis of Mao's military thought, Ch'en Po-ta explains:

Guerrilla warfare does not have the capability of deciding the outcome of a war. Final victory has to be won by means of regular warfare. However, the regular warfare phase in the Chinese revolutionary war was the outgrowth of the long period of irregular guerrilla warfare. . . . From little to big, from weak to strong—that is the general law of the expansion of revolutionary strength.[11]

These five principles constitute the essence of Mao's strategy of a people's war. In its fully developed form, the theory includes several other techniques—for example, psychological warfare, favorable treatment of prisoners of war (in order to demoralize the enemy's rank and file), and tactical use of a united front. However, the five principles listed here form the basis for all of Mao's other military-political axioms.

The Influence of the Strategy of the People's War

The influence of this strategy on contemporary Chinese Communist practice cannot be exaggerated. The men who devised it—Mao, Liu, Lin

Piao, Chu Teh, and others—conceived it as early as December 1936.[12] To them it reflected the lessons of their Kiangsi campaigns, and it constituted the blueprint which they followed to final victory. That victory —which not even Stalin believed to be possible in the post-World War II period[13]—was the most important revolutionary achievement of the twentieth century after the Bolshevik Revolution. A guerrilla army crippled and then annihilated the forces of one of World War II's "Big Five"— an army that was backed with lavish financial, material, and technical assistance from the United States. The men who led this revolution are the same men who ruled China for 15 years. Mao Tse-tung, once a guerrilla leader in south-central China, is now Chairman of the Communist Party; Liu Shao-ch'i, once Political Commissar of the New Fourth Army, was, until the Great Proletarian Cultural Revolution, Chairman of the People's Republic; Teng Hsiao-p'ing, once Political Commissar of the 129th Division, was for the first decade and a half of the new regime Secretary-General of the Communist Party; Ch'en Yi, former Commander of the New Fourth Army, is now Minister of Foreign Affairs; Li Hsien-nien, who fought as a guerrilla commander in central China, is the present Minister of Finance; P'eng Chen, who led the government in the Chin-Ch'a-Chi base, was a leading member of the Political Bureau; and this list could be extended indefinitely.

The Communist victory in China was not the only evidence the CCP had that its strategy was a genuine contribution to Communist theory of revolution. Comparable developments in Indochina, Algeria, and elsewhere suggested that the strategy was something more than the application of Leninism to China. Thus, the Chinese Communists began to argue for the relevance of their revolution as a model, and they began to venerate Mao Tse-tung as a military genius. As early as November 16, 1949, Liu Shao-ch'i stated:

It is necessary to set up wherever and whenever possible a national army which is led by the Communist Party and which is powerful and skillful in fighting the enemies. It is necessary to set up the bases on which the liberation army relies for its activities and to make the mass struggles in the enemy-controlled areas and the armed struggles coordinate with each other. Armed struggle is the main form of struggle for the national liberation efforts of many colonies and semi-colonies.[14]

Sixteen years later the Chinese Communists were still advocating the same strategy; Defense Minister Lin Piao's *Long Live the Victory of People's War*, published in September 1965, was an authoritative reassertion of Mao Tse-tung's Yenan conception of revolutionary war.[15]

There are several problems connected with the strategy, however, that the Communists have faced only obliquely. For example, they themselves were never able to obtain the mass following upon which the strategy depends until the Japanese invasion had occurred. They know that the Japanese invasion created the social conditions upon which they built their revolution, but as "scientific socialists" they cannot advocate mobilizing a population by deliberately provoked invasions. Classical Marxism leads them to maintain that the working masses are always mobilized, although their own experiences in Kiangsi do not support that belief. Nevertheless, in occasional flashes of candor they do concede that war has been the midwife of Communist revolutions. In his celebrated "On the Correct Handling of Contradictions among the People," Mao wrote:

The first world war was followed by the birth of the Soviet Union with a population of 200 million. The second world war was followed by the emergence of the socialist camp with a combined population of 900 million. If the imperialists should insist on launching a third world war, it is certain that several hundred million more will turn to socialism; then there will not be much room left in the world for the imperialists, while it is quite likely that the whole superstructure of imperialism will utterly collapse.[16]

Another difficulty of the strategy is that the wartime appeal used by the Chinese Communist Party in order to gain the support of the masses was nationalism (as it was for the rebels in Indochina, Algeria, and elsewhere). Mao has recently suggested that there is nothing incompatible between nationalism and Marxism-Leninism. In his August 1963 statement on the racial protest movement in the United States, he made the significant comment: "In the final analysis, a national struggle is a question of class struggle."[17] His basis for making this surprising leap is his concept of the masses or the people, and his belief that the people want revolution. They require leadership, and the Party—as the vanguard of the proletariat—is uniquely equipped to provide that leadership. But there has been a shift of emphasis away from both Marx's concept of the proletarian class and Lenin's concept of the vanguard party. Both concepts persist in Chinese Communist ideology, but they overlay and serve a more basic category of social analysis—namely, the people. Slowly but perceptibly, the populist stream of Maoist ideology is displacing traditional elements of Communist theory. Contradictions, antagonistic and nonantagonistic, now exist within the ranks of the people. President Kennedy's successor, we are told, is anti-Communist, antilabor, and antipeople.[18] Kuwabara Toshiji, a Japanese authority on Maoism, believes that the paper tiger theory epitomizes Mao's revolutionary optimism and that its roots lie in Mao's belief in the "almighty people."[19]

It has been recognized that the Chinese Communist theory of revolution is of great relevance to both CCP history and contemporary Chinese foreign policy. However, its relevance to domestic policy and to post-

1949 Chinese Communist ideology is equally great. The leaders of the Party did not forget, after the War, that the mobilized and organized masses of China had already accomplished one miracle: They had defeated the Kuomintang armies. If they could do that, the leaders argued, perhaps they could also overcome economic obstacles that, objectively speaking, China was not ready to overcome. Mobilization and organization—or, in the language of the mass line, "from the masses and to the masses"—therefore live on in China in a nonmilitary setting. The Party's faith in the masses, properly mobilized and organized on the old guerrilla model, has produced the scarcely disguised idealism that persists even after the reversals of the Great Leap Forward.

Compare, for example, the ideas that the Chinese Party has dared to inject into the international Communist controversy concerning strategy:

Every oppressed nation and every oppressed people should above all have the revolutionary confidence, the revolutionary courage, and the revolutionary spirit to defeat imperialism and the reactionaries, otherwise there will be no hope for any revolution. The only way to win victory in revolution is for the Marxist-Leninists and revolutionaries to combat resolutely every trace of weakness and capitulation, and to educate the masses of the people in the concept that "imperialism and all reactionaries are paper tigers," thereby destroying the arrogance of the enemy and enhancing the spirit of the great masses of the people so that they will have revolutionary determination and confidence, revolutionary vision and staunchness.[20]

Lack of technically competent personnel, or of earth-moving equipment, or of steel-making capacity, or of atomic weapons can all be surmounted by the mobilized and organized masses, just as were the tanks and aircraft of the Kuomintang.

THE COMMUNES AND AFTER

The strategies for economic development pursued by the Chinese Communists since 1949 follow a pattern roughly similar to the strategies of revolution adopted by the Party between 1921 and 1949. In the first period of the revolution, from 1921 to 1927, the CCP accepted the policies and orders of the Soviet Union. Similarly, in the first period of economic development, 1950 to 1957, the Party adopted the policy "Learn from the Soviet Union," and it slavishly copied the Soviet emphasis on the development of heavy industry. Soviet industrial experience proved to be as premature to the realities of the Chinese economy as the united front strategy had been to the realities of Chinese politics. During the Great Leap Forward, the Chinese Communist Party again turned to domestic conditions and its own experience as guides to action. It

placed the mass line in command. Liu Lan-t'ao, at the time alternate Secretary of the Secretariat of the Party's Central Committee, stated, in
1959:

There are persons who are determinedly opposed to placing politics in command, saying that as ideological and political work cannot yield grain or steel,
this task is unable to solve any practical problem. This ideology, which tends
to sever the political leadership of the Party from the practical work of the
masses and political work from operational work, aims actually at weakening
and even repudiating the role of the leadership of the Party. May we ask, are
the tremendous over-all leap forward and the great success of the people's com-
munalization program in rural areas in 1958 not historic miracles achieved by
placing politics in command and by adhering resolutely and completely to the
mass line of the Party?[21]

The Great Leap Forward was an attempt to overcome the baffling
problem of lagging agricultural productivity. During the First Five-Year
Plan, industrialization had gone ahead at amazing speed and with great
success. But the continuation of the program was threatened by the inability of agriculture to pay its bills—to provide food for the rapidly
growing urban sector, to supply an exportable surplus in order to earn
foreign exchange, and to produce the raw materials needed for light industry. The Party had neglected investment in agriculture; instead it had
assumed that collectivization on the Soviet pattern, together with the
alleged economies of large-scale production, would result in increased
output. However, according to official statistics, food grain production
rose from 182.5 million tons in 1956 (the year in which collectivization
was completed) only to 185 million tons in 1957.[22] This was the smallest
increase since the 1953 crop year (in official figures), and it placed the
1957 agricultural growth rate well below the average annual rate of
population growth.

Faced with this situation, the Communists neither abandoned the
goal of industrialization nor redirected a larger share of the country's
investable funds into agriculture. Instead they chose the policy of "walking on two legs," simultaneously advancing the modernized and traditional sectors of the economy. Industry continued to receive the lion's
share of available development funds, while the traditional sector—agriculture and handicrafts—was to increase its output via mass line techniques.

In essence, the Great Leap Forward relied on the mobilized and
organized will of the masses to overcome the enemy of stagnating agricultural productivity. Many persons have speculated on the origins of
the commune idea, and it has been variously ascribed to K'ang Yu-Wei's
utopian thought,[23] Russian experience in the war Communism period,[24]
the spontaneity of the peasants themselves, a generalization throughout

the society of the huge concentrations of labor used in the 1957 water conservation projects, and the personal left-tending Communism of Mao Tse-tung. All or none of these may have contributed to the form the communes took. Another source undoubtedly was the wartime guerrilla bases, in which a multiple-village unit also performed diverse agricultural, manufacturing, militia, and welfare functions.[25]

In harking back to the guerrilla bases, however, the Chinese found something more important than the form of the communes themselves. In their hour of need, with the Soviet model once again tarnished, they turned to the same source of power that had carried them to revolutionary victory—the masses. The mass line had been applied tactically in China from the day the Party came to power; in 1958, it was elevated to a strategy. Concerning the mass line prior to 1949, Liu Shao-ch'i has written:

In the democratic revolutionary period, the Chinese Communist Party . . . went deep into the villages and for more than 22 years led the armed revolutionary struggle, which used the villages to encircle the cities. What the Party adopted was the mass line policy of resolutely relying on the peasants' political consciousness and organized strength, mobilizing the peasants to save themselves.[26]

In 1958, the Party did the same thing, this time for the sake of economic development. Its cadres exhorted, enticed, and drove the rural members of some 740,000 agricultural producers' cooperatives into approximately 24,000 people's communes of an average size of 5,000 households each. A movement that originally was to take five or six years was completed in about six weeks. Amid a blaze of catechismic propaganda slogans—such as the "three red flags" (the general line of socialist construction, the Great Leap Forward, and the people's communes); "three bitter years of struggle"; "overtake Great Britain"; "close cropping –deep plowing"; "red and expert"; and "politics in command"—the peasantry allegedly "marched into battle" against nature, determined to overcome her.[27]

Mao's revolutionary strategy and the mass line on which it is based had been battle-tested and proved sound. If the Party were to use them successfully in analogous situations, however, it could not violate the inner logic of the mass line. In other words, mobilization was not something that the Party alone could supply. Whereas the Japanese invasion of 1937 had genuinely mobilized the population, in 1958 the Party cadres themselves were in position much like that of the Japanese invaders. In the fall and winter of 1958 to 1959, the Party discovered that organization without mobilization does not work. If the communes did not provoke open hostility (which they certainly did in some areas), at the very least they provoked a slow-down. The mess-hall Communism of the early months guaranteed food and lodging to the entire rural population regardless of how hard or how little a person worked. The consequent destruction of all incentives resulted in less production, although this fact was at first disguised by the natural bumper harvest of 1958. When the weather turned unfavorable, the weaknesses of the communes were exposed in their most glaring light—incipient starvation.

The Party has consistently blamed the food shortages of 1959 to 1962 on the worst natural disasters in a hundred years and, more recently, on the withdrawal by Russia of technical assistance. Today we know, from an unimpeachable source, that the people themselves blamed the communes. The *Bulletin of Activities* of the People's Liberation Army General Political Department, a secret Army periodical made available by the U.S. State Department to scholars in the West, documents the extent of popular dissatisfaction during the crisis period.[28] On January 1, 1961, General Hsiao Hua, Director of the PLA's General Cadres Department, told a conference of political commissars:

Because of this year's great disasters in agriculture, difficulties exist in food supply. . . . Our troops consist of peasants and workers wearing uniforms. When certain localities are troubled by agricultural crises, it is bound to be reflected among the troops. Because of these economic difficulties, political problems have greatly increased in the military units.[29]

He and other military leaders stated that "rebellious elements" existed in the Army, and he acknowledged that "destructive activities by counter-revolutionaries" in the countryside were affecting the morale of the Army's rank and file.

After an inspection trip in Honan and Shantung during late 1960, Wang Tung-hsing, a Party member and a Vice-Governor of Kiangsi province, reported that some soldiers were skeptical about the three red flags. Several men told him that, "because Mao Tse-tung is in Peking, he does not know the realities of peasant life. That is why he sends food to the cities." Another soldier thought that the distribution of food was unfair and that the Party was giving priority to industrial workers.[30] The *Bulletin of Activities* contains extensive reports on mail censorship by Army censors. One company censor found that 79.8 per cent of all the letters received by soldiers in his company contained unfavorable and discouraging news of the food crisis at home.[31] Soldiers given home leave returned to their units depressed, and more ideological problems existed among those soldiers who had been visited at the Army camp by their families.[32] General Lo Jui-ch'ing, Chief of the General Staff between 1959 and 1966, arrived in Kunming on January 20, 1961, to make a personal investigation of the situation. After inspecting Army units in Kunming, Chengtu, Chungking, and Wuhan, he reported alarming instances of murder, pilfering, and suicide, the presence of "destructive elements," weakness in the study of Mao's works, and wrong or obscure attitudes toward the three red flags.[33]

The General Political Department had no trouble in locating the source of these difficulties. Lo Jui-ch'ing found that the worst conditions existed in units composed predominantly of ex-peasants and that the communes were the specific object of the peasant-soldiers' resentment:

When questioned, the soldiers gladly talked about industrial development, land reform, and the cooperatives. However, they avoided discussing the people's communes or agricultural development. Evidently the Party's directives concerning the people's communes have not been well disseminated.[34]

Four months later, after an inspection trip in the Nanking area, General Hsiao reported that although the General Political Department had instituted an extensive campaign of indoctrination, lack of confidence in the people's communes still persisted.[35]

The Party responded to this situation by dispersing all potentially rebellious units and by launching a renewed propaganda drive in order to educate wavering soldiers. During 1960 and 1961, the Army undertook the "2-remembrances and 3-inspections" movement (i.e., *liang-i san-ch'a*), the "four-good company" movement (i.e., *ssu-hao chung-tui*), and the "five-good soldiers" movement (i.e., *wu-hao chan-shih*). The two remembrances were of class difficulties and of national difficulties; the three things to inspect were one's viewpoint, one's fighting spirit, and one's work. The four-good company movement consisted of good political ideology, good military training, good "three-eight style," and good personal discipline. The five-good soldiers movement consisted of good political thought, good productive labor, good results of study, good military and political activities, and good organization and discipline.[36]

However, the Party could not dissipate the hostility of the peasants themselves by relying solely on propaganda and indoctrination. Faced with imminent disaster for its program, and possibly for its own authority, the Party retreated. It began progressively to dismantle the communes and to turn its undivided attention to the agricultural problems that the communes had failed to solve.

The reform of the communes and the development of the succeeding agriculture-as-foundation policy took three years. The transition began at the Eighth Plenum of the Eighth CCP Central Committee in August 1959, and it ended with the formal elaboration of new economic guidelines at the Party's Tenth Plenum in September 1962. During this period, extensive and fundamental changes were made—changes that were and still are loaded with theoretical implications. Basically, the reforms can be summarized under three general categories: production team autonomy, the reopening of the cadre-peasant dialogue, and the policy that "agriculture is the foundation of the economy while industry is the guide" (*i nung-yeh wei chi-ch'u i kung-yeh wei chu-tao*).

The average size of a commune is 4,756 households, whereas the average size of a production team is 20 to 40 households. Prior to mid-1959, responsibility for agricultural production was vested in the commune administrative committee and its numerous departments and sub-committees. The commune administrative committee compensated the members of the commune for their labor in accordance with two systems of payment: fixed monthly wages of six or eight different grades; and payment in kind, in the form of free meals, housing, and so forth. These forms of remuneration and labor organization lacked incentives, since the various actual work groups simply followed the orders of the commune management committee. Neither the soundness of these orders, nor the industry of the commune members, nor the speed with which tasks were accomplished could affect the members' wages or payments in kind.

As a result of peasant opposition, Communist Party doubts, and the food crisis of 1960, the Party decentralized, by stages, the original form of commune organization. In August, 1959, at the Eighth Plenum of the Central Committee, the Party instituted the so-called "three-level" organizational pattern for communes; and it specified that ownership of land rested at the brigade level. The brigade is an intermediate level of organization between the commune and the production team. It corresponds in size to the old higher agricultural producers' cooperative (i.e., 100 to 200 households), just as the production team of 20 to 40 households corresponds to an earlier form of collectivization, the lower agricultural producers' cooperative.

The Eighth Plenum resolution declared that "the right of ownership at the level of the production brigade is basic, and the right of ownership at the commune level is partial."[37] What this statement meant, in practical terms, was that the brigade became the basic accounting unit and the brigade cadres became the basic decision-making group. The brigade henceforth determined its own crop arrangements, targets, and costs; and the cadres of the commune government could not interfere with brigade decisions. The commune became, in effect, a purchasing and supplying agent for the brigades under its jurisdiction.

The purpose of this reform was to reintroduce differential rewards for well-organized, hard-working brigades and to penalize less competently managed units. Shortly after the devolution of authority to the brigades, the Party also changed the form of labor compensation. It introduced the system of "three guarantees and one reward" (*san-pao i-chiang*).[38] Under this system, the brigade and the commune concluded an agreement specifying the brigade's output, costs, and manpower requirements for a specific production period. If the brigade exceeded its guaranteed output, it was paid a reward; if it fell short of its guaranteed output, it had to pay a penalty. In effect, poorly administered brigades paid well-run units in recognition of their accomplishments.

Beginning in the autumn of 1960, the Party further decentralized the communes by lowering the level of decision making to that of the production team. On January 1, 1962, the *People's Daily* officially announced that the production team was the basic unit of economic accounting within the three-level ownership system. The team, which corresponds to a village or a part of a village, is much closer to the pre-Communist form of agricultural management than either the brigade or the commune. Two reasons for lowering the basic accounting unit to the level of from 20 to 40 households were the need to recapture the knowledge and experience of older peasants and the desire to bring the three-guarantees-and-one-reward incentive system closer to the actual agricultural producers. Numerous reports indicate that the brigade cadres often ignored the *expertise* of experienced farmers when issuing orders to teams under their control and that production suffered as a consequence. Today a production team concludes contracts for agricultural deliveries with the commune via the brigade. If it exceeds its guarantees, it is rewarded accordingly; if it falls below, the members of the team must pay a penalty. The livelihood of production team members depends upon their contracts, their ability to produce a surplus, and the productive activities they engage in as a sideline.

There were several other features to agricultural reform. For example, private plots of land were restored to commune members; rural fairs, or markets for the sale of privately produced goods, were once again permitted; and huge numbers of ex-peasants who had gravitated to the cities were ordered to return to the countryside. Undoubtedly many of these policies are temporary. Even the granting of economic autonomy to a group as small as the production team was a pragmatic response to the agricultural crisis. Team independence cannot be reguarded as a permanent feature of Chinese economic organization:

The system of collective ownership at three levels with the production team as the foundation conforms to the present level of the peasants' consciousness and will tend to raise it. The system is the best school for conducting socialist education among the peasants, and it will remain for a fairly long time.[39]

The restoration of local control and rewards for hard, creative work helped to increase production in 1962 and 1963. Natural calamities had damaged crops in 1959, 1960, and 1961. Still, the rise in food grain output during 1964 and 1965, to the level of 1957, cannot be explained solely by changes in the weather.[40] The removal of the counterproductive features of the early communes and the encouragement of team initiative halted China's so-called descending economic spiral. One of the most intriguing questions concerning the reforms is why team-level production should be greater than brigade-level production. The three-guarantees-and-one-reward incentive system, plus the greatly expanded size of the private sector, are certainly prime causes; however, Western scholars suspect that the success of the production team may rest in part on old village and clan loyalties. The teams happen to approximate the size of a small village or part of a village.[41]

POST-CRISIS LEADERSHIP PROBLEMS

Despite China's recent recovery of economic viability, there is considerable evidence that the peasants experienced a major loss of faith in the Party's ability to lead. During the crisis period the Communist press reported that peasants were resurrecting geomancy and that rural secret societies were reappearing.[42] These items suggest that the Chinese peasantry, faced with starvation as a result of following the Party's leadership, reverted to traditional methods and forms of organization. More serious for the Party was the damage inflicted on the mass line. The cadres, instead of operating from the masses and to the masses, simply herded the people into communes regardless of popular opinion. In its retreat from the communes, the Party blamed the cadres, taking the greatest precaution to avoid criticizing either the top leadership or the formal policies. Nevertheless, the cadres are the Party's representatives at the level of actual contact with the people, and the Party cannot discredit them for long without weakening its own ability to rule.

Leadership of the Chinese command economy has always rested on a small body (that is, small in relation to the population) of dedicated supervisors, foremen, team leaders, and functionaries known collectively in China as cadres, or *kan-pu*. Estimates of the number of cadres vary greatly, but the probable figure is around 20 million, a few million more than the membership of the Communist Party.[43] These men and women may or may not be Party members, but if they are not they have usually demonstrated their progressive political inclinations as Communist Youth League members, in school, or as Army veterans. Speaking of the size of the Communist Party itself, Liu Shao-ch'i noted, on July 1, 1961, the fortieth anniversary of its founding, that it then had approximately 17 million members. Of these, 80 percent had joined after 1949, and 70 percent had joined during the First Five-Year Plan, from 1953 to 1957. In other words, only about 20 percent of the Communist elite in China can be considered hardened revolutionaries. An absolute shortage of cadres has persisted since the establishment of the regime, and many of the present 20 million cadres are deficient in ability by the Communists' own standards.[44]

Although the cadres are technically nothing more than the sergeants of the Party, the minor functionaries who carry out orders as best they understand them, it is clear that they were not entirely blameless in the failure of the communes. They were the men who, in the autumn of 1958, carried the Party's propaganda about the "entrance into Communism" so far as to confiscate even the bedding and the cooking utensils of the peasantry. They were the men who stubbornly pursued the policies of close planting and deep plowing without consulting old peasants who had farmed the same land for decades. Needless to say, they were following orders; but on the basis of recently published reports it appears as if the cadres were indeed tending to become a bureaucratic stratum or a new class. It is this tendency—the genuine divorce of the cadres from the masses—that Party policies after the Great Leap Forward were aimed at eradicating.

Between 1962 and 1966, the Party undertook a series of major campaigns, known collectively as the Socialist Education Campaign, to try to rehabilitate the cadres' reputation with the peasants and to indoctrinate the mass of the population in the fundamental wisdom of Mao Tse-tung's policies. One device for enhancing the cadres' effectiveness was to get them out of commune and brigade offices and into the fields. During July 1963, the *People's Daily* devoted most of its editorials to cadre labor, and a whole double issue of *Red Flag*[45] was given over to the subject. One article complained that:

. . . some of the hsien [i.e., county] and commune cadres, particularly the leading cadres, are always busy convening and attending meetings, listening to reports, preparing charts, and reading documents at their offices the whole year around. They are unable to mix with the broad masses, to conduct investigations, and to give personal guidance in work.[46]

According to the Party, the cadres must perform manual labor because "participation by the cadres, particularly at basic levels . . . shows the people that Party cadres are ordinary laboring people, not magistrates sitting above them."[47]

The Party is certain that part of the problem lies in the tendency of cadres to become "big shots." "Some brigade and production team cadres, and even some older Party members and cadres, say to themselves, 'We are now cadres. If we ever again take part in physical labor together with commune members, it will not be in keeping with our status.' "[48] The Party's answer to these pretensions is work in the fields, often unpleasant or demeaning work, so that the cadres may set an example for the people. Manure collection, for instance, has occupied a prominent place in the Communist press' discussions of cadre labor: "Have we not heard many basic level workers say, 'How can I complain

when the secretary of the hsien Party committee also carries manure?' "[49]
A former middle-school student, who in 1961 had returned (or been
sent) to the Nankuo commune in Szechwan province, complained to the
editor of *China Youth News* that he had been ridiculed by his production team for collecting manure. To his question, "Is manure collection
by a young intellectual 'retrogressive'?" the editor replied:

Your problem illustrates the fact that for several thousand years physical labor
was despised by the exploiting class and that their old viewpoint, according
to which scholars could not cultivate fields, is still not completely eradicated.
Now scholars go to the rural areas to cultivate fields. Their purpose is to alter
the people's way of thinking and to change their customs.[50]

A more authoritative reason for the cadre labor movement was
given in the *People's Daily*:

It is a revolution in leadership style and working methods, aimed at revising
the bureaucratic practices left behind by organs of the old society. It is a
revolution in the bureaucracy aimed at preventing and overcoming the erosive
effects of bureaucracy and safeguarding the purity of our Party and state
organs.[51]

The virulence of this campaign suggests that the Party's surrender
to localism during the food crisis was only temporary. As the economy
began to respond to team autonomy and clear-cut incentives, the Party
tried to recapture control of it, although without curtailing economic
decision making at the team level. Vigorous efforts were undertaken to
purge cadres who had become corrupt in the relatively less rigorous
post-Leap period; the most important of these efforts was the so-called
"four cleanups" (*ssu-ch'ing*) campaign of 1965. However, the Party did
not have its heart in it—or, at least, so the leader of the regime,
Mao Tse-tung, was to conclude. The Party, it seems, tried to overcome
its various, post-Leap leadership deficiencies, but because of vested interests and the increased bureaucratization that had accompanied 17
years of incumbency in China, Party members appeared to talk more
about reforming than to take actions that might work to their disad-
vantage.

By 1965, a considerable gap had appeared between the rhetoric of
the Party press and the practice of the Party in running the country. On
the one hand, the Party spoke in ever more vivid, Maoist terms of mass-
line activities, such as those allegedly employed in the model production
brigade at Tachai. On the other hand, the Party continued to rely in practice on the incentive-based economic policies that it had introduced following the failure of the Great Leap Forward. This discrepancy between

theory and practice set the stage for Mao Tse-tung's purge of the Party itself—that is, the Great Proletarian Cultural Revolution of 1965–1969.

THE SPLIT IN THE SUPREME LEADERSHIP

There are two key political institutions in any Communist government: the leader and the Communist Party. Tensions between the two are inevitable simply because of the bureaucratic characteristics of the Party. Like bureaucrats everywhere, Party leaders develop an interest in their own ruling positions and policies as they consolidate the structure of the bureaucracy over time. In Communist regimes bureaucratic tendencies are heightened by the Party's political monopoly; since it is by definition infallible, it cannot be criticized or supplanted by any non-Party political group. Bureaucratization can also have grave consequences for Communist countries because, in the event of unsuccessful policies, there is no "loyal opposition" to come in and "sweep the rascals out." Somehow a scapegoat must be found.[52]

In China, tensions between the Party and the leader have been building up for the past decade, and at least three issues have developed that are directly relevant to the so-called Great Cultural Revolution. First, Mao believes that Communism in the Soviet Union has genuinely degenerated into neobourgeois capitalism and that this Soviet "modern revisionism" is the root cause of the Soviet Union's policy of "peaceful coexistence" with the United States, including policies such as the partial Nuclear Test-Ban Treaty of 1963 and the proposed Nuclear Nonproliferation Treaty, which the Chinese Communists see as freezing the global *status quo* and working against China's national interests. China accuses the Soviet Union of using nuclear weapons as an excuse for its revisionism and its policy of *détente* with the United States; it argues that the Soviet leaders do not fear nuclear war so much as they have acquired a growing community of interests with the United States as satisfied, conservative powers.

Second, Maoists fear the growth of modern revisionism in China. This fear is fed by two specific problems. For one thing, the Maoists have remained committed to the fundamentally idealist strategy of the Great Leap Forward of 1958 and 1959, and they are appalled by the alacrity with which the population welcomed the reforms following the failure of the Great Leap *and* by the degree to which members of the Communist Party itself support these reforms as a more rational strategy of economic development than Mao's. For another, the youth of China, being innocent of the great guerrilla struggles of the revolutionary period, is effete, and likely to turn China toward revisionism after the old guard has passed away. In order to prevent this from happening, Mao has launched campaigns to develop "revolutionary heirs," criticized the

Communist Youth League, turned increasingly to Lin Piao's reformed People's Liberation Army for new Party recruits, and—most spectacularly—created the Red Guards and used them in such a way that they will gain concrete experience and the "steeling" of revolution.

A third aspect of Maoism which is related to the Great Cultural Revolution is the forward policy that China pursues against the United States and its allies and that it advocates as the proper policy for all Communist Parties and all the "progressive peoples" of the world. This policy is, of course, the sponsorship and endorsement of "wars of national liberation," and it was given its fullest elaboration in Lin Piao's *Long Live the Victory of People's War* of September 1965. According to the Chinese Communists themselves, this policy is being tested in Vietnam, and the fact that China sees the war in this ideological light is confirmed by the failure of the Sino-Soviet dispute to be patched up in order to present a united front vis-à-vis the United States. China's priorities in the Vietnam conflict appear to be: first, to oppose Soviet revisionism; second, to keep the war going as an irritant to Soviet-United States relations; and only third, to achieve the complete domination of Vietnam under Ho Chi Minh.[53]

These three immediately salient aspects of Maoism find intellectual reinforcement and authority in more abstract theories of Mao, such as the theory of contradictions, but what is more important for understanding the contemporary struggle in China is that these three ideological orientations all dictate concrete policies—opposition to the U.S.S.R., the domestic purge, and the lack of change in foreign policy toward the Third World despite major setbacks since mid-1965—and that they are all three interrelated. This interrelationship is important because it helps us to understand the launching of the purge in late 1965 and the subsequent struggle against the Communist Party itself.

During late 1965, Communist China's leadership was confronted with the need to make some basic decisions on many fronts: it had to consider what to do in light of the failure of its Afro-Asian policy the previous summer at Algiers; it had to decide whether its domestic Third Five-Year Plan (launched January 1, 1966) was to return to the Maoist strategy of the Great Leap Forward or perpetuate the agriculture-first-plus-material-incentives policy that came in to repair the damage done by the Great Leap Forward; and—most critically—it had to decide whether or not to turn to the Soviet Union for protection in case the Vietnam war spilled over into China. Some of Mao's ministers advocated changes in each of these areas, generally in a more pragmatic direction, and this precipitated Mao's decision—as soon as he realized that he was not in immediate danger of being involved in an international war—to purge and purify the Party.

The crux of the problem is this: Mao cannot change his policy in any one area, say relations with the Soviet Union, without damaging the Maoist ideological explanation for his policies in all other areas. To come to terms with the arch-revisionist Soviet leadership would at the same time destroy the rationale of domestic Great-Leap-Forward-type policies as well as his contention that waging wars of national liberation is a more "correct" Communist policy than peaceful coexistence. Moreover, and equally serious, the meeting of Party leaders that took place in Peking in September 1965 revealed to Mao that some of his own closest associates not only did not have much faith in Maoism when the going got rough but held positions similar to the small group of Party intellectuals who had been sniping at his theories in a series of transparently political plays and novels since 1961 and 1962. Mao therefore gathered a few allies around him, prepared his strategy, and the following year launched a vigorous attack on his backsliding Party comrades. To the surprise of the entire world and possibly to Mao Tse-tung himself, his critics within the highest echelons of the Communist Party fought back. Ever since the agricultural and industrial disasters that followed Mao's Great Leap Forward of 1958 and 1959, the leaders of the Party have been trying to kick Mao upstairs. Without destroying Mao's image as the Father and great revolutionary leader of his country, they would like to oust him as chief policy maker.

By way of summarizing the main issues contested in China's domestic upheaval, it may be useful to stand back from day-to-day events and attempt to make the case both for and against the central figure in the Great Cultural Revolution—Chairman Mao Tse-tung himself—in terms other than the ideological rhetoric used in Communist China. The case for Mao Tse-tung would run something like this. After 18 years of leadership in China, the Communist Party has become bureaucratized. It constitutes something of a Chinese equivalent to Milovan Djilas' "new class," a privileged stratum in society holding office for reasons connected more with being Party members than with ability. In a sense, Mao is comparing his own Party with that of his recent enemy, the Kuomintang of the 1940's, and is finding too many disturbing similarities: men holding sinecures, a continuously burgeoning bureaucracy, universities that are more havens for the privileged than training grounds for national leadership, and burgeoning corruption and venality in many walks of life. Mao appears to have said to himself that, even if it is the last thing he does, he will not let his own national revolutionary party go the way of his predecessor.

Another argument for Mao's policies is the difficulty he faces in bringing younger men into positions of leadership. As the post-1949 generation comes óf age, he must find a way of ousting many famous old guerrilla veterans who are clogging the top posts simply because of their illustrious pasts. Such a view might help explain the attacks on Chu

Teh and Ho Lung, to whose revolutionary exploits Mao himself owes so much, and against whom the Maoist charges must appear patently ridiculous to anyone but post-World War II youths, who did not participate in the revolution. If such a motive is operative, then it is not implausible to see the Chinese purges as serving a comparable function to the Stalinist purges of the late 1930's, although it must be said that Mao Tse-tung has been less ruthless in his methods up to the present time. A structural weakness of all revolutionary mobilization regimes is their inability to legitimatize routine processes of governmental recruitment and retirement.

To make the case against Mao Tse-tung, the outside observer would tend to stress first that Mao is himself China's chief obstacle to upward mobility. He is the great leader of the Chinese revolution, a man driven for 40 years by a utopian vision of a Chinese Communist society, and the father of new China, but he may have outlived his usefulness. To paraphrase Hannah Arendt, the men who make successful revolutions are seldom the best qualified to consolidate the gains of such revolutions.

Arguing against Mao's policies, one would say that the Communist Party, bureaucratized or not, is the stable, legitimate, functioning elite of contemporary China. It needs to devote its full attention to many crucially important problems, such as the Third Five-Year Plan; yet it is being continually distracted and driven off on tangents because of the unrealistic, utopian visions of a very old, possibly senile, possibly megalomanic, revolutionary leader whose very name commands tremendous power. The Party has not wanted to cross Mao Tse-tung, but it has reluctantly come to the conclusion, on the basis of practical experience, that his ideas are bad ones and that it had to fight back when Mao finally accused it of the truth: supporting him in public while doing something else in practice.

Both sides in the Cultural Revolution in China have considerable evidence to support their positions, but their open and violent conflict is producing unintended consequences that may lead to an entirely new type of Communist regime on the Chinese mainland. Even should Mao be able to oust his opponents in the Party, it seems unlikely that he can ever bring the Army—his main ally in his struggle with the Party—back under his own, or a rebuilt Party's, control. A national military regime may be emerging in China which will have more similarities to the governments of Indonesia, Burma, Pakistan, Nigeria, Ghana, and South Vietnam than to the Communist regimes of Eastern Europe and Russia. Nowhere in China has Mao been able to defeat his Party critics except by means of direct military force. The big question at the present time, therefore, is who controls the two and a half million members of the People's Liberation Army.

Mao's earliest-known pronouncement on military affairs stressed the need to keep the Army subordinate to Communist Party direction. He recognized that military leaders, regardless of their past records of loyalty and service, may easily develop interests that are contrary to those of a civilian political elite. In the course of his recent efforts to purge the Party, however, Mao allied himself with Defense Minister Lin Piao in order to make use of the Army. Mao thought that Lin Piao's reform of the Army—begun in 1959 when Lin became Minister of Defense—had made it a perfectly loyal instrument for executing Mao's own policies. In this he was mistaken.

Ever since January 1967, when Mao ordered the Army to take over his increasingly anarchic purge, the Army has behaved with a mind—or minds—of its own. China is divided into 13 military regions, and the commanders of the garrisons in these regions have been making decisions to support or not to support Mao Tse-tung independently of orders from Peking. Some Army leaders have decided to support him because it served their own interests to do so. In several cities, Army leaders have simply displaced both the Party and the Maoists and put themselves in charge. There has also been a good deal of bargaining between Peking and the military area chiefs over the nature and extent of the Army's actions. Clearly, such bargaining has strengthened the independence and political power of the military.

As of the beginning of 1968, the situation in China remained fluid and precarious, and future developments might go in any one of several directions. On December 26, 1967, Mao Tse-tung was 74 years old. Loyalty to him among the various middle-echelon Party and Army leaders has become increasingly personal, rather than doctrinal or programmatic. It is doubtful whether Mao's successor can command an allegiance anywhere approaching the adulation devoted to Mao himself, and this problem opens up the frightening prospect of a return to regionalism in China—that is, something similar to the "warlordism" that followed the death in 1916 of an earlier strongman who also commanded vast personal loyalty, President Yuan Shih-k'ai.

It is ironic that Mao Tse-tung, as he nears the end of his life, has created a succession problem in China. All Communist regimes suffer from difficulties in transferring leadership, for the simple reason that they refuse to recognize that succession is a problem. According to Party statutes, the leader of the Party is nothing more than the chairman of the Central Committee, elected by that Committee, and in the event that the incumbent dies the Central Committee need only elect a replacement. But it has never worked that way since the time of Lenin. The Party Chairman is, in dynamic Communist regimes, a virtual dictator; and the passing of a dictator always elicits a struggle among contenders for his post.

During the 1950's, it appeared as though Mao was showing commend-

able realism in recognizing this fact of life, since he had already designated his successor, President Liu Shao-ch'i. However, Liu is currently
under attack—anathematized by the Maoists as "China's Khrushchev"
—and the entire problem of succession has been reopened. Mao's present heir apparent is the Army chief, Lin Piao, but Lin has not so far
displayed the kind of political acumen that would lead an observer of
Chinese society to believe that he could fill Mao's shoes for long. Lin
is also in poor health.

The most important outcome of the purge at the present time is a per-
vasive lack of authority in the hands of any of the various hierarchies—
Party, government, or Army. The primary source of authority in China
is the thought of Mao Tse-tung—an abstract, hortatory body of maxims
that have been taught to the entire population through the publication of
millions of copies of the "little red book," *Quotations from Chairman
Mao Tse-tung*. Everyone in China has been exhorted to learn Mao's
thoughts and to use them in guiding one's own behavior *and* in scrutiniz-
ing the behavior of one's immediate superiors. The result is that mass
study of Maoism has elicited an anarchic plethora of interpretations of
what Mao really means and who is a good, loyal follower of the "Great
Helmsman." In order to get the country back to work, some authority
must be able to declare, unequivocally, that for this or that particular
task, Maoism requires this or that concrete action. Unfortunately for the
regime, there is no authority sufficiently strong to take such leadership—e.g., to say that in the present circumstances loyalty to Chairman
Mao requires that Red Guards go back to school.

The reputation of the Communist Party appears to have been permanently damaged; the governmental bureaucracy has been under continuous attack and remains working only because of the patronage and
protection of Premier Chou En-lai; and the Maoist forces themselves,
the Red Guards and so-called revolutionary rebels, continue to argue with
each other over precisely what Mao does mean and over the political
advantages of accepting one interpretation over another. The only
group in China that possesses the authority to take leadership in terms
of unblemished loyalty to Mao, and the power to take leadership, in
terms of a stable organizational structure, is the Army. The future of
the Chinese Revolution may therefore rest on the cohesion and capabilities of the political leaders of the People's Liberation Army.

THE SINO-SOVIET DISPUTE

The last great stronghold of the mass line is the People's Liberation
Army. Chinese Communist military strategy remains wedded to the belief that the support of the masses is the single most important element
in offense or defense, and the Chinese Army is trained, organized, and

equipped as if it were a giant guerrilla force. By official pronouncement, the atomic bomb is a paper tiger or, as the Army recently put it, "the spiritual A-bomb is more important than the material one."[54] The Chinese Communists do not ignore military weapons, but they believe that the technical qualities of an army are secondary to its morale, determination, and popular backing. In short, they conceive of the military arts as an adjunct to the political arts, and they explicitly reject what they call "narrow military professionalism." The Minister of Defense, Lin Piao, laid down official Chinese military policy shortly after he replaced the discredited professional, P'eng Te-huai:

At the present stage of building a modernized army, when the technical equipment of our army is being constantly improved and the mastery of technique and the raising of the technical level of our army have become more important than ever before, is the human factor still of decisive significance? Some comrades take the view that modern warfare differs from warfare in the past, that since weapons and equipment available to our army in the past were inferior we had to emphasize dependence on man, on his bravery and wisdom, in order to win victories. They say that modern warfare is a war of technique, of steel and machinery, and that in the face of these things, man's role has to be relegated to a secondary place. . . . Contrary to these people, we believe that while equipment and technique are important, the human factor is even more so.[55]

Why is it that the Chinese Communists cling so tenaciously to the mass line in their theory of military organization? As we have seen earlier, part of the answer lies in the influence of their revolutionary heritage. The Chinese Communists do not distinguish between a military and a political sphere, between war and revolution, because in their own revolutionary experience both categories were equated. They have powerful reasons for believing that these distinctions are false, and within and outside of the Communist bloc they advocate that revolutionary wars on the Chinese model are the true path to Communism. However, this is only half the reason for the persistence of the mass line in military affairs.

Although the Chinese Communist theory of revolution is one of the major causes of the Sino-Soviet dispute, the dispute itself perpetuates the mass line in the Army because China no longer has access to foreign military equipment. In advocating the mass line, the military is in part making a virtue out of a necessity. In July 1960, the Soviet Union withdrew some 1,300 experts from China, crippling such enterprises as the Ch'angch'un automobile factory. Coinciding with the failure of the Great Leap Forward, the dispute halted China's industrial growth. Since China is a predominantly agricultural country, its isolation from the Soviet Union does not necessarily spell its economic doom; however, Chinese inability to acquire modern weapons and spare parts from the

Soviet Union has had a great impact on the People's Liberation Army. The Army's air force (chiefly MiG-17 fighter-interceptors and Il-28, Tu-2, and Tu-4 bombers) is obsolete, and its ground-force equipment, virtually all of Russian specification, is greatly in need of replenishment. Guns and explosives, previously purchased from Czechoslovakia, are today unavailable.[56] Hence the chief asset of the PLA is its two and a half million men, and the continuing strength of the mass line is explained partly by the fact that China has no other choice, at least until its own munitions industry reaches a considerably more advanced level.

In 1959, several of China's high-ranking military leaders came to this same conclusion, and they argued against the dispute with Russia precisely because it would weaken China's defenses. In the summer of 1959, Marshal P'eng Te-huai clashed severely with Mao Tse-tung over a broad range of military and political issues; it was the most serious dispute among the old revolutionary leaders since 1949 and prior to the Cultural Revolution. P'eng first joined Mao in 1928, and he had served ten years as the first Minister of Defense when he was forced to resign. The People's Liberation Army accused P'eng and his chief of staff, Huang K'o-ch'eng, who was ousted at the same time, of advancing military principles at variance with Mao's ideology (the mass line strategy).[57] It seems certain, however, that military ideology was only one aspect of the disagreement between P'eng and the Maoist faction.

At the center of their dispute was the Sino-Soviet estrangement and China's decision to proceed with its development independent of the Soviet Union. P'eng and Huang appear to have favored maintaining the alliance with Russia at all costs, and they may even have entered into a Kremlin-inspired conspiracy to overturn the Chinese Political Bureau. Mao and his associates successfully turned aside P'eng's challenge, and the simmering dispute with Russia developed into the open antagonism of 1963 and after. In early 1963, Foreign Minister Ch'en Yi told a visiting Japanese delegation:

We have thought about the ideological dispute with Russia for three years. We knew that we would be attacked for our stand and that some would criticize us as being adventurous. We even ran the risk of nuclear assault by American imperialism. However, we have to defend Marxism-Leninism. We must preserve the interests of the people of the entire world even though the Chinese people have to make temporary sacrifices. We determined to endure self-sacrifice for the sake of internationalism.[58]

The Chinese Communists have cited four specific causes for the schism. The first was the failure of Russia to support China against India. In February 1963, the Chinese wrote:

How did these differences come to be exposed before the enemy? Thorez and other comrades allege that the differences were brought into the open with the Chinese Communist Party's publication of the pamphlet *Long Live Leninism!* in all languages in the summer of 1960. The truth is that the internal differences among the fraternal parties were first brought into the open not in the summer of 1960, but on the eve of the Camp David talks in September 1959—on September 9, 1959, to be exact. On that day a socialist country, turning a deaf ear to China's repeated explanations of the true situation and to China's advice, hastily issued a statement on a Sino-Indian border incident through its official news agency. Making no distinction between right and wrong, the statement expressed "regret" over the border clash and in reality condemned China's correct stand. . . . Here is the first instance in history in which a socialist country, instead of condemning the armed provocations of the reactionaries of a capitalist country, condemned another fraternal socialist country when it was confronted with such armed provocation.[59]

Needless to say, Russian neutrality in the Sino-Indian border war of 1962 poured more gasoline on this particular fire.

A second reason for the dispute was Russia's refusal to support China's atomic weapons program without at the same time controlling it. On September 6, 1963, the *People's Daily* wrote:

In 1958 [the time of the Quemoy crisis] the leadership of the CPSU [Communist Party of the Soviet Union] put forward unreasonable demands to bring China under Soviet military control. These unreasonable demands were rightly and firmly rejected by the Chinese government. Not long afterward, in June 1959, the Soviet government unilaterally tore up the agreement on new technology for national defense concluded between China and the Soviet Union in October 1957, and refused to provide China with a sample of an atomic bomb and technical data concerning its manufacture.[60]

Here, certainly, is one of the major causes of Sino-Russian antagonism. At the same time, it enables us to see in a new light Chinese statements that the atomic bomb is a paper tiger. Atomic weapons were inconsequential to the Chinese partly because they did not have any. During 1963, they adamantly opposed the Russo-British-United States Test-Ban Treaty (they called it the "tripartite pact," recalling an earlier treaty of that name), but they also insisted that they would acquire atomic weapons in the future with or without foreign assistance.[61] In October 1964, China finally revealed how propagandistic its earlier pronouncements on atomic weapons had been. Responding to intelligence disclosures by the United States and Canada, China informed selected foreign powers that it had been developing its own nuclear weapons since at least 1960, and, on October 16, it conducted its first atomic explosion. On June 17, 1967, China carried out its sixth test explosion, of a hydrogen device, confirming once and for all that elements in the regime intended to acquire a strategic nuclear capacity.

The third specific cause of friction mentioned by the Chinese is anti-Chinese subversion undertaken by Russian officials in China proper and in Sinkiang. In 1963, Japanese visitors in China were told about anti-Party activities conducted by Russian consuls in Shanghai and Nanking during 1961, and Sinkiang became the most critical arena of direct state-to-state confrontation:

In April and May, 1962, the leaders of the CPSU used their organs and personnel in Sinkiang, China, to carry out large-scale subversive activities in the Ili region and enticed and coerced several tens of thousands of Chinese citizens into going to the Soviet Union. . . . To this day this incident remains unsettled.[62]

Sinkiang, like the other two causes of the dispute, has no connection with China's avowed mission of preserving the ideological purity of Marxism-Leninism; however, Communist ideology and differences concerning the right to interpret that ideology have contributed to the dispute. In fact, a difference over ideology appears to have been the first concrete source of grievance—the catalyst that led the two partners to see each other first as competitors and then as antagonists. In September 1963, the Chinese Communist Party Central Committee wrote:

The open letter of the Central Committee of the CPSU spreads the notion that the differences in the international Communist movement were started by the three articles which we published in April 1960 under the title of *Long Live Leninism!* This is a big lie. . . . To be specific, it began with the 20th Congress of the CPSU in 1956. . . . The criticism of Stalin at the 20th Congress of the CPSU was wrong both in principle and in method.[63]

The Chinese Communists had not, of course, suffered at Stalin's hands as the Russians and East Europeans had, and they were better able to appreciate Stalin's methods because from 1956 to 1958 their own industrial development appeared to be paralleling the Soviet Union's First Five-Year Plan. Possibly most important, the Chinese Communists resented the ideological crudity of de-Stalinization as undertaken by Khrushchev. The Chinese believed that the "cult of personality" was too shallow an explanation for Stalin's excesses, and they insisted that Stalin's errors be viewed within the over-all distinction between "antagonistic" and "nonantagonistic" contradictions. In their opinion, even if Stalin had been a problem (nonantagonistic) for Soviet society, he had been effective against imperialism (an antagonistic contradiction)—and this should not be forgotten.

The fact that the Sino-Soviet dispute partly concerns Marxist-Leninist ideology poses difficult problems for the detached observer who wants to assess the function of ideology in the independent Communist nations. In my opinion, Communist ideology in China functions as the ideological rationale for its revolutionary national development. Human beings do not undertake revolutionary sacrifices lightly; they require an intellectual expression of the greatness and justness of their actions. To this end, virulent nationalist movements have always found it opportune to incorporate transnational values in order to help motivate their communicants. It should be remarked that, in characterizing the Chinese revolution as "nationalist," we are using nationalism as an analytical concept. "Communism," in this usage, is a descriptive category. Thus there is nothing incompatible between the terms "nationalist" and "Communist" any more than there is between "totalitarian" and "fascist."[64]

Clearly, the Chinese people have worked harder and made greater sacrifices since 1949 than can be comprehended solely in terms of coercive or manipulative goads. Communist ideology provides the intellectual justification for Party direction of the Chinese Revolution, and it underwrites "scientifically" the inevitability of revolutionary success. Maoism bolsters the Chinese in their attempt at rapid economic growth much as the emperor myth did in late Meiji Japan or classical liberalism in the industrializing West.

The ideological form that the Sino-Soviet dispute has taken in certain of its phases has damaged the functional value of Marxism as an integrative myth and a work ethic for both sides. Although Communist ideology functions as a national myth in the independent Communist states, its functioning is impaired if its universal, scientific pretensions become untenable. Maoism may be the concrete application to China of scientific socialism, but the Sino-Soviet dispute—or, for example, the charge made throughout China in 1963 that the Russian Communist Party was then led by a "psalm-singing, incense-burning" modern revisionist— is damaging to scientific socialism. When the Chinese Party tells the masses that the Russians have betrayed Leninism, what do the masses think of the claims for Maoism? Coming at the same time as the failure of the Great Leap Forward and the Great Proletarian Cultural Revolution, the Sino-Soviet dispute cannot have strengthened the Party's claim to infallibility. If de-Stalinization had irreversible effects within the Soviet Union, the Sino-Soviet dispute is producing comparable changes in China and in the worldwide Communist movement.

The Chinese Communist leaders are old; soon a new and unfamiliar directorate will take up the reins. Will those who follow the guerrilla leaders abandon the mass line once and for all? Will the Chinese cultural antipathy to birth control frustrate any and all economic development strategies? Will the Sino-Soviet dispute lead to something more serious than a *détente*? In C. P. Snow's *The Affair*, one of his dons inquires rhetorically over brandy, "How can China avoid becoming the dominant power on earth?" The resolution of this question will come from the Chinese people themselves; we who observe the Chinese Revolution cannot supply it.

NOTES

1. *Jen-min jih-pao* (*People's Daily*) (Peking), February 11, 1963.

2. See John Lewis, *Leadership in Communist China* (Ithaca, N.Y.: Cornell University Press, 1963); and Stuart Schram, *The Political Thought of Mao Tse-tung* (New York: Frederick A. Praeger, Inc., 1963).

3. *Mao Tse-tung hsüan-chi* (*Selected Works of Mao Tse-tung*) (Peking: Jen-min ch'u-pan-she, 1961), I, 131.

4. Mao Tse-tung, *Selected Works* (New York: International Publishers Company, Inc., 1954), III, 16.

5. Mao Tse-tung, *On Guerrilla Warfare*, trans. S. Griffith (New York: Frederick A. Praeger, Inc., 1961), p. 44.

6. Republic of China, Department of National Defense, Intelligence Bureau, *Mao-fei Tse-tung chün-chih ssu-hsiang yen-chiu* (*A Study of Mao Tse-tung's Military Thinking*) (Taipei, December 1960), p. 6.

7. *Chinese Communism and the Rise of Mao* (Cambridge, Mass.: Harvard University Press, 1958), p. 101.

8. *Selected Works of Mao Tse-tung* (Peking: Foreign Languages Press, 1961), IV, 155–56.

9. See Chalmers Johnson, "Lin Piao's Army and Its Role in Chinese Society," *Current Scene* (Hong Kong), IV, Nos. 13 and 14 (July 1 and 15, 1966).

10. Mao Tse-tung, *Selected Works* (New York: International Publishers Company, Inc., 1954), I, 239.

11. *Hsüeh-hsi Mao Tse-tung ssu-hsiang* (*Study the Thought of Mao Tse-tung*) (Hong Kong: San-lien shu-tien, 1961), II, 80.

12. See "Strategic Problems of China's Revolutionary War" (December 1936), in Mao Tse-tung, *Selected Works* (New York ed.), I, 175–253.

13. Vladimir Dedijer, *Tito* (New York: Simon and Schuster, Inc., 1953), p. 322. See the discussion of this point by Robert North, "Two Revolutionary Models: Russian and Chinese," in *Communist Strategies in Asia*, ed. A. Doak Barnett (New York: Frederick A. Praeger, Inc., 1963), pp. 42–43.

14. Speech at Trade Union Conference of Asian and Australasian Countries (New China News Agency, Peking, November 23, 1949).

15. Peking: Foreign Languages Press, 1965. See also Kao Ko, "The Victorious Road of National Liberation War," *Jen-min jih-pao*, June 3, 1963, reprinted in *Peking Review*, No. 46 (November 15, 1963), pp. 6–14; and *Selected Military Writings of Mao Tse-tung* (Peking: Foreign Languages Press, 1963), an English edition of a volume published by the Chinese Communists which brings together all of Mao's works on the subject of people's war.

16. February 27, 1957. Text in Center for International Affairs and the East Asian Research Center, Harvard University, *Communist China: 1955–1959, Policy Documents with Analysis* (Cambridge, Mass.: Harvard University Press, 1962), p. 292.

17. "Chairman Mao Tse-tung's Statement Calling upon the People of the World to Unite to Oppose Racial Discrimination by U.S. Imperialism and Support the American Negroes in Their Struggle against Racial Discrimination," August 8, 1963. Printed in *Peking Review*, No. 33 (August 16, 1963), p. 7.

18. *Jen-min jih-pao*, November 24, 1963, p. 3.

19. "Mō Taku-tō no shisō to senryaku" ("The Ideology and Strategy of Mao Tse-tung"), *Chūō kōron* (*Central Review*) (Tokyo), March, 1963, pp. 124–25. For a similar analysis, see Nomura Kōichi, "Mō Taku-tō shuseki" ("Chairman Mao Tse-tung"), *Chūō kōron*, September, 1963, pp. 55–61.

20. "The Differences between Comrade Togliatti and Us," *Jen-min jih-pao*, December 31, 1962.

21. "The Chinese Communist Party Is the Supreme Commander of the Chinese People in Building Socialism," *Jen-min jih-pao*, September 28, 1959.

22. See *Current Scene* (Hong Kong), II, No. 27 (January 15, 1964), 4.

23. See Wen-shun Chi, "The Ideological Source of the People's Communes in Communist China," *Pacific Coast Philology*, II (April, 1967), pp. 62–78. Also available as Center for Chinese Studies Reprint No. 244 (Berkeley, Calif.: University of California).

24. See Fukushima Masao, *Jinmin kōsha no kenkyū* (*A Study of the People's Communes*) (Tokyo: Ochanomizu shobō, 1960).

25. See Chalmers Johnson, "Chinese Communist Leadership and Mass Response: The Yenan Period and the Socialist Education Campaign Period," in *China in Crisis*, ed. Ping-ti Ho and Tang Tsou (Chicago: University of Chicago Press, 1968), I, 397–431.

26. *The Victory of Marxism-Leninism in China* (Peking: Foreign Languages Press, 1959).

27. "Tui-t'ien hsüan-chan" ("to declare war against heaven"). For this and many other military metaphors used in the Great Leap Forward slogans, see T. A. Hsia, *Metaphor, Myth, Ritual and the People's Commune*, Studies in Chinese Communist Terminology, No. 7 (Berkeley, Calif.: Center for Chinese Studies, University of California, 1961).

28. *Kung-tso t'ung-hsün* (*Bulletin of Activities*), No. 1 (January 1, 1961), through No. 30 (August 26, 1961), except for No. 9 (February). For a translation, see J. Chester Cheng, ed., *The Politics of the Chinese Red Army: A Translation of the Bulletin of Activities* (Stanford, Calif.: The Hoover Institution on War, Revolution, and Peace, 1966).

29. *Kung-tso t'ung-hsün*, No. 1, p. 7.

30. *Ibid.*, pp. 12–13.

31. On censors, see *ibid.*, No. 1, p. 14; No. 7, p. 18.

32. On home leave and visitors, see *ibid.*, No. 1, p. 14; No. 7, p. 18; No. 22, p. 7.

33. *Ibid.*, No. 7, p. 18; No. 11, p. 2.

34. *Ibid.*, No. 11, p. 3.

35. *Ibid.*, No. 22, p. 9.

36. See Chalmers Johnson, "Lin Piao's Army and Its Role in Chinese Society," *Current Scene* (Hong Kong), IV, Nos. 13 and 14 (July 1 and 15, 1966).

37. *Communist China: 1955–1959* (Cambridge, Mass.: Harvard University Press, 1962), p. 537 [Translation slightly altered—Au.]

38. See "Hold Fast to the System of Three Guarantees and One Reward and Strive Constantly to Improve It," *Jen-min jih-pao*, December 29, 1960.

39. Li Chien-heng, "On the Long Duration of the System of Collective Ownership," *Ta Kung Pao* (Peking), July 30, 1962. Translated in U.S. Consulate General, Hong Kong, *Survey of China Mainland Press* (SCMP), No. 2808.

40. See Michael Freeberne, "The Role of Natural Calamities in Communist China," *Current Scene* (Hong Kong), II, No. 25 (December 23, 1963).

41. Cf. John Lewis, "The Leadership Doctrine of the Chinese Communist Party:

The Lesson of the People's Commune," *Asian Survey* (Berkeley, Calif.), III, No. 10 (October 1963), pp. 457–64; and H. F. Schurmann, "Peking's Recognition of Crisis," *Problems of Communism* (Washington, D.C.), X, No. 5 (September-October, 1961), pp. 5–14. On the effects of Communist policies on village social structure, see G. William Skinner, "Marketing and Social Structure in Rural China, Part III," *The Journal of Asian Studies*, XXIV, No. 3 (May, 1965), pp. 363–99.

42. See the discussion on "brotherhood organizations" formed in Shantung, *Kung-jen jih-pao (Worker's Daily)* (Peking), September 4, 1963.

43. *Jen-min jih-pao*, July 4, 1963, p. 2; *Jen-min jih-pao*, August 29, 1963; *Three-Monthly Economic Review* (London), No. 43 (September, 1963), p. 2.

44. See James R. Townsend, "Democratic Management in the Rural Communes," *China Quarterly* (London), No. 16 (October-December, 1963), p. 149.

45. No. 13–14 (July 10, 1963).

46. "Create Favorable Conditions for Rural Party Branch Secretaries to Take Part in Labor," *Jen-min jih-pao*, July 21, 1963. Translated in U.S. Department of Commerce, Office of Technical Services, *Joint Publications Research Service* (JPRS), No. 21, 515.

47. *Hung-ch'i (Red Flag)* (Peking), No. 13–14 (July 10, 1963) (JPRS, No. 21, 795).

48. "Teaching by Words and Deeds," *Jen-min jih-pao*, July 29, 1963 (JPRS, No. 21, 515).

49. *Ibid.*

50. *Chung-kuo ch'ing-nien pao (China Youth News)* (Peking), October 15, 1963, p. 2.

51. *Jen-min jih-pao*, July 21, 1963.

52. See Chalmers Johnson, "China: The Cultural Revolution in Structural Perspective," *Asian Survey* (Berkeley, Calif.), VIII, No. 1 (January, 1968), pp. 1–15.

53. For the origins of the Cultural Revolution, see W. F. Dorrill, *Power, Policy, and Ideology in the Making of China's "Cultural Revolution"* (Santa Monica, Calif.: The RAND Corporation, RM-5731-PR, August, 1968).

54. Quoted in Ralph Powell, *Politico-Military Relationships in Communist China* (Washington, D.C.: U.S. Department of State, External Research Staff, Bureau of Intelligence and Research, October, 1963), p. 19.

55. "March Ahead under the Red Flag of the Party's General Line and Mao Tse-tung's Military Thinking," New China News Agency, September 29, 1959.

56. Economist Intelligence Unit, *Three-Monthly Economic Review* (London), No. 40 (November, 1962), p. 10.

57. Powell, *Politico-Military Relationships*, p. 5.

58. Reported by Kurota Hidetoshi, "Chū-So ronsōka no Chūgoku no hyōjō" ("The Face of China After the Sino-Soviet Dispute"), *Ekonomisuto* (Tokyo), August 6, 1963, pp. 36–39.

59. "Whence the Differences? A Reply to Thorez and Other Comrades," *Jen-min jih-pao*, February 27, 1963 (*Peking Review*, No. 9, March 1, 1963, p. 10).

60. "The Origin and Development of the Differences Between the Leadership of the CPSU and Ourselves," *Jen-min jih-pao*, September 6, 1963 (*Peking Review*, No. 37, September 13, 1963, p. 12).

61. Ch'en Yi's interview with visiting Japanese newsmen, October, 1963. Reported in the *New York Times*, Western ed., October 29, 1963, p. 1.

62. *Peking Review*, No. 37 (September 13, 1963), p. 18.

63. *Ibid.*, p. 7.

64. See Chalmers Johnson, *Peasant Nationalism and Communist Power, The Emergence of Revolutionary China, 1937–1945* (Stanford, Calif.: Stanford University Press, 1962).

SELECTED BIBLIOGRAPHY

Barnett, A. Doak, *Cadres, Bureaucracy, and Political Power in Communist China.* New York: Columbia University Press, 1967.

Berton, Peter, and Eugene Wu, *Contemporary China: A Research Guide.* Stanford, Calif.: The Hoover Institution on War, Revolution, and Peace, 1967.

Eckstein, Alexander, *Communist China's Economic Growth and Foreign Trade.* New York: McGraw-Hill Book Company, 1966.

Gittings, John, *The Role of the Chinese Army.* New York: Oxford University Press, Inc., 1967.

Johnson, Chalmers, *Peasant Nationalism and Communist Power.* Stanford, Calif.: Stanford University Press, 1962.

Mu, Fu-sheng, *The Wilting of the Hundred Flowers: The Chinese Intelligentsia under Mao.* New York: Frederick A. Praeger, Inc., 1962.

Schram, Stuart, *Mao Tse-tung.* New York: Simon and Schuster, Inc., 1967.

Schurmann, H. Franz, *Ideology and Organization in Communist China.* Berkeley: University of California Press, 1966.

Townsend, James R., *Political Participation in Communist China.* Berkeley: University of California Press, 1967.

MONGOLIA

THE FIRST COMMUNIST STATE IN ASIA

M. T. HAGGARD

The Soviet-oriented Communist Party of Mongolia has ruled Mongolia since 1921. The Mongolian Communists today have firm control of the country, having eliminated other power centers—including the Tibetan-Buddhist religious hierarchy—by the early 1940's. Sufficient economic progress has been made in the past 20 years, primarily through large-scale material and technical assistance from the Soviet Union, to make the Mongolians more tolerant of those aspects of socialization which have brought about unwanted changes in the traditional Mongol way of life. The Soviet Army enabled Mongolian Communists to gain control of Mongolia, and the Soviet Union has been the guarantor of the present Mongolian state since its inception. Soviet military assistance was important in putting down a widespread rebellion in Mongolia in 1932 and, in 1939, Soviet troops prevented the Japanese from adding Mongolia to their list of mainland conquests. In 1950, Soviet pressure resulted in Chinese Communist agreement to guarantee the independent status of the Mongolian People's Republic (MPR).

The Party and government structures established in Mongolia were patterned after those in the Soviet Union. In writing their constitutions, the Mongolians have lifted articles, sometimes whole chapters, out of Soviet constitutions, with very little change.

The present head of both the Party and government, Y. Tsedenbal, owes his position to the backing of Moscow, and the MPR under his direction has adhered closely to Soviet policies. Tsedenbal regained the top Party position in 1958, with Khrushchev's backing, and in 1959 purged six members of the Politburo. Even this major shake-up, however, did not ensure Tsedenbal complete control of the upper levels of the Party. Additional purges of Politburo and Central Committee members came in 1962, 1963, and 1964. The extent of the purge became clearer when the new Central Committee was elected by the Fifteenth Party Congress in June 1966: approximately half the members and candidate members elected at the previous Congress (in 1961) were replaced. Since the Fifteenth Congress, there have been relatively few references to internal Party difficulties, an indication that the present ruling group has eliminated its major opponents.

Tsedenbal's major opposition was accused of overstressing Mongolian nationalism at the expense of close U.S.S.R.–MPR ties and of engaging in "anti-Party factional activities." There is no evidence that these men were pro-Chinese; however, the possibility remains that they—or some of them—might have encouraged the Chinese as a means of giving the MPR more leverage in its relationship with the Soviet Union. Nationalism has been used as a rallying point for those Mongolians who dislike certain aspects of either the domestic or foreign policy of the MPR, and it has also been a cloak used by individuals seeking to replace Tsedenbal.

On major issues of dispute between Communist China and the Soviet Union, the MPR has without qualification backed the Soviet Union. However, Soviet policy frequently coincides with the professed goals of the MPR. The peaceful coexistence theme, for example, is in line with what the Mongolians consider to be their own interest. A major aspect of Mongolian foreign policy since the end of World War II has been the desire to expand contacts with all nations, and following Soviet policy is obviously more likely to contribute to the success of this Mongolian goal. The Mongolians have no ax to grind, as do the North Koreans and the North Vietnamese.

A major reason for Mongolia's firm, pro-Soviet alignment is its heavy dependence on Soviet economic assistance. More than three-quarters of all outside assistance for the development of industry and agriculture has come from the U.S.S.R. Total credits and grants extended during the past 20 years amount to well over one billion dollars. In addition, in 1962 the U.S.S.R. obtained membership for the MPR in the Council for Mutual Economic Assistance (CEMA), from which Mongolia has received considerable material and technical assistance.

There is another factor of critical importance: While many Mongolians are not completely happy with the present arrangement with the Soviet Union, they do not have the same antipathy toward the Russians as they have for the Chinese. The memories of centuries of Chinese domination are not pleasant ones, and there is no desire to see such domination reinstituted. Russian control has been more subtle.

THE MONGOLIAN PEOPLE'S REVOLUTIONARY PARTY

The official history of the Mongolian People's Revolutionary Party (MPRP) states that it was founded by the merger of two secret revolutionary groups, one led by Sukhe-Bator and the other by Choybalsan. These men are celebrated as the leaders of the 1921 Revolution, though it is probable that their role has been magnified in recent years by Mongolian and Russian historians.

Shortly after the Bolshevik Revolution, the Chinese moved into control of large parts of Mongolia. For a time, Mongolia was a battlefield, with White Russians and Chinese vying for control. However, partisan groups of Mongols were coming into being, mainly in the northeastern districts bordering the Soviet Union. These groups, purportedly led by Sukhe-Bator and Choybalsan, met near Kiakhta, in Soviet territory close to the Mongolian frontier, in March 1921, and held the First Congress of the MPRP. The Congress created a Provisional Revolutionary Government (PRG) and a People's Revolutionary Army (PRA). It also decided to ask the U.S.S.R. for assistance in removing both Chinese and White Russians from Mongolia. The PRA, backed by the Soviet Army, subsequently moved south and took Urga in July 1921. In the following months, the remaining White Russian troops were liquidated or were driven out of the country.

The MPRP, after it had been established in Mongolia with Soviet assistance, was paraded before the world as a purely national movement, independent of the U.S.S.R. In effect, however, the Soviet Union had restored the old Tsarist protectorate over Mongolia. The U.S.S.R.'s role in the establishment of an independent Mongol state was obviously one in which protection of Soviet borders and advancement of the Russian national interest were of primary concern. Soviet troops and advisers remained in Mongolia, and the Red Army did not leave until 1925, when the MPRP was firmly in power.

During the first three years of its life, the Party was cautious in its internal policy, since a difficult diplomatic war was being waged between the Soviet Union and China over Mongolia's status. As long as that was not definitely determined, it was considered necessary to keep the Living Buddha of Urga as the nominal head of the state, which had been proclaimed a constitutional monarchy. After three years of negotiations, the Chinese government finally concluded that it did not have the power to restore its control in Mongolia; in the treaty of 1924, the Chinese recognized the dominant Soviet position in Mongolia, though nominal Chinese sovereignty was continued.

On the death of the Living Buddha in 1924, the MPRP decided not to install a successor, and the Party Central Committee passed a resolution establishing the Mongolian People's Republic. The first constitution of the MPR, drafted with Soviet assistance, was patterned after the 1918 constitution of the Russian Soviet Federated Socialist Republic (R.S.F.S.R.), and the structure of the MPR's government, to a large extent, paralleled the governmental system of the U.S.S.R.

The left group in the MPRP gradually increased its strength, and it gained control of the Party at the Seventh Party Congress in 1928. Elated by their success in defeating the rightists, the leftists now argued that Mongolia could proceed directly to socialism. They attacked on every front, aiming at the liquidation of the nobility and the religious hierarchy. These policies led to open rebellion, which was quelled only with Soviet military assistance. Not only did the rural herdsmen participate actively in this rebellion, but even members of the Party and its Youth League, as well as some detachments of the Mongolian People's Army, engaged in it.

The Party later claimed that the leftist leadership "violated the Leninist principle of mass leadership and pursued a policy of separating the Party from the masses, and in so doing alienated a sizable segment of the rural population."[1] The Party also asserts that the Japanese took advantage of the discontent to organize subversive work which was in part responsible for open rebellion. The official record states that Stalin himself advised the end of the "left deviation," and, in June 1932, a plenum of the Central Committee of the Party so decided. The Party now adopted a more gradual, sophisticated approach, placing emphasis on persuasion and education.

Until the 1932 Central Committee Plenum, Choybalsan had been only one of the important figures in the MPRP. After the Plenum, however, he was clearly in the ascendancy, and he became more and more the symbol of increasingly close cooperation with the Soviet Union. By the time of the Ninth Party Congress, in 1934, the Choybalsan group was in firm control.[2]

The period of absolute control of Mongolia by Marshal Choybalsan has been compared to the Stalinist period in the U.S.S.R. This comparison is particularly apt with respect to the arbitrary nature of police rule. Choybalsan quickly moved to eliminate all opposing centers of power, the Lamaist hierarchy and what remained of the nobility being major targets. With these groups removed, Choybalsan's police moved on others, and an atmosphere of fear developed. Little was done to bring the police under tighter control until his death in 1952.

Some information on Choybalsan's role in this period has become available as the Mongolian leadership has followed the Soviet Union in carrying out a de-Stalinization program. Mongolian leaders have accused Choybalsan of fostering a personality cult, of abusing his authority as Party leader, of glorifying Stalin, of overrating his own contribution to Mongolian history, and of underrating the "deeds and efforts of the Party and the people."[3] The de-Choybalsanization campaign in Mongolia resulted in the removal of his name from the state university, from the industrial combine in Ulan Bator, and from a province in eastern Mongolia.[4] The tomb of Sukhe-Bator and Choybalsan in Ulan Bator, however, remains undisturbed. Tsedenbal has been particularly sensitive to overzealous attacks upon Choybalsan, and one of the principal charges made against high-ranking Party members removed in 1959 and 1962 was that they had used the campaign against Choybalsan to further their own careers. Some of these purged members apparently had hoped to link Tsedenbal to the personality cult charges made against Choybalsan, since Tsedenbal had been Choybalsan's protégé since the 1940's.

Tsedenbal has been the ranking member of the Party Secretariat since the 1940's, except for a four-year period from 1954 to 1958 when D. Damba was First Secretary of the Party. Tsedenbal apparently did not have the power to maintain control of the Party after Choybalsan's death in 1952. According to the official record, Tsedenbal was replaced as First Secretary "at his own request, because of his heavy duties."[5] This was also the period before Khrushchev had consolidated his position of power in the Soviet Union and when the principle of collective leadership was being stressed in the U.S.S.R. and other countries in the Communist bloc. The Damba group remained in the ascendancy until mid-1958 and, in late 1957 and early 1958, appeared to be winning. At the plenum of the Central Committee of the Party held in November 1958, however, Tsedenbal replaced Damba as First Secretary of the Party. At the next plenum of the Central Committee, in March 1959, Damba and his associates were expelled from their Party posts.

Attempts have been made to prove that Damba was pro-Chinese and that Tsedenbal's triumph represented a victory for the Soviet faction in the MPRP. It is true that Chinese influence increased considerably during the period when Damba headed the Party, but there is no evidence that the Damba faction was pro-Chinese. Damba apparently wanted to slow down the pace of the changes which were taking place in Mongolian life as a result of the predominant Soviet influence in Mongolian policy making. The pro-Damba faction of the Party, including three full members and two candidate members of the Politburo, was removed at this time. These Politburo members were charged with being "unfit in ideological and political work and unworthy in personal character." The Chairman of the Party Control Commission was also removed, charged with "having failed to cope with the work" of his office.[6]

The most notable instances of factionalism in the Party since 1959 have involved the cases of D. Tomor-Ochir and L. Tsend. Tomor-Ochir was removed from the Politburo and the Secretariat in July 1960, was reinstated in January 1962, and was again removed from these posts in September 1962. Tsend, the Second Secretary of the Party, was removed from all Party and government positions in December 1963. Both Tomor-Ochir and Tsend apparently had made bids to replace Tsedenbal as leader of the Mongolian Party and state, and their removal was in part the result of a pure struggle for power. They were perhaps more nationalistic than Tsedenbal, and Tsedenbal used this weapon against them in convincing Soviet leaders that they were a danger both to his leadership and to the continuance of the Soviet Union's dominant position.

Tomor-Ochir was charged with using the campaign against the cult of personality to further his own ambitions—that is, by trying to connect the members of the Central Committee and Politburo with the errors made by Choybalsan. He was also accused of trying to disseminate the view, in his position as Director of the Institute of Party History, "that only his leadership in Party affairs would develop the Marxist-Leninist character of the MPRP." Tomor-Ochir was further charged with trying to revise or annul a number of Central Committee decisions condemning nationalism. It was asserted that he had supported his nationalist views by seeking to elevate the role of Genghis Khan. *Unen* stated that Tomor-Ochir's nationalist views were really aimed at the relationship between the MPR and the U.S.S.R. and called such views "a feature which unfortunately has become too widespread in our country."[7] He was also condemned for taking a "dogmatic view with regard to Marxist-Leninist theory," implying some sympathy for the Chinese Communist doctrinal position. Tomor-Ochir's goal, stated *Unen*, was to replace the internationalist leadership of the Central Committee of the Party with a nationalist one.

Tsend was removed for similar reasons. The charges indicated that he had made a stronger bid than Tomor-Ochir to replace Tsedenbal, but

it took Tsedenbal a bit longer to isolate Tsend and undercut his position
Tsend was charged with attempting to move into Tsedenbal's position
permanently in the second half of 1961, when Tsedenbal was in the Soviet
Union recovering from injuries sustained in an accident. Tsend was also
accused of promoting nationalism and attempting to weaken the relationship between the MPR and the U.S.S.R. He was linked with Tomor-
Ochir in the campaign to promote nationalism and glorify Genghis Khan.
The Central Committee also listed, in great detail, Tsend's deficiencies
in carrying out his responsibilities as Second Secretary. The charge stated
that, since early 1962, "he has not done anything and has not shown
any initiative in the industrial, construction, trade, transport, and communications fields." He was also accused of interfering with the work
of the State Planning Commission and the Construction and Economic
Commission. Apparently, Tsend was made the scapegoat for the failure
of the 1963 construction plan. The charges listed above also imply that
he may have objected to the increasing role of CEMA in Mongolian
economic planning and the resulting decrease in Mongolian control
over its internal affairs.

Tsend was replaced on the Politburo by S. Lubsan, MPR's Ambassador to the Soviet Union since 1960. Lubsan has since been named
First Deputy Chairman of the Council of Ministers. It is possible that his
advancement to high rank in the Party and government can be attributed to the Soviet pressures. Discussions during Tsedenbal's long visit
to the U.S.S.R., from mid-July to mid-September 1963, may have been
related to the ultimate decision to purge Tsend and promote Lubsan.

In 1964 the ruling group moved to tighten its control of the Party,
attempting to isolate followers of Tsend and those who might question
the wisdom of Party policy which had resulted in abject dependence
on the Soviet Union and in the rapid deterioration in relations with
Peking. The resolution of the December 1963 Plenum had called on all
Party organs to resist any manifestation of nationalism capable of weakening U.S.S.R.-MPR ties and to "wage an implacable struggle against
the penetration into our midst of an ideology which is alien to Marxism-
Leninism." The resolution also called on all Party organs to suppress any
attempts to weaken Party discipline or to "violate the norms of democratic centralism and collective leadership."[8]

In late December of 1964, in the first Plenum held since the removal
of Tsend, three Central Committee members were expelled from the
Party for "anti-party factional activities." These opponents of Tsedenbal
were tagged with the usual nationalist label and it is probable that they
had questioned the MPR's slavish backing of Soviet policies. It is probable also that those purged had protested other aspects of Tsedenbal's
dictatorial rule: Tsedenbal admitted that they criticized his iron-fisted

"democratic centralism" as a survival of the Stalinist era, but claimed that nationalist elements continued to operate "clandestinely" in Mongolia. The dissension of the Party appears to have been directly responsible for a trip to Mongolia, in January and February of 1965, by A. N. Shelepin, member of the Presidium and Secretary of the Central Committee of the Communist Party of the Soviet Union (CPSU).

The Mongolian press, during 1965, claimed that implementation of ihe decisions of the December 1964 Plenum "is in progress," stressing the role of "control and inspection" by Party, government and public organizations in supervision of economic and political activities. Provincial (i.e., aymag) and city Party committees meeting in 1965 repeated the denunciations of the anti-Party group, often called the "Loohuudz group." A Plenum of the Central Committee of the Mongolian Revolutionary Youth League in 1965 urged Youth League members to be "always alert against such abnormal ideas" and to "fight against any tendency toward such deviation." Tsedenbal, in February, at a meeting honoring the visiting Shelepin delegation, stressed that the Mongolian people supported the MPRP decision to purge Loohuudz and his followers. Tsedenbal called the group a "miserable group of factionalists" who "made an attack on the unity of the ranks of our Party."

The Fifteenth Party Congress, in June 1966, revealed the extent of the turnover in the upper levels of the Party. Of the 75-man Central Committee, 31 members, plus 47 of the 51 candidate members, were new. Heavy turnover in the leadership of the provincial Party organizations was confirmed when seven aymag (i.e., Provincial) Party Committee first secretaries were added as new full members of the Central Committee and six of the aymag first secretaries became new candidate members. A close study of the Mongolian press in 1964 and 1965 made clear that a rapid turnover of aymag first secretaries was taking place.

Party Structure

Party organization and operation follow the Leninist pattern established in the Soviet Union, with its emphasis on control from the top by a small elite. Ultimately, force backs up this control, but in more recent years the Party has relied more on persuasion and education. And the Party is now able to point to some accomplishments, which serves as a means of weakening any possible trouble centers.

The supreme organ of the Party, according to the Party statutes, is the Party Congress. In practice, the Congress automatically approves decisions already made by the small executive bodies of the Party. It remains, however, one of the regime's major forums of disseminating its views to the rank and file and, indirectly, to the Mongolian people. After each Congress, Party meetings are held throughout Mongolia to ensure rapid dissemination of current policies.

During the early years of the Party, before one-man rule became the pattern, there was often real discussion of major points of policy. Party congresses met about once a year until the Eighth Congress, in 1930. The next four years, during which the Party had to quell a rebellion, were very turbulent, but by 1934 Choybalsan was emerging as the strong man. Beginning with the Ninth Party Congress in 1934, the Party Congress lost its importance as a center of power. Now, the congresses are called by the Party leaders; they are shows, under the tight control of the Politburo.

To conduct Party work between congresses, the Party Congress elects a Central Committee which ordinarily holds plenums every six months. This Central Committee, a more important body than the Congress, is also controlled by Tsedenbal and his followers. More than two-thirds of the members of the Council of Ministers, the most important government body, are members of the Central Committee. Important Party decisions between congresses are usually announced at plenary sessions of the Central Committee.

According to the Party statutes, the Central Committee "directs the activities of central state and public organizations through Party members working in them." The Central Committee "directs all Party work" establishes Party organizations as needed, and controls the use of Party members and Party funds. The Central Committee organizes a Politburo to handle political work, a Secretariat to handle organizational work and other work of an executive-administrative character for the Party, and a Central Control Commission to check on the execution of Party decisions. No other details are given on the work of the Politburo or the Secretariat, though one other article of the Party constitution does give a breakdown of departments of the Central Committee. These departments are under the direct control of the Secretariat.[9]

The election of the Central Committee by the Congress is, in effect, a formal approval of a list already selected by the Politburo. Most members are Party and government leaders or important local Party officials. It is probable that most of the members of the Central Committee are there as protégés of one or another of the ruling groups. Plenums of the Central Committee are used by Party leaders to get local reaction to Party-government policies and to maintain close contact with officials in the provinces. Plenum meetings, like meetings of the Congress, are carefully controlled by the Politburo and usually consist of the presentation of decisions already made by the ruling group. The plenums are used to announce important policy statements and are also usually the medium for official notification of purges or shake-ups in the high command.

The Politburo, though theoretically selected by the Central Committee, has selected its new members in recent years on the basis of their loyalty to Tsedenbal and their pro-Soviet views. Tsedenbal reduced the size of the Politburo when he consolidated his control, presumably to reduce the circle of those in power and thereby make it easier to maintain direct control. Prior to 1959, there were nine members and five candidate members of the Politburo. Tsedenbal reduced this number to seven members and two candidate members, and it has remained at this level.[10]

The Politburo meets frequently, probably once or more a week. Very little is known about its organization and working practices. It is likely that very close contact is maintained with the working departments of the Central Committee and that major questions of importance are funneled through these departments and the Secretariat for presentation to the Politburo.

The most important body in Mongolia for preparing plans and proposing policy is the Secretariat of the Central Committee. It ranks second only to the Politburo in the making of decisions. All five secretaries are also members of the Politburo, enabling the pro-Soviet group to maintain close control over the agencies which implement policy. While the Politburo is concerned with executive decisions, the Secretariat is the supreme administrative agency of the Party. Tsedenbal is the First Secretary, and since Tsend's removal in 1963 the Central Committee has not had a Second Secretary.

Though the secretaries are formally elected by the Central Committee in plenary session, this is merely an automatic approval of individuals already selected by the top leadership. The number of secretaries dropped from six to four when Tsedenbal regained control, but a fifth was added in 1964. Since 1959, the only changes in the Secretariat have been associated with the removal, reinstatement, and subsequent removal of Tomor-Ochir as a secretary, the purge of Tsend in 1963, and the addition of Molomjamts in 1964.

We have no information about the actual division of responsibility among the secretaries, but previous work assignments of the five members give some idea as to how duties are parceled out. Tsedenbal is concerned with the general operation of the Party and government, both in foreign and domestic affairs, and he is not likely to be tied down by any specific administrative functions within the Secretariat. N. Jagbaral, named to the Secretariat following Tsend's removal, is an agricultural specialist and presumably concerned with Party activities in the livestock raising and farming sectors of the economy. Molomjamts was responsible for coordination of CEMA activities in Mongolia prior to his election to the Secretariat and probably has a similar responsibility on the Secretariat.

The other two secretaries are in charge of Party work and agitation and propaganda. T. Dugersuren is believed to fit the first category, which apparently includes some supervision over economic development. B. Lhamsuren has been active in Party and mass organization of a propaganda character and is probably handling the agitation-propaganda function. He has been head of the Higher and Specialized Secondary Education Committee and probably has the Education Department under his supervision. He was relieved of his duties as Deputy Chairman of the Council of Ministers, ostensibly to give him more time for Party work.

One agency of the Central Committee that is likely to assume increasing importance is the Party Control Committee. The powers accorded to this committee by the Party statutes are considerable and include checking on the execution of decisions of the Central Committee. The Control Committee probes into the lives of Party functionaries and members to see if their politics and behavior are satisfactory. Tsedenbal's report to the Sixth Plenum of the Central Committee, in December 1964, severely criticized the Control Committee for its failure to carry out directives of the Party; some of the onus of internal Party difficulties was thereby transferred to the Control Committee. There were some mitigating circumstances, however, according to Tsedenbal: He claimed that some organizations of the Party, the Youth League, and the trade unions "placed obstacles" that hampered the Control Committee in its work.

Tsedenbal indicated that the role of the Control Committee would be enlarged both in the field of general Party control and in economic development. He admonished the Control Committee to "examine the activities" of any persons expected to be in league with those Central Committee members expelled in December 1964: Tsedenbal claimed that those purged had opposed the "strengthening of state, party, and public control as well as party and state discipline." He indicated that part of the problem lay in the lack of coordination between the Party Control Committee and the State Control Commission.

Party organization below the national level includes the aymag and primary Party organizations. The structure of Party organizations at these levels is roughly the same as at the national level. National Party concern with local Party operation has become more pronounced in recent years, particularly since Tsedenbal's speech to the Fourteenth Party Congress in 1961, in which he stated:

In the struggle for successful solution of the problems of economic and cultural development and of the Communist education of the workers, the role of local party organizations and of each individual party member is increasing to an immense degree. Thus the obligations of leading party organs is that of improving on a daily basis the leadership of local party organizations, raising the level of their work, and expanding their influence among the masses. It is necessary to provide constant party control over the fulfillment of the production plans of each industrial enterprise, state farm, agricultural collective, and other economic organization, making widespread use of the right to control administrative activities.[11]

Executive bodies of Party cells have been reproved for their failure to carry through decisions of the Fourteenth Party Congress and for not keeping a constant check on the performance of tasks assigned to individual Party members or to groups of Party members. Cell leaders have been criticized for making changes in the leadership of local enterprises too frequently. Criticism alone apparently did not produce the results desired and, in 1963, the MPRP made several changes in cell organization and administration to enable the primary Party organizations to cope with the increased duties and responsibilities assigned to them. The cell secretary now has an assistant, a deputy chairman, to help him in his work. Further, the basic salaries of all cell secretaries were raised 40 per cent in 1963.[12]

Membership of the Party

The MPRP remains a small elite, comprising less than 5 per cent of the total population. In 1968 there were about 50,000 members and candidate members in a population of over 1,100,000. The Party has grown only gradually in recent years, indicating an effort to keep it small enough to permit rigid enforcement of discipline and to maintain relatively high standards.

The Party has, in line with decisions of the Thirteenth and Fourteenth Party Congresses, "considerably increased the requirements on applications for Party membership." Tsedenbal, in 1961, criticized local Party organizations for not examining more closely the qualifications of each potential recruit. The Party must grow, he noted, but only "on the basis of the best members of the working class, of advanced people in industry, agriculture, and other branches of the nation's economy who by

their concrete actions have shown boundless devotion to Party affairs."
He stated that increased demands would be made on each member of
the Party and that "a number of persons were excluded from the ranks
of the Party who were undeserving of membership."[13]

The following table indicates the growth of membership in the Party:[14]

1920:	160	1930:	30,000	1954:	32,000
1924:	4,700	1932:	42,000	1956:	40,000
1925:	7,600	1934:	8,000	1957:	43,000
1926:	11,600	1939:	9,000	1961:	43,902
1927:	14,000	1940:	13,000	1966:	48,570
1928:	15,000	1947:	28,000		

Though the educational level of the average Party member is lower
than that of members of the CPSU, it is significantly higher than the
educational level of all adult Mongolians. In 1960, for example, the
Party claimed that all its members were literate, whereas the over-all
literacy rate in Mongolia was approximately 80 per cent. This contrasts
sharply with 1925, when only 50 per cent of the Party members were
literate.

The occupational composition of the membership of the Party has
generally been broken down into three groups: workers; rural workers;
and staff workers, sometimes referred to as intelligentsia. The percentage of workers in the Party has risen from 7, in 1950, to about 30, indicating both the superior role granted to the workers by Communist
philosophy and the expansion of industry in Mongolia. On the other
hand, the rural herdsmen and other agricultural workers, who still constitute over 60 per cent of the total population, comprise less than 25
per cent of the total Party membership. This is a sharp drop from 1934,
when 60 per cent of the Party's members came from the agricultural
sector, and from 1950, when they comprised 40 per cent. The third
category, the staff worker, constitutes almost half the total membership.

The position of women in the Party has improved gradually. By
1961, women comprised 18 per cent of the Party membership, over 17
per cent of the delegates to the Fourteenth Party Congress, and 5 per
cent of the Central Committee. But women headed only 41 of the
1,274 Party cells in 1961, about 3 per cent of the total.

There has been no apparent discrimination against minority groups
in the recruiting of new Party members. Party membership is approximately proportional to the total population. In 1960 the Kazakhs, for
example, constituted about 4 per cent of the total population and about
3.9 per cent of the Party's membership. Almost 5 per cent of the delegates to the Fifteenth Party Congress in 1966 were Kazakhs.

INSTRUMENTS OF THE MPRP

The major instruments of the MPRP in controlling all of Mongolia, in addition to the formal government organization, are the mass organizations, particularly the youth organizations and the trade unions, and the propaganda machinery.

The Party-controlled mass organizations have the major function of rallying public opinion behind the national policies and programs desired by the Party leadership, and they are actually the foundation for much of the control exercised by the regime over the populace. These organizations also provide the regime with at least some indication of the public temper, as well as with a means of surveillance.

Mongolian youth organizations are expected to supply recruits for the Party and to train men and women for work in all phases of the government and the economy. The Revsomol, the Party's major auxiliary, and the Young Pioneers are closely modeled after the Komsomol and Pioneer organizations of the Soviet Union.

Probably the most important mass organization, next to the youth groups, is the Central Council of Trade Unions (CCTU). The CCTU not only has control and propaganda functions, but also performs duties ordinarily carried out by government. The importance of the trade unions has increased as the MPR has placed more stress on industrialization and has given the trade unions the task of administering the government's social insurance program. A major reorganization of the CCTU, in August and September 1963, was aimed at bringing all workers, of whatever category, into one of the national trade unions. These unions include: (1) agricultural workers; (2) industrial workers; (3) trade and transport workers; (4) construction workers; and (5) cultural-educational workers.[15]

GOVERNMENTAL MACHINERY OF THE MPR

The constitution of the MPR and the government which it describes are, as in other Communist states, merely one part of the over-all control system maintained by the MPRP. The notion that a constitution serves to establish boundaries, beyond which the governing authority cannot go, has no validity in a Communist state. The Constitution itself is considered to be subordinate to the dictatorship of the proletariat, which Lenin once described as "rule that is unrestricted by any laws." The MPRP's supreme position in Mongolia is clearly stated in the preamble to the 1960 constitution: "The leading and guiding force of society and state in the MPR is the Mongolian People's Revolutionary

Party, directed in its activity by the scientific theories of Marxism-Lenin-ism."[16]

The constitution describes the Great People's *Hural* (i.e., the Mongolian legislative body) as the "supreme authority" in the MPR. It rests at the top of a pyramidal hierarchy of *hurals* which are, in almost every respect, identical to the soviets in the U.S.S.R. In practice, the Great People's *Hural* has little power; whatever power exists in the governmental structure is largely exercised by the Council of Ministers and, to a lesser extent, by the Presidium of the Great People's *Hural*. But these executive bodies of the *Hural* are merely transmitting points for the small executive bodies of the Party, particularly the Politburo and the Secretariat. The top Party men also occupy the top government posts. For example, the Chairman of the Council of Ministers, Y. Tsedenbal, is also the First Secretary of the MPRP; the Chairman of the Presidium of the Great People's *Hural*, J. Sambu, is a member of the Politburo of the MPRP; the First Deputy Chairman and the two ranking Deputy Chairmen of the Council of Ministers are all members of the Politburo.

Provincial and local government organization is similar to that of central government bodies. The major difference in the Party-government relationship at this level seems to be that Party organizations outside of Ulan Bator have a greater tendency to bypass the government machinery in carrying out Party-government directives from the national level. The Communists claim that an important feature of the provincial and local government setup is the holding of joint meetings of local Party functionaries and members of the executive committees of the local *hurals*, but even this arrangement implies Party control of policy and administration at the local level. National Party officials frequently complain that local Party leaders, particularly at the *somon* (i.e., county) level, run their areas as if they were private fiefs, without consulting local government officials and, in fact, replacing these officials arbitrarily as they see fit.

The Defense Establishment

The armed forces are an instrument of the Party, directly controlled by a special military department of the Central Committee. There have been no indications of a separate military viewpoint in Mongolia, and the armed forces are responsive to Party orders. Party control is facilitated by the high percentage of Party members, over 90 per cent, in the officer corps. The present Minister of People's Army Affairs is a member of the Central Committee of the Party. There were no changes in military representation on the new Central Committee announced in 1966: The four top military men continued as full members.

Though Mongolia's military establishment is large in proportion to the total population, it would be incapable of any effective resistance to invading forces from either Communist China or the U.S.S.R. Mongolian leaders have recognized the impossibility of a military defense of the country, and rely on their military assistance agreement with the Soviet Union to maintain the Mongolian state as an independent entity.

Because of the labor shortage, Mongolian armed forces have been used extensively in construction work and in agriculture and industry. At a military conference in February 1963, Tsedenbal declared that, as Mongolian frontiers were not in danger of aggression, Army activities were to be focused primarily on supporting the economy. Army construction units have been used in the construction of the new industrial city at Darhan. Deteriorating relations with China have, however, increased the concern of Mongolian leaders with security requirements.

THE DEVELOPMENT OF DOMESTIC POLICY

The Struggle With the Lamaist Hierarchy

The initial attempt to eliminate the power of the monasteries and the Tibetan Buddhist religious hierarchy in the period from 1929 to 1932 was a complete failure. Rebellion broke out, and Soviet armored cars and planes were used to restore order. The policies toward the monasteries were relaxed immediately following the rebellion, but this resulted in a sharp rise in the number of monasteries and lamas. Since the situation presented an effective barrier to any program of socialization the Party hoped to introduce, the Party adopted more subtle means of depriving the monasteries of their strength.

The building of new monasteries was forbidden, searches for reincarnations were prohibited, monasteries were forbidden to interfere in political and social affairs or to take upon themselves judicial or administrative functions, to enroll as lamas minors and persons eligible for military service, and to set one monastery in a position subordinate to another. Despite some resistance, these policies were effective. The number of monks in the monasteries dropped sharply and, by 1940, the Lamaist hierarchy no longer presented a major problem to the Party. Theoretically, religious activity is still permitted in Mongolia, and the state allows two small monasteries to continue religious services. These monasteries are maintained largely for the benefit of Buddhist visitors from South and Southeast Asia.

There is considerable evidence, however, that the Buddhist religion retains some support in the rural areas, the Party media still devote space to denunciations of "religious peddlers" whose "disciples . . . present obstacles to our work."[17]

The Collectivization of the Rural Herdsmen

The attempt to collectivize the rural herdsmen, carried out at the same time as the attempt to break the power of the monasteries, was also a disastrous failure. The herdsmen were not prepared for the change and they forcibly resisted the seizure of their livestock. The total number of livestock, 21,950,000 head in 1929, dropped by over 7,000,000 in the period from 1929 to 1932, as large numbers of livestock were slaughtered by embittered herdsmen and thousands of others were lost through neglect and improper care. In consequence, although the Party did not deviate from its goal of collectivization, it did adopt a more gradual, sophisticated approach which emphasized persuasion and education.

In 1958 and 1959, a stepped-up campaign apparently was successful, and the government claimed that 99.6 per cent of all rural herdsmen had been organized into collectives and state farms by the end of 1959. There is reason to believe, however, that in many areas the collective organization is a paper one, maintaining only loose control over individual herdsmen. Only 78 per cent of all livestock was state-owned in 1960; the rest were privately owned by the members of the collectives.

The collectivization of the rural areas has been a factor in Mongolia's failure to meet long-range goals to increase the number of livestock. Party leaders at first refused to admit that a reduction in the number of livestock had occurred in 1959 and 1960. Livestock, in 1960, was originally claimed to number 23,000,000 head,[18] but this figure was subsequently revised downward to less than 21,000,000.[19] By 1969 it had risen, but only to about 22,000,000.

Party leaders have listed other reasons for the drop in the number of livestock: adverse climatic conditions; incorrect organizational activities; water shortage; and so forth. High export commitments to the U.S.S.R. have also been a factor, but in 1963, the U.S.S.R. agreed to a cut in meat imports from Mongolia, as a means of assisting the Mongolians to reach livestock production goals and to prevent further depletion of their breeding stock. Extremely heavy snowfall in most areas of Mongolia in 1968 and 1969 caused considerable loss of livestock, with consequent adverse effects on agricultural and industrial plans. These continuing losses from severe winter weather point up the inadequacies of Mongolia's planning system: The programs for fodder storage and animal shelter construction regularly fall far short of the announced goals.

A Third Congress of Agricultural Cooperatives, in June 1967, concentrated on the difficulties facing the collectives and announced a new "model charter" and a reorganization of collective management. The new charter called for increases in material incentives, and Tsedenbal announced at the Congress that there would be no reduction in private herds in the immediate future. The new charter also increased the number of collective workdays required of members, to 250. This continues the sharp rise of the past dozen years, from 75 in 1955 to 150 in 1959.

Full-scale Economic Planning

Long-range detailed economic planning did not get under way until 1948, but it has since developed to such an extent that, by 1965, the Mongolians were working out plans for 1970, 1975, and 1980. Since 1962, Mongolia has maintained close liason with other CEMA nations in working out its long-range development plans.

Mongolia has had, as its primary aim, the development of the pastoral economy, but recent plans have also stressed industrial development and farming. A major goal of the planners has been to settle the nomadic herdsmen into permanent locations, both to tighten control and to allow sufficient diversification of the economy to eliminate the country's extreme reliance on livestock raising. The Third Five-Year Plan (1961 to 1965) stressed industrialization, but spectacular failures, particularly in 1964, caused the Mongolian planners to reemphasize the pastoral economy. In 1966, however, at the Fifteenth Party Congress, Tsedenbal stated that Mongolia would be transformed into an industrial-agricultural state by the end of the 1970's, thus clinging to a long-range goal despite setbacks and delays.

The Fourth Five-Year Plan (1966 to 1970), which had appeared more realistic than the preceding plan, immediately ran into trouble, and none of the major goals for 1966 were achieved. There was some improvement in 1967, but the plan still lagged far behind the goals set. The Mongolian leadership placed more blame on mismanagement than on severe winter weather and destructive floods, which in themselves were extremely costly to the Mongolian economy.

The 1966 to 1970 Plan calls for the rural areas to receive a larger share of capital expenditure, cadres, housing, consumer goods, and services. It calls for only a gradual increase in the size of the herds, to between 25 and 26 million, but places emphasis on improving their quality and on increasing the output of animal products. However, the fodder base still remains inadequate for any substantial increase in the quantity or quality of livestock, and the new Plan likely will not correct this continuing problem. The Plan also calls for all cows, sheep, and goats to have winter shelter by 1970, but the past record makes the achievement of this goal seem improbable.[20]

CEMA's emphasis on national economic specialization probably means that the MRP will remain a supplier of raw materials to other countries in the Communist bloc—in particular, a supplier of meat and other animal products. The increased role of CEMA in MPR's economic planning means even less independence for Mongolia in deciding the future course of its economic development.

Educational Policies

The educational program of the regime has been one of its major successes. The literacy rate rose, from less than 1 per cent, in 1921, to approximately 80 per cent, in 1963. The state educational system was a major weapon in the fight to destroy the power of the Tibetan Buddhist religious hierarchy, and it has continued to be used to weaken the traditional Mongol values and to replace these values with those more in conformity with Marxism.

A major reorganization of the educational system, to take seven years to accomplish, was begun in 1961, in line with the changes made in the Soviet Union and other Communist countries, as a means of ensuring a steady supply of skilled manpower for all sectors of the economy. The new system combines studies with practical labor in the secondary schools. The seven-year schools are being replaced with eight-year schools, and the graduates of these schools are either to continue their studies in eleven-year schools or receive a complete secondary education in evening schools while working full time. Separate technical and specialized secondary schools are to train skilled manpower for industry.[21]

This is the goal, but the reality is lagging far behind. Seven-year schooling is standard only in the cities, and four-year schooling generally prevails in the countryside. And although the Fourth Five-Year Plan calls for universal "incomplete," or eighth-grade, schooling by 1970, only universal seven-year schooling is likely to be achieved in that time.[22] A universal seven-year program was a goal of the Third Five-Year Plan, but was not achieved then.

MONGOLIA'S INTERNATIONAL POSITION

History and geography combine to place Mongolia between two powerful neighbors who threaten its existence as an independent political entity and who also threaten the traditional Mongol culture. Mongols have, in the twentieth century, reacted to this threat with nationalist movements aimed primarily at the formation of an independent Mongolian state. The establishment of the MPR in part answered this desire, but it did not fulfill the desires of the pan-Mongolists, who favored the union of all Mongolia into a "Greater Mongolia."[23]

There are over three million Mongols living in Asia, and approximately two million of these live in Communist China and the Soviet

Union. Over one-and-three-quarter million Mongols live in Communist China (mostly in the Inner Mongolian Autonomous Region, IMAR) and over a quarter-million Mongols live in the U.S.S.R. (mostly in the Buryat Autonomous Republic, formerly called the Buryat-Mongol Autonomous Republic). Non-Mongol immigration into these areas has steadily decreased the strength of pan-Mongolism, however. In the IMAR, the Chinese now constitute about 90 per cent of the population; in the Buryat Autonomous Republic, about 70 per cent of the population consists of Russians and Ukrainians.

The MPRP has exploited Mongolian nationalism for its own purposes, but has also been quite critical of those who have excited a feeling of nationalism in Mongols at the expense of "proletarian internationalism." The Party leadership of course subscribes to the Communist theme of the international fraternity of the working classes, but its position on Mongolian nationalism has been determined by the Soviet Union's extreme sensitivity on the subject.

Tsedenbal's close adherence to Soviet policies has been the key to his survival, but the resulting image of a Soviet satellite has caused dissension within the Party and the country. Tsedenbal seems to have weathered the serious challenge he faced from nationalists in the early Sixties, by making concessions both to his challengers and to the Soviet Union. Mongols have a strong feeling of pride in Mongolia and in past Mongolian history, and have not forgotten Genghis Khan and the long period when the Mongols dominated both Russia and China. The obverse of the coin is that Russian leaders wince at the memory of centuries of Mongol rule, and the politically astute Tsedenbal has thus found it the better part of valor to sublimate Mongol nationalist feelings and preach regularly about "proletarian internationalism." The purge of Tomor-Ochir, as we have already noted, was ascribed in part to his nationalist passions and to his idealization of the role of Genghis Khan in Mongolian, Russian, and Chinese history. Tomor-Ochir was responsible for staging the 1962 celebrations of the eight-hundredth anniversary of the birth of Genghis Khan. In the Soviet Union there was no commemoration of the anniversary, but the Chinese publicized the celebrations taking place in the MPR and organized a festival in the IMAR. The Chinese, apparently willing to forget their own humiliation at the hands of Genghis Khan, seized the opportunity to stir up trouble between the Russians and the Mongolians.

Dependence on the Soviet Union

The MPR has been, since its establishment, heavily dependent on the Soviet Union for its existence as an independent entity. Relations have not been those of equal partners and the Soviet Union has at times been heavy-handed in its treatment of the MPR. However, the relationship has not been without substantial benefits for Mongolia.

Indicative of the relationship was the gradual incorporation of a part of old Mongolia, Tannu Tuva, into the Soviet Union. In 1921, after Chinese troops were driven out, Tannu Tuva, formerly known as Urianghai, was occupied by the Soviet Union. In 1924, residents of the area declared for affiliation with the MPR, but Soviet troops successfully put down the rebellion. The U.S.S.R. did make one concession, returning to the MPR a small area west of Khobsogol, although the Tannu Tuva area still comprised about 66,000 square miles, and in 1926, the MPR reluctantly recognized the independence of Tannu Tuva. Intensive colonization by the Russians, and the introduction of a national Tuvanic written language, tightened the Russian hold on the area.[24] In 1944, the U.S.S.R. incorporated Tannu Tuva as an autonomous region, and in 1961 the area became an autonomous republic of the U.S.S.R.

On the other hand, Soviet military and economic assistance to Mongolia has been extensive. Soviet help in 1939 stopped the Japanese. This assistance was given in accordance with the Sino-Mongolian Protocol of Mutual Assistance (of March 21, 1936). In 1941, Japan signed a treaty with the U.S.S.R., agreeing to respect the frontiers of Mongolia, and peace was maintained until 1945, when both the U.S.S.R. and Mongolia declared war on Japan.[25]

Following World War II (in 1946), another Treaty of Friendship and Mutual Assistance between the U.S.S.R. and the MPR went into effect, guaranteeing Soviet assistance in case Mongolia was attacked. This Treaty remained in effect until a new one was signed, in January 1966, in Ulan Bator. The new treaty was the ostensible reason for a visit to Mongolia by Soviet Party leader Brezhnev, Foreign Minister Gromyko, and Defense Minister Malinovsky, the highest-level Soviet delegation ever to visit Mongolia. Their visit demonstrated not only the importance Moscow places on maintaining a close relationship with Mongolia but also the Soviet Union's role as an Asian power, and it certainly served to strengthen Tsedenbal's position at home.

The new Mutual Assistance Treaty states that each side will "take jointly all the necessary measures, including military ones, for the purpose of insuring the security, independence, and territorial integrity of both countries." The Treaty reportedly included a secret protocol authorizing the stationing of Russian troops on Mongolian soil, and there were numerous stories, in 1966, of the presence of Soviet troops in Mongolia, particularly in the eastern areas bordering China. Reports from the Soviet Union in 1968 and 1969 indicated that some 100,000 Soviet troops were in Mongolia. This reportedly included from five to ten Soviet divisions, mostly in the east in the Choybalsan area, equipped with both defensive and offensive missiles.[26]

Mongolia's effort, over the past 20 years, to carry out an extensive program of economic development has also been heavily dependent on the Soviet Union. The U.S.S.R. extended credits and grants amounting to from $700,000,000 to $800,000,000 from the beginning of the First Five-Year Plan in 1948 to the end of the Third Five-Year Plan in 1965. By the end of 1968, over $1,000,000,000 had been promised for the period of the Fourth Five-Year Plan, double the commitment originally made for the 1966–1970 period.

Soviet credits for the period from 1958 to 1960 were used primarily for the expansion of land under cultivation and the further development of livestock raising. During the period from 1961 to 1965, a large proportion of Soviet assistance was used in the construction of the fuel and power engineering complex being built in the Darhan area between Ulan Bator and the Soviet border. Extensive Soviet aid was also used in the virgin lands program. New Soviet credits were granted in 1964 to defray the losses resulting from severe winter weather, the drying up of Chinese assistance, and the drop in revenue received from the transit of goods to and from China. The official explanation was that the assistance was to help "overcome the temporary difficulties" facing the Mongolian economy.

The Soviet Union is scheduled to provide more than one-third of the total capital investment during the period of the Fourth Five-Year Plan, 1966 to 1970. The Darhan complex is to be completed, and Choybalsan is to be developed as the country's third major industrial center. Industrial assistance will help to build fuel and power projects, construct new foodstuff and light industrial plants, and develop transport, communications, and public utilities.

All the same, one of the principal features of the plan is a switch of resources to agriculture. A new aid agreement, signed in late 1967 (for 1968 to 1970), will be, according to *Unen*, "directed toward expansion of the material and technical base of agriculture . . . and particularly toward strengthening the fodder base for livestock breeding."[27]

Peking Attempts to Move In

Communist China was a late starter in the contest for primacy and, considering the long record of Soviet assistance, the outcome was predictable. The institutions and leadership of the modern Mongol state are Russian-oriented, and the U.S.S.R. was and is in an obviously better position to give material and technical assistance to Mongolia.

The Chinese were active in Mongolia in the early Fifties, and their influence increased noticeably during the years from 1954 to 1957. In 1955, an agreement was reached whereby 10,000 Chinese laborers were to be sent to Mongolia as construction workers. In addition, Peking advanced more than $100,000,000 in grants and credits before Mongolia was forced to take a firm stand on the developing Sino-Soviet dispute.

The high-water mark of the Chinese effort came with the visit by Premier Chou En-lai to Ulan Bator in May 1960, during which a Sino-Mongolian Treaty of Friendship and Mutual Assistance and an agreement on economic and technical assistance were signed. Under the economic agreement, Communist China agreed to provide the MPR with a $50,000,000 long-term loan (part of the $100,000,000 we referred to earlier for the construction of the industrial enterprises, water conservation projects, and public utilities).[28]

The prospect of closer ties between the MPR and Communist China seems to have spurred Moscow into action. Following a visit by Tsedenbal to Moscow in August 1960, Mongolia gradually began to make specific and public its strong support of the Soviet Union in the developing dispute between the two powers. Large-scale Soviet assistance has been flowing into Mongolia since 1960, and though there are other reasons for Ulan Bator's strong pro-Soviet stand, this heavy outpouring of Soviet material and technical assistance has been a major factor.

On the other hand, since 1960 there have been no agreements for additional Chinese assistance; moreover, the completion of projects under the 1960 agreement has been painfully slow. Even the 1955 agreement was affected; by 1964, relations had deteriorated to the extent that the Chinese workers remaining under the 1955 agreement were removed from Mongolia. Peking claimed that the workers had been returned home at Ulan Bator's request, but the Mongolian government denied this, claiming that the workers were leaving because their contracts had expired. The indications are that the Mongolians let the contracts lapse, probably under Soviet pressure (the Russians had agreed to replace the workers), and also because of a series of incidents involving the workers. Some Chinese technicians and workers remained in 1968, still working on projects connected with the 1960 agreement.

Despite Mongolia's pro-Soviet stance as the Sino-Soviet dispute was unfolding, Communist China, in December 1962, agreed to a border treaty with Mongolia which accepted in large part the boundaries claimed by the MPR and, in June 1964, the two countries signed a final protocol implementing the 1962 agreement. The boundary treaty served as another admission by Peking of the complete independence of Mongolia: Communist China had previously agreed in the 1950 Treaty of Friendship and Alliance with the Soviet Union, to a "complete guarantee of the independent status of the Mongolian People's Republic."[29]

The MPR in the Sino-Soviet Split

The MPR followed the lead of the Soviet Union in its early attacks on the leadership of the Albanian Communist Party and in its indirect attacks on the Chinese Communist Party (CCP). But the early, mild references to the CCP became progressively more bitter. The MPR endorsed the denunciation of the Albanian leadership at the Twenty-second Congress of the CPSU in 1961. In early 1962, Tsedenbal stated, "We cannot agree with the reservations on this question which, for instance, the delegation of the Chinese Communist Party made at the Soviet Twenty-second Party Congress."[30]

The speech made by Tsedenbal at a Peking rally at the time of the signing of the Sino-Mongolian border agreement (December 26, 1962) left no doubt as to where the MPR's loyalties lay. Tsedenbal was very definite in his praise of the Soviet Union's policy of peaceful coexistence and in his expressions of approval of Soviet action during the Cuban crisis. In early 1963, he reiterated Mongolian support of the Soviet Union in the Cuban crisis, and this time he directly attacked the Chinese People's Republic (CPR) for its "irresponsible and arrogant attitude."[31] The government of the MPR endorsed the 1963 Nuclear Test-Ban Treaty without reservation, and berated the Chinese Communists for denouncing it.

Subsequent attacks on the Chinese leadership in 1963 and 1964 resulted in a steady deterioration of relations between Peking and Ulan Bator. The MPR heartily endorsed the Suslov report to a Plenum of the CPSU Central Committee in February 1964, which was extremely critical of the Chinese. Ulan Bator backed the Soviet call for a Communist summit conference and a preparatory meeting to arrange the conference. Mongolia strongly supported the Soviet Union's right to participate in the Second Afro-Asian Conference held in Algiers in June 1965.

A major attack was made by Tsedenbal on the Chinese "self-reliance" policy in the lead article in the September 1964 issue of *World Marxist Review*. Tsedenbal presented a general defense of CEMA and of the benefits to be derived from "division of labor under socialism" and coordination of economic plans. He defended Mongolia's economic dependence on the Soviet Union, claiming that acceptance of extensive Soviet aid was in the best interests of Mongolia and had "helped to strengthen the sovereignty of our country."[32]

Mongolia's strident anti-Chinese stance reached a new peak, in September 1964, with abusive attacks on the CPR and on Mao Tse-tung for lingering Chinese territorial designs on Mongolia. The Soviet Union had seized on statements made by Mao Tse-tung to a group of visiting Japanese in July 1964, in which he stated that he had asked Soviet leaders in 1954 to restore Mongolian independence, and to make a general attack on Chinese territorial aspirations in East Asia. Moscow implied that Mao had asked for the incorporation of the MPR into Communist China, and claimed that Khrushchev "naturally refused to discuss this question."

Ulan Bator followed up this Soviet lead by not only denouncing Chinese designs on Mongolia but by showering abuse on Mao. Mao, the Mongolians claimed, had "exposed himself" for what he was, and the "malicious intentions" of the Chinese leaders who "have long dreamed of making the MPR an outlying region under Chinese power" were now obvious. Ulan Bator claimed that Chinese designs on the MPR gave evidence of the racist and expansionist aims of Chinese policy. Mongolian fears of Chinese domination were spelled out in the criticism of Chinese policy toward minority groups, the Mongolians claiming that Chinese control would force "our people to share the lot of the Inner Mongolians," and warning the Chinese that "we have a friend who stands on guard with us in the defense of the interests of our country."

These charges coincided with a report, by a Yugoslav news agency, of a concentration of Chinese troops along the Mongolian border. An increase in military strength along the border could have been a reflection of Chinese concern with Soviet "defense" measures in areas adjacent to the Sino-Soviet border and uneasiness as to Moscow's motives in escalating its polemical attack against so-called Chinese territorial aspirations in Asia. The strengthening of border defense could also have been part of a new effort by Peking to prevent Mongolians in IMAR from fleeing into the MPR.

Mongolia's heavy propaganda barrage against Communist China and CCP leaders stopped abruptly after the Soviet leadership shake-up in October 1964. The Mongolian radio and press were extremely cautious in their references to the purge in the Soviet Union. There was no criticism of Khrushchev. This silence reflected the equivocation of Brezhnev and Kosygin, who themselves took a soft line pending consolidation of their own position. The Mongolians continued to echo Soviet foreign policy statements, but without direct reference to the Chinese; indeed, in view of Mongolia's exposed position, many Mongolian leaders probably would have welcomed a suspension of the polemic.

Tsedenbal did not comment publicly on the removal of Khrushchev. He had maintained a close relationship with Khrushchev, and any hasty condemnation of the fallen leader could have provided ammunition for those nationalists in Mongolia who were unhappy with the satellite relationship with the Soviet Union. Tsedenbal's conferences with

Brezhnev and Kosygin after the purge resulted in a new Soviet aid agreement, an indication that his relations with Moscow remained essentially unchanged. Tsedenbal was in the midst of a tour of East European countries when the purge occurred, and the fact that he continued the tour without interruption would indicate that he was not worried about his position in Mongolia. He returned to Moscow before and after trips to Hungary and Poland, and may have served as an emissary to explain the policies of Brezhnev and Kosygin to the Hungarian and Polish leadership.[33]

In 1965, the MPR continued its lavish praise of Soviet foreign policy, but was cautious in direct comments about China. Mongolian leaders frequently called for backing of Soviet attempts to achieve "unity" within the Communist movement by the holding of a new international meeting of Communists to overcome the "difficulties" in the movement. In February 1965, at the conclusion of Shelepin's visit, Tsedenbal said their talks had affirmed a "complete unanimity of views."

There was some direct criticism of China in 1966, on an issue to which the Chinese were particularly vulnerable: united action on Vietnam. Tsedenbal reportedly stated, in November 1966, that the policy of the Chinese leadership was detrimental to the consolidation of all "antiimperialist forces in the struggle against American aggression in Vietnam." In his report to the Fifteenth Party Congress early in June 1966, Tsedenbal's references to the Chinese were relatively moderate.

Difficulties along the border were made public in the summer of 1966 when Peking (on June 20) broadcast the text of a note protesting intrusion of Mongolian "border guards" into Inner Mongolia on April 1. The note mentioned an earlier protest, made the previous December, against intrusions of Mongolian soldiers into Chinese territory. Peking claimed that in the April incident a Chinese subject was dragged across the border, "assaulted," given drugs and interrogated extensively in an attempt to obtain information about Chinese troop dispositions in the border area. All this was done, the note stated, in the presence of Russian personnel.[34]

The gloves were off in 1967 as personal criticism was hurled back and forth between Peking and Ulan Bator, and relations deteriorated to their lowest point following Red Guard action against the Mongolian embassy and against Mongolian officials in Peking. Mongolia's critical comments about the Cultural Revolution were closely monitored by Peking: The Chinese noted that in the brief period from January 25 to February 19, 1967, the Mongolian press carried more than 120 "anti China articles." In an interview in April 1967, Tsedenbal was restrained in his comments on China, but other Politburo members and the Foreign

Ministry were more blunt. D. Maydar, in an article in *Pravda* in August, wrote of the "enormous damage the policy of Mao Tse-tung and his group is inflicting upon the interests of socialism." In February, the MPR protested to Peking because of "insults" to Mongolian officials in Peking by Red Guards, condemned the use of anti-Soviet material at the Chinese embassy in Ulan Bator, and criticized activities of the Chinese resident in Ulan Bator. The Chinese during the same month, claimed that Mongolians in Ulan Bator broke showcases at the Chinese embassy containing pictures of Mao Tse-tung, and strongly protested against the MPR's "unilateral abrogation of the Sino-Mongolian non-visa agreement." Peking declared that henceforth all Mongolian citizens who traveled to China must "obtain visas from the CPR side without fail."

The situation became progressively worse in the spring and summer of 1967 as Red Guards stormed the Mongolian embassy in Peking in May and August. In the August incident, Mongolian officials were forcibly led out of the building and "subjected to brutal physical beatings."[35] The car of the Mongolian ambassador was overturned and set on fire, and the driver was beaten and arrested.

In this context, Mongolian comments about Mao and the Cultural Revolution became more harsh. Ulan Bator, in November 1967, charged that "Mao's group" had started an "unbridled and obscene campaign" against the MPR, and were "evermore exposing their great-power nationalistic attitude toward the Mongols." Premier Tsedenbal in May 1969 said that China had attempted by every means to split Mongolia from the Soviet Union. He charged that Mao had lost all connection with Marxist-Leninist principles, adding that he saw no hope of change in China's policies so long as Mao remained in power. Tsedenbal said that the Soviet-Chinese border clashes on the Ussuri River in March were the total responsibility of the Chinese and were deliberate acts of aggression.

Broadcasts from Radio Urumchi in early 1969 questioned the validity of the 1962 border agreement, claiming that it was drawn up by "opponents of Mao" and had surrendered some Chinese territory in northeastern Sinkiang.[36]

As a result, Party-to-Party relations between the CCP and MPRP are nonexistent at present and government-to-government relations are minimal. No Chinese delegation attended the Mongolian Party Congress in June 1966.

Relations with other Communist Countries.   Because of its geographical location and relative isolation, until recently the MPR's relations with other Communist countries were limited. In 1948 North Korea became the first Communist country, other than the Soviet Union, to establish relations with the MPR,[37] and for a time relations with North Korea were probably closer than they were with European members of the bloc. The pattern has been changing, however, under the impact of the Sino-Soviet dispute and with the greater ability of the European countries to assist Mongolia's economic development. This trend has accelerated since June 1962, when the MPR was admitted to CEMA.

Mongolia and CEMA

The MPR is the only Asian Communist country which has become a member of CEMA. Communist China, North Korea, and North Vietnam have been observers at CEMA meetings, not very active observers at that, and it was necessary to amend the CEMA statutes to allow the admission of a non-European state. Policy planners in the MPR view CEMA membership as a means of stepping up material and technical assistance from the European Communist-bloc countries. A CEMA meeting, held in Ulan Bator in October 1963 and attended by representatives of the U.S.S.R. and the European Communist countries, discussed Mongolian development plans for the period from 1963 to 1980 and explored the assistance CEMA countries might give to help Mongolia fulfill the 1980 plan.

In mid-1963, a CEMA agricultural committee visited Mongolia to advise the MPR on the development of animal husbandry and to assist the Mongolians to eliminate crippling livestock diseases. They also advised on the "need to try to mechanize completely" most aspects of animal husbandry. The MPR expects CEMA assistance to replace the revenue formerly derived from the Chinese trade. CEMA assistance is expected in the building of factories to process animal products, including meat, leather, and wool. Further, CEMA assistance is to be utilized for development of Mongolian mineral production, including lead, gold, and feldspar. The CEMA Permanent Commission on Geology meeting in Ulan Bator in October 1963, elected the chief of the MPR Geological Survey as its chairman.[38]

Bilateral consultations between the planning organs of the MPR and those of other CEMA countries were an important factor in drafting the Fourth Five-Year Plan. CEMA countries which will provide assistance other than the Soviet Union, include Hungary, Poland, East Germany Czechoslovakia, and Bulgaria.

Information on military cooperation between Mongolia and CEMA countries (other than the Soviet Union) is sketchy. A Moscow broad cast (September 5, 1967) carried a statement by the Mongolian defense minister that "military cooperation of the fraternal armies of CEMA countries is growing stronger." The signing of a Bulgarian-Mongolian Treaty of Friendship and Cooperation in July 1967 is indicative of some assistance. Although the   released version of that pact contained no specific defense clause, the MPR's Minister of Defense stated, in the same month, that "military cooperation" between Mongolia and Bulgaria was being strengthened and that "we have decided to exchange officers."[39]

Mongolian cultural relationships with the European Communist countries have also increased noticeably in recent years. Delegations, including some of Mongolia's foremost literary and artistic figures, have attended youth, peace, and similar festivals in Prague, East Berlin, and other Communist cities. The MPR has student-exchange programs with some of the East European Communist countries and also has exchanged Youth League and Young Pioneer groups.

Mongolia and the Non-Communist World

A major aim of the MPR, since the end of World War II, has been to extend worldwide contacts. The MPR has a number of reasons for pursuing this goal: to gain more leverage in its relationship with the Soviet Union; to disprove the charges, made in 1946 and thereafter, that the MPR was not an independent state; to increase Mongolian foreign trade; to receive technical and material assistance; and to carry on cultural and educational exchanges.

Mongolian propaganda, aimed at all the new, underdeveloped countries, has emphasized that the Mongolian techniques of economic development could profitably be used by any nation facing the problems the MPR has faced. At the Fourteenth Party Congress, for example, Tsedenbal stressed the importance of the Soviet-Mongolian relationship in the success of Mongolian policy, implying that underdeveloped countries could benefit from a similar relationship. He claimed that the Soviet-Mongolian relationship could serve as a model of equality and mutual assistance between large and small states. Mongolian propaganda frequently points to the MPR as a model for underdeveloped states to follow in going directly from feudalism to socialism.

India was the first non-Communist country to establish relations with Mongolia, in 1955, and it was followed by 25 other non-Communist countries by the end of 1968. The MPR has extended unreciprocated recognition to a number of other countries, primarily the new states in Africa. Except for Cuba, the MPR did not have relations with any country in the Western hemisphere and Canada recognized it in January 1964. The United Kingdom was the first non-Communist European nation to establish relations with the MPR (in January 1963) and to establish a permanent mission in Ulan Bator (in late 1964).

Japan. The MPR has exchanged economic and cultural missions with Japan since 1959, but formal recognition has not yet taken place. Japan and Mongolia discussed the establishment of diplomatic relations in mid-

1961, at about the same time negotiations were being carried on between the MPR and the U.S. In 1966 and 1967, Japan was actively considering a move to establish relations with Mongolia, but remained concerned about the opposition of Nationalist China to such a move. Talks between the Japanese and Mongolian Ambassadors in Moscow reportedly took place in the summer of 1966, and talks were also held between MPR Deputy Foreign Minister Chimiddorj and Japanese foreign ministry officials. The Japanese foreign minister stated, in 1966, that there was no legal obstacle to Japan's formal recognition of Mongolia. Tsedenbal, in 1967, stated that Mongolia was prepared to study all Japanese proposals, and added that the normalization of relations should not be linked with any discussions about reparations for damages inflicted during World War II.[40] Japan, by voting for the MPR's admission to the United Nations in 1961, had years ago thereby informally accepted the MPR as an independent government.[41]

The United States. Mongolia has long been interested in establishing relations with the United States, believing that American recognition would immediately open the door to expansion of contacts with the non-Communist world. Officially however, from 1945 to 1961, the U.S. questioned whether the MPR possessed the attributes of sovereignty, and direct government-to-government relations were therefore not considered. The U.S. explored the possibility of establishing diplomatic relations with the MPR in mid-1961, and the Mongolian Ambassador to the CPR reportedly stated, in March 1966, that Mongolia had been ready to establish relations in 1961, and did not understand why the United States "abandoned" the idea.[42] It has been widely reported that pressure from Nationalist China was responsible for the American decision to postpone action. There was also some opposition in the Congress. Since early 1966, the establishment of relations with Mongolia has again been "under consideration" by the United States, but the delicate situation created by the Vietnam War is an inhibiting factor for both sides.

Mongolia has made it clear since 1961 that any new initiative will have to come from the United States. Despite very harsh criticism of the American policy in Vietnam, Mongolia's objective of ultimately establishing relations with the United States probably remains unchanged.[43] Tsedenbal, in an interview in May 1969, stated that the MPR stood for "development of normal relations" between states with different social systems "on the basis of peaceful coexistence." He said that any progress on the development of diplomatic relations is up to the United States, adding that Mongolia had been prepared since the first contacts in 1961 to go forward to the establishment of diplomatic relations. Tsedenbal said that trade and cultural relations "may be established" with the United States. Tsedenbal spoke critically of U.S. foreign policy in both Vietnam and Korea.[44]

The problem created by the Vietnam War is illustrated by the fate of the American attempt to give $25,000 to Mongolia in the summer of 1966 for flood relief. The *New York Times*, in July, reported that the Mongolian Foreign Minister stated that Mongolia would be happy to accept such aid, but the Foreign Minister quickly denied this, calling the offer "a trick of the U.S. ruling quarters, which are continuing their brutal aggression in Vietnam."[45]

There are some American contacts with Mongolia, however. American tourists have visited Mongolia for the past several years under arrangements worked out by private American travel agencies and the Mongolian government, although their number has been and is likely to remain small because of the great distance and expense, made worse by a rather forbidding exchange rate in Mongolia. There is a limited amount of trade between the United States and Mongolia: it is one-sided and consists mostly of American importation of goat hair (cashmere). From 1960 to 1965, American imports from Mongolia averaged over $3,000,000 a year; during the same period, exports totaled less than $500 (all in 1964).

Membership in the United Nations

Mongolia attempted as early as 1946 to gain admission to the United Nations, but opposition by the United States and, later, Nationalist China prevented admission until an arrangement was worked out between the U.S.S.R. and non-Communist countries, in 1961, to pair the admission of Mongolia and Mauretania. Nine of the Security Council's eleven members in 1961 voted in favor of the MPR; the United States officially abstained and Nationalist China took no part in the voting.[46] Mongolia has since joined many U.N.-affiliated organizations, including the Economic Commission for Asia and the Far East, the United Nations Educational, Scientific, and Cultural Organization, and the World Health Organization.

United Nations voting records indicate that Mongolia has voted with the Soviet Union on almost every issue. This is not unusual, since Communist nations in the U.N. tend to vote as a bloc on nearly all roll-call votes.

Prospects for Mongolian International Policy

The present close relations between the U.S.S.R. and the MPR probably will continue. The internal political situation in Mongolia will remain heavily influenced by developments in the Soviet Union and Communist China. Instability in the CPSU would likely be reflected in the MPRP, but if the present ruling group maintains the confidence of the Soviet leadership and the present level of Soviet assistance continues, the pro-Soviet group is likely to remain in power.

The steady deterioration in Mongolian-Chinese relations has made Mongolia even more dependent on the U.S.S.R. and other CEMA countries. Mongolian desire to increase non-Communist contacts, particularly its desire to establish relations with the United States, as a means of improving the MPR's bargaining position with the Soviet Union and as a possible new source of technical and material assistance, is also likely to continue, with the timing of change likely to be dependent upon developments in Southeast Asia. Meanwhile, the U.S.S.R. probably will continue to encourage Mongolian activity in international organizations and in non-Communist countries because of Moscow's desire to exploit the Soviet-Mongolian relationship in its own foreign policy.

NOTES

1. Kh. Choybalsan, "Great History of the Mongol People," *Bolshevik*, No. 13, 1951. (*Soviet Press Translations*, V, No. 20, November 15, 1951, p. 618).

2. Owen Lattimore, *Nationalism and Revolution in Mongolia* (New York: Oxford University Press, Inc., 1955), pp. 73–74.

3. *Unen* (*Truth*), (Ulan Bator), March 29, 1962, pp. 8–14; February 1, 1962, pp. 3–4. Translation published by U.S. Department of Commerce, Office of Technical Service, Joint Publications Research Service [JPRS], in *Translations from Unen*, No. 18, JPRS No. 13,226.

4. *Unen*, February 25, 1962; March 22, 1962 (JPRS, No. 13,226).

5. *Izvestia*, November 26, 1954; reprinted in *Current Digest of the Soviet Press*, VI, No. 48 (January 12, 1955), p. 8.

6. *Pravda*, April 1, 1959, reprinted in *Current Digest of the Soviet Press*, XI, No. 13 (April 29, 1959), p. 21.

7. *Unen*, October 18, 1962.

8. The resolution was not published until June 1964. The Mongolians candidly state that the resolution, which was largely a polemic directed against the Chinese, was not published in December because public polemics "had been discontinued" at that time. So the MPRP Central Committee considered it advisable to refrain from publishing the resolution at that time."

9. Washington University, Far Eastern and Russian Institute, *Mongolian People's Republic*, (New Haven, Conn.: Human Relations Area Files, Inc., Press, 1956), Vol. III, pp. Pol. 48–50. (Subcontractor's Monograph HRAF-39, Wash-1).

10. Full members of the Politburo at the beginning of 1968 were: T. Dugersuren, N. Jagbaral, S. Lubsan, D. Maydar, D. Molomjamts, J. Sambu, and Y. Tsedenbal. Candidate members were: B. Lhamsuren and N. Lubsanrabdan.
    This leadership group remains comparatively young. Tsedenbal, for example, is 51, Lubsan is 55, and Lhamsuren is only 44. Members of the Politburo come from all sections of the country. Tsedenbal was born in northwest Mongolia, Lubsan in the southeast, and Lhamsuren in the northeast. Little data is available on the socioeconomic background of these men.

11. U.S.S.R., *XIV S'ezd Mongol'skoy Narodno-Revolutsionnoy Partiy* (Moscow: State Publishing House for Political Literature, 1962), p. 78. See also *Political and Economic Information on Mongolia*, JPRS, No. 17,335, January 28, 1963, pp. 97–98, trans. from *Kommunist* (Moscow), No. 11 (July, 1961).

12. *Unen*, July 20, 1963, p. 1 (in *Translations on Mongolia: No. 38*, JPRS, No. 21,276, October 1, 1963, p. 25).

13. *XIV S'ezd Mongol'skoy Narodno-Revolutsionnoy Partiy*, pp. 63–64. See also JPRS, No. 17,335, pp. 79–80.

14. Washington University, *Mongolian People's Republic*, Vol. II, p. 533.

15. *Hodolmor* (*Labor*), (Ulan Bator), September 10, 1963, p. 2; September 11, 1963, p. 2; September 14, 1963; September 17, 1963, p. 2; September 18, 1963, p. 2 (in *Translations on Mongolia: No. 41*, JPRS, No. 21,851, November 13, 1963, pp. 61–77).

16. Mongolian People's Republic, *Konstitutsiya Mongol'skoy Narodnoy Respubliki* (Ulan Bator: *Gosizdatel'stvo MNR*, 1961), p. 5.

17. *Namiin Amidral*, January, 1963.

18. Mongolian People's Republic, *Narodnoye Khozyaystvo Mongol'skoy Narodnoy Respubliki za 40 let; statisticheskiy sbornik*. Added title in English: *National Economy of the Mongolian People's Republic for 40 years: Collection of Statistics* (Ulan Bator: *Gosudarstvennoye Tsentral'noye Upravleniye Soveta Ministroy MNR*, 1961), p. 57.

19. Mongolian statistics continue to be unreliable. The MPR does not provide an over-all figure for the gross national product, simply because Mongolian planning and statistical systems are unable to provide such a figure. There has been no uniform pricing system, and statistical records of all types of enterprises are spotty. The MPR, with CEMA help, is now trying to correct this deficiency.

Soviet experts believe that Mongolia has the necessary resources to support a substantial increase in the number of livestock. Russian specialists in the MPR are working to reduce the annual livestock loss, now estimated to be some three million head annually.

20. Tsedenbal, in December 1965, said that only 40 percent of the cows and 60 percent of the sheep and goats had winter shelter.

21. *Unen*, July 7, 1961 (in *Translations from Unen: No. 15*, JPRS, No. 12,436, February 13, 1962, pp. 40–54). Also Ulan Bator, Montsame in Russian to U.S.S.R., March 1, 1963.

22. Rupen, Robert A., "The Mongolian People's Republic: the Slow Evolution," *Asian Survey*, (Berkeley, Calif.) VII, No. 1 (January, 1967), p. 17.

23. ——, "Mongolian Nationalism," *Royal Central Asian Journal*, April, 1958, pp. 157–58.

24. Friters, Gerard M., *Outer Mongolia and Its International Position* (Baltimore: The Johns Hopkins Press, 1949), pp. 143–49.

25. *Ibid.*

26. The *New York Times*, March 16, 1966; August 17, 1966; February 27, 1967; January 3, 1968; May 24, 1969. The *Washington Post*, December 11, 1966; February 19, 1967; and January 3, 1968.

Harrison Salisbury of the New York Times reported (from Irkutsk) on May 24, 1969 that between 100,000 and 200,000 Soviet soldiers were in Mongolia and that the second Soviet/Mongolian concentration point was along the southern segment of the Trans-Mongolian railroad. The Soviet troop total includes approximately 5,000 to 10,000 construction troops, distributed between the industrial areas of Ulan Bator, Darhan and Choybalsan. Salisbury reported that "most intelligence analysts" believe that the Chinese have deployed nuclear weapons on their side of the frontier, a counterthreat to the Soviet deployments.

27. Ulan Bator Radio, in Russian to the U.S.S.R., December 11, 1967, and November 27, 1967.

28. *Peking Review*, No. 23 (June 7, 1960), p. 9.

29. *Mongolian People's Republic*, Vol. II, 589.

30. Moscow, Tass, in English to Europe, January 31, 1962.

31. *Unen*, January 9, 1963 (in *Translations on International Communist Developments: No. 383*, JPRS, No. 18,025, March 8, 1963, p. 5).

32. Tsedenbal, Yumjagin, "Economic Cooperation of the Socialist Countries: A Vital Necessity," *World Marxist Review* (English ed. of *Problems of Peace and Socialism*), VII, No. 9 (September, 1964), pp. 2–9.

33. Tsedenbal spent nearly three months in the Soviet Union in 1964, visiting Moscow in April for two weeks to attend Khrushchev's seventieth birthday celebrations, and again visiting the Soviet Union for about six weeks in July and August on a working vacation. Tsedenbal has spent six to eight weeks in the Soviet Union every summer for the past several years. He made four stops in Moscow in October, and was again there for two weeks during the November 7, 1964, celebrations.

34. Peking Radio, in Mongolian to Mongolia, June 20, 1966.

35. Ulan Bator Radio, in Russian to the U.S.S.R., August 11, 1967.

36. *New York Times*, May 21, 1969; Belgrade radio, May 21, 1969.

37. Relations with other Communist countries were established as follows: Albania, May 17, 1949; Communist China, October 6, 1949; East Germany, April 13, 1950; Poland, April 14, 1950; Bulgaria, April 23, 1950; Czechoslovakia, April 25, 1950 Rumania, April 29, 1950; North Vietnam, November 18, 1954; Yugoslavia, November 20, 1956; Cuba, December 7, 1960.

38. U.S.S.R. *XIV S'ezd Mongol'skoy Narodno-Revolutsionno y Partiy* pp. 6–8 (in JPRS, No. 17,335, pp. 6–8).

39. Sofia Radio, July 16, 1967.

40. *Yomiuri* (Tokyo), April 27, 1967.

41. The *Washington Post*, June 30, 1966.

42. *Shimbun* (Tokyo), March 27, 1966.

43. *Christian Science Monitor* (Boston), July 9, 1966.

44. *New York Times*, May 21, 1969; see also *Yomiuri* (Tokyo), April 27, 1967.

45. The American offer was extended on July 19 to the Counselor of the Mongolian mission at the United Nations. The MPR did later accept a $5,000 contribution from the American Red Cross.

46. The *New York Times*, October 26, 1961.

SELECTED BIBLIOGRAPHY

Ballis, William B., "Outer Mongolia: Case Study of Soviet Colonialism" (*"Studies on the Soviet Union,"* No. 2). Munich: The Institute for the Study of the U.S.S.R., 1961.

Bawden, C. R., "Mongolian Review: October 1965," *Royal Central Asian Journal*, July–October, 1965, pp. 288–98.

Friters, Gerard M., *Outer Mongolia and Its International Position*. Baltimore: The Johns Hopkins Press, 1949.

Hart, Joe, "Mongolia: 20th Year of Economic Planning", *Asian* Survey (Berkeley, Calif.), VIII, No. 1 (January, 1968), 21–28.

Hibbert, R. A., "The Mongolian People's Republic in the 1960's," *The World Today*, March, 1967.

Langer, Paul F., *The Minor Asian Communist States: Outer Mongolia, North Korea and North Vietnam*, pp. 1–18. Santa Monica, Calif.: The Rand Corporation, 1964.

Lattimore, Owen, *Nationalism and Revolution in Mongolia*. New York: Oxford University Press, Inc., 1955.

———, *Nomads and Commissars: Mongolia Revisited*. New York: Oxford University Press, Inc., 1962.

Murphy, George G. S., *Soviet Mongolia: A Study of the Oldest Political Satellite*. Berkeley and Los Angeles: University of California Press, 1966.

Rupen, Robert A., *Mongols of the Twentieth Century* ("Uralic and Altaic Series," Vol. XXXVII). 2 vols. Bloomington: Indiana University, and the Hague: Mouton and Co., 1964.

———, *The Mongolian People's Republic* (The Hoover Institution on War, Peace, and Revolution). Stanford, Calif.: Stanford University Press, 1966.

———, "The Mongolian People's Republic and Sino-Soviet Competition," in *Communist Strategies in Asia*, ed. A. Doak Barnett. New York: Frederick A. Praeger, Inc., 1963, pp. 262–92.

———, The "Mongolian People's Republic: The Slow Evolution," *Asian Survey*, VI, No. 1 (January, 1967), 16–20.

Sanders, A. J. K., *The People's Republic of Mongolia*. London: Oxford University Press, 1968.

Titkov, Vasiliy Ivanovich, *The Government of the Mongolian People's Republic* (*Gosudarstvennyy stroy Mongol'skoy Narodnoy Respubliki*). Moscow: Gosyurizdat, 1961. Translation published by U.S. Department of Commerce, Office of Technical Services Joint Publications Research Office [JPRS], JPRS No. 17,456. Washington, D.C.: 1963.

Tsedenbal, Yumjagin, "Economic Cooperation of the Socialist Countries: A Vital Necessity," *World Marxist Review* (English ed. of *Problems of Peace and Socialism*), VI, No. 9 (September, 1964), 2–9.

———, "The Revolutionary Party and Social Changes," *World Marxist Review*, IX, No. 2 (February, 1966), 1–6.

University of Washington, Far Eastern and Russian Institute, *Mongolian People's Republic*. New Haven, Conn.: Human Relations Area Files, 1956.

STALINISM IN THE EAST

COMMUNISM IN NORTH KOREA

CHONG-SIK LEE

The Korean Workers' Party is the only ruling Communist Party in Asia (with the possible exception of the Mongolian Party) that ·has been imposed by outside forces upon a society, without substantial domestic roots. The process of consolidation of the Communist power in North Korea provides a unique example in Asia of how an alien system is transplanted outright and made to grow. The experience in North Korea also offers an example of how a small group of determined activists transformed uninitiated and disinterested masses into a disciplined, regimented, and indoctrinated people.

ORIGINS AND DEVELOPMENT OF THE PARTY

When the Soviet forces landed in North Korea in August 1945, they found a territory where Communism had made few inroads. Although most of the heavy industry of Korea was concentrated in the Soviet zone of occupation in North Korea, the proletariat was a relatively insignificant portion of the population. The result of the severe suppression by the Japanese police during the colonial period was that neither the labor nor the Communist movements had progressed beyond the nascent stage. An underground Communist movement had existed among the peasantry in a few pockets in the hinterlands, but the number of individuals affected by Communism had not exceeded a few thousand through the years, and even the idea of Communism was alien to most of the essentially conservative population. In most of the North Korean territory, the non-Communist nationalist elements which were under the influence of Christianity were much more vocal and influential.

The advancing Soviet Army was indeed greeted in various localities by self-styled Communists who had participated in some form of subversive movement before the war, but their number was still infinitesimally small and their over-all influence minute. Moreover, their quality was extremely low, in terms of general education, ideological training, and political motivation. These local Communists paid homage to a Central Committee of the Korean Communist Party (KCP) revived in Seoul (in the American zone of occupation), in September 1945, under the leadership of veteran Communist Pak Hŏn-yŏng.

The need for establishing an organizational structure that could be controlled from Pyongyang and that could be utilized for both the Soviet occupation and the creation of a political structure favorable for the Soviet Union in the future was no doubt urgent. This led to the encouragement of the local Communists to expand their forces and, in October 1945, to the creation of the North Korean Central Bureau of the KCP. The Soviet command at the same time permitted returnees from Yenan, China, to recruit followers into their Korean Independence League (later *Shinmin-dang*, i.e., the New People's Party), a group that had been nurtured by the Chinese Communists in northern China after 1941. Two non-Communist parties, the Korean Democratic Party (i.e., *Choson Minju-dang*) and the Youth Fraternal Party (i.e., *Ch'ŏng-u-dang*), were permitted to be established, but the Korean Democratic Party, led by a Christian elder, was taken over by the Communists after he was placed under custody by the Soviet command in January 1946. The Youth Fraternal Party of the *Ch'ŏndogyo* (i.e., Heavenly Way Religion) group remained on the periphery of the Communist regime, but the widespead collaboration of its members with the South Korean armed forces during the Korean War caused it to be carefully controlled thereafter.

Both the KCP and the New People's Party carried out vigorous campaigns to recruit new members and, by July 1946, the KCP had report-

122

STALINISM IN THE EAST

edly enlisted 276,000 members,[1] and the New People's Party had recruited 90,000.[2] Because of the differences in outlook, however, the two parties attracted different kinds of followers: While the KCP recruited tenant farmers and workers, the New People's Party recruited the better educated, more prosperous *bourgeoisie*, intelligentsia, and farmers. It was of course, not possible for the KCP, with largely uneducated workers and peasants, to staff and control the regional and local governments, not to mention infiltrating the masses at large.

Some form of alliance beyond the united front formula adopted toward all the non-Communist groups was needed to control and enlist the active support of the better educated and more influential elements of the society. The merger of the two parties, therefore, was executed in July 1946, and the North Korean Workers' Party (NKWP) was created. This Party became the Korean Workers' Party (KWP) in 1949, when the decimated South Korean Workers' Party, under Pak Hŏn-yŏng, was absorbed into the North Korean power structure.

The first paragraph of the Rules of the KWP defines the Party as:

. . . the vanguard, organized unit of the working class and the entire working masses in our country. The KWP represents the interest of the Korean nation [i.e., *minjok*] and the Korean people. The KWP consists of progressive fighters among all the working people of Korea including laborers, farmers, intelligentsia, etc. who support the interest of the working masses.[3]

The Party, in short, is a mass Party, similar to those in East Germany and Poland rather than to those in the Soviet Union or Communist China. Party membership, at least in theory, is not confined to any specific class of the people but rather open to:

. . . all working people who are citizens of Korea and recognize the platforms and rules of the party, struggle for the realization of them, enthusiastically carry out activities within the established party organization, positively carry out the party's decisions, and submit party membership fees.[4]

There has been no change in the Party's definition of its nature and missions, and Kim Il-sŏng has been at the apex of the Party throughout the two decades of its existence. Many of those in the leadership today have been long with the Party and have grown with it. Despite this outward stability and continuity, however, there has been a great transformation in the character of the leadership, in the style of leadership, and in the qualities of the membership. These changes, along with the changes in the international environment, have brought about corresponding changes in domestic and foreign policies.

The establishment of the KWP resulted in the coalition of three leadership groups: (1) those returning from the Soviet Union, including the so-called Soviet-Koreans born and raised in the Soviet Union (the careerists) and those who had taken refuge in eastern Siberia after 1941 after a decade of guerrilla activities in Manchuria (the Kim Il-sŏng group—the military activists); (2) the returnees from Yenan (ideologues and military activists); and (3) the Communists who had carried out underground activities within Korea before 1945 (ideologues and activists).

It was probably natural that the machinery of the Party was entrusted mostly to the Soviet-Koreans in the initial years. The members of all other groups were essentially revolutionaries accustomed to small group activities and destructive operations rather than to an orderly, structured functioning. Those from the Soviet Union, on the other hand, had been trained in a highly bureaucratic environment where the affairs of the Party were routinized.

The most prominent of these was Hŏ Ka-i, a former section chief in the Communist Party of Uzbekistan who served as the head of the Organization Department between 1945 and 1953. A number of others of similar background were placed in key positions in the Party in such fields as agitation and propaganda and cadre training.[5] It was inevitable, therefore, for the Party to pattern itself after the Communist Party of the Soviet Union (CPSU) not only in its organizational structure but in its operations. Kim Il-sŏng later charged that the leadership style of this period was that of bureaucratism, the characteristics of which could be identified as officiousness, arrogance, vainglory, arbitrariness, and rashness. Kim Il-sŏng also charged Pak Yŏng-bin, another director of the Organizational Department, of Russian origin, of having adopted the style of "detectives of the Japanese colonial police."[6] An exact replica of the Soviet secret police system was instituted in North Korea under the command of Pang Hak-se, who is reputed to have served in the NKVD system in the Soviet Union.

Party membership grew steadily. There were sufficient inducements for joining the Party, for the Communists, with the backing of the Soviet Army command, held full control of the power structure in North Korea. In July 1946, when the NKWP was organized, its membership was 366,000;[7] a year and a half later, in January 1948, its strength had almost doubled to 700,000;[8] at the end of 1952 the KWP had passed the 1,000,000 mark.[9] As of August 1, 1961, the KWP's membership was reported to be 1,311,563, including 145,204 candidate members. At the twentieth anniversary of the founding of the Party, on October 10, 1965, Kim Il-sŏng indicated that the membership exceeded 1,600,000.[10] Since the population of North Korea in 1963 was 11,568,000, the ratio of Party members to the population was 7.5 to 1, which places North Korea at or near the top of the world's Communist countries in terms of the percentage of the population in the Party."[11]

THE PURGES

The Party experienced its first serious trial during the Korean War. Although the North Korean forces (the Korean People's Army) had almost succeeded in overrunning the entire south by the end of the summer of 1950, General MacArthur's dramatic landing at Inchon reversed the situation and forced the invading army to retreat. The bitter experience of defeat showed, among other things, the defects in the Party: Those singled out by Kim Il-sŏng in December 1950, at the Third Plenum of the Central Committee, were lack of discipline, bureaucratic and formalistic propaganda and political education, and lack of creativity.[12] The problem of discipline was evidently very serious. Under the command of Organization Department Director Hŏ Ka-i, a thorough investigation of the conduct of Party members during the War was launched and, as a result, 450,000 of the total of 600,000 were disciplined.[13] The number of Party members expelled seems to have been substantial. According to the Premier's statement in April 1956, the North Pyongan Provincial branch alone expelled 18,000 members between 1948 and 1956, an average of 2,250 members a year. There are nine provinces in North Korea.[14]

Immediately after the truce was signed at Panmunjom in July 1953, a campaign to rectify the defects of the past was launched, along with a movement for economic reconstruction. In fact this campaign was to last until 1958, when the Party was purged of all elements other than those most loyal to Kim Il-sŏng. The purge was executed not only at the top leadership level but at lower levels as well.

The first target of the purge was the so-called domestic faction under Pak Hŏn-yŏng—the ideologue-activists. In August 1953, the Supreme Court in Pyongyang tried and convicted 12 leaders of the domestic faction on charges of having been American spies plotting to overthrow the leadership. This group, evidently, was to bear the onus of the military defeat. Pak, Vice-Chairman of the Party and Foreign Minister, was executed later in 1955.

The second stage of the purge was directed against the so-called Soviet-Koreans and the returnees from Yenan, and was staged between 1956 and 1958 in the aftermath of the Twentieth Congress of the CPSU and the August 1956 Plenum of the Central Committee of the KWP. Some of the leaders of these groups had called for the elimination of the one-man dictatorship and for modification of the stringent economic policies that emphasized heavy industry and demanded maximum sacrifice on the part of the population. Kim Il-sŏng's opponents evidently believed that they could muster sufficient strength at the Central Committee meeting to remove him from leadership, but they were defeated. Most of the Soviet-Koreans therefore, were ousted from the Party and returned to the Soviet Union. A few of the Yenan faction managed to flee to Communist China, but most of them suffered punishment for having had the audacity to openly challenge the leadership.[15]

These major purges at the center were followed by systematic campaigns at the lower levels. Party cadres from central headquarters were dispatched in groups to various regions, to thoroughly comb the background and outlook of the entire population. Even the slightest hint of a personal defect was attributed to the influence of "sectarian elements." Repeated confessions were demanded and exemplary trials were conducted to flush out all "anti-party" influences.[16] At the same time, an intensive campaign was launched to exalt the supreme Leader, Kim Il-sŏng, in order to fill the vacuum created by the extensive purges. A large number of Party History Study Rooms were established in agricultural cooperatives and other local units for this purpose. Histories were rewritten to castigate the anti-Kim elements and exalt the leader. Shrines, monuments, parks, and museums were established to inflate the significance of the revolutionary activities of the Premier. Kim Il-sŏng was identified not only as the flawless leader of the Party and the nation but as the personification of a glorious revolutionary tradition and the source of all wisdom. The intensity of the cult of personality that developed in North Korea after 1958 is unsurpassed by any other Communist regime.

North Korean leadership, following these successive purges and rectification campaigns, has been completely dominated either by those who had served under Kim Il-sŏng during his guerrilla days or those nurtured by him after 1945.

LEADERSHIP

At the Fourteenth Conference of the Fourth Central Committee held in October 1966, the Party adopted a plan of reorganization whereby the system consisting of a chairman, vice-chairmen, and departmental chiefs, was replaced by an eleven-member Secretariat, and a new six-member Standing Committee of the eleven-member Political Committee became the top decision-making body.[17] The fact that the members of this Committee simultaneously occupy all its posts in the Secretariat leaves no doubt about the locus of power. Directly below the Political Committee is the eighty-five member Central Committee, which, according to the Party rules, must meet at least once in four months in plenary session.

We can better understand the characteristics of the leadership of North Korea if we examine the background of the top echelon. It must never be forgotten, of course, that Kim Il-sŏng stands alone as the supreme leader. The full membership of the Political Committee and the Secretariat are presented below:

Ch'oe Yong-gŏn: Former Vice-Chairman of the Central Committee; member, Secretariat; member, Standing Committee of the Political Committee; Chairman of the Presidium of the Supreme People's Assembly. Veteran of partisan campaigns in Manchuria.

Kim Il: Former Vice-Chairman of the Central Committee; member, Secretariat; member, Standing Committee of the Political Committee; First Vice-Premier of the Democratic People's Republic of Korea. Veteran of partisan campaigns in Manchuria and a company commander under Kim Il-sŏng.

Pak Kŭm-ch'ŏl: Former Vice-Chairman of the Central Committee; member, Secretariat; member, Standing Committee of the Political Committee; Vice-Chairman of the Supreme People's Assembly. Served as liaison between Kim Il-sŏng in Manchuria and the small underground movement in the Kapsan area near the Manchurian-Korean border from 1936 to 1938.

Yi Hyo-sun: Former Vice-Chairman of the Central Committee; member, Secretariat; member, Standing Committee of the Political Committee; member of the Presidium of the Supreme People's Assembly. Brother of Yi Che-sun, who had worked closely with Pak Kŭm-ch'ŏl in the Kapsan area.

Kim Kwang-hyŏp: Member, Secretariat; member, Standing Committee of the Political Committee; Vice-Premier of the Democratic People's Republic of Korea (DPRK); Army general. Veteran of partisan campaigns in Manchuria under Kim Il-sŏng.

Sŏk San: Member, Secretariat; candidate member, Political Committee; Minister of Social Safety. Veteran of partisan campaigns in Manchuria under Kim Il-sŏng.

Hŏ Pong-hak: Member, Secretariat; candidate member, Political Committee; Army general; Deputy, Supreme People's Assembly. Veteran of partisan campaigns in Manchuria under Kim Il-sŏng.

Kim Yŏng-ju: Member, Secretariat; candidate member, Political Committee; in charge of the Organization Department of the KWP; graduate of the Higher Party School of the U.S.S.R.; Younger brother of Kim Il-sŏng. Postwar generation.

Pak Yong-guk: Member, Secretariat; candidate member, Political Committee; in charge of the International Department of the KWP; graduate of the Higher Party School of the U.S.S.R. Postwar generation.

Kim To-man: Member, Secretariat; candidate member, Political Committee; in charge of the Propaganda Department of the KWP; graduate of the Higher Party School of the U.S.S.R. Postwar generation.

Kim Ik-sŏn: Member, Political Committee; Chief Justice, Supreme Court of the DPRK (1948 to 1955, 1962 to 1966); Deputy, Supreme People's Assembly.

Kim Ch'ang-bong: Member, Political Committee; Vice-Premier; Minister of National Defense; Army general. Veteran of the partisan campaigns in Manchuria under Kim Il-sŏng.

Pak Sŏng-ch'ŏl: Member, Political Committee; Vice-Premier; Foreign Minister. Veteran of partisan campaigns in Manchuria under Kim Il-sŏng.

Ch'oe Hyŏn: Member, Political Committee; Army general; Minister of National Defense; member, Presidium of the Supreme People's Assembly. Veteran of partisan campaigns in Manchuria under Kim Il-sŏng.

Yi Yŏng-ho: Member, Political Committee. Former Vice-Minister of National Defense; Army corps Commander; and Ambassador to Communist China (1957 to 1962).

It is clear from the list that the leadership in North Korea is dominated by Kim Il-sŏng's personal followers of the guerrilla-activist type. Nine of the fifteen have been under his command since the 1930's, not including Ch'oe Yong-gŏn, who was a partisan in northern Manchuria while Kim was in the southeast. This, incidentally, helps to explain the fact that Ch'oe heads the Supreme People's Assembly, a post vacated by the Yenan group's Kim Tu-Bong. Some names are newly missing from the list. Until late 1966, Kim Ch'ang-man, of Yenan origin and an ideologue-activist, Nam Il, of Russian origin, and a bureaucratic-careerist, and Pak Chŏng-ae, an ideologue-activist of domestic origin, remained in the top leadership, but they have since been removed from the nucleus of power. The choice of personnel is obviously not based on ability but takes place by ascription.

The only non-guerrilla leaders emerging in North Korea today belong to the new generation of careerists: Kim To-man, Pak Yong-guk, and Kim Yŏng-ju are members of the Secretariat and in charge of the three key departments of the party—the Organization, Propaganda and Agitation, and International Departments. These men graduated from high-school level institutions after 1945 and later received Party training in North Korea and the Soviet Union. No doubt the importance of the younger generation will increase as time passes, but it should be noted that Kim Il-sŏng is still in his mid-fifties and that many of the former guerrillas who may be considered first-generation revolutionaries are still in their early fifties. Barring unforeseen events, monolithic and personal rule by Kim Il-sŏng is likely to continue for some time.

THE MASS LINE

Along with the concentration of power in the hands of Kim Il-sŏng and the deification of the Premier, the Party also began to adopt new styles of leadership. The points most stressed in North Korea are the so-called *Ch'ŏngsanri* spirit and the Taean Electrical Works system.

The *Ch'ŏngsanri* spirit derives its name from the fact that Kim Il-sŏng issued his rescript in February 1960 at *Ch'ŏngsanri*, an agricultural cooperative located a few miles west of Pyongyang. In essence, it is

128 STALINISM IN THE EAST

identical with the Chinese Communist *Hsia-fang* (i.e., downward) movement.[18] All cadres must, in the *Ch'ŏngsanri* spirit, regularly go down to the production level to help the workers at the lower levels. This is because, according to the North Korean theoreticians, the quantitative and qualitative growth of the workers failed to keep pace with the extraordinarily rapid growth of the economy. By directly participating in the organization of activities at the lower levels, those from the higher echelons would be enabled to make more correct plans; they would also become more familiar with actual conditions and problems at the lower levels and so become better able to provide solutions.[19] These economically couched arguments were then extended to the political sphere and the cadres were called upon to pay closer attention to the political realities below.

Implicit in the arguments behind the *Ch'ŏngsanri* spirit is the tacit admission that the cadres were ill-prepared to perform their duties, that their plans were not always based upon actual conditions, and that problems at the lower levels were too often left unsolved. Evidently these conditions were partly caused by the extensive purge of alleged anti-Party elements at both the central and local levels which had been concluded in early 1958: The new cadres lacked *expertise*. In 1960, the Party therefore launched a campaign to have all Party members attain substantial knowledge of their own fields. That Party members and cadres should be "Red" (in the North Korean context, read "loyal to the Premier") was assumed; they were now being required to become experts. Since then, all Party members have been required to devote at least two hours a day to the study of their respective fields of activities.

The *Ch'ŏngsanri* spirit is regarded in North Korea as a correct style of work applicable to all spheres of activities, and is an important element in North Korea's "mass line." The cadres are exhorted to teach and help the workers below, and to learn from the experience of working among the masses.[20] Emphasis is placed on the man rather than the material conditions. "Activities among man" and "activities of ideologically remaking the man" are given new importance.[21]

The Taean Electrical Works system, on the other hand, deals with managerial style in the factories and also reflects the experience of Communist China. As the Chinese announced in September 1956,[22] the North Koreans decided to rid themselves of one-man management of their factories and enterprises, replacing this system with collective leadership by Party Committees. "No matter how we reorganize the ministries or how brilliant a chief of the Bureau of Control we bring in, the problems cannot be solved," said the Premier in August 1962. The task of finding solutions for the problem of industrial development was laid on the Factory Party Committees. These Committees were reorganized to include Party cadres, administrative officers, engineers and "nuclei of workers" who would discuss and decide all matters dealing with production, grasp the actual conditions, guide and supervise the daily activities of the factory, and carry out the organizational and mobilization activities necessary to fulfill Party policies. Under this system, managers and chief engineers must execute the decisions of the Party Committees, but the Committees themselves must also deal with the entire Party membership and all the workers in order to fulfill the established goals.[23] Kim Il, the First Vice-Premier, asserted in October 1966, that the Taean system was designed to heighten the leading role of the Party in economic control and to "solve economic tasks by mobilizing the masses" through political education.[24] This system has been dubbed the "mass line in industry," and it is claimed that it permits the worker to participate in the planning and execution of his own work. One might add that it is another form of "politics takes command." Whether the Taean system had any impact on the failure of the Seven-year Economic Plan (1961 to 1967) cannot be determined, but evidently the Chinese, at least, have found it necessary to modify their version of the system considerably.

THE EMPHASIS ON NATIONALISM

One outstanding characteristic of North Korean postwar policies is the emphasis on nationalism. This has been reflected in its economic, political, and foreign policies as well as in its historiography. While it is difficult to offer definite explanations for the intensified emphasis on nationalism, it is possible to speculate on the motives.

It should be recalled that the Russian-armed North Korean forces almost succeeded in conquering the entire peninsula in the summer of 1950. Only the air superiority of the United States prevented the Communist troops from overrunning the Pusan perimeter south of the Naktong River before the Inchon landing in September. Is it not reasonable to assume that the leaders in Pyongyang requested air coverage by the Soviet air force in the critical summer months? This, of course, would have necessitated the overt participation of the Soviet Union in the Korean War—which, in spite of Pyongyang's insistence, Moscow strove to avoid. We can draw a striking parallel with the invasion of the Bay of Pigs.

Later in the same year, MacArthur's landing in Inchon reversed the situation, and the northern advance of the United Nations forces almost drove the Communist forces out of Korea. It is reasonable to assume that the desperate North Korean leaders requested immediate Soviet intervention during their catastrophic retreat. In the winter of

1950, direct Russian intervention seemed essential—but the Soviet Union was not willing to risk a major war to save the North Koreans. It needs to be emphasized that North Korea was definitely within the Russian sphere, not the Chinese, in 1950.

Chinese intervention in October did alter the situation on the Korean War front, but the North Korean Communists must have had some nerve-wracking moments. What if the Chinese Communists had not been able to rescue North Korea? Would the Soviet Union have intervened then? Would the Soviet Union risk danger in the future to aid its fraternal parties in a moment of extreme need? It is reasonable to assume that the North Korean leaders were compelled to sacrifice their control of the war and to swallow their pride in accepting the Chinese "volunteers" who came to the rescue. Evidence suggests that the North Korean Communists were not always in harmony with the Chinese, and one may suspect that the differences were rarely settled in favor of the Korean position. Thus, the Korean Communists had ample reasons to loathe their weaknesses—military, political, and economic.

As soon as the truce was concluded at Panmunjom on July 27, 1953, the North Korean Communists set about remedying their deplorable situation. On August 5, the Premier delivered a major policy speech at the Sixth Plenum of the Korean Workers' Party, delineating the policies to be followed. The points stressed most strongly by Kim were the strengthening of the people's democracy and the consolidation of the "democratic base" in North Korea. Kim argued that this would certainly contribute to "peaceful unification" and independence.

STRESS ON INDUSTRIAL DEVELOPMENT

Undoubtedly, the situation in North Korea was difficult in 1953. The destruction of industrial facilities had been almost complete,[25] the food shortage was severe, and consumer goods were scarce. For these reasons, some of the leaders reportedly advocated a balanced recovery and development program designed to alleviate the immediate difficulties of the populace. This group of leaders, including Ch'oe Ch'ang-ik and Pak Ch'ang-ok, evidently envisaged a program which would loosen the war-time control of the economy, import more food and consumer goods, and at the same time carry forward a moderate industry recovery program.[26] The Russian advisers evidently favored this moderate course.

But the Party's dominant group, including the Premier, emphatically rejected the moderate proposals. The sufferings of the masses were evidently the least of the leadership's concern. While praising the "patriotic mobilization of the people which greatly contributed to the attainment of victory in the war," Kim Il-sŏng admonished against any relaxation of pressure. "We must appeal to the patriotic dedication of the masses to develop mass labor mobilization in the effort to reconstruct the war-torn industrial enterprises and the educational and cultural facilities."[27]

The plan adopted in North Korea was a modified version of the industrialization policy of the Communist Party of the Soviet Union (CPSU) under Stalin. The formula, acclaimed by North Korean theoreticians as original and creative, called for the "priority development of heavy industry together with the simultaneous development of light industry and agriculture." The rapid reconstruction and development program was to be carried out through successive stages of: (1) a preparatory period of from six months to a year; (2) a Three-Year Plan from 1954 through 1956; and (3) a Five-Year Plan from 1957 through 1961. A Seven-Year Plan, for 1961 through 1967, was adopted later.

The simultaneous-development program meant, in practice, concentrated capital investment in heavy industry and a minimum allocation of capital to light industry and agriculture. Living standards were kept to the lowest level of subsistence, even by Korean standards. Production of consumer goods received little attention until 1958, and even the farmers were allowed to consume only a fraction of their agricultural products. Collectivized agriculture became an auxiliary to industry, the farmers being obliged to supply both food and industrial raw materials at the same time as they provided most of the capital for industrial development through compulsory savings. Agriculture was completely collectivized through the agricultural cooperative system, a process which was completed in 1958.

In his speech to the Sixth Plenum, in 1953, the Premier assigned priority to the following industries: steel mills, machinery production, ship construction, mining, electrical generation, chemical fertilizers, petroleum, construction materials, and cement. Textile mills and food-processing factories received only brief mention. The responsibility for the production and distribution of sundry daily necessities was relegated to the provincial committees, which in reality meant the postponement of action in these fields. As Kim Il-sŏng admitted five years later, in June 1958, even the discussion of enlarging the production of daily necessities was meaningless before that time. It was impossible, said Kim, "to raise the problem of the food-processing industry before the problem of food shortage was solved. Both food processing and the production of daily necessities required certain foundations [i.e., heavy industry]."[28]

In statistical terms, 39.9 billion won, or 49.5 per cent of the total capital investment of 80.6 billion won (price standard of January 1, 1950), were allocated to industry during the Three-Year Plan of 1954 through 1956; of this sum, 81.8 per cent was invested in heavy industry.

During the Five-Year Plan of 1957 through 1961, 55 per cent of the total capital investment of 147 billion won was allocated to industry; of this, 83 per cent was for heavy industry.[29]

Kim Il-sŏng stated, at the Sixth Plenum of the Party in 1953, that among the factors making possible the economic reconstruction and development was the "trustworthy support and assistance granted by the Soviet Union, the Chinese people and various fraternal peoples." The total amount of aid received between the end of the War and April 1963, is reported to be equivalent to 550 million U.S. dollars.[30] But, according to North Korean sources, three-fourths of all foreign aid was spent on the acquisition of the means of production (heavy and light industries), only one-quarter going to agriculture and consumer goods.[31]

Although North Korea continues to receive some aid and loans from other Communist countries, the plans succeeding the initial Three-Year Plan have had to be financed mainly by internal savings.[32] In order to finance its ambitious industrial development after 1956, it was necessary for the Pyongyang regime to enforce compulsory savings averaging 25 per cent of the national income.[33] According to Communist sources, this ratio of savings was even higher than those enforced in the Soviet Union and Communist China in comparable periods of their history.[34] The North Korean leaders demanded the utmost sacrifice and perseverance from the populace.

There is no doubt that North Korea has made significant economic gains since the War. According to official reports, North Korea had successfully shed all residues of the distorted colonial economy by 1958. It is now, in Communist parlance, an industrial-agricultural society. Table 1 shows the changing economic structure in North Korea as reported by the North Korean sources.

Table 1

COMPOSITION OF GROSS NATIONAL PRODUCT BY ECONOMIC SECTORS

	1946	1949	1953	1956	1960	1963
Industry	23.2	35.6	30.7	40.1	57.1	62.3
Agriculture	59.1	40.6	41.6	26.6	23.6	19.3
Transportation and Communication	1.6	2.9	3.7	4.0	2.2	2.8
Basic construction	—	7.2	14.9	12.3	8.7	9.8
Commerce	12.0	9.4	6.0	10.8	6.0	3.8
All others	4.1	4.3	3.1	6.2	2.4	2.0
Total	100.0	100.0	100.0	100.0	100.0	100.0

SOURCE: Chosŏn Chugnang Nyŏngam (Korean Central Annual), (Korean Central News Agency: Pyongyang, 1965), p. 477.

In 1961, the regime set up very high goals for its new Seven-Year Economic Development Plan and launched it with great fanfare, but in late 1966 the leaders announced that it would be necessary to postpone the Plan for three years. The failure was blamed on the increasing need for defense expenditures arising from the aggravation of the international situation, but more likely reasons are the aggravation of relations between Pyongyang and Moscow, unrealistic goals, mismanagement, and shortage of manpower. Table 2 presents North Korea's goals for 1967 (set in 1960), and the claims made for the years 1960, 1963, and 1966. The reader is asked to bear in mind that the data, released by the North Korean authorities, may well be exaggerated.

Table 2

PRODUCTION GOALS AND OUTPUT OF INDUSTRIAL GOODS

	Goals for 1967	Production in 1966	Production in 1963	Production in 1960
Electrical power[a]	17,000	12,500	11,766	9,139
Coal[b]	25,000,000	20,000,000	14,040,000	10,620,000
Pig iron and granulated iron[b]	2,300,000	1,500,000	1,159,000	872,000
Steel[b]	2,300,000	1,300,000	1,022,000	641,000
Chemical Fertilizers[b]	1,700,000	Not given	853,000	561,000
Cement[b]	4,300,000	Not given	2,530,000	2,285,000
Fabrics[c]	500,000	Not given	227,187	189,659

SOURCE: Democratic People's Republic of Korea, 1961, pp. 20–21. Statistical Board Release, January 17, 1964. Kim Il, "Present Tasks in the Socialist Economic Construction," Kulloja (The Worker) No. 10, 1966, pp. 56–57.

[a]In kilowatt hours.
[b]In tons.
[c]In kilometers.

INDEPENDENCE AND SELF-RELIANCE

North Korea's economic growth was immediately reflected in its internal pronouncements. Until the Three-Year Plan was completed in 1957, and while North Korea was predominantly dependent upon foreign aid, the Communists justified their policies on the ground that accelerated economic development contributed to the consolidation of a democratic base in North Korea. Thus, Kim Il-sŏng argued in 1954:

When we effectively bring about economic construction and improve the people's livelihood in the Northern part [of Korea] and make it a great paradise, no power can suppress the revolutionary forces of the South Korean people, who will long for the Northern part and oppose the reactionary regime in South

Korea. [Economic resources of the north] would also enable us to solve easily the problems of the South Korean people's livelihood when the unification of the fatherland has been achieved.[35]

As the country's economic condition improved and the international situation changed, North Korean writers began to place more emphasis on an "independent and self-reliant economy" as an essential aspect of the Party's economic program. Although the phrase was not totally new in the North Korean context,[36] it did not come to the forefront until about 1957. It is interesting to note that the Chinese Communists also began to stress this same theme about this time. By 1961, articles on the independent and self-reliant economy predominated in the Party's theoretical organ, *Kŭlloja*, replacing the former theme of the consolidation of a democratic base.

The new stress on independence and self-reliance, of course, did not come about accidentally. As the initial efforts for reconstruction were completed and North Korea's relations with the allies deteriorated, foreign aid was drastically reduced. Russian aid was not forthcoming, and the Chinese did not have enough to offer much assistance. Improvement in the economy also produced more respect and prestige for North Korea among the Communist countries,[37] and the conflict within the international Communist camp provided both the opportunity and the need for the North Koreans to speak more of independence. The simultaneous adoption of the identical theme by the Chinese and the North Koreans also suggests the possibility of Chinese influence. In any event, the North Korean Communists were gaining more self-confidence and self-respect. Kim Il-sŏng's statement of January 1958 was remarkably straightforward:

In times before, if we wanted more irrigation, we needed to buy pumps, transformers, generators, and electric motors. So, we were not able to decide on the matter by ourselves but had to ask the people who offered to provide the materials. *But we now have the right to speak and decide by ourselves.* [Emphasis supplied.][38]

The emphasis on a self-reliant economy was preceded by intense indoctrination in "things Korean." In April 1955, the Premier admonished the membership of the Party for not knowing Korean history and events connected with their own country. Party members were simply memorizing the principles of Marxism, he complained, and were not able to apply these principles. Further, on December 28, 1955, he delivered a major speech on ideological education stressing the need for "firmly establishing *chuch'e*" (i.e., self-identity). He argued that there was an urgent need to consider seriously why the ideological activities of the past had degenerated into dogmatism and formalism and why the propagandists and agitators had not been able to probe various problems deeply. The Party workers, according to Kim, had not been creative, and had only copied and memorized the ideas of others.[39]

"What should be the *Chuch'e*, or self-identity?" To answer this question, the Premier posed another: "What are we doing?"

We are engaged in none other than the Korean revolution. The Korean revolution is the theme of our party's ideological activities. Therefore, all ideological activities must be adapted to the interest of the Korean revolution. The purpose of our study of the histories of the Communist Party of the U.S.S.R. and the Chinese revolution, or the general principles of Marxism-Leninism, is entirely for the correct execution of our revolution.[40]

According to the Premier, North Korea's adulation of the Soviet Union was extreme. In the walls of the People's Army's recuperation centers hung pictures of Siberian fields. In the "democratic propaganda rooms" in the countryside hung pictorial charts of Russia's Five-Year Plan, but none of North Korea's Three-Year Plan. There were photographs of "factories of foreign nations," but none of Korean factories. Elementary schools displayed portraits of Mayakovsky and Pushkin, but none of Korean heroes.

The Premier was also emphatic in denouncing those who advocated blind imitation of the Soviet policies. For instance, he attacked Pak Yŏng-bin, then the head of the Organization and Guidance Department of the Central Committee, who had proposed that the Korean Party should remove its strong anti-American slogans because the Soviet Union was relaxing her stand against the United States. The Premier charged that this kind of advocacy not only had no common ground with revolutionary creativity, but also would paralyze "our people's revolutionary awareness." Kim ostensibly supported the "Soviet people's efforts for relaxing international tension," but argued that North Korea's "struggle against American imperialists" was in harmony with Soviet policy. Although the Premier did not elaborate on what appeared to be a unity of opposites, his implicit argument was that the strong stand taken by North Korea would soften the American imperialists and hence contribute to peace. It is worth remembering that these statements were made at the end of 1955.

In stressing the need for more study of things Korean and for a new patriotism for Korea, Kim also evoked the concept of the unity of patriotism and internationalism. To love Korea, said Kim, was to love the Soviet Union and the socialist camp. To love the Soviet Union and the socialist camp was to love Korea. That was because, according to Kim, there were no national boundaries in the great tasks of the working class of the world.

Kim Il-sŏng's speeches on ideological or doctrinal education were also devoted to attacks upon the so-called sectarian elements of the Yenan, domestic, and Russian factions. During the War, said the Premier, "Hŏ Ka-i, Kim Chae-uk, and Pak Il-u had argued uselessly over the method of political activities in the Army. Those from the Soviet Union wanted to follow the Russian way and those from China wanted to follow the Chinese way." Of course, the "Party Central [i.e., Kim Il-sŏng himself] decided that the Party should learn from both the Soviet Union and China and create methods best suited to our country's actual conditions."[41]

Kim's admonitions were well heeded by the Party's historians and propagandists, whose works on Korean history have rapidly multiplied. These writers can be grouped into three categories: (1) historians exalting the glories of ancient Korea and the virtues of the progressive scholars of seventeenth- and eighteenth-century Korea; [42] (2) pseudo-historians and propagandists apotheosizing the revolutionary past of Kim Il-sŏng; and (3) economists and propagandists praising, in greatly exaggerated form, the accomplishments of the regime. The tasks of these writers vary, but all are united in glorification of the fatherland, and those who deal with modern material are united in exaltation of the Premier.

PEACEFUL UNIFICATION OF KOREA

Nationalism has been an important theme of the Communist leaders —not only for the North Korean masses, but for the anti-Communist South Koreans as well. As we observed earlier, the peaceful unification of the fatherland was presented in North Korea as the primary justification for the frantic development of heavy industry. North Korea is to serve as the democratic base for a united Korea.

Like other policies adopted in North Korea during the postwar period, the principle of peaceful unification is not totally new. It should be recalled that the Pyongyang regime had issued strong appeals for negotiations for peaceful unification just a week before launching the attack on South Korea on June 25, 1950. The appeals were issued by the Fatherland Unification Democratic Front, the organization established to "promote the unification movement." The Fatherland Front is an apparatus of the regime for mobilizing all non-Communist democratic forces in North and South Korea; ostensibly, it is a united front of all the political parties and groups throughout Korea. The Pyongyang regime, which still adheres to the notion of a people's democracy, maintains the skeleton of a number of non-Communist parties and groups for this purpose, including the *Chosŏn Minjudang* (i.e., the Korean Democratic Party) and the *Ch'ŏndogyo Ch'ŏng-u-dang* (i.e., the Ch'ŏndogyo Youth Fraternal Party). These parties and groups are still represented in the Supreme People's Assembly, although they are believed to have almost no members.

The advocacy of peaceful unification was accepted credulously by some, both in North and South Korea, before the war. The renewed appeal after the war, however, was received with universal skepticism even in North Korea. The Communist leader spoke on this point in November 1954: "Some people think that peaceful unification is impossible and hence regard our current appeal as nothing but a formality. Even among our Party members there are those who think this way."[43]

In order to convince his subordinates that the slogan was more than an expression of vague hopes and formality, Kim treated some of the difficult theoretical problems that revealed potential areas of conflict with the positions taken by the Soviet Union, notably the question of peaceful coexistence and American imperialism.

Kim Il-sŏng asserted that there were some who extended the policy of peaceful coexistence of the two world camps into Korea and wrongly concluded that the two separate Koreas could coexist. And there were others, he said, who did not attach any hope to unification because of the obstruction posed by the American imperialists. Kim made it known that he was in complete agreement with the principle of peaceful coexistence. In fact, he said, the principle was "absolutely correct," but impossible to apply to Korea:

. . . the idea that Korea could be separated into Northern and Southern parts and that the parts should coexist with each other is very dangerous; it is a view obstructing our efforts for unification. Those holding this view would relegate the *responsibility of revolution in South Korea* to the South Korean people and relieve of the people in North Korea the *responsibility of liberating* South Korea. This is nothing more than a justification for the division of the Fatherland and for perpetuation of the division. [Emphasis supplied.][44]

The Premier conceded that the peaceful unification of the fatherland would not be accomplished in a short period because of the United States. "We cannot lightly treat the power of the American imperialists," said Kim. But the United States "would not be able to avoid the eventual destruction [destined] by the law of historical development." Kim was, of course, not going to sit idly and wait for the historical law to take its natural course: "[Our] task lies in the quickening of the process of destruction through our struggle." When this has been accomplished, argued the Premier, "even if the American imperialists strove to support the Syngman Rhee clique, we could not be restrained from attaining the great task of unifying the Fatherland." One must conclude that the policy of peaceful unification is indeed a long-range one.

With these justifications, the North Korean regime aimed an intensive propaganda campaign toward South Korea. It should be remembered that, although no North Korean publications can be obtained by the ordinary citizenry of South Korea, North Korean broadcasts are readily audible there. Basically, the North Korean aims have been to alienate the South Korean masses from the United States, to establish the North Korean Communists as the true patriots, and to organize, when possible, Communist sympathizers in South Korea. The Communist leaders seem to be aware that orthodox Communist themes have little appeal in South Korea. Only through nationalist appeals, they seem to have concluded, can the South Korean people be approached.

The Pyongyang regime's basic formula for peaceful unification has not changed since 1954, when Nam Il, then Foreign Minister, presented the North Korean position at the Geneva conference. Nam advocated the establishment of an all-Korean commission, the membership to be selected by the Supreme People's Assembly of the North Korean regime and the National Assembly of South Korea. The commission would be charged with the responsibility of making necessary preparations for a free general election and of taking "urgent measures for the economic and cultural *rapprochement* of North and South Korea."[45] Some of the later proposals would endow this commission with more power. It would, for instance, head a confederation of the two Koreas and be invested with the authority to decide on matters related to foreign affairs and national defense.[46]

As in the period before the Korean War, the Pyongyang regime continues to insist, as a prerequisite for negotiation, that all foreign troops (i.e., United States forces) be withdrawn from Korea and all military alliances dissolved. The argument is that the fate of Korea must be decided by the Koreans themselves, without the interference of outsiders. In the same vein, the North Korean regime refuses to submit to a nationwide general election supervised by the United Nations. Since more than two-thirds of the population now resides in South Korea, and since most of these are probably adamant opponents of Communism, the Communists could not hope to win a majority in a truly free election.

North Korean propaganda has sought to exploit every opportunity to create a favorable image of the Pyongyang regime in the minds of the South Korean masses. The regime has also sought to gain propaganda advantages by proposing limited intercourse between the two parts of Korea. For instance, it advocated exchange visits of "cultural and commercial personnel." It also offered to enter into "economic exchange and cooperation in order to salvage the economic catastrophe of South Korea." In addition, it advocated the exchange of mail between the two parts of Korea. It has even offered, since 1963, to provide rice to relieve the South Korean population from hunger, despite a continuing food shortage within its own territory.

It would be difficult to determine the impact of such proposals and propaganda in South Korea. It can be said, however, that the intensive campaign has placed the regime in Seoul on the defensive and that it has increased the desire of some segments of the South Korean population to open limited contacts with the north. The Pyongyang regime evidently believes that these desires can be nurtured so as to become, eventually, a strong anti-American force.

It is highly unlikely, however, that any significant segment of the South Korean population is looking north for an alternative to its present situation, arduous though it may be. For this hostility, the Communists have largely themselves to blame. Their inhumane behavior during the Korean War distilled deep and irreparable antagonism toward Communism among the South Korean masses. This fact alone would make it difficult for the Pyongyang regime to organize a revolutionary base in South Korea or to promote guerrilla operations. Atrocities committed by North Korean commando troops against innocent people in South Korea in 1968–1969 are hardly designed to make the Communists popular. The goal of "peaceful unification" is still a Communist dream.

PYONGYANG IN THE SINO-SOVIET DISPUTE

The growing intensification of the cold war within the international Communist camp has placed the Pyongyang regime in a serious dilemma. This is because the steadily worsening rift forced the North Korean Communists to choose between the two contending powers at a time when North Korea could ill afford to alienate either. Moreover, various historical, geographical, and other factors made it very difficult for the Pyongyang regime to choose one side and reject the other.

For example, the North Korean Premier and most of his cohorts owed their power and position to the Soviet Union. Although Kim Il-sŏng, in his early revolutionary days, operated in Manchuria along with Chinese Communists, it was the Soviet military command that nurtured his power in North Korea after 1945. In the initial period, Kim had to struggle against the returnees from Yenan, the group that had very close contacts with the Chinese Communist leadership. Furthermore, it was the Soviet Union that armed and trained the North Korean Army, police, and Party. Until the Korean War, North Korea was unquestionably a Russian satellite.

Geography, on the other hand, places Korea closer to China. Although North Korea shares a few miles of border with the Soviet far east, it shares a long border with Manchuria, the industrial heartland of China. And historically, China had held suzerain rights over Korea; the Middle Kingdom long had a keen interest in Korean affairs. Thus, the dispatch of Chinese volunteers in 1950 was, in certain respects, a traditional gesture. So if the Pyongyang regime owed to the Soviet Union its creation, it owed to China its survival.

Despite North Korean claims that it has attained a balanced and self-reliant economy, the support of both the Soviet Union and Communist China is vital if the country is to develop its scientific, military, and industrial facilities. The antagonism of either of the powers would weaken Pyongyang's defenses and slacken its over-all technological and economic development. The importance of these factors has been clearly shown in the vicissitude of North Korea's foreign policy.

Neutralism

Faced with growing Sino-Soviet disagreements the North Korean leaders were initially compelled to choose the policy of neutralism or non-alignment. Before 1961, before the dispute became heated, Pyongyang constantly reiterated the necessity of unity within the Communist bloc, simultaneously eulogizing both the Soviet Union and Communist China. On questions that divided the two, Pyongyang took a nebulous and middle-of-the-road attitude obviously aimed at placating the disputants: North Korea adopted an obscure position on the question of peaceful coexistence and the revolutionary struggle, as we have already mentioned, and the issues of de-Stalinization and of the communes were met in similar fashion.

Although the Chinese Communist Party took up the issue of de-Stalinization immediately after Khrushchev's secret speech, by publishing, on April 5, 1956, an article in *Jen-min jih-pao* that stressed the necessity of learning from Stalin's achievements as well as from his weaknesses, the Pyongyang regime did not mention Stalin's name for some years thereafter. *Minju Chosŏn*, the organ of government, reprinted without comment (on April 3, 1956) a *Pravda* article, "Why the Cult of Personality Does Not Have Any Relationship with Marxism-Leninism." The article did not mention Stalin by name and did not suggest that the dead hero had been disgraced. In the ensuing months, North Korean publications attacked the hero worshipers within the Party and praised "adherence to the principle of collective leadership by our Party's Central Committee headed by Comrade Kim Il-sŏng."[47] As has been suggested above, the poisoned edge of the ideological sword was directed against Ch'oe Ch'ang-ik and others, the very critics of the cult of personality centering around Kim. This emphasis upon the principle of collective leadership obviously satisfied Moscow. The policy was also one which would have been satisfactory to Peking, since Pyongyang did not attack Stalin personally. Even after the Twenty-second CPSU Congress in November 1961, Kim Il-sŏng did not choose to denounce Stalin. "The name of Stalin is well known among the Communists and the people of the entire world," said Kim. But, he continued, "The Soviet Communist Party members should know him better than anyone else. The problem of how to evaluate Stalin's activities in the U.S.S.R. belongs to the category of intra-Party problems of the CPSU."[48]

This clever neutralism can also be observed with regard to the issue of agrarian collectivization. As is well known, North Korea's agricultural collectivization program closely paralleled China's, in timing and in methods. Thus, the experimental stage was launched in August 1953; a full-scale collectivization was begun in November 1954; and the movement was completed by August 1958, when there were 13,309 cooperatives averaging 80 households each. In October 1958, after the Chinese adopted the commune system, the Pyongyang regime announced the merger of small cooperatives into larger agrarian administrative units quite similar to the Chinese communes. Instead of 13,309 cooperatives there would be only 3,843, each consisting of 300, rather than 80, households. The average acreage of a cooperative would be 500 *chŏngbo* (i.e., 1,225 acres) rather than 130 *chŏngbo*.[49]

Clearly, North Korean collectivization was modeled after Chinese. The North Korean Communists, however, seem to have exercised enough prudence to avoid offending their Russian comrades. For instance, Pyongyang retained the term "cooperative," even though the Chinese adopted the term "commune" in July 1958. Nor was any claim made in North Korean publications that the *ri* cooperatives were the "practical road of transition to communism."[50] Thus the North Korean Communists could justify their agrarian policy merely as an extension of the Soviet Union's experience with "higher-type cooperatives," or something similar to the giant cooperatives formed in 1958 in Bulgaria. No clear-cut explanations have been offered by Pyongyang.

Pyongyang Leans toward Peking

However, as Sino-Soviet relations worsened after the Twenty-second CPSU Congress in October and November 1961, and as various foreign policy issues became critical, the North Korean leaders began to adopt more distinct policies. For example, North Korea refused to follow the Russian line in denouncing the Albanian Workers' Party and its leader, Hoxha. On November 8, 1961, on the occasion of the twentieth anniversary of the founding of the Albanian Party, the North Korean leaders sent a warm congratulatory message praising its achievements and its leadership. At the enlarged Plenum of the Central Committee of the Korean Workers' Party on November 28, 1961, Kim Il-sŏng reiterated the urgency of maintaining the unity and solidarity of a socialist camp that would include the Albanian Party. He further underscored the importance of proletarian internationalism, emphasizing the equality of each Party and the principle of noninterference in the internal affairs of other Parties. Again, on November 28, on the occasion of the seventeenth anniversary of the liberation of Albania, Pyongyang sent a eulogistic congratulatory message. The North Korean position on Albania has not changed since.

On other foreign policy issues that intensified the schism, such as the Sino-Indian dispute and the Cuban crisis, North Korea stood firmly behind the Chinese. The Nehru government was condemned as an aggressor and as a reactionary force working with the American imperialists. On the Cuban issue, the Pyongyang leaders denounced the appeasement of American imperialism as futile, and they urged all friends of peace and socialism to stand firm and to force the American imperialists to "take their bloodstained hands off Cuba at once."

On the more explosive issue of revisionism, the North Korean Communists have taken a very consistent attitude since 1956. Although the March 1956 issue of the Party's theoretical organ, *Kŭlloja*, faithfully reproduced Khrushchev's speech at the Twentieth CPSU Congress, in which he praised Yugoslavia's display of "creative Marxism" and stressed the necessity for strengthening cooperation with Yugoslavia,[51] international revisionists were indirectly attacked after the August Plenum of the Korean Workers' Party's Central Committee for having aided the cause of the anti-Party, Ch'oe Ch'ang-ik, clique. The January 1957 issue of the same journal printed an article that attacked "some elements that consciously or unconsciously serve the imperialist forces by wearing the mask of a friend of Communism yet strive to split the ranks of international Communism and revise Marxism-Leninism." This was followed by two more virulent articles in February and June, 1958. Regarding the Yugoslav Ljubljana Program (March, 1958), *Kŭlloja* carried translations of two derogatory articles in the Moscow publication, *Kommunist*.

This hostile attitude toward Yugoslavia continued after the Soviet Union had begun to woo Tito in an effort to bring Yugoslavia back into the Communist camp. In 1962, even while the Russians and Tito were exchanging visits in Belgrade and Moscow, the organs of Pyongyang were blatantly attacking Tito as a subversive traitor to the international Communist movement and a faithful lackey of American imperialism. On June 23, 1963, Chairmen Liu Shao-chi and Ch'oe Yong-gŏn issued a joint statement in Peking expressing complete agreement on:

. . . the question of further consolidating and developing relations of friendship, unity and mutual assistance and cooperation between the two Parties and the two countries and on important questions concerning the current international situation and the international Communist movement.

Their joint statement on revisionism is worth quoting at length:

The modern revisionists emasculate the revolutionary essence of Marxism-Leninism, paralyze the revolutionary will of the working class and working

people, meet the needs of imperialism and the reactionaries of various countries, and undermine the unity of the socialist camp and the revolutionary
struggles of all peoples. They do not themselves oppose imperialism, and forbid
others to oppose imperialism. They do not want revolution themselves and
forbid others to make revolution. Both sides stressed that the struggle against
modern revisionism has an important bearing on the future of the revolutionary
cause of the proletariat and working people of the world as well as the destiny
of mankind. . . .[52]

Pyongyang Seeks Balance

For approximately four years, it appeared to outsiders that the North
Korean Communists would follow in the footsteps of China to the point
of a rupture of relations with the Soviet Union. On September 7, 1964,
in refuting a *Pravda* editorial on the Asian Economic Seminar held from
June 17 to 23 in Pyongyang, *Nodong Shinmun* (i.e., *Labor News*, the
organ of the KWP) went as far as to say:

What a striking coincidence of the Voice of *Pravda* with the Voice of America!
. . What a slighting attitude of contempt and arrogance this is! What over-
bearing, insolent, and shameless nonsense it is! These are the words that can
be used only by great-power chauvinists who are in the habit of thinking that
they are entitled to decide and order everything.

The North Korean regime, however, began to modify its vitriolic stand
against the Soviet Union after 1965. The downfall of Khrushchev, in
October 1964, and Kosygin's visit to Pyongyang, in February 1965, evidently had an effect. It should be noted that Khrushchev had never
visited North Korea, even though he had scheduled two visits and the
Pyongyang regime had made extensive preparations for them. An immediate product of Kosygin's visit was the signing of the U.S.S.R.-
North Korean military agreement at the end of May 1965.[53] This was
followed by the conclusion of an agreement on economic and technical
cooperation on June 20, 1966, in pursuance of which an economic and
scientific-technical consultative committee was established in October
1967.[54]

At the twentieth anniversary of the founding of the Party (October
10, 1965), Kim Il-sŏng renewed the old theme of uniting the international
socialist camp and the need for "taking joint steps in the struggle against
imperialism," even though he still adhered to his previous stand on modern revisionism.[55] A major editorial in *Nodong Shinmun* (*Labor News*),
on August 12, 1966, reemphasized the familiar theme of *Chuch'e* (i.e.,
self-identity) and attempted to put Pyongyang in a middle position,
between Moscow and Peking, on the highly sensitive issue of revisionism.
It attacked the "modern revisionists" for "distorting and revising general

principles of Marxism-Leninism under the pretext of 'situational change' or 'creative development,'" but the editorial also accused China of being dogmatic by saying:

On the other hand, we must also watch against the other erroneous tendency of emphasizing only the general principles of Marxism-Leninism, ignoring the changed conditions or specific characteristics of a country.

It must be remembered that the issue involved here is none other than that of the necessity of war as a means of revolution. Pyongyang's position on this question is ambiguous indeed.

The theme of simultaneously opposing revisionism and dogmatism and consolidating the unity of the socialist camp was reiterated by Kim Il-sŏng on October 5, 1966. The Premier denounced revisionism on the ground that it eliminated the revolutionary essence of Marxism-Leninism. Revisionism, he declared:

. . . refutes class struggle and the dictatorship of the proletariat, preaches cooperation among classes, and abandons the struggle against imperialism. Modern revisionism also spreads illusions about imperialism and obstructs in various ways the people's revolutionary struggles for social and national liberation.

Although the Premier observed that the modern revisionism is on the decline, he argued that the struggle against it cannot be relaxed because it "displays fragility before imperialism and passively reacts to the revolutionary struggles of the people."

The Premier's attack against the dogmatists (i.e., the Chinese), was much harsher in tone. He asserted:

. . . leftist-opportunism does not take into consideration the changed realities, and by dogmatically repeating individual tasks [defined] in Marxism-Leninism, it leads the people to extremist actions by taking up super-revolutionary slogans. It also isolates the party from the people, splinters revolutionary strength and makes it impossible to concentrate the attack against the main enemy.

For the Premier, it was a leftist deviation to deny unity in the name of opposing opportunism, although it would be a rightist deviation to abandon the struggle against opportunism in the name of defending unity.

The main thrust of the Premier's speech was unmistakable:

The most important thing is to create the conditions for the fraternal parties to bring about joint action against imperialism . . . Through this process, the differences can be narrowed down and the atmosphere can be created for mutual contacts. When certain conditions are produced, a conference of the fraternal parties could be convened to discuss the problem of joint anti-imperialist action.

The Premier implored the Chinese to distinguish between the enemy and the "friends who have committed errors." Narrow-mindedness was denounced. In essence, Kim was using Mao Tse-tung's dictum about the correct handling of contradictions.

The Chinese, however, showed no indication that they would take the medicine prescribed by Kim Il-sŏng. They dispatched a low-ranking delegation to North Korea's twentieth anniversary celebration in August 1965. In early 1967, the Red Guards in China angered Pyongyang by reporting, through the media of Big Character Posters, that a military *coup d'état* had deposed Kim Il-sŏng.[56] In the eyes of the Chinese to-day, Kim Il-sŏng and his cohorts are opportunists.

ROOTS OF NORTH KOREAN BEHAVIOR

The events of the postwar period and the statements issued by the North Korean regime permit us to identify some of the basic factors in recent North Korean behavior. First of all, we must note North Korea's maturity and her progressive assertion of independence. For the leaders in Pyongyang, big-power chauvinism was detestable. Khrushchev was clearly unsophisticated in this respect, and his tacit support of the anti-Kim Il-sŏng elements in North Korea in 1956, along with his support of P'êng Têh-huai in China, are not likely to be forgotten. Such interference in the domestic politics of other countries was a deadly serious matter for the North Korean leadership, in that this could have led to the loss of their power. Kosygin must have satisfied the leaders in Pyongyang that the errors of Khrushchev would not be repeated.

Closely connected with the question of the attitude of the big powers is the problem of economic development which, again, is tied to the problem of survival. North Korea has had to pay a heavy price for her previous stand on the various issues that split the Communist camp. Her Seven-year Economic Development Plan had to be postponed for three long years in 1966, and it is quite probable that the fulfillment of the original goals would have taken even longer had no Soviet aid been provided for her economy and defense. The problem would be acute, particularly because the plants and machinery brought into North Korea after 1953 were in need of parts and repair. Pyongyang must have been very receptive to Kosygin's conciliatory probings as exemplified in his visit to Pyongyang. Practical necessity dictated that Pyongyang change its course.

In arguing for the unity of the socialist camp, Kim Il-sŏng made a strong appeal to pragmatism. He argued that it did not matter why "those people who had been practicing revisionism" might want to join in the task of struggling against imperialism in Vietnam. It might be an effort to correct one's past mistakes, or it could stem from strong pressure from the people in one's country and the world. What really mattered for Kim Il-sŏng was the result—that is, to draw *all* strength into the anti-imperialist struggle.[57] One could perhaps use the same logic in interpreting North Korean behavior. What really matters for Kim Il-sŏng is the survival of the political and economic structures built in North Korea. Compared to this central concern, all other issues are secondary.

Even though the Pyongyang regime modified its stand against the Soviet Union and restored more amicable relations, its stand on revisionism is still identical with that of Communist China (with an important exception on the question of the necessity of war). Kim Il-sŏng has stressed the need for joint action against imperialism, but he has not thereby renounced the necessity of struggling against revisionism. His formula is essentially that of a united front which demands "uniting while struggling, and struggling while uniting." The similarities in the attitude of China and North Korea toward revisionism can be attributed to the similarities in the problems encountered by the two countries and in the timing of their revolutions.

Both the Chinese and Korean Communists can accept without qualification Sun Yat-sen's famous words, "The revolution has not yet succeeded." The Chinese still have Formosa, and the North Koreans still have South Korea, to "liberate." In the opinions of both the Chinese and Korean Communists, the American imperialists alone obstruct the task of unification of their respective countries. It must indeed vex the Communists in Peking and Pyongyang that the revisionists do not themselves oppose imperialism and that they discourage others from doing so. The similarities in the timing of their revolutions also create similar attitudes toward economic development. It is natural for Communist China and North Korea to desire rapid economic development and to anticipate generous aid from the Soviet Union. The withdrawal of Soviet technicians from China in 1960 was, of course, a direct affront to the Chinese, a heavy blow that they will never forgive. And the withdrawal of Russian technicians from China certainly had relevance to North Korea, where economic sanctions could also be applied. North Koreans may also have been disappointed by the limited amount of Soviet aid in the postwar era, particularly after 1957. North Korea's stress on independence, self-reliance, and on the equality of the parties (issues that concern Albania as well as North Korea) must be seen in this light.

CONCLUSIONS

North Korea has made considerable strides in the postwar era, both in the economic and the political spheres, although many problems are yet to be solved. These strides, however, have cost heavily in terms of individual dignity and human rights. This is a Stalinist era for some ten million North Koreans. Throughout this period, the Communist leaders have strongly emphasized nationalism, both in internal and foreign policies. In the foreseeable future, North Korean Communists are likely to continue these policies, demanding increased recognition in the international Communist camp. The North Korean Communists' sense of self-importance has been growing rapidly with time, and they have shown increased arrogance both at home and abroad. Posterity may record that, in the 1960's, the leaders of the Korean Workers' Party, dizzy with success, were still facing problems—both domestic and foreign—that rendered their long-range position precarious.

NOTES

1. In December 1945, its membership was 4,530. See *Kim Il-sŏng sŏnjip* (*Selected Works of Kim Il-sŏng*), (Pyongyang: Korean Workers' Party Press, 1963), Vol. I, 16.
2. Center for the Study of Party History, Central Committee of the Korean Workers' Party, *Chosŏn rodongdang yŏksa kyojae* (*Instructional Material on the History of the Korean Workers' Party*), (Pyongyang, 1964), p. 185.
3. Central Committee of the Federation of the Korean Residents in Japan, *Chosŏn rodongdang kyuyak haesŏl* (*Commentary on the Rules of the Korean Workers' Party*), (Tokyo, 1960), p. 1.
4. *Ibid.*, p. 2.
5. See Chong-Sik Lee and Ki-Wan Oh, "The Russian Faction in North Korea," *Asian Survey*, April 1968, pp. 270–88.
6. *Kim Il-sŏng sŏnjip* (1960), Vol. IV, 387–88.
7. *Kin Nichisei senshū* (*Selected Works of Kim Il-sŏng*), (Kyoto, 1952), Vol. III, 48. The total includes 73,000 laborers, 105,000 peasants, and 188,000 "others."
8. *Kin Nichisei senshū*, Vol. III, 48.
9. Kaigai jijō Chōsasho, ed., *Chosēn yōran* (*Summary Facts on Korea*) (Tokyo, 1960), p. 141.
10. *Nodong Shinmun* (*Labor News*), October 11, 1965.
11. See Franz Schurmann, *Ideology and Organization in Communist China* (Berkeley, Calif.: University of California Press, 1966), p. 138.
12. For a pungent denunciation of the defects for the Party, see Kim Il-sŏng's speech, "The Present Conditions and the Current Duties," in *Kin Nichisei senshū*, Vol. II, 105–44.
13. *Kim Il-sŏng sŏnjip* (1960), Vol. IV, 385.
14. *Ibid.*, Vol. IV, 384. As of April 1956, there were 128,157 members in the province.
15. Glenn D. Paige and Dong Jun Lee, "The Post-War Politics of Communist Korea,"

    in *North Korea Today*, ed. Robert A. Scalapino (New York: Frederick A. Praeger, Inc., 1963), pp. 17–29.

16. Personal interviews.

17. In Communist China, the Standing Committee of the Politburo was created at the Eighth Party Congress in September 1956. See Schurmann, *Ideology and Organization*, p. 145.

18. The *Hsia-fang* movement was launched in China in 1957. For details, see John W. Lewis, *Leadership in Communist China* (Ithaca, N.Y.: Cornell University Press, 1963), pp. 85–86.

19. *Ch'ŏngsanri kyoshi wa sahoe chui kyŏngje kŏnsŏl* (*The Teachings at Ch'ŏngsanri and the Construction of the Socialist Economy*), prepared by the Instructors of the Department of Economics, Kim Il-sŏng University (Pyongyang: Korean Workers' Party Press, 1962), pp. 1–8.

20. *Ibid.*, p. 7.

21. *Ibid.*, pp. 15, 164–65.

22. At the Eighth Party Congress of the Chinese Communist Party. For details, see Schurmann, *Ideology and Organization*, pp. 220–308.

23. Kim Il-sŏng, "Let Us Heighten the Role of the *Kun* (Prefecture), Further develop Local Industries and Agrarian Economy, and Markedly Improve the Livelihood of the People," (August 8, 1962), *Chosŏn Chungang Nyŏngam* (*Korean Central Almanac*) (Pyongyang: Korean Central News Agency, 1963), pp. 16–19.

24. *Kŭlloja* (*The Worker*), (Pyongyang), No. 10 (1966), pp. 79–86.

25. Electrical generation in 1953 was reduced to 36 percent of the 1949 level; fuel production, including coal, to 11 percent; chemical industry to 22 percent. The following industries were completely demolished: iron ore, pig iron, steel, lead, copper, electric motor, transformer, coke, sulfuric acid, chemical fertilizer, carbide, caustic soda, and cement. See Democratic People's Republic of Korea Academy of Science, *Chosŏn T'ongsa* (*Outline History of Korea*), (reprint ed.; Tokyo: Hak-u Sobang, 1959), Vol. III, 285.

26. See *Kim Il-sŏng sŏnjip*, Vol. V, 145, 147, 280–82.

27. *Ibid.*, Vol. IV, 39.

28. "On Enlarging the Production of People's Consumer Goods and Improving the Merchandise Circulation," June 7, 1958, *ibid.*, Vol. V, 518.

29. Cho Chae-sŏn, *Chosŏn minjujuui inmin konghwaguk sahoe kyŏngje jedo* (*The Socio-Economic System in the Democratic People's Republic of Korea*), (Pyongyang, 1958), pp. 35–36.

30. *Minju Chosŏn* (*Democratic Korea*), (Pyongyang), April 24, 1963.

31. Yi Sŏk-sim, "Construction of Independent National Economy in Our Country," *Kŭlloja* (*The Worker*), (Pyongyang), No. 19 (November, 1962), p. 140.

32. Cho Chae-sŏn, *Chosŏn Minjujuui*, p. 36.

33. An Kwang-jŭp, "Our Party's Over-all Policies in Post-War Socialist Construction of the Economy," Kim Il-sŏng taehak, *8.15 haebang 15 chunyŏn kinyŏm nommunjip* (*Essays Commemorating the 15th Anniversary of the Liberation*) (Pyongyang, 1960), p. 32.

34. The ratio of savings in the Soviet Union in 1926 and 1927 was 16–17%, although it was raised in 1932, the last year of the First Five-Year Plan, to 27%. In China the national savings in 1952 were 15.7%, but were raised to 22.8% in 1956, the last year of the First Five-Year Plan. *Ibid.*

35. "On Our Party's Policy for the Future Development of Agricultural Management" (November 3, 1954), *Kim Il-sŏng sŏnjip*, Vol. IV, 194.

36. For example, see "Thesis on the Characteristics and the Tasks of Our Revolution" (April, 1955), *ibid.*, Vol. IV, 206.

37. Kim Il-sŏng stated, on September 20, 1957, that "The heroic struggle of the

Korean people has heightened the international position of our country to an unprecedented level." *Ibid.*, Vol. V, 161.

38. "For the Future Development of Light Industry," January 29, 1958, *ibid.*, V, 284.

39. "On Eradicating Dogmatism and Formalism from Ideological Activities and Firmly Establishing *Chuch'e*," *ibid.*, Vol. IV, 325.

40. *Ibid.*, p. 326.

41. *Ibid.*, pp. 336–37.

42. These progressive scholars, known as the *silhak* (i.e., practical-learning) group, stressed, in order to restore the glory of Korea, the necessity of learning practical matters and things Korean, as against the studying of metaphysics.

43. "On Our Party's Policies for the Future Development of Agricultural Management," (November 3, 1954), *Kim Il-sŏng sŏnjip*, Vol. IV, 188–89.

44. *Ibid.*, p. 189.

45. For the initial proposal of Nam Il, on April 27, see U.S. Dept. of State, *The Korean Problem at the Geneva Conference: April 26-June 15, 1954*, Dept. of State Publication No. 5,609 (Washington, D.C.: Government Printing Office), pp. 39–40. For Minister Pyun's counterproposal, see pp. 123–24.

46. See the speech of Ch'oe Yong-gŏn, Chairman of the Presidium of the Supreme People's Assembly, "For the Further Promotion of Peaceful Unification of the Country," Supplement to *Korea News* (Pyongyang), No. 33 (1960), p. 24.

47. See for example Hŏ Il-hun's article, "Various Problems in the Correct Fulfillment of the Principle of Collective Leadership," *Kŭlloja (The Worker)*, (Pyongyang), December, 1956, pp. 92–102.

48. For the text of Kim's speech at the Enlarged Plenum of the Fourth Central Committee of the Party, see *Nodong Shinmun (Labor News)*, November 28, 1961.

49. For details, see my article, "The 'Socialist Revolution' in the North Korean Countryside," *Asian Survey* (Berkeley, Calif.) II, No. 8 (October, 1962), pp. 9–22.

50. See *Peking Review*, September 16, 1958, p. 23.

51. *Kŭlloja (The Worker)*, (Pyongyang), March, 1956, pp. 50–53.

52. See "Joint Statement of President Choe Yong Kun and Chairman Liu Shao-chi," Supplement to *Korea Today* (Pyongyang), No. 7 (1963).

53. See Joseph C. Kun, "North Korea: Between Moscow and Peking," *China Quarterly* (London), July–September 1967, p. 51.

54. Korean Central News Agency International Service (Pyongyang), October 17, 1967.

55. *Rodong Shinmun*, October 11, 1965. English text in *People's Korea*, October 20, 1965.

56. The Central News Agency in Pyongyang issued a sharp rebuttal of the rumors on January 27, 1967.

57. For the full text of Kim Il-sŏng's speech, see *Kŭlloja (The Worker)*, (Pyongyang), No. 10 (1966), pp. 2–54. For the statements quoted here, see p. 18.

SELECTED BIBLIOGRAPHY

Facts About Korea. Pyongyang: Foreign Languages Publishing House, 1961.

For Korea's Peaceful Unification. Pyongyang: Foreign Languages Publishing House, 1961.

Korea Today. Monthly magazine, published by the Foreign Languages Publishing House, Pyongyang.

Paige, Glenn D., "North Korea and the Emulation of Russian and Chinese Behavior," in *Communist Strategies in Asia*, ed. A. Doak Barnett, pp. 228–61. New York: Frederick A. Praeger, Inc., 1963.

Rudolph, Philip, *North Korea's Political and Economic Structure*. New York: Institute of Pacific Relations, 1959.

Scalapino, Robert A., ed., *North Korea Today*. New York: Frederick A. Praeger, Inc., 1963. Reprints of articles published in *China Quarterly*, April–June, 1963.

U.S. Department of State, *North Korea: A Case Study in the Techniques of Takeover*. Washington, D.C.: Government Printing Office, 1961.

NORTH VIETNAM

LEFT OF MOSCOW, RIGHT OF PEKING

JOHN C. DONNELL and MELVIN GURTOV

ince the full-scale involvement of the United States in the Vietnam
onflict, and especially with the War's extension north of the seven-
eenth parallel, the persistent slogan from Hanoi has been, "defend
he North, liberate the South, and achieve national reunification." The
logan epitomizes the fact that North Vietnam's entire productive en-
rgy, leadership capability, and foreign policy have become centered
round the preservation of the state and the accomplishment of its
rimary national objective: to recover the southern half of the country
lenied the Communists in 1954 and again in 1956. After years of pains-
aking, often shortsighted efforts at modernizing the economy and ad-
ninistration of the Democratic Republic of Vietnam (DRV), Hanoi's
eaders have been compelled to sacrifice much of the progress that
ias taken place for the sake of a larger political goal. At apparently
reat cost to their economic plant and considerable disruption to their
ociety, they have returned North Vietnam to a war footing.

In a sense, the DRV has sought to fight a three-front war: on one
ide, sustaining the spirit of struggle and high morale of Party cadres

and workers; on another, accepting the heavy damage inflicted by Amer
ican attacks in the seeming expectation that the determination of the
United States to carry on the struggle will collapse before North Viet
nam's does; and on yet a third, maintaining sole authority to deter
mine war strategy and the conditions for negotiations without alienating
the vital support of the disputing Chinese and Soviet parties. As 1968
began, none of the fronts seemed in danger of being soon outflanked
and the credit for this substantial achievement must be assigned to the
Dang Lao Dong Viet Nam (i.e., the Vietnamese Workers' Party), and
its elderly, but nonetheless agile leader, Ho Chi Minh.

HISTORICAL DEVELOPMENT OF THE
VIETNAMESE WORKERS' PARTY

The *Dang Lao Dong Viet Nam* (known as the *Lao Dong* Party), suc
cessor to the old Indochinese Communist Party, claimed in early 1968
to have a membership of 570,000, a little over 3 per cent of the North
Vietnamese population of approximately 17 million at that time. The
continuity of leadership has remained remarkably stable, enabling the
Party to surmount leadership crises without any important purges in
its top ranks for many years. A very brief recapitulation of the Party'
development will be useful.

In 1930, Ho Chi Minh, or Nguyen Ai Quoc as he was then known
succeeded in fusing three existing squabbling Communist groups into a
new Vietnamese organization redesignated the Indochinese Communist
Party. It was dissolved, in November 1945, in order to preserve unity
among, and Communist control over, the many non-Communist nation
alists backing the Vietminh fight for independence. From the time of its
formal dissolution until the advent of the *Lao Dong* in March 1951
Communist organization and indoctrination were maintained through
Marxist study groups.

The Vietminh (in full, the *Viet Nam Doc-Lap Dong Minh*, i.e., the
Vietnam Independence League) carried the banner of the war against
French colonialism. It is generally believed to have been founded
again by Ho, in Kwangsi, China, in May 1941. In February 1951, over
three years before the end of the war, the Vietminh was absorbed into
the *Lien Viet* (in full, the *Mat-Tran Lien-Hiep Quoc Dan Viet-Nam*, i.e.
the United Vietnam Nationalist Front), but the Communist component
of its membership was consolidated in the new *Lao Dong* party which
appeared the following month. The *Lien Viet* front had been launched
in May, 1946 as a broad base of support for the Revolution, and it in
cluded mass organizations, not only for youth and women but also for
non-Communist parties such as the Democratic and Socialist Parties

and for Buddhist and Catholic groups. This front was absorbed, in turn, in the still broader Fatherland Front (i.e., *Mat-Tran To-Quoc*) which emerged in September 1955, and which was calculated to appeal also to South Vietnamese disaffected with the Ngo Dinh Diem regime. It urged reunification via a transitional stage of collaboration between sovereign northern and southern governments, but it never was regarded in the South as anything more than a tactical arm of Hanoi. Although it still is in existence, it has been eclipsed by the Hanoi-dominated National Liberation Front of South Vietnam (NLFSV), which has become prominently identified with the goal of reunification.

THE LAO DONG: COMPOSITION AND CONTROL

Party membership has been recruited largely from the *petite bourgeoisie*, a fact blamed by the leadership for ideological shallowness whenever policy disputes arise. An article in the "Cominform journal" in August 1953 stated that, of 1,855 key posts in the Party, only one-fifth to one-sixth were held by persons of peasant origin, and only one-twelfth by persons from workers' families. The rest were held by intellectuals or men from bourgeois families.[1]

The *Lao Dong* has clearly experienced great difficulty in its attempt to broaden its base of support among workers and even more among peasants. It had a small membership in 1946, reported later by Hanoi to have been only 5,000 (but said in the Cominform journal article to have been 20,000). The Party underwent a purge in 1950 and 1951, but expanded rapidly following its reconstitution as a mass Communist Party so that by independence, in 1954, it totaled 400,000. Not long afterward, however, widespread peasant dissatisfaction, culminating in the peasant revolts in central Vietnam, decreased the rate of growth. By early 1963, the total still was only 570,000.[2]

The 1956 peasant uprisings were sparked by harsh land-reform measures which owed considerable inspiration to the DRV's Chinese advisers. The *Lao Dong* was eventually obliged to soften these decrees, and the Party Secretary-General, Truong Chinh, stepped down, offering self-criticism to placate internal critics. The Army, largely of peasant origin itself, had remained steadfast even to the extent of crushing some peasant groups in pitched battles. But the experience shook Army leaders, who for some time remained critical of the Party for having lost touch with the peasants to such a serious extent.

The Party never really made amends to the hundreds of thousands of peasants and other survivors reportedly victimized by the land reform measures. It apparently decided to concentrate on building its strength in urban areas among workers and intellectuals, as well as in the Army, and to count on a longer-range development of proletarian consciousness among the peasantry.

The lack of "class comprehension" among the younger industrial workers has been noted in Party statements. In 1961, "young workers accounted for about 60 per cent of the total number and even 80 per cent in some areas"[3]—that is, less than 40 per cent of the proletariat was then composed of the comparatively class-conscious old-time workers or displaced farmers who had become industrial laborers during the period of French domination.

Party leaders call regularly for heavier recruitment among youth and women.[4] The Lao Dong periodically has admitted its weakness among the ethnic minorities who live in the highlands which comprise three-fourths of the land area of the north. Thinness of Party membership is to be expected in remote areas, but a March 1962 statement claimed that 35 per cent of the highland communities lacked Party cells.

Lax direction of Party cells also attracts continuing criticism. In early 1962, one Party spokesman criticized comrades in "some regions" for failing to convene any meetings for six months at a time or any criticism sessions for two years.[5] The most astonishingly candid critique of Party weaknesses in recent times was published in the Party journal in March 1963. In this article, it was openly admitted that the Party had been seriously damaged over the past few years by slack security precautions, so that bourgeois groups, "anti-Bolsheviks," and enemy ("U.S.-Diem") agents had "succeeded in infiltrating leading organs to carry out sabotage." This resulted in the destruction of "some basic party organs" and "leading organs," as well as in "the arrest or death of some cadres." The impression given here was that this anti-Party activity had occurred mostly in the past. More recently, however, during an "ordinary investigation conducted in the party's ranks, a number of persons were unmasked who falsely claimed to be party members and who attended party meetings or fulfilled party tasks for years."[6] The role of "U.S.-Diem agents" in this picture was obviously emphasized to dramatize the external threat and to gloss over more routine organizational failings. But the threat of infiltration has evidently caused growing concern as the DRV's own involvement in the Viet Cong insurgency has increased.

At the same time, the extension of the War to the North meant that organizational lines had to be tightened if the society was to hold together under the impact of "imperialist" attacks. Consequently, during 1966 and 1967, numerous articles appeared, stressing on the one hand the importance of close Party relations with the masses and, on the other, the necessity for cadres to maintain absolute discipline so long as the threat to the national security remained.

On the first score, there has evidently been some concern in *Lao Dong* Party circles that cadres, as in the past, have become overly bureaucratic and authoritarian. In late 1966, Le Duc Tho, a member of the Central Committee Politburo, reported instances of corruption and immoral personal behavior and charged that "a small number of cadres and party members, who are entrusted by the party and people with leading functions in the party, state organs, and mass organizations, have degenerated into bureaucratic, dictatorial, and arbitrary elements concerned only with their private and individual interests." Instead of having a "high sense of responsibility to the party and people," he wrote, these functionaries were superficially going about their jobs.[7] A movement was therefore undertaken to improve the "mass line" by encouraging more open criticism of cadres by the masses and by reemphasizing self-criticism among all Party workers.[8] On the related second point, stricter Party control of the Army was promised to combat tendencies toward "individualism and liberalism" among political and military cadres. Inasmuch as the armed forces, in a war situation, have to set good examples for others, it was argued, Army cadres were urged to abide by the strictest discipline and to work closely with the masses.[9]

Party Leadership: The Question of Factions and Identity

The striking tradition of political unity among Vietnamese Communist leaders has been a factor of inestimable strength to the Vietnamese movement. When important differences of opinion have arisen, the identity of the opposing personalities and the nature of the opposing standpoints have been carefully concealed. Nevertheless, analysts of North Vietnamese politics tend to identify key Party figures by their supposed pro-Soviet, pro-Chinese, or neutral affiliations, a breakdown which seems to distort the nature of the debates that take place in the Politburo by implying that ranking Vietnamese officials give first priority to non-Vietnamese interests in reaching decisions. In recent years, members of the Politburo appear to have divided on such questions as military strategy, economic policy, and perhaps the timing of negotiations, but it is important to realize that such differences have been thrashed out within the context of North Vietnam's interests, rather than Moscow's or Peking's. The ultimate criterion, in other words, has always been the furtherance of Hanoi's objectives; disputes have apparently revolved about the best *means* to achieve them, even though the question of means frequently runs parallel to the question of whether the "line" of China or the Soviet Union most promotes North Vietnamese ambitions.

Decision making is, of course, the exclusive property of the *Lao Dong* Party. The Party's Central Committee appears to have about 100 members, although the only official membership list published (in 1960) named only 71. Forty-three are full members and the others are alternates.[10] The Politburo has had 10 regular members since the death in 1967 of General Nguyen Chi Thanh, whose replacement, if any, is unknown. The membership includes President Ho Chi Minh (but not the aging figurehead, Vice-President Ton Duc Thang), and two alternates who serve *ex officio* from their top posts in the security apparatus. The 10 full members are:

Ho Chi Minh: Chairman of the *Lao Dong* Central Committee; President of the DRV.

Le Duan: First Secretary of the Party; chief of the Vietminh resistance in South Vietnam from 1949 to 1951.

Truong Chinh: former Secretary-General of the *Lao Dong*; Chairman of the National Assembly Standing Committee; Chairman of the Nguyen Ai Quoc training school for Party cadres.

Pham Van Dong: Premier.

Vo Nguyen Giap: Minister of Defense; Commander of the Vietnamese People's Army; a Vice-Premier.

Le Duc Tho: chief of the Vietminh resistance in South Vietnam from 1951 to 1954, after clashing with Le Duan, the earlier chief.

Nguyen Duy Trinh: a Vice-Premier and Foreign Minister.

Pham Hung: a Vice-Premier.

Le Thanh Nghi: a Vice-Premier who heads the Industrial Board under the Premier's office.

Hoang Van Hoan: specialist in international affairs and diplomacy; former Ambassador to China, now Vice-chairman of the Standing Committee of the National Assembly.

Ho has always been the moderator of factional tension, although he himself has been regarded as particularly friendly to the Soviet Union ever since his original training there in the early 1920's. He has had the political sagacity to plot an independent Vietnamese course between the Sino-Soviet antagonists whenever possible, and has even made strenuous attempts to mediate between Mao and Khrushchev, as at the 1960 Congress of the 81 Communist Parties in Moscow. At this writing, Ho is 77 and has spells of poor health; he still appears in public, but his participation in important diplomatic trips abroad and the enunciation of important policy statements in his own right has declined.

Le Duan, a founding member of the Indochinese Communisty Party, has risen rapidly in Party councils since 1951 (when he was relieved of his command of the Vietminh resistance in the South and replaced by Le Duc Tho), and particularly since 1957. He has traveled abroad, as member and leader of DRV delegations to important conferences, and he led the early 1964 delegation to Moscow (with stops in Peking) to negotiate the ticklish business of seeking increased material support from the Soviets while the DRV was responsive to the Chinese line in the dispute within the Communist bloc. His policy statements have been accorded the prominence due a very powerful Party leader. Whereas his speeches have hinted at support for the Chinese line, as in 1963 and 1964, he has been careful to give the Soviet Union its due for earlier revolutionary inspiration and for diplomatic and economic assistance to the DRV. He has continued to express hope for Sino-Soviet solidarity and to direct moderate pleas to Moscow to see the error of its "modern revisionism." Le Duan and Le Duc Tho are known to have retained a mutual antagonism dating from their earlier clash in the South, but the implications of this in the context of the rift in the Communist bloc are not clear.

Truong Chinh (an alias meaning "long march"), the Party's leading ideologist, cultivated a strong following in the Party during his lengthy tenure (from 1941 to 1956) as Secretary-General. Later he developed his new post of Chairman of the Standing Committee of the National Assembly into one of new authority.

General Vo Nguyen Giap, the brilliant soldier, retains the strong affection of the people of the North as the hero of Dien Bien Phu. He and Truong Chinh, once close collaborators, are now considered to be arch foes. Giap may be the chief architect of present Viet Cong-North Vietnamese Army strategy in South Vietnam.

Premier Pham Van Dong is a diligent administrator identified mainly with carrying out policy for Ho, apparently including Ho's balancing of Party factions. He does not have a personal following in the Party, but is evidently respected by others who do. Dong is also an experienced negotiator (he represented the Vietminh at Geneva in 1954) whose presence at future peace talks would seem fairly certain.

Whatever the precise areas of disagreement among these top leaders, there seems to be unanimous concurrence among them that the *Lao Dong* Party has developed from an organization dependent for advice and guidance on Moscow and Peking to one of extraordinary ideological and practical creativity. Since 1963, but particularly after the spring of 1965 when the maintenance of a balance between Moscow and Peking became especially important, the North Vietnamese have been proclaiming that *their* Party has correctly adapted Marxist-Leninist principles to the special conditions prevailing in Vietnam. In 1963, for instance, Le Duan praised Mao Tse-tung for having created the theory that revolution is led by the peasant class in agriculturally based countries. Under such circumstances, Duan wrote approvingly, the peasantry is "the main force of the revolution" rather than, as in industrially advanced

nations, an important but secondary ally of the proletariat.[11] Duan's interpretation of Maoist theory lasted until 1966 when, in a speech significantly
not published for five months, he proclaimed that the peasants in Vietnam never have led and never could lead the revolutionary struggle,
and that, while numerically the most numerous class, they must be led
by the working class.[12]

This important theoretical departure—which, as we will see later, had
relevance to Sino-Vietnamese differences—was coupled with another relating to the doctrine of "people's war." Although the Chinese have consistently harped on the originality of Mao's military theory, the North
Vietnamese have laid claim to sole responsibility for Communist successes in South Vietnam. In the most remarkable such instance, Brigadier General Hoang Minh Thao wrote, in 1967: "The people's war outlook of our party is a new, creative development of the Marxist-Leninist
ideas of revolutionary violence and revolutionary war." He referred
only to "our theory" on people's war and gave no credit to Mao or Lin
Piao, China's Defense Minister.[13] In short, Hanoi has stressed that its
historic struggles against foreign domination have succeeded because the
Lao Dong's leadership has itself pursued the correct revolutionary
course.

Leading Party members have publicized these "unorthodox" views not
only to make clear the DRV's ideological independence but also to
infuse in Party workers and cadres a sense of "Vietnameseness," although
the departures from Soviet and Chinese experiences have been made
slowly. In a speech late in 1963, for instance, Le Duan attacked certain
Party members who believed that the *Lao Dong*, "a small party born in
a former colony with a backward agriculture and low cultural level . . .
can hardly understand Marxist-Leninist science and complex international problems."[14] But the authoritative journal *Hoc Tap* went much further in 1966, when it specifically enjoined Party personnel from slavishly
producing theoretical documents on the basis of the experiences of
foreign Parties. Whereas previously the Party was merely declared capable of dealing with complex problems on its own, the thesis now was
that while some "selected" experiences of fraternal parties could benefit
theoretical work, the primary reference should be to Vietnam's unique-
nesses and the Party's inventiveness. The *Lao Dong* was thus declared
to be:

. . . a creative party, creative in the association of the universal truth of
Marxism-Leninism with the reality of the Vietnamese revolution. Formerly,
sometimes faced with difficulties, a few unstable people contended that our
party lacked creativeness and theory. Let us ask: If our party were not creative,
how could Vietnam, the first colonial country, have raised high the spirit of
self-reliance, have defeated Japanese fascism, and have seized power in the

entire country? How could it then have defeated the French aggressors? And
how could it at present be defeating the U.S. aggressors? . . . The comrades
who had the above-mentioned erroneous concepts failed to understand the
simple truth that each revolution has its creativeness. This is a rule. Without
creativeness, a revolution cannot succeed. With dogmatism, a revolution will
fail.[15]

Thus, one of the more interesting developments in the *Lao Dong* Party
has been a growing independence of mind with regard to the theory
and practice of Marxism-Leninism, a development that has been assisted by the competition between Peking and Moscow for influence
over Hanoi, and one to which the Chinese, in particular, no doubt
take strong exception.

ECONOMIC DEVELOPMENT OF NORTH VIETNAM

The DRV and its allies in the Communist bloc have been determined to make North Vietnam a showcase for Communism in Southeast
Asia. Toward that end, as well as toward building a socialist North,
emphasis was initially placed on industrialization. Thus the First Five-
Year Plan, for 1961 through 1965 (which followed a preliminary Three-
Year Plan), "sharply reflect[ed] our Party's line concerning . . . particularly heavy industry." The priority accorded industrialization aroused
some dissent within the Party at the same time as it gave rise to certain large projects, showpieces which apparently cannot always be defended on rigorous economic grounds. The Five-Year Plan was to increase capital investment in industry from 36 per cent of the total to
about 49 per cent, and about 80 per cent of that investment was to
be in the production of goods. The investment in agriculture was to
be almost doubled to 28 per cent. Total food production was to rise
by 32 per cent; most of the increase, however, was to be in secondary
crops—corn, sweet potatoes, beans, manioc, and so forth. The potential
increase in rice production has been leveling off, even with wider use
of fertilizer and planting of multiple crops, and the campaign begun in
1964 to move one million Vietnamese from the Red River delta to the
sparsely populated highlands can enlarge only the cultivation of other
crops.

Industrial production was supposed to increase annually by 20 per
cent, and agriculture by 10 per cent, but the norms for 1963, a year of
calamitous weather, had to be cut to 17 per cent and 6.4 per cent, respectively. An average annual food increase of 6.4 per cent is not
large, considering the present low rate of consumption and the fact
that little of the increase will be in rice, which is greatly preferred
over the secondary foods. There was to be a similarly modest increase,
6.7 per cent, in other consumer goods.

Even at the time of the war's extension to the North, the DRV had a spotty record of economic attainment. The production of rice, at the end of the preliminary Three-Year Plan in 1960, was about 50 per cent less than the planned increase. In 1963, it was claimed, industrial output rose 6.5 per cent, far short of the original goal of 13 per cent and even of the revised goal of 7.9 per cent. The totals for rice and all other food production, moreover, dropped about 13 per cent below the 1962 level. Consequently, per capita food production was apparently the lowest since 1954 when the war in Indo-China ended.[16]

Le Duan said, in April 1962, that a peasant's average monthly income was about ten *dong*, about $34 dollars per year. Workers averaged 27 to 100 *dong*, he said (the equivalent of $92 to $340 per year), but still suffered more shortages than peasants—a fact, he added ruefully, which the peasants often did not understand.[17] The regular monthly rice ration was supposed to be 15 to 18 kilograms (33 to 40 pounds) per person, depending on his age, physical condition, and so forth, but the ration has been decreased when harvests are poor.

The War has produced some radical changes in the economy of North Vietnam.[18] Most significantly, American air strikes have forced the regime to drastically decentralize the internal distribution system. As life in the main towns was disrupted, the recourse was a major evacuation to the rural areas, a move begun in the summer of 1966. Those persons remaining in the cities were reported to have been gripped by a food shortage, especially of fish, milk, and flour; the Chinese sent foodstuffs, but evidently not in sufficient quantities. Still, on the average, monthly rations did not markedly decline: Most persons received roughly 28 pounds of rice; students got 33 pounds; and soldiers, 44 pounds. During 1966, the regime announced that tighter measures needed to be imposed to guard against speculation and hoarding; at the same time, all-out action was begun to organize the society for maximum civilian participation in tasks related to defense and economic production.

Production statistics are hard to come by, of course. In 1965 and 1966, the regime claimed an increase in the production of rice, but 1967 brought a major drought and a poor harvest. The Soviet Union responded with monthly shipments of 20,000 to 30,000 tons of wheat or wheat flour which, together with Chinese shipments of rice, gave the DRV some 500,000 tons of additional food.[19] Severe damage to industrial facilities doubtless eliminated any plans to inaugurate a new five-year program. Factories reportedly were dismantled for reassembly in safe rural areas; but no figures are available on the extensiveness of this program of "regionalization" or on its impact on production. Interestingly, whether because of or in spite of the bombing, the government's emphasis has again shifted, from industrialization to agricultural production. In late 1966, for

nstance, the call went out to institute a "technical revolution," which was
lefined as giving priority to agriculture so as eventually to develop a
mechanized industrial base.[20]

Collectivization

The DRV's agrarian program has been in trouble for years because of
popular resistance or apathy toward the vaunted benefits of collectiv-
zation and because of the frequently deplored lack of technical and
administrative skills to carry it out effectively. The DRV has followed
China's example in its progression from labor exchange teams of 30 or 40
members, to lower and then higher-level cooperatives, and finally to state
arms, but it has not attempted to introduce communes. The emphasis
on consolidation of the cooperatives during 1962 to 1964 added 2 per
cent to the number of farmers involved in cooperatives, bringing the to-
al to 87 per cent. Of the almost 30,000 cooperatives, one-third are of
he more fully socialistic, "higher" type. By early 1964, over 10,500 of
these comprised entire hamlets and 208 consisted of entire villages,[21]
but the average cooperative in early 1963 was said to have 85 members. State farms were introduced in late 1955, and by 1962 there were
55, the majority operated by the Army.[22]

Some of the highest ranking members of the Party, including Ho
himself, have visited cooperatives to encourage greater effort and, in
he process, have made some exceedingly candid remarks about recent
difficulties. In 1962, in a visit to Nghe An (where peasant outbreaks
occurred in 1956), Le Duan acknowledged that, the previous year, the
peasants had complained to him about being compelled to join. He
responded frankly that the gradual erasure of the private plots which
had been distributed earlier was a necessary consequence of low acreage
cultivation and production.

The highlands, which cover three-quarters of North Vietnam, have
posed special problems for the cooperative campaign and for the Five-
Year Plan to move a million lowland Vietnamese to a half-million hectares of new farmland there (this goal was reduced to 450,000 hectares
in 1963). The earliest groups of settlers were relocated in existing
communities of ethnic minority peoples, but this caused considerable
friction. Later, migrant groups were assigned to separate areas but the
terrain and soil were often less favorable, and the result was greater
hardship and lower production. By the fall of 1963, only about 50 per
cent of the land reclamation and 17 per cent of the manpower adjustment (resettlement) goals had been achieved.[23]

Poor leadership and organization by government cadres have figured
prominently in the weaknesses of the collectivization program. The re-

gime admitted, for example, "In analyzing the cases of cooperatives which had to close down in early 1963, we have noted that the main cause was mostly that of Party commissioners who gave up their leadership."[24]

To combat these weaknesses, the Party launched a movement for the improvement of cooperative management and for strengthening state leadership in agriculture during the final two years of the 1961 through 1965 Plan. It decided to assign a large force of administrative cadres to a relatively small percentage of cooperatives to devise a simple but more effective planning and management routine during the first 18 months and, then, during the final 18 months, to spread the new techniques to the rest of the cooperatives.[25]

The thorny question of incentives for farm production drew conflicting recommendations from Party spokesmen in 1963, reflecting the debates in Party councils—between the gradualists and the anti-revisionists—on Vietnam's ideological position in the dispute among the Communist countries and on domestic policies consistent with that position. Proponents of the hard line publicized instances of poor performance and failure in cooperatives, where private cultivation and incentive payments were said to have gradually eroded the collectivist spirit. Yet despite the many difficulties in implementing the collectivization program—including, in the past year, accusations by Party officials of "commandism" and "bureaucratism" among cadres responsible for administration of the collectives—the economy as a whole has been flexible enough to withstand the combined pressures of military attack from without and ineptitude from within.

Aid from Other Communist Countries

As we have already noted, the war over North Vietnam has enhanced the DRV's bargaining room position vis-à-vis its Soviet and Chinese partners even as the bombing has sharply curtailed its production and caused it to modify its supply system. Not only have the North Vietnamese leaders become able to assert a Vietnamese road of revolution; they have also proved skillful at exacting substantial economic and military assistance from their more powerful allies. Under the banner of "proletarian internationalism," the DRV has at various times spoken out against "modern revisionism" (without specifying the Russians), but at the same time it has upheld Russian appeals for unity in the face of the enemy.[26] Hanoi's request for unity has been ignored by Communist China, but this has not kept DRV spokesmen from harping on the theme, lauding the support of Moscow and Peking, and reaping the benefits of the competition.

Some mention has already been made of the food provided by the

Soviet Union and China. Additional Soviet assistance, for the most part in direct grants, has included medicines and nonmilitary vehicles that are labeled gifts from the Russian people.[27] The DRV's industrial program has been significantly assisted by Soviet funds, reflecting to some extent Moscow's program of economic integration of the Communist bloc and specialized production by its members (the DRV is not a member of CEMA, the Council for Economic Mutual Assistance). Along with some of the East European states,[28] the U.S.S.R. has also provided credits for agricultural development and mining, as well as more advanced types of assistance to the economic infrastructure (e.g., electric power and communications facilities, and machinery for heavy industry). In October 1966 a broad new aid agreement was announced from Moscow, and while details were omitted, it was apparent that the Soviet Union's recalcitrant position on aid, which followed on the DRV's refusal to sign the Test-Ban Treaty, had disappeared, to be replaced with total (military and economic) assistance in excess of the $500,000,000 granted in 1965.[29]

The "vast and effective" aid of the Soviet Union has not been matched in dollars by the Chinese, but Peking has contributed immensely nevertheless. In the economic sphere, the Chinese early provided basic construction materials for irrigation and transportation systems, and for light industry. Peking has also dispatched more technicians than the Soviet bloc: Over 5,000 Chinese were said by Ho Chi Minh to have come to Vietnam by May 1963 and, since that time, roughly 45,000 more have been sent, primarily for road and railway construction, freeing North Vietnamese troops for other duties.[30] Chinese aid has also included, besides the large deliveries of rice already mentioned, funds (usually outright grants) to develop the large Thai Nguyen industrial complex of plants producing pig iron and allied products, fertilizers, soft coal, and light machinery. Finally, the DRV Transport Minister noted, during 1967, that China had been training Vietnamese for, and equipping, technical research institutes, professional colleges, and vocational high schools. "The Chinese Communist Party and the Chinese Government," he said, "have sent many outstanding scientific and technical cadres and many skilled technical workers to directly help our Vietnamese communications and transport cadres and workers in various fields."[31] Hoang Quoc Viet, a high-ranking Party official speaking in the capacity of president of the Vietnamese-Chinese Friendship Association, summed up the DRV's gratitude for Chinese assistance when he called it "generous, selfless, timely, and thorough." "The important political and military successes which the people in the northern and southern areas of our country have won in succession," he continued, "are inseparable from the great support given by the Chinese people."[32]

In military assistance no less than in economic aid, the DRV has been able to extract from its fraternal Communist Parties the kinds of materials they are best suited to provide. Thus, from the Russians have come such sophisticated equipment as surface-to-air missiles, radar, jet aircraft, and anti-aircraft artillery, most of these items having been shipped following the beginning of daily air attacks by the United States. Moreover, the Russians have, apparently since late 1966, been training North Vietnamese to fly the huge MI-6 helicopters.[33] The Chinese, meanwhile, have concentrated their military aid on weapons and ammunition, and since 1965 they have added MIG-15, MIG-17, and even scarce MIG-21 jets. During 1967, Washington officials also revealed that China was not only training North Vietnamese pilots but was also permitting DRV fighter planes to be based in airfields in southern China.[34]

The North Vietnamese are well aware of the tremendous value of Sino-Soviet aid to their war effort; but they also realize that the greater the aid, the more open they are to compromises on complete control of policies governing war and peace. This point was made in a document captured in South Vietnam in January 1967, and attributed to General Nguyen Van Vinh, a *Lao Dong* Party member and Deputy Chief of Staff of the North Vietnamese Army (NVA). Vinh also said, according to the document, that were it not for the Sino-Soviet dispute, victory would come sooner; he admitted the danger that the rift might someday hinder the shipment of aid from both allies, leading him to conclude that it is necessary to gain a decisive victory in the South "within the four coming years" (by 1971) while maximizing support from the Communist bloc. The concern evident in the Vinh document about how long the North Vietnamese can continue to count on such aid—a concern that must have mounted with the onset of the Cultural Revolution in China— dictates that the DRV leaders maintain absolute neutrality in their praise of Chinese and Soviet assistance, even if certain of them happen to prefer one or the other side's position in international affairs.[35]

THE DRV IN THE SINO-SOVIET SPLIT

In tracing the DRV's necessarily zigzag course in the highly volatile Sino-Soviet debate, some points made earlier might profitably be repeated. Hanoi has not been ideologically neutral in the debate, but has chosen positions geared to best serving the interests of the DRV. Inasmuch as North Vietnam's primary concern is that the NFL succeed at "liberating" South Vietnam, it behooves Hanoi to placate both Communist powers, where placation seems called for, but without jeopardizing its freedom to decide its own over-all foreign policies, primary among which now are questions of war and peace. As we observed in our discussion of the DRV's leadership and of aid from the Communist bloc, North-Vietnamese attitudes toward the rift in Moscow-Peking relations seem to have a common denominator in the single-minded dedication of Party spokesmen to the goal of national reunification, even though differences of viewpoint over tactics doubtless exist. Particularly as the war has expanded in scope and intensity, the Hanoi regime has recognized and exploited the different motivations of China and the Soviet Union to assist North Vietnam's struggle—and it is precisely in this context that the appearance Hanoi sometimes gives, of being "pro-Peking" one year and "pro-Moscow" the next, must be understood.

Between 1954, when independence was formally secured at Geneva, and 1960, when the NLFSV was officially formed, Hanoi's reactions to Chinese and Soviet views of the world situation seemed to swing pendulum-like through periods of inclination toward one or the other,[36] with Ho Chi Minh evidently playing the role of moderator. During 1959 and 1960, however, when various DRV leaders—notably, Ho and Le Duan, at the Third Party Congress in September 1960—indirectly averred an interest in accelerating the southern anti-Diem revolution, Hanoi's interests clearly dictated a move in Peking's direction. The Russians, after all, were proffering a policy of peaceful coexistence and evolutionary advancement of the Communist cause, a view that Hanoi could hardly have found attractive given the necessity of backing a militant liberation campaign in the South. The Chinese, on the other hand, could only welcome the North Vietnamese determination to encourage and support the Viet Cong, inasmuch as such action would advance Peking's claims concerning the inevitability of armed struggle against the imperialist camp and would hold out the possibility of ousting American influence from an important area of Southeast Asia. By 1961, then, when North Vietnam opened a "Southern branch" of the *Lao Dong* as the NLF's vanguard element—the People's Revolutionary Party (PRP)[37]— and increased the flow southward of ex-Vietminh resistors who had been regrouped in the North between 1954 and 1955, Chinese support was certainly more to Hanoi's interests than the kind of reluctant backing for national liberation movements Khrushchev had expressed in his speech of January 6, 1961 to a meeting of organizations of the Communist Party of the Soviet Union (CPSU).

What is significant for a proper understanding of Hanoi's position at this time, and since, is that even when North Vietnamese interests dictated heightened support for China (as from 1960 to the spring of 1963), Hanoi was careful to leave ground for retaining close relations with the Soviets. North Vietnam specifically supported the Chinese position toward India and Laos for example. The DRV became furious with the Indians when the Indian delegate sided with the Canadian member against the Pole, in an investigation by the International Control Commission (ICC) for Vietnam. The ICC, charged under the 1954 Geneva accords with investigating and reporting violations of those accords, condemned the DRV, in June 1962, for subversion in South Vietnam through the dispatch of men and munitions. The sudden change of heart of the Indian representative paved the way for the DRV's sympathy for the Chinese in the Sino-Indian border war that October, and for its subsequent endorsement of Chinese policy in the Himalayas.

Even more important, Soviet policy in Laos had brought about an air corridor for military supplies through Hanoi to Kong Le, and this favorable situation ended with the new Geneva accords which formally concluded the Laotian conflict in July 1962. The Russians, after lending direct support to the Lao insurgents, had led the Communist negotiators at Geneva in the quest for a formula to guarantee a "neutral, sovereign and independent" Laos. The DRV undoubtedly could foresee that the new state of affairs would permit its troops to continue to infiltrate Laos and thence proceed into South Vietnam, but even so, it may well have concluded that the settlement expressed a limitation on the degree of Soviet willingness to assist the Vietnamese national liberation struggle at that time.

The DRV's stance in favor of China was also revealed indirectly in discussion of the heated topic of "modern revisionism." Hanoi had followed Moscow's lead in its reconciliation with Tito, but when Tito published his Draft Program in 1958, his brand of revisionism was savagely attacked in North Vietnam. Then, in 1962, when the Chinese made Titoism the scapegoat for their thinly veiled diatribes against Khrushchevism, the *Lao Dong* Party joined in with zeal. An article in the November issue of *Hoc Tap* flailed away at peaceful coexistence on the basis that: "The transition to socialism is not a spontaneous . . . phenomenon but is the result of a fierce class struggle between the socialist and capitalist systems and . . . of socialist and national liberation revolutions . . ." Revisionism was labeled "the principal danger at present," and dogmatism and sectarianism were called only secondary dangers. Always hedging their bets, however, the Party was careful not only to avoid attacking the Russians directly, and even continue to emphasize the value of Russian power. "The force protecting world peace is now formed by the socialist countries, of which the U.S.S.R. is the core," *Hoc Tap* added.

North Vietnam's unwillingness to go as far as China in scoring the U.S.S.R. was demonstrated again in late 1962, when Hanoi supported the Soviet withdrawal of missiles from Cuba as well as the demands in

Castro's "five points." Moreover, the visits of two important pro-Soviet delegations to Hanoi also brought expressions of favor. In December 1962, a military group under General Batov, along with members of the U.S.S.R.'s Supreme Soviet, traveled to the DRV capital, and in January 1963 Czech President Novotny joined with President Ho in a final communiqué that contained pro-Soviet overtones. The Chinese showed their dissatisfaction with this state of affairs by ignoring the February anniversary of the founding of the *Lao Dong*. This, together with a deterioration of Sino-Soviet relations at the East German Party Congress in January—to a point where both antagonists appeared determined to widen the rift inexorably—seems to have shocked the DRV Politburo into remedial action. A statement was drafted, appealing to the Communist countries for unity, recommending an end to recriminations, and calling for a world conference of Communist Parties, to be sponsored by the Soviet Union and China. The DRV's Politburo revealed that it had made the first two proposals in letters to Communist Parties in January 1962, and it repeated its determination to continue playing the strongest possible role in the quest for unity. The statement was careful to pay roughly equal compliments to both the Russians and the Chinese, although it still called the CPSU "the vanguard of the international Communist movement."

This statement was the DRV's first official acknowledgment of the seriousness of the Communist split. It served to heighten political and factional tensions at various levels, within and outside the Party, to such a point that Vo Nguyen Giap, considered by some analysts the leader of the pro-Soviet faction, released an article apparently intended to confirm that the Politburo's statement had truly expressed the unified sentiments within the leadership.[38]

A Sharper Turn Toward China: April 1963

China's disturbance at the course Hanoi was following evidently produced a reaction within the *Lao Dong* Party leadership in favor of more open avowals of support for the Chinese views. Such expressions did not come easily, it would seem, for as Nguyen Chi Thanh admitted in a speech on March 14, 1963, "leftist" as well as "rightist" tendencies within the Party existed. The dilemma, as well as the fact that at least some Party leaders still wished to straddle the fence between Moscow and Peking, was reflected in Le Duan's address in Hanoi on March 13. Yugoslav revisionism was strongly castigated; but peaceful coexistence remained "a form of class struggle" between different social systems, and was not in conflict with struggles for liberation. While armed struggle to gain power could never be ruled out (and Khrushchev had not done so at the 1960 Moscow meeting), peaceful transition to power was regarded as the best tactic "even when there is one chance in a hundred. . . ."[39]

Le Duan's middle-of-the-road formulation was, nonetheless, not entirely at variance with Pham Van Dong's speech to the National Assembly, in late April, in which he reiterated the DRV's agreement with China on the Sino-Indian border conflict, Taiwan, and U.N. membership. The culminating move to heal any breach with Peking remained for May, however, when CPR Chairman Liu Shao-ch'i and Vice-premier Ch'en I arrived in Hanoi for a six-day visit that was the occasion for great fanfare and warm displays of Sino-Vietnamese amity. The visit, perhaps Hanoi's way of mitigating Chinese anxiety over the Russian and Czech visits to the DRV in previous months, provided a platform for aggressive, but still veiled, anti-Soviet statements from the Chinese. The DRV backed some, but not all, of these, hewing to the line set down by Pham Van Dong in his April speech. Liu gave two major talks, one at a mass rally and the other at the Party's Nguyen Ai Quoc School for cadres. He attacked Khrushchev's modern revisionism on grounds of crucial importance to his hosts—"whether the people of the world should carry out revolution or not, and whether the proletarian parties should lead the world's people in revolution or not." The second speech, particularly, was a fiery one which frankly avowed that the fight against revisionism would be "protracted and complicated."[40]

The joint communiqué issued by Ho and Liu at the end of the visit revealed that certain tensions remained unresolved. The DRV went along with the Chinese attack on revisionism as the "main danger" (the Yugoslav version of revisionism was overtly excoriated), but a paragraph also explained why "it is also necessary to combat dogmatism." The principles of "unity," "independence and equality," and "unanimity" were held to govern relations and policy decisions within the Communist bloc (a pro-Chinese position, since the Soviets had substituted "a single view" for "unanimity" in their reporting of the *Lao Dong* Politburo statement of January). Both sides desired "the development of nuclear superiority by the socialist countries"—the plural form here anticipating the DRV's later rejection of the Soviet Union's argument for acceptance of the Test-Ban Treaty, that it could furnish single-handedly whatever nuclear capability might be required for the defense of countries in the Communist bloc.

Liu's statement of support of the war in South Vietnam was significant because it remained essentially the Chinese position into early 1964, when the Vietnamese tried to secure more specific guarantees. The communiqué said:

The Chinese people firmly support the heroic South Vietnamese people's just and patriotic struggle against U.S. imperialism and the Ngo . . . clique, and regard this struggle as a brilliant example for the oppressed nations and peoples . . . fighting for liberation.[41]

In their editorial comment on the visit, the Chinese stressed the importance of struggles for national liberation so heavily as to give the impression that the DRV had agreed with the sharp opposition expressed by Liu to the Soviet conception of peaceful coexistence. The actual treatment given these two key concepts in the communiqué was as follows: "[Socialist countries] must strive for peaceful co-existence with countries having different social systems on the basis of the Five Principles, and must support the revolutionary struggles of all oppressed nations and peoples." The DRV did not come around to the bellicose Chinese position until July, when an unsigned article in the Party journal (described later) expressed a harshly militant stance on revolutionary struggle.

In striking contrast to the outpouring of pro-Chinese sentiment during Liu's visit was a newspaper article, by Vice-president Ton Duc Thang printed one week after Liu's departure. The occasion was the thirteenth anniversary of the founding of the Vietnam-U.S.S.R. Friendship Association, and the title was of particular poignance, given the situation: "May Vietnam–U.S.S.R. Friendship Last Forever." The article injected a wishful implication into Soviet policy when it thanked the U.S.S.R. for supporting the South Vietnamese people's struggle and then went on to pledge that the DRV would stand with the U.S.S.R., China, and other socialist countries to struggle for the success of the national liberation movement.

In May, however, there appeared another in the series of militant statements by Nguyen Chi Thanh, the authoritative tone and comprehensiveness of which indicated that Thanh had regained considerable power in the Party during its shift toward the Chinese position. In his pronouncements, Thanh was pressing his earlier demand for ideological struggle, making only passing references to the secondary leftist dangers of dogmatism and sectarianism. Thanh spoke during his inspection of the military and political institute of the Army, especially warning "middle- and high-ranking officers" against any slackening of revolutionary militancy, any tendency toward softness and corruption. As might be imagined, Peking found this speech to its liking.[42]

The DRV's muted treatment of the Sino-Soviet talks in Moscow in July reflected its desire to minimize the ugly fact of disunity as well as its determination to maintain what degree of independence it could, even while its radio and press reports clearly showed decreasing optimism. On July 3, Radio Hanoi and the newspapers summarized parts of the CPSU resolution of June 21 and the declaration of the Communist Party of China of July 1 concerning the talks to begin on July 5, and expressed the usual hopes for unity. These news stories admitted that Sino-Soviet relations had deteriorated, but they were too brief and bland to convey a real understanding of the issues and the bitterness of the antagonists.

Meanwhile, the negotiations for a partial Nuclear Test-Ban Treaty had served to impel the DRV even further toward the Chinese position. Official Vietnamese antagonism to the Treaty emerged much more gradually than Chinese, again suggesting protracted intra-Party debates on the relative merits of the Chinese and Soviet positions. Hanoi had supported a Soviet Union initiative toward unilateral action to stop nuclear testing in the spring of 1958,[43] but six years later the Soviet role in test-ban negotiations perhaps appeared much more threatening in the event Hanoi should ever have need of a nuclear deterrent.

A further leftward impulse in the *Lao Dong* position was registered in the unsigned article in *Hoc Tap*, in July 1963, to which we referred earlier, which adopted the Chinese rationale for class struggle and "just wars," including wars for national liberation. This article, "The Renegade Tito again Spews the Venom of Revisionism," decried Titoist and, implicitly, Khrushchevian theories of peaceful coexistence, describing as an acceptable version of the doctrine one closely akin to the Peking line. It adopted also the Chinese view of the aftermath of a possible nuclear war: ". . . it would bring about extremely grave consequences," but it would result in the eradication of imperialism rather than the human race. Virulent as this commentary was, it still maintained a discreet vagueness in one brief passage which hinted that the test-ban negotiations probably were the major, or at least the latest, provocation.

The news of the initialing of the Treaty in Moscow was announced in the DRV in a radio broadcast on July 27, in a brief, factual statement. Three weeks later, however, the domestic radio service gave the signing of the treaty unusual coverage, including excerpts from the Chinese and Soviet statements of July 31. An editorial in *Nhan Dan* emphasized the attempts of "U.S. and British imperialists" to use the test-ban negotiations to "split the socialist camp," implying that the U.S.S.R. had been a dupe of the imperialists. And in mid-August, Hanoi further revealed its distaste for the Treaty by announcing its approval of the Chinese call for a conference of all nations to discuss total nuclear disarmament. But again, leaning to the side of China on most international issues still did not lead to frenzied attacks on Moscow.[44]

Through 1963 and into early 1964, Hanoi's relatively firm position on problems affecting the international Communist movement remained consistent, falling just short of open attack of the CPSU. The DRV's criticism extended also to a favorite theme exploited by the Chinese: the decisive role in war of men rather than weapons, including nuclear ones. Thus, General Hoang Van Thai, deputy chief of staff, wrote in the September 1963 issue of *Hoc Tap*—in contrast, it might be added, to views he had expressed three years earlier—that the modern revisionists, preaching "weaponism," were "relying on their nuclear arsenal to revise the fundamental principles of Marxist-Leninism concerning class struggle." The general decried the notion, attributed to the U.S.S.R. by China, that superior weaponry determines victory in war. Later, in December, Le Duan expressed similar views. Speaking at the Central Committee's Ninth Session in December, Duan stated the importance of not being mesmerized by nuclear weapons and so falling into a "defensive strategy." The socialist world was already sufficiently superior to the capitalist world, he said, to justify revolutionary struggle without being hamstrung by fear of instant world war.[45]

The DRV's closeness to the Chinese international line was clearly to its own interests, given the optimistic state of the Viet Cong insurgency in the South. Nevertheless, at this time as before and since, state policy did not receive blanket endorsement from all leaders and Party cadres. This much is clear from the admissions in DRV literature that there remained sharp differences of opinion on such questions as private landholdings, the place of ideological training in a society requiring economic development, and the danger of revisionism.[46] A division seems to have occurred in the Party hierarchy, between those militants like Nguyen Chi Thanh who assigned first place to the Viet Cong's struggle and those more managerially oriented leaders who, according to Thanh, were primarily concerned with increasing agricultural production by drastically modifying the Party's industry-first program and its methods for organizing cooperatives.[47] The unusual delays in the publication of important documents arising out of the Central Committee meetings in December, capped by the indefinite withholding of a major speech by Truong Chinh,[48] seemed to reaffirm the existence of factional disputes. Final testimony to the strife within the Party appeared in the differences between the Central Committee communiqué (issued January 20, 1964) and Le Duan's December speech (not published until February). The communiqué, primarily concerned with achieving unity in the Communist camp, drew a clear distinction between Titoist revisionism, which had to be exposed, and the "error of [Soviet] revisionism or right-wing opportunism," which necessitated "struggle for the sake of unity." Le Duan, on the other hand, upheld Chairman Mao's claims to theoretical creativity, pointed out the validity of the Chinese revolutionary model for many Communists in Asia, Africa, and Latin America," and called for "constant attacks" as the best way to weaken the imperialist camp while protecting world peace.

Intensification of the War and
Moves toward a Rapprochement with Moscow

As we suggested earlier, the Soviet Union, apparently in response to Hanoi's marked affinity for such Chinese positions as opposition to the Test-Ban Treaty, sharply cut back aid to the DRV. Aware of the need for Russian assistance at a time when the Viet Cong seemed on the road to victory, the DRV sent to Moscow a delegation, headed by Le Duan, which visited there from January 31 to February 10, 1964. Politburo members Le Duc Tho and Hoang Van Hoan (as well as To Huu and Nguyen Van Kinh) accompanied Duan and held "many meetings" with CPSU officials, including a lengthy conversation with Khrushchev, according to a subsequent brief communiqué from Hanoi. But, to judge from the weak wording of the final communiqué, Le Duan's mission had failed to obtain the requisite Soviet commitment of moral and material support for the war in South Vietnam. An editorial in *Nhan Dan* subtly phrased the meaning of the new Soviet pledge: "We clearly see that, *transformed into practical deeds*, this statement *will be* a valuable contribution not only to the revolutionary cause of our people but also to the national liberation movement in the world as a whole [emphasis supplied]."

Between February 1964, when Le Duan's mission returned home apparently empty-handed, and February 1965, when the United States began daily air attacks on the DRV, relations with Moscow remained rather strained. At the same time, Peking took advantage of the situation, especially following the Tonkin Gulf incidents in August 1964, by hinting that they would send troop support across the border if the United States committed (ground) "aggression" against North Vietnam. Hanoi's interests, however, dictated moving rightward toward Moscow, once the War was carried to the North. Hanoi suddenly needed air defense and other military support against a new kind of war being waged by the United States, and the Russians were hard put to refuse given the fact that a fraternal socialist state was now fighting for survival. Thus the North Vietnamese apparently found no real difficulty in switching from a stanchly pro-Chinese position to one more closely in keeping with the theme of unity that the DRV's leaders had often expounded.

Soviet re-engagement in Vietnamese affairs, and the inauguration of a new period of harmony between the DRV and the U.S.S.R., coincided with the American air attacks. A high-ranking Russian delegation, under Premier Kosygin, had arrived in Hanoi during January 1965; the air attacks, coming when Kosygin was still there, may have played into the *Lao Dong* Party's hands by compelling the Soviet leader to commit his country to further aid. The joint communiqué of February 11, in any event, reflected the Soviet Union's concern over the fate of the DRV by promising "the necessary aid and support" in view of the American threat to the DRV's security. Further negotiations included a trip to Moscow by Le Duan, and Soviet deliveries of jet fighters and surface-to-air missiles began by the end of May.[49]

Since that time, Hanoi has made certain to give appropriate thanks to both partners for their assistance. Proletarian internationalism, rather than modern revisionism, has been the most prominent theme in remarks by Hanoi on the international Communist movement. And much as the U.S.S.R. would probably prefer a negotiated settlement that removed the danger of further escalation and possible new demands for support, she has been adamant in publicly backing the DRV's well-known "four points" for ending the war[50] and the DRV's subsequent insistence that the United States must first cease bombing North Vietnam before meaningful peace talks can get under way. In return, the DRV's leadership has supported Moscow's persistent call for unity in the international Communist movement in view of the American threat and has, in defiance of Peking's wishes,[51] refrained from committing itself against *Soviet* revisionism even while remaining firmly opposed to the Titoist version.[52]

North Vietnam's appreciation for Soviet aid has been paralleled by noticeably cooler relations with Communist China. Not that Hanoi has in any way criticized Peking's policies, as it did Moscow's in earlier years; rather, Hanoi has mixed its praise of the Chinese with efforts to make clear that its military strategy and tactics flow from decisions of the *Lao Dong* Party and not from the advice or ideology of Mao Tse-tung. More positive support has been expressed by lauding the contributions of China to the world revolutionary movement and by greeting every Chinese advance toward the acquisition of an arsenal of nuclear weapons with praise for Chinese science and claims that the defense of the socialist world is thereby enhanced.[53] Also, in contrast to the Soviet Union, the DRV has maintained its friendship with the Albanians. Finally, despite growing Chinese caution over the Vietnamese War (since early 1966, Peking has turned from talk of possible intervention to the view that the prosecution of the War is entirely a Vietnamese struggle), Hanoi continues to rejoice in the "lips-to-teeth" closeness of the Chinese leadership and the spirit of sacrifice of the Chinese people for the sake of Hanoi's struggle.

Nevertheless, important differences appear in the respective approaches of the DRV and the CPR to the War. First, with regard to negotiations, Hanoi has made clear that its four points are meant to form an agenda should peace talks take place, whereas the Chinese have maintained that the granting of the "four points" must be a condition of such talks. Moreover, the DRV has refused to consider the Geneva accords inapplicable since the onset of the American attacks, while China, on the other hand, has spoken of events since August 1964 as having "trampled [the accords] underfoot," the implication being that no new Geneva conference can logically be convened to settle the fighting. Indeed, when the DRV's Foreign Minister, Nguyen Duy Trinh, implied, on January 28, 1967, that only America's cessation of the bombing stood between the two sides and negotiations, Peking, after considerable delay, responded with a vigorous reprimand that sought to remind Hanoi that *only* a full-fledged American withdrawal from South Vietnam should pave the way for discussions.[54]

A second important issue has concerned military theory and tactics. The Chinese revolutionary model lauded by Le Duan in 1963 is no longer alluded to by Hanoi leaders. Instead, as we have already observed, the DRV now claims its own creativity in conducting a people's war. Interestingly, the DRV has seemed to borrow the Chinese rationale: Just as Lin Piao stressed in his famous article "Long Live the Victory of People's War!" (September 3, 1965), that revolutionary movements must rely primarily on their own strength to succeed, so have the North Vietnamese stressed since then the importance of being self-reliant and the secondariness of having international support. As General Van Tien Dung stated Hanoi's position recently:

In the fight against the war of destruction [waged by the U.S.], we must rely mainly on our own strength and, at the same time, strive to struggle for international assistance, especially the assistance of all countries in the socialist camp. These two things are closely connected and insure victory. International assistance is very important, but no matter how great it may be, it must be utilized through our efforts in order to develop its effect. This is the objective rule of revolutionary war. Our party and people themselves have solved all problems concerning the lines, policies, aims, strategy, and tactics of our people's war in a correct and creative manner. . . . All our armed forces and people must be fully conscious of the "rely mainly on our own strength" ideology. . . .[55]

In practice, Hanoi's disavowal of indebtedness to Mao or Lin Piao for military doctrine has evidently been geared to an independent assessment of the tactical requirements for "correct" struggle in South Vietnam. The Chinese, through the news media, have consistently played up the *guerrilla* victories of the Liberation Armed Forces (LAF, the combined North Vietnamese Army and the Viet Cong), thereby indirectly indicating their disapproval of the North Vietnamese tendency to rely, under certain circumstances, on regional and large main forces and to engage American units in conventional, costly battles. China evidently believes—but has failed to convince North Vietnam—that the

large-scale presence of well-equipped Americans necessitates a rever-
sion to protracted, primarily guerrilla warfare in order to wear down
the United States.

A third major source of disagreement between the *Lao Dong* Party
and the Chinese Communist Party has arisen since the beginning of, and
conceivably in direct response to, China's Cultural Revolution. This difference concerns varying interpretations of Marxist-Leninist ideology
and its meaning for revolutionary societies such as China and North
Vietnam. First, as we have noted, Le Duan came forth and reversed the
position he took in 1963 on the role of the peasantry in revolution, by
speaking of working-class leadership of the overwhelmingly peasant-
based Vietnamese revolution.[56] Secondly, the North Vietnamese have refused to respond affirmatively to the Maoist cult sweeping mainland
China. Rarely have DRV leaders so much as mentioned the Cultural Revolution, at home or abroad. Even on those few occasions when they
have, they have shied away from any endorsement of its aims and
from any attempt to link it to China's social and technical progress.[57]
Indirectly, moreover, at least one Hanoi spokesman has gone as far as
to attack the Maoist cult by pointing to President Ho as a model leader,
one who has not needed to be deified because he has always been
close to the masses, advocated policies designed to ensure the indivisi-
bility of the Party and the masses, and preferred collective to individual leadership.[58] The North Vietnamese have evidently become wary
of emulating the all-out Chinese assault on the Party and the intellectuals at a time when unity and tight organization are essential to the
war effort.

Finally, the Chinese must find irksome North Vietnam's repeated calls
for Communist unity. Not only has the DRV reoriented its position since
1964, and moved toward a more genuine neutrality; it has also retained
firm relations with the Japanese, Mongolian, and North Korean Communist Parties at a time when Peking has attacked them for likewise appealing for united action in Vietnam. Thus, as the Chinese find themselves increasingly isolated in both the Communist and non-Communist
communities of Asia, the North Vietnamese have proved able to exploit
the War to improve their position with the Soviet Union, to steer clear of
untoward Chinese influence, and to maintain friendship with other Communist Parties.

NORTH VIETNAM, THE NATIONAL LIBERATION FRONT, AND THE WAR IN THE SOUTH

Whether or not differences between Hanoi and the leadership of the
National Liberation Front (NLF) actually exist—an oft-debated point
that may only become known once negotiations begin—there can be

little doubt that the DRV is broadly responsible for the strategic direction and material support of the Viet Cong. Working through the Central Office of South Vietnam (COSVN) and at least eight NVA generals known to be operating in South Vietnam, Hanoi is able to ensure that its directives are carried out. From captured documents,[59] for example, we know that after the large-scale introduction of American troops into the war zone in mid-1965, the *Lao Dong* Party decided (at its Twelfth Conference, in December) that the American "special" war had become a "limited" one. The Conference's decisions—to stick to protracted struggle, but also to seek a "decisive victory in a relatively short period of time"; to build up a total force of about 1,000,000 in the South during 1966; but to put 50,000 U.S. troops out of action while eroding South Vietnamese strength by one-half—were adopted by the Fourth COSVN Congress in April 1966. From then on, Hanoi's assessment that the long-awaited "general uprising and general offensive" would have to be temporarily postponed became Viet Cong strategy.

Nevertheless, North Vietnam has gone to considerable lengths to stress the independence of the NLF. Beginning in 1962, Hanoi fully backed the NLF's claim to be the sole legitimate representative of the South Vietnamese people. In the four points, it will be recalled, the Party specified that the NLF's program should determine the nature of the peace settlement in South Vietnam, and that the question of reunification should be subject only to negotiation between northerners and southerners. Until 1966, however, Hanoi's view of the Front as independent was not paralleled by any effort to promote the notion of autonomous governmental authority in the South. Then, in December, Nguyen Van Tien was appointed permanent Front delegate to Hanoi —but again, the NLF was not treated as a separate entity with provisional or *de facto* diplomatic status.[60] Consequently, Hanoi's policy has been to maintain the notion that South Vietnam will remain independent after the peace until reunification is accomplished; and in line with that policy, the North Vietnamese have insisted that if the Americans wish to negotiate matters relating to South Vietnam, they must deal with the NLF, not with Hanoi.

For its part, the NLF, no doubt reacting to the publicity attending the local and national elections in South Vietnam and their at least partial success, has attempted to regain the political initiative by offering the people a wide-ranging program of reform. After periods in which it did not actively portray itself as a true cross-section of Vietnamese political life, the Front, in mid-1966, again stressed that a new national government would comprise "representatives of all social classes, all religious communities, and all patriotic groups," thus omitting only key figures in past and present Saigon governments.[61] The front elaborated on its position in its August 1967 program. Assertedly, under Front control, the government of South Vietnam would be neutral, independent, free of all alliances, and prepared to enter into diplomatic relations with all countries on the basis of the principles of peaceful coexistence. Redistribution of the land would be carried out, but not collectivization of the land or socialization of industry and commerce. Foreign investments and assistance would be accepted from all quarters. North-South relations would be renewed, in the interim preceding reunification, to permit travel, postal exchange, trade, and cultural exchange between the zones.[62] Spokesmen for both Hanoi and the Front have publicly asserted that there need be no haste in reunifying the country.[63]

Of some importance is the fact that Peking has, as might be expected, given the Front considerable attention and publicity in precisely the period when North Vietnam has ignored Chinese tactical advice. In December 1967, for example, it was announced from Hanoi that the permanent NLF Mission to Peking had been granted full embassy status as an official diplomatic mission.[64] Thereafter, a large NLF delegation visited Peking and subsequently, during December and January 1968, toured several of China's major cities amidst great fanfare and laudation. Front leaders no doubt find the hard Chinese position on negotiations much more suited to circumstances in the South than Hanoi's conditional acceptance of negotiations—and it is perhaps for this reason that Nguyen Duy Trinh's speech in January 1967, and others since, have not been given special attention in the clandestine broadcasts of the Front's Liberation Radio.

The available evidence seems to demonstrate, however, that the Front is independent to about the extent Hanoi wishes to it to be. By playing up the Front's representative nature, Hanoi hopes to diminish the importance of its own significant contributions to the Viet Cong effort; and by insisting that the Americans talk directly with the Front, Hanoi evidently believes it can control the outcome without disturbing the image of an independent, Communist-dominated coalition that will eventually control the Southern zone. As General Vinh commented in the captured document cited earlier, when negotiations come, either the DRV will do the talking while the LAF continues to fight, or "South Vietnam will *participate* in negotiations but continue to fight [emphasis supplied]." Another North Vietnamese general has corroborated this view of a DRV-controlled negotiatory process when he told the NVA Seventh Division (in August 1966): "Negotiation or diplomatic struggle is the work of the Central Headquarters and the Politburo [of the *Lao Dong*]. . . ."[65] Clearly, when serious negotiations do occur, the NLF is destined to play a role subordinate to that of the North Vietnamese.

As the statements by ranking North Vietnamese military leaders clearly indicate, they regard serious negotiations, if and when they occur, as part and parcel of the ongoing struggle in South Vietnam. In that struggle, they believe they are fighting a defensive war against the American invaders who have linked up with a despotic, unrepresentative regime in Saigon to foil the dream of reunification. As the North Vietnamese view the war,[66] the fact that the Americans have intervened with huge amounts of materiel and great numbers of men can only temporarily postpone their own inevitable triumph, for the "enemy" camp is riven with internal "contradictions" that will eventually erode his will to fight and compel him to withdraw. Protracted struggle combined with pushes for dramatic victories (perhaps small Dien Bien Phus) is the requisite strategy, then—not only because numerous casualties inflicted on the enemy will wear down his fighting capabilities, but equally because the contradictions he has created between himself and the Vietnamese people and the Saigon regime will multiply. The comment of leaders such as General Vinh, that "attack and negotiation at the same time is a rule of war," is consequently understandable within the framework in which Hanoi operates: Once the enemy is weakened, military superiority on the battlefield will yield a favorable political outcome at the bargaining table, for negotiations are merely an extension of the protracted struggle.

CONCLUSION

The prospects for the internal development and external stability of communist North Vietnam obviously hinge on how and when the War is settled. The slow but identifiable advances North Vietnam seemed to be making toward industrial and agricultural expansion have naturally been blunted to a considerable extent by the toll the war has taken of its economy and its manpower. Yet the regime's unalterable commitment to the War in South Vietnam has made those tolls bearable for the Party's leadership, even though strains have begun to appear in the society's capacity to withstand the disruptive effects of the bombing and to mobilize resources effectively for the southern front. Few can deny, however, the leadership's great ability to endure pressure, an endurance sustained by the full, if somewhat reluctant, support of China and Russia. In Hanoi's view, the costs of the War are probably outweighed by the inevitability of victory, by its image of itself as the defender of Vietnamese sovereignty, and by its proven ability to maintain its ideological independence and its control over vital questions of war and peace.

The subordination of economic and social progress to long term political considerations seems to be accepted by the Party's leaders. Whatever their individual views about proper tactics, the members of the Po itburo evidently share Ho Chi Minh's determination to continue the struggle in the South rather than again accept a divided country. At the beginning of 1968, the prospects for peace were cloudy, and it seemed evident that South Vietnam's destiny also involved, as far as Hanoi was concerned, Laos and Cambodia. Pathet Lao forces employing, if not dominated by, North Vietnamese soldiers and cadres, began a new offensive against the government of Prince Souvanna Phouma; while in Cambodia, the Viet Cong's use of Prince Sihanouk's country for sanctuary and resupply was making Cambodian neutrality exceedingly tenuous. As in the early 1950's, when the Vietminh operated throughout much of the three Indochinese states, the North Vietnamese and their allied forces were posing, to their opponents, the difficult choice between localized and regional fighting.

Late in 1967, there was some evidence, from captured documents, that the North Vietnamese command was considering a major strategic shift from a protracted war to inauguration of the "general offensive."[67] The likelihood that such a shift did occur was strengthened by a broadcast from Radio Hanoi on February 2, 1968 (in the name of the previously unpublicized Command Headquarters of the South Vietnam People's Liberation Armed Forces) that greeted widespread Viet Cong attacks on key cities in the South with the comment: "the long-awaited general offensive against the Thieu-Ky puppet administration has come. . . We would like to tell our compatriots that we are determined to overthrow the Thieu-Ky puppet administration."[68] But whether the shift, presuming it is genuine, presaged a major military push in advance of negotiations, was a bid to recapture the initiative on the battlefield, or was an attempt to bolster the morale of war-weary cadres remains to be seen. Whatever the case, there can be little doubt that it is chiefly in North Vietnam's hands that the decision when and how to cast the die rests.

NOTES

1. Cited in Bernard B. Fall, *Le Vietminh: La République Démocratique du Viet-Nam: 1945–1960* (Paris: Librairie Armand Colin, 1960), p. 173.
2. Nguyen Huu Khai, Article, *Hoc Tap* (*Studies*), March, 1963. *Hoc Tap* is the Communist Party journal.
   Titles of articles from Vietnamese periodicals are omitted from the citations because of their frequently great length and the fact that the author's name and date of journal issue suffice for the location of the materials in question.
3. Duong Huong, Article, in *ibid.*, September, 1963.
4. Le Duc Tho, quoted in *Tien Phong*, June 19, 1963.
5. Vu Duong, Article, *Hoc Tap* (*Studies*), February, 1962.

6. Nguyen Huu Khai, Article, in *ibid.*, March, 1963

7. Le Duc Tho, Article, *Nhan Dan (The People)*, November 7, 1966. *Nhan Dan* is the official Hanoi newspaper.

8. Vu Oanh, Article, in *ibid.*, August 29, 1967. Translation published by U.S. Department of Commerce, Office of Technical Services, Joint Publications Research Service [JPRS], *Translations on North Vietnam, No. 259*, October 9, 1967, pp 12–16.

9. Lt.-Gen. Song Hao, Article, *Hoc Tap*, May, 1967 (in *Translations from Hoc Tap*, JPRS, No. 41,648, June 30, 1967, pp. 53–64).

10. P. J. Honey, *Communism in North Vietnam: Its Role in the Sino-Soviet Dispute* (Cambridge, Mass.: The M.I.T. Press, 1963), p. 21.

11. Le Duan, *Some Questions Concerning the International Tasks of Our Party* (Peking: Foreign Languages Press, 1964), pp. 12–13.

12. Le Duan, Article, *Hoc Tap*, May, 1967 (in *Translations from Hoc Tap*, JPRS No. 41,648, June 30, 1967, pp. 9–35).

13. In *Hoc Tap (Studies)*, December, 1966.

14. Le Duan, Article, in *ibid.*, February, 1964. (The article was based on a speech delivered in December, 1963.)

15. *Hoc Tap*, September, 1966 (in *Translations from Hoc Tap*, JPRS, No. 38,660 November 16, 1966, pp. 4–5).

16. These calculations are based on data announced in a Hanoi domestic broadcast in Vietnamese on January 31, 1964.

17. This speech was serially published by *Nhan Dan (The People)* on July 13 to 15 1962. The exchange rate used here is 3.55 *dong* to the U.S. dollar. Other exchange rates, used by Vietnamese and foreign (including some American sources, range from 1.2 to 4 *dong* to a dollar.

18. For information on North Vietnam's economy, see *Far Eastern Economic Review 1967 Yearbook* (Hong Kong, 1967), pp. 286–288; and Harrison E. Salisbury "North's Economy Badly Disrupted," *New York Times*, January 1, 1967, p. 1.

19. *New York Times*, August 31, 1967, p. 2.

20. See, for example, Nguyen Van Tran, Article, in *Tuyen Huan (Propaganda and Training)* (Hanoi, periodical), October, 1966 (in *Translations on North Vietnam: No. 96*, JPRS, February 2, 1967), pp. 28–30.

21. Vietnam News Agency, editor's note introducing a Hanoi English-language broadcast, January 15, 1964.

22. Hanoi, Vietnamese-language broadcast, March 5, 1963; and Bernard B. Fall, *The Two Vietnams* (New York: Frederick A. Praeger, Inc., 1963), p. 161.

23. Nguyen Duong Tam, Article, *Hoc Tap (Studies)*, September, 1963.

24. Truong Ngoc, Article, *Hoc Tap (Studies)*, October, 1963.

25. Hanoi, Vietnamese-language broadcast, March 10, 1963.

26. For example, Ho Chi Minh declared, in a letter of greeting to the Soviet Communist Party, that the American threat "requires that fraternal Socialist countries, Communist and Workers parties and all forces of peace, democracy and progress in the world unite closely to oppose United States imperialists . . ." Characteristically, Chinese and Soviet aid to the DRV was praised with equal fervor. See *New York Times*, April 1, 1966, p. 6.

27. The official Soviet news agency, Tass, broadcast on August 27, 1967, for instance that goods valued at over one million rubles were being sent out of Soviet "peace funds" (donations from the Soviet people).

28. During 1965 and 1966, for example, Hanoi received aid from Hungary (long-term loans) and Bulgaria (interest-free loans to purchase equipment). *Far Eastern Economic Review: 1967 Year Book*, p. 287.

29. *New York Times*, October 4, 1966, pp. 1, 10.

30. See the report in *New York Times*, August 12, 1966, p. 4, which gives the estimate of American officials that Chinese troop strength had reached 50,000 uniformed soldiers, most of whom were said to be engaged in repairing and improving the Sino-Vietnamese supply lines.

31. Hanoi, domestic service broadcast, October 2, 1967.

32. Broadcast over Peking domestic service radio, December 31, 1965.

33. *New York Times*, January 9, 1967, p. 13.

34. *Ibid.*, March 14, 1967, p. 3, and August 27, 1967, p. 1. So far as is known, however, North Vietnamese aircraft operating from bases in China have not engaged American jets.

35. The extent to which the DRV must go in its "neutral" position on aid from Moscow and Peking was lucidly illustrated during 1966, when the Russians charged that Soviet aid destined for Hanoi was being delayed *en route* in China (some reports saying the Russians had accused the Chinese of taking equipment or making blueprints for themselves). In rebutting the charges, the Vietnam News Agency, in a broadcast on December 10, 1966, cited them as stemming from "Western news agencies."

36. For further information, though in somewhat exaggerated fashion, on these shifts of position, see P. J. Honey, *Communism in North Vietnam*, pp. 40 ff. See also Le Duan, *On Some Present International Problems* (Hanoi: Foreign Languages Publishing House, 1964). The text of Le Duan's speech to the *Lao Dong* Party's Central Committee (in December 1960, after returning from the Moscow meeting of 81 Communist Parties) illustrates the difficulty the North Vietnamese were experiencing in seeking to harmonize Sino-Soviet differences while simultaneously translating them into meaningful statements of DRV policy.

37. This admission was made in a "top secret" resolution issued by the Central Office for South Vietnam, the headquarters of the PRP and the NLF. The resolution was captured by American forces during 1967 and released to the press by the U.S. Embassy, Saigon, on August 18, 1967. The PRP, in fact, was consistently referred to as the *Lao Dong's* "Southern branch" and as an organ "closely led by the [Hanoi] Party Central Committee."

38. Vietnam News Agency, February 21, 1963.

39. Le Duan, *Hold High the Revolutionary Banner of Creative Marxism: Lead Our Revolutionary Cause to Complete Victory!* (Peking: Foreign Languages Press, 1964).

40. New China News Agency, May 15, 1963.

41. *Ibid.*, May 16, 1963.

42. The text was published in *Quan Doi Nhan Dan* (*People's Army*), May 25, 1963, and broadcast by Radio Peking in English on June 8. *Quan Doi Nhan Dan* is the Vietnamese Army's newspaper.

43. Honey, *Communism in North Vietnam*, p. 59.

44. See, e.g., an unsigned article in *Hoc Tap* (*Studies*), September, 1963.

45. Le Duan, *Some Questions*, p. 20.

46. See, for example, Hoang Minh, Article, in *Hoc Tap* (*Studies*), October, 1963.

47. Thanh's scathing attack on the opposition is in *Hoc Tap* (*Studies*), October, 1963.

48. We know from Le Duan's speech that Truong Chinh recapitulated the Central Committee debate and introduced a draft resolution. That resolution was also never published.

49. Charles B. McLane, "U.S.S.R. Policy in Asia," *Current History*, XLIX, No. 290 (October, 1965), p. 219.

50. The "four points" were made public by the Vietnam News Agency on April 13, 1965, in a broadcast citing a Report made the same day to the second session of

the Third National Assembly by Premier Pham Van Dong. The points are: (1) that the United States, in accordance with the Geneva agreements, must recog nize Vietnamese territorial integrity and unity, withdraw all forces and dismantl all bases in South Vietnam, and "stop its acts of war against North Vietnam. . . ." (2) pending peaceful reunification, the two zones of Vietnam "must refrain from joining any military alliance with foreign countries," including refraining from permitting foreign bases and forces on their respective territories; (3) South Vietnam's internal affairs must be settled by its people "in accordance with the program of the NFLSV without any foreign interference"; and (4) the Vietna mese of both zones will alone settle the matter of peaceful reunification.

51. The former General Secretary of the Chinese Communist Party, Teng Hsiao p'ing, implicitly attacked Hanoi's "neutrality" in the Sino-Soviet dispute when he said, during the visit of an Albanian delegation in May 1966: "There can be no centrist line in the struggle between Marxism and Leninism and revisionism." *New York Times*, May 12, 1966, pp. 1, 11.

52. Thus, when Hoang Van Hoan represented Hanoi at the Fifth Congress of the Albanian Workers' Party in late 1966, he praised Albania's policies (thus antag onizing the U.S.S.R.) and spoke only of the DRV's opposition to the "Tito re visionists." *Nhan Dan*, November 6, 1966 (in *Translations on North Vietnam No. 72*, JPRS, December 7, 1966, pp. 23–24).

53. E.g., in a Radio Hanoi broadcast, October 28, 1966; also, "The Great CCP," in *Nhan Dan* (*The People*). This article was carried by the Vietnam News Agen cy's international service on July 1, 1967, the forty-sixth anniversary of the Chi nese Party. Significantly, the DRV has not gone so far as the Albanians in attrib uting the technological accomplishments of the Chinese People's Republic (CPR to "the thought of Mao Tse-tung."

54. Observer, Article, in *Jen-min jih-pao* (*People's Daily*), (Peking), February 20 1967, as broadcast by New China News Agency (Peking), domestic service, on the same day.

55. Third installment of an Article, broadcast by Radio Hanoi, domestic service, June 15, 1967.

56. See Le Duan, Article, *Hoc Tap*, May, 1967 (in *Translations from Hoc Tap* JPRS, No. 38,660, November 16, 1966).

57. Typical were the speeches of the DRV's representatives at celebrations of Com munist China's Eighteenth National Day, held at Hanoi. At a reception, profuse praise of Mao's thoughts as being responsible for all of China's successes (in speech by Lu Wei-chao, CPR *chargé d'affaires ad interim* to the DRV), con trasted sharply with Pham Van Dong's passing reference to the Cultural Revolu tion in a speech devoted mainly to North Vietnam's resistance struggle. Pham Van Dong's speech was reported, importantly, by the Vietnam News Agency in an international service broadcast, on September 29, 1967.

At the Peking celebration, things were different, according to the New China News Agency (Peking). There, Le Thanh Nghi followed Chou En-lai to the rostrum with reportedly vigorous applause for China's Cultural Revolution "to prevent a capitalist restoration and insure that China will never change her color." The text of Le Thanh Nghi's speech was broadcast by the New China News Agency on September 29, 1967.

58. Hong Chuong, *Hoc Tap* (*Studies*), May, 1967. Hong Chuong is the deputy editor of *Hoc Tap*, and his article commemorated Ho Chi Minh's seventy-seventh birthday.

59. In particular, a letter sent from Le Duan, in March 1966, to high-ranking cadre in South Vietnam for dissemination to the COSVN and other Viet Cong agencies The letter was captured in January 1967, and released to the press by the U.S Embassy, Saigon.

60. *Nhan Dan* (*The People*) commented on the establishment of the permanent rep

resentation in an editorial, December 13, 1966, broadcast by the Vietnam News Agency, international service, on the same day. On December 13, *Quan Doi Nhan Dan (People's Army)* proclaimed, in an editorial: "The Front has actually performed the functions of a genuine state of the southern people." *Quan Doi Nhan Dan's* editorial was broadcast by Hanoi Radio's domestic service on the same day.

31. Interview with the President of the Front, Nguyen Huu Tho, *Le Monde* (Paris), December 14, 1966, p. 3.

32. The complete political program of the Front, said to have been adopted at an Extraordinary Congress convened by the Central Committee in mid-August 1967, was broadcast approvingly by the Vietnam News Agency on September 1, 1967. See also an interview between Nguyen Huu Tho and Wilfred Burchett, the pro-Communist Australian writer, in the *New York Times*, February 11, 1967, p. 4; and further comments on the August program by a member of the Presidium of the NLF Central Committee, Dang Tran Thi, in *Hoc Tap (Studies)*, September, 1967.

33. See, for example, an interview of Premier Pham Van Dong by the chief editor of the *Asahi Evening News* (Tokyo), April 24, 1967.

34. Vietnam News Agency, international service broadcast, December 10, 1967.

35. Major General Tran Do's statement was part of a lengthy tape-recorded speech captured by U.S. forces in January, 1967 and made public by the U.S. Embassy, Saigon. Tran Do is Deputy Commander of the Viet Cong and an alternate member of the Central Committee of the *Lao Dong* Party.

36. For a fuller discussion of Hanoi's perception of the war and negotiations, see Melvin Gurtov, *Hanoi on War and Peace* (Santa Monica, Calif.: The RAND Corporation, P-3696, 1967).

37. Joseph Alsop, "Captured Documents Indicate a Major Red Strategy Shift," *Washington Post*, December 15, 1967.

38. *New York Times*, February 2, 1968, p. 2. A similar statement, under the same authority, was broadcast the previous day by Liberation Radio (clandestine), which identified the new Command Headquarters as "the commanding organ of various patriotic South Vietnamese armed forces."

SELECTED BIBLIOGRAPHY

Burchett, Wilfred G., *North of the 17th Parallel* (2nd ed.). Hanoi: Privately published, 1957.

Fall, Bernard B., *Le Viet-Minh: 1945–1960*. Paris: Librairie Armand Colin, 1960.

——, *The Two Vietnams: A Political and Military Analysis*. New York: Frederick A. Praeger, Inc., 1963.

Gurtov, Melvin, *Hanoi on War and Peace*. Santa Monica, Calif.: The RAND Corporation, P-3696, 1967.

Hoang Van Chi, *From Colonialism to Communism*. New York: Frederick A. Praeger, Inc., 1964.

Honey, P. J., *Communism in North Vietnam: Its Role in the Sino-Soviet Dispute*. Cambridge, Mass.: The M.I.T. Press, 1963.

——, ed., *North Vietnam Today: Profile of a Communist Satellite*. New York: Frederick A. Praeger, Inc., 1962.

Lacouture, Jean, *Vietnam: Between Two Truces.* Translated by Konrad Kellen and Joel Carmichael. New York: Random House, Inc., 1966.

Ojha, Ishwer C., "China and North Vietnam," *Current History,* LIV, No. 317 (January, 1968), pp. 42–47.

Salisbury, Harrison E., *Behind the Lines—Hanoi: December 23, 1966–January 7, 1967.* New York: Harper & Row, Publishers, 1967.

Tanham, George K., *Communist Revolutionary Warfare.* New York: Frederick A. Praeger, Inc., 1962.

Tongas, Gerard, *J'ai vécu dans l'enfer communiste au Nord Vietnam et j'a choisi la liberté.* Paris: Les Nouvelles Editions Debresse, 1961.

Trager, Frank N., ed., *Marxism in Southeast Asia.* Stanford, Calif.: Stanford University Press, 1959.

Zagoria, Donald S., *Vietnam Triangle: Moscow, Peking, Hanoi.* New York: Pegasus Publishers, 1967.

THE PATHET LAO

A "LIBERATION" PARTY

BERNARD B. FALL

FOREWORD

Death in Vietnam prevented Bernard Fall from revising his chapter on "The Pathet Lao: A 'Liberation' Party," originally written in 1965. Although this excellent piece of scholarship stands up remarkably well under the test of time, new data have since become available to the student of Lao politics. They suggest a few corrections in Fall's presentation and point to certain modifications in the trends he observed two years ago.

An analysis of our admittedly incomplete data on the Pathet Lao indicates that the role played by the ethnic minorities of Laos is perhaps in some respects less significant than Fall thought at the time. While complete and reliable statistics are unavailable, it appears that ethnic minority elements form a substantial part of, but apparently not the bulk of, the Pathet Lao fighting forces. It is also true that quite a few minority persons have gradually been moving from the ranks into middle-level positions of the Pathet Lao military and civilian hierarchy. However, they are still only a small fraction of the Pathet Lao's leadership and are apparently less significant in decision making than even their limited number would suggest.

This is not to deny that one of the insurgent movement's great strengths in Laos is the support it finds among the hill tribes, especially in the south, where hatred of lowland Lao rule has a long history. Enlightened Pathet Lao policies toward these hitherto economically and culturally disadvantaged victims of Laotian discrimination have been reinforced by an acutely felt need on the part of the Communist leaders to build a firm base in the mountainous areas of Laos along the borders of Vietnam—areas where the ethnic minority groups are heavily concentrated.

Although new information regarding the evolution of the Pathet Lao movement has come to light, the history of Communism in Laos remains more murky than that of most Asian countries. In fact, until quite recently, it could be argued that no Communist Party existed in Laos and that the Neo Lao Hak Sat, headed by Prince Souphanouvong, somehow functioned both as a broad national revolutionary front and a Party. Russian sources, for example, assert that in this instance the two terms can be and are used interchangeably. They make no reference to a Communist Party organization in Laos. On the other hand, there have long been indications that a small, secret Communist apparatus operates in Laos and acts as the controlling element within the Pathet Lao movement. This organization has been given various names, but most frequently it has been referred to as *Phak Khon Ngan* (i.e., Laotian Labor Party)—a term also used by Bernard Fall and, significantly, the exact Lao translation of the Vietnamese Communist Party organization's designation.

In recent years, evidence has confirmed that a Communist Party organization does indeed exist in Laos, if clandestinely; that its leadership overlaps, but is not identical with that of the Neo Lao Hak Sat front; and, that its name is not the Laotian Labor Party, but rather *Phak Pasason Lao* (i.e., Lao People's Party). To mention but one piece of such evidence: the official Japanese Communist monthly *Zen'ei* (*Vanguard*), in its special December 1966 issue on the occasion of the Party's Tenth Congress, carried a message of greetings from Sam Neua (Laos), dated October 24, 1966, and signed by the "Secretary General of the Central Committee of the Lao People's Party" rather than by the leader of the Neo Lao Hak Sat, Prince Souphanouvong. The message contained such passages as, "under the correct leadership of the Lao People's Party, we the Lao people have firmly united within the Neo Lao Hak Sat . . . ," thus making a clear distinction between the two organizations. A similar message was more recently sent to the Communist National Liberation Front in Vietnam. It too was signed by Kaysone Phomvihan rather than by Prince Souphanouvong, founder and nominal leader of the Pathet Lao. Kaysone appears to be today the single most important individual in the Lao Communist movement, probably followed closely in that respect by Nouhak Phoumsavanh. It seems clear that, although Souphanouvong stated, in 1967, for the first time (at least in public) that he now considers himself a Communist, the major role in the Pathet Lao revolutionary movement is played by elements identifying themselves more closely with the North Vietnamese than does the Prince. Both Kaysone and Nouhak have, over the past two decades, spent much of their time in Vietnam, they have shunned contact with such Royal Lao Government leaders as the neutralist Premier Souvanna Phouma, and they have generally been considered particularly close friends and associates of the North Vietnamese. Kaysone, moreover, is of mixed Vietnamese-Lao parentage.

In 1965, when Bernard Fall wrote, the international relations of the Pathet Lao movement and the role played in it by outside Communist influences were not as clear as they are today. More information regarding the decreasing Soviet and the mounting Chinese weight in the Communist areas of Laos and among its leaders is now available. Both rival powers' influence is overshadowed, however, by that of North Vietnam, to whom China, at least for the time being, appears to have conceded jurisdiction over Lao affairs. The testimony of prisoners and defectors—both Lao and Vietnamese—made public in Vientiane during 1967, as well as related documentation, confirms not only the Pathet Lao's heavy reliance on North Vietnamese military, economic, political, and ideological support, but also sheds light on the specific ways in which the North Vietnamese support program is carried out and its control maintained. If anything, the central role played by the North Vietnamese in Laos has grown since the days when Bernard Fall made his assessment.

Paul F. Langer

In large measure, the Laotian Communist movement appears to be based not on the ethnic Laotian lowlanders but on many of the minorities of Laos—Thai, *Meo*, and Malayo-Indonesian [i.e., *Kha*, Lao for slave] peoples.

Whether this situation is the result of deliberate decisions by the Laotian Communist leadership or their Vietnamese sponsors or whether it arose out of the natural circumstances that the bulk of the Laotian territory under Communist control is located in minority areas, is not clear at present. In any case, the ethnic composition of the Pathet Lao adds a complex and fascinating factor to the study of this movement.

ORIGINS

Throughout the entire period of French colonial domination, Laos constituted a political and administrative backwater. There was only a single *lycée* in Vientiane which dispensed a full French high-school education. Only 14,700 Laotians had attended French-type primary schools by 1945, and less than 100 (mostly from noble families) had received an advanced Western education. Such an education usually began for Laotians with the equivalent of junior college studies in neighboring North Vietnam which, during the colonial period, housed at Hanoi the only full-fledged university then existing in Indochina. This explains why quite a few of Laos' senior leaders, regardless of political hue, speak Vietnamese and have a particular affinity for Hanoi as a center of culture. Some, notably Prince Souphanouvong, the titular leader of the Pathet Lao, also found Vietnamese wives there. A very few—the most notable examples were perhaps Prince Souvanna Phouma and Prince Souphanouvong—went on from Hanoi to a full college education or even graduate work in France.

It is, therefore, not surprising that political consciousness should have reached the Laotians via Hanoi or France. This was particularly true of the Communist movement. Until the creation of the specifically Vietnamese *Dang Lao Dong* (Workers' Party) on March 6, 1951, there existed only an Indochinese Communist Party (ICP) created in January, 1930, which supposedly also included Laotian and Cambodian elements. As early as 1936, it was known that the ICP's Central Committee included a Laotian member, Kham Seng.[1]

Kham Seng allegedly was a relative of a tribal leader, Kommadam (or Komadome), from the southern Laotian Boloven plateau who had been killed by the French colonial forces at the end of the extremely bloody Boloven uprising of 1936 and 1937. The Boloven had been in an almost permanent state of insurgency against the French since 1910, and tribesmen from the area eventually provided, as will be seen, an impressive number of guerrilla and political leaders to the Pathet Lao—just as the neighboring Lao lowland area, Savannakhet and Paksé, was to provide Vientiane with a goodly number of right-wing politicians: Prince Boun Oum, Katay Sasorith, and Generals Kou Abhay and Siho, among others. Prince Boun Oum allegedly participated in the French repression of the Boloven revolt, since the Boloven were located on the territory of his principality of Champassak. This overlay of ancient ethnic hatreds, beyond doubt, plays a certain role today in the relationships between the right-wing Laotians and their Pathet Lao opponents.

Nevertheless, the most important Laotian left-wing leader was an ethnic Lao lowlander of princely origin, Souphanouvong. The youngest of 20 sons of Prince Boun Khong of Vientiane, who had several wives, Souphanouvong stood little chance of acquiring a position of great importance within the feudal structure of his country. His eldest half-brother was Prince Phetsarat. Prince Souvanna Phouma was somewhere in between. Phetsarat, who had obtained an engineering degree abroad with a specialty in printing machinery and who, as Viceroy of the Kingdom of Luang-Prabang, resided at Vientiane,[2] advised Souvanna and Souphanouvong to study abroad and thus acquire knowledge which would permit them to rise to high posts within the colonial administration.

Both princes, after *lycée* studies at the Albert Sarraut *lycée* in Hanoi,[3] went to highly competitive French engineering schools and did extremely well. Souvanna took a triple engineering degree in marine, electrical, and construction engineering. Souphanouvong took a civil-engineering degree at the well-known *École des Ponts et Chaussées* in Paris.

It was during his stay in France that Souphanouvong became interested in left-wing politics. The year was 1937. France was ruled by the Popular Front, and French universities seethed with sympathizers for the Spanish Republic in its fight against Franco and his Nazi and fascist supporters. According to Communist sources, Souphanouvong took the unusual course, for a man of his background, of working during college vacations. As a dock laborer in Le Havre and Bordeaux, he came to know the French working class and its problems and "was caught up in the spirit of the great days of the Popular Front."[4]

Upon his return to the Far East in 1939, Souphanouvong was appointed to the Public Works Department of the French colonial government (Souvanna Phouma went into the civil administration of Indochina), married a Vietnamese girl from Hanoi who is said to have been a committed Communist even then, and began to build roads and bridges throughout North Vietnam and Laos. That job not only put him in everyday touch with a great number of local inhabitants—Lao uplanders, lowland Laotians, and Vietnamese—but also gave him intimate knowledge of the topography and local resources of his own country. It was to stand him in good stead later, during his guerrilla days. To this day, a certain type of bridge with round culverts is known in Laos as "*pont* Souphanouvong."[5]

When Japan occupied Indochina in 1941, Souphanouvong, as well as other Laotians, Cambodians, and Vietnamese throughout the peninsula saw the moment ripe for shaking off French colonial rule. Whether myth

or not, another Communist source asserts that Souphanouvong met Vietnamese Communist leader Ho Chi Minh in south China and asked him
for advice as to what to do next. Ho's answer allegedly was: "Seize
power from the colonialists."[6] Souphanouvong supposedly heeded the
advice and returned to Vientiane, where he began to organize young
members of the *bourgeoisie* into an anti-French resistance group. He
failed, however, to make extensive contacts with upland chieftains, and
this proved to be a serious error.

On March 9, 1945, the Japanese overthrew whatever remained of
the French colonial administration in Indochina and invited the rulers
of Cambodia, Laos, and Vietnam to proclaim their countries' independence under Japanese aegis. King Sihanouk and Emperor Bao-Dai took
advantage of the offer. King Sisavang Vong of Laos refused at first,
arguing that "independence under duress" would be just as politically
meaningless as independence under colonialism itself. But the King
relented when the Japanese arrested his heir (now King) Savang Vatthana
and held him prisoner in Saigon, and Laos was formally proclaimed to
be independent on April 8, 1945.

Prince Phetsarat, who, as Viceroy, had assumed the function of
prime minister, set up a provisional Laotian government in Vientiane
and created, on August 18, 1945 (three days after Japan's surrender), a
Lao Issara (i.e., Free Laos) committee which became the nucleus of a
Laotian political party. Both of his well-known brothers and other
members of the Vientiane upper classes joined the new group. However,
the arrival of French paratroop teams,[7] dropped into Laos along with
British teams from Force 136, brought a clash between the King and
Phetsarat: The King felt that he had been right in not accepting independence from the now-defeated Japanese and he dismissed the Viceroy
from his post on October 10, 1945.

That dismissal brought about a miniature revolution in Vientiane.
A People's Committee formed in that city proclaimed a new revolutionary government under Khammao, an old civil servant, on October
12, and dismissed King Sisavang Vong from the Laotian throne on October 20. Souvanna Phouma took the post of Minister of Public Works—
a rather unimportant post for someone of his background—while his
younger brother Souphanouvong cumulated the key posts of Minister
of Defense and of Foreign Affairs and was appointed Commander of the
Laotian Army.[8] Katay Sasorith, a Laotian southerner of humble (and
partly hill-tribe) origin, whose father owned a *bistro* in Paksé, became
Minister of Finance. Nhouy Abhay, Laos' only Bachelor of Letters, became Minister of Education. This situation already contained the makings
of a typical Laotian crisis: the King isolated in Luang-Prabang; a government in Vientiane representing little else but itself and made up of the

traditional elite; and the bulk of the country at the mercy of whoever
wanted to seize it.

The seizing was done by the French. Backing up the returning French
was Prince Boun Oum of Champassak, who had withstood the Japanese
invasion with a mixed Lao-French guerrilla force and who now began
to march slowly north with the help of French paratroops. The political
tide had turned against the Free Laotians in Vientiane, because Ho
Chi Minh's Democratic Republic of Vietnam had, on March 6, 1946,
arrived at a modus vivendi with France which provided for the return
of French troops to North Vietnam. Souphanouvong's hastily marshaled
troops were no match for the French in a pitched battle. On March 21,
1946, at Thakhek, the *Lao Issara* forces were decisively defeated. Souphanouvong himself tried to flee in a pirogue across the Mekong into Thai
territory, but was caught in mid-river by a French Spitfire fighter and
strafed. He was badly wounded and most of his companions were killed,
but the pirogue reached Thailand and Souphanouvong was nursed back
to health in Bangkok. The *Lao Issara* movement had lost the first contest
with France. The Vientiane regime, with Khammao, Phetsarat, Souvanna
Phouma, and Katay, fled to Thailand and, on April 23, 1946, King Sisavang
was crowned King of Laos once more. On the 24th, French forces entered
Vientiane. On May 13, 1946, a French paratroop force under Colonel
Imfeld, which had been dropped earlier on Luang-Prabang, linked up
with French troops from Vientiane and the French reconquest of lowland Laos was complete.

FROM LAO ISSARA TO PATHET LAO

The *Lao Issara* refugees in Bangkok continued to style themselves
the Laotian government-in-exile, but as the French yielded at least some
of the appearances of power to a Laotian government at home, certain
Lao Issara members began to support a compromise solution that would
permit them to return home. Khammao resigned from his premiership-in-
exile in favor of Phetsarat, who now called himself "Regent." But he
and his brothers began to drift apart. Phetsarat adopted a sterile wait-
and-see policy which was to lead to ten years wasted in exile before he
returned home in 1957, to become Viceroy again but only to die a few
months later. Souvanna Phouma returned to Vientiane when the *Lao
Issara* government-in-exile officially declared itself dissolved on October
25, 1949, after Laos formally gained its independence from France. But
Souphanouvong had already chosen a more dangerous course.

He had been in Hanoi late in 1946 and had seen Ho Chi Minh's
preparations for resistance against the French. After the outbreak of the
Indochina War on December 19, 1946, he had watched with great

interest how the lowland Vietnamese of Ho successfully withdrew into the mountain tribal areas to keep up the fight that was to lead them eight years later to full victory over the French. Souphanouvong now began to make contacts with the anti-French tribal leaders in southern Laos. His unbending will to resist the French militarily, as well as his extreme political views, led to his expulsion from the *Lao Issara* on May 16, 1949. But Souphanouvong was no longer interested in the fate of the dying movement. He was on his way through the jungles of Laos and Vietnam, to join Ho Chi Minh's mountain redoubt at Tuyên-Quang, north of the Red River delta. The split between the nationalist and pro-Communist factions of Laos began at this point. It was still wide open almost 20 years later.

At Tuyên-Quang, Souphanouvong convened a congress of hard-core Laotian rebel leaders on August 13, 1950. Among those present were: Sithone Kommadam, representing the southern *Kha* tribes; Phai-Dang (Faydang) of the *Meo*; and Nouhak Phoumsavan. The congress, with the obvious encouragement of the Democratic Republic of Vietnam (DRV), proceeded to elect a new resistance government of what it called the State of Laos, or Pathet Lao. Souphanouvong was, of course, the Prime Minister of the new regime. Rejecting the traditional royal Laotian flag with its tricephalous elephant, the new Pathet Lao regime displayed a flag very similar to North Korea's except for a missing red star: a red field bordered by two dark-blue horizontal stripes with a white disk at its center.

A subsequent meeting held in North Vietnam in November, 1950, provided the Pathet Lao with a new political movement, the *Neo Lao Issara* (i.e., Free Laos Front) and a new political program whose tenor was bound to appeal to every Laotian: equality of all races in Laos; united struggle against the French; and abolition of unjust taxes.

While the Pathet Lao could still claim national autonomy to some extent, its subordination to the DRV and the total coordination of its operations with those of the Vietnamese Communist movement soon became apparent. Between March 3 and 11, 1951, when the DRV set up its own, specifically Vietnamese, Communist Party (and no doubt at the same spot in the jungle), a meeting took plate among Vietnamese, Laotian, and *Khmer* (i.e., Cambodian) Communist leaders. Among those present were Ton Duc Thang (since 1960, Vice-president of the DRV); Souphanouvong; and Sieu Heng (head of the *Khmer* Liberation Committee). Burchett gives us a clear picture of the important results of that conference:

It was decided to set up a Viet Nam-Khmer-Lao Alliance which called on the people of the three countries to coordinate their fight to defeat the colonialists. It was on the basis of these decisions . . . that Vietnamese volunteers later

entered Cambodia and Laos to fight side by side with the Khmer Issarak forces
. . . and the Pathet-Lao.[9]

The March 11, 1951, agreement must be regarded as a key step in
the subsequent relations between Laos and North Vietnam, for it provides a semblance of a legal rationale for the commitment of North
Vietnamese volunteers to fight on the side of the Pathet Lao, just as
Chinese "people's volunteers" had fought alongside the North Koreans
in Korea. Burchett does not underestimate the importance of this North
Vietnamese support when he writes[10] that the "Pathet-Lao received a
powerful stimulus when Vietnamese volunteers swept into Laos early
in 1953."

Indeed, it was the Laotian invasion of 1953 and 1954 by North
Vietnamese forces supported by elements of the Pathet Lao which provided the essential local contacts and intelligence, which finally broke
the back of the French in Indochina. After all, lest it be forgotten, the
battle of Dien Bien Phu was fought in order to save Laos from Vietnamese invasion. In March 1953, the first Laotian provincial capital,
Sam Neua, had fallen into Vietminh hands and had been handed over
to Souphanouvong as a seat for his government. By July 20, 1954, when
the first Geneva cease-fire agreement was signed, the Vietnamese Communists and the Pathet Lao controlled roughly the same area as they
controlled ten years later: the bulk of the Laotian uplands (i.e., two-
thirds of all of Laos) with the exception of the *Plaine des Jarres*, then
solidly French-held.

Nevertheless, the Pathet Lao had suffered a serious defeat at the
Geneva conference. Neither Russia nor Communist China had succeeded
in getting the Laotian or Cambodian rebel regimes accepted as conference participants—a privilege granted the DRV without the slightest
question. As Phoui Sananikone, the Royal Laotian delegate, told the
conference:

We have said, and we repeat, that the military operations in Laos are the
work of Viet-Minh troops, that is to say troops foreign to the country by race,
tradition and ideology. We maintain that the so-called "free government,"
which by a gross misuse of language they [the North Vietnamese] misterm the
"Laos Resistance Government," has been fabricated lock, stock and barrel by
the foreign invaders.

The conference adopted that view, and the Pathet Lao was not
heard from directly at Geneva in 1954. However, unlike Cambodia,
which had won its military battle against the *Khmer Isaara* and thus did
not have to yield a regroupment area to them, Laos had to pay in part
the price of military defeat: Two northeastern provinces, Phong Saly and
Houa Phan (Sam Neua) and a connecting corridor between them were
assigned as a regroupment area to the Pathet Lao forces, their capital

to be in the town of Sam Neua (in Houa Phan).[11] But it was not a full-fledged victory for Souphanouvong, either. As Burchett remarks:

Thus, in return for a promise of nation-wide elections in which the Pathet-Lao would take part like any other political party, the Pathet-Lao forces agreed to withdraw from their old resistance bases in the centre and the south and concentrate in the two northern provinces . . . This was a hard decision to make; it was especially bitter to pull out of the Komadome [Kommadam] country in the provinces of Attopeu and Saravane and the Bolovens Plateau. But it was accepted.[12]

According to the Final Declaration of the 1954 Geneva Conference, a nationwide election would be held in Laos during 1955, and the political reintegration of the Pathet Lao into the Laotian nation would be achieved on that basis. In the meantime, however, the Pathet Lao movement had acquired a permanent home base in two provinces; a recognized *de facto* military force, the Pathet Lao Fighting Units (henceforth better known by their French initials UCPL, for *Unités Combattantes Pathet-Lao*); and the legal means for nationwide political agitation.

It was the latter gain that was to prove fatal in the long run to the non-Communist Laotian central government.

THE PATHET LAO POWER STRUCTURE

Like almost all Communist movements in underdeveloped countries, the Pathet Lao consists of an extremely small Communist hard-core group and a vast united front movement covering all strata and all age groups of the population. The core party in Laos is the *Phak Khon Ngan Lao* (i.e., Laotian Labor Party or PKNL) which, according to the extremely sketchy information available,[13] was created late in 1952, in North Vietnam, as a Laotian adjunct to the *Lao Dong*.

By 1953, it was thought to have only 17 members; Prince Souphanouvong was not its head, but merely one of its Central Committee members; Nouhak Phousavan was thought to have been its real leader as late as 1959. The PKNL has continued to be an elite cadre unit. Seven years after its creation, its total known membership was 62, including 8 women. Its main job is "political preparation." It carries out no guerrilla activities or overt sabotage of any kind, but it probably acts as a political coordinator with the North Vietnamese and Thai Communist organizations. Some of its members have at times been reported by the Thai police as having been seen in northeastern Thailand, particularly among the Vietnamese refugees who have lived at Mukdahan for the past 20 years. Its main job inside Laos is to direct the activities of the broad support organizations grouped inside the Laotian Patriotic Front (i.e., *Neo Lao Hak Xat*, or NLHX), which was created on January 6, 1956.

It is probably the background existence of the PKNL which permitted the NLHX to continuously emphasize the nationalist character of its program, as Souphanouvong himself was to explain to an East German journalist in 1959:

We are no Communist Party, as is being asserted quite often, but members of the national liberation movement which is called Pathet-Lao abroad. Our movement called itself Neo Lao Issara, Laotian Freedom Movement. The program of that movement was national independence and peace—and that, too, is the program of the Neo Lao Hak Xat.[14]

With a solid political and military base, the Pathet Lao has rarely lost its momentum in Laos since 1955. Already, on the eve of the Bandung Conference on April 13, 1955, the Royal Laotian Government, headed then as later by Prince Souvanna Phouma, issued a long and detailed report describing the activities in violation of the 1954 agreements of the Pathet Lao and of Vietnamese people's volunteers who apparently had not departed from Laos.[15] Contrary to expectation, the administration of the two northeastern provinces had remained totally in Pathet Lao hands. Military and civilian schools in Sam Neua had begun to turn out trained cadres for further operations. In short, the Pathet Lao (PL) behaved, in the apt image of a Rand Corporation report, as if its position were, "though on a much reduced scale, similar to that of the Chinese Communists in 1945 . . ."[16] That is, it was preparing itself in a remote military and political base for the showdown that was to come when all conditions for it were ripe. As a Laotian government report said at the time: "In their immense majority the NLHX cadres stand up under the stress, lower their heads under the storm, but refuse to yield." That was particularly important in those provinces which officially had been returned to Royal Laotian Government (RLG) control, but where the infiltrated PL cadres remained at their posts.

Within the regroupment areas (where they operated openly as the civil and political administration) and in the provinces under theoretical RLG control (control that was to become more and more theoretical as time went on), the Pathet Lao set up full-fledged paragovernmental structures (Chart 1). These were largely patterned on what the North Vietnamese regime had done between 1945 and 1954 and were eventually operated with a similar degree of fairly high efficiency.

The structure is based on the rule-by-committee system from the top to bottom of the scale, with a special watchdog apparatus controlling the whole structure for the benefit of the central leadership. The committee system shown in Chart 1 repeats itself at all echelons, with the committee members of the higher echelons being at the same time the leaders of the lower echelons. For example, most of the *Kommakan* (i.e., Committee Members) of the provincial echelon will be in fact the

Chart 1

PATHET LAO ADMINISTRATIVE STRUCTURE

Central: Neo Soun Khang   (Chairman, Central Committee)

Provincial: Nanhok Neo Khoueng (Chairman)
                      Neo Khoueng ⤛   Long Nanhok (Deputy)
                                            Kommakan (Committee Members,
                                            1 Secretary)

District: Neo Muong ——— (Same organization)

Township:
                      Neo Tambol, ⤛   Houa Na Neo (Chairman)
                      or Tasseng   Pho Kong Tin (Administrator)
                                            Tha Han Ban (Self-defense chief)

Village: Neo Ban ——— (Same organization)
Affiliated Groups: Samakhom

┌──────────────────────┬──────────────────────┬──────────────────────┐
    Sao Hay   Sati   Say Noum, etc.
    (Farmers)   (Women)   (Youth)
├──────────────────────┴──────────────────────┴──────────────────────┤
                              Nouey
                              (Cells)
└───┘

Nanhok Neo Muong (Presidents of subordinate district front committees), and so forth. The key echelon is that of the township (i.e.,
tambol, or *tasseng*); the best-trained Communist cadres are said to operate there. Very often, the NLHX village administrative official (i.e., *Pho
Kong Tin*) is at the same time the official village head for the Royal
Laotian Government. In other words, the local administration in Laos is
often completely entwined with the Communist underground organization. Thus has developed a system of "parallel administration" which
is harder to bring under control than the more usual situation where the
legal administration is under open attack.

The whole Pathet Lao administrative system is under the constant
control of ubiquitous and completely secret *Kene sane* (i.e., he who sees),
roving inspectors directly appointed by Nouhak, who constantly report
on how the regular Communist administrative echelon performs. Each
kene sane can, in turn, appoint several deputies who do not know each
other and, thus, unknowingly also report on the activities and performance of their own colleagues.

Strength of the Pathet Lao

Estimates of the over-all numerical strength of the movement are
widely divergent. The 1959 consensus, based on extensive surveys and
interviews throughout Laos, was that there were at least 1,500 full-time
armed Pathet Lao guerrillas. By 1964, there were estimated to be about
20,000 Pathet Lao troops in the country, backed up by perhaps 5,000

North Vietnamese regulars. At least 10,000 Laotians and mountaineers left Phong Saly and Houa Phan provinces for North Vietnam when they were temporarily integrated with the rest of Laos in November, 1957. Table 1 shows the estimated strength of the permanent cadres of the NLHX administrative structure in 1960. The figures are very unlikely to have been revised downward by 1965.

Table 1

NUMERICAL ARRANGEMENT OF PATHET LAO ADMINISTRATION

Lan-Xang (provinces of Luang-Prabang, Nam-Tha, and Sayaboury)	500
Vientiane (city and province)	700
Tran-Ninh (Xieng-Khouang and eastern Vientiane)	400
Central Laos (Khommouane and Savannakhet)	1,000
Southern Laos (Bassac and Attopeu)	400
	3,000

In addition, small groups of specialists are being trained abroad. Soviet and Communist Chinese sources mention Laotian students in Moscow and Peking, some of whom are *Meo* (also, *Miao*) mountaineers. Their total number seems never to exceed 100, and another 100 study in North Vietnam. Recent reports speak of military specialists (a large proportion of them tribesmen from central and southern Laos) who are being trained in North Vietnamese military schools, in addition to those being trained in PL schools at Sam Neua and Khang Kay in Laos. While those figures may not seem impressive at first glance, they are sufficient —within the Laotian context of scarce and poorly trained leadership material—to tilt the balance of strength dangerously to the PL side.

By 1965, the *administrative* hold taken by the PL power structure over large areas of Laos was, in fact, more dangerous to the survival of a non-Communist Laos than the military situation, although Western observers usually blithely disregard it. As of 1965, there existed at least 11 full fledged PL provincial administrations (out of a total of 16 Laotian provinces), and these successfully overshadowed the legal but ineffective RLG administration. There even exists an openly known PL Governor of the province of Vientiane: Say Pethrasy. Significantly, all those PL-held provinces abut directly on North Vietnam, and actual PL control limits itself to the mountainous areas for the time being. However, it is sufficiently flexible to expand or retract, according to the fortunes of the political and military situation, without losing its structural integrity.

In those provinces which PL forces do not entirely control, they nevertheless maintain base areas (i.e., *Phun Than*) composed of village groups that are solidly under the control of the NLHX or the PL forces.

This does *not* mean that they no longer are accessible to Royal Army forces or even to periodic inspections by government civil servants. On the contrary: Such personnel is received politely, but with sufficient reserve to show that such visits from outsiders are unwelcome. Gifts are refused, and offers of help are turned down with the explanation, "No aid is needed. We're helping each other and can get along very well without your aid."

In a base area, Communist indoctrination is continuous. The schools are Communist-run. There generally exists a dispensary and at least one good radio receiver capable of listening to the Lao-language programs of Radio Hanoi and Radio Peking. Some bases have their own short-wave transmitters. Propaganda periodicals and newspapers are edited, printed, and distributed. For a time, the *Lao Hak Xat*, with a print run varying between 25,000 to 40,000 copies, was by far the largest Lao-language publication in the country.

A friendly Asian military observer who had an opportunity to tour parts of backcountry Laos in the spring of 1960 reported, upon his return, that "the Pathet Lao in hundreds of villages has almost reached the stage of political organization that enabled the Vietminh to defeat the French in Vietnam."

That, unfortunately, turned out to be no exaggeration.

THE OPEN CONTEST

It is not within the scope of this study to recount in detail the incredible sequence of erroneous estimates, overoptimism and maladministration which eventually led Laos to its parlous state in 1965. These factors alone would probably have sufficed to destroy all chances of the survival of a non-Communist Laotian state. The rising efficiency of the Pathet Lao and of its Communist-bloc mentors added to the peril.

After two years of arduous negotiations, the two enemy brothers, Souvanna Phouma and Souphanouvong, finally reached a mutually acceptable agreement on November 2, 1957. It provided for the reintegration into the Laotian national fabric of the two PL-controlled provinces; the absorption into the RLG administration of PL civil servants; and the integration into the Royal Laotian Army of 1,500 UCPL officers and men. In exchange, the PL accepted RLG administrators in the northeastern provinces; the surrender of its excess military equipment; and the total departure of North Vietnamese "volunteers" and "experts." In addition, free elections were to be held in several provinces of Laos, to add 21 legislators to the 38-man National Assembly. Two Cabinet posts went to the PL: Souphanouvong himself became Minister of Planning (for which, as an engineer, he was well suited) and one of his chief aides, Phoumi

Vongvichit, became Minister of Religious Affairs (as which, as a pro-Communist, he was expected to be able to do little harm).

Prior to the elections, which were set for May 1958, the Pathet Lao even agreed to surrender its weapons. In a special ceremony held on February 18, 1958, at the *Plaine des Jarres*, 1,501 UCPL soldiers were officially accepted as Royal Army personnel, while another 4,284 UCPL soldiers and 1,479 dependents and civilian personnel were officially discharged. The UCPL also surrendered 4,773 weapons, including 23 machine guns, 10 automatic rifles, and 65 mortars. Since the total number of UCPL forces at that time was officially estimated at 6,199, the number of weapons surrendered, while obviously not amounting to total disarmament, was impressive.

The May 1958 elections that followed were a farce. As one high RLG official admitted later (and without arousing the slightest ripple of indignation anywhere), corruption, as well as internal division, was rampant on the anti-Communist side:

Candidates who had been rejected for the sake of unity demanded to be reimbursed for their campaign expenses, which in some cases reached astronomical proportions: two or three hundred thousand *kip* [then about $10,000], and even more. In contrast to the pettiness and rather sordid quarrels occupying the government factions, the two opposition parties[17] had formed an alliance and were presenting a solid disciplined front.[18]

The NLHX and its neutralist ally *Santiphab* not only presented a united front; they also presented a wide range of candidates, including two princes, one woman, and one *Kha* mountaineer. And thus out of the 21 seats at stake, they gained 9 for the NLHX and another 4 for the *Santiphab*. That was proportionally less Communist or fellow-traveling representation than, for example, existed in the French or Italian Parliaments at that time. The situation appeared alarming to Washington, however, and the immediate American reaction was to throw support to Laotian civilians and military men of extreme right-wing persuasion in the hope of creating a strong government that would be able to cope with the Pathet Lao menace. That proved to be not only a miscalculation, but a fatal error.

It is, of course, fruitless second-guessing to try to assess whether Souphanouvong, if given a chance in 1958, would have preferred to obtain a strong PL position with a unified non-Communist Laotian regime and thus shake off his North Vietnamese mentors—to have taken a Tito-like position, as has sometimes been suggested—or whether, under any circumstances, he was determined to make a bid for undivided power under PL control. The fact remains that the coup-like reactions of the Vientiane government to the PL victory and its radical departure from

Souvanna Phouma's neutralism (he was compelled to resign on July 22, 1958) played its part in the open clash between the RLG and the NLHX that was to follow. This writer fully shares the view of the authors of the previously cited Rand Corporation report, who appraise the outbreak of the 1959 fighting in Laos as follows:

In retrospect it is apparent that the [right-wing] Sananikone government precipitated the final crisis that led to war in Laos; it also is apparent that while the Sananikone government knew, at the time, that it was running a serious risk of open conflict with the NLHX and its mentors in Hanoi, the pattern of Communist behavior up through mid-May [1959] had not been sufficiently belligerent to deter it.[19]

In sum, the Laotian right wing totally underestimated the Pathet Lao's intrinsic strength and its capacity for sustained resistance. Worse, Vientiane also underestimated the ability of the Pathet Lao to secure outside aid, while it overestimated its own ability to make effective use of the large-scale foreign support it had been guaranteed in advance.

After unilaterally denouncing the Geneva agreements of 1954 in February 1959 (an often-forgotten fact is that it was the later neutralist Souvanna Phouma who had succeeded in getting the International Control Commission [ICC] to cease its activities in Laos on July 18, 1958), the Sananikone government attempted to deal militarily with the problem of integrating PL Battalions Nos. 1 and 2—the first stationed at Xieng-Ngeun near Luang-Prabang, the second at the *Plaine*. Integration had been stymied because of the dilatory tactics of the PL, which chose to interpret the November 1957 agreements to mean that integral PL units, with their own officers, would be maintained within the Royal Army; the RLG, for obvious reasons, wished to disperse PL adherents throughout other units. Also the PL demanded a higher ratio of officers than is usually required for a two-battalion force.

On May 11, 1959, Battalion No. 2, surrounded at the *Plaine* by five government battalions, slipped through the encirclement with its women and children and reached North Vietnam unscathed. Battalion No. 1 made a pretense at submission and melted into the jungle on August 8. Prince Souphanouvong and all the other senior PL leaders, however, were arrested and jailed in Vientiane during May and July, which further confirms the view that the Pathet Lao, at least in the spring of 1959, was not bent on provoking a military showdown with the Vientiane government. As Sisouk na Champassak, who certainly is no friend of the PL, said later:

Although the Neo Lao Hak Xat leaders in Vientiane launched the rebellion, they soon were powerless to stop it . . . Not only were they from the beginning under surveillance and completely cut off from their troops, but with the start of guerrilla warfare, the military leaders naturally held the reins. After May 15, it was no longer Souphanouvong who led the rebellion, but men like Kayson and Cham Nien and their lieutenants.[20]

The events of May 1959, were to have a deep influence on all subsequent events in Laos. When the Pathet Lao was deprived of its regular political leaders, who were accustomed to the rules of the political game in Vientiane,[21] the initiative fell to the PL military leaders, such as Colonel Singkapo, and Kaysone, and to their troops, largely composed of tribal mountaineers who had old scores to settle with the Laotian lowlanders. These events made the PL leadership extremely suspicious of working and negotiating in Vientiane. They felt they had been betrayed in Vientiane[22] in 1959, and hence they were not willing to make the same mistake in 1963 or 1964. This explains PL insistence, in 1963, on transferring the seat of government to Luang-Prabang (farther away from pro-Western Thailand, which is just across the river from Vientiane; and closer to the PL-held jungles), and repeated PL proposals for negotiating in neutralized areas to which all three sides would bring only a fixed number of armed men. In view of the military coup of right-wing generals Abhay and Siho on April 19, 1964, the senior PL leaders must have again congratulated themselves for not having accepted an earlier invitation of neutralist Premier Souvanna Phouma to return to Vientiane for further negotiations.

The notorious failure of the Laotian Royal Army, then 25,000 men equipped with tanks, artillery, and airplanes, to annihilate 1,501 ill-armed UCPL members burdened with women and children, destroyed Vientiane's last chance of achieving victory on its own terms. The reaction of the Communist bloc (then still acting as a united force) was as swift as it was effective: North Vietnamese aid again began to flow to the Pathet Lao. Within less than three months (as this writer saw for himself, since he was in Sam Neua during this period) the two UCPL battalions had wreaked havoc throughout northern Laos. They were able to rout far larger Laotian units, which had finally begun to believe their own government's propaganda about a North Vietnamese invasion and who now fled in front of the smallest UCPL unit when the cry, "Vietminh," was raised. By August 1959, the Sananikone government was driven to the wall and forced to ask for a United Nations investigation of the North Vietnamese invasion.

The United Nations investigation mission concluded, on November 5, 1959, that "The ensemble of information submitted to the Sub-Committee did not clearly establish whether there were crossings of the frontier by regular troops of the D.R.V.N."[23]

Subsequently, a combination of external factors led to a period of quiescence lasting almost a year. The United States contributed a show of strength by sending elements of the Seventh Fleet to Bangkok. The United Nations continued to make its presence felt, leaving a Security Council representative in Laos after its subcommittee departed. It may also be that the Pathet Lao did not desire to risk everything it had gained at Geneva in 1954 and in the Vientiane agreements of 1957.

But inside Laos itself, the carefree days of the past were fading with the old leaders. Viceroy Prince Phetsarat, the oldest of Laos' three princely stormy petrels, died on October 14, 1959, followed by King Sisavang Vong on October 29. Sisavang had reigned for 55 years. And Katay Don Sasorith, probably the most resourceful and energetic of Laos' pro-Western politicians, died on December 29. New, less experienced and more radical leaders began to take the helm.[24]

THE NEUTRALIST EXPERIMENT

A new phase of the Laotian crisis began when all of the Pathet Lao leaders detained in Vientiane's maximum security prison escaped on May 22, 1960, taking with them the warders whom they had converted to the Pathet Lao cause.

This proved extremely important to the *Neo Lao Hak Xat* command. For Souphanouvong, even *if* he is no longer the real center of power, as certain sources have repeatedly asserted,[25] is nevertheless a national figure in both the traditional and the revolutionary senses. During the year of his absence, the NLHX had, on the whole, held its own but neither Nouhak, with his hard-core PKNL, nor Phoumi Vongvichit nor Kaysone, had been able to do much more than hang on defensively to back-country strongholds. Contrary to expectations, the escaped Souphanouvong initially held back his men. For three months after his disappearance into the jungle, no one heard of him or, for that matter, of the Pathet Lao. Radio Hanoi, which had been extremely vocal on his behalf, remained silent. So did Peking.[26]

That silence was shattered by the neutralist coup of Captain Kong Lê's 2nd Paratroop Battalion, which overthrew Lao's right-wing regime in favor of a return to a neutralist policy, on August 9, 1960. Prince Souvanna Phouma, in semi-exile in France as ambassador of Laos, returned to the premiership.

The Kong-Lê coup was immediately hailed by the Central Committee of the NLHX in a communiqué:

This uprising becomes part of the patriotic movement of the Lao people standing up to American imperialism, and proves that the tenacious struggle of the Neo Lao Hak Xat for national salvation already has produced a powerful awakening of the national conscience among all layers of the population, up to and including the officers and men of the Royal Army.[27]

The program presented by Souvanna Phouma to the Laotian Parliament on August 31, 1960, bore a marked resemblance to the NLHX platform. Its internal aims were a "policy of national union and an end to
fratricidal wars among Laotians," and its external political aims were:

1. Pursuing a policy of neutrality in accord with the aspirations of the Lao
people.
2. Respecting all international engagements, the [1954] Geneva Agreements
included.
3. Accepting aid from any nation, providing it is not burdened with political
and military conditions.
4. Establishing friendly relations with all neighboring countries, tightening al-
ready-existing relations, and seeking to establish relations with [other] peace-
loving countries.

Souvanna Phouma and Kong-Lê were apparently attempting to return to the *status quo* established in the November 2, 1957, accords. But
they failed to take into account the fact that the Laotian right wing,
which in 1957 had had almost no external assistance, now had powerful
outside supporters determined to keep in power in Vientiane a regime
which was—in the words of an official commentator in Washington—
"willing and able to resist Communist aggression and subversion."
The resulting policy took the form of a countercoup based on right-
wing forces, grouped around Prince Boun Oum of Champassak and General Phoumi Nosavan, in southern Laos, beyond the scope of this study
to describe. The Pathet Lao, sensing that a military second round was
about to be unleashed, in turn sought to draw the neutralist Vientiane
regime to its side. In this, it was aided by the fact that the Soviet Union
had openly come out in favor of Souvanna Phouma and had entered the
Laotian scene in October 1960, by appointing an Ambassador to Vientiane for the first time. On October 27, Soviet economic aid to the
Kong-Lê forces and Vientiane began by an airlift of supplies from Hanoi.
Communist-bloc involvement in the Laotian situation, covert for 15 years,
had finally come out in the open.
In a very small way, the Laotian crisis now began to resemble, not
the Chinese model of 1945 (as the Rand report we have cited averred),
but rather the Spanish Civil War. Outside powers on both sides began to
use various Laotian factions as proxies for their own confrontation on
Laotian soil. Faced with a direct military threat as the right-wing forces
slowly fought their way northward along the Mekong, Souvanna Phouma
met his half-brother face to face at the latter's headquarters at Sam Neua
on November 18, 1960, and endorsed an accord between neutralists
and the NLHX which provided for a "government of national union"
including the NLHX, approved the establishment of diplomatic relations

with the U.S.S.R., and expressed "satisfaction at the government's promise to accept aid from People's China and the Democratic Republic of Vietnam . . ."[28]

As in the latter days of the Spanish Civil War, polarization was taking place on both sides, with the hard-core left wing taking control of its side and, in the absence of any other effective foreign aid, becoming the major funnel for Soviet support. On December 9, 1960, as right-wing forces were approaching Vientiane, Colonel (later General) Kou Abhay, the regional military Commander, defected from Souvanna Phouma to the right wing. A few days later, Souvanna Phouma fled into exile to Cambodia, and Kong-Lê and his veteran paratroops slowly withdrew northward. Thanks to the unbelievably inept Laotian right-wing military leadership, he was able to occupy the key *Plaine des Jarres* airstrips (there are three of them) on New Year's Day, 1961, and thus provide the Communist bloc with an excellent logistic and military base in the heart of Laos. Soon a round-the-clock airlift from Hanoi was to provide Kong-Lê with the necessary equipment to match the right-wing military buildup. Moreover, the reopening of the vital Route 7 (closed since 1945) between North Vietnam and the *Plaine* brought Kong-Lê and his new-found Pathet Lao allies medium Soviet armor and field artillery.

Politically also, the NLHX soon proved that it had not lost its pace. A Committee for Peace, Neutrality, Concord, and National Union was set up in Vientiane in November 1960, under the joint presidency of Souvanna Phouma and Souphanouvong, and similar local committees were established throughout the country wherever possible, thus further broadening the relatively narrow front structure of the NLHX. How effective those organizations could become in a relatively short time was shown by the Committee for Peace-Loving Youth of Vientiane. When it appeared that Souvanna Phouma was being pressured by the then President of the Laotian National Assembly, Somsanith, to negotiate with the right-wing leaders at Savannakhet, the Peace-Loving Youth, rapidly marshaled on December 2, 1960, invaded the Parliament building and compelled the legislature to cancel the session where such feelers toward the right were being debated. Souvanna Phouma, unable to withstand the pressure, yielded to the mob and all peace feelers were withdrawn. On December 12, 1960, the Pathet Lao proclaimed a general mobilization of its forces (which brought back to it all those UCPL members who had been discharged in 1958, and more). With new Soviet equipment and North Vietnamese "instructors" now freely flowing to the *Plaine*, new Pathet Lao and neutralist battalions began to appear throughout Laos.

The Kong-Lê forces, ironically, now styled themselves the "Roya legal forces," while the UCPL units retained their own separate command structure, although both forces cooperated under the unified command of Kong-Lê (later promoted directly to Major General) and Colonel Singkapo Chunamali Sikhot, a member of the Central Committee of the NLHX, as are most UCPL senior commanders.[29] Kong-Lê's title, President of the Supreme Military Council (of all the anti-Vientiane forces) had little practical effect except to further enhance the role of the NLHX and UCPL as a legal force fighting to reestablish a legal government in Laos.

By the spring of 1961, the right-wing forces had not only been almost completely defeated militarily, but they had also lost effective administrative control of nearly all of upland Laos with the exception of a few Meo strongholds faithful to such Meo right-wing leaders as Toubi Ly-Foung and Colonel (later General) Vang Pao. But right-wing and American attempts at organizing the mountain tribes in favor of Vientiane after hundreds of years of oppression, came too late to be fully effective. The Pathet Lao, whose policy of securing tribal support had been firmly established by Souphanouvong in 1946, had too great a start. The first cease-fire line established on May 2, 1961, shows an incredibly close concordance with the traditional dividing line between lowland Laotians and tribal uplanders. The disappearance of neutralist strongholds in Phong Saly and on the *Plaine* in the course of the mid-1964 Pathet Lao offensive changed little in that situation.

OUTSIDE COMMUNIST INFLUENCES

It is difficult to say at what precise point in time the Pathet Lao lost control over its own operations to become a mere pawn of the policy objectives of other Communist powers interested in the area—*if* the Pathet Lao is indeed a pawn.

To direct *anything* in Laos by remote control is, as the West has found out, not an easy game. In sheer physical terms alone, it is easier for the West to supply Laotian right-wing forces from nearby Thai railways and airstrips than it is for the Communists to supply even the *Plaine des Jarres* across the whole North Vietnamese upland jungle with its washed-out roads (when they exist at all) and the monsoon climate which is notoriously inhospitable to airlifts. Thus, of sheer necessity, much must often be left to the local initiative—not only the initiative of Souphanouvong himself, but even the initiative of his own local commanders.[30] Many a group claiming to be Pathet Lao may, in reality, be little more than a Laotian version of a warlord band.

The increased severity, at least for the time being, of the Sino-

Soviet split has added to the complications of the Laotian situation. This has shown up clearly in the diverse Russian and Sino-DRV reactions to negotiations to restore the precarious neutralist regime established in the wake of the 1962 Geneva negotiations.[31] The fact that the West itself is about as badly split as the Sino-Soviet bloc (France holds a more conciliatory position than the United States and Britain) certainly does not make the situation less confused.

From 1959 to late 1960, the Soviet bloc unanimously asked for the mere reconvening and reactivation in Laos of the International Control Commission (ICC), no doubt inspired by fears that the well-armed right-wing forces would totally destroy the NLHX. As the military shoe switched to the other foot and destruction was more likely to befall the Vientiane regime, the still unified Communist position was to make the granting of cease-fire conditional upon the convening of a Geneva conference that would almost rule out any chance of reestablishing a right wing regime that could be militarily supported by the West. As Modelski was to observe, such a settlement also did "necessarily prevent the immediate and outright victory of the Pathet-Lao faction and the Souvanna Phouma group then allied with it. Each of the great powers thus settled for less than their maximum objective."[32]

The agreement which was signed at Geneva on July 23, 1962, after a new flare-up of fighting in Laos had resulted in further large-scale defeats of the right-wing forces at Nam-Tha and Ban Houei Sai,[33] followed fairly predictable lines: A troika-type neutralist government under Souvanna Phouma was installed in Vientiane with Cabinet members of all three factions; an eventual reunification of the three armed forces and administrations was to be negotiated; all foreign military advisers (except, for a time, French) were to be withdrawn; and the ICC was restored its inspection prerogatives.

If the purpose of the agreement was merely to defuse the explosive situation in the Mekong valley for a time, then it must be considered at least a partial success. General Phoumi's right-wing forces, numbering over 50,000, were saved from utter destruction and given time to reorganize. The Pathet Lao, solidly entrenched in the northeast, began to take hold solidly of the mountainous part of the Laotian panhandle abutting on South Vietnam. And Souvanna Phouma, as he had twice before, in 1954 and 1959, began the thankless task of putting the Laotian pieces together again.

That he failed in the attempt is due in large part to factors over which he had little, if any, control and for which (locally, at least) the right was as much to blame as the Pathet Lao. Externally, the Sino-Soviet rift had great influence over the Laotian situation. In fact, i could be said that thus far (and until the Vietnam situation degenerates into a Korean type of war engulfing both north and south) Laos is the *major victim* of the Sino-Soviet rift. All sides involved can point to a long list of violations of the 1962 Geneva agreements by their adversaries—from murders of leading neutralist figures in Vientiane (probably by right-wing elements) and on the *Plaine* (probably by UCPL elements) to actual military attacks from extremists on both sides. An agreement of November 27, 1962, to set up tripartite military and police forces of equal strength was blithely disregarded by both left and right, and so was an agreement which directed the right wing to turn over its total control of Vientiane to tripartite control. Without this agreement the Pathet Lao leaders, for reasons shown earlier, felt highly reluctant to work in the city.[34] A series of gangland-style killings, such as that of Souvanna's left-leaning neutralist Foreign Minister Quinim Pholsena on April 1, 1963, in Vientiane, further drove home the point.

At the same time, the deepening Sino-Soviet split began to affect Russian supply deliveries to the neutralists, until they allegedly stopped altogether in the spring of 1964. The Russian embassy in Vientiane as much as openly admitted that it was no longer in a position to actively influence Pathet Lao actions. And Hanoi, under Chinese pressure, denied the Russians access to the roads and airports into Laos, or in any case, saw to it that Russian supplies went to the Pathet Lao faction rather than to the Souvanna and Kong-Lê forces. In fact, under attack by rebellious pro-PL neutralist forces led by Colonel Deuane, Kong-Lê lost the central *Plaine* airfield of Xieng-Khouang on April 20, 1963, thus beginning an attrition process that was to see the Kong-Lê troops completely driven off the *Plaine* about one year later.

Those attacks by the Pathet Lao, as well as the lack of Soviet spare parts and ammunition for his Russian armored vehicles, eventually drove Kong-Lê back into a position of *de facto* integration with the right-wing coup in Vientiane on April 19, 1964; polarization on the two extremes was again taking place—and this time, the process was at least implicitly encouraged by the military actions taken by the PL.

What contributed to strengthening China's and Hanoi's new preeminence in the Laotian struggle was the progressive tying-in of the PL-held regions with neighboring areas of China and North Vietnam. Red China had begun a significant road-building program linking the important Yunnan garrison town of Sze-Mao with the northern Laotian provincial capital of Phong Saly.[35] That road was completed in May 1963. Together with Road 7 going into North Vietnam, it now gives Laos better land communications with its two Communist neighbors than with its anti-Communist neighbors to the south. Moreover, the conquest of the *Plaine* airfields of Xieng-Khouang, Phong-Savan, and Muong Phan (not to speak of smaller airstrips elsewhere) and of the key central Laotian field at Tchépone, provides the Pathet Lao with more than adequate outside communications. While it is not probable at this stage that Red China has an important stake in Laos, it is obvious that North Vietnam does: Laos abuts on 700 miles of highly vulnerable North Vietnamese border area and provides the best avenue of approach to South Vietnam. Both factors are vital in the present South Vietnamese insurgency.

Thus, North Vietnam has a stake of the most direct kind in keeping Laos divided, as long as the one faction friendly to it, the Pathet Lao, continues to be the strong military buffer which it has been since 1952. This will remain true as long as the Pathet Lao political leadership sees no chance to gain a controlling share in the nationwide political power emanating from Vientiane—and that will, in all likelihood, continue to be the case so long as there are anti-Communist regimes in Thailand and South Vietnam. To them, the loss of part of the Mekong valley to a Communist force would be an almost mortal blow. And it is likely that even neutral Cambodia would view such a presence at its borders with great discomfort. That the Pathet Lao could be considered as such a threat—not only as a puppet of its North Vietnamese allies, but in its own right—is perhaps best evidenced by the fact that, since the late 1950's, Thai police and intelligence keep picking up evidence of a Pathet Lao political subversive network among the Lao-speaking peoples of northeastern Thailand. How truly effective such Pathet Lao propaganda has been is unknown, but its persistence is in itself an ominous sign.[36]

Structurally, the Pathet Lao now seems well adapted to its limited offensive mission. Surely, the NLHX is not a mature Communist Party even within the Asian context, but it is far from being a rabble of illiterate tribesmen, as some of its adversaries like to claim. Its leadership is battle-tested; and if Prince Souphanouvong may not be the all-powerful leader[37] of his movement (with the exception of the Chinese and Albanian leaders, one may well ask *who* is such a leader in the Communist Parties of today), he is nevertheless recognized by his followers as the only Laotian Communist leader to have nationwide appeal. The reported creation in Hanoi of a joint operations staff for Laos and Vietnam with Chinese, North Vietnamese, and Pathet Lao "military and political officers,"[38] is, if true, another indication that the Pathet Lao is more than a mere adjunct of the Vietnamese Communist Party.

The Pathet Lao, like other Communist Parties in this era, may well develop purely national objectives of its own. For the time being, in any case, it has become an important and, perhaps, critical factor in the tangled destinies of the Indochinese peninsula.

NOTES

1. Western transliteration of Lao is at best approximate. Kham Seng is also referred to as Kham Xang or Xang Kham.

2. Southern Laos was directly administered by France until 1941. Only with the Franco-Laotian treaty of August 29, 1941 did France recognize the King of Luang-Prabang as King of all Laos.

3. In 1965, the Albert Sarraut *lycée*, still named after a French colonial Governor, was the last French educational institution operating in Communist North Vietnam.

4. Wilfred G. Burchett, *Mekong Upstream* (East Berlin: Seven Seas Publishers, 1959), p. 223. Burchett has been a reporter for the British Communist organ, *The Daily Worker*.

5. Another story about Souphanouvong's bridges is that many of them were built in advance of the roads between them, with the result that many of them bridge a river only to connect two pieces of equally unpassable jungle. Some people feel that this image fully applies to the political situation in Laos as well.

6. Anna Louise Strong, *Cash and Violence in Laos* (Peking: New World Press, 1961), p. 35.

7. For an account of French paratroop operations in Laos, see the largely unknown book by Major L. H. Ayrolles, *L'Indochine ne répond plus* (Saint-Brieuc: Armand Prud'homme, 1948).

8. Part of the information contained here comes from my book manuscript *Crisis in Laos* (Washington, D.C.: Public Affairs Press).

9. Burchett, *Mekong Upstream*, pp. 89–90.

10. *Ibid.*, p. 91.

11. Article 14 of the Agreement on the Cessation of Hostilities in Laos of July 20, 1954.

12. Burchett, *Mekong Upstream*, p. 243.

13. Based on field research in Laos in 1959 under a Southeast Asia Treaty Organization (SEATO) research fellowship. SEATO is, of course, in no way responsible for the facts and opinions presented here.

14. Georg Krausz, *Von Indian bis Laos* (East Berlin: Verlag Volk und Welt, 1960), p. 327.

15. B. Fall, *Le Viet-Minh* (Paris: Armand Colin, 1960), p. 131.

16. A. M. Halpern, and H. B. Fredman, *Communist Strategy in Laos* (Santa Monica, Calif.: The Rand Corporation, 1960), p. 4.

17. The *Neo Lao Hak Xat* and the *Santiphab* (i.e., Neutrality Party). The latter was a left-leaning group under Bong Souvannavong, which later supported Souvanna Phouma again.

18. Sisouk na Champassak, *Storm Over Laos* (New York: Frederick A. Praeger, Inc., 1961), p. 62. It is worthy of note that Sisouk, until 1962 representative of his country to the UN, is a member of the Laotian right-wing faction.

19. Halpern and Fredman, *Communist Strategy in Laos*, p. 51.

20. Sisouk, *Storm Over Laos*, p. 83.

21. See the excellent studies by Joel Halpern on the *Lao Elites* (Los Angeles, Calif.: University of California, 1960), mimeographed, and his *Government, Politics, and Social Structure in Laos* (New Haven, Conn.: Yale University Southeast Asia Studies, 1964).

22. For example, Thao Khé, one of the UCPL battalion commanders, had come down to Vientiane under a safe-conduct pass. He was arrested upon arrival.

23. United Nations, Security Council, *Report of the Security Council Subcommittee under Resolution of 7 September 1959*, No. S/4236 (New York, November 5 1959), p. 31.
24. Fall, *Crisis in Laos.*
25. For a sober analysis of that period, see Arthur J. Dommen, *Conflict in Laos: The Politics of Neutralization* (New York: Frederick A. Praeger, Inc., 1964).
26. Halpern and Fredman, *Communist Strategy in Laos*; and Chen Yi *et al.*, *Concerning the Situation in Laos* (Peking: Foreign Languages Press, 1959).
27. Quang Minh, *Au pays du million d'éléphants* (Hanoi: Editions en langues étrangères, 1961), p. 72.
28. *Ibid.*, p. 86.
29. For example, Thao Tou (Pa Tou), Commander of the 2d UCPL Battalion, is a Meo chieftain from northern Laos, and a member of the NLHX Central Committee. Sithone Kommadam, the Boloven chieftain from southern Laos, is Vice-president of the NLHX Central Committee.
30. For example, several British officials captured by Pathet Lao forces in central Laos found the local commanders reluctant to accept Souphanouvong's orders for their release.
31. See the excellent study by George Modelski, *International Conference on the Settlement of the Laotian Question 1961–62* (Canberra: The Australian National University, 1962).
32. Modelski, *Ibid.*, p. 2.
33. Fall, "Laos: Who Broke the Cease Fire?" *The New Republic* (New York), June 18, 1962.
34. For a brief but excellent account of the progressive degradation of Laos in 1962 and 1963, see Stuart Simmonds, "Laos: A Renewal of Crisis," *Asian Survey* (Berkeley, Calif.), January, 1964, pp. 680–684. See also Parke Fulham, "A Million White Elephants," in *Far Eastern Economic Review* (Hong Kong), May 28, 1964, pp. 420–421.
35. Fall, "Red China's Aims in Asia," *Current History*, September, 1962, pp. 140–141.
36. Seth S. King, "Thais Report Rise in Reds' Activity," *The New York Times*, January 9, 1965.
37. The *Washington Post* (Washington, D.C.), May 30, 1964, spoke of the possibility of the creation of a PL-controlled neutralist government in which Souphanouvong would be Vice-premier and left-wing neutralist Khamsouk Kéola would be Premier. See also Fulham, *A Million White Elephants*, p. 421.
38. The *Washington Post*, May 31, 1964.

SELECTED BIBLIOGRAPHY

Anon., *Der Befreiungskampf der Völker von Vietnam, Khmer and Pathet-Lao* East Berlin: Dietz Verlag, 1954.

Ayrolles, L. H., *L'Indochine ne répond plus.* Saint-Brieuc: Armand Prudhomme, 1948.

Berval, René de, ed., *Kingdom of Laos.* Saigon: France-Asie, 1959.

Blume, Isabelle, *De la frontière du Laos à la rivière Bên Hai.* Hanoi: Editions en langues étrangères, 1961.

Burchett, Wilfred G., *Mekong Upstream: A Visit to Laos and Cambodia.* East Berlin: Seven Seas Books, 1959.

Chalermnit Press Correspondent, *Battle of Vientiane, 1960.* Bangkok: Niyomvithaya Printing Press, 1959.

Chen Yi et al., *Concerning the Situation in Laos.* Peking: Foreign Languages Press, 1959.

Dommen, Arthur J., *Conflict in Laos: The Politics of Neutralization.* New York: Frederick A. Praeger, Inc., 1964.

Epstein, Israel, and Elsie Fairfax-Cholmeley, *Laos in the Mirror of Geneva.* Peking: New World Press, 1961.

Fall, Bernard B., "The International Relations of Laos," *Pacific Affairs,* XXX, No. 1 (March, 1957).

——, "The Laos Tangle," *International Journal* (Toronto), XVI, No. 2 (January, 1962).

——, *Crisis in Laos.* Washington: Public Affairs Press.

French Government, *Convention générale franco-laotienne du 19 juillet 1949 et Conventions annexes du 6 février 1950.* Saigon: Imprimerie d'Extrême-Orient, 1950.

Halpern, Abraham M., and H. B. Fredman, *Communist Strategy in Laos.* Santa Monica, Calif.: The Rand Corporation, November 15, 1960.

Halpern, Joel M., *Government, Politics, and Social Structure in Laos.* New Haven, Conn.: Yale University Southeast Asia Studies, 1964.

——, *The Role of the Chinese in Laos Society.* Santa Monica, Calif.: The Rand Corporation, December 15, 1960.

Katay D. Sasority, *Le Laos.* Paris: Berger-Levrault, 1953.

Krausz, Georg, *Von Indien bis Laos.* East Berlin: Verlag Volk und Welt, 1960.

Modelski, George, *International Conference on the Settlement of the Laotian Question 1961–62.* Canberra: The Australian National University, 1962.

Okonitnikov, A. P., *Gosudarstvenyi stroi Laosa.* Moscow: Yuridicheskoi Literaturyi, 1959.

Quang Minh, *Au pays du million d'éléphants.* Hanoi: Editions en langues étrangères, 1961.

Report of the Security Council Subcommittee under Resolution of 7 September 1959. United Nations, Security Council: No. S/4236, November 5, 1959.

Sisouk No Champassak, *Storm Over Laos.* New York: Frederick A. Praeger, Inc., 1961.

Strong, Anna Louise, *Cash and Violence in Laos.* Peking: New World Press, 1961.

Zukrowski, Wojcech et al., *Sous le ciel du Laos.* Hanoi: Editions en langues étrangères, 1961.

THE JAPANESE
COMMUNIST PARTY

YOYOGI AND ITS RIVALS*

HANS H. BAERWALD

The Japanese Communist Party (JCP) is an anomaly. According to clas
sical Marxist doctrine, Japan's advanced state of industrialization, the
superior organization of her labor union movement, the early origins o
the Party itself (1922), and the extent to which Marxist though
has penetrated Japanese academic circles should make this society rip
for the culmination of the processes of historical materialism. Yet
among the 486 members of the House of Representatives only 5 are
Communists; and in the 250-seat House of Councillors, only 5 are ad
herents of the JCP.[1] Although this limited statistical evidence does no
tell the whole story, the fact remains that despite the attention lavished
upon the JCP by the Japanese government, by the Allied Occupation dur
ing its later years, and by foreign observers since the peace treaty, the

*Yoyogi refers to the headquarters of the Japanese Communist Party, as distinct from
the location of various dissident groups.

212

Party is impotent by comparison with the governing Liberal-Democratic Party and its principal opposition, the Socialist Party.

Two major factors have contributed to the JCP's powerlessness. In the 1920's, the movement floundered in a morass of seemingly endless doctrinal disputes.[2] Some of these could be attributed to extraordinarily inept direction from the Comintern, some to the fact that the movement's leadership in Japan was drawn largely from the ranks of academicians who were more concerned with theoretical correctness than with the arduous tasks of building a popular mass base and gaining power. The repressive policies of the Japanese government also weakened the movement in the prewar period. No sooner would the movement begin to have the semblance of an effective organization than the government would jail the leaders or cause them to flee into exile. Under the circumstances, the conspiratorial character of the movement began to be accepted as a constant by those who remained.

During the 1930's, the movement ceased to exist as an organized force in the politics of Japan. What remained was a leadership either in jail or in refuge abroad and a disorganized, largely underground remnant existing in an extremely hostile environment and, as a consequence, seeking external support—support to which were attached ideological strings which further alienated the movement from the mainstream of Japanese thought. It is in many respects a tribute to the persuasiveness of ideas and the tenacity of a few true believers that the movement survived at all.

HISTORY OF THE JAPANESE COMMUNIST PARTY

The history of the JCP as an organization actively participating in Japanese politics really begins in the fall of 1945, subsequent to the defeat of Japan in World War II. On October 4 of that year, the Supreme Commander for the Allied Powers (SCAP) issued a directive to the Japanese government which abrogated all laws restricting freedom of thought and assembly. Furthermore, the same directive ordered the release of all political prisoners.[3] One month later a Congress of the Party was convened under the leadership of Tokuda Kyūichi and Shiga Yoshio, both old-timers who had spent years in prison. In January 1946, Nosaka Sanzō [4] joined them upon his return from exile in China. During the war Nosaka had beamed propaganda broadcasts from Yenan urging his compatriots to end the war against the United States, and in these efforts had the support of the American government's Office of War Information. He had also indoctrinated Japanese POW's in a school set up for that purpose.

Understandably enough, the JCP welcomed the Allied Occupation as a liberating force and Nosaka proclaimed that the JCP should be a "lovable party," implying that it should not resort to tactics of violence The Party also attempted to create a united front with the socialists in which efforts it was rebuffed. On the question of strategy and tactics the Party adopted the line that Japan would have to go through a two stage revolutionary process—first, the bourgeois revolution leading to the establishment of a democratic government, which process was being sponsored by the Occupation and should be supported; second, the socialist revolution led by the JCP, concerning the consummation of which some violence might be necessary. The basic thrust of the Party' program, however, was to rely on the processes of peaceful change.

This honeymoon between the JCP and the Occupation was not to last long. A number of factors contributed to the alienation. First wa the Occupation's decision to retain the Emperor, whose removal, as wel as the dismantling of the Emperor institution, had long been advocated by most leaders of the Party. More important was MacArthur's decision to ban the general strike scheduled for February 1, 1947.

Under the authority vested in me as Supreme Commander for the Allied Powers, I have informed the labor leaders, whose unions have federated for the purpose of conducting a general strike, that I will not permit the use of so deadly a weapon in the present impoverished and emaciated condition of Japan, and have accordingly directed them to desist from the furtherance of such action.[5]

The organization of this strike had represented one of the JCP' major efforts to capture control of the burgeoning trade union movement Despite the generally adverse economic conditions then existing in Japan and despite the growing disparity between wages and the inflationary spiral of prices, the Socialist Party and the labor leaders allied with i had been reluctant to make common cause with the JCP in organizing the strike. Their lack of eagerness was influenced by advice from genera headquarters (GHQ), SCAP, that the strike would not be permitted to take place, advice which the socialists had listened to with greater car than the Communists. As a consequence of the failure of this gamble the JCP lost considerable support within the trade-union movement, and the somewhat hesitant united front that had come into existence for the purposes of the general strike disintegrated quickly.

Direct action having proved a failure, the Party returned to a program of supporting those social, economic, and political reform sponsored by the Occupation with which it agreed, although it recog nized that there was an increasingly apparent divergence of basi goals. Such a position developed in the final months of the reform era The 1947 general elections brought to power a coalition cabinet con sisting of representatives of the Socialist and Democratic Parties, initiall under the Prime Ministership of socialist Katayama Tetsu and subsequently under democrat Ashida Hitoshi. In many respects, the Katayama and Ashida Cabinets were the high-water mark of the reform era under the Occupation. Toward the end of this period—the summer of 1948—there was a clear indication that the "reverse course" (so termed by the Japanese to indicate the change in emphasis of Occupation policies from reform to recovery and/or reaction) had begun.

In this instance too, a trade-union issue serves as a convenient bench mark. The controversy at hand was the denial of the right to strike on the part of ". . . persons holding a position by appointment or employment in the public service of Japan or in any instrumentality thereof. . . ."[6] At least two major trade unions—the Government Transportation Workers and Communications Workers—had their operations seriously restricted by this quasi-directive which was aimed at undermining the growing influence of Communists within the ranks of trade-union leaders.

Communists were not the only ones affected by the resultant amendments in the Japanese government's Public Service Law. These amendments had to be sponsored by a Cabinet in which the socialists held at least a share of power. Furthermore, scandals involving the Cabinet besmirched the reputation of the socialists. Thus, in the election of January 23, 1949, the Communist Party's popular vote jumped from the 3.7 per cent it had obtained in the 1947 election to 9.7 per cent and, instead of only 4 members in the House of Representatives, as in 1947, 35 Communists became members of the lower house.[7]

Neither before nor since has the JCP managed to make such a respectable showing at the polls. A substantial portion of Japan's renovationist-oriented voters had turned from support of the socialists, whose ideological commitments were presumed to have been tarnished by their participation in the Katayama and Ashida Cabinets. The implication of certain socialists, such as Nishio Suehirō (long-time leader of the Democratic-Socialist Party) in the Showa Denko scandals had not helped the socialist cause. The socialists' share of the popular vote plummeted downward by over 11 per cent (from 26.2 per cent in 1947 to 15.5 per cent in 1949). Instead of electing 143 members of the House of Representatives, it sent only 48 to Diet posts in 1949, a drop of nearly 100 seats. The disaster suffered by the Socialist Party in the 1949 election was matched by a substantial decline (from 121 to 69 seats in the House of Representatives) in the conservative Democratic Party and a comparable rise in the electoral fortunes of the equally conservative Liberal Party (from 131 to 264 seats).[8] The Japanese electorate appeared to be turning away from the center of the political spectrum to its extremes, and many observers feared that a polarization of politics in Japan was imminent.

The JCP's electoral triumph of January 1949 proved to be short lived. Within 18 months, the Party had the misfortune of being hit from two diverse directions. First there was criticism from the Cominform and just as the Party's leadership had managed to readjust itself to the new line there came the body blow dealt in concert by the Occupation and the Japanese government. Each of these deserves brief elaboration as they helped to determine the Party's subsequent fortunes, which have been none too good.

Of the two events, the Cominform criticism is the more inexplicable. An observer would have thought that the Party's leadership had done rather well. Here was the JCP, which had been in effective existence only for about four years, more than doubling its popular vote in 21 months and increasing its Diet representation nearly tenfold. One might suppose that such a record would have pleased Stalin, who was then still directing the international Communist movement. Instead, Nosaka's tactics of having the JCP be a lovable party were assailed as "anti-dem ocratic," "anti-socialist," and as serving "the imperialist occupiers in Ja pan and the enemies of independence."[9]

Nosaka recanted; in all probability, this was the price he had to pay for remaining as a major Party leader.[10] While the recantation made possible his survival, it clarified for the Japanese people the extent to which the Party's leadership was subservient to international control. Substantial repercussions were felt by the Party, especially among its intellectual supporters. It is at least possible that elements less subservient to Moscow within the ranks of Party leaders wanted to use this oppor tunity to seize control from the mainstream leadership of Nosaka and Tokuda Kyūichi.[11] Certainly there was fierce infighting between the com paratively moderate mainstream group and the more militant interna tionalists led by Shiga Yoshio and Miyamoto Kenji. Before these effort could bear fruit, the second blow fell, this time at the Occupation's in stigation.

In response to the Cominform's criticism of Nosaka, the JCP in creased the intemperance of its outbursts against the Occupation and turned toward acts of violence in the achievement of its goals. As a con sequence, GHQ began issuing a series of warnings to the JCP, designed to keep the Party's activities within limits acceptable to the Occupation authorities. Specifically leading up to the first warnings were a serie of articles in the Party's newspaper, Akahata (i.e., Red Flag), severely criticizing the Occupation, and remarks of a similar tenor made on the floor of the Diet by one of the Party's representatives.[12] General Whitney Chief of GHQ's Government Section, made the following comments in his meeting with representatives of the JCP:

I have summoned you to give you warning, and through you to warn your associates in the Communist Party that lying statements concerning the Occupation will not be tolerated. Your statement [by JCP Representative Sunama Ichirō in the Diet] was in direct violation of a long standing Occupation directive with which you and your fellow party members are fully familiar. Its obvious purpose is to use the legislative forum as an instrument of propaganda directed against the Occupation. The *Akahata* . . . likewise is moving steadily toward the line beyond which it cannot go without similarly violating the Occupation directive.[13]

This warning by General Whitney was reinforced by General MacArthur a few months later. The JCP's leadership would not, or could not (because of pressure from the Cominform), adjust its public stance. Given the nearly limitless power of the Occupation at that time, the confrontation between the Party and SCAP moved to a predictable climax.

On June 6 and 7, 1950, General MacArthur, in two letters addressed to the then Prime Minister Yoshida Shigeru, ordered the Japanese government to purge from public office the entire Central Committee of the JCP and the editorial staff of *Akahata*.[14] Even these relatively drastic steps proved to be of little avail in halting the publication of what Occupation authorities viewed as scurrilous material. On the day after the outbreak of the Korean War, MacArthur ordered *Akahata* to suspend publication for one month and, even before the month was over, GHQ ordered the Japanese government to suppress the publication of "all Communist newspapers and all offending party-line publications of whatsoever nature."[15]

Japanese government suppression of Communist publications and harassment of hard-core Communists and alleged sympathizers reached prodigious proportions in the year that followed. Not only was there a systematic weeding out of suspects from government employment, but the purge made substantial inroads into the ranks of those employed in private industry. Like the purge which had been initially (in 1946 and 1947) applied to large numbers of individuals for their participation in the war effort, the red purge of 1950 and 1951 cut deeply and not always with a sense of discrimination or fair play. It need only be added that while many issues in the realm of civil liberties were raised by these actions, their full elaboration would take one very far afield.

Whatever views one may hold as to the justifiability of the actions taken by the Occupation and its agent, the Japanese government, in suppressing the JCP in 1950 and 1951, the Party has not yet recovered from the consequences. On the eve of the peace treaty between Japan and the United States, the JCP was almost where it had been at the time of Japan's surrender in the late summer of 1945. It was barely legal, and much of its leadership was barred from public office and either operating clandestinely or back in self-imposed exile.

The JCP's efforts during the 1950's were designed to help it to recover and to rebuild its shattered forces. In these tasks, it has fared none too well. Its extremely slow and painful efforts to rehabilitate itself and become an effective force can be seen from Table 1.

Table 1

ELECTORAL STRENGTH OF THE JAPANESE COMMUNIST PART\

House of Representatives	1952	1953	1955	1958	1960	1963	1967
Per cent of popular vote:	2.6	1.9	2.0	2.6	2.9	4.0	4.76
Seats in House of Representatives (of 467):	0	1	2	1	3	5	5

House of Councillors	1953	1956	1959	1962	1965
Per cent of popular vote:					
National constituency	1.1	2.1	1.9	3.1	4.4
Prefectural constituencies	0.9	3.9	3.3	4.8	6.9
Seats in House of Councillors (of 250):					
National constituency	0	1	1	2	2
Prefectural constituencies	0	1	0	1	1
Total	0	2	1	3	5

Source: Figures for House of Representatives from Jichisho Senkyokyoku, *Shugiin Giin Sosenkyo Kekka-Shirabe (Results of the General Election for the House of Representatives)*, March, 1967, pp. 10–14. Figures for House of Councillors from Jichisho Senkyokyoku *Sangiin Giin Tsūojō Senkyo Kekka-Shirabe (Results of the General Election for the House of Councillors)*, March, 1966, pp. 8–9, 15.

PARTY LEADERSHIP AND ORGANIZATION

Despite, and very possibly also because of, the vicissitudes that have beset the JCP for most of its existence, there has been remarkable continuity in its leadership for most of its history. One of the triumvirate that resuscitated the Party in the postwar period, former Secretary-General Tokuda Kyūichi, died in self-imposed exile in China subsequent to the red purge. Nosaka Sanzo, Chairman of the Party since 1955 and member of the House of Councillors since 1959, has retained his intellectual acumen despite having had to adjust to innumerable changes in Party doctrine. He remains the Party's most respected spokesman, but respected more by those outside than those within the movement. The years (he is now 79) are beginning to take their toll.

Shiga Yoshio, until the spring of 1964 second only to Nosaka in seniority, was the Party's most elected parliamentarian, having been a member of the House of Representatives since 1946 (with the sole exception of the red purge years). A graduate of Tokyo's Imperial University, h too added intellectual luster to the Party. Repercussions of the Sino-Soviet dispute contributed to his downfall.

Shiga, bolting Party discipline, voted for ratification of the Partial Nuclear Test-Ban Treaty in the Diet on May 20, 1964, and as a consequence, the JCP Central Committee voted to remove him from all Party posts. He subsequently organized the JCP Voice of Japan with a few of his former comrades (including Nakano Shigeharu and Kamiyama Shigeo) and, allegedly, the help of Moscow. This splinter movement, the first overt split in the Party during the postwar period, never managed to achieve organizational strength. Shiga's own political career may have come to an end in 1967, when he ran as an "independent" Communist candidate in the general election. He lost his seat and many well have contributed to the defeat of the Yoyogi-backed candidate, Kanzaki Toshio, for their combined vote would have been 69,347, more than sufficient to be elected in the three-man Osaka 6th district.[16] Shiga's activities and his ties with Moscow have contributed to the difficulty of reestablishing cordial relations between Yoyogi and the Kremlin.

In the mid-sixties, the Party's Secretary-General, Miyamoto Kenji, gradually solidified his control over the Yoyogi mainstream. Another Tokyo University graduate, he joined the Party in 1931 and spent the greater part of the prewar period in jail. In fact, a long jail sentence (unless one was abroad, as was Nosaka) remains one of the guarantees of loyalty to the Party and, hence, a guarantee of eligibility for a position of trust within it. His exact role during the period when Yoyogi first began to seriously grapple with the issues raised by the Sino-Soviet dispute remains a matter of some controversy. He was reported either to be neutral or to lean toward Moscow. He is now generally accepted as the main architect of the current *jishu-dokuritsu-ron* (i.e., autonomously independent line) and as the Party's true leader.

Miyamoto's emergence has led to the relative downgrading of certain other Party leaders. For example, Hakamada Satomi, who had previously been reported to be Miyamoto's principal rival, especially during the years when Yoyogi's relations with Peking were close and cordial, is now regarded as a lieutenant of Miyamoto. Hakamada is one of the leaders with an authentic proletarian background: His formal education ended with the completion of primary school, but was subsequently filled out by attendance at the University for the Toilers of the East (i.e., KUTV, or *Toyo-Kinrosha-Kyosanshugi-Daigaku*) in Vladivostok.

Miyamoto's control over the Party was also strengthened by the appointment of Oka Masayoshi as editor of *Akahata* and by the prominence accorded to the Ueda brothers at the Tenth Party Congress in October 1966. The last-named ideologues, Ueda Kōchirō and Ueda Tetsuzō (who uses the pen-name Fuwa Tetsuzō) are loyal lieutenants of the Secretary-General. They, as well as Oka, have the additional advantage of

being Tokyo University graduates. The *Todai* tie is far more than neck
wear, carrying with it prestige and certification of intellectual brilliance
   Factional strife has continued to beset the JCP, however, despite in
creased unity within Yoyogi itself. Shiga's Voice of Japan has declined
in influence, to be sure. On the other hand, a left-deviationist (from the
current Yoyogi vantage point) JCP "liberation front" has made its ap
pearance. This wing of the Party is probably dominated by the pro
Chinese members of the JCP.[17] Most of their group had participated in
the rash of violence in the early 1950's and had subsequently fled to
China for five or six years of study. Some of them may have retained
their membership in the Chinese Communist Party in the intervening
years, but if this is so it would have been in violation of JCP regula
tions.
   Activists inside the so-called China lobby were also occasionally
dubbed the Young Officers (an oblique reference to the militants who
precipitated the Japanese militarist era of the 1930's, goading their
seniors into taking increasingly radical action). A number of these pro
Peking militants (such as Nishizawa Ryuji and Anzai Kuraji) were actually
expelled from the JCP and have reportedly taken refuge in Peking. Fur
thermore, Yoyogi has taken pains to bring the dissident elements at
prefectural and local levels to heel. Most noteworthy among these ef
forts was the suppression of the Yamaguchi Prefectural Chapter, which
had been dominated by a group of Peking loyalists.
   Such internal troubles should not lead one to conclude that the JCP
is poorly organized. At the center, an elaborate Party machinery (Presi
dium, Central Committee, Secretariat and special bureaus) sits atop a
network of 46 prefectural, 271 district, and 254 local organizations. At the
base of the pyramid are the cells, estimated at between 8,500 and 9,000
in which there are probably 250,000 dues-paying, card-carrying mem
bers.[18] If the figures on Party membership are correct (and there is
every reason to believe that the Japanese government is well-informed)
there has been a spectacular membership increase in the 1960's. In July
1959 it was believed that Party membership had fallen to 37,000. Seven
years later more than a sevenfold increase had taken place.[19] The Party
has finally managed to retain and surpass the numerical strength it had
had in 1947!
   Blue-collar factory workers constitute an important but by no means
exclusive element in the Party's membership. We have noted the influence
of intellectuals, especially of Tokyo University alumni, at the Central
Committee level. Over 30 per cent of the Central Committee members
are university graduates, and another 25 per cent have attended either
a university or an old-style high school, which would have included
junior college. Most Central Committee members have occupational

backgrounds which involved some intellectual activity (e.g., public service, teaching, newspaper reporting). Only one-third are classified as
workers.[20] In most respects, the education and occupational background
of the Central Committee are a reflection of the Party's general membership.

One large group—persons engaged in agriculture, forestry, and fishing—has not managed to enter the leadership in proportion to its membership. This group makes up over 11 per cent of the total membership, yet only 2 per cent of the Central Committee members are farmers
and fishermen.[21] Land reform, which was accomplished under the aegis
of the Occupation, did much to blunt peasant dissatisfaction; indeed, to
the extent that there is grumbling in the villages, it is by landlords who
lost part of their holdings during the reform. These individuals are
hardly likely to turn to the JCP for redress of their grievances. The
one major exception is the predominantly rural prefecture of Nagano,
whose third electoral district was the only nonurban area to elect a
Communist, Hayashi Hyakurō, to the Diet in the 1963 and 1967 general
elections.[22]

The JCP's electoral strength is centered in the major urban areas. Of
Hayashi's four Party colleagues in the current House of Representatives,
one comes from Tokyo, one from Kyoto, one from Osaka, and one from
Kita-Kyushu—all industrial cities. In prefectural and local elections, the
Party showed that it had strength throughout the islands by polling
nearly two million votes in the local elections of 1963 and close to three
million votes in 1967, electing 603 and 964 members of local assemblies
in the respective contests. (The reader should compare these figures
with the more than twenty million votes polled by the Liberal-Democratic Party and the close to ten million votes polled by the Socialist
Party.) The JCP did considerably less well in the election of executives
(prefectural governors and city mayors). In 1967, however, its candidate for the mayoralty of Shiojiri City (again, in Nagano Prefecture)
was successful, thus becoming the only Communist mayor in all of Japan.
In addition, JCP members helped to elect, as Governor of the world's
largest metropolis—Tokyo—Minobe Ryokichi (son of the famous Con-
stitutionalist, Minobe Tatsukichi). Minobe has since made it clear that
while he was appreciative of Communist Party support, he is not in any
sense amenable to its dictation. It would still seem correct to say that
the Japanese people, to the limited extent that they cast their ballots
for Communists, are more likely to support Communists running for
posts within a general assembly in which their views would have to be
mingled with representatives of other parties than to vote to elect them
to positions in which they might exercise sole authority.[23]

All these activities of the JCP require money. Political fund-raising is a murky area no matter what party is involved. It becomes doubly so if there is the possibility, as in the case of the JCP, that irregular sources might be involved. The most interesting of these suspicions involved kick-backs from the trade of the firms friendly with the Chinese People's Republic. Allegedly, a certain percentage of their profits was allocated to Yoyogi so long as relations with Peking remained cordial. Rumors of the amounts involved vary so widely that it is not possible to make even a tentative estimate, but some indication that substantial sums entered party coffers is provided by the guesses of cynical observers who speculated that the break between Yoyogi and Peking could be partially traced to the difficulties encountered in the trading relationship.[24]

On the other hand, certain Party-run enterprises such as *Akahata* have prospered. Its daily circulation was nearly 300,000 and its Sunday edition sold well over one million copies in the summer of 1967.[25] The Special Investigation Bureau found one interesting example of the manner in which the Party used an increase in *Akahata*'s circulation to accomplish two purposes simultaneously. In a certain (unnamed) city hall in Kagoshima prefecture, the local Party initially induced some of the higher officials in the city government to subscribe to *Akahata*. City officials were not anxious to accede to the Party's wishes, but they hoped that by subscribing for a short time they could placate the local Party leaders whose various demands had made the running of the city more and more difficult. Once the higher officials had subscribed, Party activists advertised this fact among lower-ranking officials and clerks who could easily be convinced that subscribing to *Akahata* would not hurt their careers and might even be helpful.[26] With such techniques, it is no wonder that the Sunday edition of *Akahata* has provided the Party with a local source of income.

One known instance of Peking's financial assistance to its comrades in Japan was a contribution made not directly to the Party but to the *Nihon Minshushugi Seinen Domei*, often referred to as *Minseido*, the Japanese Democratic Youth League. At the time of the struggle against the revised U.S.–Japan Security Pact in 1960, it is reported, the Chinese Party's Youth League's Central Committee sent 5,500,000 yen (about $15,000) to their friends in Japan.[27]

FRONT ORGANIZATIONS

The strength and influence of the JCP cannot, of course, be assessed solely on the basis of its official membership or its popular support in elections. The Party has made strenuous efforts to establish subsidiary organizations and to penetrate, and ultimately to control, others already in existence. One major goal, control of the trade union movement, has eluded the Party. To be sure, Party members have, on occasion, been able to acquire positions of leadership in one union or another (currently the Party is believed to control the Day Workers' Union, *Zennichi-jirō*). However, *Sōhyō* (i.e., the General Council of Trade Unions), the largest and certainly most powerful labor union federation, has been constant in its support for the Socialist Party. Indeed, *Sōhyō's* hostility toward the JCP has been so pronounced that Japanese government observers have at times believed that the JCP might try to form a separate trade union federation rather than continue in their efforts to penetrate *Sōhyō's* leadership. There is no indication as yet that the Party is taking such a drastic step.

For a time, in the late 1940's and early 1950's, the Party was reasonably successful in achieving considerable control over the major student organization, *Zengakuren*, which achieved international notoriety by playing an important role in the movement to oppose revision of the Security Pact between the United States and Japan. By 1960, however, the Party was able to control only a faction inside the student federation: Their leaders had been expelled from or had left the JCP two years earlier, when the students wanted to continue to pursue tactics of violence while the Party, very possibly under the impact of the anti-Stalin campaign, desired a return to moderation. The recent situation inside *Zengakuren* can only be described as chaotic. One faction remains relatively loyal to Yoyogi, but there are at least four major factions which are strongly opposed to the current mainstream of the JCP, and three of these are loosely united in the *Sampa Rengō* (i.e., Federation of Three Factions) which, in its public behavior, is far more militant than the Yoyogi loyalists. Its ideology seems to be a mixed bag of classical Marxism and anarchosyndicalism, though that is hardly the way in which they themselves would describe it.[28] The disaffection of university students from people over thirty also afflicts the JCP.

The Party has had more success with a more broadly based youth organization, the *Minseido*, a successor to the *Kyosan Seinen Domei* (i.e., Young People's Communist League) which came into existence in 1951. During the greater part of the 1950's it did not amount to very much as an organization, but in 1959, possibly because of the deviationist tendencies that were coming to the fore in *Zengakuren*, the Party began to pay more attention to *Minseido*. In December 1959, *Minseido* had a reported membership of 4,000; by the fall of 1963, its membership had come close to 100,000, a target of 300,000 having been set at its Sixth National Congress in 1961.[29] At the JCP's Central Committee meeting in 1960, it was decided that *Minseido* should become the reservoir of future Party members. It remains to be seen whether *Minseido* will fulfill its assigned role or whether, like *Zengakuren*, it too will develop factional conflicts which will limit its usefulness.

A third segment of Japanese society that the Party has tried to manipulate is the peace movement. By far the most popular and best-organized peace group has been the Japanese Council for Banning Atomic and Hydrogen Bombs (i.e., *Gensuikyō*), and at the last five annual worldwide rallies conducted in Hiroshima, there has been an increasingly severe clash between the Japanese Socialist Party (SJP) and the JCP for control. The Ninth World Rally, held during the first week of August 1963, resulted in the virtual disintegration of *Gensuikyō*, a process that had begun at the rally held one year earlier. To the clash between the JCP and the JSP *Sōhyō* alliance was added the spectacle of delegates from China and the Soviet Union denouncing each other. At one point, Soviet delegates turned their backs to the podium during a speech by the principal Chinese delegate.[30]

Conflict within the peace movement has continued to confound the organizers of the Hiroshima Rallies. Support for and opposition to the Partial Nuclear Test-Ban Treaty was only the beginning of the split between the socialist *Gensuikyō*-ites and the Communist *Gensuikyo*-ites. With the turn away from Peking in 1966, controversies within the JCP became an added factor, in turn complicated by the pro-Chinese proclivities of the Japan Socialist Party during the latter part of Sasaki Kozo's chairmanship, especially in 1966 and the first half of 1967.

Similar issues plagued other organizations which were partially dominated by or affiliated with the JCP. Disputes arose inside the Japan-China Friendship Association as well as in the Afro-Asian Solidarity Committee in Japan. Similarly afflicted were the Japanese Congress of Journalists and the New Japan Women's Association. In essence, the issue was always the degree to which Peking should be looked to for leadership, rather than whether an alternative external source of inspiration, such as Moscow, would be a better point of reference.[31] All elements of the Japanese left have thus become more deeply factionalized due to the Sino-Soviet cleavage, as disputes have seeped into the JCP, organizations allied with the Party, and the JSP as well.

IDEOLOGY AND TACTICS

A variety of ideological controversies, plus their inevitable overtones concerning strategy and tactics, helped to slow the rebuilding of the Party in the 1950's.[32] Apparently, Khrushchev caught the JCP leaders by surprise with his denunciation of Stalin at the Twentieth Party Congress of the Communist Party of the Soviet Union (CPSU), and it was some years before the JCP managed to begin the task of accommodating itself to the new complexities that gradually manifested themselves in the international Communist movement. The climax came just prior to the JCP Eighth National Conference held in July 1961, and it produced the ouster of the Kasuga Shōjirō.

Kasuga and his supporters had argued, in effect, that the JCP's principal enemy was monopoly capitalism in Japan and that the coming socialist revolution would therefore be a one-stage process which could be achieved through peaceful means. (It is believed that Kasuga was strongly influenced by Togliatti's views on structural reform, which are being advocated by a major faction of Japan's Socialist Party, thereby adding to the over-all confusion.) Kasuga's opponents in the JCP won the intra-Party debate, contending that the Japanese society is confronted with two enemies, American imperialism as well as Japanese monopoly capitalism, and that Japan, though highly developed industrially, is nevertheless still subordinated to American imperialism. Thus a two-stage revolution is envisaged, the first being the removal of the shackles of American imperialism, and only the second and later stage being the socialist revolution in Japan. Opponents of this thesis, including Kasuga, maintained that too much stress was still being placed on American imperialism as the prime enemy and that insufficient emphasis was being placed on the possibilities of a peaceful transformation of Japanese society.

Ambiguities abound in Kasuga's formulation which, in its essentials, is a papering over of two radically different viewpoints and, at best, is a return to the ideological posture of the JCP in the initial postwar, lovable-Party period. His opponents did not have sufficient support to press their case at the Seventh National Party Congress in 1958, and they might have lost again at the Eighth, but Kasuga's group departed after its failure to prevail at the Central Committee meeting in March 1961. This Central Committee meeting settled the issue within the Party.

The defeat of Kasuga and his supporters had obvious tactical consequences. It signified that emphasis would still be given to opposing: (1) the presence of American military forces in Japan; and (2) remilitarization. In this effort the JCP has sought to create a broadly based united front, but it has been relatively unsuccessful in the last eight years, as the trials and tribulations of *Gensuikyō* and events within *Sōhyō* would indicate.

The Party advocates a host of specific subsidiary policies which, in broad outline, are not too far removed from policies advocated by the socialists. The JSP, too, stands adamantly opposed to Japan's remilitarization. Socialists, too, are opposed to revision of the constitution, the revival of an oppressive police force, and the reintroduction of nationalistic propaganda in the schools. The list can be lengthened, but the main point is that the JCP has often found itself in the position of having its thunder stolen by the JSP. Relations between the two parties have run warm and cool, especially on matters such as joint campaigns on issues or joint support of candidates. On occasion the parties have even reversed their respective roles, the socialists becoming more radical than the

226   THE JAPANESE COMMUNIST PARTY

Communists. One year the JCP may attack Eda Saburo, a major figure
in the JSP, for being an exponent of "right-wing social democracy,"
"revisionism," and "petty-bourgeois opportunism."[33] Another year, certain
JSP leaders may sponsor the Japanese edition of *Quotations from Chairman Mao*,[34] while the JCP removes pictures of Mao Tse-tung from Yoyogi
and local Party headquarters. Such shifts, symbolic though they may be,
have their origin in the dispute between Moscow and Peking, and possibly in the desire of the Japanese to maintain open lines of communication with one and all so that if a door closes to one group, another
avenue of approach might be found.

THE SINO-SOVIET CLEAVAGE AND THE JCP

Since 1962, the many ideological and factional struggles within the
JCP have been brought into sharper focus as the Party finally began
grappling with the Sino-Soviet dispute. The JCP's dilemma was summed
up in an interview of Shiga Yoshio.[35] He contended, as late as August
1963, that newspaper and magazine reports of a split inside the JCP
were grossly exaggerated, possibly deliberately so, by individuals (especially inside the Japanese government's security police, the Special
Investigation Bureau of the Attorney General's Office) who could take
satisfaction in picturing the Party as being in a state of disarray. Japan,
Shiga argued, is a highly industrialized country, comparable to Italy and
possibly even France in its economic development, but its geographical
location is Asia. Shiga's analysis gave one the impression that the JCP
was having some difficulty in determining which of these considerations
should be given greater weight in the determination of Party policy.

The interview was conducted shortly after the negotiations in Moscow leading up to the Partial Nuclear Test-Ban Treaty and within two
weeks of the *Gensuikyō's* ninth rally, which had been the scene of so
much confusion. When questioned on the JCP's position concerning
the Moscow treaty, Shiga responded with the statement that neither he
nor his Party really opposed the treaty. It was a case of wanting to alert
the Japanese people to the possibility that the treaty was a sham if it
did not lead to total disarmament and if it left unresolved such issues as
the maintenance of military bases by the United States in Japan or having
American nuclear-powered submarines call at Japanese ports. (The JCP
subsequently criticized the Test-Ban Treaty, as we shall see.)

Shiga was probably seeking to reflect the views of the Party's leadership because he was conversing with a foreigner in the presence of a
member of the Party's Secretariat. In any event, he cast his vote in
favor of the Treaty's ratification, in contrast with the rest of his colleagues
in the House of Representatives. It is possible that he was already con-

sidering this step in the late summer of 1963, though he was still observing the formalities of Party discipline.

Implicit in the views of the leadership was the continued effort to downgrade the significance of the Sino-Soviet dispute, thereby permitting the JCP to have close fraternal ties with both Moscow and Peking. The maintenance of these ties had been a cardinal principle for the JCP ever since the divergence of viewpoint between Mao and Khrushchev became manifest. In the autumn of 1963, however, there were signs that the JCP was beginning to line up with Peking on most issues. Indeed, some Japanese government observers had noted this process earlier, particularly in the emergence of Hakamada and the so-called China lobby inside the JCP.

In the view of the Japanese government, by 1963 there was a substantial amount of evidence which pointed to the conclusion that the JCP had become Peking-oriented. The following factors were considered indicative:

1. The JCP delegates to the Twenty-second Party Congress in Moscow expressed no opinion when Khrushchev criticized Albania. But upon returning home, Party leaders expressed views similar to those voiced in Peking, i.e., that Khrushchev's attack on the Albanian Party was a violation of the Moscow Declaration of 1957.

2. On the issue of the Sino-Indian border controversy, the JCP supported their Chinese comrades, reproducing the complete text of China's denunciation of Nehru in *Akahata*.

3. During the Cuban missile crisis, the JCP, understandably enough, maintained a barrage of criticism against American imperialism. The "victory of reason" propounded by Khrushchev to justify the withdrawal of the missiles did not receive any words of praise. Indeed, *Akahata*, in its coverage of the crisis, paid almost no attention to the position of the Soviet Union. Subsequently, *Akahata*, according with the views of the Chinese Communists, appealed for the maintenance of a constant struggle against American imperialism and emphasized the dangers of relying on American good sense.

4. The JCP was considerably more friendly toward its Albanian than toward its Yugoslav comrades. *Akahata*, for example, reprinted the whole of the CCP's attack on Tito.[36] *Akahata* also carried a long article celebrating the fiftieth anniversary of Albanian independence and had not as yet made any reference in its columns to the Stalinist orientation of the Albanian Party.

5. Possibly the most crucial indicator of the pro-Peking proclivities of the JCP was the position that the Party ultimately took with respect to the Partial Nuclear Test-Ban Treaty. *Akahata* published an article in October 1963 (subsequently reprinted in *Zen'ei*) strongly opposing the Treaty.[37] Interestingly enough, Soviet participation in the agreement was barely mentioned, the brunt of the criticism being directed against the United States.

It was argued that: (1) the agreement represented an attempt to contain the Chinese People's Republic; (2) it attempted to weaken the true peace-loving forces who espouse the complete abolition of nuclear weapons; (3) it did not provide for a check against the further dispersal of nuclear weapons by the United States; and (4) it was a facade behind which the United States could continue to pursue its aggressive policies.[38]

Nevertheless, as late as the summer and early fall of 1963, the JCP still seemed to be making an effort to steer a neutral course between China and the Soviet Union. This effort was consonant with the resolutions adopted at the Fifth Central Committee meeting held between February 13 and 15, 1963, the first meeting at which first official cognizance was taken of the existence of the dispute. The JCP declared that an open dispute between Communist Parties was a violation of the Moscow Declaration of 1957 and justified its nonparticipation in the dispute by noting that the less said about it in public the better it would be for all concerned. The JCP desperately sought to straddle the fence, stressing on the one hand the importance of the ties that united the Communist Parties in Asia with the CCP as their center, and adding, on the other, that both the CCP and the CPSU were the two great Communist Parties in the world. By the summer of 1964, however, there seemed to be more than sufficient evidence that the JCP had lined up with Peking. An extraordinary exchange of letters between Yoyogi and the Kremlin was published in the CPSU's semi-monthly magazine *Party Life*, and their vituperative tone indicated the extent to which a spirit of fraternal comradeship was lacking between the CPSU and the JCP.

In retrospect, it does not seem clear that merely because the JCP was on less than friendly terms with Moscow its relations with Peking were extremely cordial. If such cordiality prevailed, it lasted a relatively short space of time.

Even in 1964, during the earlier presumed height of cordiality between Yoyogi and Peking—at least to the extent that relations with Moscow were cold—there were signs of trouble. Secretary-General Miyamoto's conversations with Mao did not go well; furthermore, during his absence from Tokyo, the JCP's so-called China lobby sought to undermine his position. In effect, both Mao and his JCP supporters sought to influence the Japanese to take a more militant stance, especially vis-à-vis the American involvement in Vietnam. The JCP held back. Its decision to do little was justified, from its own point of view, one year later, by events in Indonesia. For the Japanese the failure of the attempted coup and the demise of Comrade Aidit became an object lesson against blind acceptance of Peking's revolutionary ardor. Miyamoto's next visit to Peking, in February 1966, further conversations with

Mao, and an inspection trip to the front lines in North Vietnam, confirmed the JCP in its position that Peking was being unrealistic in not wanting to cooperate with Moscow.[40] The JCP would appear to face the same dilemma—in its relations vis-à-vis Moscow, Peking, and Hanoi—as the conservative Liberal-Democratic Party faces in its relations with Washington and Saigon. Verbal commitment and visits to the respective capitals are permissible and may even be desirable, but the interests of Japan, even if viewed from very different perspectives, come first.

SUMMARY AND CONCLUSION

Yoyogi, or the official JCP, is currently reflecting its own particular brand of nationalism—and it is doing so when Japan itself is beginning to attempt to define its own interests and to give them preference over competing international ties. This view is clearly set forth in the Central Committee Report to the Tenth JCP Congress held in October 1966:

The unfortunate split of the Party in 1950 and the serious errors committed subsequently have something to do with open criticism from without—criticism by some of the foreign brother parties and international organizations. They are also connected with various forms of high-handed interference in the internal affairs of the Party. All this, coupled with a tendency to blindly accept and misapply the then-prevailing international theory and tactics concerning the liberation struggles in colonial nations still dependent on foreign powers, complicated the situation more and made the errors even more serious.

In view of the bitter experiences gained from the split in 1950 and subsequent developments, the Party [JCP] has realized with confidence how important it is to maintain, *as an independent Party responsible for revolutionary movements in Japan, an independent position which is free from any foreign influences*, but which is based on Marxism-Leninism and proletarian internationalism. [Emphasis supplied.][41]

In its essentials, this statement summarizes Miyamoto's formulation of his *jishu-dokuritsu-ron* (i.e., autonomously independent line). Marxism-Leninism is still important, but of equal importance is the objective situation in Japan.

Whether the JCP can maintain its autonomy is an open question. Throughout its history it has been peculiarly vulnerable to foreign influences. Furthermore, Yoyogi, under Miyamoto's leadership, is beset at home with challenges from both the (temporarily?) defeated China lobby and the increasingly less important Voice of Japan faction. It is just possible that the JCP has matured sufficiently to be able to stand on its own feet and make good on its promise to devote itself to the domestic problems of Japan (housing, water, sewage, public transportation, and the host of other bread-and-butter issues of politics). Should it be able to do so, the JCP may prove to be a formidable challenge to the much larger Japanese Socialist Party in carving for itself a respectable niche in Japanese left-wing politics.

NOTES

1. *Sankei Shimbun* (*Sankei Newspaper*), January 31, 1967, p. 3.
2. For comprehensive histories of the JCP in the English language, see Rodger Swearingen and Paul Langer, *Red Flag in Japan* (Cambridge, Mass.: Harvard University Press, 1952); and Robert A. Scalapino, *The Japanese Communist Movement: 1920–1966* (Berkeley and Los Angeles: University of California Press, 1967).
3. For the full text of this directive, see General Headquarters, Supreme Commander for the Allied Powers [SCAP], *Report of Government Section: Political Reorientation of Japan* (Washington, D.C.: Government Printing Office, 1949), Vol. II, 463–65.
4. Nosaka's name is often transliterated as Nozaka.
5. "Statement Calling Off General Strike," (January 31, 1947), in SCAP, *Political Reorientation of Japan*, Vol. II, 762.
6. General Douglas MacArthur's letter to the Prime Minister (Ashida Hitoshi) of Japan. See "Amendment of the National Public Service Law," July 22, 1948, in SCAP, *Political Reorientation of Japan*, Vol. II, 581–83.
7. Jichisho Senkyo-kyoku (Autonomy Ministry, Election Bureau), *Kekka-Shirabe* (*Examination Results* [*of House of Representatives Elections*]) (Tokyo, 1960), pp. 11–14.
8. *Idem.*
9. Swearingen and Langer, *Red Flag in Japan*, pp. 199 ff.
10. Nosaka Sanzō, "My Self-criticism," *Zen'ei* (*Vanguard*), (*Tokyo*), March, 1950.
11. This possibility was suggested to me in private conversation by an individual who was a sympathizer (though not a member) of the JCP at that time. Also see Yamabe Kentarō, "Sengo Nihon No Kyōsanshugi Undo" ("The Postwar Japanese Communist Movement") in *Chuō Kōron* (*Central Review*), December, 1963, pp. 138–49. This issue of the magazine is devoted to "Contemporary Communism."
12. Details for this section are taken from an unpublished typescript entitled "Control of Antidemocratic Elements," prepared by Government Section, General Headquarters, Supreme Commander for the Allied Powers. The typescript bears no date, but is believed to have been written in late 1951 or very early 1952. See particularly pp. 36 ff.
13. *Idem.* The Occupation directive referred to is SCAPIN 33, of 19 September 1945, according to the terms of which nothing could be printed which might "disturb the public tranquility" or which constituted "false or destructive criticism of the Allied Powers."
14. *Idem.* There is reason to believe that some Occupation officials considered these actions to be too mild and recommended that the Party be outlawed. Until more of the Occupation's official records become part of the public domain, it is not possible to completely confirm this view.
15. *Ibid.*, pp. 41–42.

16. *Shugiin Giin Sosenkyo Kekka-Shirabe*, p. 231.

17. Hirotsu Kyosuke, "Trouble Between Comrades," *Current Scene* (Hong Kong), March 15, 1967, V, No. 4 (March 15, 1967), pp. 7–8.

18. This estimate was provided by an official in the Public Security Agency of the Japanese government during an interview on August 22, 1967. The membership figure is as of December 1966, and is possibly low.

19. Naigai Josei Chosakai (Domestic and Foreign Conditions Investigation Organization), *Kokunai Josei Kaisetsu* (*Comments on Domestic News*), November 15, 1963, p. 18. This magazine is published with subsidies from the Japanese government.
    Much of the rural membership of the Party is believed to be made up of hired hands in family enterprises.

20. Occupational classification of members of the Central Committee of the JCP: workers, 32.0%; public service employees, 20.4; school teachers, 4.9; students, 9.7; farmers and fishermen, 1.9; office clerks of companies and shops, 14.6; liberal professions, 10.7; newspaper reporters, 3.9; other, 1.9. SOURCE: Public Security Investigation Agency, Ministry of Justice, Japan, *Current Situations in the Japan Communist Party*, 1962, p. 145.

21. Occupational classification of party members: Professional Party members, 2.15%; factory workers, 13.58; general workers, 10.51; casual workers, 5.27; public service employees, 12.75; teachers, 6.64; persons engaged in agricultural, forestry, and fishing industries, 11.35; office workers, 9.25; dealers, 7.20; company managers, 0.76; liberal professions, 4.26; others, 3.66; persons without regular occupations, 4.55; unknown, 6.52. *Source*: Public Security Investigation Agency, Ministry of Justice, Japan, *Current Situations in the Japan Communist Party*, 1962, p. 135. "General Workers" are workers such as carpenters, plasterers, and furniture makers employed in factories and workshops considered to be small and medium enterprises.

22. *Shugiin Giin Sosenkyo Kekka-Shirabe*, p. 226.

23. Jichisho Senkyo Kyoku (Autonomy Ministry Election Bureau), *Chihō Senkyō Kekkacho: Sokuhō* (*Investigation of Local Election Results: Initial Report*), (Mimeographed, 1963), pp. 27–33; also, mimeographed material from the Public Security Agency, n.d., but prepared during summer of 1967.

24. For one estimate of JCP income and expenditure, see Scalapino, *The Japanese Communist Movement: 1920–66*, p. 327.

25. Mimeographed material from the Public Security Agency, n.d., but prepared during summer of 1967.

26. *Kokunai Josei Kaisetsu* (*Comments on Domestic News*), November 15, 1963, pp. 9, 20.

27. *Sayoku Dantai Jiten* (*Dictionary of Leftist Organizations*), (Tokyo: Musashi Shobo, 1961), p. 63.

28. For background material on Zengakuren, see George R. Packard, III, *Protest in Tokyo* (Princeton, N.J.: Princeton University Press, 1966), especially pp. 94–105.

29. *Kokunai Josei Kaisetsu* (*Comments on Domestic News*), November 15, 1963, p. 22.

30. Japanese Press Coverage, *Asahi, Mainichi, Yomiuri, Sankei Shimbun* (Tokyo), August 7, 8, 9, 1963.

31. *Current Scene* (Hong Kong), p. 10.

32. The beginnings of the turn away from violence by the Party can be traced to the Sixth National Party Conference, held in July 1955. At this Conference there was a good deal of soul-searching concerning the leftist adventurism that had played such an important role in the early 1950's. It is interesting to note that in this instance the JCP anticipated the changes brought about by Khrushchev's denunciation of Stalin at the Twentieth Party Congress of the CPSU in 1956.

See Murakami Kanji, *Nihon Kyosanto* (*The Japanese Communist Party*) (Tokyo: Hobunsha, 1956), p. 183. Also see the program adopted at the Eighth JCP Conference (July, 1963), printed in *Zen'ei* (*Vanguard*) (Tokyo), September, 1961, pp. 97–108.

33. *Asahi Nenkan* (*Asahi Yearbook*) (Tokyo, 1964), p. 332.
34. Mō Toku-tō (Mao Tse-tung), *Joroku* (Quotations) (Tokyo: Miyakawa Shobo, 1966).
35. Interview with Shiga Yoshio in his Diet office, August 20, 1963.
36. "Let Us See the Corruption of Modern Revisionists" was originally published in *Jen-min jih-pao* (*People's Daily*), September 17, 1963, when Khrushchev was attempting, with some success, to improve his relations with Tito, and was reprinted in *Akahata* (*Red Flag*) three days later.
37. *Akahata* (*Red Flag*), October 8, 1963; and *Zen'ei* (*Vanguard*) (Tokyo), December, 1963, pp. 22–27. See also Hirotsu Kyōsuke, "The Communist Party of Japan: Its Present Strength and Revolutionary Policy," *Review: A Journal for the Study of Communism and Communist Countries* (Tokyo: Ōa Kyokai), May, 1964, pp. 35–57.
38. Material for this analysis is based on Hirotsu Kyosuke, *Chūsō-Tairitsu to Nihon Kyosan-to oyobi Kakushin Jinei e no Eikyō* (*The Sino-Soviet Conflict and Its Impact upon the JCP and the Renovationists*), Mimeographed (Tokyo, 1963); and Naigai Josei Chosakai (Domestic and Foreign Conditions Investigation Committee), "*Chūsō Ronsō no Gekika to Nihon Kyōsanto no Dōkō*" ("The Intensification of the Sino-Soviet Dispute Dating from October 1961 and the JCP's Responses Thereto"), November, 1963.
39. For English translations of some of these letters, see *Peking Review*, July 31, 1964 and September 18, 1964.
40. *Current Scene* (Hong Kong), March 15, 1967, pp. 3–8; Hirotsu Kyōsuke, "Isolation of Communist China and [the] Japan Communist Party," *Review*, March, 1967, pp. 1–28.
41. *Akahata* (*Red Flag*), October 25, 1966. For further background and analysis see Tawara Kōtarō "*Nikyo 'Jishu Dokuritsu' Rosen no Haikei*" ("The Background of the JCP's 'Autonomously Independent Line'"), *Gendai no Me* (*The Eye of the Present*), September, 1966, pp. 64–73; and Kōancho (Public Security Investigation Agency), *Nihon Kyosan-to Dai Jiukkai Taikai ni tsuite* (*Concerning the JCP's 10th Party Congress*), March, 1967.

SELECTED BIBLIOGRAPHY

American Embassy, Tokyo, *Daily Summary of the Japanese Press* and [Weekly] *Summaries of Selected Japanese Magazines*. These often contain translations of Japanese Communist publications.

Kublin, Hyman, *Asian Revolutionary: The Life of Sen Katayama*. Princeton, N.J.: Princeton University Press, 1964.

Langer, Paul, "Communism in Independent Japan," in *Japan Between East and West*, ed. Hugh Borton. New York: Harper & Row, Publishers, 1957.

———, "Independence or Subordination: The Japanese Communist Party between Moscow and Peking," in *Communist Strategies in Asia: A Comparative Analysis of Governments and Parties*, ed. A. Doak Barnett. New York: Frederick A. Praeger, Inc., 1963.

Packard, George R., III, *Protest in Tokyo.* Princeton, N.J.: Princeton University Press, 1966.

Scalapino, Robert A., *The Japanese Communist Movement: 1920–1966,* Berkeley and Los Angeles: University of California Press, 1967.

Swearingen, Rodger, "Japanese Communism and the Moscow-Peking Axis," *The Annals of the American Academy of Political and Social Science,* November, 1956, pp. 63–75.

———, and Paul Langer, *Red Flag in Japan: International Communism in Action, 1919–1951.* Cambridge, Mass.: Harvard University Press, 1952.

Tsukahira, Toshio G., *The Post-war Evolution of Communist Strategy in Japan.* Cambridge, Mass.: Center for International Studies, The Technology Press of the Massachusetts Institute of Technology, 1954.

COMMUNISM IN SINGAPORE AND MALAYSIA

A MULTIFRONT STRUGGLE

FRANCES L. STARNER

From September 1963, when Malaysia was formed from Malaya, Singapore and the Borneo states of Sabah and Sarawak, through most of 1965, her existence was threatened as a result of confrontation by Indonesia aided by subversion from within. Djakarta's abortive coup of September 30, 1965, which led eventually to a military takeover there, also led gradually to the end of hostilities between Indonesia and Malaysia and a tapering off of overt acts of subversion within the Malaysian states. Even before the *Gestapu* affair, however, Malaysia lost the most heavily populated and the most advanced of the new states—Singapore—as a result not of subversion or outside pressure but of conflict between the political leadership of Singapore and that of the Federation.

During the almost two years that Singapore was part of Malaysia, the Federation was forced to combat Communist activity on the Thai-

Malayan border, in Singapore, and in Sarawak, and in each of these places Malaysia was presented with a separate problem. Even though the active threat of Communism had been eradicated in Malaya in the mid-1950's, in Malaysia it challenged the government both above ground and underground and, in Sarawak, offered the reality of armed subversion. Even after the separation of Singapore from Malaysia, Communism in the two countries maintained a unique identity, attributable only in part to their common colonial heritage.

Communism in Malaysia and Singapore is today, as it was through most of its history in Malaya and the Straits settlements, an almost exclusively Overseas Chinese phenomenon. Its aspirations, its occasional successes, its frustrations and, above all, its limitations have generally reflected the fact that it has been essentially a movement appealing to the Chinese ethnic community. This is not to say that the more than four million Chinese in Singapore and Malaysia show, as a whole, a predilection for Communism; indeed, it would be erroneous to contend that the Malaysian and Singapore Chinese have been united in their views either of their own interests or of the correct attitude to take toward Peking. Both for historical and political reasons, however, Marxism-Leninism established a foothold within the Chinese community; and its failure to gain permanent ground among the Malays and Indians has reflected not so much a lack of effort on the part of Malayan Communist leaders as an inability to create, except for brief periods, a basis of mutual interest with the other Malayan nationals. At times, it is true, the movement has suffered from an excessive preoccupation with issues centered on China or in the resident Chinese communities—issues with little appeal for non-Chinese. More often, it has been hampered because the interests of Malays and Indians have been regarded as competitive with, rather than complementary to, those of the Malayan Chinese.

In order to gain perspective on recent activities of the Communist movements of Malaysia and Singapore, one must view the time line of developments in the region against this constant ethnic factor. In large part, one might conclude that Communist policies in the two states in the past five years have been a relatively direct response to the tide of events which reached its high point in the formation of the Malaysian Federation on September 16, 1963, and its low ebb in Malaysia's partial break-up in August 1965. Even the reaction of the Malayan Communists to the Sino-Soviet quarrel was explicable in terms of their felt need for the revolutionary instrument to be used against "neo-colonialism" or the threat of renewed Western domination most recently manifested in the American involvement in neighboring Thailand. Here, the natural inclination of the Communist Party of Malaya to side with the "parent" Chinese Party could be interpreted as simply reinforcing a position dictated by conditions prevailing in Malaysia and Singapore, and in Southeast Asia generally. It must be borne in mind, however, that the Communist response to current events is also heavily conditioned by events of the past; in particular, the Party's ability to react to the threat posed by Malaysia, as well as those from Thailand and Vietnam, has been severely circumscribed by its continued involvement in the "war of national liberation" launched in 1948. Communist movements in the two states, as distinguished from the Malayan Communist Party itself, are certainly less inhibited by prolonged involvement with the past. Nevertheless, the unresolved "war" has continued to place strictures on both Party and movements, as have the ruptures within the united front in Singapore, which began when the People's Action Party split in 1961.

It needs to be pointed out here that the Communist Party has always regarded Singapore as an integral part of Malaya and therefore has never distinguished organizationally, between the two. If its spokesmen did not accept the formation of Malaysia as valid, neither did they accept the subsequent separation of Singapore from the peninsula as having any reality. However, since the British had separated Singapore and Malaya for purposes of governance, and since, in addition, there have been important differences in the economic and social patterns of Singapore and the Malay states, the forms of Party activity on the two sides of the Causeway frequently diverged, from a fairly early date. There is, therefore, justification for talking about a movement in Singapore as distinct from that in the Federation, if one bears in mind that nominally they both serve one Party. In contrast, the Borneo states—designated by the government today as East Malaysia—have never been acknowledged by the Communists, or by the Socialist Front of Singapore, as a part of the Malayan state. The Communist movement there, which has assumed significant proportions only in Sarawak, and only in the last eight to ten years there, appears to have been assisted informally by the Singapore movement in the past but organizationally to be autonomous. Whether a Communist Party of Borneo actually exists is not clear even at the present time. The existence of a clandestine organization with avowed Communist purposes and with international Communist ties is amply documented, however, and evidence of the intent to form a Borneo Party was captured in 1959.

A BRIEF HISTORY OF THE COMMUNIST PARTY OF MALAYA

It appears that the Indonesian Communist, Tan Malaka, first brought Malaya to the attention of the Communist International. The first agent sent to work there, however, was reportedly a special representative of the Chinese Communist Party, Fu Ta Ching, who arrived in Singapore in 1925. Until the Kuomintang-Communist split in China in 1927, Communist activity in Singapore and Malaya took place under the umbrella of the local Kuomintang organs (which were themselves proscribed by the colonial government at that time). Following the split in China, Communist activity was not renewed among the overseas Chinese until early in 1928, when the Nanyang (i.e., South Seas) Communist Party was organized, with headquarters in Singapore, to direct activities in most of Southeast Asia.[1] Two years later, the Nanyang Party gave way to the Malayan Communist Party, which had jurisdiction chiefly in Malaya and Thailand. This new party was in turn virtually obliterated in 1931, as a result of police raids in Singapore which had repercussions throughout the Asian Communist movement. Nevertheless, by the mid-Thirties, the Malayan Communist Party, focusing—as the Malayan movement had from the beginning—on labor action, was again a force with which to reckon. Aided by the worldwide economic depression which had drastically curtailed Malay's export trade, Communist-led unions embarked on a program of militant strike activity which seriously embarrassed the colonial government; at one point, strikers even succeeded in establishing a workers' soviet at a coal mine in Selangor, which they held briefly.

The Japanese conquest of Manchuria, in 1931, marked the beginning of anti-Japanese activity among the Malayan Chinese, and the Communists attempted, from an early date, to capture the movement. The Party therefore had little difficulty in adjusting its aims, from 1935 onward, to conform with the Comintern's policy of a united front against imperialism. And it succeeded remarkably well in putting itself in the forefront of the anti-Japanese effort, in spite of the difficulties arising from its simultaneous anti-British activities. Significantly, it was on orders from the Chinese Communist Party that the efforts to obstruct the British war effort were abandoned, nine months *before* the Soviet Union was invaded.

Thus, when the Japanese took over Malaya, the attitude of the Malayan Communists was clearly defined, and their underground forces were therefore in a position to move more decisively than other nationalist movements in the area. It is generally conceded that, in 1945, they were in a position to command the postwar settlement. Their position was without parallel in Southeast Asia, but they did not choose to capitalize on the advantages they had gained during the war. The Party's failure to use these advantages to seize the governmental machinery and to block the return of the British has been the subject of much conjecture; generally it has been attributed to lack of direction from the international Communist movement and to indecisive leadership.[2] Whatever the reason, the blow which might have been struck in 1945 was delayed for almost three years while the Party, able to operate above ground for the first time, returned to open activities to strengthen its base. During this interval, there was a real attempt to link up with Malayan radicals to establish a multiracial party. It is true that the movement, which concealed the identity and whereabouts of its top leaders even from British liaison forces during the War, continued to maintain underground cadres and caches of arms during the brief period of its legal existence. Nonetheless, by the time the call for armed insurrections went out, the Communists had lost virtually all of the tactical advantage they enjoyed in 1945, and much of the popular support as well.

When the emergency began in June 1948, the aim of Party strategists, relying upon the writings of Mao Tse-tung, was to strike for a clear-cut victory and to avoid a war of attrition. In this, they seriously overestimated their own strength among the Malayan people, including the Chinese, and they seemingly underestimated the determination of the British. From the British standpoint, it was a costly campaign, involving not only the commitment of troops to treacherous jungle operations but also the resettlement of 450,000 Chinese—mostly squatters— from the edges of the jungles into new villages. This factor may have made the insurrection a success, from the point of view of the international Communist movement at that time.[3] From the viewpoint of the Malayan movement, however, it can only be rated a failure, since the British had the superior resources to win a war of attrition, whereas the guerrillas of the Malayan National Liberation Army,[4] increasingly cut off from sources of supply, had not. By 1951, the Party was admitting that the terrorist tactics had failed, and was stressing the need to rebuild popular support through techniques of persuasion.

By 1955, the Communists in Malaya recognized that they were about to lose the initiative they had once held in the independence struggle and upon which they counted heavily for popular support. Accordingly, the Party's Secretary General, Chen Ping, proposed a meeting with Tengku Abdul Rahman and other Malayan political leaders to negotiate an end to hostilities. The meeting, which took place at Baling in December, failed when the Tengku refused to accept the Communist terms. In 1957, an attempt by Chen Ping to reopen negotiations made even less headway.

Surprisingly, the Communist "war of national liberation" is still in progress. At least, the Central Committee of the Party commemorates the anniversary each year and, from time to time, proclaims to fraternal Parties its continued involvement in the armed struggle for independence. The Malayan government proclaimed the end of the emergency in 1960, but it admits the continued threat of the Liberation Army from its base on the Thailand border.

THE SINGAPORE COMMUNIST MOVEMENT

Although Singapore experienced its own Communist-inspired crises in the decade and a half before it joined Malaysia, it was not the scene of armed insurrection. Some Singapore Communists joined the guerrillas in the Malayan jungles, but others went underground to direct anti-British activity through various front organizations. Much of the unrest which characterized Singapore in the 1950's was fomented by the organizers of "general labor unions," a device which had been utilized by Communist agents for political purposes in Singapore since the 1920's. It is noteworthy, however, that after the War the Indians were active in the Party and in the labor front for the first time. And, at the intellectual level, the Party was joined by a number of Eurasians and Europeans who functioned largely through the Anti-British League. In addition, the Chinese middle schools played a key role in Communist action in the mid-Fifties, not only serving as a training ground for new cadres but also providing the base from which antigovernment riots were launched. Finally, when 14 persons were killed in the October 1956 riots, the elected government of Lim Yew Hock took steps to arrest the instigators and to dissolve some of the chief front organizations. In the following year, the government followed up with widespread arrests of subversives in labor organizations and in key positions in leftist Parties, and on this occasion it issued a command paper detailing the techniques and the extent of Communist penetration of united fronts, particularly of the People's Action Party (PAP), a radical left group.[5]

Victories for the People's Action Party at the polls in 1957 and in 1959, which carried with them the responsibilities of governing, contributed to a change in Communist tactics. Undoubtedly, the overdue realization that Singapore's future was in real jeopardy was also a factor on the side of change. As indicated earlier, the Communists—and most non-Communists in Singapore, also—had never recognized the island as having an existence apart from Malaya; and yet their excesses, as regards both labor and Chinese education and culture, created a real barrier to merger with the Federation. From 1957 onward, Singapore's Chinese could no longer hope to wrest favorable terms for Malayan union from the British but could only try to persuade the conservative Malay-dominated government of its wisdom. And to Kuala Lumpur, Singapore's record of extremism was anything but reassuring.

Paradoxically, at the same time that the PAP was achieving its greatest success at the polls, it was not only harassed from without by police action but also divided within on questions of leadership and on ultimate aims. Its stability as a political front appears to have rested less on the compatibility of the moderate and extreme left forces who comprised it than on the demands of political expediency, and these lost much of their validity once the PAP came to power. Lee Kuan Yew, the British-educated leader of the moderate faction, owed much of his own political ascendancy to his key position in the PAP at the time when Lim Chin Siong and other leaders of the militant left were detained and hence unable to stand in the 1959 elections. After the elections, Lee fulfilled his campaign promise of forcing the release of the detained men before he would form a government, but he did not, as some observers expected, pave the way for their reentry into politics. Instead, the Lee government moved steadily toward the day in 1961 when the left wing of the PAP withdrew, taking with it a major segment of the Party's labor support, to form the new *Barisan Sosialis*, or Socialist Front. And it has been chiefly from within the *Barisan*, again freed of any responsibility for governing, that Communist political action has taken place since the PAP split.

COMMUNIST ACTIVITY IN SARAWAK

Reportedly, some Communists who fled China at the time of the 1927 purge by the Kuomintang ultimately settled in Sarawak. There is no evidence, however, that such persons engaged in overt Communist activities there before the Japanese war. Moreover, in contrast with the major resistance effort of the Communists in Malaya, the effort against the Japanese of the Sarawak Anti-Fascist League was relatively insignificant. The Communist takeover on the Chinese mainland, however, provided the impetus for a wave of Communist activity in Sarawak which, assisted by local conditions and utilizing the independence issue, has reached substantial proportions. The current movement may be dated roughly from the formation of the Sarawak Overseas Chinese Democratic Youth League, in October 1951.

According to the colonial government, the Democratic Youth League was "poorly led by inexperienced men lacking in discipline, without direction and having sufficient knowledge of Communist theory to enable them to interpret and exploit any situation arising."[6] The League participated, from its inception, in student strikes and other provocative acts against the government, with the result that an emergency was proclaimed briefly in 1952 and a number of League leaders were either deported or fled to avoid arrest. However, although the League disintegrated, a nucleus of leadership remained to become the seasoned leaders of subsequent Communist groups. In 1954, the Sarawak Liberation League became the center for Communist indoctrination work, apparently to be superseded, from 1956 onward, by the Sarawak Advanced Youths' Association. The latter described itself in these terms:

A mass organization of the progressive elements, that will serve and struggle for the realization of complete freedom and democracy in Sarawak. All its members must energetically study and practice the theories of Marxism-Leninism and the ideology of Mao Tse-tung, and use them for the education of the masses and for elevating, with positiveness, the level of politics and ideology of ourselves and the masses with a view to becoming one of the proletarian elements.[7]

It is not known with any certainty whether the Communist Party of Borneo, which was in the blueprint stage in 1958 to 1959, was ever actually established or whether, as seems more probable, its formation was inhibited by the disclosures of government intelligence forces. The Sarawak Advanced Youths' Association is known to be in existence today, as is the North Kalimantan National Liberation League; and the Malaysian government designates the Youth Association as the Sarawak Communist Organization (SCO).

It is surely no accident that the Communist appeal in Sarawak was initially to the youth in the Chinese middle schools or that Communism continues to gain many recruits among this group today. For at a time when the proportion of Sarawak Chinese with middle-school education is rising rapidly, Sarawak—never a land of great opportunities—has had less and less to offer the educated youth, particularly those in the Chinese language stream. As a result, there have been large numbers of middle-school graduates who were either unemployed or not suitably employed; and there have been others who remained in school beyond the usual time because of the lack of employment opportunities, and who became the nuclei of subversive activities. Among educated Chinese youth, therefore, unrest and dissatisfaction with the prospects for the future have been high. Under the circumstances, it would be surprising if some of Sarawak's young Chinese did not see an escape from their own frustrations in the successes of Communist China or pin their hopes for a brighter future on the establishment of Chinese Communist hegemony in Sarawak.

As elsewhere, the Communists in Sarawak also undertook to penetrate the trade unions, concentrating particularly on this field of activity in 1958 and 1959. (In Kuching, for example, the goal for 1958 was to train 100 cadres and 500 additional activists.) In August 1961, the organization reported that the working masses had "stepped on the stage," and become the "mainstay for the direction of the socialist movement"; and the government concedes that the Communists control "large and predominantly Chinese Unions" in Sarawak.

Organizational efforts among the farmers are more recent. A decade ago, the Communists admitted that the farmers were not ready to be organized since they did not suffer from exploitation and oppression by landlords. Equally important, the peasantry in Sarawak, described in recent documents as "narrow-minded, selfish, conservative, believing in fatalism and entertaining some other ideological defects,"[8] were, by and large, not Chinese and therefore not particularly susceptible to recruitment by Chinese Communists. Nevertheless, by 1960, spurred on by its successes in education, labor, and politics, the organization undertook to organize the peasants into a Farmers Association, a move which specifically received the imprimatur of Peking.[9] Although the Council Negri (i.e., State Council) refused to register the Association on the grounds that it was a Communist front, and although it had negligible success among the 85 per cent of the farmers who are not Chinese, it has continued to function underground and appears to have made some headway among Chinese farmers, who have a number of genuine grievances. (The government's discriminatory policy in the allocation of lands, for instance, has been felt particularly by Chinese smallholders in rubber in the Third Division, where population growth, declining yields, and slumping rubber prices have contributed to economic stagnation since the end of the Korean War boom.)

Politically, the Communists of Sarawak launched their major effort in 1959, when they supported the effort of a number of prominent Sarawak Chinese to organize the Sarawak United People's Party (SUPP), the first political party in the colony. Although the men who organized the Party were in most instances professionals and property owners, and not extremists in their political views, the Communists were able to infiltrate it quite extensively by making use of their student and trade union support. Moreover, although the moderates of the SUPP (like Ong Kee Hui, who is its Chairman and President of the Kuching City Council) have been increasingly disturbed over their inability to give direction to the Party, they have continued to cooperate with the radical left—perhaps partly in the hope that they may regain control, but also because they share its views on a number of questions affecting the Chinese community. For a number of reasons, Singapore's withdrawal—or ouster—from Malaysia constituted such a question.

STRENGTH AND ORGANIZATION

The Federation and the Thai Border Area

When the Malayan National Liberation Army (MNLA) found itself increasingly hard-pressed by the British military effort in 1953 and 1954, it shifted its operations northward, finally digging in along the Thai-Malayan border. Here in mountainous jungle terrain, virtually impenetrable by conventional police operations, Chen Ping and the Party Secretariat established their headquarters. And it is here, on the Thai side of the boundary, that the Communist Party of Malaya (CPM) has established a "geographical terrain," an area over which it exercises considerable control. Some observers, indeed, regard this region as having almost reached the stage of a "liberated area." By this move, the Party leadership secured itself and its revolutionary arm against continuous harassment by military and police forces of the Malayan government. Moreover, although the Thai and Malayan governments have mounted joint offensives from time to time to flush out the terrorist army, the MNLA's policy has been, at least until very recently, to avoid contact when possible, so that these joint operations have produced negligible results. Indeed, from 1963 to 1965, it appeared probable that even these operations would shortly cease. In the absence of evidence that the fugitive forces intended to disrupt peace and order in the country where they were domiciled, the Thailand government adopted the view that the joint border control no longer served a useful purpose, in spite of Malaysian efforts to convince them otherwise. However, since the stepped-up campaign by the Communists in Northeast Thailand, the Thai government has shown renewed interest in eliminating those operating on its border with Malaysia. Indeed, following indications in June 1968 that the border insurgents were reverting to armed struggle at Peking's instigation, the Thai and Malaysian governments have made a concerted effort to root out the border elements. Significantly, in December 1968, Thailand agreed, for the first time, to the use of airplanes against jungle positions on her side of the line.

In this border area, the number of known Communists, these so-called charted terrorists, number between 500 and 600 men. However, they have unquestionably built up considerable support among the Thais in the area (particularly those of Chinese extraction), on whom they rely both for supplies and intelligence. Additionally, the Malaysia government has claimed that up to 1,000 youths in the border area have had guerrilla training and constitute a reserve force. It should be borne in mind however, that the chief propaganda efforts of the Communist Party are directed not at the Thais, since active subversion would jeopardize the Party's base of operations, but across the border at Malaya.

If the isolation of the jungles north of the Thai border provides highly effective cover from a security standpoint, it is less than ideal as the nerve center of underground activities in the Malay states. Intelligence gathered during the emergency indicated that even at the height of Communist activity in the Federation, there were delays of up to a year in the transmittal of directives from headquarters to regional commands and to the units in the field. At the present time, it would appear that the communications network has been almost completely disrupted and that local Communist activity in the Federation originates in the satellite organizations or in local cells and lacks central direction. Some propaganda is, of course, disseminated from the border area, chiefly into the adjacent states, and according to government sources, there has been at least one recent campaign to orient, briefly, selected representatives of socialist front Parties in the border area itself. It is also known that some communications are transmitted through the regular mails, since these are not easy to check on. In the absence of sustained recruitment and indoctrination efforts within the states, however, the propaganda and study materials emanating from the border are probably no more effective and much less certain than those emanating from Communist China itself. It would, in fact, be reasonable to assume that Communist organs in Malaya and Singapore currently depend far more on Peking for guidance than they do on the Party leaders along the Thai border.[10]

Communist strength in the Federation, then, is extremely scattered, with known Communists and activists centered chiefly around the capital, in Penang, and in urban centers in Johore, Negri Sembilan, and similar places. Some 500 persons are known to be members of the underground satellite organizations. However, since they are under close police surveillance and their contacts are closely watched, the scope of their activities is severely circumscribed and the opportunities for them to enlarge their spheres of influence are very limited. It is generally conceded that these men are engaged in watchful waiting and that they are a threat only if external conditions shift in their favor.

The Communist Party of Malaya underwent extensive reorganization shortly before, and no doubt preparatory to, the talks at Baling in 1955. Since that time there appears to have been no formal reorganization, although the constriction of the Party's effective sphere of activity has undoubtedly induced practical changes. Under the 1955 reorganization, Chen Ping was confirmed as Secretary-General; a Malay, Musa Ahmad, was named Chairman; and an Indian, Balan, was named Vice-Chairman. (Balan had been under detention at that time for seven years, however.) Yeong Kuo, who remained behind when the Party moved to the border, was named Vice-Secretary to Chen Ping. Balan renounced Communism when he was subsequently released, and Yeong Kuo was killed in 1956. Chen Ping and Musa Ahmad, however, apparently continue to hold the same positions in the Party hierarchy today, although Central Committee documents are no longer issued in their names as they were until five or six years ago.

The Central Committee, which once had from 11 to 15 members, probably now consists of 10 or less. Whether all the Central Committee is in the border zone, or whether part of it is in China, is not known. It is highly likely, however, that Committee members with prior experience in China have returned there and serve in a liaison capacity to the People's Republic. (One Politburo member, Li On Tung, was believed to have gone to China in 1953, and several years later was reported to be back in south Thailand with Chen Ping.) The Political Bureau, which appears to be the only functioning organ of the Central Committee, certainly consists of Chen Ping and no more than two or three close associates. It is doubtful if an organization bureau exists at all; if it does, it is probably identical with the Politburo. Of two Departments of Work set up at the time of the move to the border, one, the Indian Department, no longer exists. The Department of Malay Work, however, appears to be quite active, and it is believed today to be achieving greater results among the Malays than had been achieved at any previous time in the history of the Malayan Communist movement.

The Malayan National Liberation Army, which formerly consisted of 12 regiments—none of which was full regimental strength—is now reduced to 3: the Eighth, or west, regiment; the Twelfth, or central, regiment; and the Tenth, in the east. The Tenth, which was originally the Malay regiment—composed of Malays backed up by Chinese cadres —now serves as the Department of Malay Work. Chen Ping, whose rise in the Communist movement during the Japanese war was attributable to his contribution as a strategist in the Malayan People's Anti-Japanese Army (MPAJA), is no doubt still Supreme Commander of the Malayan National Liberation Army. This is conjecture, however, as is much that is said about the forces operating from within Thailand.[11]

Organizationally, Malaya was formerly divided into three regions— northern, central, and southern, each under the direction of a Party Bureau. With the disruption of the Communist movement in the Federation, however, none of these has any significance today except the northern region, which included Penang, Perak, Kedah, and Kelantan. In recent years, this Northern Bureau has been superseded by two Border Committees—the Penang-Kedah committee, which serves the western extremity of the border, and the Kelantan-Perak committee, which functions on the eastern extremity. The propaganda function of the Party, which apparently comes under the border committees, is in the hands of Chen Tien, a close associate of Chen Ping, for whom he served as interpreter at Baling.

Since 1965, much of the external propaganda work of the Malayan Communist Party has been carried on by "missions" of the Malayan National Liberation League—in Djakarta in 1965, and in Peking since January 1966. The League, described by the Malaysian government as the political arm of the CPM, celebrated its eighteenth anniversary on February 1, 1967, although the uninterrupted existence from 1949 of such an organization can be seriously doubted.

Singapore

The size of the Communist movement in Singapore is more difficult
to assess, both because conclusive evidence of Communist involvement
is often lacking and because the distinction between the Communists and
other groups with similar aims and sympathies is blurred. Communist
leaders have apparently solved part of their problem of eluding the police
by virtually eliminating their records and files—at least in Singapore—
and as a consequence, the documents which would link specific persons
to the Communist network in many cases do not exist. Moreover, in the
propaganda field, popular front materials have almost entirely replaced
the proscribed Communist publications which once constituted a significant part of the evidence of Communist activity. At the same time,
Communism has been allied in Singapore with a number of more or less
popular causes—the end of British rule, propagation of Chinese education
and culture, Malayan union (as opposed to Malaysian federation), guarantees for labor, and improved standards for welfare—and it would certainly serve no useful purpose to lump together all those who espouse
these causes under the label of Communists or even Communist sympathizers. What makes the line even more difficult to draw is the presence
in Singapore of large numbers of Chinese, chiefly in the Chinese language
stream, who admire and take pride in the achievements of Communist
China. Communism and Chinese chauvinism are not the same thing, but
they are not always easy to distinguish when they serve the same causes.
     Intelligence sources document a number of "known Communists"
on the basis of dossiers dating back many years, although in some cases
they do not know either the whereabouts or the present activities of
these persons. The rolls of those who have, from time to time, been
detained under the Preservation of Public Security Ordinance (PPSO),
give some clue to the identities of known and suspected Communists, but
it must be borne in mind that the government does not allege that all of
these are guilty of Communist activities. Rather it describes those held
under preventive detention—at times in recent years in excess of 200—
as Communists and Communist sympathizers;[12] but security agents also
suggest that some roundups of leftists have been aimed at crushing the
united front rather than at curbing strictly Communist activity. The
Malaysian Minister of Internal Security, late in 1963, claimed the existence of a "well-established network of underground Communist cadres
in Singapore."[13] Today, Singapore officials dispute the existence of such a
network, at least operating within the state, although they admit that
there are at least several hundred Communist activists serving in the
open front. (Security agencies are reluctant to even speculate on the
number of persons in Singapore who could be said to deliberately and

actively serve the Communist cause.) How effective the Malaysian and Singapore governments have been in reducing Communist strength in Singapore by actions directed against left-wing unions and rural associations, by purges within the Chinese schools, and by arrests of persons connected with Nanyang University and of *Barisan Sosialis* leaders is even now not clear. Lim Chin Siong—detained without trial since February 1963—offered Singapore's militant left a quality of leadership which Dr. Lee Siew Choh, the present *Barisan* leader, apparently does not possess. Additionally, differences among the *Barisan's* elected representatives on tactical questions have split the movement and kept it, at times, from rallying effective opposition to the PAP government. Whether or not the Front's decision, in 1966, to abandon the role of opposition in Parliament in favor of the struggle in the streets—a move which cannot be separated from the struggle taking place in China—was a sound one remains to be seen. Although security officials tend to deprecate the strength of the radical left in Singapore today, they admit that the underground has shown a high degree of resourcefulness and flexibility in adjusting to changes in circumstances in the past. Reflecting its concern on the security question, the PAP government has continued, by repressive measures, to tighten its control over education and over labor.

Organizationally, then, the Singapore movement appears to have been, for several years, in a state of flux. When the Southern Bureau was still functioning, Singapore was nominally under it, together with Johore, but Singapore undoubtedly exercised a great deal of autonomy in Party affairs even then. The Town Committee, which directed activity in Singapore when the CPM enjoyed legal existence, was destroyed by police action around 1951. Until the recent military takeover in Indonesia, direction of the Singapore movement apparently derived from the underground, with key personnel operating from the comparative safety of the Rhio Islands and only entering the city for brief periods.[15] (It is possible, because of the remoteness of the Rhios from Djakarta, that there are still Singapore Communists operating from there.) In recent years, those serving in the open front have generally maintained no contacts with the underground, even if they once served in it, and rules against illegal printed matter have been rigidly enforced on front premises. Nevertheless, as a result of the deregistration of the radical leftist Singapore Association of Trades Unions (SATU) in 1963, and simultaneous actions taken against the *Barisan* and other components of the united front, it appeared for a time that the front itself might be superseded. In early 1964, there were indications that mass action was being abandoned and that underground satellite organizations, formed along functional lines, would be set up to direct above-ground activities in the various fields. By 1967, however, it was clear that street action had again become a major part of the struggle. How much underground direction this activity received was in doubt; here, as in other parts of Southeast Asia, the exhortations of Radio Peking were sufficient to account for at least a part of the disturbances which occurred.

Sarawak

In Sarawak a third set of conditions obtains. Since few restrictions were placed on Chinese-language activities until 1963 and supervision of these was slight, the precautions taken by the Communists to conceal underground work were not very thorough and even above-ground publications often advanced the Peking line. Moreover, although the Sarawak government acted, in the last few years of British rule, to eradicate Communist subversion, substantial quantities of Communist propaganda materials and a number of documents continued in circulation, being found frequently on persons detained for questioning. Beginning in the middle of 1963, there was new evidence of Communist activity. Ammunition and home-made guns were seized, and small groups of Chinese youths, hiding in huts on the jungle fringe while undergoing indoctrination, were captured. Sarawak Chinese youths, trained in guerrilla warfare in Kalimantan, also participated in raids on border villages and in skirmishes with security forces. This latter force, still operating on the Kalimantan-Sarawak border in 1967, apparently with some logistic support from Chinese in the area, was equipped with Sten guns, grenades, and substantial quantities of ammunition.

An Indonesian officer claimed, in 1963, that approximately 1,600 Sarawak youths had been trained in Kalimantan, although some of these undoubtedly belonged to non-Communist rebel groups such as Azahari's *Tentera Nasional Kalimantan Utara* (TNKU).[16] A campaign undertaken by the Malaysian government, in July and August 1966, to induce insurrectionists to surrender and bring in their weapons, resulted in the surrender of some non-Communist remnants but produced negligible results among the Communists. How many of the latter returned to their homes without surrendering is, however, only a matter of conjecture. Since confrontation has ended, and particularly since August 1967, when diplomatic relations between Malaysia and Indonesia were restored, Indonesia has made some effort to aid Malaysia in rooting out guerrilla elements dug in on the Kalimantan side of the border. An Indonesian general has estimated these at four to five hundred, although there were some reports that "Chinese Communist guerrillas" from elsewhere were shifting to the Pontianak area to augment the local Communists.[17] In mid-1967, Malaysian official sources placed the total number of insurrectionists in the field—that is, on both sides of the border—at between seven hundred and one thousand, and they estimated the number of active Communists in Sarawak at somewhere between one thousand and fifteen hundred. (As of May 31, there were 737 persons detained under the PPSO in the two Borneo states, but admittedly a number of these were not Communists.) In addition, the government estimated that there were from fifteen to twenty thousand open front activists operating in East Malaysia, almost all of whom were centered in the cities of Kuching, Sibu, and Miri, in Sarawak.

Although Sarawak's militants have gained some experience in guerrilla operations and in underground activities since 1963, it should be observed that these are not the veteran revolutionaries of the Thai border area nor the hard-core Communists who have been tested in Singapore's jails. As we indicated earlier, the Sarawak Communist organization apparently has had no official ties with either the Malayan Communist Party or the Communist Party of Indonesia (PKI). Unofficially, however, the Sarawak movement, which the government describes as "100 per cent Chinese," is much closer to the Chinese and Singapore Communists than it ever was to the PKI. On questions of internal organization, there is evidence that the Sarawak Communists have utilized the works of Mao Tse-tung and Liu Shao-chi on organization and strategy, some of which were used by the Communists in Malaya 15 to 20 years ago.[18]

According to reports of the Sarawak government,[19] the Communist organization is directed by a Central Committee which operates through four Departments of Work: namely, Labor Movement, Peasantry, Students, and Political Party. (In 1956, there were also sections for Racial Work and Literature and Culture.) As in Communist organizations elsewhere, a Political Bureau and an Organization Bureau function within, and give direction to, the Central Committee. The pyramidal structure, which adheres to the principle of democratic centralism, moves upward from cells, to branches, to district committees, to area and town committees, to divisional committees, to the Central Committee at the top. In addition, and coinciding with the appearance of the Malayan National Liberation League Mission in Indonesia, a North Kalimantan National Liberation League made its appearance in Sarawak, apparently with the same object, that of creating the impression of a popular front against colonialism. On the military side, the "people's forces" were designated as the *Pasokan Guerrilla Rakyat Sarawak* (PGRS).

Considerable evidence has been amassed concerning the operation of the *hsueh-hsih* or study cells which constituted a major phase of the Communist program during the organizational period; the reproduction and transmission of documents and study materials; the selection, training, and recruitment of cadres; and the periodic purges, of which there have been at least three. There is some evidence also of the relationship between the underground and the open front; in Sarawak, unlike Singapore, a number of key individuals are known to have occupied positions at both levels. It does not appear, however, that the government knows with certainty either the identities of the persons who fill the key slots in the organization or the way in which they function. A few high-level people were removed earlier by detention or deportation, and the labor and political fronts have been damaged by police action. Nevertheless, it appears doubtful that much headway has been made against the underground, and it is probable that no documentary evidence concerning organizational structure and personnel exists today.

THE COMMUNIST LEADERSHIP IN MALAYSIA AND SINGAPORE

In its early days, the Malayan Communist movement was forced to rely on leadership from outside the area—frequently, as we have seen, with disastrous results. Later, the Party came to depend on locally trained leaders, although these were augmented from time to time by revolutionaries from China. Within Singapore and the Federation, there were two main streams from which leadership was recruited—the trade-union movement and the Chinese middle schools. Of these, the schools proved to be the more rewarding source for the top echelons of the Party: according to a Party document,[20] 60 per cent of those who have risen to Central Committee rank came to the Party by way of the student movement, and this trend was only slightly less evident on the second rung of leadership. It should be observed, however, that these two streams are not mutually exclusive: A significant number of labor leaders, such as Lim Chin Siong, were not bona fide unionists but rather Party men or united front men directed into labor organization.

There was, in addition, a group within the Singapore leadership from 1950 onward, not numerous but conspicuous, who were English-educated. Most of these were non-Chinese who entered Communist ranks by way of student action at the university, and frequently, also by way of the anticolonialist front organizations. One of these was P. V. Sarma, an Indian expelled from Singapore in 1952, who has recently emerged as head of the Malayan National Liberation League (MNLL) mission in Peking. These organizations, particularly the Malayan Democratic Union and the PUTERA–All Malayan Council for Joint Action, were also the source for what Malayan leadership the movement acquired. On the whole, however, the Malays, even those with radical predilections, inclined toward the Indonesian nationalist movement rather than toward the Malayan Communists.[21]

There were few Malayan Communist leaders, then, without some middle-school education, although the number who completed senior middle school would not seem to have been very high. (Some were expelled for their political activities before they completed their studies. These included such men as Siew Chong, who became a Politburo member and is probably now in China, and Chiam Chung Him, variously identified as a courier and as a high-ranking official in the Singapore underground.) A few of those with Chinese education also had a little English education; these were found chiefly in Singapore. Most of the Communist leaders attended school in the Federation or in Singapore—and some in both places—although a significant number were educated in China.

Generally the leadership had its origins in the lower middle class—that is, their parents were small shopkeepers, at least able to provide some education for their children. Chen Ping's father, for example, owned a bicycle shop in Sitiawan, and Lim Chin Siong's father has a sundries store in Singapore. A few Party officials have come from the propertied class: Wu Tien Wang, a Singapore town committee member who represented the Party at the empire Communist conference in London in 1947 was a member of a proprietary family in Sitiawan;[22] and Eu Chooi Yip, also a former member of the Singapore town committee, who emerged from the underground in 1965 as a member of the MNLL mission in Djakarta, was the son of a landed proprietor, too. At the other extreme, a few Party leaders have come from extremely poor economic circumstances and have themselves been employed at very menial tasks. The parents of Lam Tat, who was a Politburo member before he was killed in 1960, were hawkers; Lam himself was a member of the Democratic Servants Union, and is believed to have been employed as a cook or a manservant to a European family before the War, about the time he affiliated with the Party. Another prominent Communist, active in the Malayan Races Liberation Army (MRLA) in Negri Sembilan at the time he was killed in 1956, worked as a cook and houseboy for the manager of a large oil palm corporation in Johore before the Japanese invasion.

The local Chinese have been of greater value to the movement than those born elsewhere, because they were more familiar with local conditions and also less exposed and therefore less vulnerable than their counterparts born and educated abroad. But they have been handicapped in the quality of their education. Standards in the Chinese schools in Sarawak and in the Federation have been deplorably low, and they are only somewhat better in Singapore. The Malaysian-born Communists have also suffered in the quality of their Party indoctrination and training, because the Party has never been able to maintain free communication with more flourishing parties elsewhere. On the other hand, the China-born Communists have never been more than a limited asset to the movement because of their extreme vulnerability. Unlike the Malaysian-born worker who could be arrested, serve a few years in jail, and return as an experienced veteran, the China-born Communist was liable to deportation at the first sign of questionable political activity.

In spite of this, there have been a number of China-born Chinese who have occupied critical positions in the Communist movement in Singapore, in the Federation, and in Sarawak. Probably because of their superior education, a high proportion of these served in some aspect of the public opinion or communications fields. Few are left in Malaysia today, but a number are known to serve in Peking as advisers on overseas affairs or in a liaison capacity for the Malayan Communist Party. Li On Tung, who was born in China but brought to Singapore at an early age, became a Party member in 1935, a Central Committee member in 1946, a member of the Politburo by 1948. Li, who was responsible for propaganda in the Party, reportedly left for China in 1953 but apparently returned to the border area where he now serves with the Secretary-General's group.

Two men, apparently China-born and educated, who edited the Party-controlled *Min Siang Pao* in Kuala Lumpur between 1945 and 1948 and were members of the Central Committee, now serve in Peking. Lam Fong Sing, a veteran newspaper editor,[23] appeared in China as early as 1951, where he was assigned as Assistant Director of the South Seas Research House attached to the Commission on Overseas Chinese Affairs. Liew Yit Fun, a Eurasian who was detained in 1948 and deported in 1955, was assigned to the Chinese Party's United Front Work Department. Another prominent Malayan Communist who was born in China and apparently received some education there was Lu Cheng, who commanded the 4th Regiment of the MPAJA and was active in the Communist-dominated labor front before his deportation in 1946. In China, he subsequently worked with the propaganda section of the All-China General Labor Union. Later he joined the Communist Party of Malaya's Representative Group in China and for some years has been prominent in overseas Chinese affairs in Peking. The Malayan Group in China, incidentally, was joined in 1962 by a half-dozen Sarawak Chinese who were either deported or who requested permission to leave after being placed under restricted residence orders. These included Wen Ming Chuan, the editor of *Sin Wen Pau* of Kuching and an Assistant Secretary-General of the SUPP, and Bong Ki Chok and his wife, both officials of the SUPP, in whose possession was found a quantity of Chinese Communist documents.

It is hardly surprising that J. H. Brimmell found the leaders of the Malayan insurrection, whom he described as "much inferior to Mao and his associates," lacking in efficiency, adaptability, and finesse.[24] Chen Ping, like most of his colleagues, was deficient in formal education and limited in his understanding of the realities of the Communist revolution in China, which he tried to imitate in Malaya; apparently his outside contacts were confined to a few months' residence in Hong Kong not long after the Japanese War.[25] Whether the CPM leaders have been able to remedy their deficiencies during their exile in Thailand is not clear. They have apparently learned the value of caution, and reports indicate that they have gained valuable experience in working among the Malay peasantry. (The head of the MNLL mission in Djakarta, Ibrahim Muhammad, was a former member of the Department of Malay Work; however, detention of the mission by the Indonesian government between November 1965 and January 1967 makes it difficult to draw any conclusions about its members.) At the same time, however, their isolation from outside contacts have been reinforced and their ranks depleted. And it appears unlikely that any substantial leadership group has been developed within the reserves of the border area.

The problems of leadership in Singapore, although somewhat less acute than on the peninsula, have steadily grown. For a decade, defections in the non-Chinese sector have been high, with the result that this phase of activity seems to be at a standstill. Within the Chinese movement, defections have been somewhat lower, although the number of detainees opting for "Hollywood contracts"[26] to secure release has increased sharply in the last year or so. The substantial pool of potential leaders coming from Nanyang and the Chinese middle schools has undoubtedly dwindled as a result of continued government pressure on both schools and students. But it continues to exist.

The evidence is too fragmentary to allow a proper evaluation of the quality of leadership in Sarawak. Undoubtedly, many of the Sarawak Party officials suffer from the same handicaps that the insurrectionary leaders in Malaya did and, even today, they are far less schooled in terrorist tactics than their Malayan counterparts were in 1948. Nevertheless, it appears that their indoctrination has been quite thorough and at times they have had the advantage of fairly substantial assistance from outside.

Ironically, the cream of the Malaysian Communist leadership appears to be in none of these places, but in China itself, where the top echelon of the Malayan Communist movement may render valuable services to the overseas movement but certainly cannot provide the essential day-to-day direction.

RECENT COMMUNIST POLICY IN MALAYSIA

The Campaign for a Patriotic Front

We noted earlier that, from 1951 onward, the Communist Party of Malaya recognized that armed insurrection was not achieving its objectives and therefore initiated a campaign of mass action intended to regain popular support. This campaign, carried out by the *Min Yuen*, or civil arm of the Liberation Army, undertook to infiltrate "grey" organizations, to build new organs of support, and to foster the idea of a national united front against imperialism. Secret documents of this period indicate that the Party was not abandoning its reliance on armed struggle but, rather, seeking mass support for it.

The peace feelers of 1955[27] which led to the Baling talks were a tacit admission that the armed struggle could not much longer serve a useful purpose. The failure of the talks at Baling constituted a failure to effect the united front with patriotic elements which Chen Ping sought and it denied to the Communists the opportunity to move from illegal and secret, to open and legal, forms of struggle.

By 1960, the Malayan Communist Party and the Liberation Army were still committed to the two-pronged policy of violent struggle to be undertaken side-by-side with legal and open struggle where possible. The Party continued at this time, however, to advocate an end to hostilities and to seek popular support to compel the Malayan government to negotiate. And it insisted that it had made numerous efforts in recent years to reopen peace talks, all of which had been sabotaged by the British. Indeed, at this point the Communists were insistent that the British had started the war and that all Malayan political parties wished to see it ended—by negotiations between the "opposing forces locked in armed conflict," and without foreign interference of any kind. Recognition of the "right of self-determination" for all Malayans, including Communist Party and MNLA personnel, was also to be a condition for any negotiations.[28]

In one of the important policy papers of 1960, Musa Ahmad, on the thirtieth anniversary of the founding of the Malayan Communist Party, reiterated the five points of the Party's 1957 program. This appears to be the most recent program formulated by the Party, and apparently is still considered valid today:

1. Strengthen and safeguard the independent status of our country; pursue an independent and self-determined foreign policy of peace and neutrality; establish diplomatic relations with all countries; oppose war and uphold peace; refrain from joining any military bloc; unite and cooperate with Afro-Asian countries; strive for the reunification of Singapore with the Federation of Malaya.
2. Foster unity and mutual support among the Malays, Chinese and Indians, etc. with the Malays as the pivot; protect the legitimate rights and interests of the various nationalities in the country.
3. Safeguard the democratic rights and liberties of the people; release all patriotic prisoners; extend legal status to all political parties and public organizations which pledge loyalty to the Malayan fatherland.

4. Protect and develop national industries, agriculture and commerce; improve and develop culture; enforce universal education and ameliorate the living conditions of the people.

5. Terminate the war; repeal the Emergency Regulations and restore internal peace.[29]

It should be noted, however, that the thesis of Musa Ahmad's statement was that the Alliance government was thwarting this program by adopting policies hostile to China and other socialist and Afro-Asian countries, by disciminatory policies aimed at the Chinese and Indians (and poor Malays), by creating myths about the Communist threat, and by protecting feudal interests and encouraging foreign monopoly capitalists.

A manifesto issued on the fourth anniversary of the Baling talks shows clearly the emphasis of the Party's propaganda efforts through 1960. The Baling talks had failed because all nationalities of the country had not developed a broad enough patriotic and anti-imperialist national united front based on a worker-peasant alliance. The manifesto therefore called on:

. . . people of all nationalities and strata, irrespective of their political affiliations, political views and religious beliefs, to unite under the banner of the patriotic and anti-imperialist united front and strive unflinchingly for bringing an end to the anti-people's colonial war, for attaining complete national independence, for realizing full democratic rights and for reunifying Singapore with the Federation of Malaya.[30]

The Communists denied that events were going against them at this time. The *Malayan Monitor* insisted that the National Liberation Army had continued to strike hard at the imperialists in 1960 and that the Party's policy and line of action had been vindicated in the important advances made by the national liberation movement. The *Monitor* outlined two objectives for 1961: (1) continued struggle for national liberation, unification, peace, and democracy through a united front; and (2) "fighting for a clear-cut anti-imperialist foreign policy," again along united front lines.[31]

It should be observed that, in spite of the Party's protestations, its terms for ending the armed conflict were hardly a measure of its negotiating strength at that time. Even if the government had been willing to amnesty the guerrillas who surrendered, there was little reason for expecting that it would accord legal status to the Malayan Communist Party or rights of self-determination to Liberation Army personnel. One may conjecture that Party spokesmen were well aware of this and used the campaign to end hostilities more for its propaganda value than in the expectation of achieving peace. However, it is significant that, with the development of the Malaysia controversy in 1961, the Party ceased to call for the cessation of the armed struggle, although it did step up its campaign for an even broader front against imperialism and neocolonialism.

The Threat of Malaysia

The issue of Malaysia has been intimately tied in with the question of the delicate balance of Malays and Chinese in the Federation and the anticipated effect upon this balance of the addition of Singapore's predominantly Chinese population. This threat to racial balance weighed heavily with the Federation's conservative leadership against direct union, as did also the extremist nature of Singapore politics. On the other hand, Singapore's vulnerability, both economically and militarily, argued strongly for *some* type of political union with the Federation as an alternative to independence as a city-state.

The Alliance government in Kuala Lumpur viewed uneasily the prospects of having an independent Singapore, perhaps under Peking's influence, as an immediate neighbor, and the Malayans were extremely cool to the campaign in Singapore for reunification. In Singapore, however, there was no significant segment of the population which opposed merger. The possibility that independence might well mean the severing of all economic and political ties with Malaya was one that even the militant left-wing Chinese could view only with dismay, however much they might resent the alternative of Malay hegemony.

The break within the ruling People's Action Party in Singapore came, then, not on the issue of Singapore's joining the Federation but on the nature and extent of the concessions which the Lee government was to grant to gain merger. A Malaysian federation in which Sarawak, North Borneo, and Brunei were to serve as counterbalances to Singapore was Tengku Abdul Rahman's answer to appeals that Singapore be allowed entry in the Malay federation. Even this was not to constitute a direct merger of the five territories, however. Instead, Singapore was to be granted autonomy in certain fields, and some concessions were to be made to her in regard to economics and finance. In return, however, her citizens were to be denied the privileges of citizenship in other parts of Malaysia, and Singapore's representation in the federal parliament was to be scaled down considerably compared to that of other parts of the projected federation. It was over these terms of merger that Singapore's militant left parted company with Lee Kuan Yew and the PAP and set up a new Party and a new trade union federation, the Singapore Association of Trades Unions (SATU).[32] In the fight over Malaysia which followed, Lim Chin Siong and the *Barisan Sosialis* were able to gain a substantial following, not only among the Communists and others of the militant left, but also among non-English-speaking, non-Communist Chinese upon whose fears for the future the Communist leadership was able to capitalize. Significantly, the Front also gained allies among the Sarawak Chinese and in the Brunei Party *Ra'ayat*, and—for different reasons—in the Indonesian government.

It was not until several days after the new Federation was inaugurated that the Malayan Communist Party issued a statement on Malaysia. At this time, the Party took a stand vigorously opposing Malaysia as a neocolonialist intrigue, and supported the people of "North Kalimantan" in "their sacred right to national self-determination," thereby giving CPM approval to the Borneo separatist movement.[33] However, the Communist position had been earlier defined by the *Malayan Monitor*, which treated the new Federation as not merely a British plot but also as one in a complex series of intrigues by the imperialists to "extend their global anti-Communist anti-national liberation, anti-national sovereignty and anti-peace bloc." Specifically, the Bangkok headquarters of the Southeast Asian Treaty Organization (SEATO) had ordered the setting up of the Association of Southeast Asia as a link with "Rahman's 'Greater Malaysia' alignment."[34] Nor was this the full extent of the intrigue; for "Japanese 'Panzers' . . . armed and nurtured by American imperialists in Okinawa for 'duties' in Southeast Asia" were ready to move, apparently to infiltrate the Asian Common Market.

The "popular demand for genuine reunification" of Malaya, the *Monitor* contended, contained somewhat different ingredients:

Unite all forces in both territories of Malaya [i.e., the Malayan Federation and Singapore] to secure the immediate withdrawal of all foreign military forces; the dismantling of all foreign bases; the abolition of the imperialist-dominated "War Council" in the Malayan Federation and of the "Internal Security Council" in Singapore; and dissociation of both territories of Malaya from SEATO and all its adjuncts; the scrapping of the unequal humiliating and extremely dangerous "Treaty of Military Alliance and Mutual Assistance" between Britain and the Malayan Federation; the abolition of the so-called "Internal Security" legislation imposed by the imperialists on both territories of Malaya.[35]

This program of struggle was to lead to a new national constitution guaranteeing "all political Parties and individuals the right to elect a national Parliament" and the rights of freedom of speech, assembly, organization, and publication.

During the two years which elapsed between the Lee-Rahman talks and the realization of Malaysia in September 1963, the Communist mood fluctuated between outrage at the fresh indignities which the imperialists were attempting to perpetrate and elation at the difficulties which Malaysia encountered. There was consternation over the split within the PAP, particularly over Lee Kuan Yew's exposé of the militant left as Communist-led. Faced with a "new 'monster' called the People's Socialist

Front," the *Monitor* said, Lee wanted "to 'prove' that the Front is 'Red'; everybody opposing him is 'Red'."[36] Consternation mounted in November 1961, when the initial merger agreement was signed in London, with its extension of the existing United Kingdom-Federation defenses agreement. This agreement, it was said, had extended the foreign military occupation of Malaya, intensified the "joint Rahman–Commonwealth–SEATO operations" against the Malayan and Bornean liberation movements and increased the "cynical use" by the Malayan government of racial antagonisms.[37] Later it was charged that the Malaysia plan would not only stir up racial troubles by setting Malay Malayans against Chinese Malayans but also encourage chauvinism by arrogantly imposing the "imperialist 'greater nation' dictate on the people of the 3 Borneo territories."[38]

Neither the Communists nor the People's Socialist Front in Singapore could draw much comfort from the results of the plebiscite held in Singapore, in September 1962, on the merger agreement. The *Monitor* was, however, able to cite the editorial opinion of the *London Times* in support of its contention that there was not, properly speaking, a referendum on the agreement at all. As for the *Barisan*, Lim Chin Siong announced that it would not accept the results of the "sham referendum," since it did not reflect the true wishes of the people, whom the government had intimidated.[39]

The involved series of events, which commenced with the abortive Brunei rebellion in December 1962 and climaxed with the Manila summit conference at the end of July in the following year, was generally received as evidence that the east wind was indeed prevailing. The elation of the anti-imperialists was somewhat subdued, however, following the large-scale arrests in Singapore in February 1963, which led to the detention of Lim Chin Siong, Fong Swee Suan, and many other top officials in the *Barisan* and the SATU unions and of a number of Nanyang University students and graduate officers. The Communists, from the Thai border[40] to Peking, hailed the Brunei rebellion as a genuine national liberation effort directed against the neocolonial Malaysia intrigue[41] and, as such, requiring the support of all fellow anticolonialists. Indonesia's confrontation of Malaya, and subsequently of Malaysia, was welcomed as the courageous reaction of an "enraged giant" to the imperialist threat of encirclement by Malaysia.[42] Finally, Brunei's decision to remain outside of Malaysia, and the difficulties which arose in the last-minute negotiations between Singapore and the Federation in London, were taken as a vindication of the Communist position that the Malaysia scheme had been doomed to failure from the start. In June, Malaysia was "in shambles"[43] and by August, when its inauguration was postponed, the "rotting corpse" was only awaiting burial.[44]

Not all the barriers erected in the path of Malaysia, however, met the anticolonial test. The Philippine claim to North Borneo was a machination of the "Yankee imperialists" who coveted Kalimantan's resources and "openly incited the Philippines to make a claim to Brunei [sic]."[45] Nor were the two Manila conferences or the agreement on Maphilindo greeted with enthusiasm. Both the Federation and the Philippine governments were too well-known for their anti-Communist views to be accepted into the Afro-Asian circle by the Communists.[46] For the record, the *Monitor* opposed the alignment on the grounds that Indonesia was the only one of the Maphilindo powers which had attained sufficient national independence and sovereignty to be able "to possess and use the democratic machinery to record the sovereign will of the people."[47] True, two of the three Maphilindo states opposed Malaysia. The Philippine motive for opposition was suspect, however, being based not on anticolonialism but on an unproved claim to Brunei which, "the world knows for a fact," had been "incorporated into the Unitary State of Kalimantan Utara." The idea of Maphilindo confederation was doubtful also because a number of its advocates saw it as a counter not to Malaysia but to the anti-Malaysia movement, that is, "A kind of 'Balkan Federation' of the imperialist-*cum*-Tito mould aimed not at the imperialists but at giving the imperialists a foothold within the anti-imperialist threshhold!"[48] Ironically, the decision taken at the Manila summit to make use of a United Nations fact-finding mission to ascertain the views of the people of the two Borneo territories was greeted as a "victory for the popular forces who had resolutely and ceaselessly hammered at 'Malaysia'."[49]

Such internal consistency as the Communist arguments possessed derived in large part from the *Monitor's* thesis that SEATO was the chief agency of imperialist intrigue in the region and that Malaysia constituted only one, albeit a key, aspect of the SEATO plot. According to this thesis, Malaysia's chief *raison d'etre* was to give the SEATO powers bases from which to launch their operations against national liberation forces in Southeast Asia, and Abdul Rahman and Lee Kuan Yew were merely puppets of the imperialists in this enterprise. Because the Treaty Organization was "hated throughout the length and breadth of Malaya," the Tengku could not commit Malaya to it openly. Nevertheless, it was charged, he had made facilities available to train personnel for antiliberation campaigns in Vietnam, Laos, and the Thai border region, and Lee and Abdul Rahman had allowed Malayan bases to be used as staging grounds for troops and combat aircraft committed to SEATO operations outside Malaya.[50] Although an "Asian Coalition," which included Indonesia and the Soviet Union, replaced SEATO—"fast disintegrating and discredited"—as the key agency of Western intrigue from

1966 onward,[51] the plot and the characters changed very little. Regarding the relations of Singapore and Malaysia, the imperialists had aided Britain's "divide and rule" policy, and by mid-1966 they were ready to move on to a "unite and rule" policy, in which "the two highly dramatized 'antagonists' are brought together again for 'closest cooperation.' "[52]

For a time, the SEATO test was also a convenient one for identifying the friends and foes of the Malayan Communists. However, it frequently required peculiar extensions and, after the Gestapu affair in Indonesia, was generally replaced by the "Malaysia" test.[53] Prior to October 1965, Indonesia's identification as an anti-imperialist ally was well-established, and the Malayan Communists went to some lengths to demonstrate their support for her West Irian claim. Subsequently, however, they found that Sukarno had never been a reliable ally and that treachery in the NASAKOM front in Indonesia went back as far as 1963.[54] On the other side, Germany became a part of the SEATO plot (like Japan, by a process of association), in this instance by way of the Association of Southeast Asia (ASA) and the North Atlantic Treaty Organization. On the question of India, the convolutions became even more involved. In spite of Nehru's long association with anti-colonialism, his government was discredited, as far as the Communists of Malaysia were concerned, by the Sino-Indian dispute; and by late 1963, it was thoroughly implicated, by the *Monitor*, in both the "British imperialist 'Malaysia' plot" and in SEATO. As to the Indian government's links with the Malaysia scheme, "its policy of 'non-aligned' alignment with U.S. and British imperialism against China and Pakistan," it was said, was clearly "being extended into the 'Malaysia' region (via the Nicobars and the Andamans) on promise of a jackal's share of the spoils should the imperialist plot in Asia succeed."[55] On India's role in SEATO, the *Monitor* asserted:

It is now known that the enforcement of "Malaysia" is part of the Western imperialist scheme to extend the operational range of SEATO, one flank of which is being extended in league with the Nehru Government (via the Nicobar and Andaman Islands), while the eastern flank is being widened by the direct participation of the American 7th Fleet in the "encirclement" of S.E.A. [Southeast Asia].

The assignment to SEATO of a major role in the Malaysia plot has, it will be noted, had the interesting corollary of elevating the United States to a leading part of the production. According to the *Monitor*, American imperialists had a threefold interest in Malaysia: (1) "to join in 'strangling' Indonesia"; (2) "to 'assist' Britain in 'strengthening' 'Malaysia' " in the hope of gaining the proprietary role there when British imperialism collapsed; and (3) to acquire a "military-economic base" near Indochina to stave off their imminent defeat in Laos and Vietnam. How prevalent this idea of American interest at work in Malaysia was could be seen in the Singapore elections of September 1963, during which the *Barisan* charged that American dollars were being used to split the vote of the extreme left in order to defeat *Barisan* candidates.[56] In addition, the uneasiness caused in Malaya by the United States government's policy of releasing stockpiled rubber and tin, and thus holding down world prices, has been exploited by the Communists. However, this issue has been used chiefly for its value as an irritant, with only awkward attempts being made to fit the American policy in with the plot thesis.

"What is Necessary at this Stage"

It appears that the Communists' strategy was to foster opposition to the Malaysia plan, from any direction possible, but to avoid actual commitments until they were reasonably sure of adequate assistance from non-Communist quarters. The available evidence also suggests that, until July 1963, they pinned their hopes on Malaysia being thwarted without overt Communist intervention. Beginning at that time, however, they began to advocate a more open program of resistance and they received overt support from Peking in this advocacy.

Singapore's open front had, of course, attempted to block Singapore's participation in Malaysia by utilizing the legal channels. At least, in the referendum of September 1962—in which there were three alternatives, but no way of voting against the merger—they tried to induce voters to register a protest by submitting unmarked ballots. (Contrary to its previously announced policy, the government did not count blank votes as votes for the Lee-Rahman agreement, but tallied them separately.) Subsequently, some of the *Barisan* leaders, including Lim Chin Siong, held conversations with Sheikh Azahari when the latter was laying the groundwork for the Brunei rebellion, but apparently they decided against offering him any form of assistance. The *Barisan* did, however, offer public support for the rebel cause after the rebellion began, a fact which was utilized by the Internal Security Council when it instituted the massive arrests of February 1963. In the aftermath of Operation Cold Stores, *Barisan* efforts to regain the initiative were seriously hampered, chiefly because the Front was deprived of its most competent leaders. Both in the elections and in their wake, the left-wing parties were consistently outmaneuvered by the government, which had admitted its readiness to use Communist tactics to suppress Communism. By the end of October, Dr. Lee Siew Choh, the *Barisan* chairman, reminded a rally that Lim had called for constitutional struggle as long as there were "constitutional means left" for their struggle, but Lee concluded that the PAP was doing everything possible to "close all doors of constitutional struggle." But his public conclusion, that future emphasis must be on the organization and education of the masses,[57] hardly seemed to be the alternative which Lim had in mind.

In contrast with the situation in Malaya, there were a number of factors in Sarawak which inclined the Communists there toward armed struggle. One of these was the acuteness, for Sarawak, of the issue of independence versus merger with Malaya. Many of Sarawak's citizens, both Chinese and Ibans, felt that Malaysia was sprung upon them without warning and that their future was being committed without their being given a voice in the matter; and neither group relished the idea of Malay hegemony, which they associated with the old Brunei sultanate. The timing of Malaysia, which was designed to prevent the opposition from mobilizing, required, from the Communist point of view, that action to keep Sarawak out of Malaysia be immediate. In a second sense, also, the Communists were impelled toward armed subversion by the course of events, since both the Brunei revolt and Indonesia's confrontation offered fortuitous assistance which any avowed revolutionary movement would have found difficult to resist. But it is also a fact that the general situation in Sarawak and the nature of the movement there particularly inclined the Sarawak Communists toward armed struggle. As we have noted earlier, this movement was characterized by the extreme youth of both its organization and its membership; and the degree of frustration, both intellectual and economic, was extremely high among its members. Under these circumstances, a high proportion of the Sarawak Communists were emotionally attuned to revolutionary activity.[58]

The Communist organization and the labor and political fronts through which it operated presented a solid front of opposition to Malaysia at a time when there was little informed opinion in other segments of the populace on the subject, and they employed some of their most colorful invective to describe it:

Seeing their approaching doom, the colonialists are terrified. When the Malaysia Plan was proposed these degenerated politicians and the slaves and running dogs of the British in the 5 states behaved as if they had come across a precious jewel. They immediately cried out and sprawled before the Tengku begging for the preservation of their lives as dogs. . . . We want to remind this group of slaves and running dogs that we shall be able to clean away this whole group of political rubbish.[59]

Whether or not the Sarawak Communists were informed beforehand of the Azahari plot concerning the Borneo states, they did not take part in the rebellion in December 1962. Rather, it appears that the decision to embark on a limited armed struggle dated from that event, although suppression of the constitutional struggle for independence from that time on was cited as the justification for the new course of action.

At the same time, however, the Borneo organization was not willing to commit the error, committed by the Party in Malaya in 1948, of cutting itself loose from the legal phase of activity. In another document on the organization's purposes in contesting the elections in 1963, we find these significant assertions:

One hand actively preparing for armed struggle, another hand continuing to carry out constitutional struggle, this is our proposal today. We, in laying stress on the road to arms have not and cannot, under the present day circumstances, let go our constitutional struggle. Therefore we must and should participate in this year's elections and at the same time fight for victory in the elections. . . .

When the people are still backward (especially the natives) they are infatuated with constitutional struggle (especially the bourgeoisie). As regards the armed struggle, at a time when they either know nothing or little about it, or become very frightened, to let go constitutional struggle will mean giving up the fight to win the people over and lead them, isolating ourselves and damaging the racial united front.[60]

On the question of the future of the united front, this document was equally candid. The left wing of the Sarawak United People's Party had been weakened by security action. Therefore, for the present, the Communists must continue to work with the "reactionaries" led by the "Ong XX" group,[61] in the meantime, however, exposing them and preparing, if necessary, to form a new party. It is quite obvious that Azahari's rebels, who specifically sought to restore the Brunei sultanate for all of northern Borneo, were operating at cross-purposes with the Sarawak Communists, and the Communists were presumably aware of this fact. However, it was less obvious that the cause of Indonesian confrontation was not the cause of Sarawak Communism. It appears, for example, that hundreds of young Communists who crossed the border expecting to be welcomed fraternally by members of the PKI faced disillusionment on the other side. Instead of PKI agents, the border recruits found Indonesian Army men training them in guerrilla warfare and hardly according them the treatment they had anticipated. What was particularly remarkable, however, was that the spokesmen for Malayan Communism, from London to Peking to the Thai border, blandly asserted the legitimacy of the Azahari "unitary state" without weighing the effect of this claim on the Sarawak movement; Sarawak Chinese could hardly be expected to fight for the domination of Brunei as an alternative to Kuala Lumpur, and yet this is precisely what the endorsement of the Azahari claim implied.

In September, when Malaysia came into being, the *Monitor* abandoned its policy of caution and boldly proclaimed a program of action which was to include all elements opposing Malaysia. Significantly, in this they received extensive support both from the press and radio in Peking. The

Monitor, in an editorial entitled, "The 'Malaysia' Explosion," indicated that what was both necessary and feasible at that stage of the anti-Malaysia, anti-imperialist struggle was a "broad united front of the people within each given country concerned, coupled with a broad, closely coordinated movement among the peoples of the various countries directly concerned." There were to be four aspects to this program:

(a) the consolidation and extension of the broad anti-'Malaysia', anti-imperialist united front on a national scale in Malaya;

(b) the consolidation and extension of the broad anti-'Malaysia', anti-imperialist united front on a national scale in the three Borneo territories, coupled with the extension of the guerrilla war carried out by the Kalimantan Utara National Army;

(c) the consolidation and extension of the broad anti-'Malaysia', anti-imperialist struggle programme of confrontation on a national scale as outlined by the Indonesian Government and people.

(d) the setting up of a joint operation council or command to coordinate the day-to-day implementation of the common strategy of the anti-'Malaysia', anti-imperialist campaign throughout the region.

This editorial was quoted extensively in the Peking *People's Daily* on October 8, with the conclusion, "What is Necessary at this Stage," cited in full, and a much condensed version of the same editorial was broadcast on Radio Peking a day later.[62] However, in spite of continued exhortations to struggle, and scattered incidents of Indonesian-directed terrorism on both sides of the Causeway, the Malayan Communists were themselves unable to form a consolidated front or to unite effectively with other anti-Malaysia elements. In Singapore, the fact that the *Barisan* constituted the parliamentary opposition led to disagreement in Party ranks over the use of militant tactics and, in 1964, to Dr. Lee's temporary withdrawal from the Party. It was only in 1965 that the MNLL issued a call for "a strong united front" of "all patriotic political parties and organizations opposing Malaysia"—open and clandestine, internal and external. On March 15, through its "mission" in Djakarta, the MNLL announced an eight-point manifesto,[63] intended to appeal to a broad cross-section of "national groups" and not differing in substance from the 1957 program.

Singapore's withdrawal from Malaysia in August and the military take-over in Djakarta in October virtually ended the anti-Malaysia campaign, except on the Sarawak border. In November, the MNLL mission itself was incarcerated. Ironically, the results were exactly the opposite of those intended by the anti-Malaysia forces; Singapore was again constitutionally separated from Malaya and the Borneo states were not. And undoubtedly the militant left has been hurt by the suspicion that it was in part responsible for Singapore's ouster from the Federation. In Sarawak, armed revolt continued. However, according to a document seized at Sijijak in August 1966, the emphasis was not to be on guerrilla activities:

. . . besides practicing racial work as the central duty, to do well racial work with great effort and to develop underground work with great endeavor through various forms (open, secret, legal, illegal, in the councils, and outside the councils), to educate and organize the masses extensively, guerrilla war will be carried out by gradual steps with careful planning and under favorable circumstances, if necessary—this is the new content of the present general policy.[64]

The Malayan Communist Party and the Sino-Soviet Dispute

Nowhere has the Communist Party of Malaya shown its complete subservience to the Chinese Communists so much as on the question of the split within the international Communist movement. In fact, on this question it appears that the Malayan Communist line may be literally made in Peking. This requires little elaboration. The Central Committee itself is on record, in a series of letters to fraternal Parties, as supporting Peking's position against Moscow's.[65] Mao's thinking is the "common treasure of the international Communist movements and of all oppressed nations throughout the world," illuminating the way for the "peoples of Asia, Africa and Latin America in their struggle against imperialist oppression and enslavement and for freedom and liberation." Comrade Mao's conclusion that "imperialism and all reactionaries are paper-tigers," and his idea that one must slight the enemy strategically while taking full account of him tactically had "heightened the Malayan people's confidence in victory and helped them to better grasp the art of struggle."[66] The 1957 Moscow Declaration and the 1960 Moscow Statement are the common programs for the international movement. The modern revisionism of Tito is the main danger facing the international Communist movement. Although the Malayan Communists hoped, in 1963, that a reasonable solution to the Sino-Soviet differences could be found in accordance with criteria established in the 1960 Moscow Statement,[67] a year and a half later, in the most complete statement in a single issue it had issued for several years, the Central Committee of the CPM bitterly attacked the "Krushchov [sic] revisionist group" and charged the leadership of the Soviet Party with "clinging to Krushchov's revisionist line, notwithstanding the collapse of Krushchov."[68] And paradoxically, at a time when Malayan Communists were trying to utilize fronts domestically, the Party assured the Albanian Party of Labor:

Our experience proves that in order to defeat imperialism and achieve national liberation it is imperative to draw a clear line between ourselves and the social democrats and reformists of every hue, and carry out a relentless struggle against them politically and ideologically; at the same time it is absolutely necessary to crush the modern revisionists and refuse to have anything to do with their "united action."[69]

The *Malayan Monitor* expounded at greater length on specific aspects of the controversy, publishing, for example, a six-page defense of China's position on the three-power Nuclear Test-Ban Treaty[70] and tilting with modern revisionists on the Sino-Indian border dispute. Significantly, the *Monitor's* views on these issues have been cited at some length by Radio Peking. The *Monitor* also involved itself deeply on the side of China in the split within the Afro-Asian Peoples Solidarity organization, although here the "test" of Malaysia was also a factor. Steps taken by the Soviet Union to establish diplomatic relations with Malaysia and Singapore in the first half of 1967 further confirmed Malayan Communists in the view that the USSR was aligned with the imperialists.[71] In June 1968, the Party's dependence on Peking was again made apparent when, on the occasion of the twentieth anniversary of the War of National Liberation, Peking and the MNLA jointly underscored the importance of the event. In an unusual departure, Peking took note of the occasion not only by broadcasting the exchange of messages between the Central Committees of the CPM and the Chinese Communist Party on Radio Peking; in addition, the *People's Daily* of Peking devoted substantial space on its front page on successive days to this exchange of messages.[72] Yet not even this new evidence of dependence on the Peking line added any new dimension to the quarrel, since the Malayan position was, and continues to be, the Peking position. After all, the *Monitor* had found, as early as 1963, that the modern revisionists had joined with the imperialists and their stooges, "certain heavily aligned 'non-aligned' 'neutralists'," and the "raggle-taggle brigade of faint hearts" in suggesting that confrontation be ended.[73]

CONCLUSION

The circumstances which surrounded the inauguration of Malaysia were hardly auspicious. Nevertheless, her birth marked the end of the era of British colonialism in Asia and, with it, most of the advantage the Communists had had in the fight for independence. Singapore's subsequent removal from Malaysia, which might in other circumstances have been exploitable by the militant left there, was not so in actual fact; for Singaporeans generally accepted the view that membership in Malaysia, with all its inequities, was decidedly superior to no ties at all. Similarly, the leftists might have profited from the economic dislocations accompanying the separation, but any advantages they gained in this way were more than offset by the loss at this time of Indonesia as a base from which to operate and as an ally. Strangely enough, Singapore's withdrawal from Malaysia, with the attendant losses of revenue to the Federation, had, and continues to have, political repercussions in the Borneo states, particularly Sarawak. However, here also the events in Indonesia have more than offset the propaganda advantages gained by the militant left.

The issue of Chinese chauvinism is another matter. So long as there is evidence that the Chinese are victims of discriminatory policies, whether culturally or politically, they will be potential targets for Communist propaganda. As we have noted, Communism in Malaysia and Singapore has thrived most of the time almost exclusively within the Overseas Chinese communities, and the temptation for the Communist leadership to appeal to Chinese sentiments is therefore overwhelming. The issue of Chinese nationalism is, nonetheless, not a simple one for the Communists. Chinese sentiment has itself undergone a radical change during the lifetime of the Malayan Communist movement; the desire to preserve things Chinese remains, but the sense of expatriation has virtually disappeared. Malayan Chinese may take pride in China's position today, but they are Malayans as well as Chinese and therefore concerned primarily with conditions in Malaya; Sarawak Chinese are similarly oriented to their state of residence. And for better or for worse, Singapore Chinese today have their own state; although for a number of reasons, the government prefers not to emphasize this fact.

The demands of expediency, then, as well as their ideological commitments, prevent the Communist leadership in either Singapore or Malaysia from fully exploiting Chinese chauvinism. A program which threatened to disrupt the present relations among ethnic groups in either state would cost the Communists support both at home and in the Afro-Asian world. Nevertheless, the issue remains. Between 1964 and 1969, there have been bloody riots with racial overtones from Singapore to Penang, and the Chinese question could become crucial if economic conditions, for example, or an expanded Chinese involvement in Vietnam accentuated existing racial differences.

The Communists appear to be tied down on the peninsula and in Singapore. In Sarawak, their threat is substantially diminished by their lack of sanctuary in Indonesia, although Sarawak's continued tie with the Federation remains a potentially explosive political issue. Prosperity in the two states is a deterrent to any significant resurgence of Communist strength. Conversely, unemployment in Singapore and threats of even greater unemployment in the near future—(as British bases are phased out) help keep the movement alive and cast a shadow on the future. What happens in Singapore and Malaysia will undoubtedly be influenced also by events in China: echoes of the Cultural Revolution have already been heard in the cities of the two countries. It would be a mistake to underestimate the number of Communists and Communist sympathizers either in Singapore, in Sarawak, or in Malaya; any change in the economic situation which carried with it an increase in unemployment and a decrease in the rate of government expenditures would certainly bring renewed Communist activity. And a further spread of insurgency through peninsular Southeast Asia, stemming from the conflict in Vietnam, might well produce the same result.

NOTES

1. That is, in Burma, Indochina, Indonesia, Malaya, and Thailand.
2. Virtually the entire prewar leadership was wiped out by the Japanese in mid-1942, in separate actions in Singapore and the peninsula; and it remains in doubt whether the Party Secretary, Loi Teck—who survived the war—wanted the Party to succeed. In any event, he was subsequently charged, after he had absconded with the Party's funds, with having betrayed the Party to the Japanese.
3. J. H. Brimmell, *Communism in Southeast Asia* (London: Oxford University Press, 1959), p. 82, alleges that it was the interests of the Soviet Party, rather than those of the local Parties, which led to the call for insurrection in 1948. It is supremely important, of course, to recall the 1948 Calcutta Communist conference in which the signal for a switch to militant tactics was given by Cominform agents. This had almost immediate repercussions—in terms of stepped-up guerrilla warfare—in all parts of Southeast Asia.
4. Also known as the Malayan Races Liberation Army.
5. Singapore Legislative Assembly, *The Communist Threat in Singapore*, Cmd. 33 of 1957, 15 pp.
6. *The Danger Within* (Kuching: Sarawak Information Service, 1963), p. 3.
7. *Ibid.*, p. 5.
8. Cited from a captured document entitled, "How to Educate the Masses," in *Communism and the Farmers* (Kuching: Sarawak Government, 1961), p. 4.
9. That is, it was given recognition on Radio Peking. *Ibid.*
10. A variety of contacts with China are possible by both direct and indirect means, and Radio Peking can be readily picked up anywhere in Malaysia. Radio Peking undoubtedly furnishes much of the Communist study material used in the area; it also may provide an important medium for transmission of CPM policies within Malaya. See note 28 (p. 269), on *Malayan Monitor*.
11. Chen Ping's own presence in the border area has not been definitely established. There have, however, been indications which point to his presence there, such as reports from surrendered terrorists about persons assigned as Chen's bodyguards, and so forth. In 1963, a newspaper report from Alor Star indicated that police sources there believed that the Communist guerrillas were split into two groups and that Chen Ping was with the elite group which operated in the deep jungle. *Sunday Mail* (Singapore), September 8, 1963.
12. See speech by Dato (Dr.) Ismail bin Dato Abdul Rahman, Minister of Internal Security, on Television Singapura, November 3, quoted in *Straits Times* (Singapore), November 4, 1963. Ismail said on this occasion that he could "assure" his listeners that the powers of preventive detention would only be used on "Communists, their sympathizers and others who threaten the security" of the country.

13. *Ibid.*
14. Although the Rhios are very close to Singapore, they are Indonesian-owned.
15. *Straits Times* (Singapore), November 17, 1963.
16. The North Kalimantan National Army.
17. Reports from Antara and from the (Indonesian) *Armed Forces Bulletin*; in *Straits Times* (Singapore), September 2, 1967.
18. A reproduction of a speech by Liu Shao-chi on organization and disciplinary self-cultivation was among the Communist materials found in the possession of a Chinese couple from Kuching who submitted to deportation in 1962. Copies of this speech, published in Malaya, were captured in the Federation 15 years ago, although it does not appear to have ever been published in China. See H. F. Schurman, "Organizational Principles of the Chinese Communists," *China Quarterly* (London), Vol. I (1960).
19. *The Danger Within*; also *Subversion in Sarawak* (Kuching: Council Negri, 1960).
20. A history of the Communist movement in Malaya, seized in December 1962, which was apparently prepared in the border region for indoctrination purposes.
21. See, e.g., Brimmell, *Communism in Southeast Asia*, pp. 97 ff., 330 ff. Brimmell comments that the Communist insurrection took on in many ways the "aspect of a concealed war between Malays and Chinese."
22. Wu reportedly has been with the Twelfth Regiment in southern Thailand since 1956.
23. He edited *Nanyang Siang Pao* before the Japanese war and is the author of a book entitled *Problems of Malaya*.
24. *Communism in Southeast Asia*, pp. 320–39 *passim*. Brimmell comments, for example, that their 1955 program was "certainly far too subtle" for them to have evolved—and probably also to have carried out—unaided.
25. Chen Ping's destination on this occasion was China, where he expected to confer with Party leaders. Circumstances in China prevented his going beyond Hong Kong, it is believed; however, it is not known who his contacts there were.
26. That is, confessions and exposés taped for use on radio and television.
27. Originating in the so-called Ng Heng letter, of May 1, to Malayan political leaders.
28. *Malayan Monitor* (London), June 30, 1960. See also "For a Just Settlement of the Malayan War," a CPM statement of September 1959, *ibid.*, January 31, 1960.
    The *Malayan Monitor*, although not an official publication, publishes policy statements of the Central Committee of the CPM, as well as Party greetings to fraternal Parties and Communist governments. Moreover, it is recognized as an authoritative spokesman for Malayan Communism in London, where it is published, and in Peking. On current questions, it has the advantage of access to sources denied to the Party itself; moreover, it appears to reflect Singapore Communist preoccupations far more than does the Central Committee. Lim Hong Bee, its publisher through 1965, helped organize the Malayan Democratic Union in Singapore in 1945, and went to London in 1947 as a representative for the PUTERA-AMCJA front. He has since been barred from re-entry.
29. "Forward Along the Path toward Complete Independence," statement of April 30, 1960, *ibid.*, September 30, 1960. Contrary to usual practice, this statement was not issued in the names of Chen Ping and Musa Ahmad jointly, but only in Musa Ahmad's.
30. "Manifesto of the Communist Party of Malaya on the Fourth Anniversary of the Baling Talks: December 28, 1955," *ibid.*, April 30, 1960.
31. This was to be a foreign policy "in keeping with the national aspirations and the interests of the Malayan people: namely, a foreign policy which strictly upholds the five principles of peaceful coexistence among nations with different

social systems, respects the U.N. charter, develops and extends friendship and mutually beneficial intercourse with all friendly countries, and which entirely dissociates Malaya from SEATO and all other imperialist-sponsored 'hot' or 'cold' war commitments." *Ibid.*, January 31, 1961.

32. The SATU was deregistered in 1963.

33. "Malaysia: Statement of the CP of Malaya," *Malayan Monitor*, January 31, 1964, pp. 1–2.

34. *Ibid.*, August 31, 1961. The *Malayan Monitor* not only blurs the distinction between organizations with some deliberation, but is also guilty on occasion of glaring errors in fact—whether accidentally or not is unclear. Thus, on numerous occasions, it has asserted that the Philippine claim was to Brunei rather than North Borneo; and recently it claimed that the ill-fated Southeast Asia Friendship and Economic Treaty superseded ASA when, in fact, it preceded it.

35. *Ibid.*

36. *Ibid.*, October 31, 1961.

37. *Ibid.*, November 30, 1961.

38. *Ibid.*, April 30, 1962.

39. *Ibid.*, September 30, 1962.

40. A statement on Brunei attributed to the Central Committee of the CPM and dated December 15, 1962, was published by the *Malayan Monitor* in the same month, together with statements on the Sino-Indian dispute and on the Cuba incident, both dated November 30. The fact that these documents, and particularly the Brunei one, were issued by the Central Committee and released abroad so soon after the events to which they relate raises interesting questions about their origin, particularly since none of them was signed. It is significant that translations of these documents, both in Chinese and in *Jawi* (i.e., Malay script), were sent from the Thai border area into the Federation, but only some months after the London release.

41. The *Malayan Monitor*, December 31, 1962, explained that after the Azahari forces achieved their "initial purpose," they "withdrew to prearranged areas, leaving the oil installations, all properties and all personnel taken prisoner unharmed."

42. *Ibid.*, November 30, 1963.

43. *Ibid.*, June 30, 1963.

44. *Ibid.*, August 31, 1963.

45. *Ibid.*, December 31, 1962.

46. The *Malayan Monitor* noted critically a statement by the Tengku that, *en route* to his meeting with Sukarno in June 1963, he had agreed in Manila that the Philippines and Malaya should jointly contain Communism. Curiously, however, no notice was taken of the press reports from Manila, at the close of the Foreign Ministers' meeting, that the three powers had agreed to cooperate in solving their Chinese problems.

47. *Ibid.*, September 30, 1963.

48. *Ibid.*

49. *Ibid.*, August 31, 1963.

50. In May 1962, for example, a flight of British fighters and bombers was allegedly sent from Singapore to Thailand "for direct aggression against Laos." *Ibid.*, May 31, 1962.

51. *Ibid.*, April 31, 1966.

52. *Ibid.*, June 30, 1966. See also MNLL statement of August 15, 1965, published August 31 in the *Monitor*.

53. As early as June 30, 1964, the *Monitor* described Malaysia, in an editorial com-

memorating the sixteenth anniversary of the "Malayan People's Armed Struggle," as the "acid test" of friend or foe.

54. See, e.g., " 'Malaysia'—Sukarno Shows His Hand—New Situation Analysed," *Ibid.*, May 31, 1966.

55. *Ibid.*, October 31, 1963.

56. *Barisan* campaign posters and streamers graphically portrayed an American tank from which the Statue of Liberty held aloft a missile, Uncle Sam handing out dollars to the head of another left-wing party, and other propaganda of this nature.

57. *Malayan Monitor*, November 30, 1963. In another message, printed in *ibid.* on February 28, 1963, Lim had written:

> There can be no harmony, no development, and no progress for our nation so long as the left-wing is excluded from the arena of constitutional politics by police repression. Only with the free and unhampered participation of the progressive forces can the constructive energies of the people be released. However, the ruling clique in the Federation are heavily committed to the imperialists and will pursue an anti-democratic policy in the hope of maintaining themselves in power indefinitely.
>
> If the forces in the Federation who are pressing for increased recourse to police terror have their way, then a turning point in this country's political development will have been reached. The country will then be set on a course that must lead to a fascist and military dictatorship. The left-wing forces must then make the necessary judgement on the matter. [Emphasis in original text.]

58. The emotional appeal to armed struggle is apparent in a number of the captured materials, such as this poem found in possession of a female cadre:

> The graceful and beautiful rivers and mountains of the fatherland
> Lie across North Kalimantan,
> Bordering the South China Sea in the North and Indonesia in the South.
> British imperialism sucks dry our blood and sweat
> Oh, the labouring people suffer from hunger and hardship.
> The heroic and brave people
> Have to pick up shotguns to fight them.
> We want to chase away British imperialism
> With determination and perseverance.

59. From an issue of the *Workers' and Farmers' News*, seized in June, 1962, quoted in a press release, Sarawak Information Service, August 22, 1962.

60. Press release, Sarawak Information Service, July 31, 1962.

61. A reference to the moderates within the SUPP, led by Ong Kee Hui. Ong, who was educated in the English stream, was of considerable importance to the SUPP because he had the contacts, through many years of government service as an agriculturist, to bring large numbers of Ibans to the Party rolls. (Although claiming to be multiracial, the SUPP was in fact effective only among the Chinese at the polls.)

62. Simultaneously, the bimonthly *World Knowledge* (China) published two articles on Malaysia. The first, entitled "Oppose the 'Federation of Malaysia' Which Has Been Assembled by Imperialism," gave China's three-point stand against Malaysia. The second, " 'Malaysia': A Product of Neo-Colonialism," accused the United States of trying to take over British interests in Malaya.

63. *Malayan Monitor*, July 31, 1965.

64. *Carrying Out Guerrilla War by Gradual Steps: This Is the New Content in the Development of Revolution and the New Content of the Prevalent General Policy* (a duplicated document).

65. This was true, for example, even when other Parties in the area were denying that the rift was significant. See, e.g., "The Communist Party of Malaya Greets

the 7th (Extraordinary) National Congress of the Communist Party of Indonesia," *Malayan Monitor,* June 30, 1962.

66. "Greetings of the Communist Party of Malaya to the Communist Party of China on its 40th Anniversary" (June, 1961), *ibid.,* October 31, 1961.

67. "Letter of the Delegation of the Malayan Communist Party to All Delegates Attending the Sixth Congress of the German Socialist Unity Party" (January 17, 1963), *ibid.,* April 30, 1963.

68. "Statement of the Central Committee of the Malayan Communist Party on the International Communist Movement," *ibid.*

69. *Ibid.,* Letter of October 15, 1966, published January-February, 1967. The *Malayan Monitor* was reorganized at the end of 1966.

70. *Ibid.,* August 31, 1963.

71. The Soviet recognition of Malaysia, in April 1967, was worse, according to the *Malayan Monitor,* than "the double-dealing recognition of all other puppet regimes" because it involved "the calculated and wholesale betrayal of the fraternal Party and Liberation movement and the people of the plundered state" by a supposedly Marxist-Leninist body, *ibid.,* April, 1967.

72. I.e., On June 19 and 20. The CPM statement on this occasion placed heavy stress on the importance of armed struggle, asserting:

In the final analysis, the practice of armed struggle during the past twenty years has confirmed that Mao Tse-tung's thought, Marxism-Leninism of the present era, is the guide to the Malayan revolution, and that the integration of the universal truth of Mao Tse-tung's thought with the concrete practice of the Malayan revolution is the only guarantee for achieving victory in the armed struggle of the Malayan people.

Citing the "rising tide of struggle," etc., it concluded that "the outbreak of a new revolutionary storm is inevitable."

73. *Ibid.,* November 30, 1963. The *Malayan Monitor's* charges against the modern revisionists bore a strong resemblance to charges aired in Hanoi by the weekly *Thong Nhat* (*Reunification*). This "organ of struggle for the liberation of South Vietnam" was quoted in the *Saigon Post,* March 16, 1964, as identifying the opponents of Hanoi's war effort as "the revisionists and rightist opportunists who have been so frightened by America's nuclear force that they have highly publicized the bourgeois pacifist thoughts about these mass-destruction weapons."

SELECTED BIBLIOGRAPHY

Brimmell, J. H., *Communism in Southeast Asia: A Political Analysis.* London: Oxford University Press, 1959.

Communism and the Farmers. Sarawak, Kuching, 1961.

Hanrahan, Gene Z., *The Communist Struggle in Malaya.* New York: International Secretariat, Institute of Pacific Relations, 1954.

Malayan Monitor (London).

O'Ballance, Edgar, *Malaya: The Communist Insurgent War, 1948–60.* London: Faber & Faber, Ltd., 1966.

Pye, Lucian W., *Guerrilla Communism in Malaya: Its Social and Political Meaning.* Princeton, N.J.: Princeton University Press, 1956.

Subversion in Sarawak ("Sessional Paper," No. 3). Kuching: Council Negri, 1960.

The Communist Threat in Singapore. Singapore: Legislative Assembly, Cmd. 33, 1957.

The Communist Threat to Sarawak. Kuala Lumpur, Malaysia: Ministry of Home Affairs, 1966.

The Communist Threat to the Federation of Malaya. ("Paper," No. 23). Kuala Lumpur: Federation of Malaya, Legislative Council.

The Danger and Where It Lies. Kuala Lumpur, Federation of Malaya: Information Services, 1957.

The Danger Within. Kuching: Sarawak Information Service, 1963.

The Militant Communist Threat to West Malaysia. Kuala Lumpur, Malaysia: Ministry of Home Affairs, 1966.

Thompson, Robert, *Defeating Communist Insurgency: Experiences from Malaya and Vietnam.* London: Chatto & Windus, Ltd., 1966.

THE RISE AND FALL OF
THE COMMUNIST PARTY
OF INDONESIA

GUY J. PAUKER

FROM PERSECUTED FACTION TO MASS PARTY

The Communist Party of Indonesia, in its pursuit of power, has been led by several generations of political activists, all of whom made fatal mistakes and were consequently destroyed by antagonistic forces.[1] Students of Indonesian Communism will eventually have to explain why different generations, whose political consciousness was shaped under a variety of circumstances, namely Dutch colonialism, Japanese military occupation, and an independent nationalist regime, ended equally in disaster. Here I will only attempt to explain the circumstances that led to the fall of the PKI in 1965.

Addressing a Chinese audience in Canton in September 1963, the Chairman of the PKI, D. N. Aidit, divided the development of his Party into four periods:

1. the period of the founding of the Party and the struggle against the first white terror (1920–1926);

2. the period of underground struggle and the anti-fascist united front (1926–1945);

3. the period of the August Revolution in 1945 and the struggle against the second white terror (1945–1951);

4. the period of the national united front and the building of the Party (since 1951).[2]

Two years after Aidit's speech, the ill-fated PKI entered another historical period, that of the third white terror. It resulted in the destruction of the largest Communist Party in the world, after those of China and the Soviet Union, and caused the death of numerous cadres, including most members of the PKI's Politburo and of hundreds of thousands of followers.

The PKI was outlawed on March 12, 1966, by a decree signed in the name of President Sukarno by General Suharto, who was at that time Commander of the Army in charge of security operations, following the failure of the Communist-initiated September 30 Movement. The teaching of Marxism-Leninism was prohibited in Indonesia by a decree of the Provisional People's Consultative Assembly (MPRS) of July 5, 1966. Today the PKI is a clandestine movement, divided into factions and constantly and effectively repressed by the security agencies of Indonesia.

The history of the PKI begins with the creation of the first Marxist organization in the Netherland East Indies, the *Indische Sociaal Democratische Vereniging* (The Indies Social Democratic Association), founded in Surabaya on May 9, 1914 by H. J. F. M. Sneevliet, a young Dutchman who had arrived in the Indies the preceding year. Later, under the pseudonym Maring, he played an important role in the international Communist movement. The Indies Social Democratic Association (ISDV) brought together some 60 Social-Democrats. At its Seventh Congress, held in Semarang on May 23, 1920, the ISDV changed its name to *Perserikatan Kommunist di India*, which thus became the first Asian Communist Party. On December 25, 1920, at another conference in Semarang, the Party decided to join the Third International. At its Second Congress, held on June 7, 1924, in Djakarta, the name of the organization was changed to *Partai Komunis Indonesia* (the Communist Party of Indonesia), which reflected the nationalist aspirations active among the politically conscious population. At the same time, official headquarters of the Central Committee were transferred from Semarang to Djakarta.[3]

The first generation of Indonesian Communists was destroyed by the Dutch colonial authorities following the failure of the 1926–1927 armed Communist rebellion. The rebellion led to the arrest of 13,000 persons, of whom a few were executed, 5,000 were placed in preventive detention, 4,500 were sent to prison, and 1,308 were deported to Boven Digul in Western New Guinea. The PKI was declared illegal in 1927. Ruth McVey, the historian of the early period of the PKI, writes that "this action put an effective end to Communist activity in the Indies for the remaining period of Dutch rule."[4]

The next Communist generation grew up during a period of repression by the Dutch of all nationalist manifestations. Then came the united front against fascism initiated by Georgi Dimitrov as Secretary General of the Comintern in 1935. In the Indies, that period was marked by the creation of the "Illegal PKI" by Musso, who returned for that purpose in April 1935 from several years of exile in the Soviet Union.[5] Little is known about the activities of the PKI in that period, or during the Japanese occupation, except that during the war years some Communists cooperated with the Allies in the struggle against the Japanese.

After the war, Musso's name was linked with the New Road policy, which was announced immediately following his second return from the Soviet Union in August 1948. He was killed by the Indonesian Army during the PKI's second unsuccessful armed rebellion which broke out at Madiun in East Java on September 18, 1948. That venture ended with the imprisonment of up to 36,000 PKI members and sympathizers, and the summary execution of 11 top PKI leaders, including 5 members of the Politburo. The implementation of the New Road policy was left to D. N. Aidit and his associates, who took over the leadership of the PKI in 1951.

Although the early months of Aidit's leadership were marred by the arrests in August 1951 of at least 2,000 PKI members and sympathizers by the Masjumi Prime Minister Sukiman, the Party thereafter met few obstacles and grew phenomenally. By the time of its Fifth National Congress in March 1954, the PKI claimed 165,206 members and candidate members. Five years later, at its Sixth National Congress in September 1959, the figure had increased nearly tenfold, to about one and a half million.

Between 1954 and 1959, the PKI scored other remarkable successes. At the September 1955 elections for Parliament it obtained 6,176,900 votes, 16.4 percent of all votes expressed. During the summer of 1957, the elections for regional assemblies in Java, Sumatra, and Riau brought the PKI 7,760,000 votes which, with 504,300 votes in other areas, as Chairman Aidit proudly stressed, amounted to an increase of 34 percent in electoral strength over 1955.[6]

The PKI leaders had reason to expect even more from the next general elections, which according to law were to be held in 1959. Many observers believed at the time that the PKI would emerge as the country's strongest political party, thus entitled by constitutional practice to form the new cabinet. If this had happened, the PKI would have been the first Communist party anywhere in the world to gain control of a national government by legal, peaceful means. Such victory would have been an epochal confirmation that a "parliamentary road to socialism," officially endorsed by Premier Khrushchev at the Twentieth Congress of the Communist Party of the Soviet Union in February 1956, was indeed possible. But the Army, on which President Sukarno depended for protection against the *Pemerintah Revolusioner Republik Indonesia-Perdjuangan Semesta* (PRRI-*Permesta*) rebellions in Sumatra and Celebes that threatened his regime, was not prepared to permit a Communist electoral victory and requested in May 1958 that elections be postponed for six years. Aidit attempted to counteract the fear of a PKI victory in an interview published on May 22, 1958:

It is not true to assert that one party will be able to get the majority of seats in Parliament through the forthcoming elections. The PKI has estimated that it will obtain not more than 25 percent of all the votes. . . . The PKI will not fight for more than it is struggling at present, i.e. the formation of a National Coalition Cabinet.[7]

These assurances were not satisfactory, and general elections were postponed. Then, in July 1959, Indonesia's parliamentary system was replaced by an authoritarian regime backed by the Army, Sukarno's so-called "guided democracy." Showing considerable political agility, the leaders of the PKI decided to make the most of a bad thing and began to cultivate President Sukarno in his new role as a dictator, while continuing to try to reopen the "parliamentary road."

For five years, from 1958 to 1963, domestic and external crises made it easy for the Indonesian power elite to justify the postponement of general elections. The PRRI and *Permesta* rebellions, and the fanatic *Darul Islam* movement as well, threatened the survival of the state and the unity of the nation. The sharpening conflict with the Netherlands concerning the *terra irredenta* of Western New Guinea conjured the specter of war until international pressures led to a peaceful solution in Indonesia's favor in the summer of 1962.

COMMUNIST POLITICAL STRATEGIES

With the miraculous disappearance of all major foreign and domestic foes, circumstances seemed auspicious for political normalization and, in February 1963, the PKI, showing a good sense of timing, requested elections "at the earliest possible date." The First Plenum of the new Central Committee appointed by the Seventh National Congress of 1962 stated that "there are at present no reasons whatsoever to procrastinate."[8]

But the forces anxious to prevent a Communist takeover prevailed, and President Sukarno announced at the Congress of the Indonesian Nationalist Party (PNI), on August 28, 1963, in Purwokerto, that "no elections will be held if this splits the unity of the Indonesian people."[9] Undaunted, the PKI reiterated its demands in a resolution adopted by the Second Plenum of the Central Committee held from December 23–26, 1963. Picking up the theme of national unity, it argued that the "time had come . . . to carry out a general election campaign which supports national unity and the Political Manifesto as hoped for by President Sukarno."[10]

The Political Manifesto was a speech given by President Sukarno on August 17, 1959, under the title "The Rediscovery of our Revolution," in which he justified his *coup d'état* of July 5, 1959. In September 1959 a committee of the Republic's Supreme Advisory Council, headed by Aidit, recommended that the speech be made into the state's official policy guideline. That proposal, enacted by decree in January 1960, marked the beginning of an intensive effort to indoctrinate the Indonesian nation with Sukarno's ideology. The PKI was able to argue many of its demands in terms of these officially ratified political slogans. Particularly useful was the recognition of the concept of "enemies of the Revolution," which made it possible to purge (or as Sukarno called it "retool") his opponents, who were in most cases also the enemies of the PKI.[11]

While attempting to keep the parliamentary road open, the PKI increased its options after 1959 by building up an alternative road which I described in 1961 as seeking to come to power by "acclamation":

. . . building up [the Party's] prestige as the only solid, purposeful, disciplined, well-organized, capable political force in the country, a force to which Indonesia will turn in despair when all other possible solutions have failed. In building up this image, it is important that the PKI demonstrate its power, skill, and influence at all levels of public life.[12]

To establish their legitimacy, the PKI leaders worked hard to appear to the masses as Sukarno's most faithful disciples and therefore his most deserving political heirs. This unorthodox and novel strategy seemed in keeping with the independent frame of mind manifested by Aidit early in his career, when Stalin was still alive and Communism was far from polycentric. At a time when deviant Communists were executed in Eastern Europe and China was still accepting Soviet leadership, Aidit showed real courage as leader of a then minor Communist Party, stating on May 23, 1952:

The people of Indonesia must be oriented toward the socialist Soviet Union and not toward imperialist America. This does not mean that the state structure

of the Soviet Union, that is, the Soviet system, should be followed by all nations, including Indonesia. Certainly not. On the contrary, *each nation will
travel its own road toward socialism*, on the basis of the development of its
national situation, its political situation, its economy, and its culture. [Emphasis
supplied.][13]

In courting Sukarno's favors as an alternative road to power, in case
the parliamentary one was to remain closed, the PKI leaders were trying
an imaginative but dangerous gambit. For their own political purposes
they were drawing on the unique popularity of Sukarno, who had
used modern techniques of mass manipulation to bolster his charisma as
the nation's leader, endowing himself with the aura surrounding traditional monarchs, whom most of the population considered to be possessed of divine, magical powers.

As the leading nationalist agitator of his country for almost four decades and as principal national spokesman and leader for over 20 years,
Sukarno had attained the summit of political power. The Provisional
People's Consultative Assembly had proclaimed him, in May 1963, President for life, a decision which received enthusiastic Communist support.[14]

The Communist leaders spared no efforts to establish in the public
mind their closeness to the President. The statements of Aidit and his
associates were replete with reverent quotations from Sukarno's pronouncements, which seemed to be recited as frequently as passages from
the Communist classics.

By mid-1965 it looked as if Aidit were about to be proclaimed the
political heir of the aging President. The forty-fifth anniversary of the
PKI on May 23, 1965, was celebrated at the Djakarta Stadium as if it
were a national holiday. In the presence of cabinet members, foreign
diplomats, and various dignitaries, 120,000 spectators heard Sukarno describe Aidit as the "bulwark of Indonesia." The President then confirmed
Aidit's statement that the PKI had three million members, the Communist youth organization *Pemuda Rakjat* another three million, and that
altogether Communism had twenty million sympathizers.

This incredible figure, representing one-fifth of the total population
of Indonesia at that time, does not appear farfetched even though many
persons must have belonged to more than one organization. After all,
in 1964 the Communist Federation of Labor Unions (SOBSI) claimed
more than three and a half million members; the Indonesian Farmers'
Front (BTI) eight and a half million members; the Women's Front
(GERWANI) one and three-quarter million members; and smaller front
organizations formed by groups such as artists (LEKRA) and students
(CGMI) enough additional members to bring the total to twenty million.

This enormous mass movement provided Sukarno with huge enthusiastic audiences wherever he went—audiences which he thoroughly enjoyed, especially since he lacked an organization of his own to mobilize
support for his agitational politics. Understandably, at the end of his
speech at the forty-fifth anniversary of the PKI, Sukarno exhorted the
Communists, as in 1962 at their Seventh Congress, "PKI, go ahead! Onward, onward, onward, never retreat."[15]

SUKARNO'S AMBIGUOUS ROLE

The true nature of Sukarno's relationship with the PKI lends itself
to fascinating speculations. Reactionary politicians and colonial authorities have always been prone to pin the Communist label on nationalists
fighting against imperialism. Therefore one ought to approach this subject with great diffidence. Yet there are a number of puzzling questions,
answers to which would cast new light on the events of the last years of
Sukarno's political career.

Was there special significance in the fact that as a student, in March
1923, Sukarno had addressed the "Congress of the PKI and Red Sarekat
Islam," convened in Bandung by the Communists?[16]

Was Sukarno revealing a major influence on his political career when
on July 25, 1965, at the thirty-eighth anniversary of the PNI, he praised
the 1926 Communist rebellion and related that "one of the PKI leaders
from Tjiamis, who had been sentenced to death by hanging, left a
note exhorting me to carry on the struggle"?[17]

Concerning the banning of the PKI after the 1926 uprising, Sukarno
had stated in his book *Sarinah*, published in 1947:

At that time, Dutch imperialism had just lashed ferociously at the pure heart
of the Communists. Severe blows were inflicted upon the Indonesian Communist Party and the People's Union. Thousands of their leaders were thrown into
jails or banished to the Upper Digul. To carry on the revolutionary struggle
I then founded the Indonesian National Party.[18]

Was the PNI founded by Sukarno in July 1927, a few months after
the PKI had been destroyed by the Dutch following the 1926-1927 rebellion, created as a political shelter for Communists who had escaped
detection? Was Sukarno, as an imaginative young revolutionary, pursuing in his own way the same political objectives as the banned PKI?

In 1926, Sukarno published in *Suluh Indonesia Muda* an article entitled "Nationalism, Islamism, and Marxism." Was his thesis developed
independently, the thought of a young nationalist eager to see all na-
tive political forces join against the common colonialist enemy, or was
Sukarno simply reiterating in Aesopian language the "united front from

above" strategy advocated by the Comintern from 1920 to 1927? Sukarno was obviously familiar with the Comintern's strategy when he wrote in that article:

The new tactics of Marxism do not reject cooperation with nationalists and Moslems in Asia. They even support true Nationalist and Moslem movements. Marxists who are hostile to Nationalist and Moslem movements in Asia do not follow the spirit of the times and do not understand the changed Marxist tactics.[19]

I do not interpret these items as circumstantial evidence that Sukarno was a crypto-Communist who rose, under PKI guidance, to the presidency of Indonesia. His personality and his career make it unlikely that he ever accepted orders from others, much less the harsh discipline of a conspiratorial movement. Sukarno was his own man, pursuing his political fortunes according to his own judgment. But his basic political vision was that of left-wing radical nationalism, even though his romantic temperament and taste for high living, as well as political considerations, prompted him to behave, as President, in the style of an Oriental potentate.

Yet, despite such behavioral inconsistencies resulting from character defects that his political beliefs were not able to eradicate, Sukarno cannot be dismissed as a shallow opportunist. He went down with the PKI which he had favored, rather than accept the transfer to the anti-Communist forces that became dominant in the aftermath of the September 30 Movement of the enormous political capital represented by his popularity.

This is not the place for an essay on Sukarno's political behavior, but I believe that a crude, personalized version of Marxism had conditioned him against accepting the role of a "bourgeois nationalist." The revolutionary heroes who had captured his youthful imagination must have implanted the desire, which became stronger after he had passed his prime, to be remembered as a true revolutionary leader. The PKI capitalized on these traits successfully, up to a point, but in the end its reliance on Sukarno had catastrophic results.

Yet all this does not warrant the facile conclusion that Sukarno was the tool of a protracted Communist conspiracy. There are striking discontinuities in his political career. When armed Communist units rebelled against the Republican government in September 1948 at Madiun, Sukarno—though only after intensive prodding by nationalist officers—lent his popularity to the Indonesian Army and appealed by radio to the Indonesian people to choose between him and the Communist leader Musso.[20]

In 1951 Sukarno was still being attacked by the PKI as a "false and demagogic Marxist," "playing a primary role in the Madiun Affair" and "selling out his country to the Dutch in the Round Table Conference Agreement."[21]

Only after D. N. Aidit and his young associates Lukman, Njoto, and Sudisman, took over the leadership of the PKI did Sukarno's relations with the Communists become increasingly cordial. Under his protection the PKI then grew from less than 8,000 members in 1951 to a gigantic mass organization in 1965. In the 1960s, Aidit, Njoto, and Lukman became ministers of State. Then the three Communist leaders met their death, as did many thousands of their followers, and Sukarno's career ended ignominiously, as the result of one of the most bizarre political episodes of contemporary history.

THE SEPTEMBER 30 AFFAIR

On the night of September 30 to October 1, 1965, six senior generals of the Indonesian Army were either shot down in their homes or taken to a place on the perimeter of the Indonesian Air Force base Halim Perdanakusuma and murdered there. The only target of the conspirators who escaped, by jumping over the wall and hiding for several hours, was Defense Minister and Chief of Staff of the Armed Forces General A. H. Nasution. Those who lost their lives were Commander of the Army, Lieutenant General A. Yani, and five senior members of the General Staff, Major General Soeprapto, Major General S. Parman, Major General Harjono, Brigadier General D. I. Pandjaitan, and Brigadier General Soetojo Siswomihardjo.

Hours after these assassinations, at 7:15 on the morning of October 1st, the Djakarta radio station, which had been occupied by rebel troops, broadcast a long statement which began as follows:

On Thursday, September 30, 1965, a military move took place within the Army in the capital city of Djakarta which was aided by troops from other branches of the Armed Forces. The September 30th Movement, which is led by Lieutenant Colonel Untung, Commandant of a Battalion of the Tjakrabirawa, the personal bodyguard of President Sukarno, is directed against Generals who were members of the self-styled Council of Generals. A number of Generals have been arrested and important communications media and other vital installations have been placed under the control of the September 30th Movement, while President Sukarno is safe under its protection. Also a number of other prominent leaders in society, who had become targets of the action by the Council of Generals, are under the protection of the September 30th Movement.

The Council of Generals is a subversive movement sponsored by the CIA and has been very active lately, especially since President Sukarno was seri ously ill in the first week of August of this year. Their hope that President Sukarno would die of his illness has not materialized.

Therefore, in order to attain its goal the Council of Generals had planned to conduct a show of force (*machtvertoon*) on Armed Forces Day, October 5 this year, by bringing troops from East, Central and West Java. With this large concentration of military power the Council of Generals had even planned to carry out a counter-revolutionary coup prior to October 5, 1965. It was to prevent such a counter-revolutionary coup that Lieutenant Colonel Untung launched the September 30th Movement which has proved a great success.[22]

Far from being a great success, the September 30 Movement failed to secure power, led to the death of those involved in it, and reversed the course of Indonesian history, by precipitating the destruction of the PKI.

Many students of Indonesian politics, including the present writer, found it at first difficult to believe that the PKI had anything to do with that brutal and clumsy plot. The leaders of the PKI seemed to be skillful and patient operators who had been able to build their party into a formidable political organization and had acquired in the process considerable stature in their own country and in the international Communist movement. Their past caution made it implausible that they would repeat the mistakes of 1926 and 1948, which had temporarily destroyed their party.

Before October 1965, considerable controversy prevailed among foreign experts with regard to the future of the PKI. It was claimed by some that the apparent strength of the PKI was illusory.[23] In that view, Communist leaders were being absorbed into the Indonesian ruling class, whose way of life they were emulating, while failing to develop among their followers the militancy required for a revolutionary take-over. Therefore, Communist victory appeared to those observers as an unlikely possibility.

By contrast, the present writer concluded, in the first half of 1964, that the PKI had outmaneuvered all major rival political organizations and, because of Indonesia's urgent need for better government, would come to power in the near future, by a combination of three factors: Sukarno's active support, lack of political competitors within the framework of an increasingly radical political milieu, and gradual elimination of all effective opposition, an operation justified in part by a militant foreign policy that equated all actions of the regime with the national interest.[24]

Those who saw no future for the PKI were convinced that it would never dare confront the Army, which would therefore be able to block indefinitely the PKI's road to power. Alternatively, I believed that the prevailing atmosphere of radical nationalism, under a leadership pursuing an aggressive, ego-gratifying foreign policy, claiming for Indonesia the role of "lighthouse" of the Third World, would induce the military establishment to accept the PKI as partner in the common pursuit of national glory.

Communist leaders and Army officers were, after all, members of the same generation, whose lives had been dominated by the struggle against colonialism and by strong anti-imperialist sentiments. They were not divided by genuine class antagonisms, but came from the same social background, in a country that lacked both substantial landowners and indigenous capitalists.

Communist leaders and members of the officer corps might have been brought together by Sukarno's patient policy of reconciliation, in the name of shared national aspirations. In this task, the PKI at first helped Sukarno. Although they were attacking the officer corps as "bureaucratic capitalists," a pejorative term borrowed from Communist China, the PKI leaders were also courting the military by offering cooperation through the National Front, making repeated appearances at the war colleges and incessant appeals for common action in pursuit of nationalist aspirations.

Although past states of mind are difficult to reconstruct, especially after the upheaval of 1965, the military could hardly have avoided being ambivalent toward the Communists, who seemed so successful and had such powerful friends, not only in Sukarno but also abroad. It could not have escaped the attention of the military that the PKI had abstained from using its influence with the Communist Party of the Soviet Union (CPSU) to block the Soviet military assistance programs initiated around 1960. The relationship between the two forces was not as simple as it appears in retrospect .

PKI RADICALISM AFTER 1963

What has to be explained is why, after 1963, the PKI committed, first the strategic mistake of adopting new policies which placed it on a collision course with the Army and then the tactical mistake of making a showdown unavoidable by initiating the assassination of the Army leadership. Were the PKI leaders dizzy with success? Their fatal self-confidence seems to have grown inordinately after Sukarno decreed the abolition of martial law on December 19, 1962, effective as of May 1, 1963. From then on they seem to have overestimated their victory against the military, and perhaps also the strength of their following inside the Armed Forces.

There was, of course, some factual basis for their overconfidence. Security operations since October 1965, and especially in the summer of 1968, revealed that the PKI had made serious inroads within the

Army, including senior officers whose affiliation was so well concealed
that they still occupied positions of trust two years after the PKI had
been banned.

Besides, in the political climate prevailing in Indonesia in 1964 and
1965, even persons secretly hostile to Communism may have given
the impression of being friendly toward the PKI or at least neutral.
Sukarno, who constantly denounced what he called "Communist-pho-
bia," had not only managed to make anti-Communism appear politically
dangerous, but he also presented it as bad form, something just not
done in his country.

Aidit and his comrades may have overestimated the weight of their
support in the Armed Forces and also the "revolutionary situation" in
the country as a whole. They may have believed their own statistics,
according to which roughly one-fifth of the total population, or almost
one-half of the adult population, appeared friendly to the PKI. If so,
they committed the fatal mistake of equating friendly inclinations with
militancy.

In November 1963, a field grade Army officer concerned with Territorial Affairs told me that PKI's membership drives were successful
largely because people had much free time in the villages and slums of
Indonesia and were starved for news and entertainment. A membership
card opened to the holder participation in meetings where newspapers
were read, matters of general interest were discussed, and intellectual
stimulation was provided. According to that officer, membership figures
did not measure the PKI's strength as a militant organization.

At the time, impressed by the PKI's dynamism, which contrasted so
strikingly with the apathy of other political parties, I discounted the
argument. I realized that aggressive, fanatic, dedicated cadres are a
small minority in any movement, but I assumed that the sheer weight
of numbers would protect the PKI and was bound to make itself felt
in the political life of the country. Naturally, in free elections members
of Communist-controlled organizations were likely to vote for the PKI,
however lacking they might be in militancy. If a new government were
to be appointed by Sukarno, in an extra-parliamentary setting, the size
of the PKI and the disarray of its political rivals was a powerful argument in favor of the Communists. Even in case of internal war it
could be assumed that those who had Communist sympathies would
at least passively favor PKI guerrillas against their enemies. Finally, it
seemed difficult to visualize the destruction of a party with such a
broad mass base. In November 1964, I had written:

Were the Communists to lose Sukarno as a protector, it seems doubtful that
other national leaders, capable of rallying Indonesia's dispersed and demoralized anti-Communist forces, would emerge in the near future. Furthermore,

these forces would probably lack the ruthlessness that made it possible for the Nazis to suppress the Communist Party of Germany a few weeks after the elections of March 5, 1933, an election in which the Communist Party still won five million votes, almost 13 percent of the total. The enemies of the PKI, including the remnants of various right-wing rebellions, the suppressed political parties, and certain elements in the armed forces, are weaker than the Nazis, not only in numbers and in mass support, but also in unity, discipline, and leadership.[25]

The assassination of the six Army generals by the September 30 Movement elicited the ruthlessness that I had not anticipated a year earlier and resulted in the death of large numbers of Communist cadres. Then, social tensions created in the countryside by Communist agrarian and other policies exploded in large-scale massacres triggered by the Army's anti-Communist mopping-up operations. Thus, contrary to my forecast, the PKI was destroyed as an overt organization and up to 300,000 persons were killed.

Aidit's change of strategy during the year 1963 may have been based on similarly erroneous assumptions. His Political Report to the First Plenum of the Seventh Central Committee presented on February 10, 1963, entitled "Dare, Dare, and Dare Again!" sounded the keynote for a new policy.[26] The strategy pursued by the PKI under Aidit's leadership between 1951 and 1963 had been to change slowly and cautiously the balance of power between political forces. In May 1953, he had stated:

The PKI uses Marxism-Leninism as a constant guide in determining the character of its policy; it also bases its decisions on the existing balance in social forces. The PKI is obliged to continuously calculate the balance in the unstable social forces in Indonesia.[27]

After the failure of the PKI to obtain seats in a coalition cabinet, even though it had established itself as one of the country's four major parties and was willing to cooperate with the other three, the Communist leaders probably reviewed their strategy, which Aidit then explained to the Fourth Plenary Session of the Fifth Central Committee in July 1956 in these words:

The PKI's work is not limited solely to the parliamentary struggle, but consists also, and primarily, in activity among the masses of workers, peasants, intelligentsia, and all other democratic masses. Basically, the PKI's activity is to change the balance of power between the imperialists, landlords, and other comprador bourgeoisie on the one hand, and the people on the other, by arousing, mobilizing and organizing the masses.[28]

During this period the PKI concentrated on signing up anybody who was willing to join, in the hope of creating a bandwagon effect. This is the strategy which I described as the road to power by acclamation, based on creating the impression of an irresistibly dynamic movement which also had the endorsement of the unchallenged national leader Sukarno. But after almost eight years this stratgy had not yet succeeded, despite the fact that the PKI's major enemies among the political parties, namely the *Masjumi* and the PSI, had been banned by Sukarno in August 1960, and Indonesia had moved very close to the international Communist orbit.

Aidit and his associates were apparently under increasing attack from younger cadres who were beginning to lose confidence in the strategy of protracted struggle and were also viewing with suspicion the mingling of Politburo members with the "bourgeois establishment." This problem came to the surface in Aidit's remark at the First National Conference of the PKI, on July 3, 1964:

The internal contradictions in the Party cannot be avoided but must be faced, taken care of and terminated. In settling in the right way the Party's internal contradictions, the skill and quality of the leadership increases. Bringing to an end the internal contradictions of the Party is an absolute condition for increasing the ability of the Party to terminate external contradictions.[29]

But Aidit and his senior comrades were themselves increasingly disenchanted with the Soviet Union, which had capitulated on Cuba in October 1962, had refused economic aid for the rapid development of Communist China, and had not been able to help the PKI achieve its domestic objectives despite massive military and economic aid to the Sukarno regime. The February 1963 Political Report reflected the growing impatience of the PKI leadership, which was under pressure from the more militant younger PKI cadres and probably also from its Chinese friends:

Although the demand for the formation of a Gotong-Royong Cabinet with NASAKOM as the fulcrum[30] is scientific, objective, democratic, and patriotic, the Indonesian Communists must be fully conscious of the fact that the question of its formation is one of the balance of forces, and that there is no class that voluntarily wants to share power with another class. Not only is the reactionary bourgeoisie reluctant to share power with another class, but the national bourgeoisie too, unless compelled to do so, is reluctant to share power with the proletariat.[31]

CHINESE INFLUENCES ON AIDIT

Although the conclusion that even the national bourgeoisie must be compelled to share power with the proletariat was expressed publicly in February 1963, marking the beginning of the PKI's new militancy, the policy of the party seemed still to be vacillating a few months later when Aidit made several speeches in China, following visits to several other Communist countries, including the Soviet Union. In a report delivered to the Higher Party School of the Central Committee of the Communist Party of China on September 2, 1963 , he argued that

. . . the state power of the Republic of Indonesia is a contradiction between two opposing aspects: The first aspect is that which represents the interests of the people. The second aspect is that which represents the interest of the people's enemies. The *first aspect* is embodied in the progressive attitude and policy of President Sukarno which enjoys the support of the CPI and other sections of the people. The *second aspect* is embodied in the attitude and policy of the rightists and the diehards; they are the old established forces. Today the popular aspect has become the *main aspect* and plays a leading role in the state power of the Republic of Indonesia, meaning that it guides the course of the political development in the state power of the Republic of Indonesia.[32]

The impression conveyed by this passage is that Aidit assumed that the balance of power had tipped in favor of the PKI. Yet he obviously still had doubts and hesitations, and he expressed them in an obscure passage in which he claimed that "the antipopular aspect has ceased to be the main aspect," but "it is still the dominant aspect." What this could perhaps mean is that he believed that the anti-Communist forces no longer had real influence on the formulation of Sukarno's policies, but were still a dangerous obstruction blocking the PKI's road to power.

Two days later, on September 4, 1963, at a mass rally in Peking, Aidit stated that he expected the struggle for power in Indonesia to be a lengthy one:

On the basis of an analysis of Indonesian society and of the Indonesian revolution, the Constitution of the CPI [sic] stresses that the Indonesian revolution is a protracted and complex one. To be able to guide the revolution, the CPI must carry the people's revolutionary struggle forward by using the tactic of advancing steadily, carefully and surely. In the course of the struggle, the CPI must consistently oppose two trends: capitulationism and adventurism.[33]

It would seem that while preparing his September 2 and 4 speeches Aidit was still hesitating between the peaceful and the violent road to power, a dilemma which—as will be seen below—was apparently solved during the following three weeks of his stay in China. On September 4 the main thrust of the PKI's strategy seemed yet to be in line with the Party's past policy, based on the concept of the two aspects of state power in Indonesia, the popular aspect and the anti-popular aspect:

Indonesia must carry out the revolution from top to bottom and from bottom to top. By "from top to bottom" we mean that the CPI has to urge the state to adopt various revolutionary measures and carry out reforms in personnel and in state organs. By "from bottom to top" we mean that the Party has to arouse, organize and mobilize the people to realize these reforms. By these methods the Party is changing the balance of forces between imperialism, the bureaucrat-capitalists, compradors and landlords on the one hand and the people on the other.[34]

Aidit found it still necessary to argue, in intellectually rather unconvincing terms, that his policy was different from the Italian Communist Party's doctrine of "structural reform," which was viewed at that time in the Communist world as the epitome of gradualism and had occasioned the vigorous denunciation of the Italian Communist leader Palmiro Togliatti by the Communist Party of China.[35] He probably still felt rather defensive on this issue, particularly in China.

We know, from a statement made by the Italian Communist leader Giuliano Pajetta after a visit to Djakarta in April 1963 that he was surprised to find the views of the PKI to "differ markedly" from those of his own party. Pajetta confessed that he failed to understand the Indonesians' "prejudice against the 'peaceful paths.'"[36] This is useful testimony, from a visitor who had probably lengthy doctrinal discussions with the PKI leaders. It corroborates the statement made to the February 1963 Plenum, which we discussed earlier. But altogether, the speeches in Peking on September 2 and 4 seem to express uncertainty about the future course the PKI should take, probably because the Communist leaders feared the reaction of the military. How Aidit was hoping to deal with this crucial problem is reflected in the following passage of his September 4 speech in which he contrasted the struggle against the Dutch with the present:

Today there are no enemy armed forces in Indonesia; there are only the armed forces of the Republic of Indonesia which were born shortly after World War II in the anti-fascist struggle and the national democratic revolution. In building these forces, the working class and the CPI played an important role. They are not reactionary armed forces. It can be seen from their inception that they have been anti-fascist, democratic, and anti-imperialist in character. The duty of the CPI is, therefore, to closely unite the people and the armed forces, so that in any crisis the armed forces, or their greater part, will stand firmly on the side of the people and revolution. . . .[37]

ON COLLISION COURSE WITH THE ARMY

We have no way of knowing whether the words of Aidit's September 4, 1963, speech represented more than the expression of hope that the PKI and the Army would eventually join forces. But we do know that a year later Aidit initiated concrete steps to translate this thought into reality. The investigations and trials conducted by the Indonesian military authorities in connection with the September 30 Movement revealed the existence of a clandestine organization created by Aidit in November 1964, which was known to a few Communist leaders as the Special

Bureau (*Biro Chusus*), to others as the Contact Board (*Badan Penghubung*), or as the Contact Bureau (*Biro Penghubung*).

This organization consisted of a small group of trusted cadres whose primary mission was to establish close personal relations with individual military officers, indoctrinate them patiently if they seemed friendly and willing to help the PKI, and use them eventually for Party purposes.

Officers were not invited to fill out membership forms and become card-holding Communists, as military personnel were not supposed to have party affiliations. Furthermore, officers "managed" by members of the Special Bureau were not put in contact with each other ("horizontal organization"), but were only in touch with the PKI cadre who was assigned to maintain contact with them. When an officer was transferred from one locality to another, the Special Bureau arranged, through carefully guarded channels, that he be contacted by another PKI cadre.

The Central Special Bureau managed a number of military officers stationed in Djakarta. It also set up Regional Special Bureaus in the provinces.

This whole clandestine network was not linked organizationally with the rest of the PKI, but existed under the personal supervision of the Party Chairman, D. N. Aidit, and reported only to him. Although it is not entirely clear how much other members of the PKI leadership knew about the Special Bureau, it would seem that even at the very top, among members of the Politburo, this information was strictly guarded on a need-to-know basis, following a division of duties in mid-1964 that left all military matters exclusively to Aidit.

In the provinces, the head of the Regional Special Bureau was responsible directly and exclusively to the Central Special Bureau and functioned outside the overt organizational structure of the PKI. The PKI structure itself consisted of 27 Greater Regional Committees (*Comite Daerah Besar* or CDB), responsible for major provinces or metropolitan areas, which were subdivided into Section Committees at the regency (*Kabupaten*) or city level. These, in turn, supervised Subsection Committees responsible for districts (*Ketjamatan*), smaller towns, or urban sectors. Only the CDB First Secretary, as the highest provincial representative of the PKI, knew in some cases the name of the Special Bureau representative, but even the First Secretary was apparently unfamiliar with the details of the Regional Special Bureau's operations.

As head of the Special Bureau, Aidit appointed a trusted personal aide, one Kamarusaman bin Achmad Moebaidah, known to participants in the September 30 Movement as Sjam. The first significant indications that the PKI was involved in the coup came from the interrogations of Lieutenant Colonel Untung and other conspirators, who stated that a representative of the PKI named Sjam participated in their planning sessions in September 1965.

Sjam was captured on March 9, 1967, and tried by an Extraordinary Military Tribunal in Bandung a year later. I attended his trial, and most of the information used here is derived from the statements made in my presence before the court and from the records of Sjam's preliminary investigation which I have studied. According to his statements in court, the Special Bureau had recruited about 40 to 50 PKI sympathizers in the Armed Forces in Djakarta, 80 to 100 in West Java, around 250 in Central Java, 200 in East Java, 30 to 40 in North Sumatra, and 30 in West Sumatra. All participants in the September 30 Movement were recruited through the Special Bureau and followed its instructions.

Sjam said that he was put in charge of the Special Bureau because, as early as 1957, Aidit had asked him to find a solution to the problem of how to deal with officers who wanted to be sympathizers or members of the PKI, despite the fact that there was a ban on military personnel joining any political party. The Special Bureau was established in 1964 as a way to solve the organizational problem of how to utilize pro-Communist officers.

The establishment of the Special Bureau was a major, covert, manifestation of the new militancy that became dominant among the leaders of the PKI in late 1963. As mentioned above, Aidit still seemed hesitant at the time of his speeches in Peking on September 2 and 4. Then, during the following three weeks, which he must have spent in consultation with the Chinese leaders, something seems to have happened. At the end of his visit, speaking in Canton on September 25, 1963, Aidit stated that the PKI "must have confidence in its own strength" and announced that the PKI "will always be on the side of Marxism-Leninism and oppose revisionism."[38] This, in context, could only be interpreted as a firm commitment to support China, given in a form the PKI had previously avoided.

Yet, despite the increased militancy discernible in Aidit's speeches between September 4 and September 25, they were still very cautious statements compared with what he was to say in his Political Report to the Second Plenum of the Seventh Central Committee on December 23, 1963, at which time the PKI's new line was openly proclaimed. Many clues indicate that Aidit discussed his doubts about the PKI's previous strategy with the Chinese leaders, came back strengthened in his belief that a new line was necessary, and proclaimed it after obtaining the agreement of his colleagues in the Politburo. For instance, the Partial Nuclear Test-Ban Treaty had been signed in Moscow on August 5, 1963, and Aidit had a chance to denounce it during his visit to China, where such a posture would have been warmly welcomed. Yet Aidit made no public mention of it, in China, but then attacked it strongly in his December 1963 Report to the Second Plenum.

Aidit also openly attacked the Soviet Union for the first time. He warned that "it is a great mistake to think that the restoration of capitalism cannot take place in Socialist countries." He deplored the fact that "there are also Socialist countries whose state leaders are striving to eradicate or in the very least to gloss over the contradiction between Socialism and imperialism by speaking fine words about U.S. imperialism." He argued that "there should be no question about the Socialist countries assisting the national independence struggle because this should be something quite automatic. A country is not a genuine Socialist country if it does not genuinely assist the struggle for national independence." He denounced the viewpoint of "modern economism in the international Communist movement," which is "calling upon the people in the newly independent countries to halt their revolutionary struggle and to rely completely upon economic aid from the Socialist countries while sitting by and gazing in wonderment at the economic construction in those countries." He pleaded:

. . . between the victory of Socialism in one country and the victory of the world Socialist revolution there is an inseparable connection. The Socialist revolution that has already been victorious in one country must not be turned into a self-contained entity and cut off from the rest; it must be turned into an assistant or means in order to speed up the victories of revolutions in other countries.[39]

Beyond doubt, by December 1963 there was complete agreement between the leaders of the PKI and the Maoists concerning the Soviet Union. Aidit had chosen to become an enemy of the Kremlin, abandoning the previous posture of careful neutrality in the Sino-Soviet conflict.

The same militancy characterized Aidit's new attitude toward the Indonesian Army. In the December 1963 Report there were no kind words for the military, unlike the September statement previously quoted. This time Aidit denounced "the counter-revolutionary adventurers" in sharp words:

They have long striven to bring about the downfall of what they call the "Sukarno regime." They have tried by means of *coup d'état*, by means of counter-revolutionary rebellion, by attempting to assassinate President Sukarno, by attempts to brand President Sukarno as "communist" so as to draw the more backward religious sections over to their side.[40]

It should be noted at this point that the September 30 Movement was created two years later by the PKI's Special Bureau by convincing a number of managed officers that the counter-revolutionaries were preparing a coup against Sukarno. Equally significant in Aidit's statement of December 1963 was the fact that he no longer seemed interested in cooperation with the military in the context of Indonesia's ambitious and aggressive foreign policy. The leaders of the Army had endeavored, throughout 1963, to make militant statements against Malaysia and against Western imperialism. Aidit dismissed all such statements contemptuously as part of a devious plot:

In public, the counter-revolutionary adventurers are fond of publishing "fiery" statements about "Malaysia" with the result that foreign observers who do not grasp the question frequently get all confused, and the gullible ones are easily deceived, because the words the adventurers used are the same as those used in statements made by the Communists and other revolutionaries. This confusion quickly disappears, after the real motive behind their "fiery" words is explained, namely fishing for limited military action by the British so as to arouse panic at home which they hope will present them with a good opportunity to put an end to the "Sukarno regime" or at the very least to make Bung Karno [i.e., Sukarno] their political captive, willing to sign whatever they present him with, and then finally establish good relations with "Malaysia" and the British as well as presenting their victory to the U.S.A.[41]

These statements suggest that, by December 1963, Aidit was consciously engaging the PKI on a collision course with the Army. The officers were no longer treated as acceptable partners in Indonesia's chauvinistic foreign policy. Indeed they were accused of being "imperialist agents," a charge which appeared again in the initial proclamation of the September 30 Movement.[42] The same defiant mood against his opponents prevailed throughout 1964 and culminated in Aidit's great strategic mistake on January 14, 1965, when he requested the arming of peasants and workers "in reply to the large-scale military build-up of the British imperialists in Malaysia."[43]

Even though, on the same day, Sukarno told foreign correspondents that he had rejected the demand, Aidit repeated it publicly at a meeting of the National Front on January 17:

I have submitted a proposal to President Sukarno to arm immediately the workers and peasants, the pillars of the revolution. No less than 5 million organized workers and 10 million organized peasants are ready to take up arms. This is the only correct reply to the British and American aggression.[44]

In thus trying to acquire a paramilitary capability, the PKI was challenging a cardinal principle of the Army. From the early days of the struggle for independence, when a multitude of armed groups had been established by spontaneous social action, the Army had been hostile to irregular military formations, some of which were affiliated with political parties. Efforts to bring all these formations under the control of the General Staff led to the September 1948 Madiun rebellion, in which the Army suffered and inflicted heavy casualties at a time when the very existence of the Republic of Indonesia was in jeopardy. The memory of that violent episode was a crucial factor in the lasting hostility of the officer corps toward the PKI. The specter of new Communist paramilitary formations was bound to be totally unacceptable to the Army. In his State of the Union address on August 17, 1965, Sukarno noted "heated discussions" concerning this idea, which he now presented not as Aidit's but as his own:

I feel gratified for all the support that has been given to my idea. We always have to set out from the facts. The facts are that NEKOLIM[45] are aiming the tip of their sword and the barrel of their gun at us. The facts are that the defense of the State demands a maximum of effort from us all while, according to Article 30 of our 1945 Constitution: "Every citizen shall have the right and the duty to participate in the defense of the State." After an even more thorough consideration of this question, I will make a decision on this matter in my capacity as Supreme Commander of the Armed Forces.[46]

CLASS STRUGGLE IN THE COUNTRYSIDE

Aidit did not limit the PKI's militancy to a confrontation with the military. The agrarian policy proclaimed in December 1963 abandoned, for all practical purposes, the united front strategy followed since 1951 and launched an appeal for class war in the countryside:

All talk about modernizing Indonesia and about completing the revolution is also nonsense so long as there is not the courage to implement radical land reform. Indonesia is an agrarian country where feudal survivals still predominate. It is for this reason that the Indonesian revolution is in essence an agrarian revolution, a revolution of the peasants.[47]

This analysis of the Indonesian situation, in line with Maoist doctrine, was no idle verbal exercise. The PKI, through its Indonesian Farmers' Front, which claimed at that time over seven million members, had already initiated in the countryside, especially in over-populated East and Central Java, the Unilateral Action Movement (*Gerakan Aksi Sefihak*), inciting the Javanese peasants to take the law into their own hands and implement the 1960 basic agrarian law and the law on crop-sharing agreements. Until then, the local authorities had paid lipservice to the idea of agrarian reform, while actually siding with the existing vested interests. Now, in his December 1963 Report, Aidit stated that "revolutionaries must enthusiastically welcome and encourage unilateral actions taken by the peasants."[48]

Unilateral actions took such proportions that Acting President Dr. Johanes Leimena found it necessary, on June 15, 1964, to order the Department of Home Affairs to prevent such actions by seeking the best possible settlement of agrarian disputes through mutual consultations.[49]

The Farmers' Front, in defiance of the Government's appeal, announced that it was planning more intensified and consolidated actions against the landlords, and demanded the dismissal of officials who took a tough attitude toward the peasants. The first National Conference of the PKI, held in Djakarta from July 3 to 5, 1964, adopted a special resolution supporting the unilateral actions of the peasants in strongest terms and condemning "the despicable slanders of the despotic landlords and their apologists who are against the basic agrarian law and the law on the crop-sharing agreement." It also requested the establishment of land reform courts that would include representatives of communist peasant organizations, and the release of arrested peasants.[50]

On July 10, 1964, a special court in Klaten, Central Java, opened the trial of a group of members of the Farmers' Front who were arrested after violent clashes with the police. President Sukarno, in his August 17, 1964, Independence Day address, while avoiding explicit endorsement of the Unilateral Action Movement (Aksi Sefihak), conveyed his sympathy for the Movement, expressed his concern with the fate of the peasants, and ordered the immediate completion of the basic agrarian law on Java, Madura, and Bali. On September 24, 1964, the Cabinet Presidium created a committee to expedite agrarian affairs, consisting of Police Brigadier General Mudjoko and PKI Vice-Chairman Njoto, both Ministers attached to the Presidium, and R. Hermanses, Minister for Agrarian Affairs. The same day, the establishment of land reform courts that included peasant representatives was announced.

These efforts on the part of the Government did not stop unilateral actions in Java. Clashes between Farmers' Front members and local authorities continued throughout the last months of 1964. Particularly violent riots over the distribution of public forest lands involving 2,000 peasants led by the Farmers' Front took place at Indramaju, West Java, on October 15 and 16. Several policemen were injured and sixty-four peasants were held for trial.

By May 1965, the class struggle in the countryside seems to have worried Aidit. In his Political Report to the Fourth Plenum of the Seventh Central Committee in May 1965, he remarked that "in some places Farmers' Front cadres, because of their desire to increase peasants' actions, have acted impulsively." And although he noted with obvious satisfaction that the Farmers' Front now had a membership of "about nine million peasants," he warned that "the peasant movement must proceed in a framework of strict discipline."[51]

If Aidit had already decided, by May 1965, to eliminate the anti-Communist leadership of the Army, he may have considered it undesirable to intensify further the revolutionary situation in the countryside, as these actions increased the risk that the PKI's enemies might combine to crush the Party. In other words, if the September 30 Movement was already taking shape in Aidit's mind as a preventive measure against future anti-Communist moves by the military, it made sense to keep the PKI's enemies from closing ranks prematurely.

But the decision to stop "unilateral actions" came too late. The PKI was soon to suffer the consequences. In my opinion, by disrupting the harmony (*rukun*)[52] of the Indonesian village community, the Farmers' Front unilateral actions set the stage for the gruesome massacre of hundreds of thousands of Communists in the aftermath of the September 30 Movement.[53]

THE COUP THAT FAILED

The detailed story of the events that led to the destruction of the PKI does not belong here. Some details are still missing and may never be established. What happened: In May 1965, rumors circulated in PKI and Indonesian intelligence circles that a Council of Generals (*Dewan Djenderal*) was planning a coup against Sukarno. The origin of these rumors is not easy to establish, though there are various speculations. But it was an open secret at the time that the Commander of the Army, Lieutenant General A. Yani, and his informal "brain trust," consisting of Major General Suprapto, Major General S. Parman, Major General Harjono, and Brigadier General Sukendro, were discussing "contingency plans" to prevent chaos should Sukarno die suddenly.

For several years President Sukarno's health and age had been the central preoccupation of all those concerned with the politics of the "post-Sukarno period."[54] After the resignation of Vice-President Hatta in December 1956, there was no clear line of legitimate succession to the presidency. This situation encouraged innumerable ambitions and generated endless political maneuvers.

Early in August 1965, Sukarno had a brief illness which made Aidit rush back from a visit to Peking, bringing with him two Chinese doctors who had previously treated Sukarno's chronic kidney condition. The doctors apparently informed Aidit that Sukarno might soon die or be permanently incapacitated. From the investigations and trials of Communist leaders in connection with the September 30 Movement, we know that the political implications of this medical assessment were discussed by the Politburo of the PKI, which was already in a very militant state of mind. As Sudisman told the Extraordinary Military Tribunal on July 5, 1967, in open court, the Politburo, following the Fourth Plenum of the Seventh Central Committee (May 1965), was already implementing the decision to "step up to the utmost" the revolutionary situation. Thus, when on August 28, 1965, Aidit introduced the issue of Sukarno's health and its possible consequences for the PKI, the Politburo unanimously approved a pre-emptive military operation against the Council of Generals, and the formation of a Revolutionary Council that would lead to a change of Cabinet.

Interrogation by the judges brought out the facts that Sudisman had no information about this Council of Generals other than what Aidit had told the Politburo, that the plans for the September 30 Movement remained unchanged even after Sukarno had recovered from his early August illness, and that, while Sudisman accepted full responsibility as a member of the Politburo who had participated in the crucial August 28 decision, he, personally, was not involved in the actual planning of the military operations, which was exclusively Aidit's responsibility.[55]

The PKI leaders were probably genuinely afraid, and in my opinion rightly so, that if Sukarno died before the political balance of forces had been changed, the Army would re-establish martial law, take charge of the government, and set back or even ban the PKI. Worrying, like the PKI, about the "post-Sukarno period," the Army General Staff had obviously made contingency plans. The officer corps had always considered themselves the custodians of their new nation, and Sukarno's policies had created a succession crisis in that the country lacked legitimate procedures for the replacement of the President in case of sudden death or incapacity.

These contingency plans of the Army, about which there is little concrete information, were turned into the May 1965 rumor that a Council of Generals was planning a coup *against* Sukarno. The legitimate hierarchy of the Army was made to appear as a conspiratorial junta, and the contingency plans of a group of senior officers who had not violated their oath of loyalty to the Commander-in-Chief were made to seem a plot against him.

In October 1965, events were to disprove these malicious rumors. If the Army leaders had actually planned to overthrow Sukarno it would have been much easier for the survivors to carry out this plan after October 1 when public opinion would have supported their action. But in fact no action was taken against Sukarno until March 1966, and his rule was only terminated in March 1967, after he had made defiant efforts to protect the PKI and to obstruct the Army's security operations.

Any explanation of the role of the so-called Council of Generals in prompting Aidit to organize the September 30 Movement hinges on the question of what the chairman of the PKI really believed at the time. If the rumor that such a Council of Generals was ready to depose Sukarno was launched by others, Aidit may have believed it, panicked, and organized the September 30 Movement as a counter-move, after his return from Peking in August.

But I am inclined to believe that Aidit was preparing his own offensive against the Army leadership before the rumors about a Council
of Generals began to spread in late May 1965, which suggests that those
rumors were actually initiated by him, as part of a scenario that would
also have taken advantage of Sukarno's next health failure in order
to maximize the PKI's chances of obtaining the support of the officers
managed by the Special Bureau that he had created in November 1964.
In this context, there is an intriguing statement made by Aidit in his
Political Report to the Fourth Plenary Session of the Seventh Central
Committee, May 11, 1965. The Report, delivered on the eve of the
grandiose celebration of the forty-fifth anniversary of the PKI, included
the following passage:

With the strength of the national front based on Nasakom we succeeded in
delivering heavy blows to the enemies of the people, and the masses are further
convinced that the enemies can certainly be beaten. However, life itself proves
in a definite manner that the enemy still has a power we cannot trifle with. It
is, therefore, the duty of all revolutionary people, Communists in particular,
to hold firm to the principles of national unity based on Nasakom and *to determine in a better manner the smallest possible target at a given moment
while maintaining the broadest possible front. Finding the smallest possible
target means a concentration of attacks on the most obstinate enemies of the
revolution* [emphasis added].[56]

The smallest possible target was, logically, the top leadership of the
Army, which opposed a Nasakom Cabinet and which was capable of doing serious harm to the PKI, especially after Sukarno's death. If the
plan to eliminate the Army generals existed already in Aidit's mind
when he addressed the Central Committee in these terms in May 1965,
then Sukarno's brief illness in August 1965 and the rumors about a
Council of Generals were not causative factors that precipitated an im-
provised PKI action, but parts of a predetermined scenario. We may, of
course, never know with certainty whether Aidit panicked and moved
hastily, or acted in cold blood but bungled the operation.

My own impression is that the latter explanation is the correct one
I am particularly intrigued by a macabre detail which suggests that
Aidit was already carrying the plans for the September 30 Movement
in his head when he gave his Political Report on May 11, 1965. He
ended his statement, which lasted for seven hours and twenty-three
minutes,[57] by quoting a verse written by Central Committee member
and Head of its Cultural Affairs Department, Banda Harahap: "Nobody
intends to turn back, though death is awaiting."[58] This was the last po
litical report Aidit ever made to the Central Committee of the PKI. The
Party had indeed embarked on a road of no return. After the failure of
the September 30 Movement, Aidit fled to Central Java on a plane

provided by the Commander of the Air Force, Omar Dani. He then wandered around Central Java until November 22, 1965, when he was captured and summarily executed by the Army. His death was never officially announced.[59]

Njoto, the Second Deputy Chairman of the PKI, was captured and killed in early December 1965. Lukman, the First Deputy Chairman of the PKI, was killed in May 1966. Politburo member Sakirman was killed in October 1966, and Politburo member Rewang, in July 1968. Politburo members Njono and Sudisman were tried by the Extraordinary Military Tribunal, sentenced to death, and executed in October 1968. Candidate Politburo member Peris Pardede may have been executed soon after he was sentenced to death. Candidate Politburo member Anwar Sanusi also was arrested. Only Politburo member Jusuf Adjitorop escaped, having been in Peking since 1964 as Head of the Delegation of the Central Committee of the PKI to the Communist Party of China.[60] This means that only one out of the ten men who were Politburo members or candidate members in May 1965 escaped.

The Central Committee had been expanded by the First National Conference, held in July 1964, to fifty members and five candidate members.[61] If the ten members of the Central Committee who were also on the Politburo are included in the count, it appears that, as of July 1968, at least ten members of the Central Committee were dead and at least nineteen were under arrest. At most, twenty-six, or less than half, may have escaped the dragnet of the Army's security operations. Not a single Central Committee member's name other than Jusuf Adjitorop has been mentioned in the propaganda emanating from Peking. It would therefore appear that Communist China has not assisted any Communist leaders in escaping from Indonesia.

THE PKI UNDERGROUND

At the third and fourth sessions of his trial, on July 6, 1967, Sudisman admitted that after the failure of the September 30 Movement he met six times with Sujono Pradigdo, Head of the Central Verification Committee of the PKI, who was later arrested, and with Sukadi, Deputy Secretary of the Djakarta Raya Greater Regional Committee. They planned the clandestine rebuilding of the Party, on the basis of three-man groups. Their discussions started before the PKI had been formally banned on March 12, 1966, but continued thereafter. Sudisman told the court that those two men were the only ones with whom he could meet, and that it was difficult to hold a meeting of more than three men at one time.

In June 1966, they examined the situation of the Party and concluded that "subjectivism" was beginning to prevail among their comrades, who "feeling comfortable and secure refused to think about other comrades and did not conduct Party work actively." They also decided that in their struggle they should "not have any illusions about Bung Karno but be politically independent" and that the PKI must be rebuilt, "which is difficult to accomplish because of the security roundup conducted by the government."[62]

In trying to reorganize itself, the underground PKI is not only harassed by the Army but also divided on doctrinal grounds. Survivors of the official leadership of the PKI, speaking for the old Politburo of the Party, circulated statements in Java in 1966 characterized by the old independent spirit of the PKI. A group of PKI refugees, led by Politburo member Jusuf Adjitorop, keeps issuing declarations from Peking. The latest major public pronouncement of that group, which calls itself "the Delegation of the Central Committee of the PKI," is dated May 23, 1968, commemorating the 48th anniversary of the founding of the Party. It praises "the Indonesian Marxist-Leninists" for

the unfolding of guerrilla warfare, by establishing rural revolutionary bases, by arousing the peasant masses to undertake agrarian revolution, and by persevering in protracted armed struggle to encircle the cities from the countryside and eventually seize the cities and win national liberation.

Unlike the statements issued by Sudisman in the Javanese underground in 1966, those of the PKI refugees in Peking (and perhaps also those of the leaders who replaced Sudisman in Java) are characterized by outspoken adulation of Mao. The May 1968 statement contains the following passage:

From their own experience, the Indonesian Marxist-Leninists regard Mao Tsetung's thought as the sole guiding ideology of the PKI in building itself into a Marxist-Leninist party capable of leading the Indonesian revolution. In its May 23, 1967, statement the Political Bureau of the Central Committee of the PKI stressed: "The Indonesian Marxist-Leninists unhesitatingly recognize Mao Tsetung's thought as the peak of Marxism-Leninism in the present era, and are determined to study and use it as an effective weapon in the struggle for the liberation of Indonesia, which inevitably will have to follow the road of people's war as shown by Comrade Mao Tse-tung."[63]

A third group, distinctly pro-Soviet, appealed in 1967 for a return to the united front program of 1954 and attacked the pro-Chinese party leaders. The mimeographed PKI weekly, *Suara Pemuda Indonesia* (Voice of Indonesian Youth), published in Peking by the Indonesian Students Association in China, referred to this group in November 1968 as the "Thomas Sinuraja-Ali Chanafiah renegade clique." I do not know whether this group operates within Indonesia or abroad.

Of all the various statements issued, the three documents circulated in

1966 in Java in the name of the Politburo of the PKI are likely to be of lasting significance. All analyzed the Party's past mistakes and weaknesses. The first was dated May 23rd, to commemorate the forty-sixth anniversary of the PKI and the second was issued on the occasion of the twenty-first anniversary of the Proclamation of Independence on August 17. The third and most important statement, published in September, was entitled "Build the PKI Along the Marxist-Leninist Line to Lead People's Democratic Revolution in Indonesia (Self-Criticism of the Political Bureau of the Central Committee of the PKI)." We know, from his July 1967 trial, that the third statement was written by Sudisman, who, until he was captured in December 1966, acted as the *de facto* leader of the Party, being at that time the ranking Politburo member at liberty to direct the Communist underground.

The three statements were first published abroad in English translation in the *Indonesian Tribune* printed in Tirana, Albania.[64] The August statement was then reproduced in March 1967 in *People's Democracy*, the weekly of the pro-Chinese Communist Party of India CPI(M), published in Calcutta. Curiously, Peking did not give these documents circulation until July 1967, at which time they were broadcast by the New China News Agency, featured in the *Peking Review*, and discussed editorially in *Hongqi (Red Flag)*.

Another analysis of the September 30 Movement has been circulated by "The Marxist-Leninist Group of the PKI," which, despite its name, is clearly a pro-Soviet group. The earliest abridged version that has come to my attention was printed in New Delhi in March 1967, in *Main Stream*, the weekly publication of the pro-Soviet Communist Party of India. A full English version appeared in November 1967, in the *Information Bulletin* of the *World Marxist Review (Problems of Peace and Socialism)*, edited in Prague under Soviet direction and published in Toronto.

As was to be expected, these statements have a polemical purpose in the context of the Sino-Soviet doctrinal debate. The pro-Soviet group claims that the Chinese point of view "was instrumental in paving the theoretical way for the gamble known as the September 30 Movement."[65] The pro-Chinese groups retort that the PKI's downfall was caused by weaknesses resulting from Soviet revisionist doctrine. It should be noted that all these statements have been issued anonymously. The various factions are obviously competing for supremacy in the Indonesian underground and prefer to let the surviving cadres believe that they represent the whole Party.

In "Self-Criticism of the Political Bureau" Sudisman accused "the PKI leadership," meaning Aidit, of "adventurism," and wrote: "Violating organizational rules they had easily involved themselves in the September 30 Movement that was not based on the high consciousness and conviction of the masses." Sudisman meant obviously that Aidit acted

without the consent of the official policy-making organs of the Party
and misjudged the militancy of the rank-and-file. He also condemned:

. . . the mistakes in the organizational field, in particular those concerning the
style of work which gave the Party leadership the power to build their own
organizational channel beyond the control of the Political Bureau and the Central Committee.[66]

This was clearly a reference to the Special Bureau set up by Aidit
under the leadership of Sjam. At his trial, Sudisman admitted publicly
that the Special Bureau was directly under Aidit and that its functions
"were never mentioned because its nature was special." He also stated
that he did not know exactly what Sjam's functions were, either in general or in the September 30 Movement, but knew that he was very
close to Aidit.[67] Sudisman, who acted with great dignity at his trial, accepting collective responsibility as one of the top leaders of the PKI,
had good reasons to criticize Aidit if, as he stated in the "Self-Criticism,"
the Politburo had not been fully informed about Aidit's plans.

Some observers have dismissed Sudisman's confessions and those of
other defendants before the Extraordinary Military Tribunal as worthless products of a "show trial." In my opinion nothing could be further
from the truth. Sudisman's public statements in court confirmed the
"Self-Criticism," which he had written at a time when he was still free
to speak his mind and had no way of knowing whether he would be
captured and, if so, whether, unlike his comrades, he would survive
and be permitted to testify publicly.

Sudisman obviously used his trial for the same purpose for which he
had written the "Self-Criticism," namely to give the remnants of the
PKI an explanation of why the Party had failed and to establish a correct line for the future. When asked by one of the judges to state
his political objectives, Sudisman answered that they were to establish people's democracy, a first stage toward socialism, and then Communism, through an armed revolution of peasants under the leadership
of the working class. He then explained that "conducted peacefully,
the people's democratic revolution would take the form of democratic
general elections in which the people could vote directly, secretly,
and freely." But "now that the PKI has been banned in Indonesia,
adoption of peaceful means is no longer possible and consequently the
people's democratic revolution will have to be conducted through an
armed agrarian movement led by the working class."

He then stated the three principles (the term he used was TRIPANDJI,
i.e., Three Banners) that should guide the PKI in the future, namely:
(1) creation of a Marxist-Leninist Party free from opportunism and
modern revisionism; (2) armed revolution conducted by the peasants

under the leadership of the working class; and (3) a united front under the leadership of the working class.[68]

Exactly the same policy guidelines were given in the "Self-Criticism,"[69] which is still playing a major role in the Communist underground of Indonesia as Sudisman's political testament. After a lengthy and bitter denunciation of the many errors and weaknesses of the group that led the PKI from 1951 to 1965, Sudisman told the survivors that now "the Party has to work under completely illegal conditions and the organizational structure of the Party must, therefore, be adjusted according to the new conditions." He then warned that "so long as the ideology of subjectivism is not completely eradicated from the Party, or worse still, if it is still to be found among the Party leadership, then our Party will not be able to avoid other mistakes." To combat and liquidate subjectivism (or, as we would say, "wishful thinking"), which in Sudisman's opinion was the main cause of the PKI's fall, he urged the next generation of Communists to be better prepared ideologically:

The Party must educate its members to apply the Marxist-Leninist method in analyzing the political situation and in evaluating the forces of the existing classes, so that subjective analysis and evaluation can be avoided. The Party must draw the attention of the members to the importance of investigation and to the study of social and economic conditions, in order to be able to define the tactics of struggle and the corresponding method of work. The Party must help the members to understand that without an investigation of the actual conditions they will get bogged down in phantasy.[70]

THE FUTURE OF THE PKI

Events since Sudisman's arrest in December 1966 suggest that, even after three major setbacks in 1926, 1948, and 1965, Indonesian Communists remain incapable of learning from experience. A new Politburo, probably self-appointed on the basis of Article 70 of the PKI Constitution concerning emergency situations, took over in 1967. It included Rewang of the old Politburo, Oloan Hutabea, former Rector of the highest party school, the Aliarcham Academy, Tjugito of the Central Committee, Munir, former chairman of the Communist federation of trade unions SOBSI, and Suripto (Iskandar Subekti), a member of the Special Bureau and a covert member of the Central Committee. This group proceeded to rebuild the underground PKI in accordance with the Three Banners principles formulated by Sudisman.

Details on these covert activities are neither clear nor easy to obtain, but it would seem that the Greater Regional Committees (CDB) of the legal PKI, which had jurisdiction over provinces as large as East or Central Java, have been replaced in the new underground by Re-

gional Bureaus (*Biro Daerah* or BIRDA) responsible for areas equivalent to the smaller administrative entities called residencies.

Each Regional Bureau is responsible for the organization of armed
struggle in its territory. It creates revolutionary bases (*Basis Revolusi*
or BASREV) in the countryside, operating through rural Project Committees (*Komite Projec* or KOMPRO), which are paramilitary structures. Each KOMPRO sets up guerrilla training centers (*Sekolah Per-
lawanan Rakjat* or SPR) and forms regional guerrilla units (*Detasemen
Gerilja* or DETGA) and village guerrillas (*Gerilja Desa* or GERDA).
The pattern seems to follow that of the Viet Cong guerrilla organization
in South Vietnam.

In urban areas the new organizational structure is based on the City
Trio (*Trio Kota* or TRIKO), responsible for underground PKI activities in the cities on lines similar to those of the old overt Party, but
not responsible for guerrilla activities. The TRIKO does not establish
guerrilla training centers and controls no guerrilla units, which shows
that the emphasis of the new PKI's armed struggle is clearly rural.

Apparently the new leaders of the PKI underground decided to establish a major revolutionary base in East Java, where the population
was considered particularly friendly to the Communists. A sparsely populated strip of forested hills south of the town of Blitar, running about
100 Km along the Indian Ocean coast, was chosen probably because
access by land was rendered difficult by very poor roads, while at sea
strong currents and heavy surf impeded navigation. The area was criss-
crossed by Viet-Cong style underground caves and tunnels. The new
Politburo leaders Tjugito, Rewang, and Hutabea decided to use the
South Blitar area as their headquarters from which to direct the rebuilding of the PKI.

Although there seems to have been agreement among the new PKI
leaders on the necessity of preparing for armed struggle along Maoist
lines, the old incapacity for sustained discipline manifested itself again.
While some of the leaders argued that armed struggle be undertaken
only after the PKI's underground structure was rebuilt on a strong mass
basis, others engaged in isolated terroristic attacks on the Army and on
Moslem civilians who had been involved in the anti-Communist massacres of early 1966. This brought the South Blitar area to the attention of the East Java Army Command and resulted in security operations which culminated in the June-July 1968 killing of Hutabea and
Rewang, the capture of Tjugito, and the destruction of the South Blitar
guerrilla base. Altogether about 2,000 members and leaders of the PKI
underground were killed during the summer months of 1968, leaving
the Party again adrift.[71]

The epitaph on the latest period of the PKI's stormy history was
offered by Radio Moscow in a broadcast in Mandarin to Southeast Asia

on September 19, 1968. After deploring the destruction of the Communist underground organization in East Java by the Indonesian Army, the Russian commentator related that

in accordance with Mao Tse-tung's instructions, a group of Indonesian splittists in Peking announced the formation of a new PKI based on Mao Tse-tung's thought in the spring of 1967. This new PKI accepted Mao Tse-tung's adventurist strategy of so-called people's war, founded a party which was alien to the people, and attempted to besiege the city from the countryside.

With biting sarcasm, Radio Moscow then asked:

What about the weapons of the Indonesian insurgents who were ordered by the agents of the Maoist splittist clique within the PKI to rise up in struggle and take over the regime? After the destruction of this underground organization it was revealed that their arms amounted to forty locally-manufactured, second-rate firearms.

As noted earlier, the Chinese Communists do not seem to have made any efforts after the failure of the September 30 Movement to rescue the leaders of the PKI. If it is also true, as the Russians inform us, that the PKI underground of 1968, although guided by "Mao's thought," received no material support from its Chinese patrons, it is doubtful that Peking will retain in the long run a decisive voice in the affairs of Indonesian Communism.

This leaves us with the intriguing but currently unanswerable question of whether the Russians will find new ways to assert influence over the future PKI, assuming that this ill-starred movement has a future. The appeal of Communism in Indonesia will be weak in the period ahead unless the present regime fails abysmally in responding to the basic needs of the long-suffering Indonesian people.

NOTES

1. At the Seventh (Extraordinary) National Congress of the PKI in April 1962, Djoko Sudjono, a member of the PKI Secretariat and one of the founders of the "Illegal PKI" of 1935, stated that delegates from all the generations that created the Party participated in the Congress: the Founders' Generation (1920–1926); the 1926 Generation (1926–1935); the Anti-Fascist Generation (1935–1942); the Anti-Japanese Generation (1942–1945); the 1945 Generation (1945–1948); the New Road Generation (1945–1951); the 1951 Generation (1951–1954); the Fifth National Congress Generation (1954–1959); the Sixth National Congress Generation (1959–1962). See *Harian Rakjat* (*People's Daily*), Djakarta, May 9, 1962.

2. D. N. Aidit, *The Indonesian Revolution and the Immediate Tasks of the Communist Party of Indonesia* (Peking: Foreign Languages Press, 1964), pp. 111–112.

3. Historical Branch of the PKI "Concise Chronology of the PKI," *Harian Rakjat*, May 22, 1965.

4. Ruth T. McVey, *The Rise of Indonesian Communism* (Ithaca, N.Y.: Cornell University Press, 1965), p. 353.

5. Arnold C. Brackman, *Indonesian Communism, A History* (New York: Frederick A. Praeger, Inc., 1963), p. 30.

6. D. N. Aidit, *Pilihan Tulisan* (*Selected Works*), Vol. II (Djakarta: Jajasan Pembaruan, 1960). Translation published by U.S. Department of Commerce, Office of Technical Services, Joint Publications Research Service (JPRS), No. 8886 (1961), p. 288.

7. Aidit, *ibid.*, p. 323.

8. *Antara* News Agency, Djakarta, February 19, 1963, English edition, A/p. 11.

9. Departemen Penerangan, *Penerbitan Chusus 282, Amanat P. J. M. Presiden Sukarno* (*Department of Information, Special Publication 282, A Speech By His Excellency President Sukarno*), pp. 8–9.

10. *Harian Rakjat*, January 18, 1964, p. 3.

11. See *Dewan Pertimbangan Agung, Tudjuh Bahan 2 Pokok Indoktrinasi* (*Supreme Advisory Council, Seven Basic Indoctrination Materials*) (Djakarta, 1961), pp. 86–87.

12. Guy J. Pauker, "Current Communist Tactics in Indonesia," *Asian Survey* (Berkeley, Calif.), May 1961, p. 30.

13. D. N. Aidit, "Menempuh Djalan Rakjat" ("Embarking on the People's Road"), speech to commemorate the thirty-second anniversary of the PKI, in *Selected Works*, Vol. I (1959). JPRS, Translation No. 6551 (1961), p. 43.

14. See *Harian Rakjat*, May 20, 1963.

15. *Ibid.*, May 24, 1965.

16. See Ruth McVey, *op. cit.*, p. 155.

17. *Harian Rakjat*, July 26, 1965.

18. Quoted by Aidit in *The Indonesian Revolution, op. cit.*, pp. 5, 113.

19. Sukarno's article seems to have been forgotten until it was reprinted in a collection of his early papers entitled *Dibawah Bendera Revolusi* (Under the Flag of the Revolution), I (1959), 1–23, published in Peking. It was then reprinted as a pamphlet by the PKI in 1963, probably in support of its claim for participation in the government of Indonesia. On the united front from above strategy, see Ruth McVey, *op. cit.*, p. 68. For the quote from Sukarno's 1926 article, see *Nasionalisme, Islamisme dan Marxisme, Jajasan Pembaruan* (Djakarta, 1963), p. 25.

20. See George McT. Kahin, *Nationalism and Revolution in Indonesia* (Ithaca, N.Y.: Cornell University Press, 1952), p. 292. Kahin describes the episode, but does not mention that Sukarno acted under Army pressure.

21. Donald Hindley, *The Communist Party of Indonesia 1951–1963* (Berkeley and Los Angeles: University of California Press, 1964), p. 53.

22. *Harian Rakjat*, October 2, 1965. Translation in *Indonesia*, Vol. I (April 1966), published by the Modern Indonesia Project, Cornell University, p. 134.

23. Ruth T. McVey, "Indonesian Communism and the Transition to Guided Democracy," in A. Doak Barnett (ed.), *Communist Strategies in Asia* (New York: Frederick A. Praeger, Inc., 1963), p. 149; Herbert Feith, "Dynamics of Guided Democracy," in Ruth T. McVey (ed.), *Indonesia* (New Haven, Conn.: Human Relations Area Files, Inc., Press, 1963), pp. 340–41; Donald Hindley, "President Sukarno and the Communists: The Politics of Domestication," *American Political Science Review* (December, 1962), p. 915; Daniel S. Lev, "The Political Role of the Army in Indonesia," *Pacific Affairs* (New York), Winter 1963–1964, p. 355, note 13.

24. My views were expressed in *Communist Prospects in Indonesia*, The RAND Corporation, RM-4135-PR (November 1964), and in "Indonesia in 1964: Toward a 'People's Democracy'?" *Asian Survey* (Berkeley, Calif.), February, 1965.

25. Guy J. Pauker, *Communist Prospects in Indonesia*, The RAND Corporation, RM-4135-PR (November, 1964), p. 22.

26. Significantly, this was the first PKI document published in English translation by the Foreign Languages Press in Peking (1963), 91 pp.

27. D. N. Aidit, "Menudju Indonesia Baru" ("Toward a New Indonesia") speech on May 23, 1953, to commemorate the thirty-third anniversary of the PKI, in *Selected Works*, Vol. I (1959), JPRS Translation No. 6551 (1961), p. 88.

28. D. N. Aidit, "Bersatulah Untuk Menjelesaikan Tuntutan Revolusi Agustus 1945" ("Unite to Complete the Demands of the 1945 August Revolution"), General Report to the Fourth Plenary Session of the Central Committee of the PKI, July 1956, in *Selected Works*, Vol. II (1960), JPRS Translation No. 8886 (1961), p. 50.

29. D. N. Aidit, "Dengan Semangat Banteng Merah Mengkonsolidasi Organisasi Komunis Jang Besar" ("With the Spirit of the Red Buffalo Consolidate the Big Communist Organization"), in *Harian Rakjat*, July 6, 1964, p. 3.

30. The concept of a Gotong Royong (Mutual Aid) Cabinet was launched by Sukarno on February 21, 1957, when he tried unsuccessfully to form a cabinet in which all four major parties would be represented. NASAKOM was an acronym later coined by Sukarno to signify the political cooperation of all three major ideological currents in Indonesia, namely Nationalism, Religion, and Communism.

31. D. N. Aidit, *Dare, Dare, and Dare Again!* Foreign Languages Press, Peking (1963), p. 50.

32. Aidit, *The Indonesian Revolution, op. cit.*, p. 42. This English translation published in Peking uses "CPI" instead of the standard "PKI."

33. *Ibid.*, p. 65.

34. *Ibid.*, p. 86.

35. *The Differences Between Comrade Togliatti and Us*, Foreign Languages Press, Peking (1963).

36. Giuliano Pajetta, article in *Rinascita*, Rome, June 8, 1963, pp. 14–15. JPRS No. 22592 (1964), p. 13.

37. Aidit, *The Indonesian Revolution, op. cit.*, pp. 69–70.

38. *Ibid.*, pp. 129–30.

39. Quotations from D. N. Aidit, *Set Afire the Banteng Spirit! Ever Forward, No Retreat!* Foreign Languages Press, Peking (1964), pp. 80, 81, 92, 93, 104.

40. *Ibid.*, p. 40.

41. *Ibid.*, pp. 40–41.

42. See above, p. 282.

43. *Antara* News Agency, January 14, 1965.

44. *Harian Rakjat*, January 19, 1965.

45. NEKOLIM is an acronym for neocolonialism, colonialism, and imperialism.

46. "Reach to the Stars: A Year of Self Reliance," Address by President Sukarno, August 17, 1965, *Antara* Special Edition, English translation, Djakarta, p. 26.

47. Aidit, *Set Afire the Banteng Spirit!, op. cit.*, p. 29.

48. *Ibid.*, p. 27.

49. *Antara* News Agency, June 24, 1965.

50. *Harian Rakjat,* July 15, 1965.

51. D. N. Aidit, "Perhebat Ofensif Revolusioner Disegala Bidang!" ("Intensify the Revolutionary Offensive on All Fronts!"), *Harian Rakjat,* May 12, 13, 14, 15, 1965, JPRS Translation No. 31,451 (1965), pp. 26, 59.

52. On this concept see Hildred Geertz, *The Javanese Family: A Study of Kinship and Socialization* (New York: The Free Press, 1961), pp. 47–49.

53. I first stated this hypothesis in "Toward a New Order in Indonesia," *Foreign Affairs* (New York), April, 1967, p. 504, and developed it further in "Political Consequences of Rural Development Programs in Indonesia," *Pacific Affairs* (Vancouver), Fall, 1968.

54. I had already noted, in early 1962, that "private political discussions in Indonesia today center on the more distant future, the so-called 'post-Sukarno period.' " See "The Soviet Challenge in Indonesia," *Foreign Affairs* (New York), July, 1962, p. 8.

55. *Mahkamah Militer Luar Biasa,* "Berkas: Berita Atjara Persidangan Perkara Sudisman" (*Extraordinary Military Tribunal*), "File: Records of Sessions in the Case of Sudisman," Vol. II, Typescript, Djakarta, 1967, pp. 34–35, 68.

56. Aidit, "Intensify the Revolutionary Offensive," *op. cit.,* p. 4.

57. *Harian Rakjat,* May 12, 1965.

58. *Hariat Rakjat,* May 15, 1965, p. 3. The Indonesian words are: *Tak seorang berniat pulang walau mati menanti!* Dr. Walter Slote of Columbia University in a personal communication interprets this statement as suggesting that Aidit expected subsconsciously the failure of his plans.

59. An alleged confession by Aidit after his capture was published by the Japanese newspaper *Asahi Shimbun* in early 1966. For details see John Hughes, *Indonesian Upheaval* (New York: David McKay Company, Inc., 1967), pp. 167–72.

60. On December 26, 1967, Jusuf Adjitorop sent a letter of congratulation to Chairman Mao on his 74th birthday. He addressed him as "our most distinguished and beloved leader." See *Indonesian Tribune* (Tirana, Albania), II, No. 1, 44.

61. See *Harian Rakjat,* July 8, 1964, and May 14, 1965, for the last official changes in the governing bodies of the PKI. The current status of PKI Central Committee members was estimated by the author from a variety of reliable Indonesian sources.

62. *Extraordinary Military Tribunal,* "Case of Sudisman," *op. cit.,* pp. 65, 103, 104.

63. "Solidly United Under the Great Red Banner of Mao Tse-tung's Thought, the Communist Party of Indonesia is Leading the Indonesian People to March Onward on the Road of People's War!" Statement of the Delegation of the CC of PKI, in *Indonesian Tribune,* Vol. II, N. 4–5, 1968, p. 3.

64. The May and August statements in Vol. I, No. 1, November, 1966, and the September statement in Vol. I, No. 3, January, 1967. I have seen in Djakarta the original Indonesian text of the September statement, which circulated as a stenciled pamphlet. It was not identified as an issue of *Mimbar Rakjat,* the clandestine PKI journal in which, according to Sudisman, he published the "Self-Criticism." See Extraordinary Military Tribunal, "Case of Sudisman," *op. cit.,* p. 100.

65. *Information Bulletin,* World Marxist Review Publishers, Toronto, 1967, No. 106 (18), p. 58.

66. *Indonesian Tribune,* I, No. 3 (January, 1967), 6, 23.

67. Extraordinary Military Tribunal, "Case of Sudisman," *op. cit.,* pp. 22, 36.

68. *Ibid.,* pp. 37–38.

69. See *Indonesian Tribune, op. cit.,* I, No. 3, 28.

70. *Ibid.,* p. 26.

71. See *The New York Times,* July 12 and October 29, 1968.

THE COMMUNIST
PARTIES OF BURMA

JOHN H. BADGLEY

In the three decades since the Communist movement was born, two competing insurgent Communist Parties have flourished, while one proto-Communist Socialist Party has passed into history. Within each organization, long-existent personal dissension has been exacerbated by the Sino-Soviet split. None of the Communist Parties have obtained Cabinet seats since Burma achieved independence. Perhaps this is chiefly because of Communist belligerence and, also, skillful governmental manipulation of the competition with Communist leadership. Directly below Ne Win's Revolutionary Council, however, there are civilian advisers who have been active in the Communist movement and who model their developmental programs after those of Communist states. Some of these advisers encourage authoritarian measures resembling steps taken in Eastern Europe during the early Communist years, namely, imprisonment of political opposition, suppression of the critical press, nationalization of industry, and reorientation of the educational system to emphasize Marxist doctrine.

Despite these indications of leftist influence, it would be an error to consider the current Burmese government Communist, or, at least, Communist in any traditional sense. The government belongs to no Communist military alliance, maintains a neutral foreign policy towards the Soviet Union and the United States while diplomatically opposing Communist China, supports the arms control negotiations and Test-Ban Treaty; encourages China to accept India's demands in the Sino-Indian border dispute; and imprisons and harasses Communist leaders within Burma. In short, the current strength of Communism in Burma rests more on the inherent persuasion of Communist ideology expressed by independent Marxists than it does on the group of splintered Party organizations; and the indigenous development program reflects more the influence of general socialist ideas than the power of a monolithic Communist Party.

ORIGINS AND DEVELOPMENT OF THE
COMMUNIST PARTIES IN BURMA

The current weakness in the organization of the Communist Parties in Burma is an accentuation of organizational difficulties which appeared in the 1930's, when Communist ideas were first introduced into Burma. At that time, diverse extremist ideologies were seized upon by younger Burmese nationalists who regarded dyarchy and the continued British presence as the greatest of political evils. A number of radical organizations were founded, although no Communist Party appeared until 1943. Communist activity began with study groups instigated by Thakin Kodaw Hmaing and other publicists after the Saya San rebellion in 1933. Active agitation can be dated from the late Thirties, when students boycotted the university, and from the Indian riots of 1936. Communist classics first appeared in translation in those years.

The most active student political group, the Thakins, was influenced by the radical writings of Marx, Lenin, and Stalin, as well as those of European Fascists and socialists. Some called themselves Communists, but no Party discipline was imposed and no widely accepted leadership emerged to unite these self-styled Communists. Hence, a broad organizational base was not created. Kadaw Hmaing, then in his early fifties, and Thakins Soe, Ba Hein, and Pe Htay, who were in their late twenties were among the first committed Burmese Communists, but none of these men sought to synthesize Communist theory to fit the indigenous circumstances, as did M. N. Roy in India, Tan Malakka in Indonesia, and Ho Chi Minh in Indochina. No Burmese traveled to Moscow or established ties with the Communist International; indeed, in the Thirties,

Burma's Communists were relatively isolated from foreign Communists and the Comintern.[1]

Communism in Burma took root untended and unappreciated by the outside world. This unique quality set the movement on a stormy course from which the Burma Communist Parties have yet to recover: a course plagued by lack of cohesive leadership and almost devoid of international legitimation.

Notwithstanding difficulties encountered in creating a single Communist authority, the movement did prosper at the intellectual level in Rangoon. The imprisonment of boycott and riot leaders in 1936 threw the few Communists into jail with students who, during subsequent months, were tutored and enlisted in various Communist causes. For example, U Nu, Aung San, and Than Tun were persuaded by Thakin Soe to assist in translating *The Communist Party of the Soviet Union* and the *Communist Manifesto* into Burmese.[2] A Marxist study-group, formed by 13 Thakins in 1938 near Rangoon University, may be considered the first Communist cell in Burma as well as the initial core of the Communist Party of Burma.[3] Thakin Ba Hein published *The Capitalist World* in 1939, and provided through it an indigenous Communist interpretation of colonialism as it affected Burma. Although the government confiscated those Communist materials they could find, most of the younger active nationalists had read tracts by Lenin prior to the Japanese invasion of 1942.

Japanese involvement in the Burmese independence movement, which commenced in 1940, precipitated the first basic division among the Communists. The embryonic Communist movement found itself seriously divided over the strategy to obtain independence, and trouble developed when many Thakins decided to seek foreign support for a proposed insurrection against the British. One key Japanese agent, Colonel Suzuki (Bo Mo Gyo), encouraged the notion and promised military aid, an option which caused a three-way division among the Thakins: One small group favored an appeal only to the Chinese Communist Party; another supported the Japanese proposal; and a third element—the Soviet-oriented Communists—opposed fighting the British on the grounds that Japan should first be defeated.[4] Thakin Kodaw Hmaing and the Premier, Dr. Ba Maw, met secretly with the Japanese, in March 1940, to work an arrangement whereby the Japanese would train cadres for an independence army. Subsequently Dr. Ba Maw encouraged the young Thakin, Aung San, to establish contact with Japanese agents in China.[5] Meanwhile, the more radical political parties—including the Thakin Party, the Fabian Party (a moderate Marxist group), the People's Revolutionary Party (subsequently the Socialist Party), and the nationalistic Myochit Party of U Saw—clandestinely espoused a variety of strategies to achieve independence by violent means. Speaking of this period after the War, Aung San wrote:

It was true that I was one of the original members of the Communist Party. But that party at first existed more or less in name, its members being exceedingly small. Than Tun, who is today one of its leaders, did not belong to it at that time . . . [Later] when I met Thakin Soe secretly in August 1944 to hammer out the anti-Jap movement and organization, he urged me to join the Communist Party formed by him [the previous year]. I agreed to join it finally, but I left it afterwards as I disagreed with some of his views and with his sectarianism.[6]

In Aung San's statement rests the fundamental problem of Party discipline, namely, the lack of a consensus among the leadership. Only briefly, from August 1944 to October 1946, did the Communists work together as a part of the united front Anti-Fascist People's Freedom League (AFPFL) in the drive for freedom. Within the AFPFL, over which Aung San presided, clustered political, communal, and functional organizations. The Chairman of the Communist Party of Burma (CPB), Thakin Soe, hoped eventually to dominate the coalition, for the CPB had earned the goodwill both of the British and many Burmese by actively fighting the Japanese throughout the War. However, Soe's aspirations were frustrated when the Socialist Party, the core of the AFPFL leadership, agreed to negotiate rather than fight for independence.

Thakin Soe withdrew his faction of the CPB, a group henceforward called the Red Flags, early in 1946, and some months later took a small band underground to initiate the insurrection which he continues to fight 23 years later. Thakin Than Tun then formed a new Burmese Communist Party, the White Flags (BCP) which continued to cooperate with the government until August 1947, when U Nu, the Premier-designate following Aung San's assassination, refused to include any Communists except Thein Pe Myint, a deviant CPB member, within his shadow cabinet. Militancy gained the ascendancy within the BCP Politburo thereafter, and in March 1948, only three months after independence, Than Tun announced that he would follow Thakin Soe underground,[7] leaving Thein Pe Myint without a Party affiliation.

The White Flags quickly amassed a substantial guerrilla force. The Party had extensive contacts in the districts because of its wartime anti-Japanese activities. After 1951, it operated in loose alliance with the Red Flags as well as with the People's Volunteer Organization (PVO), an ex-militia led by rurally oriented politicians who, like the two Communist Parties, had broken with U Nu over the distribution of Cabinet posts. These three insurgent forces, with a fourth group of several thousand Karen insurgents, dominated central and southern Burma between 1948 and 1952, controlling the countryside and most small towns, fighting together in the early years but, after establishing sectors of control for taxation purposes, becoming increasingly suspicious of one another. Gradually, a revitalized Burmese Army, under the command of Ne Win, reasserted Rangoon's control over the towns and transport routes. By 1954, the two Communist Forces had been driven from their most valuable economic bases and had begun to retrench. By 1958, 38,000 insurgents, about a quarter of whom were Communists, had surrendered or been amnestied.

Meanwhile a group of radical Socialists, members of Parliament who had remained loyal to the government, split from the AFPFL over the issue of Burma's support for the United Nations' policy in the Korean War and formed a new political party in January 1951. This new Burma Workers and Peasants Party (Red Socialists, or BWPP) competed with the AFPFL in the next two elections, retaining its seats in Parliament and generally demonstrating that a Communist, or at least a radical socialist, position could obtain wide support. Two popular newspapers, the *Mirror* of Rangoon and *Ludu* of Mandalay, publicized BWPP policies.

Prior to the 1956 elections, the BWPP joined the loosely structured National United Front (NUF), obscuring their own Communist orientation within a relatively moderate platform. The NUF was indeed successful, capturing over 40 per cent of the popular vote, but the Red Socialists were unable to improve their positions in Parliament. Of 239 contested seats, the NUF captured only 48. The next election, which was delayed by the Ne Win caretaker government, was held in February 1960, and despite a split with the AFPFL and U Nu's creation of his own National Union Party, the NUF lost electoral support and won only 30 seats. NUF influence in Parliament declined, and the old problem of divisiveness within Communist leadership returned to split the BWPP into moderate and radical factions, some loyal to Moscow, others pursuing the Peking line, and a significant minority independent of any foreign line.

During the same decade that the Red Socialists were building their organization, another faction of the White Flags, originally led by Than Myaing, had taken residence in China and established Burma's first close relationship with a foreign Party. Some 32 members of this faction, led by Bo Zeyya and Yebaw Htay, returned in three groups to Burma in July and August 1963, to help in the negotiations for termination of the Communist insurrections. The meetings broke down in November, and Yebaw Htay took the Peking group into rural Burma to join and eventually to dominate Than Tun's White Flags. The Red Flags, long since isolated from the rest of the Communist movement, were branded as Trotskyites by other Communists and were destined to obscurity. For a brief period in 1964, a split developed within the White Flags, and a faction led by Goshal allegedly joined the Red Flags in opposition to Than Tun, perhaps reflecting a conflict between the Maoist-oriented Than Myaing and Goshal, whose ties had been with Indian Communists. The execution of Goshal and another non-Maoist Politburo member in 1967 confirmed the nature of the conflict and the success of the Maoists.

COMMUNIST LEADERSHIP AND ORGANIZATION

The diverse leadership within the several Communist organizations should not obscure the dominant position held by the White Flags since 1950. This position was partially legitimized by contact with the Indian, British, and Soviet Communist Parties. Than Tun established relations with the Communist Party of India (CPI) through his theoretician, Thakin Ba Tin (i.e., Goshal), a Burmese of Bengali extraction who associated with the Ranadive faction of the CPI during the Japanese occupation. Goshal retained his Indian Party membership and was for several years the chief liaison between the CPB and the CPI. Then, in 1946, a Chinese Communist visiting India, Thang Fa, sent official felicitations from Mao Tse-tung. The Soviets established communications through the Yugoslavs attending the 1948 Calcutta conference and maintained this channel through a series of Burmese Communists in Moscow, the first of whom was Yebaw Aung Gyi, a member of the White Flag Politburo.

Than Tun himself remained inside Burma and was neither internationalist in outlook nor particularly concerned about foreign assistance. His strongest qualities, from the outset, were his ideological flexibility and his capacity to attract better-educated Burmans to his cause. All but two or three of his Central Committee members had attended universities. Tun had these men teach in his Central Political School for cadres, which offered dialectical materialism, Marxist economics, and the philosophy of the Cominform as major courses; subsequently they instructed Party organizers at district and township levels. The White Flags proselytized students at Rangoon University and in district high schools, and from these students came the cadres to serve as their political militia.

After the insurrection began, the White Flag structure resembled the Chinese Communist guerrilla organization. Key village areas were established as economic bases. The Central Committee represented regions, and within each region were district, township, and village circle cadres. Each command position was shared by a military and political leader, and local leaders who were sympathetic to the White Flags were usually made chairmen of the People's Courts. Than Tun also maintained liaison officers with the Red Flags and the PVO command in Pyinmana district during 1949, in Prome district in 1950, and in Pakokku and Lower Chindwin districts thereafter. However, the Central Command Post actually exercised little influence over the other insurgent groups.

The Red Flags were much more bound to a singular leader than were the other Communist Parties in Burma. Thakin Soe was the first Burmese to publish translations of the Lenin and Stalin classics, but his faith in his own dogmatic interpretation of this literature became intolerable to his contemporaries and, between 1946 and 1952, his Red Flag forces were relatively isolated from the other Communists. Then, following the formal alliance of the Communists in 1952, Than Tun met frequently with Thakin Soe, while the Communists' influence waned in the face of the government's increasing control over towns and major villages. Soe proposed creation of a single liberation army and, nominally, this proposition went into effect. In practice, however, no single command chain was established. After 1951, both the above and below-ground Communists espoused a popular democratic front idea; again, however, words and deeds differed, for both the White and Red Flags continued to follow the tactics of militancy, rejecting all government overtures.

The division between Burma's two insurgent Communist Parties made military victory more difficult and was clearly endangering the entire Communist movement by 1954. The two Politburos, however, persisted in their rigidity. Personal rivalries were also a significant factor preventing unification. Than Tun was accused of being unrealistic and excessively theoretical by second-line leaders, who began to surrender in increasing numbers. "He organized the party, not the masses, and made slow headway in raising the political consciousness and establishing a people's army."[8]

The underground Communists attacked both the domestic and foreign policy of U Nu's government, especially the American aid program, and sought to associate it with alleged American aid to the Kuomintang forces in the Shan States. This latter issue was widely accepted as a legitimate grievance, but other insurgent propaganda was clearly false, for it denied specific government accomplishments in the economic sector, further alienating the insurgents from the public.[9] The government restricted trade between Army-controlled and insurgent territory, placing the villagers in Communist districts on a subsistence existence. Finally, surrendered White Flags complained that the rural cadre generally fell short of even minimum qualifications as "good Communists." Few were effective among the villagers; those assigned this most basic task were often "unsuited for any other activity," since village work was the least prestigious job in the Party organization. In my own interviews, village leaders complained of terrorist practices by both Communists and AFPFL organizers, but the brutality of the Red Flags was most outstanding in the minds of villagers a full decade after the Red Flags had evacuated north-central Burma. The refusal of the better-educated workers to live and serve within village communities was, therefore, a general problem that plagued Communist and non-Communist parties alike.

Burma's third proto-Communist Party, the Burma Workers' and Peasants' Party, was, as we have already noted, popularly known as the Red

Socialists. Their major support came from one faction of the trade unions, although they also claimed to be a peasants' party. Rural factions of the PVO, as well as BWPP town organizers, were able to win votes for Red Socialist candidates who campaigned on a platform more akin to Khrushchev's Communism than to Mao's or Stalin's. The top leadership resided in Rangoon and normally traveled to their districts only before elections; thus BWPP influence rested on their relationships within the elite rather than on powerful rural associations such as the PVO and the White Flag organizations had. The more prominent Red Socialists were scarcely distinguishable from the socialist faction of the AFPFL, in terms of their education; most were lawyers in Rangoon. Only their ideology was markedly dissimilar, for it displayed considerable Soviet influence, particularly in later years. The BWPP gained its greatest influence shortly before the 1956 elections, when it allied with other opposition groups to form the National United Front, and again for a few months in 1958, when U Nu retained his Premiership only through their support in Parliament. Ne Win's caretaker regime, U Nu's brief return, and the Revolutionary Council all worked against the BWPP organization. In December 1962, the old BWPP and NUF combined to form a new leftist Party, the National Democratic United Front. In November 1963, most of the Rangoon and district organizers were arrested, disintegrating the Party structure, and, in March 1964, this Party, along with others except the Lanzin-Burma Socialist People's Party (BSPP), was declared illegal. However, two key leaders of the Red Socialists, U Ba Nyein and Thein Pe Myint, shifted their support to the BSPP, an organization formed by the Army.

The proto-Communist student associations in Rangoon and Mandalay universities were a fourth leftist group in Burma. The tradition of radical student associations extends back into the 1920's. However, as Communist-dominated organizations, their history began in 1951, when they first contested the elections for the Rangoon University Students Union. They were defeated the initial year by U Kyaw Nyein's socialist-supported student association. The following year, the several factions of Communist students united to form the Progressive Students Organization (PSO) and staged a successful strike against the University administration. This group won the student elections at Rangoon University in 1953 and then began the construction of a national organization among district students.

However, the Progressive Students Organization, like the senior Communist Parties, was unable to retain its unity. In 1954, it split along the three major Communist Party lines then existing in Burma, namely, the Red Flags, White Flags, and Red Socialists. Rather than publicly reveal the cleavage, the leaders formed the Rangoon University Students United Front (RUSUF), a more autonomous association of "sympathizers and neutrals" to replace the PSO. The new slate of Communist candidates again defeated the government-backed student organization and continued to control official student government until the Army came to power in 1958, at which time the leadership was imprisoned. These students were released during the 1960 to 1962 administration of U Nu. In July 1962, the RUSUF-led students rioted on the campus, and Ne Win dispatched troops who fired upon the massed students, killing some 30 of the demonstrators. The Army then dynamited the Student Union building, symbol of organized student opposition, reducing it to rubble. All student political activity was then banned by the Revolutionary Council, and the universities were twice closed, in 1963, to destroy the students' organization. The University itself was reorganized into Institutes and the mass-based student movement channeled into *Lanzin* Party activities.

The students of Burma were the most volatile of all politicized groups, for they had been deeply affected by the vast social change enveloping the land. Within their ranks was the specific discontent of unemployment: They were a group educated for a modern society yet living in a traditional agrarian state. This very practical problem was directly related to the successful recruitment of Burma's Communists until after 1963, when the educational system was changed to fit the economic conditions.

THE SOCIOECONOMIC CHARACTER OF THE COMMUNISTS

Interviews of town and village leaders in central Burma in 1962 revealed a typology of the Communist leadership. Even though I was unable to meet with any active White or Red Flags, and the interviews were confined to NUF leaders, these sources and the press interviews of amnestied Communists published over the past decade provided relatively clear distinctions. The majority of Communist leaders, apart from the Red Flags, have been educated to the high-school level or beyond. All higher leaders come either from higher-income village families, merchant families in towns, or, as in the cases of Ba Nyein and Thein Pe Myint (both of whom were independent Communists and now serve as civilian "theorists" for the Revolutionary Council), are sons of clerks in the British civil service. In their youth, therefore, these men enjoyed a much higher status and standard of living than the normal villager or townsman. Nearly all prominent leaders in the White Flag organization were political activists in high school or university and joined the CPB as students or soon after leaving school.

Even at the district level, the older Communist leaders are not peasants, although the ranks of both the White and Red Flags have been filled with villagers who served as militia. Younger leaders, usually recruited in town high schools, are sent to villages to organize cadres or militias, a policy differing from that practiced by the PVO and all former legalized Parties which built upon the existing village power structure or a minority faction within the village.

The Red Flags, the more extreme of the two Communist Parties, have attempted to dissolve the traditional family and village structure in their drive to achieve a complete revolution. In areas under Red Flag control, Buddhist priests have either relinquished their authority or have been shot, in the same fashion that landowners have either donated their property to the party or have risked death. Such terror has been sanctioned by Thakin Soe, who has preached militant egalitarianism, elimination of Buddhism, and the imminent attainment of Communism in Burma. The Red Flag cadres have operated as military units seeking to mobilize entire village, both men and women, into a Communist militia. Thakin Soe promoted a number of women to high rank in his army; indeed, his chief negotiator with the Ne Win regime was a woman, and his advocacy of female equality has become one of his most spectacular policies. Like an evangelist, Thakin Soe recruited devotées, not members, and defections from his organization have been incredibly few, considering the hardship and failure that have characterized its history. For two decades, the Red Flag forces have been driven from village to village in the poorest section of Burma, and finally separated from all popular support. In a certain sense, the Red Flags echo the rebel tragedy of a century ago, when Burman guerrilla fighters fought along the fringes of the Arakan Yomas and Chin Hills against the British for a quarter of a century before they were extinguished.

While the insurgent Communists operate more as armies than as political parties, the Red Socialists functioned as a Party striving to win votes on issues and personalities. As the major opposition for 12 years, the BWPP was not able to gain the financial support that the AFPFL or U Nu's Union Party obtained; consequently its organization was always limited by financial stringency. Members of the Party, if not the organization itself, turned to the Chinese and Soviet embassies as well as to Chinese merchants for aid, and their press made abundant use of Tass and *Jen-min jih-pao* materials. The Russian defector, Kaznacheev, reports a fascinating method of planting imaginative, but false, stories about Burma in the other Asian papers, then republishing them in the Burmese *Botataung* and the *Mirror* as reliable foreign reports concerning capitalist imperialism within Burma.[10] Of course, there was also evidence that the right-wing faction of the AFPFL and the anti-Communist press in Burma were not without foreign aid. Propaganda from both sides filled the bookstores throughout the country until the Revolutionary Council banned foreign propaganda in 1963.

The problem of financing political parties may well have been the immediate reason for the collapse of Burmese democracy in 1962, and the earlier corruption that resulted from the scramble for the limited funds available for Party coffers became most apparent within the BWPP. The Red Socialists seem to have set out to be an independent, nationalist-Communist front. They attracted to the lightly disciplined BWPP many of the leftist intellectuals in Burma. The heritage of this group of college graduates, lawyers, and professionals was similar to that of the top AFPFL leaders except for their personal wealth. Eventually, however, the BWPP became so compromised by its dependence upon outside support that Burmese untutored in the Khrushchev-Mao debate had difficulty discerning the difference between Red Socialist and White Flag ideology.

CURRENT IDEOLOGIES AND RELATIONS
WITH OTHER POLITICAL FORCES

In considering the variety of Burmese Communists, some observers have wondered whether the apparent complexity of the movement was merely a guise concealing a basic unity. Such a strategy was pursued successfully by Ho Chi Minh and by several Eastern European Communist Parties. From 1952 to 1967, moreover, the Chinese Communists have strongly urged such an approach for all national liberation movements. Since the BCP (the White Flags) has had intimate relations with the Chinese, is it not probable that Chinese tactics do indeed prevail? There can be little doubt, however, that the cleavages among the Burmese Communists are real and politically significant. Therefore, until April 1967, when the White Flag Central Committee split over the Chinese request to launch a Red Guard movement, the conclusion must be that the Chinese did not prevail over the movement.

The top leaders have been unable to tolerate the discipline of a single Party because of the higher value they have placed upon their own absolute command. In this respect, the Communists have behaved like other Burmese politicians, all of whom have had extreme difficulty in defining political authority. Who is entitled to power within any party? The question remains unanswered over two decades after independence. In Burma, modernity is still so seriously challenged by traditionalists that every political party represents nothing less than a replica of the total culture. Thus, contestants for power must operate within two key institutions, the village community and the central regime, those two monarchal traditions later reinforced by British colonial policy. As yet, the political party has no legitimate function as a nexus of conflicting interests which can be compromised. No method whereby politicians and lobbyists can agree to disagree and thus coexist within a single organization has been accepted within the Burmese political process. If one can neither command nor follow, then one withdraws.[11] The official *Lanzin*

Party has rewarded participation by "candidate" members, who numbered about 200,000 by 1968, but as Burma is a single-party state, with frequent imprisonment of opposition leaders, we have no evidence that this party can compromise conflicting interests.

In the splintering of the Communist Parties, ideological positions are often connected with personal rivalries and are frequently taken to rationalize a pre-existing antagonism toward another leader. For example, Thakin Soe renounced Kodaw Hmaing's support in 1940 over the single issue of acceptance of Japanese aid, and he never again heeded the old man's authority, even though the difference of opinion became irrelevant after the War and Kadaw Hmaing eventually received the greatest international Communist recognition awarded a Burmese, the Lenin Peace Prize. Thakin Than Tun split with the more senior Thakin Soe over the British negotiation issue, yet even after both leaders were underground and jointly attacking the government, they could never be successfully reunited. Thakin Lwin, a leading Red Socialist, dissented from Than Tun's insurrection policies; still, in later years, after the BWPP became a proto-Communist Party and both leaders were propagating an ideology that was markedly similar in content, neither man was willing to join the other's organization. U Ba Nyein, for a decade Thakin Lwin's colleague in the BWPP, split with him in 1962 over the question of supporting the Revolutionary Council: Ba Nyein became adviser to the Finance Ministry and Thakin Lwin went to jail. In short, questions of power, of gaining or retaining command, and of personal relations have often been more significant than ideology.[12]

Despite the qualification just placed upon the meaning of ideology, however, there are differences in Party lines. Once these are identified, one can see clearly the deep cleavage between the White Flags, the major group, and the other left and right-wing Parties within the movement.

Since 1950, the White Flags have propagated, in foreign affairs, an ideological position nearly identical to Peking's. In that year they published, in Burmese, a 36-page document edited by U Ba Win and entitled "The First Year's Journey of the New Republic of China," which argued that "500 million Chinese are now ready to take action in any condition of foreign interference in the Far East." The White Flags consistently opposed economic aid from any Western power and, like the Chinese Communists, were particularly incensed over the United States' presence in the Southeast Asia Treaty Organization (SEATO), Korea, Vietnam, and Laos. U. Nu's and Ne Win's neutral positions, and Burma's role in the test-ban and arms control negotiations, were condemned in White Flag statements. Except during the four months of amnesty negotiation in 1963, the White Flags' radio and pamphlet propaganda considered the Revolutionary Council a "fascist dictatorship."

The Red Flags have advocated the same policy towards the West, and have been even more vitriolic in their condemnation of the various Burmese governments. However, Thakin Soe has been most bitter in his denunciation of the Russian policy of coexistence, and has even admonished Mao Tse-tung for not actively supporting liberation movements since the 1948 uprisings. He has advocated a united peasant revolution throughout Asia and Africa, to cast out the capitalist influence which he believes still controls politics outside of China. This stance has earned Thakin Soe the epithet of "Trotskyite"; nevertheless he views himself as the only legitimate heir to Lenin's revolution.[13]

Most Red Socialists have supported close economic and political ties with the socialist camp but have followed the Soviet Union's lead in favoring peaceful coexistence and the Test-Ban Treaty. In domestic policy they have differed even more with the insurgent Communists, for they were willing to operate in the open within the bounds of the 1948 Constitution, until its demise in the 1962 coup. The Red Socialists initially declared their support for the Revolutionary Council, an action refused by the more leftist Parties, and they indicated a willingness to join in one monolithic Party, the Lanzin-BSSP, in which several ex-PVO leaders would have high civilian positions. Red Socialist participation in the BSPP was strongly opposed by the underground Parties and a majority of the BWPP finally pulled out and sought to reestablish their own district organizations. The arrest of the entire BWPP leadership in November 1963, and the outlawing of all parties within the National Democratic United Front in March 1964, destroyed their influence and, of course, convinced the White Flags even further that they had no hope of cooperating with the military regime.

The dramatic collapse of the negotiations between the several Communist Parties, and the confinement of over 500 BWPP politicians, opened a new phase in the extended Communist-nationalist conflict in Burma. For the first time since March 1948, a clear division existed between the socialist and Marxist theorists who were essentially nationalists and those Communists with undetermined and varied loyalties to foreign interpretations of Communism. Internment of all significant politicians, including leaders of the National Union Party and the National United Front, cut off the insurgent Communist Parties from any potential political support within Rangoon, except from military factions or the BSPP. However, there was scant opportunity for the Communist Parties to influence or permeate this remaining legitimate Party. Several key Colonels, particularly Tin Pe and Than Sein, and their advisers, were as sensitive to Communist subversion in Burma as any individuals Ne Win could have selected for such key posts, thanks to their own socialist commitments and their fifteen years of experience in fighting White Flags. By way of example, consider one adviser, Bo Htein Lin.

Bo Htein Lin was one of the two leading PVO commanders during the PVO nine-year insurrection. He attempted to work with the Red and White Flags for four years after the insurrection commenced. PVO guerrillas eventually flushed the Communists out of north-central Burma, after rejecting further cooperation because of their efforts to penetrate the PVO and their excessive dependence upon violence during the insurrection. Many PVO commanders were schoolmates of the new Burmese Army commanders, some had been Thakins, and most had fought together in the Burmese Independence Army against the Japanese in 1945. Thus, although the Burmese Army constructed by Ne Win after 1949 was theoretically fighting the PVO as well as the Communists, and although PVO propaganda was flavored with Marxist jargon, there were seldom major engagements between PVO forces and Army companies. From 1953 onward, moreover, the forces lived in mutual respect of one another, encouraging commerce across one another's territory and eventually developing a situation of mutual trust which enabled them to work out a mutually advantageous amnesty.[14]

Ne Win called Htein Lin and other key socialist politicians (subequently another Htein Lin, from lower Burma, also joined the BSPP as a journalist, causing some confusion among foreign observers) to Rangoon two weeks before the March 1962 coup, to serve as political advisers. By 1965, the BSPP had expanded its organization into rural towns across central Burma and even into some Karen territory in the delta and in Karenni State. District politicians from other parties have had no choice except to cooperate with or fight the BSPP. Given the intimate ties between the military and the BSPP leadership, moreover, there has been little opportunity for any political opposition to form, apart from a few isolated demonstrations arranged by Buddhist monks opposing the secular, authoritarian development program.

Both the Red Flags and the White Flags seemed, for a period, to be allied with the communal political forces. After the November 1963 break, they apparently sought to exploit the tensions that have matured among the Shans and Kachins as the Burman military has consolidated its grip on the central government. The current relationship between the Communist Parties and the non-Burman insurgent forces may be summarized as follows: During most of the 1950's, Thakin Soe's Red Flags were allied with the delta faction of the Karen National Defense Organization (KNDO), the Karen nationalists who went underground in 1949. Thakin Soe allegedly converted to Communism Mahn Ba Zan, the delta Karen commander, and was able to utilize the superior arms and numbers of the Karens for many of the Red Flag operations against the Burmese Army. The Mahn Ba Zan faction called itself *Kaw-*

thule (i.e., Karen National Union Party, KNUP). Later a leftist faction of hill (or Red) Karens organized around Ba Aung Than Lay, calling itself the National Progressive Party. Tiny front groups of Chins and Mons also worked with the KNUP. Following the 1962 coup, Ne Win opened a new series of negotiations with the KNDO and KNUP, and offered amnesty terms which included significant contributions to the economy of the Karen State. The KNDO commander, Saw Hunter, continued discussions for over a year, finally in June 1963, coming to Rangoon, where he has remained. However, Mahn Ba Zan, who headed the tripartite discussions and who renounced his allegiance to Thakin Soe, later returned to his insurgent delta Karen force and cooperated with the White Flags in raids until mid-1967. Since then the right-wing Karen Freedom Congress, which operates out of the Thai border area, and the KNUP may have been working together.

To the north, however, the military faces an incredibly nationalistic Kachin Independence Army (KIA) which controls much of the Kachin State and which became very militant after the collapse of the government's negotiations with the Karens and the Communists. As was once the case with the Karens, one or another of the Communist Parties seems to be in a position to exploit the separatist sentiment and, until the Revolutionary Council can offer satisfactory conditions for amnesty, the KIA is likely to remain a chronic and serious political opposition to any unifying efforts in northern Burma.

The White Flags could obtain unlimited armaments from the Chinese if Peking chose to exploit this weakness on her border by funneling arms to the Kachins. Some Kachin leaders who fled to Yenan a decade ago have returned to command positions in the KIA. Confirmation of some assistance has seriously undermined the Chinese effort to identify themselves with nationalist sentiment in Burma. More significance, to date, should be attached to the American arms captured in Vietnam or sold in Thailand or Assam, which have been purchased by Kachin agents. Certainly, any hint of American support of the KIA would be equally serious for American relations with Burma. The American aid that at one time reached the Kuomintang Chinese forces in the Shan States still haunts American efforts to cultivate Burmese friendship.

There has been no evidence of cooperation between the several insurgent forces in the Shan States and any of the Communist Parties. There is little chance, however, that the Shan separatist movement can be broken without major changes in the structure of Burma's government, for the depth of the Shans' distrust and antagonism toward the Burmans, reawakened by the internment of leading Shan politicians between 1962 and 1968, and is rooted in precolonial history. Meanwhile, a younger Shan leadership is emerging within the underground forces operating out of northern Thailand, and the slim possibility exists that these men might align themselves with one or both Karen factions—the KIA, or the White Flags.

The key to the eventual solution of the communal difficulties, from the Kachin and Shan vantage point, obviously does not lie in the creation of a Chinese satellite in Burma. Burmese minority groups are in an excellent position to learn of the outcome of Chinese policy toward national groups from refugees who have fled across the border in the past 15 years. In the long run, the border minorities should seek a solution through a government in Rangoon, and this cannot be a Maoist-type Communist government if they are to achieve their goals. Therefore, it is most likely that the KIA and Shan insurgents, like the KNDO before them, will try to use the Communist Parties, if at all, for their own ends. Once the government in Rangoon offers terms politically and economically acceptable to the minority leaders in these semi-autonomous states, the Communist Parties will have lost this remaining bastion of popular support in Burma. Until such terms are offered, however, popular leaders dedicated to the cause of their particular ethnic group will continue to push the campaign against Rangoon, frequently aligning themselves with other dissidents.

IMPACT OF THE SINO-SOVIET SPLIT

Perhaps the growing division in the Communist world did not have the same significance for Burma as for other Southeast Asian states, because the Burmese Communists were already divided between Khrushchev, Mao, and Thakin Soe, although it seems very likely that the White Flags have been strongly influenced, though not totally controlled, by a Peking faction since 1952.

Competition for influence over the BWPP commenced in Burma with the visits of Chou En-lai in 1954, of Bulganin and Khrushchev in 1955, and of Chou En-Lai again the same year. Kaznacheev reports that the Chinese were exceedingly cool to the Russian efforts to aid the Red Socialists, and it may be that the legalized Burmese Communists felt the first impact of Sino-Soviet competition. Both Soviet and Chinese agents attempted to work with the BWPP, and both achieved limited success. Later, and all within one year, there occurred the attempted defection of the Russian military attaché, the Southeast Asian Tass representative's bumbling attempt to libel a leading newspaper editor as having accepted a bribe from the United States, and finally the successful defection of Kaznacheev. Soviet influence over the Burmese Communists could scarcely have been lower at the time. Since 1963 the Russians have eschewed any covert support for non-government forces. On the other hand, the most significant question concerning White Flag relations with Peking was answered by Thau Tun's assassination on September 24, 1968, and the subsequent domination of the Politburo by Maoist returnees.[15]

There is reason to believe that the Chinese have long given active encouragement to the Peking faction of the Burmese Communists. Yebaw Htay and Bo Zeyya flew into Rangoon from China only a few months after Liu Shao-ch'i's visit to Burma in April 1963, which suggests that Ne Win may have brought some pressure to bear upon the Chinese to help solve the problem of Communist insurgence within Burma in exchange for Burmese understanding in the Sino-Indian border conflict. Subsequent action by Ne Win, who flew to Delhi apparently to act as an intermediary between Nehru and Chou En-lai, supports this hypothesis. The Chinese Communists may well have taken a leaf from their experience in Laos, where a coalition government was created in 1962, and sought to encouage in Burma a united front government in which the White Flags would participate as the Pathet Lao did in Laos. But Ne Win sent the Peking faction of the White Flags packing two months after their return from China, thus possibly placing the Chinese in an awkward position, their strongest pressure group within Burma having been publicly discredited.[16] From that point on, relations between Peking and Rangoon deteriorated sharply. By June 1967, Peking was roundly condemning the Ne Win government as fascist, a policy that persists to date.

SUMMARY

The Communist movement in Burma in the late Sixties consist of three heads (Thakin Soe, the White Flag and the imprisoned Red Socialist leadership), four arms (the Red Flags, White Flags, Red Socialists, and shattered Politburo student organizations), and no body or legs upon which to move. Like other political parties in this still traditionalist country, the Communists have failed to bridge the gap between peasant and government, tradition and modernity, and leader and follower. They have suffered from disciplinary problems and ideological confusion even more severely than the non-Communist Parties. This is not to say that the Communists have not drawn intelligent, capable leaders into their movement; indeed, one of the most plaintive comments I have heard in Burma is the observation that "our best leaders have followed the wrong cause." Deeply felt ethnic Burman nationalism remains the dominant political mood of Burma today. Any variety of international Communism or unusual loyalty to any foreign political system is sufficient cause to create suspicion, official distrust, and even confinement.

However, those aspects of Communism that could be mixed with

Burmese nationalism as it develops under military leadership have gained acceptability. It is significant that some deviant Marxists from the BWPP and the PVO have secured power within the Ne Win military regime. A clear line has been drawn between internationalists and nationalists among the Communists, and only the national Communists have achieved respectability. The essential position of these leaders, that the central government must assume responsibility for all production if Burma is to progress economically, is similar to that of the current Revolutionary Council. In agriculture, as in industry and services, these leaders have advocated a guided economy, and for five years their policies have been followed. Since 1965, nonetheless, such policies have not yielded larger harvests and more rapid industrial growth. If improvements are not forthcoming, there will eventually be a reaction against rash revolutionary measures from within the military itself, as well as from the alienated business community.

The influence gained by the few national Communists (Red Socialists) has not modified Burma's foreign policy; on the contrary, there seems to be a heightened awareness of the dangers of "neo-imperialism" as practiced by the Soviet Union and the Chinese People's Republic, as well as by the United States. Both the Soviet and Chinese consulates have been removed from upper Burma, in Mandalay and Lashio, and foreign Communist propaganda is missing from the bookstalls. Burma has intensified its diplomatic activity with its non-Communist neighbors, and continues active participation in the Colombo Plan, ECAFE, the Geneva arms control discussions, and, of course, the United Nations. The bedrock of Burma's foreign policy, independent neutralism, has been shaken by the Chinese verbal onslaught, yet the military leadership continues its support for a nationalist philosophy that will be compatible both with its desire for modernity and its continuing commitments to Burman culture.

NOTES

1. Young Thakins were most influenced by writings of Indian and British Communists in the late Thirties. There was contact with the Indian Party, but we have little documentation of the extent of communication.
2. Thakin Mya Than, *The Return From Two Islands* (Rangoon, 1962).
3. An interview by the author with Than Maung, editor of the *Mandalay Sun*, February, 1958.
4. Aung San, *Burma's Challenge*, address delivered in Rangoon, August 29, 1945, mimeographed by Defense Service Historical Institute (DSHI). Personal copy received from U Thein Naing, Research Director, DSHI.
5. Hachiro Takahashi, "The Great Asia War History: Secret of Establishing A Country" (English translation in Defense Service Historical Institute). Aung San resided in the International Settlement at Amoy for two months prior to his

move to Tokyo. He made a feeble effort to contact the Chinese Communists, but failed, and was finally traced by Japanese intelligence and given free transport to Japan. Also, Dr. Ba Maw, *Breakthrough in Burma* (New Haven: Yale University Press, 1967).

6. Aung San, "President's Statement," March 3, 1946, in Archives, Defence Services Historical Institute, Rangoon.

7. From March to May, 1948, U Nu and Than Tun negotiated intensively in an effort to resolve the issue. Nu extended a 15-point proposition which promised the White Flags more than the AFPFL was prepared to give. Thein Pe Myint played a key role in these discussions, earning the permanent enmity of the insurgent Communists in so doing. Earlier, in December and January, Thakin Than Tun and other Southeast Asian Communists met in Calcutta with Eastern European and Russian Party delegates who encouraged the uprisings that occurred the following spring throughout Southeast Asia. See my article, "Burma's Radical Left," *Problems of Communism*, March-April, 1961.

8. Chit Than Tun, former member of the Central Committee, White Flags, quoted in *The Nation* (New York), January 14, 1954.

9. Burma's economy has failed to advance as rapidly as its population growth over the past two decades. However, land reclamation, crop diversification, and small-scale industry have been moderately successful projects. For a detailed study, see Louis Walinsky, *Economic Development in Burma: 1951–60* (New York: Twentieth Century Fund, 1963).

10. Aleksandr Kaznacheev, *Inside a Soviet Embassy* (Philadelphia: J.B. Lippincott Co., 1962), pp. 173–78.

11. See Lucian Pye, *Politics, Personality, and Nation Building* (New Haven, Conn.: Yale University Press, 1962), pp. 177–207. Pye, in exploring this tendency, offers the hypothesis that male child-rearing techniques cause such behavior. My own observations of Burman family life cause me to reduce the importance of this factor and to suggest that this political phenomenon derives from a more fundamental cause, an ethical system which demands that any individual reject secular authority when it seems to challenge his integrity or self-identity. Theravada Buddhist emphasis upon self-realization and concern for future existence provides sanction for the individual who acts to reject or overwhelm any secular authority which seems to threaten his will. The courage to take such a step is a highly prized virtue and is expected in a leader. Thus, the more powerful the leader, the more compulsion from his followers that he should assert his will.

12. Perhaps the best example of ideological flexibility in Burma is Thein Pe Myint, who has undertaken government-sponsored tours in the Soviet Union, China, and the United States. He has assumed an incredible variety of ideological postures since publishing his first Marxist essay just before World War II, and at one time or another has been on close terms with most of Burma's major Communists, as well as being available for conversations with visiting political observers who want inside information about Burmese politics. All of Thein Pe Myint's major works are in Burmese. The most significant of his recent publications include *Experience in Politics*, 1956; *The Eastern Sun Is Rising*, 1958; *Kyaw Nyein: A Political Biography*, 1961; and *Experiences as a Candidate*, 1962. More recently, he has been a major theorist for the *Lanzin's* Political Science Academy.

13. Following Stalin's death, Thakin Soe claimed his mantle of authority and, during the 1963 amnesty discussions with the government, Soe met the press with a framed picture of Stalin on the desk before him. He criticized Peking for lack of courage in denouncing Khrushchev: "While it dared to make repeated attacks on the treachery of Tito, it failed to attack the real culprit of Soviet revisionism by name." Also, Thakin Soe blamed China for double-talk when it condemned the Twentieth Congress of the Communist Party of the Soviet Union, but still subscribed to the 81-Party Declaration which was based on that Congress. Press Conference, August 13, 1963, reported in *The Nation* (New York), p. 1.

14. Information about the PVO was gained through interviews in Lower Chindwin district and Burmese government documents in the Rangoon Defense Services Historical Institute. I met with Bo Htein Lin on several occasions prior to, and following, the coup.

15. See my analysis, "Burma's China Crisis: The Choices Ahead," *Asian Survey* (Berkeley, Calif.), VII, No. 11 (November, 1967). Than Tun was assassinated on September 24, 1968, by a Chin aide in the White Flags. The assassination was a reprisal for the execution, the previous week, of several underground student leaders. Several Peking-returned Burmese Communists then seized control (*The Guardian*, September 27, 1968).

16. The Revolutionary Council published the entire transcript of the Internal Peace Parley, which was conducted between June 11 and November 11, 1963. See Bibliography.

SELECTED BIBLIOGRAPHY

Ba Maw, U, *Breakthrough in Burma: Memoirs of a Revolution, 1939–46.* New Haven: Yale University Press, 1968.

Butwell, Richard, *U Nu of Burma.* Stanford, Calif.: Stanford University Press, 1963.

Cady, John, *A History of Modern Burma.* Ithaca, N.Y.: Cornell University Press, 1958.

Johnstone, William, *Burma's Foreign Policy.* Cambridge, Mass.: Harvard University Press, 1963.

Pye, Lucian, *Politics, Personality, and Nation Building.* New Haven, Conn.: Yale University Press, 1962.

Revolutionary Council, Union of Burma, *The Philosophy of the Burma Socialist Programme Party.* Rangoon: Government Printing Office, 1962.

————, The Peace Parley. Rangoon, 1963. Mimeographed.

Shway Yoe, *The Burman: His Life and Notions* (4th ed.). New York: The Macmillan Company, 1963.

Tinker, Hugh, *The Union of Burma.* London: Oxford University Press, 1965.

Trager, Frank, *Burma: From Kingdom to Republic.* New York: Frederick A. Praeger, Inc., 1966.

Walinsky, Louis, *Economic Development in Burma: 1951–60.* New York: Twentieth Century Fund, 1962.

REVISIONISTS AND SECTARIANS

INDIA'S TWO COMMUNIST PARTIES

RALPH H. RETZLAFF

In its drive to attain power in the world's second most populous nation, the Communist movement in India has undergone major internal conflicts as it has sought to respond to the ideological demands and controversies in the international Communist movement, while also seeking to retain a legitimate status within India's freedom movement and post-independence political system. By 1964, the conflict over the appropriate strategy and tactics to be adopted in respect to both the international and domestic problems became so intense that a formal split occurred in the Communist Party of India (CPI).[1] Since then, two rival Parties have competed vigorously for control over the Communist movement in India, often to their mutual detriment.

The rightist, pro-Soviet faction within the former undivided Party continues to be designated as the Communist Party of India, (CPI), while the leftist, ostensibly pro-Chinese, faction within the Party calls itself Communist Party of India (Marxist) (or CPI-M). The breakdown of unity within the Indian Communist movement is directly traceable to the breakdown of ideological unity within the international Communist movement and to the Sino-Soviet dispute, but it is also rooted deeply in the Indian movement's past, and stems in part from the political, social, and economic context within which the Indian movement has functioned. This essay is an assessment of the past events and conditions which have shaped the present situation and which will influence the prospects of Indian Communism in the immediate future.

During the early phases of the development of Indian Communism in the 1920's, the movement, as elsewhere, was largely under the direction of the Communist Party of the Soviet Union (CPSU), but a pattern developed whereby this control was exercised indirectly through the Communist Party of Great Britain (CPGB). The ties between Indian and British Communists were extremely important. They covered not only matters of ideology, strategy, and tactics, but also the supply of funds, trained organizers, and other agents. Prior to the formal organization of the CPI,[2] the Communist movement operated within India through a series of regional parties and front groups. Foremost among those was the Workers' and Peasants' Party which had units in Bengal, Bombay, the United Provinces, and Punjab. The movement also contacted and drew recruits from several revolutionary and terrorist groups in Punjab and Bengal,[3] and elements of these groups continue down to the present day as recognizable and important factors in the Punjab and West Bengal state units of the CPI.[4]

As the Party developed, both the quasi-federal character of the Indian polity as well as the regional variations in Indian society exercised an influence over its organizational structure and operation. The result has been that the most strategic operational units of the CPI have been at the state rather than at the national level. In certain respects the national Party, particularly down to 1964, was an aggregate of these state units. They formed the power base from which Party leaders in different regions competed for control over the national units of the Party. Whenever national CPI leadership was weak or divided, state units sought to assert a degree of autonomy from central control, particularly with regard to Party tactics. The continuing pressure for flexibility within the Party was reinforced by the fact that the state Party units were more sensitive to the need to define the relationship of the CPI to other political parties and social groups in their particular areas: This was especially true with respect to the formation of alliances for purposes of mass agitation, electoral contests, and parliamentary activity. It continues to be the case even after the 1964 split.

THE DEVELOPMENT OF THE CPI

The formation of the CPI, in late 1928, from the loosely related regional groups and organizations which had been active in the Communist movement, was followed less than six months later, in mid-1929, by the arrest and detention of 31 leaders of the Party. As a result, the Party's operations were seriously hampered for several years. Thus from 1928 to 1935, the CPI, under Comintern direction, followed the united-front-from-below tactics which implied an antagonistic posture toward the Indian National Congress (INC) and other nationalist groups. Nevertheless, during this period it won the sympathy of a small but influential leftist segment within the INC. In 1935, when the Comintern dictated the shift to the united-front-from-above tactics, the CPI readily moved to more active cooperation with the nationalist movement. Its members joined the Congress Socialist Party (CSP) and over a period of time were highly successful in infiltrating positions of leadership within it, especially in south India.[5] In 1939, when the CPI members were expelled from the CSP for disruptive tactics, the CPI was able to take with it the bulk of the cadres in areas now comprising the three south Indian states of Andhra Pradesh, Kerala, and Madras.

In addition, during the early 1940's, the CPI successfully extended its control over substantial segments of the most important peasant, labor, and student organizations then existent in India.[6] The bulk of the non-Communist nationalist leadership was either imprisoned or underground at the time, as a result of the 1942 Quit India agitation launched by the INC, and they remained there until 1944. This greatly facilitated Communist infiltration of mass organizations, since the CPI was granted legal status by the British in 1943. On the eve of Indian independence, the CPI had increased its membership from an estimated 5,000, in 1942, to 53,000 in 1946,[7] and it had recruited most of the leaders who currently control the national and state units of the Party. It had developed disciplined, experienced cadres in several regions of India, able to serve as a matrix around which later expansion could take place.

These modest gains, however, were counterbalanced by the fact that it had alienated the leadership of the entire nationalist movement, particularly Gandhi. In 1939, following the outbreak of World War II and the signing of the Hitler-Stalin pact, the CPI faithfully carried out the "anti-imperialist-war" line set down by the CPSU. Many CPI leaders were arrested and detained. Its position at this juncture was somewhat comparable to that of the INC, which also opposed the involvement of India in the War, though for quite different reasons. When the international Communist line shifted radically in the wake of the Nazi invasion of the Soviet Union, however, the CPI began to call for cooperation with

the British and support for "the people's war," and a complete rupture
of relationships between the CPI and the INC took place. This was
further intensified in 1942, when the INC began the Quit India agitation
while the CPI was calling for full cooperation in the War effort. As the
War began to draw to a close in late 1944, and many INC leaders were
being released from jail, the CPI sought a reconciliation with the INC,
but to no avail. As a result, its influence in Indian politics on the eve of
independence was negligible. In the elections to the provincial legisla-
tures held in 1946, it succeeded in capturing only 3.6 per cent of the
valid votes polled, and 8 of 1,477 seats.[8]

During the period immediately prior to the granting of Indian
independence, the CPI was forced to face the need to define precisely
its position in Indian politics and, in particular, its attitude toward the
INC. In the absence of clear guidance from the CPSU or the CPGB, a
split began to develop within the Party. A radical wing, which called
for a turn away from positions of cooperation or conciliation with the
INC and for the adoption of a militant line, emerged. It advocated a
reversal of the wartime policy of restraining mass activity of a revolutionary character, and called instead for a policy of insurrection and
guerrilla activity. The Zhdanov speech of September 1947, which sig-
naled the advent of cold-war policies by the CPSU, and the advice of
the Yugoslav Cominform delegates who attended the Second CPI Congress (in February and March 1948, in Calcutta) and strongly urged
militant action, set the seal of international approval on insurrectionary
tactics. As a result, B. T. Ranadive, the prime exponent of this view,
replaced P. C. Joshi as General Secretary, and the CPI embarked upon
an adventurist line of action which did not end until 1951. Ranadive was
strongly influenced by the Russian model of revolution and consequently
directed principal attention to the urban working classes. Thus, shortly
after India attained independence, and while the Nehru government was
struggling to consolidate and stabilize its position, the CPI launched
a series of violent agitations and once again placed itself in direct opposition to Indian nationalism.

It was during this adventurist phase that one of the earliest indications of a potential basis of Sino-Soviet controversy over the ideological
direction and control of the CPI emerged. The Andhra Pradesh unit of
the CPI, under the direction of C. Rajeshwar Rao, came out in vigorous
criticism of Ranadive's adherence to a Russian-style revolution, calling
instead for emulation of the Chinese experience under Mao's concepts of
"new democracy." In June 1949, when the CPSU gave tentative approval
to this latter approach as applicable to Asian Communist Parties, its move
was interpreted as supporting the replacement of Ranadive as General
Secretary. This was carried out in May 1950. While the emphasis under
Rajeshwar Rao, who became the new General Secretary, shifted from

urban to rural areas, the use of violent insurrectionary tactics continued. Party membership declined sharply throughout this adventurist period, and several of the state units of the CPI were declared illegal.[9]

Several factors facilitated the shift away from adventurism. First, the widespread failure of militancy in Asia (the Philippines, Malaya, Indonesia, Burma, Japan, and India), together with the internal changes in the U.S.S.R. after Stalin's death, led to conditions in which such a shift was called for, or at least strongly urged by, the CPSU. In addition, while Stalin was still alive, the Soviet Union's attitude toward India began to undergo a change in the light of India's position on the Korean War. R. P. Dutt, of the CPGB, directed a letter to the CPI which advised a shift away from adventurism and a reassessment of the Nehru government. Also, within India, the imminence of the first general elections to be held since independence under universal adult suffrage, forced the CPI to consider participating. Inside the CPI, an attack was directed at the adventurist line by P. C. Joshi, the former General Secretary, and several other important Party leaders, including S. A. Dange and Ajoy Ghosh. Ultimately, Ajoy Ghosh was elected General Secretary, replacing Rajeshwar Rao, and the Party began its first tentative steps toward a return to "constitutional Communism."

The role of Ajoy Ghosh, who continued as General Secretary of the CPI to the time of his death in January 1962, should not be underestimated.[10] He derived his strength with the Party from the balancing role which he played at the national level. He was not closely identified with any state unit of the Party, nor with its emerging left and right factions. Under his leadership the CPI gradually, albeit reluctantly, came to support the view that Communism could come to power in India through peaceful parliamentary means. This position was formally adopted by the Party in the wake of its electoral triumph in Kerala in the 1957 elections.

THE SHIFT IN CPI POLICY FROM 1951 TO 1958

The gradual shift in the attitude of the Soviet Union toward the Nehru government in India between 1950 and 1955 had two perceptible effects upon the CPI. First, it brought about a gradual and very reluctant reorientation of the CPI's official line toward the Nehru government. As late as 1950, the CPI officially denounced both the foreign and domestic policy of the Nehru government in the strongest possible terms. Gradually, under pressure from the CPSU and with the abandonment of the CPI's adventurist phase, it came to acknowledge that there were some positive aspects in what was still generally viewed as an undesirable foreign policy. Subsequently, its emphasis shifted to the view that while the Nehru government's foreign policy was good, its domestic policy was bad. Finally it came to the position of acknowledging that there were favorable features in both the domestic and foreign policies of the Nehru government.

The policy shift regarding the Nehru government was not accomplished without considerable internal conflict within the CPI, however. Even in 1957, a hard-core left faction remained unconvinced that either the domestic or foreign policies of that government merited CPI support. As the right faction within the Party gradually adjusted itself to the CPSU line, it was increasingly separated from the left faction, which refused to acknowledge the validity of the CPSU assessment, although at this point it did not directly challenge Soviet authority.[11]

In 1954 and 1955, Nehru exchanged visits with both the Soviet and Chinese leaders. During this period, several important statements appeared in international Communist Party journals, causing considerable debate within the CPI. The first of these was an article by R. P. Dutt, of the CPGB, which appeared in October 1954.[12] In it, Dutt implied strong support for both the domestic and international policies of the Nehru government. Since the article had been written by the CPGB's main spokesman on India, it threw the CPI into a quandary. At first, the Central Committee of the CPI almost rejected the Dutt article. It argued that the line which emerged from it was one of increasing support to the Nehru government and of "lining up behind it on a plea of national freedom, . . . [which] . . . would have weakened the movement for full freedom and . . . the economic and political struggles of the masses."[13] Subsequently, in a second resolution, the Central Committee took a wait-and-see attitude, seeking further guidance in the hope of resolving the deep internal dispute that had developed.[14]

The second article which influenced CPI policy was an editorial in *Pravda* on January 26, 1955. It praised not only the foreign-policy accomplishments of the Nehru government, but also commented favorably on his domestic policy. This article appeared one month before the special elections in Andhra Pradesh in February 1955, and was used widely by the INC, to the detriment of the CPI, which was badly defeated.

In 1956, another article caused deep consternation within CPI ranks.[15] Written by Modeste Rubenstein and appearing in *New Times*, it went even further than previous Soviet statements and adopted the view that for many years the Nehru government had been following a peaceful path to socialism, strongly implying that it, rather than the CPI, might lead the way to socialism in India. Ajoy Ghosh, then General Secretary, who had played a key role in bringing the CPI around to limited support of the Nehru government, took strong exception to the Rubenstein article.[16] The CPSU withdrew from the extreme position taken in the Rubenstein article, which had failed to acknowledge a possible constructive role for the CPI in the development of Indian socialism; however, the tendency characterized by the Dutt and *Pravda* articles, toward recognizing some positive aspects of the Nehru government, carried with it the strong implication that the CPI should play a constructive and cooperative role vis-à-vis the INC. As we mentioned earlier, a segment within the CPI comprising, in part, those who were identified with the adventurist period, such as B. T. Ranadive, strongly resisted this pressure for a shift in attitude which emanated from the CPSU. Throughout this entire period, inner Party differences continued to grow in strength and to pervade all aspects of Party operation and activity.

By the Fifth Congress of the Party in 1958, however, the leadership of the CPI exuded confidence that the parliamentary takeover in Kerala could be repeated in other states, and eventually, at the center. It expressed support not only for the foreign policy of the Nehru government, but also for substantial segments of its domestic policy. The militant leftist faction of the Party viewed this dual tendency—to support constitutionalism and parliamentary action, coupled with support given specific INC policies—with increasing disfavor. Rather than rejoicing in the CPI electoral victory in Kerala, it felt that this victory restricted its ability to engage in militant mass activities in other parts of India where this was regarded as essential. Nevertheless, the internal situation made it necessary for the leftists to bide their time.

THE SHATTERED IMAGE OF THE CPI

The adoption by the CPI of its new constitution at Amritsar in 1958 marked the culmination of a process whereby the Party gained increasing respectability on the Indian political scene. The liabilities which the Party had incurred in the past as a result of its antinational stands and its adventurist phase faded from public consciousness. Under Ajoy Ghosh's leadership, the CPI gave increasing evidence of being able to cope successfully with the conflicting demands of national and international loyalties.

In 1959, however, three events brought about a marked transformation of the political scene and served to shatter the image of respectability which the CPI had built up. By the end of 1959, the CPI once again found a very broadly based and active hostility directed toward it within India. This, in turn, provided the basis for the reemergence of vigorous intra-Party conflict.

The uprisings by Khampa tribesmen in Tibet, which culminated in the flight of the Dalai Lama to India in April 1959, resulted in the expression of widespread concern within India about the Tibetan situation. In mid-March, Nehru made two statements in Parliament. He sought, on the one hand, to assure Indian public opinion of the government's concern over events in Tibet; on the other hand, he sought through cautious wording, not to arouse the Chinese. However, in late March, the official Chinese news agency issued a communiqué that set off a wave of anti-Chinese sentiment in India. First, it stated that the Tibetan rebellion was being directed from Kalimpong on Indian soil; and second, it charged that reference to developments in Tibet made in the Indian Parliament amounted to an interference in the internal affairs of China by India. With the exception of the CPI, all political parties joined the Prime Minister in a vigorous denial that Kalimpong was being used as a base for subversive activities by the Indian government and supported Nehru's view that the Indian Parliament had the right to discuss any matter which it found fit for such discussion.[17] The Secretariat of the National Council of the CPI, however, issued a statement on the Tibetan situation essentially supporting both of the Chinese charges.[18] This resulted in criticism of the CPI and the assertion that the Party was playing an antinational role in Indian politics.

Even as the controversy over the CPI's position on Tibet developed a second attack upon it began to take shape. The actions of the Communist Ministry which had taken office in the state of Kerala in 1957 were strongly criticized. The focal point of the controversy was the Kerala Education Bill, which proposed basic changes in both public and private school administration in Kerala.[19]

In January 1959, after the Act received the assent of the President of India, the Nair Service Society, a caste Hindu organization, spearheaded a statewide campaign against it. In May, it convened a conference of all communities and non-Communist political Parties and, acting in concert they initiated a mass agitation. The ostensible purpose was to cause the withdrawal of the Act, but in fact (as later admitted by the leader of the Nair Service Society) the true aim was to bring about the downfall of the Kerala government. Widespread violence occurred throughout the state in connection with the antigovernment agitations in June and July Finally, over the vigorous objections of the Kerala government and the national CPI, the President of India, acting under the emergency provisions of the Indian Constitution, signed a proclamation dissolving the state legislature and dismissing the government. The Governor took over administration of the state and retained control until February 1960 when a united front of anti-Communist parties succeeded in defeating the CPI in a special election.

These events strained the CPI's continued adherence to the Amritsar thesis and the acceptance of parliamentary democracy as the principal avenue through which the Party would secure power in India. Nehru's affirmation at a press conference that the Communists could rule again if they won the elections in Kerala was clearly aimed at encouraging continued CPI adherence to democratic methods. And, in the wake of the

CPI's defeat, E. M. S. Namboodiripad, the former Chief Minister, indicated that the Party in Kerala would continue to function as a constructive and responsible opposition in the Assembly.[20] Nevertheless, the successful overthrow of a Communist government by anti-Communist forces gave added support to the leftists within the Party who argued that the INC would never allow a Communist government to institute a program of socialist reforms.

While the flight of the Dalai Lama and the overthrow of the Kerala government were incidents to which the CPI was capable of adjusting, albeit with some difficulty, the third aspect of the changing scene in 1959 posed a much graver challenge. For some time there had been indications that differences about the demarcation of the border existed between India and China. In August 1959, the Chinese occupied Longju in the Northeastern Frontier Area (NEFA), and the dispute became serious. Shortly afterward, the Secretariat of the National Council of the CPI issued an equivocal statement "regretting" the incident.[21] Subsequently, the Central Executive Committee (CEC), meeting at Calcutta, adopted a resolution on the border issue in which it advised the government of China not to insist upon the acceptance of its maps and advised the government of India not to press for the McMahon line. The CEC expressed its confidence that socialist China could never commit aggression against India, just as India had no intention of committing aggression against China.[22] The resolution was designed to meet the mounting pro-Chinese sentiments of the leftist faction, but also stressed that the CPI stood with the rest of the people of India for the territorial integrity of the nation, thus establishing its *bona fides* as a true national party. However, the resolution did not satisfy the external critics of the Party nor its left or right factions. Intra-Party tensions continued to mount.

Ajoy Ghosh, the General Secretary of the CPI, led a five-man delegation to China in early October to participate in the anniversary celebrations of the founding of the Chinese People's Republic. Upon his return to India on October 18, he stressed that the Chinese leaders were extremely anxious that the border dispute be settled as quickly as possible. With a timing that succeeded in seriously embarrassing Ghosh, the Chinese attacked an Indian patrol in the Konga Pass in the Ladakh region of Kashmir (on the 21st of October). By the end of that month, intra-Party conflict within the CPI emerged into public view. S. A. Dange, a leading rightist, explained to a public meeting that he was not in full agreement with the Party's views on the Sino-Indian question. He urged that the CPI recognize the McMahon line in order to meet the increasing criticism leveled at it and to stop the estrangement of the Party from the rest of Indian. The CPI National Council, meeting in Meerut in mid-November, formally accepted the McMahon line and stated that the areas south of it were and should remain a part of India.[23] This represented a clear victory for the right, even during the tenure as General Secretary of Ajoy Ghosh, who still sought to maintain a centrist position in the Party. It failed to stop the dissatisfaction voiced by the leftists within the Party, who felt that the CPI was abandoning the requirements of proletarian internationalism. By late 1959, the CPI leadership was on the defensive.

THE SINO-SOVIET DISPUTE

The rise of the Sino-Soviet dispute and the consequent breakdown of ideological unity in the international Communist movement has had a marked effect upon the CPI, leading ultimately to the formal split within the Party in 1964 and the formation of the CPI-M. The evolving position of the factions within the CPI regarding this dispute can best be seen against the background of the Twentieth Congress of the CPSU in 1956, the 1960 Congress of 81 Communist Parties in Moscow, and the Twenty-second Congress of the CPSU in 1961.

Two major lines set forth at the Twentieth Party Congress of the CPSU were the concept of peaceful transition to socialism and the de-Stalinization campaign. Both were sources of major discussions and controversy within the CPI. After hearing Ajoy Ghosh's report on the actions taken at the Twentieth Party Congress of the CPSU, the Fourth Party Congress of the CPI adopted a resolution which, recognizing the gravity of the issues raised by the CPSU, called upon all Party committees to discuss Ghosh's report and, in conjunction with this, required that the Central Committee of the CPI make available to all Party members an editorial which appeared in the Chinese Communist Party (CCP) organ, the *People's Daily*, on April 5, 1956, entitled "On the Historical Experience of the Dictatorship of the Proletariat," which supported and justified many actions taken by Stalin in the Soviet Union.[24]

In an exchange of correspondence with Jaya Prakash Narayan, a former Socialist Party leader, Ghosh elaborated his views on the de-Stalinization campaign:

We agree that we were wrong in idealizing everything in the USSR. We should have paid more attention to the criticism of the USSR made by Socialists and non-Communist democrats. We agree that among us and in other Communist Parties, the tendency developed of defending everything done by the USSR, of condemning everyone who criticized any aspect of Soviet policy. We are deeply conscious of the damage this has done to the cause of Communist-Socialist unity and even to the cause of Socialism. We are determined to abandon this attitude.[25]

In the context of the Sino-Soviet dispute, the implication of Ghosh's remarks suggested a desire on his part to support a much more flexible and nationalist line.[26] Despite the Party's electoral triumpn in Kerala, the left faction within the CPI continued to oppose the support extended by Ghosh to the possibility of a peaceful transition to socialism and to the de-Stalinization campaign. The events of 1959 and, in particular, the surfacing of the Sino-Indian dispute greatly exacerbated inner Party conflict. As was only natural, the two contending factions sought to buttress and legitimize their internal quarrels by seeking support from the external debate between CPSU and the CCP. Thus, in 1960, as the Sino-Soviet dispute emerged into full view and competition began for the loyalties of the world's Communist Parties, the CPI factional quarrels, which had been heightened by the events of 1959, took on an added intensity and were interwoven into the international Communist quarrel.

The World Federation of Trade Unions (WFTU) meeting in Peking in June 1960, and the Bucharest conference held in conjunction with the Third Congress of the Rumanian Workers Party in the same month, provided indications of the conflicting positions held by groups within the CPI on the Sino-Soviet dispute. Interestingly, whereas the CPI delegation to the WFTU meeting in Peking was headed by S. A. Dange, a leading rightist, the CPI delegation at the Bucharest Conference consisted of two leftists who were members of the CPI Central Secretariat, namely, Basavapunniah and Bhupesh Gupta.[27] While Dange is reported to have strongly supported the CPSU at the Peking Conference, the leftists at the Bucharest Conference reportedly avoided taking an open position on the Sino-Soviet quarrel.[28]

At the 1960 Congress of 81 Communist Parties in Moscow, Ajoy Ghosh delivered a lengthy speech in which he sought to explain the position of the CPI with respect to both the Russians and the Chinese.[29] In his speech he sought, to a limited extent, to conciliate the CCP and to assure it of the cooperation of the CPI; nevertheless, he made it unmistakably clear that he strongly supported the CPSU in the internal conflict in the Communist world and that he opposed the CCP in the Sino-Indian border dispute. By mid-1960, factional quarrels within the CPI had reached a point where several of the state units of the Party began to consider resolutions concerning the attitude of the CPI toward the CPSU, the CCP, and the border dispute.[30]

Among all the CPI units, the most staunchly leftist has been the largest, that in West Bengal. This fact was not lost upon the Chinese. Reportedly, a two-man CPI delegation attended the Vietnamese Communist Party Congress in September 1960. It consisted of H. K. Konar, a leading West Bengal leftist, and K. Damodaran, a rightist from Kerala. While snubbing Damodaran, the CCP sought out Konar, and reportedly explained to him the nature and character of the Chinese position in the Sino-Soviet dispute.

In late 1961, when the Twenty-second Congress of the CPSU took

place, Ajoy Ghosh led a seven-man delegation consisting of both rightists
and leftists. Upon his return from Moscow, he admitted at a press conference that serious differences continued to exist within the ranks of
the CPI over the intensified de-Stalinization campaign in the Soviet
Union. The differences soon broke out into the open. E. M. S. Namboodiripad, in a press conference in Calicut, Kerala, remarked, "We
Indian Communists have experienced only the result of what is positive
in Marshal Stalin."[31] Shortly afterward, the Secretariat of the West
Bengal unit of the CPI accused the leadership of the CPSU of a "direct
violation" of the principles of the 1957 Moscow Declaration in its attack
on the Albanians.[32] Party divisions on matters of basic ideological importance found the center group, led by Namboodiripad, and the left group,
led by the West Bengal CPI unit, ranged in open opposition to Ghosh,
who had the support of the right group led by Dange. These divisions,
moreover, were a reflection of the open split which had manifested itself
within the CPI at its Vijayawada Congress earlier that year.

The Breakdown of Party Unity

In the spring of 1961, the CPI had held its Sixth Party Congress.
The events of the Congress, as well as those leading up to it in the
Central Executive Committee and in the National Council, gave ample
indication that neither the left nor right factions within the Party were
in a mood for compromise. While the rightist faction of the Party had a
majority in both the Central Executive Committee and the National
Council, it did not feel that its position was sufficiently strong either to
purge the left faction or to force its ideological position upon the entire
Party.[33] Thus, when the National Council completed its meeting on
February 22, 1961, prior to the Vijayawada Congress, it adopted, with
only minor modifications, the political thesis sponsored by Ajoy Ghosh,
the General Secretary of the Party. This was a thesis supported by the
Dange group. But the Council also agreed that the rejected thesis of the
leftists headed by B. T. Ranadive should be circulated to the Party
Congress as a minority document. In fact, a third document, prepared
by E. M. S. Namboodiripad and critical of both the extreme right and
left, was also circulated at the Congress.[34]

The principal distinctions among the three draft resolutions placed
before the CPI at Vijayawada centered on the Party's attitude toward the
INC and the Nehru government. The official draft, put forward by Ghosh
and supported by the rightists, argued that the INC could not be regarded as a force of reaction. It advanced Ghosh's view that the CPI
should oppose INC measures considered to be reactionary and support
those considered to be progressive. The leftist draft, sponsored by B. T.
Ranadive and others, gave credit to the INC for some of the work which

it had done, but nevertheless regarded it as a force of reaction and consequently urged vigorous opposition. The Namboodiripad draft sought to create a distinction between two sections of the *bourgeoisie* within the INC. It argued that, although one section had obvious connections with both foreign and indigenous monopoly capitalism, another section was clearly anti-imperialist and antifeudal in its outlook, and that it was with this section of the national *bourgeoisie* that closer contacts should be forged in order to win them to the side of the CPI.[35]

The conflict at Vijayawada over the ideological line to be adopted by the Party was paralleled by a comparable struggle for organizational control. This ultimately resulted in an expansion of the National Council from 101 to 110 members, the additional members being evenly divided between the right and left factions.[36]

In June 1961, the National Council chosen at the Vijayawada Conference elected a 25-member Central Executive Committee.[37] An examination of the new, outgoing, and continuing members reveals that the right faction continued to maintain a slight position of dominance within the Party but faced a fairly substantial leftist opposition.

The split within the CPI over internal issues was reflected in the stands taken by the right and left factions in the growing dispute within the world Communist camp. The CPI was thus obliged to turn its attention to the Third General Elections, scheduled for the spring of 1962, in a state of deep division. Ajoy Ghosh, in his election statement, remarked:

. . . our attitude toward the Government of India's foreign policy is . . . one of general support, together with the demand that it should become firmer and more consistent.

. . . [In regard to domestic policy] the Communist Party considers that in the forthcoming elections it is of utmost importance that the "anti-people" policies of the Congress are exposed, the damage done by them is explained and the people rallied to weaken—and where possible to break—the Congress monopoly of power. . . . That would be for the good of the Congress itself since it would help honest Congressmen to fight the evils that have crept in with greater chances of success. . . . We do not, however, advocate the breaking of the Congress monopoly of power for its own sake and by any methods. We do not want merely the defeat of the Congress—no matter at whose hands. Our attitude toward the Congress has nothing in common with the attitude of parties, groups and elements of the extreme Right. . . . In contrast to [them] . . . we combat the policies of the government with a view to bring [sic] about a move to the Left—toward democracy, social advance and consistent anti-imperialism.[38]

Ghosh's views were honored in the breach as CPI state units each sought to secure that balance of electoral alliances and mass action most in keeping with the demands of the local situation. While the CPI's support of V. K. Krishna Menon was consonant with this position, the actions of state units in Andhra Pradesh, Madras, Punjab, and West Bengal, for example, were much less unambiguous. To some extent, the CPI was aided in its electoral campaign by the fact that mass attention had been diverted from the Sino-Indian border dispute by the Indian government's occupation of Goa. The CPI strongly supported the Goan action, a move that had also brought forth warm praise from the Soviet Union. The outcome of the Third General Elections showed that the CPI did not suffer a setback in mass support; rather, with few exceptions, it continued its modest but steady gains in percentage of votes polled throughout the country. In three states, Andhra Pradesh, Kerala, and West Bengal, the CPI remained a major factor in the political scene.

Far more serious, however, was the death of Ajoy Ghosh in mid-January of 1962, on the eve of the elections. The intensity of intra-Party conflict between the left and right factions, as well as the unsettling conditions which existed during the elections, seriously complicated the search for Ghosh's successor. It was not until a meeting of the National Council on April 29, 1962, that a compromise was reached between the left and right factions. A new position, Chairman of the Party, was created. It was given to S. A. Dange, the leading rightist; and E. M. S. Namboodiripad, the centrist, was made the General Secretary.[39] This proved to be an uneasy and ultimately unsuccessful maneuver.

The Chinese Invasion of India

Throughout early and mid-1962, as the right and left factions of the Party continued to jockey for control, signs of an approaching conflict between India and China in the border regions increased. Finally, on October 20, 1962, Chinese troops invaded Indian territory in both NEFA and Ladakh and pressed onward into previously uncontested territory in NEFA. The ties of Indian nationalism and of proletarian internationalism were directly and intensely confounded. The main offices of the Party in New Delhi were stoned and sacked by mobs, and demands were raised by opposition parties that the CPI be abolished as an antinational group.

Three days before the Chinese invasion, the National Council had adopted a resolution on developments in NEFA in which it strongly supported the notion that the McMahon line was the border of India and that Chinese forces which had reportedly crossed it had thus violated Indian territory. The CPI had nevertheless refused to condemn China as an aggressor.[40] Even Dange, on October 19, 1962, the day before the Chinese invasion, refused to label Chinese action on the border "aggression," preferring rather to speak in terms of Chinese violation of Indian territory.

The intensity of the split within the CPI over the invasion is indicated by the fact that it was not until November 1, 1962, almost two weeks later, that the National Council was able to adopt a resolution on the Chinese invasion.[41] In it, the Party specifically termed the Chinese action "aggression" and called upon all sections of the Indian People to "unite in defense of the motherland."[42] The adoption of the November 1 resolution had an immediate impact on the inner Party conflict. Jyoti Basu (of West Bengal), P. Sundarayya (of Andhra Pradesh), and H. K. S. Surjeet (of Punjab)—three leading leftists—resigned from the Central Secretariat immediately after the adoption of the resolution.

On November 20, 1962, the Central Secretariat addressed to all fraternal parties throughout the world a letter in which it sought to explain and justify the stand taken in its November 1 resolution. In particular, it attempted to meet criticism directed at it by the leftists of the Party that it had violated the rules of proletarian internationalism through its attack upon the CCP. The letter asserted that the CCP had acted in "total disregard" of CPI advice on the Indian situation. It further charged that "it is evident that at the root of their understanding and policy lie certain narrow nationalistic considerations and some distorted and incorrect approach and line following thereon."[43]

Two features of the letter were particularly noteworthy: First, the extent to which the CPI Central Secretariat justified and supported *all* aspects of the foreign policy stand taken by the Nehru government in the Sino-Indian border dispute; second, the fact that the letter was signed not only by Dange, Bhupesh Gupta, Z. A. Ahmed, M. N. Govindan Nair, and Yogindra Sharma, all rightists, but also by the important centrist, E. M. S. Namboodiripad.

In mid-November, the government of India began a selective crackdown on the CPI left wing, arresting 957 top and middle cadres of the Party in almost all the states by January 10, 1963. Significantly, Namboodiripad, who was taken into custody on November 22, was released one week later.[44] All opposition parties continued to mount an attack on the CPI, which was virtually in a state of collapse. By mid-December, there were indications that the CPI front organizations had for the most part either declined or disappeared.[45] From December 9, 1962, to January 6, 1963, Dange went abroad on an "explaining mission" in which he visited both Moscow and London. Reportedly, in Moscow, Khrushchev strongly criticized Dange for falling "easy victim to the chauvinism of the reactionary forces." He condemned the CPI resolution of November 1, which had accused the Chinese of committing aggression. He is said to have argued that it would rather have been advisable for the CPI to charge Peking with "misconceiving a situation on its border and invading India."[46] Immediately thereafter, Dange went to London. At a public meeting there, he said that both India and China had accused each other of aggression. In general content, his speech marked a return to the pre-November 1 National Council position on China. This caused considerable consternation among the rightists in the CPI.

Dange's Dispute with the CCP

It is at this juncture, early 1963, that a radical transformation took place within the Party. In the wake of the Chinese invasion, the West Bengal unit had been seriously affected by the large-scale arrests of its members. The Central Secretariat, therefore, took steps to create a Provincial Organizing Committee (POC) which superseded the formal state Party unit. A similar reorganization took place in Punjab, and there is indication that reorganizations had taken place in Andhra Pradesh and Madras prior to the arrests of CPI members.[47] The West Bengal POC was clearly controlled by rightists who supported Dange. The left faction was not slow in reacting. First in West Bengal and subsequently in other states, they set up a parallel organization, called the PCZ, in West Bengal.[48] In early February 1963, as the organizational splits within the CPI continued to deepen and the situation regarding the factional loyalties of many of the Party members remained fluid, the National Council met in an eight-day session and adopted, over the strenuous objections of the party leftists, most of whom were in jail, two resolutions, two resolutions which served to worsen relationships between the CPI and the Chinese Communist Party.

The first resolution, "On Certain Ideological Questions Affecting the Unity of the International Communist Movement,"[49] clearly aligned the formal leadership of the CPI with the position taken by the CPSU in the Sino-Soviet debate. Specifically, the National Council resolution charged the CCP and the Albanian Party of Labor (APL) with violating the 1957 Moscow Declaration and the 1960 Moscow Statement, and also with violating the norms of proletarian internationalism with respect to relations between the fraternal parties.[50]

The second resolution, "On the Political Situation," dealt with a wide range of national and international issues. It supported Khrushchev's actions in the Cuban missile crisis and reiterated the specific charge that the Chinese had committed aggression against India, although significantly the charge was made in a much less strident tone. The National Council once again strongly supported Nehru's position on international issues, while attempting to isolate certain domestic policies of the Nehru government for criticism and specific opposition.[51]

Less than a month later, on March 9, 1963, the Chinese Communist Party unleashed its strongest attack up to that point on the CPI. It published an editorial in *People's Daily* titled "A Mirror for Revisionists."[52] In it, the Chinese referred to "the Dange clique" which had:

. . . seized the leadership of the Communist Party of India . . . [and] betrayed Marxism-Leninism and the proletarian revolution, betrayed the revolutionary cause of the Indian proletariat and the Indian people and embarked on the road of national chauvinism and class capitulationism, thus creating complete chaos in the Indian Communist Party.[53]

It specifically charged Dange with: (1) replacing the theory of the class struggle by the slogan of class collaborationism; (2) replacing proletarian socialism by bourgeois socialism; (3) defending the dictatorship of the *bourgeoisie* and the landlords; (4) giving unconditional support to the Nehru government in its policies of hiring itself to United States imperialism; and (5) of trampling underfoot the friendship of the Chinese and Indian peoples and acting as buglers for Nehru's anti-China campaign.[54] In closing, the editorial made a thinly disguised bid for support from the leftists in the CPI:

The Chinese Communist Party and the Chinese people have a deep concern and a profound sympathy for the Indian Communists who are persisting in their struggle for the Communist cause and for the Indian proletariat and the Indian people who have a glorious revolutionary tradition. No reactionaries, no revisionists can block the advance of the Indian people. . . . History will prove that those who are firmly upholding truth and justice and firmly adhering to Marxism-Leninism and proletarian internationalism are the genuine representatives of the interests of the Indian people and the Indian nation. India's future is in their hands. . . . In the last analysis nobody can undermine the friendship between the peoples of China and India or the friendship between the Chinese Communists and the Indian Communists.[55]

On April 21, 1963, a month and one-half later, *New Age* published a reply by Dange, titled, "Neither Revisionism nor Dogmatism Is Our Guide."[56] Dange's reply to the CCP attack bears close reading by all students of the Sino-Soviet split. In a most frank and open fashion, Dange reviewed in great detail not only the Sino-Indian border dispute which served as the catalyst for the breakdown in relations between the CCP and the CPI, but also placed it in the context of the fundamental differences which had evolved in the world Communist movement. Addressing himself directly to the Chinese bid for support of the CPI leftists, he argued:

Contrary to the interests of the world Communist movement, the Chinese leadership has, through [its] . . . allegations virtually given a call for a split within the ranks of the Communist Party of India. . . . We, of the Communist Party of India, will leave no stone unturned to defeat every splitting move and uphold the banner of Communist unity.[57]

But Dange was unable to match his statement with actions. The situation with the CPI was progressively deteriorating as the leftists continued to develop their parallel organization outside the disciplinary channels of the main CPI structure.

The Battle for Institutional Control

The spring and early summer of 1963 was a period of intense maneuvering within the Party. Immediately following the National Council session on February 12, E. M. S. Namboodiripad submitted his resignation as General Secretary of the Party. Presumably no final action was taken on the matter until the National Council meeting of June 26 to July 6, when it was announced that he had formally resigned and that the duties of the General Secretary would be taken over by Chairman Dange. At that meeting, which preceded the ill-fated Sino-Soviet ideological discussions of July in Moscow, the National Council of the CPI proceeded to take up several matters. One was the organizational problem posed by the actions of the left group within the party; the other was the adoption of a political resolution.[58]

The main attention of the National Council session centered on the organizational issue. The resolution on organizational problems, put forward by M. N. Govindan Nair and Yogindra Sharma, strongly urged that the leftist faction was no longer an innocent minority. It had started functioning as a rival all-India party with its own discipline, organization, and leadership. It had been issuing circulars in West Bengal asking members of the CPI to defy the National Council and the POC appointed by it. The resolution further charged that the PCZ was distributing anti-Khrushchev literature among CPI members and was bringing out several weeklies in various parts of India to preach the "dogmatist sectarian line." Despite this and other evidence presented at that time, Dange and the rightists were unwilling to move directly against the entire leftist faction and risk an open split. Instead, the matter of a parallel party was referred to the Central Control Commission for investigation, and a showdown was thus postponed.

Dange did move in a limited fashion against the left by having the National Council take notice of the complaints against A. K. Gopalan. The charges against Gopalan were that he had been visiting several states and holding meetings with CPI members without consulting the official leadership of the Party, and acting in general in support of the leftist faction within the Party. It did not, however, take any formal action against Gopalan at that time.[59]

Emboldened by the inability and unwillingness of the rightist-controlled National Council to precipitate an open split, the left forces supporting the PCZ in West Bengal intensified their activity. The first step was a secret meeting, called on September 1st at the Muslim Institute in Calcutta, organized in violation of a POC directive.[60] Subsequent to this, a mass public rally was held by the PCZ in Calcutta, again organized in defiance of a directive from the POC and addressed by A. K. Gopalan.[61] Even before Gopalan addressed the rally a move had been underway to dislodge him from his position of leadership of the 31-member CPI delegation in the central Parliament.[62] In addressing the rally he forced the Dange group to confront a painful choice—either strict enforcement of Party directives and policies at the risk of a split, or continuance of the Party as a faction-ridden organization. As the rightist group contemplated making formal charges of Party indiscipline against Gopalan, reports continued to appear in the press of the growing strength of the PCZ groups in Kerala, Andhra Pradesh, Punjab, Madras, and West Bengal. In each case, it was apparent that the PCZ had been successful in gaining the support of a substantial segment of the state Party unit.

When the National Council met in New Delhi in mid-October, it had available to it five punishments which it could levy against Gopalan— warning, censure, temporary suspension, removal from post, and expulsion from the Party. Originally, the demand had been made that Gopalan be removed from his position of leadership of the CPI in Lok Sabha and suspended from membership on the National Council. At the National Council session, a resolution was moved which demanded public censure and temporary suspension of Gopalan. The final action taken clearly showed that Dange, while still in nominal control of the CPI, dared not go beyond a certain point. The resolution adopted by the National Council, by a vote of 49 to 22, was a simple public censure.[63] As one commentator noted, the vote was most revealing in regard to the situation within the Party.

That it could not suspend [Gopalan] . . . from the party or take some other drastic action has been interpreted as proof of the inherent strength of the pro-Peking group in the party. A too reckless wielding of the disciplinary rod will break the party to pieces and Mr. Dange knows it only too well.[64]

Shortly after the National Council session, Gopalan, in company with E. M. S. Namboodiripad, toured Kerala and vigorously attacked the Nehru government's policies.[65]

By December 1963, it was clear that the Party contained two parallel organizations. One, the rightist faction, controlled the formal units of the Party; the other, the leftist faction, was operating a parallel Party center and commanding the loyalty of significant segments of virtually all of the state Party units. Within West Bengal, the two principal factions coexisted with a much smaller, centrist group. Jyoti Basu, who had been a member of the left and associated with its leaders in jail, upon his release sought to contact Namboodiripad, reportedly with the proposal that together they should "gather a third force which might help in building up party unity."[66] Namboodiripad flew to Delhi from Kerala and began conversations with a range of Party leaders.

The leaders of the leftist faction met in Delhi prior to the meeting of the Central Executive Committee, reportedly drew up a ten-point indictment of Dange, and planned to issue it at the session of the CEC, thereby forcing a split in the Party. This they did not do. Two important factors undoubtedly conditioned the tactics of the CPI left wing at this juncture. First, the sudden, serious illness of Prime Minister Nehru; second, a secret directive, attributed to Peking, which called for a split in the world Communist movement.[67] At the CEC session a number of issues were considered, each of which elicited sharp debate along factional lines.

The debate on the convening of a Party Congress was critical. Many saw it as intimately related to the increasing demand by Peking for a split within the CPI. The leftists in the Party were unanimous in demanding that the Congress be held in April 1964.[68] They also demanded that the 1960 membership rolls be the basis for the election of delegates of the Congress, rather than the 1962 membership rolls, which would have worked to their detriment. On both these issues, they were defeated. The CEC voted to convene the Party Congress in October 1964, and to hold it on the basis of the 1962 membership rolls.[69]

Throughout the CEC meeting, reports persisted that Namboodiripad made an unsuccessful attempt to achieve a *rapprochement* between the two principal factions of the Party in view of the desperate need for Party unity.[70] The CEC appointed a commission to draft documents on ideological, political, and organizational issues to be placed before the National Council and the Party Congress to be convened in October. The commission was comprised of the Central Secretariat and six other members from the Central Executive Committee. Among the latter, reportedly, were three leftists, Jyoti Basu, P. Ramamurthi, and M. Basavapunniah. All three are understood to have refused to serve.[71]

The National Council meeting in New Delhi, in April 1964, was the scene of a full-scale effort by the leftists and several centrists to oust S. A. Dange and Party Chairman. The immediate issue was a letter that Dange had purportedly written to the British authorities prior to independence, offering to work for the government in exchange for his release from prison. The National Council's refusal to consider this allegation led to a walk-out by 32 members, including all the hard-core leftists as well as Namboodiripad and Jyoti Basu, who issued an appeal to Party members to repudiate "Dange and his group" and their "reformist political line" and "factional" organizational methods. On April 15, the National Council suspended from Party membership all the signatories of this appeal. This marked the final split in the Party, even though several unsuccessful efforts were made in the next three months to bring the two factions together.

The Formation of the CPI-M and the Final Party Split

In July 1964, the left faction of the Party met at Tenali, in Andhra Pradesh, and took steps to formally establish a separate Party structure, through one which claimed to be the legitimate Communist Party of India. It was called the Communist Party of India (Marxist) (CPI-M). In September, the Central Executive Committee of the CPI, now dominated solely by the rightist faction, struck off the Party rolls the names of all those who had participated in the Tenali meeting or who had joined the new Party subsequently.[72] Thus, in the last quarter of 1964, India witnessed the spectacle of two Communist Parties both holding the Seventh All-India Congress of the Communist Party of India. The CPI held its meeting in late December and early January, in Bombay, and the CPI-M met in Calcutta in the first week of November. In its convention the CPI-M, while repudiating the Party's 1948 policy of armed insurrection, nevertheless significantly amended the Party constitution by dropping the preamble (adopted at the Amritsar Session of the CPI) which had emphasized the possibility of a peaceful transition to Socialism.[73] The leftists denied that the establishment of their Party had been instigated by the Chinese, stressing rather that it was the result of differences that had existed within the CPI since 1947 on the role of the *bourgeoisie*. However the Party's stand on the 1962 Chinese invasion of India, which it described as merely "the October clashes on the Border" did little to mitigate its reputation as a pro-Peking Party within India.

At the rightist-dominated Party Congress held in Bombay, the "sectarianism" of the CPI-M's political program was denounced. It was evident from the political resolutions which they adopted that the rightists differed significantly with the leftists on the character of the *bourgeoisie* and, in particular, on the role of the Indian National Congress in the contemporary political situation and the changes which were taking place within the INC.[74]

In late December, the Government of India proceeded to arrest more than 750 members of the CPI-M. Home Minister Nanda defended the Government's actions by charging that the CPI-M had been organized "to serve as Peking's instrument in creating conditions of instability in the country and to facilitate the promotion of Chinese designs against India," by promoting an "internal revolution to synchronise with a fresh Chinese attack."[75] The mass arrests of the CPI-M leaders came to a critical juncture, since mid-term elections were soon to be held in Kerala, a state which was acknowledged to be one of the main areas of strength of the CPI-M.

350   REVISIONISTS AND SECTARIANS

The Kerala elections were the first immediate test of strength between the two Communist Parties. Even though the CPI-M was, at the outset, recognized as the stronger of the two in Kerala, the results of the mid-term elections were disappointing to the CPI. The Kerala legislative assembly had 120 seats. The CPI-M put up 74 candidates, 39 of whom had been jailed. The CPI put up 79 candidates. In the elections, 40 members of the CPI-M won, while only 3 members of the rightist CPI were elected, and the CPI-M became the largest single Party in the legislative assembly. Shortly after the elections, on the advice of the Governor of Kerala that a stable government commanding a majority of the legislature could not be formed, the Union Government invoked the emergency powers of the Constitution and instituted President's rule once again.

Following the Kerala elections, pressures arose from centrist forces in both Parties to find areas of agreement between the CPI and the CPI-M in order to minimize the competition between segments of the Communist movement. Agreement was sought on a minimum program of mass protest on immediate economic and political issues up through a maximum program for achieving unity and the eventual reintegration of the two Parties. The most vocal centrist spokesman in the CPI was Bhupesh Gupta, whose efforts accomplished little; this led him to resign from the Secretariat and the Executive Committee of the CPI in April 1965. Within the CPI-M, the main centrist spokesmen were E. M. S. Namboodiripad and Jyoti Basu. While tensions mounted between the two Communist Parties, it was clear that there was still some reluctance to make the split within the movement permanent. One principal indication of this was the reluctance of both Parties to bring about a split in the main Communist trade union and peasant mass organizations—the All India Trade Union Congress (AITUC), and the All Indian Kisan Sabha (AIKS).[76]

In September 1965, representatives of the CPI and CPI-M met to discuss the possibility of joint operational programs, leaving aside the question of unity, but these talks failed. E. M. S. Namboodiripad, in analysing the differences between the parties at that juncture, is reported to have remarked: "Theoretically it is possible, if for the moment we leave out international questions, and confine ourselves to internal issues, there can be agreement [sic]."[77] While agreement on short-range tactics of opposition to the Congress government was conceivable, still each Party was having considerable difficulty in establishing within itself a consensus about the main political and ideological issues. In March 1966, P. Sundarayya, the leading theoretician of the CPI-M, went to Moscow for talks, and upon his return he expressed views somewhat critical of China's contention that the Soviet Union was ganging up with the U.S. to crush China. As additional leaders of the CPI-M were released from detention by the Government of India, differences within the CPI-M became more evident, and it therefore formally initiated intra-Party discussion on a number of issues, including the state of Party organization and ideological questions concerning the international Communist movement. The division on the international issues was so intense that it took the CPI-M more than a year to agree on a formal statement. Even so, there are still divisions of opinion on some aspects of the international movement, particularly in relation to the Chinese Communists. Still another indication of the indecision and turmoil within both Parties took place in mid-1966, when the governing bodies of the two main mass organizations, the AITUC and the AIKS, met. Each of these organizations contained members from both Parties, the AITUC being largely dominated by the CPI, and the AIKS by the CPI-M. At each session attempts were made to challenge the majority in control of the organization, but in neither case was a formal attempt at a split carried out.

The Fourth General Elections

At the same time as both the CPI and the CPI-M were confronted with internal differences over organizational matters and ideological issues, they were faced with the necessity of preparing for the fourth all-India general elections which were to be held in the spring of 1967. As they attempted, at the national level, to minimise the inter-Party competition, the critical role of the state units within both Parties once again became clear. This may be seen by comparing the situations in the states of Kerala and West Bengal.

In Kerala, where the CPI-M was led by E. M. S. Namboodiripad, an Anti-Congress Party United Front, composed of seven opposition parties, was formed, and constituencies to be contested were allocated to each of the seven parties within the Front. Thus the CPI-M was allocated 61 constituencies, and the CPI 24, and contests between the two Parties were avoided. The attempt was to capture a majority of the state's 120 seat legislative assembly. By contrast, in West Bengal, where there was a very strong extremist faction within the CPI-M, attempts to work out an agreement broke down. Each of the Communist Parties formed its own united front group, and in a number of constituencies the two parties contested each other directly, splitting the Communist vote. A similar situation developed in Andhra Pradesh, the other of the three states in which observers had accorded the Communists a chance of making substantial gains in the fourth general elections.

The results of the elections came as a distinct surprise to most observers of the Indian political scene. The Indian National Congress had been expected to come back with a slightly reduced majority at the center, and possibly to lose power in a few states. In fact, the Congress

Party secured a majority of less than 30 seats out of the 521 in *Lok Sabha*, the lower house of the Union Parliament, and lost control of five states. In Kerala, West Bengal, Bihar, and Orissa it was defeated by opposition coalitions; and in Madras it lost to a regional party, the Dravidia Munnetra Kazigham. Shortly after the elections, in four more states —Uttar Pradesh, Madhya Pradesh, Punjab, and Hayana—defections from the Congress Party enabled opposition groups and coalitions to form non-Congress governments.

In the face of the serious decline in strength of the Indian National Congress, the split in the Communist movement and the inability of the CPI and the CPI-M to work out effective cooperative agreements on an all-India basis has had important consequences for the Indian political system. On an all-India basis, the CPI and the CPI-M emerged from the fourth general elections roughly equivalent in strength. In the Parliamentary elections, the CPI won 22 seats and polled 7.1 million votes (roughly 4.80 per cent of the votes polled); and the CPI-M won 19 seats and polled 6.4 million votes (roughly 4.28 per cent). A summary for all states and Union territories shows the position reversed at the level of state legislative assemblies. The CPI-M won 127 seats and polled 6.4 million votes (roughly 4.60 per cent of the votes polled); and the CPI won 121 seats and polled 5.9 million votes (roughly 4.23 per cent).[78] A closer analysis of the state-by-state election results shows that the distribution of Party strength throughout India, of both the CPI-M and the CPI, is quite uneven. The strength of the CPI-M is concentrated largely in three states, Andhra Pradesh, Kerala, and West Bengal. In two of these, Kerala and West Bengal, the CPI-M was the largest single Party in the united front governments which were formed after the elections. By contrast, the CPI, while not a major political force in any single state, had some support in almost every state, and in five states it succeeded in entering into coalition arrangements with the united front governments formed in the wake of the elections, i.e., Bihar, Kerala, Punjab, Uttar Pradesh, and West Bengal.

The decision to enter the non-Congress coalition governments proved to be a critical one for both Communist Parties, one which exacerbated the differences within each. In the CPI National Council meeting at Calcutta in the post-election period, a shift in the domestic position of the Party came about when the original political draft resolution, which called for the formation of a "left democratic government" at the centre, was modified to call for a "non-Congress democratic government." The Party was also sharply criticised for its failure to make adjustments with a number of regional political parties that had previously been characterised as rightist or regionally chauvanistic. The post-election dispute within the CPI-M was equally intense. The resolution on international ideological issues, which had been called for a year earlier, was still being circulated in draft form among the leadership and had not been adopted or released to the members. In assuming the major role in the governments in Kerala and West Bengal, the CPI-M opened up major fissures within its own Party. In West Bengal, the extremist segment felt that the Party's participation in government sharply restricted their ability to engage in mass agitation and thus to build a mass base for the Party.

Conflict Within the CPI-M

In the late spring of 1967, armed insurrectionary activities began in northern West Bengal, in an area adjacent to both Pakistan and Nepal which serves as a corridor to Indian territory in the remainder of northern West Bengal, Assam, Nagaland, Manipur, Tripura, and the North-East Frontier Area. This was the Naxalbari area of Silighiri District. What began as a peasant movement for land redistribution, sparked by the CPI-M Land Revenue Minister, H. K. Konar, soon developed into armed insurrectionary activity. It took on grave overtones when Peking Radio began to describe the actions in Naxalbari as those of "revolutionaries of the Indian Communist Party spearheading a phase of the peasant armed struggle" and went on to forecast a people's revolution in India.

The position of the CPI-M in the united front government in West Bengal soon became extremely difficult. Unlike Kerala, where E. M. S. Namboodiripad headed a CPI-M dominated government, West Bengal had selected a dissident Congress Party leader, Ajoy Mukherjee, the compromise choice for Chief Minister. In order to maintain its position within the united front government, the CPI-M sought to play down the significance of the Naxalbari uprising, but its failure to openly advocate and support the cause of the Naxalbari insurrectionists, plus its continued participation in the united front government, created a most ironic situation within the Party. The extremist faction of the CPI-M began to call openly for the removal of Party officers such as P. Sundarayya, B. T. Ranadive, Jyoti Basu, and E. M. S. Namboodiripad. The Party also found itself being criticised by the Chinese Communist Party, which it had been supporting in the international Communist controversies, although with increasing reservation. In late 1967, the CPI-M expelled a number of members connected with the Naxalbari incidents, and these expelled members immediately called for the formation of a third Communist Party, purportedly along strictly Maoist lines.[79] Little is known about the relationship between the Naxalbari extremists of the CPI-M in West Bengal and yet another Peking-oriented activity known as the Red Flag movement. Elements of this movement have been active in Madras, Kerala, Punjab, and West Bengal for approximately two years, but in each state they have a membership numbering only in the hundreds, according to published reports.[80]

The confusion generated in the Communist movement as a whole by the Naxalbari uprising was further heightened by the dismissal of the united front government in West Bengal by the State Governor late in 1967, reportedly with the consent of the Congress Party–controlled central government. The constitutionality of the Governor's action in dismissing the West Bengal united front government has been questioned, but its most important aspect may be the effect it had in undermining the position of those within the Communist movement who supported the notion of a peaceful, constitutional transition to socialism within India.

In early 1968, in a major coup, the rightist CPI captured control of the peasant mass organization within the Communist movement, the All-India Kisan Sabha, and ousted the CPI-M leadership from the AIKS Committee, the organization's highest body. This led to a formal split, with both Parties claiming control of the AIKS and holding separate annual conferences. A similar split in the AITUC, the Communist movement's labor mass organization, and the All-India Students Federation will probably ensue.

CONCLUSIONS AND FUTURE PROSPECTS

The present period is one of extreme flux and uncertainty within the Communist movement in India. Both Communist Parties contain serious internal divisions; moreover, the *raison d'être* of each as a separate party has been seriously compromised or otherwise altered by recent events. The CPI's faith in a peaceful transition to socialism and in the ability of left-wing parties to hold power at the state level while the Congress Party retains power at the center—one of the ideological cornerstones of the CPI's Amritsar constitution—has been badly shaken, particularly by the dismissal of the united front government in West Bengal. Equally serious for the Party was the fact that once it began to share power, its rightist segments manifested further "revisionist" tendencies by calling for modifications in the Party's position toward conservative and regional parties in order to enable the CPI to participate in additional government coalitions. The desire manifested by some of its members, to share political power at the expense of the Party's ideological stance, has exposed the CPI to charges of revisionism.

For the CPI-M, the period since the fourth general election has been equally stressful. In August 1967, the Party finally adopted its resolution on organizational, political, and ideological matters.[81] In its resolution, its Politburo directed major criticism at "modern revisionism," which it held to be the main danger to the world Communist movement, but it also sharply criticised "certain dogmatic and left-sectarian trends in

some parties on certain issues connected with the revolutionary movement of the proletariat." It rejected the theory that armed uprising
was a form of struggle always obligatory, under all conditions, and in
doing so further alienated the extremists within the CPI-M who continued to support the Peking position.

It would be correct, therefore, to characterise the Communist movement in India as badly divided and in danger of even further fragmentation. To this assessment must be added an equally important consideration, namely that the Indian Communist movement has been completely
unable to bring about a radical expansion in its mass base during
the last two decades. Its electoral support is a good example of the
static character of the movement. Apart from 1952, when a part of
the Party was still under ban and it polled only 3.3 per cent of the
vote, its share of the votes polled for candidates to the central Parliament has remained relatively fixed. The CPI polled 8.9 per cent in 1957;
9.9 per cent in 1962; and the sum of the votes for the two Parties in
1967 was 9.1 per cent. At the state level, the movement as a whole is
able to come consistently within striking distance of forming its own
government in only one state, Kerala; and in only two other states does
the sum of the votes for both Parties exceed 10 per cent, i.e., Andhra
Pradesh and West Bengal. The bulk of the non-Congress Parties, at both
the national and regional levels, are conservative in character and unlikely to participate in actions which would further the cause of the
Communist movement. This will be particularly true as long as an expansionist China, under Communist control, continues to menace India's
borders. Constitutional Communism, as a vehicle for an eventual Communist takeover in India, is no longer as attractive a prospect as it was
in 1957.

On the other hand, armed insurrection, given the movement's present
level of support, is not a major strategic option for securing power. The
failure in Telengana in 1948, and the quashing of the extremists in
Naxalbari in 1967, twenty years later, testify to the effectiveness of the
Indian Army and the state and central Police, who have remained completely loyal.

Thus neither the Soviet nor Chinese ideological alternatives for securing power have proved effective in contemporary India. The main poten-
tiality of the Communist movement in India today is to create conditions
of political instability and to mobilize mass discontent, but it should be
noted that the potential of the Communists is no greater than that of a
number of other parties or of the dissident elements of the Congress
Party. Where either Communist Party has given evidence of seeking
to subvert state government institutions and powers, the Central Government, using its emergency powers under the Constitution, has

been more than able to cope with it. Moreover, even the limited potentialities of the Communist movement will be blunted as long as it continues to be split between revisionists and sectarians.

NOTES

1. The positions taken by both parties at the time of the split in 1964, when both claimed to be holding the Seventh Congress of the Communist Party of India, are set forth in several publications. The views of the rightist, pro-Soviet CPI are contained in *Proceedings of the Seventh Congress of the Communist Party of India* (Bombay, 13–23 December, 1964), Vol. I, *Documents;* Vol. II, *Greetings;* Vol. III, *Discussions* (New Delhi: Communist Party of India, 1965). Among other items, Vol. I contains the Party program, its political resolution, its organizational report, its constitution, and a resolution on ideological controversies and unity in the international Communist movement. Vol. II contains detailed reports of the commissions which drafted each of the aforementioned statements and documents.

    The views of the leftist, pro-Chinese CPI-M are contained in *Fight Against Revisionism: Political-Organizational Report, Adopted at the Seventh Congress of the Communist Party of India, Oct. 31–Nov. 7, 1964, Calcutta* (Calcutta: E. M. S. Namboodiripad, on behalf of the Central Committee of the Communist Party of India, 1965); *Programme of the Communist Party of India: Adopted by the Seventh Congress of the Communist Party of India, Calcutta, Oct. 31– Nov. 7, 1964* (New Delhi: Desraj Chadha, on behalf of the Communist Party of India, n.d.); *Communist Party of India: Resolutions Adopted at the Seventh Congress, Oct. 31 to Nov. 7, 1964, Calcutta* (Calcutta: E. M. S. Namboodiripad, n.d.).

2. Most students of Indian Communism agree that the CPI was organized in December 1928. See G. D. Overstreet and M. Windmiller, *Communism in India* (Los Angeles, Calif.: University of California Press, 1959), pp. 133–34. Some sources date the founding from May 1933, and credit P. C. Joshi, who became the CPI's first General Secretary, with an important role in its formation. S. A. Dange, the present Chairman of the CPI, was one of those involved in the events in 1928. A statement in *New Age* (New Delhi weekly), June 9, 1963, cited December 26, 1925, as the date, a move some observers took as critical of P. C. Joshi. See *Thought* (New Delhi weekly), June 15, 1963, p. 4.

3. In Bengal the Anushilan Samiti and the Jugantar Party; in Punjab the Ghadr Party and the Hindustan Socialist Republican Army. Overstreet and Windmiller, *Communism in India*, pp. 44, 235.

4. For an analysis of the role played by these elements in the leadership struggle within the West Bengal Communist Party unit, see Asok Mitra, "Plebian Revolution," *Seminar* (New Delhi), No. 51 (November, 1963), pp. 33–36. See also N. C. Bhattacharyya, "Leadership Problems in the Communist Party of India: With Special Reference to West Bengal," Paper presented at International Political Science Association, Round Table, Bombay, January 4–10, 1964 (mimeographed), *passim.*

5. The CSP had been formed in 1934 as a separate Party within the Indian National Congress. Its leadership at that time was predominantly Marxist.

6. The All-India Kisan Sabha, the All-India Trade Union Congress, and the All-India Students Federation, respectively.

7. Overstreet and Windmiller, *Communism in India*, p. 357.

8. Asoka Mehta, *The Political Mind of India* (Bombay: Socialist Party, 1952), pp. 84, 86–87.

9. CPI membership declined from an estimated 89,263 in 1948, to 20,000 in 1950. By 1954, after the Party had rejected the adventurist line, its membership once again climbed to 75,000, and by 1957 it had reached 125,000. Overstreet and Windmiller, *Communism in India*, p. 357.

10. See *Link* (New Delhi weekly), January 21, 1962, pp. 12–14, for a perceptive and sympathetic analysis of Ghosh's role in the CPI. See also the interesting comments by E. M. S. Namboodiripad in *World Marxist Review*, VI (March, 1963), pp. 74–77. This periodical is now titled *Peace, Freedom, and Socialism*.

11. This growing gap between the right and left in the CPI could be seen in the Third Party Congress at Madurai, 1953. See *Communist Conspiracy in India* (Bombay: Democratic Research Service, 1954). The Fourth Party Congress at Palghat, 1956, provided additional substantiation. See *Communist Double-talk at Palghat* (Bombay: Democratic Research Service, 1956).

12. "New Features in National Liberation Struggle of Colonial and Dependent Peoples," *For a Lasting Peace: For a People's Democracy* (Moscow), October 8, 1954.

13. "Draft Resolution for the Emergency Session of the Central Committee, New Delhi, October 29, 1954," in *Communist Double-talk at Palghat*, pp. 139–44.

14. "Central Committee Resolution on Comrade R. P. Dutt's Article, New Delhi, November 6, 1954," in *Communist Double-talk at Palghat*, p. 145.

15. Modeste Rubenstein, "A Non-Capitalist Path for Underdeveloped Countries," *New Times*, Nos. 28 and 32 (July 5 and August 2, 1956). Reprinted in *New Age* (New Delhi monthly), October, 1956, pp. 19–28.

16. Ajoy Ghosh, "On India's Path of Development," *New Age* (monthly), October, 1956, pp. 6–18.

17. See *The Hindu* (Madras), March 31, 1959.

18. *New Age* (weekly), April 5, 1959, pp. 1, 20.

19. The Kerala Education Bill, one of the first measures adopted by the Communist-controlled Kerala legislature, was passed on September 2, 1957. After considerable legal delay, the President of India gave his final consent to the Bill in January 1959, and it was then published as the Kerala Education Act in the *Government Gazette*. The situation came to a head in March 1959, when the government published rules framed under the Act which, among other things, sought to prohibit school teachers and students from taking part in antigovernment agitations. For an analysis of some problems which arose within the Kerala CPI and the Party in general on this issue, see N. C. Bhattacharyya, "Leadership Problems in the Communist Party of India," p. 15.

20. *Hindustan Times* (New Delhi), February 19, 1960, p. 9.

21. *New Age* (weekly), September 20, 1959, p. 1.

22. See "Resolution Adopted by the Central Executive Committee of the CPI, Calcutta, 25 December 1959," in *The India-China Border Dispute and the Communist Party of India* (New Delhi: Communist Party of India, 1963), pp. 8–11. Marked "For Party Members Only."

23. *The India-China Border Dispute*, p. 15.

24. The text of Ghosh's report to the Fourth Party Congress of the CPI is in *Communist Double-talk at Palghat*, pp. 104–27. The report was printed in a pamphlet by the CPI, along with the *People's Daily* editorial and the resolution of the CPI Fourth Party Congress specifying their joint distribution. See *On the Twentieth Congress of the CPSU* (Delhi: Communist Party of India, 1956).

25. See *New Age* (weekly), November 18, 1956, p. 7, and November 25, 1956, pp. 1, 8–9, for the texts of the Narayan-Ghosh letters.

26. For an interpretation which supports this point of view see *Link* (New Delhi),

27. During this period, Bhupesh Gupta took an essentially opportunist position within January 21, 1962, pp. 12–14.

the Party, shifting his allegiance in accordance with his estimate of group strength at the state and national levels, and his judgment of how his own prospects were affected. The rapidly changing character of developments within the West Bengal unit of the CPI added to this tendency to change allegiances.

28. *Link* (New Delhi), July 31, 1960.

29. The text of Ghosh's speech at this conference is now available in *The India-China Border Dispute*, pp. 28–52.

30. An instance of this took place on October 22, 1960, when the West Bengal unit of the CPI adopted, by a vote of 67 to 10, a resolution which rejected the Moscow line of peaceful coexistence. See *Indian Affairs Record* (New Delhi), VI, No. 10, p. 229. For other examples, see *Indian Express* (New Delhi), June 22, 1960; and *Hindustan Times* (New Delhi), November 14, 1960.

31. *Indian Affairs Record*, VII, No. 11, p. 253.

32. *Ibid.*, VIII, No. 1, pp. 8–9.

33. One report gave the strength of the three factions as follows: right, 56; left, 36; and followers of E. M. S. Namboodiripad (at the time a centrist), 18. See *The Hindustan Times* (New Delhi), April 17, 1961, pp. 1, 6. When the actual split in the Party took place, however, only 33 members of the National Council sided with the leftists. This discrepancy is most probably due to several factors: (1) an overestimate of leftist and centrist strength within the Council; (2) a shift in position by those whose loyalties to the left group were less intense; and (3) an unwillingness on the part of some, despite their pro-leftist convictions, to face the prospects of actually going "into the wilderness."

34. A year earlier, at a meeting in Calcutta of the Central Executive Committee, Ghosh had remarked to a press correspondent: ". . . we differ from a *bourgeoisie* party. We never fall apart because of differences among us; the minority always yields to the opinion of the majority." Quoted in *The Statesman* (New Delhi), May 6, 1960. By the time of the 1961 Congress, this interpretation of democratic centralism was being severely strained.

35. For a discussion of the Vijayawada Congress, see Savak Katrak, "India's Communist Party Split"; also *Indian Affairs Record*, VII, Nos. 4–5, p. 771; and the *Hindustan Times* (New Delhi) and *The Hindu* (Madras), April 7 to 17, 1961. The full text of the final version of the political resolution adopted is contained in *New Age* (weekly), May 7, 1961, pp. 5–8, 13–16. It explicitly sets forth Ghosh's view that the relationship between the CPI and the INC ". . . will inevitably be one of unity and struggle . . ." It acknowledges that, while the INC is the organ of the national *bourgeoisie* as a whole, it is necessary for the CPI to forge links: ". . . independent mass activity . . . combined with fraternal and genuine united front approach so that on each issue the maximum possible support is mobilized—such has to be the tactics" (p. 14).

36. While no fraternal delegation attended from China, a formal delegation from the CPSU, headed by Mikhail Suslov, attended for the first time in CPI history. Suslov's role at the Party Congress is believed to have been one of counseling moderation to the dominant right faction, urging it to avoid an open Party split.

37. See *New Age* (weekly), July 2, 1961, p. 6, for the composition of the new Central Executive Committee and the new Central Secretariat.

38. S. L. Poplai, ed., *1962 General Elections in India* (New Delhi: Allied Publishers, 1962), pp. 46–47, 50. This volume contains several useful documents, including the statement on the Third General Elections, prepared by Ajoy Ghosh less than three weeks before his death, from which we have quoted. It also contains the CPI election manifesto and the resolutions adopted at the Amritsar and Vijayawada Conferences.

39. See *New Age* (weekly), May 6, 1962, pp. 8–9; and May 27, 1962, pp. 1 and 4, regarding CPI resolutions on these changes. The change in leadership of the Party was followed a few months later by a change in editorship of the weekly

and monthly editions of *New Age*. P. C. Joshi, who had been editor of the weekly was replaced by Namboodiripad. B. T. Ranadive, who had been editor of the monthly edition, was replaced by S. A. Dange.

40. For a text of the National Council resolution of October 17, 1962, "On Developments in NEFA," see the *India-China Border Dispute*, pp. 61–62.

41. Many commentators refer to this as the resolution of November 2, but in fact it was adopted on November 1. See *New Age* (weekly), November 4, 1962, pp. 1 and 12, for the text. The Chinese, in their attacks upon Dange and the CPI, refer to it as the resolution of November 1.

42. One of the most serious charges made against the Chinese by the CPI was omitted in the published version of the November 1 resolution (quoted here from *The India-China Border Dispute*, p. 67: "The behavior of socialist China toward peace-loving India has most grossly violated the common understanding in the communist world arrived at in the 81 Parties' Conference in 1960 in relation to peaceful coexistence and attitude to newly liberated countries and the question of war and peace. Socialist China has fallen victim to narrow nationalistic considerations at the cost of the interests of world peace and anti-imperialism, in its attitude towards India."

43. *Ibid.*, p. 87.

44. In subsequent factional disputes, the left-wing leaders of the Party charged that the Home Ministry and the police were acting on lists supplied by the right wing of the Party, which sought to use this opportunity to destroy the left wing. For a breakdown, by state, of persons arrested under the Defense of India Rules, see *New Age* (weekly), February 24, 1963, p. 4.

45. *Thought* (New Delhi), December 22, 1962, p. 4.

46. *Ibid.*

47. Dange, after a meeting of the National Council on February 12, 1963, indicated that steps were being taken to organize the work of the Party in West Bengal since the majority of the members of the State Council were in jail. See *New Age* (weekly), February 17, 1963, p. 3. A report in *Thought* (New Delhi), January 26, 1963, indicates that Party reorganizations had taken place in four states: West Bengal, Punjab, Andhra Pradesh, and Madras. In Andhra Pradesh and Madras, the reorganizations were of an *ad hoc* character and presumably had taken place before the widespread government arrests.

48. Among those involved in the creation of the parallel Party were: Promode Das Gupta, Jyoti Basu, Muzaffar Ahmad, and H. K. Konar (all of West Bengal); H. K. S. Surjeet (of Punjab); B. T. Ranadive (of Maharashtra); P. Ramamurthi (of Madras); and P. Sundarayya (of Andhra Pradesh). Information available to the Dangeite leadership of the CPI in late December indicated that at that time there were parallel Parties in at least five states: Andhra Pradesh, Kerala, Punjab, Madras, and West Bengal. Each had its own officers, couriers, and agitation-propaganda machinery. In addition, the leftists brought out the following regional weekly newspapers in vernacular languages: *Desh Hitaishi* (West Bengal); *Janashakti* (Andhra Pradesh); *Spark* (Madras); and *Chinta* (Kerala). See *Thought* (New Delhi), January 25, 1964, p. 4.

49. For the text, see *New Age* (weekly), February 17, 1963, pp. 1, 12. The CPI also reprinted, in the same issue of *New Age*, an editorial appearing in *Pravda* of February 10, "For Marxist-Leninist Unity of the Communist Movement: For Cohesion of Countries of Socialism," which was a sharp attack on the CCP.

50. *Ibid.*

51. For the text, see *New Age* (weekly), February 24, 1963, pp. 5, 10.

52. The text is available in *Peking Review*, March 18, 1963. It was also reprinted by the CPI in *New Age* (weekly), March 31, 1963, pp. 5, 14.

53. *Idem.*

54. *Idem.*
55. *Idem.*
56. Supplement to *New Age* (weekly), April 21, 1963, p. xiv.
57. *Idem.*
58. For a report of the events surrounding these National Council meetings, see *Link* (New Delhi), June 30, 1963, p. 9, and July 7, 1963, pp. 9–10. See also the columns by Sathi in *Thought* (New Delhi), immediately before and after the National Council session, for a very detailed discussion of internal developments. The political resolution finally adopted, while emphasizing the danger of right reaction, called for the unity of all progressive elements, including Congressmen. An alternative political resolution, put forward by a left-wing delegate, Ram Piara Saraf of Jammu, charged that the Nehru government had shifted rightward, had made heavy concessions to reactionary vested interests, and had adopted anti-people policies. It was overwhelmingly rejected.
59. Note that at the June and July session of the National Council, approximately 54 of the 110 members, less than a majority, are reported to have attended. Of these, 6 are said to have voted for the alternative political resolution put forward by Ram Piara Saraf. Thus Dange was no longer able to muster an absolute majority in support of his position in the National Council. See *Indian Affairs Record*, IX, No. 8, p. 259.
60. *Thought* (New Delhi), September 7, 1963, p. 4.
61. Press reports indicated that many of the speeches were directed as much against the attitude of the Party leadership, under Dange, toward the *détenus'* fate, as against the West Bengal government which had imprisoned them. See the *Times of India* (New Delhi), September 30, 1963, p. 1.
62. *The Tribune* (Ambala), September 26, 1963, p. 1.
63. *The Tribune* (Ambala), October 23, 1963, p. 4. A slightly different breakdown is given in *Thought* (New Delhi), November 16, 1963, p. 4. Thirty of the 110 members of the National Council were in jail. Of the remaining 80, 52 voted in favor of the resolution, 21 voted against, 3 abstained, and 4 absented themselves at the time of voting.
64. *The Tribune* (Ambala), October 23, 1963, p. 4.
65. *Times of India* (New Delhi), October 22, 1963, p. 3.
66. *The Statesman* (New Delhi), December 28, 1963, p. 13.
67. *Thought* (New Delhi), January 25, 1964, p. 4. An earlier indication of Peking's position on the matter of a split in the international Communist movement appeared in the *New York Times* (West Coast edition), January 6, 1964, p. 1, which reported that a line calling for "the establishment of separate splinter groups or parties" was laid down in an ideological speech made by Chou Yang, Deputy Director of the Propaganda Department of the Central Committee of the CCP, before an October meeting of Chinese Communist ideologists and intellectuals. See also the *New York Times* (New York edition), February 4, 1964, p. 1, where reference is made to an editorial published in *Hung Chi*, the ideological journal of the Central Committee of the CCP, which laid down a theoretical justification for the formal break with Moscow and the formation of an independent Communist movement.
68. *The Statesman* (New Delhi), January 18, 1964, p. 1.
69. *Ibid.*, January 19, 1964, p. 1.
70. *Ibid.*, January 15, 1964, p. 9.
71. *The Statesman* (New Delhi), January 19, 1964, p. 9; and *Thought* (New Delhi) March 7, 1964, p. 4.
72. The CPI and the CPI-M issued conflicting claims regarding the support they

had within the movement in India. See the documents mentioned in ftn. 1 for the claims made by each Party at the time of the Seventh Congress.

73. *Amrita Bazar Patrika* (Calcutta), November 2, 1964, p. 7.

74. See the documents mentioned in ftn. 1, in particular the respective political resolutions adopted by the CPI and the CPI-M.

75. *The Hindu Weekly Review* (Madras), January 11, 1965, p. 5.

76. For a good discussion of some of the problems of the AITUC see Harold Crouch, *Trade Unions and Politics in India* (Bombay: Manaktalas, 1966), Chap. 7. The best published discussion of the AIKS is still in Overstreet and Windmiller, *Communism in India*, pp. 384–95.

77. *Indian Recorder and Digest* (New Delhi), September, 1965, p. 8.

78. *Ibid.*, March, 1967, pp. 5–6.

79. *The Statesman Weekly* (New Delhi), November 18, 1967, p. 1. The designation used by this group to identify itself is "Communist Party of India (Naxalbari)." It is uncertain how much of the extremist segment has gone over to it and opted for a separate Party structure as opposed to continuing the struggle within the CPI-M. They felt that the Naxalbari movement, which had been "betrayed" by the CPI-M, should guide all revolutionary action in the rural areas, and they expressed extreme criticism of the CPI-M as "a collaborator and friend of American imperialism, Soviet revisionism and the reactionary government in India." In Kerala since the beginning of 1968 a third Communist Party, along "Naxalbari lines" has been formed by extremists who were expelled from the CPI-M; see *The Hindu Weekly Review*, January 29, 1968, p. 13. For an example of the recent attempts by the "Naxalites" (as they have come to be called) to launch armed insurrection in Kerala see *The Statesman Weekly* (New Delhi), November 30, 1968, pp. 1 and 16.

80. *Statesman Weekly* (New Delhi), July 1, 1967, p. 8. The publication and distribution of pro-Peking literature seems to be the main function of the Red Flag groups. Their common thesis is that both the right and left Communist Parties in India are revisionist and "tools of the Soviet-American reactionary clique."

81. See *Central Committee's Draft for the Ideological Discussion: Adopted by the Central Committee of the Communist Party of India (Marxist) Medurai, August 18 to 27, 1967* (Calcutta: Desraj Chadha on behalf of the Communist Party of India (Marxist), n.d.). Two other important documents containing resolutions adopted by the CPI-M at the Central Committee session at Madurai in August 1967 are *On Left Deviation or Left Opportunism: Central Committee Resolution adopted at Madurai, August 18–27, 1967*; and *Central Committee Resolution: Divergent Views between Our Party and the CPC on Certain Fundamental Issues—Political and Economic Developments in Our Country and Our Tasks* (both, Calcutta: Desraj Chadha on behalf of the CPI-M, n.d.). These three documents set forth in most poignant form the position of the CPI-M today between the Scylla of revisionism and the Charybdis of Maoism.

SELECTED BIBLIOGRAPHY

Communist Conspiracy in India. Bombay: Democratic Research Service, 1956.

Communist Double-talk at Palghat. Bombay: Democratic Research Service, 1956.

Dange, S. A., "Neither Revisionism nor Dogmatism Is Our Guide," *New Age* (New Delhi weekly), April 21, 1963, Supplement.

The India-China Border Dispute and the Communist Party of India. New Delhi: Communist Party of India, July, 1963.

Kautsky, John H., *Moscow and the Communist Party of India: A Study in the Post-war Evolution of International Communist Strategy.* Cambridge, Mass.: The Technology Press of the Massachusetts Institute of Technology, 1956.

Masani, Minocheher Rustom, *The Communist Party of India: A Short History.* London: D. Verschoyle, 1954.

Overstreet, Gene D., and Marshall Windmiller, *Communism in India.* Berkeley, Calif.: University of California Press, 1959,

COMMUNISM UNDER HIGH ATMOSPHERIC CONDITIONS

THE PARTY IN NEPAL

LEO E. ROSE

Nepal, uncomfortably situated between Asia's largest and most dynamic Communist and democratic powers, would seem to be a logical arena for a major confrontation between these two conflicting ideologies. That such a confrontation is still in an embryonic stage despite the border clashes between India and China is due to a unique and complex combination of historical, political, and international phenomena that have contrived so far to keep Nepal out of the mainstream of developments—a happy situation that cannot be expected to continue. One intangible factor that may influence to some extent the course of events in this potentially strategic area is the Communist Party of Nepal (CPN), the subject of this essay. Probably no Communist Party in Asia not in control of the governmental machinery—with the possible exception of the Indonesian Communist Party prior to 1965—has enjoyed such favorable conditions for growth and development. And yet the results to date have been unimpressive, even on a comparative scale. To explain why this is the case, we shall briefly survey the history of the Communist movement in Nepal and analyze the factors that have made it habitual for the Party to waste opportunities and concentrate on nonessentials.

Most contemporary Nepali political movements had their origin in India in the years immediately following World War II, as the situation under the autocratic Rana regime inside Nepal was scarcely conducive to political activity. A large number of Nepalis resident in India prior to 1947 participated in the Indian struggle to oust British rule on the assumption that independence for India was the necessary prerequisite to the ouster of the Ranas in Nepal, in view of the vital support the regime had long received from the British rulers of India. It is also probable, however, that many Nepalis, both in Nepal and India, were emotionally involved in India's struggle for independence because of the close historical and cultural ties between the two peoples. And, indeed, vociferous as Nepali Communist criticisms of India may often be, it is nevertheless Indians (and not just their Indian comrades) with whom Nepali Communists have the most in common and with whom communication is most simple and comprehensible. It is for this reason, presumably, that Communist verbiage in Nepal tends to be a close reflection of that currently preoccupying the Communist movement in India, for the arguments and symbolisms used are frequently borrowed directly from the Indian Communist Party even though they may not be particularly relevant to objective conditions within Nepal.

The close relationship between the two Parties extends back into the pre-independence period when a few Nepalis were admitted to membership in the Communist Party of India (CPI). This occurred most widely in a few urban centers such as Calcutta, Banaras, Gorakhpur, and Patna, where there were a number of Nepali students, and in the tea-plantation areas of Darjeeling district, where there were large communities of migrant Nepali workers among whom Communist-dominated labor unions had made some inroads.

Subsequently, there emerged a subtle divergence in attitude between these India-trained Nepali Communists and the other leaders of the Party who had confined their political activities to Nepal during the Rana period. Divisions within the Party since 1951 would sometimes appear to have been influenced by this factor. It is probably not entirely coincidental that most of the Nepali Communist leaders currently in exile in India had been active in India in the period from 1947 to 1951, while most of the leaders who have remained in Nepal since the banning of all political parties, in December 1960, are those who did not affiliate with the Party until after the overthrow of the Ranas in 1951.

This is not to imply, of course, that the Nepali Communist leaders currently in India are pro-India and that those in Nepal are anti-Indian. Indeed, the Communist faction in exile is the Party group to which is usually attributed pro-China sentiments. What may be significant in this instance are the close ties that were developed between Nepali and Indian Communists during this earlier period. These appear to have continued despite wide subsequent differences in their tactics and ideology. According to reports, for instance, a leader of the extremist, reputedly pro-China, faction of the Nepali Party now in exile in India has his closest personal relationship with a leader of the moderate, pro-Soviet and anti-China wing of the CPI.

Moreover, the CPI appear to maintain the closest ties with all Nepali Communist factions, whether in Nepal or India. The establishment of Russian and Chinese embassies in Kathmandu may have provided the Nepali Communists with alternative channels of contact and financial support with the world Communist movement, but it is doubtful that these have yet completely superseded the old established relationship with the Indian Communist leadership. All parties are illegal in Nepal today, and it would certainly be embarrassing to the embassies to be approached too openly or too frequently by Communist leaders. It is also somewhat ironical that most of the reputedly pro-China Communist leaders are currently in exile in India and are, thus, denied easy access to the Chinese either in India or Nepal, except possibly through the pro-China faction of the CPI, which may not be too reliable or eager a channel.

THE EARLY YEARS

By 1947, Nepali members of the CPI were active in Nepal, participating in a "no-tax" campaign among the tenants in the eastern Terai (a plains area at the foot of the hills) and in a strike among mill workers at Biratnagar in southeastern Nepal.[1] The Nepali Communists were also actively attempting to infiltrate other Nepali political organizations in India, in particular the Nepali National Congress (NNC) which had been founded in Calcutta in 1946. Most of the leaders of the NNC, however, were closely associated with the socialist wing of the Indian National Congress—a group that had turned bitterly anti-Communist because of their betrayal by the Communists during the united front period prior to World War II and by the Communist prowar policy after the German invasion of the Soviet Union in 1941. Rejected by the NNC, the Nepali Communists finally decided to establish their own Party. On September 15, 1949, five Nepalis[2] met in Calcutta and formed the Communist Party of Nepal.

The new Party continued to reiterate the necessity for a united front of all anti-Rana political organizations, but met with an unenthusiastic response from the Nepali Congress, which had been formed in

March 1950 by a merger of B. P. Koirala's NNC and the Nepali Democratic Congress headed by Subarna Shamsher. Their overtures having once again been ignored, the Communists denounced the Nepali Congress as representative of the "national-capitalist *bourgeoisie*" and as a tool of the "reactionary" Nehru government in India.[3] The anti-Rana revolution launched by the Nepali Congress, in November 1950, placed the CPN in a quandary. The Party met the situation squarely by straddling the fence—the CPN never formally announced its support of the movement, but a number of Communists participated, apparently on a personal basis, in the struggle. The Party's position on the compromise agreement that terminated the conflict in February 1951 was somewhat more forthright. The Nepali Congress was accused of having betrayed its own revolution by agreeing to join a coalition Cabinet headed by the Rana Prime Minister. It was alleged that this solution had been imposed upon Nepal by the government of India and "Anglo-American imperialists."[4] The Communists did their best to encourage dissident forces within the Nepali Congress, such as the K. I. Singh group in western Nepal, which refused to accept the cease-fire agreement and continued the struggle. The suppression of these factions by Indian constabulary and military forces at the request of the new Home Minister, B. P. Koirala, added volumes to Communist criticisms of the Nepali Congress and the Indian government.

Despite their discontent with the political compromise that ended the revolution, the Communists immediately hastened to Kathmandu once the new government had removed the ban on Party activity and had released political prisoners. Aware of its own intrinsic weakness, the Party moved to strengthen its position in two ways: by agitating for a united front of all "progressive forces" opposed to the Nepali Congress-Rana coalition government[5] and by forming a number of front organizations through which the Communists could work more effectively in certain segments of Nepali society.[6] During Nehru's visit to Kathmandu in June 1951, the Communists cooperated with Tanka Prasad Acharva's *Praja Parishad* Party and some elements of the pro-Rana *Gorkha Dal* in organizing a "black flag" demonstration. Student demonstrations were also organized in the fall of 1951, culminating in the arrest of several Communists. The united front policy achieved its most notable success in October 1951, with the formation of the *Jatiya Janatantrik Samyukta Morcha*, or National Democratic United Front, by the CPN, the *Praja Parishad*, and a number of Communist front organizations, as the basis for a "national front of all progressive forces."[7] In its Manifesto, the *Morcha* denounced the newly established Nepali Congress government, headed by M. P. Koirala, as a tool of the Nehru government and condemned the "expansionist war-mongering camp of America and Britain."[8] Except for some of the usual anti-Rana clichés, the manifesto was diffident on the subject of a domestic program, probably a reflection of the basically different composition of the *Praja Parishad* and the CPN.

The first serious setback to the Communists resulted, ironically enough, from a situation that was primarily not of their own making. In February 1952, some supporters of K. I. Singh in the Nepali Congress military unit, the *Raksha Dal*, organized a coup against the M. P. Koirala government. From available sources, it would appear that the CPN played no part in the planning and launching of the coup but that it did attempt to take advantage of the situation. Announcing its support of the K. I. Singh demand for an all-party government, the CPN hastily organized a few demonstrations that did little except to confuse the situation further. K. I. Singh and several of his followers fled to Tibet on February 24, and the coup collapsed. On the following day, the CPN was banned because of its complicity in these events, and the Party leaders had to go underground to avoid arrest.

Though illegal, the Party still had several avenues for legal activity through the various front organizations that had not been banned, and through the united front. Tanka Prasad found the alliance with the CPN an obstacle to his efforts to form alliances with other political factions, however and, in October 1952, the *Praja Parishad* withdrew from the *Morcha*. Deprived of its two main components, the united front was eventually discarded. Isolated in the Nepali political spectrum, the CPN temporarily reduced the emphasis on the united front policy in favor of unilateral action. A new political front organization, the *Jana Adhikar Surakshi Samiti* (i.e., the People's Rights Protection Committee, or JASS), was founded. The JASS devoted comparatively little attention to civil-liberty issues, however, and concentrated its attention on questions of foreign relations, helping to organize anti-American demonstrations in August 1954 and anti-Indian demonstrations the following month.

The illegal status of the CPN did not seriously hamper the activities of the Party leaders and workers, most of whom were only nominally underground since the government seldom attempted to enforce the warrants for arrest that had been issued.[9] The Party openly supported a number of candidates in the Kathmandu municipal elections in September 1963, and six of their candidates won. This was the largest number from any party and an unexpected show of strength in the nation's capital. A few months later, in January 1954, the First All-Party Congress of the CPN was held in Kathmandu, with representatives from many parts of Nepal present. A constitution was adopted, outlining the Party's organizational structure (see Chart 1) and specifying the conditions under which members were to be recruited. The Congress also approved a Party program which included three controversial provisions: (1) "continuous struggle" against the "feudalist" royal regime; (2) replacement of the monarchy by a republican system framed by an elected constituent assembly; and (3) confiscation of large and middle-sized land holdings without compensation.[10]

Chart 1

ORGANIZATIONAL STRUCTURE OF THE NEPAL COMMUNIST PARTY UNDER THE 1954 PARTY CONSTITUTION

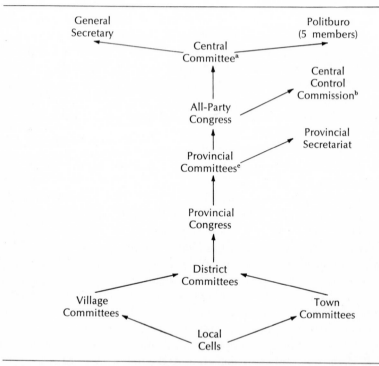

[a] The size of the Central Committee is left to the discretion of the All-Party Congress; so far it has had 17 to 19 members.
[b] The Central Control Commission is given the task of maintaining Party discipline, guaranteeing that all Party units implement the decisions of the higher-level committees.
[c] There are seven Provincial Committees: (1) East Kosi; (2) West Kosi; (3) North Gandak; (4) South Gandak; (5) Middle Gandak; (6) West Gandak; and (7) Karnali.

The Party's critical attitude toward the monarchy was expressed in a resolution passed by the Politburo shortly after the conclusion of the Party Congress, which declared that "The King, who represents the feudal landlord interests as well as the former ruling Ranas, has opposed any advancement of the cause of democracy in the country."[11] In the current Nepali political context, these were bitter words indeed.

The left-sectarian character of the 1954 platform contributed substantially to the further political isolation of the CPN. The demand for the abolition of the monarchy, particularly, alarmed other political leaders, who were then busily currying favor with the palace on the assumption that this was the most plausible route to high office. In adopting this platform, the CPN was implicitly admitting that two announced objectives—a united front with progressive forces and an all-party coalition Cabinet—were unfeasible. It is also probable that the platform served to dissuade the government from even considering lifting the ban on the Party.

It was soon apparent to several CPN leaders that the 1954 platform had been a serious mistake. At their insistence, an All-Party Conference[12] was held in November 1955, to reconsider policy questions. A new political resolution was adopted. As interpreted in a widely circulated article by the Central Committee entitled "Why the Changes in the Party Program?"[13] this resolution marked a substantial transition toward a more moderate policy. The Party admitted that its attitude during the 1950 revolution, its policies of continuous struggle against the subsequent governments, and the demand for an all-party coalition government had been serious errors which had only served to strengthen the power of the monarchy and other feudalist elements. While still maintaining that "the republican idea [is] more suited to Nepal than monarchy or constitutional monarchy," the Party admitted that it was futile to raise antimonarchial slogans "as long as the peasants and the majority of the people . . . are not united for a struggle against the monarchy."[14] The Party's position on monarchy and upon land confiscation were admitted to be major obstacles to the formation of a "broadbased joint front." It was stated that such a front was the prime objective of the Party, and that "controversial measures that are unnecessary and impractical at present" should not be given undue emphasis.[15]

LEGAL ONCE AGAIN: 1956 TO 1960

The trend toward moderation in the CPN's policy received added stimulation in January 1956, when King Mahendra appointed Tanka Prasad Acharya, the Party's old ally in the united front of 1951 and 1952, as Prime Minister. The chances for the legalization of the Party were greatly enhanced and, indeed, Tanka Prasad entered into negotiations with CPN leaders on this question shortly after assuming office. As the price for lifting the ban, the new Prime Minister insisted upon the acceptance of constitutional monarchy by the Party.

The CPN Central Committee was still badly divided on this question. The majority, moderate wing headed by Keshar Jang Rayamajhi was ready to accept constitutional monarchy, but a minority faction headed by Pushpa Lal Shrestha insisted that the goal of a republic should not be totally abandoned. The Central Committee finally agreed on a compromise by which the Party tentatively accepted constitutional monarchy, leaving the ultimate decision to the Constituent Assembly which was scheduled for election in 1957. While this statement did not precisely meet Tanka Prasad's conditions, the Prime Minister advised the King to legalize the CPN, and the ban was lifted in April 1956.

Operating openly once more, the CPN adopted a dual tactical approach primarily intended to improve the Party's position in the long-awaited general elections. Tacit support was extended to the *Praja Parishad* government throughout its period in office, particularly in foreign relations issues, since Tanka Prasad's abandonment of the special relationship with India for equal friendship with India and China was enthusiastically endorsed by the Communists. At the same time, the CPN sought to end its isolation within the Nepal political movement. An alliance with the *Praja Parishad* might have seemed logical but in fact was precluded by the *Praja Parishad's* own efforts to establish working relations with other, more conservative political factions. In these circumstances, the *Praja Parishad* would have found an alliance with the CPN an embarrassing encumbrance, as well as likely to raise questions about the governing party in the royal palace. The Communists, therefore, had to look elsewhere for potential allies and, as usual, it was the Nepali Congress that received the first overtures. In August 1956, the CPN Central Committee instructed lower units of the Party to cooperate with the Nepali Congress's political action program. The Congress was no more inclined towards cooperation with the Communists now than it had been in the past. Indeed, the CPN was almost completely ignored, both by the palace and the political parties, in the dramatic political developments surrounding the dismissal of the Tanka Prasad Cabinet, in August 1957, and the appointment of K. I. Singh in his place.

The vacillation evident in the Party's tactics at this time was probably a reflection of the serious rifts that had long divided the Central Committee. These centered around the question of policy toward the monarchy and, as the necessary corollary, the Nepali Congress, still the major political party in the country. The moderate Rayamajhi faction argued that the Party should accept constitutional monarchy, at least temporarily, since conditions under a royalist regime were more conducive to the growth of Communist strength than a government headed by the Party's main rival, the socialist Nepali Congress. Alliances with the Congress for limited purposes might be feasible under certain conditions, but only if this served the ultimate purposes of the Party. The extremist faction headed by Pushpa Lal maintained that the destruction of all "feudalistic" remnants, including the monarchy, should be the immediate as well as the ultimate goal of the Party and that the CPN should align itself with all "progressive" forces that might contribute to the fulfillment of this task. Not all factions of the Party aligned themselves on exactly this basis, of course, but this was the general pattern. The Rayamajhi faction, with broad support throughout Nepal, usually controlled a majority on the Central Committee. The leftist opposition was centered in the powerful North Gandak Regional Committee, which includes Kathmandu, but it also received substantial support from other regional and local Party units, particularly in the eastern Terai.

The struggle within the Party reached a critical stage at the Second All-Party Congress, held in Kathmandu in May and June 1957. The Central Committee presented to the Congress a draft resolution which reflected essentially the views of the Rayamajhi faction. The most controversial items in the draft were the clauses that condemned the "permanent revolution" concept as "adventurist" and "suicidal" and which termed "infantile leftism" the demand for nationalizing land without due consideration of the interests of the middle-class peasant. This was a direct challenge to the left sectarians, who were bitterly critical of the draft and who were apparently able to prevent its adoption by the Congress, at least in the form presented.[16]

In his opening remarks to the Congress, the Acting Secretary-General, Keshar Jang Rayamajhi, stated the moderate position very clearly:

In prevailing backward conditions, it is not only impractical but foolish to talk of socialism. As long as the basis for the exercise of democracy by the people is not created, that is, as long as capital is not accumulated in the country through industrial development, it would be difficult to find the way to republican democracy, not to talk of socialism or communism. Therefore, at present it will be the aim of the Communist Party to bring about the development of democracy.[17]

That the leftists had not accepted Rayamajhi's thesis was clearly demonstrated when, shortly after the close of the Second Congress, Pushpa Lal told a public meeting at Kathmandu that the CPN would place a resolution before the Constituent Assembly, when elected, calling for the abolition of the monarchy.[18]

King Mahendra's postponement of the first general election caused another uproar in Nepali politics in the last quarter of 1957. The Democratic Front—originally organized by the Nepali Congress, the *Praja Parishad* and the Nepali National Congress to oppose the K. I. Singh government—decided to launch a civil disobedience movement in December to protest the King's decision. The CPN applied for admission to this select group, but once again was coldly rejected. The Communists deplored this "political narrow-mindedness," but nevertheless the Central Committee, under leftist pressure, decided to pledge its support to the movement.

Over Communist objections, the Democratic Front terminated its campaign on December 15, after King Mahendra had agreed to new dates for the election. Having failed to influence the Democratic Front parties, the Central Committee of the CPN suddenly switched tactics and virtually came out in support of King Mahendra. In explaining the new Party policy, Rayamajhi declared:

We believe in constitutional monarchy. We are against any action which will affect the prestige of the Supreme Leader of the nation. The date that he has fixed for the election is quite reasonable. Attempts by the Democratic Front to resume the civil disobedience movement should be considered as mischievous.[19]

To show that his support of constitutional monarchy had not been a slip of the tongue, Rayamajhi repeated the substance of his argument in the Party journal, *Navayug*, asserting that the sovereignty of the King was inevitable under prevailing conditions, since the King was the Supreme Leader of the country.[20]

Naturally, the leftist faction was not prepared to accept Rayamajhi's statements. The controversy became even more intense when King Mahendra suddenly issued a proclamation on February 1, 1958, stating that the elections, then scheduled for February 1959, would not be for a constituent assembly, as he and his predecessor had promised, but for a parliament that would function under a constitution bestowed on the country by the King. Some leftists argued that the Party should refuse to contest the elections under these conditions, and should instead launch a movement to force the King to hold the elections for a constituent assembly. The North Gandak (Kathmandu) Regional Committee met on February 4 and approved a resolution to this effect. On March 2, however, the Central Committee rejected this proposal and voted to accept the Royal Proclamation with some reservations. In its resolution, the Central Committee declared that "The combined efforts of the democratic forces in the country can turn a Parliament into a powerful body. In order to achieve this objective, the Communist Party's slogan from now on will be that the constitution to be granted by the King must be democratic."[21]

A second plenary session of the Central Committee, held in Rautahat in June, once again endorsed the decision to contest the election,[22] though only over the strong opposition of the North Gandak Regional Committee representatives. The moderate policy attained an unexpected political reward when, in June 1958, the King appointed two Communists to the Advisory Assembly set up to advise the government until the election had been completed. It was the first time any Communists had received direct recognition of this sort from the palace.

The Central Committee met once again, in September 1958, to discuss election tactics and to complete the Party's election manifesto. It was decided to support "democratic" candidates in constituencies in which the CPN did not have a candidate. As this policy actually worked out, however, only a few friendly political leaders, such as Tanka Prasad, and several independents received Communist support. At one stage, the CPN had approached the Nepali Congress for an election alliance but had met with the usual negative response. No Nepali Congress candidate received Communist support, even in constituencies in which the Congress' main opponent was the reactionary *Gorkha Parishad*. Indeed, most of the CPN's election propaganda was directed against the socialist Nepali Congress rather than against more conservative parties. The CPN's election manifesto was innocuous in the extreme for a Communist Party, not even mentioning the monarchy or some of the more radical land-reform programs previously supported.[23]

The election results were a tremendous victory for the Nepali Congress, which won over two-thirds of the seats, and a bitter disappointment to the Communists who ran 46 candidates but won only 4 seats. Party leaders have usually attributed their lack of success to a shortage of funds, but this is probably more an excuse than a reason. It would appear that the rift in the Party leadership, which by now extended down to the local units in some areas, was a more important factor in the defeat of Communists in several constituencies where the prospects had seemed encouraging.

The poor showing of the Party in the elections led to increased criticism of its moderate leadership. Nevertheless, the Rayamajhi faction was able to retain a tenuous control at the plenary session at Janakpur in June 1959. It was decided that the Party's attitude toward the Nepali Congress government should be one of selective support or opposition, depending upon the issue at stake. In point of fact, most of the Communist Party's criticism of the B. P. Koirala government was directed at its foreign policy, which was alleged to be pro-Indian. Usually the Communist M.P.'s supported the economic, social, and administrative reform measures of the Nepali Congress, though describing them as inadequate. This was also a relatively peaceful period, internally: Even the September 1960 meetings of the Central Committee which formulated draft resolutions for the Third All-Party Congress, scheduled for February 1961,[24] did not result in the usual wrangle. The Party made no progress, however, in its constant search for political allies, as was demonstrated in November 1960, when all the opposition parties in the Parliament except the Communists held a series of meetings in an effort to form a united opposition to the Nepali Congress government.

THE CPN DIVIDES

A new crisis occurred on December 15, 1960, when King Mahendra suddenly dismissed the Nepali Congress government and arrested all of the Congress Ministers and many other political party leaders in Nepal.

Ten days later, the King placed a total ban on all parties and political activities—a move that probably affected the other parties more adversely than the Communists, since the CPN had years of experience in operating underground. In fact, the Palace appeared to be more concerned with the destruction of the Nepali Congress organization, and paid comparatively little attention to the CPN and other parties. Several Communist leaders were arrested at the time of the coup but, with the important exception of Manmohan Adhikari, they were released shortly thereafter.[25] Warrants were issued for several others, but no real effort was made to apprehend them. Many Party members were allowed to continue their political activity virtually undisturbed. This gave the CPN a tremendous advantage over the Nepali Congress, many of whose workers, even on the district and local level, were imprisoned or forced into exile.

Despite these initial advantages, however, the Communists have not been able to reap full benefit from the situation, primarily because of their chronic inner struggle for power.[26] The first signs of a fundamental disagreement within the Party over the 1960 coup became evident early in 1961. The Communists had been as surprised by the King's action as had the other parties, but they appear to have recovered their poise more quickly. Before long, the Party was operating underground in much the same fashion as it had prior to 1956.

Because of Rayamajhi's absence in Moscow at the time of the coup, the first public reaction of the Party to the King's move reflected the views of the Pushpa Lal faction. On December 24, 1960, a cyclostyled circular was distributed, ostensibly in the name of the Politburo, demanding the cessation of "military terror" and a conference of all parliamentary parties. By mid-January 1961, however, Rayamajhi and other moderate Communists had returned to Nepal, and the struggle for control of the Party machinery began in earnest. The moderate faction was able to gain approval for a more cautious policy toward the new royal regime. In the latter part of January, the Party issued another press note, this time reflecting the views of the moderate faction. While cautiously critical of the December coup and demanding the release of political prisoners, the lifting of the ban on political activity, and the restoration of fundamental rights, the note did not insist on the reconvening of the Parliament, thus by implication accepting the new regime.

The dispute reached a critical stage at a secret plenary session of the Central Committee (held at Darbhanga, India, in March 1961) which was also attended by 54 delegates representing 24 district units of the Party.[27] In these stormy meetings, the Rayamajhi faction argued that the Party's immediate objectives should be limited to: (1) the restoration of fundamental rights; (2) the release of political prisoners; (3) the withdrawal of the ban on political parties; and (4) the election of a new

Parliament in the near future. The Pushpa Lal faction, supported by the Party organization of North Gandak (Kathmandu), Gorkha, and Bandipur, demanded the reconvening of the dissolved Parliament (that is, the restoration of the Nepali Congress government) and, if necessary, the launching of a Communist-led movement to achieve this objective. A third, minor faction, led by the Piuthan Party unit, demanded the election of a constituent assembly to draw up a new constitution, and the eventual establishment of a republican form of government. For all practical purposes, the second and third factions were aligned against the moderates.

The plenary session ended in a virtual stalemate, although the Rayamajhi faction was able to retain control of the Central Committee. Eleven of the seventeen members of the Central Committee were reported to be Rayamajhi supporters, while six followed Pushpa Lal's leadership. However, three members of the Rayamajhi faction were in prison in Nepal and a fourth resigned from the Central Committee during the session, thus reducing the pro-Rayamajhi majority at the Darbhanga session to one.

To negotiate the differences between the two factions, the Plenum appointed a joint committee which was assigned the thankless task of chalking out a compromise Party program. This proved to be impossible, however, and the two factions continued their bitter debate over the royal regime.[28] There are some reasons for suspecting that the struggle in the Party was not strictly verbal. There were persistent allegations in Kathmandu, in July 1961, that a colleague had attempted to assassinate the leader of the moderate faction.[29] A few days later, Rayamajhi was apprehended by the Kathmandu police under very curious circumstances. What actually occurred has never been clarified, but one Nepali journal with close ties to the Communists implied strongly that opposition elements in the Party had betrayed Rayamajhi to the police.[30] Equally intriguing is the government's sudden arrest of the leader of the promonarchy faction of the Nepal Communist Party while the leader of the extremist faction was allowed to wander around Kathmandu, only indifferently disguised. Whatever the reasons may have been, the government apparently reversed itself quickly for, scarcely one month later, Rayamajhi was released from prison, without having had to sign the declaration of loyalty to the King that had been required of other political prisoners.

Rumors of collaboration between Rayamajhi and certain members of the government circulated even more widely in the Kathmandu bazaar in September 1961, when the Communist leader was given a passport and allowed to visit Moscow for medical treatment. His departure did nothing to reduce the tension in the Party, and indeed may have been partially responsible for bringing matters to a head. The moderates, bolstered by the return of the three members of the Party's Central Committee who had been released from prison at approximately the same time as Rayamajhi, decided to issue a strong warning to the extremists. Pushpa Lal and his associates were threatened with expulsion if they did not mend their ways, accept the decision to support the royal regime, and work within the existing institutional framework.

A serious clash occurred between the two factions at a Central Committee meeting at Kathmandu, held in late November or early December 1961. Pushpa Lal insisted that the King's rule was "feudalistic" and had to be overthrown by any means required, even revolution. The "bourgeois and reactionary" Indian government was only a slight improvement over the royal regime, Pushpa Lal agreed, but in the circumstances New Delhi could be expected to favor and support "democratic forces" in their struggle to free Nepal from the "King's dictatorship." He also favored an alliance with the Nepali Congress as the necessary prerequisite for a successful revolution. These views were totally unacceptable to the moderates, and the extremists were threatened with expulsion from the Party if they did not cease their anti-Party activities. Shortly thereafter, Pushpa Lal and several colleagues fled to India.

On arriving in India, Pushpa Lal made two tentative offers of cooperation to the Nepali Congress.[31] These were received cautiously by Subarna Shamsher and his colleagues, though it would appear that no outright rejection of the proposal was made at that time. For nearly three months Pushpa Lal toured areas of India in which there were substantial settlements of Nepali migrants—followed very closely, it should be noted, by D. P. Adhikari, then a member of the moderate faction of the Party. Pushpa Lal announced, in early April 1962, that a "Congress of the Communist Party of Nepal," would be held the following month, ostensibly to formulate policy for the Party but actually to set up what amounted to a parallel Communist Party. The announcement brought forth an immediate denunciation from the Rayamajhi wing of the Party. Speaking on behalf of the Central Secretariat, Kamar Shah issued a statement in Kathmandu (it should be remembered that the Party was illegal in Nepal and all political activity was theoretically proscribed) accusing the Pushpa Lal group of "actively conspiring against central leadership, violating the Leninist standard of party life and indulging in factional activities to undermine the very unity of the party."

Despite their "anti-Party" activities, the announcement continued, the Central Committee was "confident that the rank and file of the party, educated in Leninist principles, will defeat the nefarious designs of the Pushpa Lal group to split party unity, and the party will advance further in its goal to serve the people and the country in its glorious past tradition."[32]

The Pushpa Lal group ignored the warnings that accompanied Kamar Shah's statement. Meetings, termed an *Adhibeshan* (i.e., General

Congress) of the Party, were held in Banaras in mid-May 1962, and drew representatives from 8 of the 35 districts of Nepal.[33] Seven resolutions were passed, the most important of which called for a revolution against the King's regime. A second resolution expelled ten moderate members of the Central Committee, including Rayamajhi, Shambhu Ram Shrestha, Kamar Shah, D. P. Adhikari, and P. B. Malla, on charges of betraying the Party by supporting the King's "anti-democratic" steps. In their place, a new 19-member Central Committee, including only 4 members of the old Committee was elected. In addition, a 51-member National Council was formed, and most of these were also newcomers.

The Banaras meetings were an open declaration of the split within the CPN. In late May, the Central Committee (the Rayamajhi faction) issued a statement condemning the violent activities of the "anti-national elements" in India: "No democratic movement succeeds through violence and terroristic activities. It can succeed only through a mass movement launched inside the country. Violent actions weaken the mass movement. The Communist Party therefore condemns such activities."[34]

This statement, astonishing in view of its source, would seem to be directed more at Pushpa Lal and his supporters in the Party than at its ostensible object—the Nepali Congress. By the summer of 1962, all efforts to prevent the formalization of the split within the Party leadership had come to naught. Finally, in September, the Central Committee expelled Pushpa Lal, Tulsi Lal Amatya, and Hikmat Singh from the Party. Other members of the Party who supported these three "deviationists," it was stated, would be dealt with by the appropriate committees of the level on which they worked.

With the revolutionary path to Communism discarded, presumably temporarily, the Rayamajhi faction reemphasized the old policy of a "united front of all democratic forces" in Nepal. One of the first indications of the new direction of Communist policy was the article in a pro-Communist weekly[35] complaining that "no united and organized front had yet been established to meet the challenge" of the "Indian-American puppet forces led by Subarna and Bharat."[36] As the government's ban on political activity was a serious, possibly insurmountable obstacle to the formation of a united front, much of the Communists' persuasive talents were employed in a campaign to convince the King that the dynamics of such a movement were basically in conformity with his own political objectives. In terms slightly exotic even for Nepali Communists, one Party spokesman wrote:

In view of its historical necessity and its probable nature, the leadership of the national front must necessarily be undertaken by His Majesty who is not only the propounder but also the symbol of national unity. The entire country and Nepal's real friends abroad have full confidence and faith in His Majesty. As it would prove highly beneficial to the interest of national unity to utilize His Majesty's great personality, it is in the fitness of things that he should announce the formation of a national front and guide it. Only through such a front will it be possible to achieve the national goal on the basis of a minimum program by establishing political unity in the country. As the national front will not be a political party, His Majesty's leadership thereof will never mean that there will be political partisanship. Rather, this will foster equality of treatment and thus promote the cause of national unity.[37]

To emphasize even further the "royalist" character of the proposed united front, the Central Committee of the Communist Party suggested that the King should call a political conference at the royal palace to discuss the nature of the united front and added: "All nationalistic and democratic forces standing for different ideologies and policies, with a program for the solution of national problems" should be invited.[38] The use of the adjective "nationalistic" is particularly significant, since in current Nepali political parlance, the Nepali Congress and affiliated "anti-national" elements were automatically excluded. The term "democratic," on the other hand, is interpreted so broadly in Nepal that it is doubtful if any organization could reasonably be excluded on this basis, thus permitting any of the forces representing traditional and vested interests to join at their discretion.

The relationship between the front and the government was also a delicate question upon which the Communists attempted to reassure the King. The front would not be a political party, the Party said, nor would it be entrusted with the task of running the government:

Of course, it would be indispensable to maintain close contact and hold consultations between such a front and the government. Each will have to respect the other as otherwise there will be no national unity. In case such a front is formed, it will not be able to assume the form of a "party" though its members following different ideologies and principles may work for nationalism, for the country's development and for democracy. Instead, such a front may put an end to mutual rivalry and opposition for the sake of opposition, and pave the way for a healthy competition for constructive work and service to the country.[39]

As described so enthusiastically by the Communists, the front would be another instrument through which the government could implement its political and economic programs. Needless to say, there was some skepticism in official circles in Kathmandu concerning the sincerity of the Communist position. It was noted that a body of the type proposed would have several obvious advantages for the CPN. It would provide the Party with an organization within which the Communist cadres could legally operate even while the Party itself was still banned. Furthermore, the Communists would be assured easier access to such administrative institutions as the local, district, and national *panchayats* and class organizations which they had been assiduously attempting to infiltrate. Finally, the Party could use its participation in the front to seize a central and possibly dominant position among the remnants of the political Party movement in Nepal, in preparation for the time when it might again have to compete for popular support with the Nepali Congress.

RECENT DEVELOPMENTS

China's aggression against India, in October 1962, had a drastic impact on the Nepali Communists—on internal policy disputes as well as on attitudes toward the international situation. In the wake of the Sino-Indian conflict, the Nepali Congress leader-in-exile, Subarna Shamsher, terminated the terrorist campaign that had been launched against the royal regime nearly a year earlier. Pushpa Lal's group, which had been active in this campaign, though on an autonomous basis, found itself in a difficult situation. Pushpa Lal's policy had been based on the proposition that the overthrow of King Mahendra should be the primary objective of the CPN, even if the immediate result was a regime dominated by the Nepali Congress. With the collapse of the campaign, it was obvious that this policy was unrealistic and that these tactics had been unavailing.

The decision to cancel the "nation-wide movement" that had been scheduled for November 1962, and the total collapse thereafter of all armed resistance to the royal regime, demoralized the ranks of the CPN-in-exile. A meeting of the Executive (Extended) Committee of the Party met in India, in April 1963, to consider the situation and to devise new tactics, and there the rift between Pushpa Lal and his successor as Secretary General, Tulsi Lal Amatya, first came into the open. The resolution on organization and tactics submitted by Pushpa Lal was criticized by Tulsi Lal and adopted only after some amendment.

Thereafter a propaganda struggle ensued between these two factions of the CPN-in-exile, mainly around questions of tactics and political objectives. In his main theoretical statement, *"Hamro Mue Bato"* (i.e., "Our Main Road"), Pushpa Lal argued that a political struggle against the royal regime was impractical under objective conditions, and that the CPN should instead seek to exploit economic grievances to attain political goals—defined as the revival of parliamentary democracy and the restoration of fundamental rights. Pushpa Lal was even prepared to accept the *Panchayat* system for the time being if the Party could thereby gain the right to operate openly in Nepal. In his reply, Tulsi Lal attacked this thesis as "the main road to revisionism." He insisted that the tactics adopted should be directed at the achievement of "national democracy," defined as the first stage in the establishment of a Communist society, rather than "parliamentary democracy," which he equated with "capitalist democracy."[41] He argued that alliances with other democratic parties should be sought only when these advanced the Party's long-term political goal, national democracy, and not merely for short-term expediency.[42]

This debate over tactics is not quite so sterile and devoid of reality in the Nepali context as might appear on the surface. Adopting Raya-majhi's approach in practice if not in theory, Pushpa Lal has encouraged his followers within Nepal to infiltrate *panchayats* and class organization, while the organization in exile concentrates on propaganda activities. Tulsi Lal, while not ignoring the possibility of infiltrating the *panchayat* system, is reportedly also training his group in guerrilla warfare tactics.

Tulsi Lal would appear to have retained a small majority among the exiled Communists. At the Party's Central Committee meeting at Banaras, from January 26 to February 3, 1967, Pushpa Lal's criticism of Tulsi Lal's policy as Secretary-General was rejected. The victory of the group supported by the Nepali Congress over the CPN group in the important Nepali Student Federation elections at Banaras Hindu University in 1967 was a further setback for Pushpa Lal. It is indicative that the main center of CPN activity has shifted from Banaras, Pushpa Lal's headquarters, to Darbhanga, which is Tulsi Lal's stronghold.

Since 1962, the Rayamajhi faction has not fared too badly, as rewards for their "loyalty" to the royal regime have been forthcoming from the Nepal government. Rayamajhi was appointed to the prestigious if power-less *Raj Sabha* by King Mahendra; CPN members or sympathizers have usually been included in the ministries formed since 1963; an estimated 15 to 20 per cent of the membership of the National *Panchayat* (i.e., central legislature) was Communist or pro-Communist; and royalist Communists have even infiltrated into the Palace intelligence service, according to reports.

Despite this progress, the Rayamajhi approach has been challenged on occasion even within his own faction. In 1963, two of the three Joint Secretaries, D. P. Adhikari and Shambhu Ram Shrestha, decided to move a resolution censuring Rayamajhi at the Central Committee meeting scheduled for July. Rayamajhi reportedly informed on his two colleagues through the Palace intelligence unit. Shambhu Ram Shrestha was arrested and D. P. Adhikari had to flee to India, where he denounced Rayamajhi in very strong language.[43] Other Communist leaders, including Shailedra Kumar Upadhyaya, have also attempted to challenge Rayama-jhi's strategic position as contact man with both the Palace and the Soviet embassy, but with no apparent success.[44]

Rayamajhi's tactics have gained tangible benefits for his small group of adherents as well as a degree of viability for his Party within Nepal. However, this has been achieved at the cost of the modicum of public support the Party once enjoyed, particularly among students. It would appear that only the Pushpa Lal and Tulsi Lal factions have even a limited capacity for enlisting popular participation in their occasional agitational activities in Nepal. It is generally accepted that only one Communist leader, Manmohan Adhikari, could possibly unify all the CPN factions behind his leadership. For this reason, presumably, the Nepal government is prudent enough to keep Adhikari in prison.

INTERNATIONAL COMPLICATIONS

From the preceding analysis it is apparent that internal factors have been primarily responsible for the serious divisions within the CPN, but that international developments, such as the Sino-Indian border conflict and the competition between Russia and China for influence within Asian Communist movements, have also had a preceptible impact. It would probably be inaccurate to divide the CPN into intransigent pro-Soviet or pro-China factions and expect to find any high degree of consistency in their statements and behavior. Like most other Asian Parties, the CPN finds it extremely embarrassing to have to make a choice between the two Communist giants. The position of the Nepali Party is made doubly difficult by the reality of a major Sino-Indian struggle for influence throughout the Himalayan area, which has now become inextricably enmeshed in the Sino-Soviet dispute and in the division of the Indian Communist Party into ostensibly pro-Soviet and pro-China factions.

With commendable caution, the major Nepali Communist leaders have avoided any open alignment with either side in the quarrels currently dividing the Communist world. Pushpa Lal and Tulsi Lal are known to have strong pro-China leanings, but their position as exiles in India makes it imprudent for them to stress this aspect of their program publicly. And, indeed, it is doubtful whether Peking would openly welcome them into the fold. Despite its vocal advocacy of radical revolutionary tactics, the Chinese Communists have generally discouraged overt opposition to King Mahendra as inconsistent with their own intensive courting of the royal regime. There were some indications in mid-1967 that this policy might be under reconsideration in Peking, but there is no substantial evidence as yet of a change in the nature of the relationship between the Chinese government and the more extremist elements in the CPN.

The pressure on Rayamajhi is not nearly so great, but an overtly pro-Soviet alignment might well alienate many Party members who are emotionally anti-Indian and, thus, staunchly pro-Chinese. In the present context in Nepal, no clear line is drawn between pro-Soviet and pro-

Indian positions. Rayamajhi has, therefore, assumed a neutral position in the Sino-Soviet fracas and has carefully refrained from commenting publicly on any of the issues in dispute. His contacts have been mainly with Moscow, however, and presumably his wing of the CPN would line up with the Soviet Union if ever it became absolutely necessary to choose sides. The Rayamajhi group would appear to follow the Soviet Party's lead on such questions as the Test-Ban Treaty, the proper method for settling disputes between Communist Parties, and the attitude to be adopted towards the national *bourgeoisie* in still unliberated areas.

THE CPN IN RETROSPECT

As we have noted, the Nepali Communists have not fared as well as might perhaps have been expected, even accepting the thesis that Nepal is still in a primitive stage of political consciousness and is not prepared for anything as modern and sophisticated as dialetic materialism. In this essay, it has been suggested that the inadequacies of the leadership, and its division on what are essentially tactical rather than ideological questions (the dividing line is not always too precise), have torn the Party asunder, absorbing the workers' energies and attention.

But perhaps such factionalism inevitably stems from the nature of the leadership. For a Party that prides itself upon an egalitarian and cosmopolitan character, casteism, regionalism, and ethnocentricism seem to play a very important role. Virtually all the top Party leaders are from the three most prosperous high-caste communities in Nepal: the Brahmans of the Terai and Kathmandu; the Vaisya (commercial) castes of the Newar community in Kathmandu Valley; and the *Chettri*, or Kshyatriya (warrior, now mostly landowning) castes of the Terai and lower hill areas.[45] The current divisions within the Party leadership are not drawn solely on caste lines, but it is impossible to avoid the impression that caste antagonisms, and particularly those between Brahman and Newar, are a contributing factor.

Such predominance of high-caste leaders is the general pattern within all political parties in Nepal. A list of the 20 most important political leaders in Nepal in 1959, for instance, gives this breakdown, by caste: 10 Brahmans; 3 Newar Vaisyas; 6 *Chettris* (including 3 Ranas); and 1 Christian (from Darjeeling). As in most of Asia, there is a high positive correlation between political leadership in Nepal and social and economic position and, perhaps more important, education. It was the high-caste communities who were in a position to obtain education and then, subsequently, participate in the anti-Rana movement which, after 1951, provided most of the top political leadership in Nepal.

Presumably, this pattern is in the process of transformation because of the broad expansion of educational opportunities and the gradual nationalization of politics, which has been further stimulated by political developments since December 1960. One would expect such changes to become manifest in the CPN at an early stage, in view of its emphasis upon peasants and workers. And, indeed, Communist leaders have claimed that the bulk of the Party's rank and file outside Kathmandu Valley is drawn from the peasant class, though the term appears to include middle-landowning groups. The list of members of the CPN District Committees (c. 1959) indicates that in some areas, particularly in the western hills, recruits from local tribal communities are in a majority.[46] But these were usually areas in which the Party was weak and where, perforce, local leadership was left in local hands. In the real centers of Party strength—that is, Kathmandu and the Terai—local leadership would appear to have been the prerogative of the powerful high-caste communities which have long dominated these areas.

A survey of the CPN candidates in the 1959 general elections supports this conclusion. The Party ran candidates in 46 of the 109 constituencies. Most of these were concentrated in Kathmandu Valley, the Terai, and a few foothill constituencies,[47] presumably the areas in which Party structure was substantial enough to support candidacies. Of these 46 candidates, at least 15 were Brahmans, 10 were Newar Vaisyas, and 12 were *Chettris*. In addition, there was 1 Muslim, 3 members of local ethnic groups, and 5 candidates whose caste or ethnic affiliation cannot be determined from available data.[48] The small number of candidates from local ethnic groups, which often constitute a majority in their areas, is very striking. Even in the several eastern hill constituencies contested, where Limbus and Kirantis are in the majority, most of the Party's candidates were Brahmans, who in this area are often large landowners. In the Terai constituencies, most of the Party's 27 candidates were Brahmans or *Chettris*; there was nary a peasant in the lot despite the long period in which the Communist-dominated *Kisan Sangh* had been active in parts of this area. The Newar Vaisyas provided the candidates for Kathmandu Valley, as well as for a number of western hill constituencies in which Newars have long been the most prominent merchant community.

All this illustrates another major weakness of the CPN—its failure to emerge as a truly national party with operational units in all sections of the country. Party activity was concentrated in Kathmandu and the Terai. There were units in some hill areas, but only in a few places such as Palpa and Dharan could the Party muster any kind of significant support. This was apparent not only in the 1959 elections but also from a survey of Communist agitational activities prior to 1960, which showed that these were effective only in Kathmandu and the Terai.

Reportedly, the Communists have been able to augment their strength in the hill areas since the ouster of the Nepali Congress regime in December 1960. The inauguration of local, district, and zonal *panchayats* has provided the CPN with a valuable channel for organizational activity which it has not been slow to exploit. In the elections of the National *panchayat* in 1963, for instance, 18 Communists were reported to have won seats; in contrast, 4 succeeded in the 1959 parliamentary elections. Since all candidates ran as independents and not as Party members, it has not been possible as yet to obtain full information on the successful Communist candidates. But the limited data available shows that in the election of the National *panchayat* in 1963, 1965, and 1967, the Communists won in areas where they had shown strength in 1959 as well as in several places where they had run a rather poor second to the Nepali Congress in the first general elections. The Communist victories in these areas are probably attributable to the thoroughness with which the royal regime has destroyed the Nepali Congress organization while leaving the CPN virtually untouched. From the long-range viewpoint, this may be one of the most hopeful signs for the Communists' future.

Another weakness in the Party, and one on which the Communists lay considerable emphasis, is the alleged lack of adequate financing. In view of the lack of even remotely reliable data, this question cannot be discussed in any detail. Bazaar rumors are, of course, numerous, but they are usually unverifiable and often inconsistent. There is little doubt, however, that the Soviet embassy in Kathmandu is a regular source of income for the Rayamajhi faction and that the Chinese Communist embassy provides some financial assistance to Pushpa Lal and Tulsi Lal. The Chinese would seem to furnish just enough funds to keep the two factions in existence, but not enough to encourage them to expand their activities substantially.

One final comment on the composition and character of the leadership of the CPN may help explain its tactics and attitude. It has sometimes been asserted that membership in a Communist Party leads to social and intellectual isolation, including the severance of relations with family, caste, and non-Party friends. This may be the case in other parts of Asia, but it would not seem to be so in Nepal. Naturally, Party work absorbs the interests and time of the Party workers, but far from totally. One Communist leader estimated that only one-fifth of the members are full-time workers, while the rest go on with their regular activities. Nor is the social and intellectual climate in Nepal such as to lead to expulsion from a family for anything so unessential as political beliefs. Indeed, one would suspect that it is a rare high-caste Kathmandu family that does not have at least one member in most major political camps, all coexisting with relative congeniality and ensuring the family against total exclusion from the rewards of any conceivable political changes. Nor is it unusual to see Communists participating in family, caste, and religious ceremonies. It might well be difficult for many Communists to put into practice some of their "progressive" ideas about society and social relations, even were they in a position to do so.

THE PRESENT AND POTENTIAL STRENGTH OF THE CPN

If the protestations of the Rayamajhi wing of the CPN were taken seriously, there would be no reason to discuss the present situation of the Party. According to their official statements, there have been Communists in Nepal since December 26, 1960, but there has not been a Communist Party, since all political activity has been banned since that date and no good Communist would consider violating one of His Majesty's ordinances. Objective conditions in Nepal, it is argued, are such that there is as yet no scope for an organized Party. The most Communists can do is to work to create conditions which would eventually permit the emergence of an organized Communist movement. No one takes these protestations too seriously, of course, and even some of the CPN leaders prefer to ignore rather than deny the obvious contradictions between such statements and some of the readily apparent examples of Party activity.[49] To operate under and within the partyless *panchayat* system, it is necessary to make this disclaimer; otherwise, Communists who have attained positions in government and *panchayat* institutions could be disbarred and imprisoned. All available evidence indicates, however, that the CPN structure has been maintained intact since 1960, if on a considerably reduced scale because of the dissension within the Party.

Any estimate of the size of the Party in Nepal must be purely speculative. Rayamajhi was reported to have claimed that there were 6,000 full members and 2,000 cadets in 1959.[50] In addition, large numbers of Nepalis were affiliated with various front organizations at one time or another. The *Kisan Sangh*, for instance, once claimed over 125,000 members (undoubtedly a gross exaggeration), and the Communist students' organization also had attracted wide support within the student community. These fronts served as valuable vehicles for the recruitment and training of potential members. The abolition of all class organizations in 1961, and the establishment of government-supervised organizations of peasants, labor, women, students, youth, children, and ex-servicemen may have disrupted the Party's recruiting tactics temporarily. But if the infiltration tactics employed by the CPN achieved any significant results, the new class organizations may eventually prove to be valuable recruiting agencies for the Party. As yet, this has not been the case, and the number of Party activists is undoubtedly much reduced over what it was a decade earlier. One Nepali source estimated, in 1967, that there were not more than 500 active workers in all factions of the

CPN. This may be an underestimation, but perhaps not too far off the mark.

From the viewpoint of future development, possibly the most important objective of the CPN is the further isolation of the Nepali Congress and of the democratic-socialist political movement it represents. The CPN and the Nepali Congress are the only two parties in Nepal that have demonstrated any political potential, for they alone seem to have any conception of the role of parties in modern political systems. It was these two parties that contended for influence in social and class organizations prior to December 1960, and it is often their party workers, now functioning nominally as independents, who are involved in the new class organizations. A similar contest, though incipient and seldom verbalized, is also evident in the *panchayats*, even though party politics are still officially in abeyance. When party politics once again emerge in Nepal, it is likely that the real struggle for power will lie between the Nepal Congress (or some similar organization) and the Communists.

Obviously, the policies followed by King Mahendra since December 1960 have given the CPN a decided advantage in its rivalry with the Nepali Congress. But it is probably still too early for dire predictions. Indeed, the Rayamajhi Communists may eventually find their proroyalist label an embarrassment, even if the existing political system demonstrates a greater capacity for survival than the other experiments that have been tried since 1951. It is still questionable whether the Communists constitute a serious menace to the present regime, or to any successor government that might be established in the next few years. It would appear to be too isolated and too fractionalized to offer a real alternative—unless of course, its rule were imposed on Nepal by an external power. In the current political context, it would be possible for a comparatively small but determined group to overthrow the regime and fasten its control on the country, *but only* if it had substantial support from the officer corps of the Army. Despite recurring reports that the CPN is earnestly endeavoring to establish a base of influence among the younger officers, there are no indications that they have met with any success as yet, and this is one group over whom the King keeps a careful surveillance.

The greatest scope for Communist advancement would still seem to lie in the infiltration of political and social institutions, and it is success or failure in this sphere that will largely determine the Party's prospects in the foreseeable future. If permitted an unchallenged opportunity to shape these institutions to their own purposes, which the government's present policy has virtually assured, it is not implausible that the Communists could emerge eventually as one of the feasible alternatives to the royal regime.

There were some indications, in late 1967, that the Nepal government's policy of leniency toward the CPN did have limits. A number of Tulsi Lal's followers in Nepal were arrested, reportedly because they were planning to emulate their Indian comrades in Naxalbari by resorting to violent tactics. The Pushpa Lal and Rayamajhi factions were not affected, however, and they continue their efforts to infiltrate political and administrative institutions in Nepal without much serious interference from the Kathmandu authorities. Nevertheless, the CPN is still a negligible and manageable element in Nepali politics, and the Party's efforts to dominate a significant segment of the political spectrum in that country have met with only limited and usually transitory success.

NOTES

1. *Jatiya Andolanma Nepal Kamyunist Party (Contribution of the Nepal Communist Party in the National Movement)*, Text of the Report of the General Secretary at the First Conference of the Nepal Communist Party, September, 1951 (Kathmandu: Nepal Communist Party, 1951), pp. 3–4.

2. Niranhan Govind Vaidya, Narayan Vilash, Nara Bahadur, Durga Devi, and Pushpa Lal. See *ibid.*, p. 16. Of these, only Pushpa Lal subsequently achieved a prominent position in the Party's leadership. However, a number of other Nepalis, such as Man Maohan Adhikari, were already active in Communist circles in 1949, and apparently were associated with the new Party from the beginning.

3. *Ibid.*, p. 5. During this period the Indian Communist Party was still taking an uncompromisingly hostile attitude toward the Nehru government.

4. See the May Day, 1951, call for a People's Front by the Party's Central Committee. *May Divash ko Avasarma Kamyunist Party ko Ghosanapatra (Manifesto of the Communist Party on the Occasion of May Day)* (Kathmandu: Nepal Communist Party, May, 1951), pp. 4–6.

5. *Ibid.*, pp. 4–6.

6. In addition to the all-Nepal Peace Council which had been founded in India, the Communists set up the *Kisan Sangh* (i.e., Peasants' Organization), the *Mahila Sangh* (i.e., Women's Organizations), a Students' Federation, and several other similar organizations, in 1951.

7. Letter from Pushpa Lal to Tanka Prasad, July 4, 1951, *Jagaran* (Nepali weekly), July 12, 1951, p. 19.

8. *Jatiya Janatantrik Samyukta Morcha ko Ghosanapatra (Manifesto of the National Democratic United Front)* (Kathmandu, November, 1951), pp. 3–5.

9. In 1954, for instance, a Communist wedding "was the social event of Kathmandu." Both the groom and the bride were wanted by the police, but nothing was done to interfere with the widely publicized ceremonies. "Nepal in Ferment," *Statesman* (Calcutta), November 27, 1954, p. 12, col. 4.

10. *Nepal Kamyunist Party ko Karyakram [Masauda] (Draft Program of the Nepal Communist Party)* (Kathmandu: Communist Party of Nepal, 1954).

11. *Text of the Resolution of the CPN Politburo Passed at its February 20, 1954 Meeting in Kathmandu* (unpublished typescript copy, circulated only to Party members).

12. It is difficult to ascertain the exact differences between the two All-Party Congresses (1954, 1957) and the two all-party conferences (1951, 1955). The 1954 Party constitution makes no provision for such conferences, and their legal basis

is unclear. It would seem that the regular biennial Party meetings are termed Congresses and that special Party meetings called at the instigation of the Central Committee are designated as conferences.

13. *Political Resolution of the Nepal Communist Party*, Adopted at the second all-Party conference, November 22, 1955 (Bhagalpur, India: Sharada Press, 1955); and Central Committee of the Communist Party of Nepal, *Party Karyakram ma Parivartam Kina?* (*Why Changes in the Party Program?*) (Benares, India: Azad Press), 17 pp. For Party members only.

14. *Why Changes?*, pp. 16–17.

15. *Ibid.*, pp. 12–13.

16. The course of events at the Second Party Congress has never been made public. Apparently the Congress did not accept the draft presented to it by the Central Committee, and this political resolution, unlike all previous resolutions, was never published in its entirety. Indeed, the only excerpts from the draft appeared in several strongly critical articles published in the leftist-controlled weekly, *Masal*. See A. N. Rimal and P. N. Rana, *"P.B. Dastavejena Hamro Motaved"* ("Politburo Memorandum: Our Opinion"), *Masal*, May 16, 1957; and Pushpa Lal Shrestha, *"Prathan Mahadhevisar le pas Gariyeko Karyakram Prati Mero Vichard"* ("My Views on the Program Approved by the First Congress"), *Masal*, May 30, 1957.

17. *Samaj* (Nepali daily), May 29, 1957.

18. *Diyalo* (Nepali daily), June 11, 1957.

19. *Naya Samaj* (Nepali daily), December 26, 1957.

20. *Navayug* (Nepali weekly), January 5, 1958.

21. Text of the "Central Committee Resolution on the Royal Proclamation: Adopted at the Central Committee Meeting at Janakpur on March 2, 1958," *Naya Samaj* (Nepali daily), March 8, 1958.

22. Test of the "Resolution Adopted at the Plenum Session of the Central Committee" (held at Gaur, Rautahat, from June 3 to 6, 1958), *Halkhabar* (Nepali daily), June 13, 1958.

23. *"Nepal Kamyunist Party ko Chunao Ghosanapatra"* ("Election Manifesto of the Nepal Communist Party"), *Navayug* (Nepali weekly), November 26, 1958.

24. The history of the Third All-Nepal Party Congress suggests the difficulties imposed on the Party by the rift in the leadership. Initially scheduled for Biratnagar in November 1958, the session was postponed until after the 1959 elections. Rescheduled for February 1960 at Chitaun, the session was once again postponed, and a new date and locale—February 1961, at Narayangarh—was announced. The royal coup of December 1960 intervened before the Narayangarh Congress could be held, however, and a plenary session of the Central Committee was held at Darbhanga, India, in March 1961, instead.

25. None of the 5 members of the Politburo and only 3 members of the 17-man Central Committee were arrested in the three months following the December coup.

26. It has been charged that the well-publicized division of the CPN's leadership into pro- and antimonarchy factions is nothing but a gigantic hoax, deliberately contrived by the leaders of both factions to guarantee the Communists maximum maneuverability no matter what the trend of political developments. While this possibility cannot be discounted, there is no substantive evidence to support it. The issues dividing the CPN, and the policy and tactical arguments advanced, are similar to those disrupting most Asian Communist Parties today. It is also questionable whether the Communist leadership in Nepal is sufficiently subtle and unimpassioned to employ such sophisticated tactics for an extended period, particularly since their own Party workers could not be made privy to the game and would be as badly misled as their political opponents and the royal regime.

27. Source materials on the Darbhanga session of the Nepal Communist Party are both meager and unreliable. The most detailed account of the proceedings was published in the pro-Communist Nepali weekly, *Samiksha* (March 23, 1961). The reliability of this source is somewhat lessened by the fact that it reflects the views of the Rayamajhi faction of the Party. Shorter interesting comments on the Darbhanga session can also be found in: *Halkhabar* (Nepal daily), March 29 and 22; *Dainik Nepal,* March 27, 1961; and *Nepal Samachar,* March 22, 1961.

28. *Nepal Sandesh,* June 28, 1961.

29. *Motherland,* July 9, 1961.

30. *Pravartak,* July 12, 1961. It is interesting to note that the day after Rayamajhi's arrest, a leader of the extremist faction, Tulsi Lal Amatya, told reporters in Darjeeling that the Communists had divided Nepal into five zones and that he had been given the task of organizing the revolution in the eastern districts. See *Nepali,* July 9, 1961.

31. P. N. Chowdhury, the General Secretary of the Nepali Congress, reported that the Pushpa Lal group had "assured us that it would soon join the movement." See *Nepal Today,* I, No. 9 (April 1, 1962), p. 93.

32. Statement by Kamar Shah on behalf of the Central Secretariat, *The Himalayan Sentinel,* April 16, 1962, p. 4.

33. For one of the most complete reports on this meeting, see C. Kesari Prasai, "Nepali Communists in Wilderness," *Janata* (Journal of the Praja Socialist Party of India), XVII, No. 23 (July 1, 1962), 4:1–3.

34. *Nepal Samachar,* June 1, 1962.

35. As all parties are banned in Nepal, there are no longer any official party organs. However, the *Samiksha,* a Nepali weekly published by a former member of the CPN, adheres closely to the policy positions taken by one faction of the Rayamajhi group.

36. Madan Mani Dikshit, *"Rashtriya Prajatantric Yekta"* ("National Democratic Unity"), *Samiksha* (Nepal weekly), August 23, 1962. It should be noted, however, that at least a year and a half earlier, Communist leaders had discussed the necessity of a united front that would exclude the Nepali Congress. See *The Statesman* (Calcutta), March 13, 1961, p. 6, col. 5.

37. *Samiksha,* October 14, 1962.

38. *Ibid.*

39. *Ibid.*

40. According to *Nepal Today,* the CPN-in-exile adopted a *Tatkalik Karyaniti* (Short-term Program) in 1963 which in essence accepted the Rayamajhi approach on tactics. See "A Communist *Volte* Face," *Nepal Today,* II, No. 19 (September 1, 1963), p. 178.

41. Tulsi Lal, *Janavadi Kranti Ya Samshodhan Vad?* (*People's Revolution or Revisionism?*), (Communist Party of Nepal: no press or place of publication cited, September 15, 1966).

42. Tulsi Lal, *Kun Bato?* (*Which Road?*) (Kathmandu: Prajatantra Press, on behalf of the Communist Party of Nepal, n.d.). (The article is dated February 15, 1965.) The press and place of publication cited may be a stratagem, as it is probable that the pamphlets published by the Tulsi Lal group are printed at an Indian press.

43. Communist Party of Nepal, "More on Raimajhi's Anti-Party Activities" in *Report of the Third Executive (Extended) Committee of the Communist Party of Nepal* (Banaras: Arya Bhushan Press, 1963), p. 19.

44. Reportedly, Damodar Shamsher J. B. Rana, a Communist sympathizer and former Royal Ambassador to the Soviet Union, has been one of the principal channels between the palace and the Rayamajhi faction of the CPN in recent years.

45. Only one person from outside these three groups—a member of a well-to-do Kathmandu Muslim family—has as yet achieved a prominent position in the CPN hierarchy.
46. This would not necessarily mean that these members were drawn from the lower economic stratum, however, since there are many landowning families within these tribal communities.
47. The Communist candidate in Kathmandu Valley withdrew in favor of Tanka Prasad Acharya, the Party's old ally and benefactor. This turned out to be a mistake, since Tanka Prasad lost badly, while the CPN candidate might well have won.
48. With some exceptions, the caste identification of the candidates has been based upon their names, a procedure which, among the highly structured high-caste groups in Nepal, is a relatively simple proposition. In the name of egalitarianism, however, some Nepali Communists have dropped the use of caste names. The five unknowns on this list belong to this category, though from their given names it is probable that they were all Brahmans or *Chettris*.
49. In one interview, a prominent Communist leader in Kathmandu commenced our discussion with the usual statement that the Party had been disbanded in December 1960. With a barely perceptible pause, he then went on to discuss some of the Central Committee's plenary sessions that had been held since that date.
50. *Samiksha* (Nepali weekly), June 11, 1963.

SELECTED BIBLIOGRAPHY

A Nepali, "Political Parties in Nepal," *Economic Weekly*, July 19, 1952, pp. 736–39.

Chakravarty, Nikhil, "Nepal's Unfinished Revolution," *New Age*, VI, No. 10 (October, 1957), pp. 54–64.

Gupta, Anirudha, *Politics in Nepal: A Study of Post-Rana Political Developments and Party Politics*. Bombay: Allied Publishers Private, Ltd., 1964.

Jain, Girilal, *India Meets China in Nepal*. New York: Asia Publishing House, 1959.

Joshi, Bhuwan Lal, and Leo E. Rose, *Democratic Innovations in Nepal: A Case Study of Political Acculturation*. Berkeley: University of California Press, 1966.

Mihaly, Eugene B., *Foreign Aid and Politics in Nepal: A Case Study*. London: Oxford University Press, 1965.

"Nepal in Ferment," *The Statesman* (Calcutta), November 26-December 3, 1954. A seven-part article.

Red'ko, I. B., *Nepal Posle Vtoroi Mirovdi Voiny. Antifeodol'noe I Antiimperialisticheskol Dvizhenie, 1945–1956*. (*Nepal after the Second World War: The Anti-Feudal and Anti-Imperialist Movement, 1945–1956*). Moscow: Izdatel'stov Vostochnoi Literatury, 1960.

Rose, Leo E., *Nepal: Government and Politics*. New Haven, Conn.: Human Relations Area Files, Inc., Press, 1956.

"The Soviet Union and Nepal," *Central Asian Review*, X, No. 3 (1962), pp. 294–96.

THE COMMUNIST PARTIES
OF CEYLON

RIVALRY AND ALLIANCE

ROBERT N. KEARNEY

Communism has not been a powerful force in the politics of Ceylon. After decades of mutually debilitating rivalry with other Marxist parties, the Communists were split into two fiercely antagonistic Parties, each proclaiming itself the legitimate Ceylon Communist Party. Membership has been small, electoral successes have been few, and little change in Communist strength has occurred since independence in 1948. Ceylonese Communists suffer from the unique humiliation of facing a much stronger Trotskyist Party, which regularly wins more than twice the popular vote of the Communist Party. Nonetheless, despite their failure to create a large Party or attract great electoral support, the Communists are vigorous and vocal participants in Ceylonese politics and play a prominent if limited role in the rivalries and alliances of the highly competitive and pluralistic political struggle of Ceylon. The stronger of the two Communist Parties, the pro-Moscow Party, has allied itself with two larger parties in a coalition which constitutes the major opposition and a plausible alternative to the present Government and membership in the coalition potentially greatly enhances the Party's position and influence.

MARXISM IN CEYLON

Marxism became an organized political movement in Ceylon in December 1935 with the formation of the *Lanka Sama Samaja* Party (i.e., Ceylon Socialist Party), or LSSP, dedicated to independence and socialism. The Party was founded by a small group of young men from middle-class families, most of whom had returned from study at British universities a few years earlier and plunged into labor and nationalist causes.

A tendency to splinter, and acrimonious competition between rival claimants to Marxist legitimacy, has characterized the Ceylonese Left for three decades. Soon after the commencement of World War II, a breach developed between the Sama Samajists with Trotskyist leanings and those who supported the Third International, the latter including about 70 of the LSSP's small membership.[1] After an intra-Party battle, a resolution condemning the Third International was adopted by the LSSP's Executive Committee, and the opponents of the resolution were expelled from the Party, reversing the usual climax of Trotskyist-Stalinist contests. The remaining Sama Samajists followed the Fourth International's line of opposition to the War even after the Nazi attack on the Soviet Union; as a result, the Party was proscribed by the colonial government and its leaders arrested or driven into hiding.

In November 1940, those members who had been expelled from the LSSP for defending the Third International established the United Socialist Party, which was transformed into the Ceylon Communist Party in July 1943. Following Russia's entry into the War, the Communists cooperated in the prosecution of the "people's war against Fascism" and in 1943 joined the eminently respectable and non-radical Ceylon National Congress.

The fragmentation of Ceylonese Marxism continued after the War and independence. A split in the LSSP in 1950 produced a third Marxist Party, the *Viplavakari Lanka Sama Samaja* Party (VLSSP). After participating in a united front with the Communist Party for several years, the VLSSP combined with the non-Marxist *Sri Lanka* Freedom Party (SLFP) and some minor groups in a coalition called the *Mahajana Eksath Peramuna* (People's United Front), which triumphed in the 1956 election and formed the Government until it broke up in 1959. After the collapse of the coalition, the VLSSP assumed the coalition's name and subsequently has called itself the *Mahajana Eksath Peramuna* (MEP).

In 1963, the Communist Party underwent a schism which produced two separate political organizations, one praising Moscow's leadership of world Communism and the other looking to Peking for inspiration.[2] The following year, when the LSSP formed a coalition Government with the SLFP in defiance of Fourth International directives, a small group of orthodox Trotskyists broke with the LSSP and formed the fifth self-proclaimed Marxist Party, called the *Lanka Sama Samaja* Party (Revolutionary), or LSSP(R).

In the early years of independence, the Marxist Parties constituted the principal organized opposition to the conservative, Western-oriented United National Party (UNP) which governed the island from independence to 1956. The rise of the *Sri Lanka* Freedom Party, coinciding with the growth of language and communal issues, deprived the Marxists of their expectation of replacing the UNP in power. The SLFP became the main spokesman for newly aroused popular social and communal discontent, and was the major beneficiary of growing political awareness among the rural masses. The SLFP either formed the government or was the dominant coalition partner from 1956 to 1965, except for a few months in 1960. Faced with cultural, linguistic, and religious issues instead of class issues, the Marxists saw their electoral strength stagnate and decline slightly. They won about one-fifth of the total vote in the first two parliamentary elections and, except in March 1960 when they presented a record number of candidates, their proportion of the vote subsequently has dropped to about one-seventh. Except in the March 1960 election, when the MEP momentarily made a strong showing, the majority of the Marxist vote has gone to the LSSP. The Communist Party has consistently attracted less than half the popular vote of the LSSP (see Table 1).

Table 1

PERCENTAGE OF POPULAR VOTE WON AT PARLIAMENTARY ELECTIONS BY MARXIST PARTIES

Party	1947	1952	1956	March, 1960	July, 1960	1965
Communist Party	5[a]	6[b]	4	5	3	3[c]
Lanka Sama Samaja Party	17[d]	13	10	10	7	8[e]
Mahajana Eksath Peramuna[f]	....	....	....	11	3	3

[a] Includes vote cast for two Communists contesting as independents.
[b] Vote cast for the Communist-VLSSP united front.
[c] Vote cast for candidates of the pro-Moscow Party. Pro-Peking Communist candidates received 0.1% of the total vote.
[d] Includes two factions contesting the election separately.
[e] Does not include votes cast for LSSP(R) candidates, who received 0.2% of the total vote.
[f] Called the *Viplavakari Lanka Sama Samaja* Party until 1959. The VLSSP fought the 1952 election in a united front with the Communist Party, and contested the 1956 election as a part of the *Mahajana Eksath Peramuna* coalition.

Marxist political strength is heavily concentrated in the relatively ur-
banized and modernized southwest corner of the island. Most of the
parliamentary seats won by Marxists since 1947 have been along the
southwest coast, from Colombo to the southern tip of the island, and
inland from Colombo toward the Kandyan highlands. May Day rallies, which are now held by nearly all Ceylonese political parties and
have become major demonstrations of strength, repeatedly reveal the
strong position of the Marxists in the Colombo area. This concentration
is attributable to a number of factors. The southwest coast is the area
which has had the longest and most extensive contact with the West,
and economic, social, and ideological changes have been most extensive there. Literacy is appreciably higher than in any other area of the
island except the Northern Province. The Marxists have devoted their
principal organizational and ideological efforts to the southwest ever
since the Left movement originated, more than three decades ago. Many
leading Marxists have been active in local government there, especially
in Colombo. Most of Ceylon's urban population lives in the southwest,
and Ceylon's small non-agricultural labor force is largely located there.
Commencing before the founding of the LSSP, the Marxists have ex-
pended tremendous energy in developing trade unions, and their greatest successes in labor organizing have been among the urban workers.
(Marxist efforts to win support among laborers on tea and rubber estates, on the other hand, have met with only limited success, although
a large proportion of the estate laborers are organized in non-Marxist
unions.) Ceylon's relatively large bureaucracy, situated principally in
the Colombo vicinity, has provided the Marxists with an important source
of support. Marxist influence is particularly strong among the government clerks, who occupy an unenviable position in the rigid class structure of the bureaucracy and who are among the more radical groups in
politics and labor relations.[3]

The Marxists' hostility toward the social *status quo* and their advocacy
of the destruction of caste distinctions have enabled the Left to profit
politically from the various protests against the caste system. Minority castes are particularly strong and articulate along the coastal belt ex-
tending south from Colombo. Caste protest in Ceylon usually takes the
form of opposition to the social and political domination of the Goyi-
gama caste, which is both the highest in status and the most numerous
of the Sinhalese castes. The United National Party has been thought to
be Goyigama-dominated, particularly during the first decade after independence. As the Marxists were virtually the only organized opposition
to the UNP immediately after independence and have continued to
constitute the major opposition to the UNP in the urban and semi-urban
areas of the southwest, votes reflecting caste protest ordinarily have
gone to the Left parties.[4]

A major element in Marxist strength is the personal esteem and re-spect accorded individual Marxist leaders. The support the Marxists re-ceive in the villages of the southwest is often attributed to the personal appeal of their leaders and candidates. Nearly all the prominent Marxists are themselves low-country Sinhalese from this area, and many belong to locally prominent families. Regular Communist successes in the South-ern Province commonly are credited to the respect accorded Dr. S. A. Wickremasinghe, the Party's President, and his family in that area.

While the Marxists have been unable to win a strong island-wide following, the concentration of their strength in the strategic Colombo area gives them an element of extra-parliamentary political power. Marxist influence in the southwest was demonstrated dramatically in 1953, when a Left-organized hartal resulted in widespread destruction and disorder. Marxist trade union strength in the Colombo vicinity has been evident in a number of bitter labor disputes, commencing with general strikes in 1946 and 1947. Avowedly political strikes were called by the LSSP in 1959 and by the Communists, the LSSP, and the SLFP in 1964 and 1966.

COMMUNIST LEADERSHIP, ORGANIZATION, AND SUPPORT

The Ceylonese Marxist leadership, like that of most of the formerly colonial areas of Asia, is drawn primarily from the urban, Westernized, middle-class intelligentsia. The Left leaders of Ceylon are mostly low-country Sinhalese of wealthy families, as noted earlier, who have been educated at British universities or Inns of Court. Several are respected far beyond the ranks of their own Parties for their intellectual bril-liance and their devoted efforts and personal sacrifices on behalf of the "common man."

For most of its 25-year history, the Communist Party has been domi-nated by two men, Pieter Keuneman and Dr. S. A. Wickremasinghe. Keuneman has been General Secretary of the Party since its inception, except during a period of Party factional strife between 1948 and 1950.[5] Dr. Wickremasinghe was a principal founder of the *Lanka Sama Samaja* Party, and he led the fight against the LSSP's condemnation of the Third International. After his expulsion, he was instrumental in organizing the United Socialist Party and the Communist Party, and has been President of the Communist Party since 1952. Dr. Wickremasinghe, a member of a very wealthy and prominent family of high traditional status from the Southern Province, is a medical doctor who studied and engaged in stu-dent politics at the University of London. He served briefly in the pub-lic service, but lost his post in a reduction of force at the onset of the Great Depression and entered private medical practice. In 1931, he was elected to the colonial legislature. When he failed to win re-election in 1936 he returned to Britain, where he developed ties with British Communists. Many years later, he attributed his radicalism to witnessing the stern suppression of communal disturbances by British and Indian troops in 1915, when he was 13 years old.[6] Although defeated in several earlier attempts to enter Parliament, he has served as an M.P. since 1956.

While Dr. Wickremasinghe occupies an important position as the Party's founder and a veteran Marxist, Keuneman apparently has provided the vigorous leadership of the Party. Born in 1917, Keuneman is about a decade younger than the other Marxist leaders. He is a member of a prominent family of the small Burgher community, of Dutch and Ceylonese extraction, and his father was a respected judge during the colonial period. Like many of the leaders of the Left, Keuneman had a brilliant record as a student in Britain. He won Bachelor's and Master's degrees from Cambridge University and was elected president of the Cambridge Union, then worked briefly as a journalist before turning his full attention to politics. The only Communist to serve continuously in Parliament since 1947, Keuneman is a skillful debator and probably has made more frequent and effective use of the question period than any other Member of Parliament. He has been elected to Parliament in six consecutive elections, and sat for a dozen years on the Colombo Municipal Council. His loss of that seat is the only defeat of his political career.

Other Communist leaders have attracted considerably less public attention. M. G. Mendis, one of the Party's founders and veteran leaders, has been a principal organizer of the Communist trade union movement. He narrowly missed winning a seat in Parliament in 1965. A brother of Dr. Wickremasinghe has been repeatedly elected to Parliament from the Southern Province. A Buddhist *bhikkhu*, the Ven. U. Saranankara, who died recently, was long active in the Party and for many years was a Central Committee member. N. Sanmugathasan, who since the 1963 schism has headed the pro-Peking Communist Party, became a full-time official of the Communists' Ceylon Trade Union Federation immediately after his graduation from the University of Ceylon in 1943 and has been the Federation's General Secretary since 1957. Sanmugathasan is one of the relatively few leading Communists who is a member of the Island's Tamil ethnic minority.

While the top Party leadership is predominantly composed of middle-class professionals and intellectuals, Party workers and trade union organizers apparently are frequently recruited from the lower-middle-class clerical employees of the public service and private business firms and, occasionally, from the working class. K. P. Silva, who has served as the Party's National Organizer and has been a full-time Party professional for some years, is one of the few Party officers of working-class origin. The Communists frequently stress the participation of working-class members in the Party. At the Seventh Congress of the pro-Moscow Party, 40 per cent of the delegates were claimed to be industrial or plantation workers and 9 per cent clerical employees. Of more than 400 delegates, only 18 were said to be university graduates and only 140 had completed secondary or comparable schooling.[7]

Both Ceylon Communist Parties are organized along typical Leninist lines, with democratic centralism and rigorous Party discipline the cardinal organizational principles. Prior to the 1963 split, and in the pro-Moscow Party subsequently, the two chief officers have been the General Secretary and President. Control of the Party apparatus and responsibility for the conduct of day-to-day Party affairs appear to be concentrated in the hands of the General Secretary,[8] although it is doubtful that in practice there is any marked specialization or clear division of responsibilities between the top officers. The National Congress formally is the most powerful Party organ. Congresses are supposed to meet in normal circumstances every two years, but they have in fact met considerably less frequently. The 1964 Congress was the seventh held in 21 years, but between 1950 and 1964 only two Congresses met.[9] Control of the Party between Congresses is vested in the Central Committee, which appoints the Party officers, a Secretariat and the Politburo, in which plenary power is lodged between meetings of the Central Committee.[10] Branches, which have replaced cells as the basic organizational unit, are formed on the basis of workplace or residence, the latter reportedly being more numerous.

The pro-Peking Party formally follows a similar organizational pattern, although in practice there seems to be a more personal leadership and relatively little organizational structure. At the pro-Peking Party's Seventh Congress, in 1964, Premalal Kumarasiri was named General Secretary but the following year he left the Party. Since the meeting of an Eighth Party Congress in 1965, the Party has been headed by a three-man Secretariat which includes N. Sanmugathasan. Public statements are issued by the Secretariat or by Sanmugathasan in the name of the Secretariat, and in practice, Sanmugathasan's individual and personal control seems to be complete. The Party's organization and activities are closely intertwined with those of the Ceylon Trade Union Federation.

Only a rough estimate can be made of the membership of either of the Communist Parties, and estimates are likely to be valid only briefly. Although the Party's constitution describes an elite cadre of activists schooled in Party history and Marxist-Leninist doctrine,[11] the 1960 Congress called for the Party's "transformation to a mass Communist Party."[12] Remarkable claims of highly successful membership drives are frequently made, to be followed in a few years by the leaders' self-criticism for failing to expand the Party satisfactorily. It is likely that membership actually fluctuates considerably. Several Communists who were elected or sought election to Parliament as Party candidates have subsequently deserted the Party, and, presumably, commitment to the Party is even more tenuous at the lower levels. More than one-third of the total membership at the time of the 1960 Congress reportedly had joined the Party since the preceding Congress in 1955.[13] In the early 1950's many members left the Party because of its failure to endorse Sinhalese as the only official language. Another decline in membership has probably occurred in the last few years, in part because of the internecine conflict associated with the Party schism in 1963, and in part because of some post-1965 positions of the pro-Moscow Party which alienated Tamil members. The U.S. Department of State which estimated the Ceylon Party's membership at 4,000 in 1961, stated the probable membership of the pro-Moscow Party to be 1,100 and that of the pro-Peking Party to be 800 at the beginning of 1967.[14] The figure for the pro-Moscow Party may be somewhat low, and that for the pro-Peking Party is probably exceedingly generous.[15]

Communist influence has been extended beyond the narrow bounds of Party membership by a number of ancillary organizations. The relatively large but amorphous All-Ceylon Federation of Communist and Progressive Youth Leagues has served as a mass organization and recruiting ground for the Party. Other organizations, such as the Afro-Asian Solidarity Association, the Ceylon Peace Council, and the Lanka-Soviet Friendship League, have brought non-Party members into Communist-supported "anti-imperialist" and "peace" campaigns and have served as public forums for Communist spokesmen. The 1963 Party schism and the rivalry between hostile Communist groups seriously disrupted the federation of youth leagues and has probably reduced the influence and membership of the other organizations. The pro-Peking Party maintains a Ceylon Youth League Federation and an All-Ceylon Peasant Congress.

Of considerably greater significance as a source of Party strength is the carefully cultivated Communist trade-union movement. In December 1940, before the Communist Party was inaugurated, Communists had brought together into the Ceylon Trade Union Federation (CTUF) the unions which they led or influenced. Although surpassed in size within a few years by the LSSP's Ceylon Federation of Labor, the CTUF continued to be an important trade union center. In 1963, immediately before the Party split, the CTUF included 31 affiliated unions which claimed a membership totalling 68,130.[16] When the Party split, the Federation was captured by the pro-Peking Communists led by the CTUF's General Secretary, N. Sanmugathasan, and the pro-Moscow Party leaders formed a new organization, called the Ceylon Federation of Trade Unions. Communists have also exercised considerable influence in other labor organi-

zations, the most important of which is the 100,000-member Public Service Worker's Trade Union Federation, the Island's largest organization of
public servants. This Federation remained oriented toward the pro-
Moscow Party following the Communist split.

In addition to publishing Sinhalese, Tamil, and English weeklies intended for the Party faithful and sympathizers, the pro-Moscow Communists launched, in December 1964, a Sinhalese-language daily newspaper, Äththa (Truth), which was intended for a broader audience.
Although the number of copies distributed is probably modest, the
newspaper apparently has succeeded in reaching a significant number of
readers, especially among the lower classes in the Colombo area.
Äththa was believed to have profited considerably when the government banned the pro-LSSP Jana Dina (People's Daily) in 1967, which
left Äththa as the only opposition daily.

Although vigorously active in every parliamentary election since 1947,
the Communist Party has not succeeded in capturing impressive electoral support. The Communist vote, which has remained near 100,000
for two decades, has neither indicated a significant core of popular
support nor displayed a tendency to rise. Only a handful of Communist
candidates have been victorious at each election (see Table 2), and
the Communist victories have been narrowly concentrated in two areas.
All but one of the parliamentary seats won by the Party in the six elections since 1947 (the Party won three seats in each of the first four
elections and four in the last two) have been in Colombo or in a small

Table 2

COMMUNIST ELECTORAL STRENGTH IN PARLIAMENTARY ELECTIONS

Election	Number of candidates	Votes polled	Percentage of total vote	Number of M.P.'s elected[a]
1947[b]	15	92,529	5	5
1952[c]	19	134,528	6	4
1956	9	119,715	4	3
March 1960	53	141,857	5	3
July 1960	7	90,219	3	4
1965				
Pro-Moscow Party	8	109,684	3	4
Pro-Peking Party	3	3,912	—[d]	0

[a] Ninety-five seats in the House of Representatives were at stake in the 1947, 1952, and 1956 elections, and 151 seats in 1960 and 1965.
[b] Includes two Communists contesting the election as independents.
[c] Includes the VLSSP, contesting the election in a united front with the Communist Party. Three Communists and one VLSSP member were elected.
[d] Less than 0.1%.

area of the Southern Province near the southern tip of Ceylon. Keuneman has been elected consistently as one of the three Members from the Colombo Central constituency, and in July 1960 a seat in the Colombo suburbs went to the Communists. Two seats in the South were captured by Communist candidates in each election except 1956, when they secured only one, and 1965, when Communists won three seats in the Southern Province and failed by a narrow margin to carry a fourth. The only constituency outside the Colombo area or the pocket in the South ever won by a Communist was a constituency at the extreme north of the Island, captured in 1956.

RIVALRY AND ALLIANCE

The Communist Party has been constantly involved in competition and cooperation with other political parties. As a small group with limited electoral appeal within a sharply competitive and fragmented political party system, the Communists seem to have looked to their relationships with other parties as the key to influence and to have turned their energy and attention relatively more to tactics of maneuver among other political parties than to organizational activities or questions of public policy. The narrow parliamentary majorities frequently held by governments, and the close balance of votes in many constituencies, have made even the limited strength of the Communist Party of possible significance and have provided the Communists with some bargaining power. Keuneman recently boasted that while the Communists had never participated in a government, "the influence that the Communist Party has exerted on the aims, tactics, unity and development of the progressive movement as a whole over the past 24 years has been considerable."[17]

For nearly two decades after the founding of the Communist Party, the Communists were locked in sharp and often acrimonious competition with the Sama Samajists of the LSSP, and their rivalry frequently emerged in elections and was a perpetual feature of Ceylonese trade unionism. A few years after independence, a Sama Samajist leader charged: "The C.P. actually holds that its *first task* today is to destroy Trotskyism! . . . It claims a monopoly of Leftism."[18] In the 1947 and 1952 elections, the LSSP accused the Communists of supporting candidates of the "capitalist" parties against those of the LSSP.[19] The Communists replied with accusations that the LSSP, in collusion with the right-wing UNP, sought to divide the Left and isolate the Communist Party.[20] Reflected in the rivalry between the two Parties were the views each held of the other: The Communists looked on the LSSP as representing the more privileged elements of the working class and the English-educated clerks who embraced Trotskyism as a device which allowed them to be both anti-capitalist and anti-Communist;[21] the LSSP held the Communist Party to be a tool of the Soviet bureaucracy, more concerned with the needs of Soviet foreign policy than with the interests of the Ceylonese masses.[22]

Nonetheless, a realization that disunity greatly weakened the Left, plus a shared antagonism toward the UNP, which both Communists and Sama Samajists identified as the party of the implacable class enemy, created recurrent demands for cooperation. In the 1956 election, the Communist Party and the LSSP, together with the SLFP, agreed on a "no-contest" pact to avoid contesting the same seats and dividing the anti-UNP vote. The arrangement was repeated during the July 1960 election. A short time later, the Communists noted that confidence built by the electoral cooperation and rectification of "certain errors arising from the cult of the individual" by the international Communist movement after 1956 had reduced the barriers dividing the Parties, and they issued a call for united action with the LSSP aimed at "the creation of a single socialist party, based on Marxism-Leninism."[23] The electoral agreements of 1956 and 1960 did not end the frequent disagreements and considerable trade-union rivalry between the two Marxist Parties, but Trotskyist-Communist antagonisms gradually receded as each Party became more pragmatic and more preoccupied with parliamentary politics. The two Parties and the MEP joined in forming a United Left Front in 1963, but it collapsed abruptly the following year when the LSSP decided to join the SLFP in a coalition government without its United Left Front partners.[24] However, the LSSP and the pro-Moscow Communist Party, the larger of the two Communist groups which had emerged by this time, were soon drawn together again by the 1965 election and the Communists' admission to the SLFP-LSSP coalition.

If the Communist Party has alternated between competition and cooperation with the LSSP, for more than 15 years, it has fervently sought to ally itself with the *Sri Lanka* Freedom Party. The most consistently voiced objective of the Communist Party in the post-independence period has been the unity of all "progressive" forces. In the view of Ceylonese Communists, Ceylon is passing through the first of two revolutionary stages, the national-bourgeois, or anti-imperialist and anti-feudal, stage which must precede the socialist stage of revolution. As appropriate to this stage, the Party has advocated limited measures of a "democratic" and "progressive" nature, and has sought close association with the "progressives" among the "national *bourgeoisie*." The Party has never totally abandoned its claim to be a proletarian Party, but it has simultaneously sought to embrace "progressive" and "nationalist" support; thus, the Party's 1960 election manifesto claimed: "The Communist Party is based on the working class and defends the interests of all progressive sections of the people. . . . It combines the principles of scientific socialism with all that is progressive in national traditions."[25]

Shortly after independence, the Communists adopted a policy of total opposition toward the governing UNP, which was identified as the Party of the *compradore bourgeoisie* to whom the British colonial rulers had handed political power. The 1950 Party Congress issued a call for "unity of the working class and the national-bourgeois forces to defeat the reactionary alliance between imperialism and the UNP,"[26] a theme that has been repeated subsequently with monotonous regularity. In 1951, the *Sri Lanka* Freedom Party was founded by S. W. R. D. Bandaranaike; although the SLFP stressed language and religious appeals, it claimed to be a socialist party seeking equality of opportunity and a classless society.[27] It was also anti-UNP. To the Communists, the SLFP clearly represented the "national *bourgeoisie.*"[28] Since 1952, with rare lapses, they have insistently sought cooperation with the SLFP. Communists supported SLFP candidates in the 1952 election and had no-contest agreements with the SLFP in 1956, July 1960, and 1965. They supported the SLFP–dominated coalition government formed in 1956, the SLFP Government which came to power in July 1960, and the SLFP–LSSP coalition government of 1964 to 1965. The only prolonged periods of Communist disengagement from the SLFP were in 1959, following the breakup of the *Mahajana Eksath Peramuna* coalition, and from 1962 to 1964, when the Communists expressed sharp criticism of the SLFP leadership.[29]

Communist support of the SLFP seems clearly related to a marked preference for the foreign policy of the SLFP-dominated governments. The UNP governments in power from independence to 1956 maintained generally close and friendly relations with the West and did not disguise their hostility toward Communism. A defense agreement provided for British military assistance if needed and allowed the British to maintain naval and air bases in Ceylon. With the creation of the SLFP, an alternative foreign policy was presented. Neutralism, the maintenance of diplomatic and economic relations with the Communist bloc, and avoidance of security ties with the West have been basic elements of SLFP policy. Soon after Bandaranaike came to power in 1956, he arranged for the liquidation of the British bases and established diplomatic relations with the Soviet Union and Communist China. Subsequently, trade and economic assistance agreements were negotiated with several Communist states. The SLFP has remained committed to the neutralist foreign policy of Bandaranaike.[30] The Communists have been lavish in their praise of SLFP foreign policy, hailing the shift in Ceylon's foreign relations as the most significant consequence of the change of government in 1956. The Communist Party organ declared:

The defeat of the UNP in 1956 marked an important change in the role that Ceylon played in world affairs. As a result of the election victory of the late Mr. Bandaranaike, Ceylon ceased to be a reserve of imperialism and its war plans, as she was under UNP rule, and became an active force fighting for world peace and against imperialism and colonialism.[31]

THE REGULAR PARTY AND THE COALITION

Since 1965 the regular Communist Party has enjoyed a position it has sought for more than 15 years. Following the 1965 election, the Party found itself firmly consolidated in a coalition with both the SLFP and LSSP. The Party thus became a component of the opposition coalition which, although out of power at the moment, constituted the alternative to the government and held a reasonable prospect of securing power at the next election. The SLFP–LSSP coalition, from which the Communists had been excluded in 1964, accepted a renewal of the "no-contest" arrangements with the Communists which had linked the three Parties in earlier elections. In 1965, the regular Communist Party and the LSSP did not issue individual election manifestos, but adopted the manifesto of the SLFP, which was based on the coalition program formulated the preceding year.[32] Following the election, the Communists became a recognized component of the coalition.

Although it lost the election, the coalition remained in existence and appears to have gained substantially in cohesion. The split in the LSSP and the departure of the orthodox Trotskyists who subsequently formed the LSSP(R) eliminated the wing of the LSSP which had been opposing cooperation with the SLFP for years. The right wing of the SLFP, long cool to association with the Marxists, had undergone a steady attrition since 1959, and in late 1964, most of the remaining members of the right wing left in protest against the coalition. Mrs. Sirimavo Bandaranaike, the SLFP leader and widow of S. W. R. D. Bandaranaike, who was once critical of the Marxist leaders and was accorded slight respect by the Marxists, became a vocal champion of the coalition and was accepted by the Marxists as the popular symbol of the "progressive" movement among the masses. Since the election, a joint committee of leaders of the coalition Parties has met regularly to coordinate activities, the parliamentary delegations of the Parties have formed a single group, and most political rallies and meetings have been staged jointly by the three Parties. In 1967 a common program was drafted. The appointment in 1967 of T. B. Subasinghe as General Secretary of the SLFP is claimed to have further strengthened the coalition. Subasinghe, once a member of the LSSP who later served in Parliament as an independent socialist, is looked upon by many coalitionists as a bridge between the SLFP and its Marxist allies.

Fundamental to the cohesion of the coalition is the acceptance by the Marxists of the forces of Sinhalese national resurgence as the progressive mass movement of the period, which has required a reorientation of attitudes toward linguistic, religious, and cultural issues. Resurgent Sinhalese group self-consciousness is closely associated with the official-language issue which exploded into the political arena in the early 1950's. The issue arose largely as a protest against the privileged position of the English-educated classes, but as sentiment developed to declare Sinhalese the sole official language it increasingly became a communal contest between the Sinhalese-speaking majority and the Tamil-speaking minority. The SLFP had risen to power in 1956 promising to make Sinhalese the only official language and championing the demands of the Sinhalese Buddhists.

For more than a decade the Marxists had experienced great difficulty with the language issue and the rise of communal consciousness in politics.[33] The Communist Party and the LSSP had advocated both Sinhalese and Tamil as official languages and continued to adhere to this policy for some time, but both Parties lost members and suffered a decline of popular support as a result of their stand against the rising "Sinhalese-only" tide. By the time of the 1960 elections, the Communist Party had shifted to acceptance of Sinhalese only, and at the Party Congress later that year, the Communists confessed that "when the struggle over the official language matured in 1956, the Party endorsed wrong slogans and adopted incorrect tactics which temporarily isolated it from the developing movement." The policy of advocating both Sinhalese and Tamil as official languages, the Communists conceded, resulted from "a cosmopolitan and not a Marxist-Leninist understanding."[34] The Sama Samajists accepted the principle of Sinhalese as the only official language in the joint program of the United Left Front in 1963 and their endorsement became more unequivocal in the coalition program of 1964.[35]

In the 1965 election, the political leaders of the Ceylon and Indian Tamil minorities supported the Marxists' perennial enemy, the UNP, and following the election, helped to form a "national" government. The UNP was the government's largest component, but included were the Federal Party and the Tamil Congress, the two parties of the Ceylon Tamils, and additional support came from the Ceylon Workers' Congress, an Indian Tamil organization. The Left coalition commenced an attack on the government for its reliance on minority support and concessions to the minorities, and an explicit and almost exclusive appeal to the Sinhalese Buddhists, who comprise about two-thirds of the island's population, became the basis of the coalition's strategy.[36]

Marxists argue, in explanation of the reorientation of attitudes toward Sinhalese language, cultural, and religious appeals, that the Sinhalese

resurgence touched off by the language issue a decade earlier constitutes the genuine mass movement of the period and contains progressive elements, particularly as it represents the class revolt of the Sin-
halese-educated masses against the privileges of the English-educated
upper classes, as well as containing "reactionary" divisive and obscurantist
elements. The Marxists claim that in the present context of Ceylonese
politics the strength of this movement is so great that opposition to it
is futile and progress can be made only by accepting it and guiding it
into "progressive" channels.[37] The willingness of the LSSP and Communist Party to join in explicit appeals to the Sinhalese and Buddhists
brings the two Marxist Parties closer in policy to the SLFP and gives
unity and coherence to the coalition; it also substantially widens the
gap separating the LSSP from the LSSP(R), and the regular from the
pro-Peking Communists.

The coalition represents a major opportunity for the regular Communists, as it provides them with the possibility of influencing the policies
and behavior of a political formation with vastly greater political strength
and popular support than the Communist Party alone ever possessed
or had any prospect of gaining. Participation in the coalition brings
the Communists from the margin to the center of Ceylonese politics.
Communist leaders are prominent in virtually all the coalition's public
activities, and the Party has probably gained substantially in prestige
and legitimacy by association in the coalition. The Communist Party
appears, however, to be clearly the junior partner of the coalition. As
the smallest of the allied Parties, the Communist Party probably exercises only a restricted influence on the coalition and often must itself
adjust to the demands of its partners. The coalition was formed without
the Communists and presumably could continue without them, while the
withdrawal of either of the other participating Parties would almost
certainly mark the coalition's end. The two positions the Communists
reportedly have most adamantly insisted upon are the isolation of the
pro-Peking Party and a foreign policy of nonalignment containing liberal criticism of the United States and moderate friendliness toward the
Soviet Union.[38] The preoccupation of the regular Communists with the
coalition seems to submerge them more deeply in nonrevolutionary
electoral and parliamentary politics.

THE PARTY SCHISM

In 1963, the Ceylon Communist Party was jolted by a split which produced two violently antagonistic Parties, each professing to be the legitimate Ceylon Communist Party. The differences which divided the Party
have largely been argued in the vocabulary of the Sino-Soviet breach in
international Communism, and the rupture took the form of a revolt by

some second-level leaders and rank-and-file members against the un-equivocal pro-Moscow stand taken by the top Party leadership. It prob-ably also reflected conflicting personal ambitions and outlooks, and pos-sibly dissatisfaction with the leadership provided by the veteran heads of the Party.

A firmly pro-Soviet position had been assumed by the leaders of the Ceylonese Party at the first indication of divisions within international Communism. At the Twenty-Second Congress of the Communist Party of the Soviet Union in 1961, Pieter Keuneman echoed Khrushchev's at-tack on the Albanian Party of Labor and praised the Russian Party's Twentieth Congress as a turning point in the history of the entire Com-munist movement.[39] In 1962, the Central Committee of the Ceylonese Party proclaimed unequivocal support for the Soviet Union in its devel-oping contest with Albania and, indirectly, China.[40] In September 1963, the Ceylon Communist Party reaffirmed its staunch support of the Soviet Union's position on issues separating the Russian and Chinese Commu-nists. In a lengthy statement issued by the Central Committee, the Cey-lonese Communist leaders delivered a sweeping denunciation of Chinese views, professing to be "deeply pained, surprised and alarmed at many of the political positions and deeds of our Chinese comrades in recent times." The statement sharply criticized as "both erroneous and dan-gerous" Chinese attitudes on the inevitability of war, peaceful coexis-tence, and disarmament, and attacked the Chinese stress on the role of national liberation struggles and de-emphasis of the likelihood of a peaceful transition to socialism. Chinese suggestions that the Soviet Communists were revisionists were labeled as "unfounded and unworthy slander."[41]

A partial explanation of this strong support for Moscow may lie in the personal ties and preferences of the Party's top leaders. Keuneman and Dr. Wickremasinghe have been frequent travelers to Moscow, presum-ably know the Soviet Party officials, and for many years seemingly have identified their fortunes with the Soviet Party. They do not appear to have had similar contacts with the Chinese. In addition, China is not in a good position geographically to aid or influence the Ceylonese Communists. To the Ceylonese, China is as distant as the Soviet Union. Keuneman has disclaimed any special lessons for Asian Communists from the Chinese experience, which he has attributed to unique his-torical circumstances in China.[42]

As the Central Committee was restating its support of Moscow, the dissension which had been rumored for some time erupted into public view and touched off factional struggles within both the Party and Com-munist-controlled organizations. N. Sanmugathasan, a leading Com-munist trade unionist and Politburo member, was expelled from the Party in October 1963 for promoting the Chinese line in defiance of

Party policy and for attempting to separate the CTUF from the Party. A short time later, a second Politburo member, Premalal Kumarasiri, also was expelled for advocating the Chinese line. The dissidents publicly challenged the Ceylon Communist Party leaders in a reply to the Central Committee's pronouncement in support of Moscow the preceding month. The statement, dated October 27, 1963, and signed by ten Central Committee members including Sanmugathasan and Kumarasiri, accused the Central Committee majority of "dutifully obeying the baton" in siding with the Soviet Party. The Sino-Soviet ideological controversy was attributed to Russian attempts "to revise the basic tenets of Marxism-Leninism at the 20th Congress of the CPSU and since."[43] The following month a declaration entitled "To All Marxist-Leninists Inside the Ceylon Communist Party," reportedly signed by 118 Party members, leveled a series of 12 charges against the Party leadership and announced the formation of an organizing committee to convene a Party Congress.[44]

Early in 1964, the two groups held separate Party Congresses, each claiming to be the Seventh Congress of the Ceylon Communist Party. The Congress of the pro-Peking group was held in January and reportedly was attended by 399 delegates and 149 observers from 109 Party branches.[45] A resolution repudiating the pro-Moscow statement of the Central Committee the preceding September, and endorsing the reply by ten Party members in defense of the Chinese positions on the questions in dispute, was approved.[46] The following April, 422 delegates gathered for the Seventh Congress convened by the pro-Soviet Party leaders. Keuneman told the gathering that the Party had withstood the onslaught of "an unprincipled anti-Party group of splitters and renegades . . . who were encouraged and supported in an impermissible way by the leadership of the Chinese Communist Party."[47] He traced an abrupt break of relations with the Chinese Party to 1962, when the Ceylonese Party differed with the Chinese on the Cuban missile crisis and the Sino-Indian border fighting.[48]

The Communist-led trade unions quickly became the principal battleground of the contending groups. The pro-Peking Communists, led by Sanmugathasan, who was General Secretary of the Ceylon Trade Union Federation, succeeded in wresting control of the Federation from the regular Party leaders. The regular Communists immediately formed a rival federation, the Ceylon Federation of Trade Unions, and launched a counterattack against the pro-Peking group. Keuneman, M. G. Mendis, and other regular Party officers conducted an exhaustive campaign, going from workplace to workplace attempting to persuade groups of workers to shift from unions affiliated with the CTUF to unions formed by the new Federation, and their efforts apparently were largely successful. The new Federation won a major proportion of the rank-and-file membership, but the cadre of trade-union activists generally remained with Sanmugathasan and the CTUF. By mid-1965, the regular Communists' Federation claimed 70 to 80 per cent of the former membership of the CTUF,[49] and although the claim is disputed by the pro-Peking Communists, it is almost universally substantiated by non-Communist trade unionists and other observers.[50]

A further test of strength between the two Communist Parties came with the 1965 election, and the result was scarcely encouraging for the pro-Peking Communists. Sanmugathasan sought election from the Colombo Central constituency in an attempt to attract sufficient left-wing votes to deny to Keuneman the seat in Parliament he had held for nearly two decades. The attempt failed, and the pro-Peking leader secured only 2,400 of the more than 200,000 votes cast, while Keuneman won 41,500. Two other candidates of the pro-Peking Party sought election, both from constituencies in the Tamil-speaking North, and each polled less than 5 per cent of the votes cast in these constituencies. The regular Party, campaigning in alliance with the SLFP and LSSP, suffered no apparent electoral decline as a result of the split.

The disagreements between the two groups of Communists extend from the ideological to the personal level. The most bitter ideological disagreement concerns the relative emphasis to be placed on the peaceful and the revolutionary paths to socialism. The regular Party leaders have stressed the possibility of obtaining power by parliamentary and other nonviolent means. Although not ruling out the possibility of "extra-Parliamentary struggles," the Party in 1960 proclaimed that it "seeks to establish full democracy and socialism in Ceylon by peaceful means."[51] In 1967, Keuneman defended two decades of Communist parliamentary activity, claiming that the Party "has never agreed with the ultra-Left[ist]s who proclaim that Parliament is a mere talking-shop and that work within it is useless and a waste of time."[52] A typical example of the attitudes of the veteran Communist leadership is provided in a description by Keuneman of a claimed Communist triumph. In 1959, he asserted, a reactionary *coup d'état* was about to occur. The plot was foiled not by an armed uprising, a general strike, or mass demonstrations but because "the Communist Party and other progressive forces fearlessly exposed in Parliament the foul conspiracy."[53]

The pro-Peking Communists' most scathing denunciations of the regular leaders have been for their lack of revolutionary zeal and excessive reliance on the parliamentary path to power. In their reply to the Central Committee in October 1963, the pro-Peking dissidents charged that the veteran Party leaders had "turned their back on the revolutionary struggle and pinned their hope exclusively on the parliamentary method of achieving victory for the working class."[54] Sanmugathasan has argued: "The basic reason for the present degeneration of the bulk of the left movement was their departure from Marxism-Leninism and their capitulation to parliamentarianism and to the theory of peaceful transition to socialism through parliamentary means, particularly after 1956."[55] The newspapers of the pro-Peking group are regularly adorned with quotations from Mao Tse-tung extolling the role of violence and military force in achieving revolution, one of the favorites being the Maoist assertion that "political power grows out of the barrel of a gun."

Each side questions the integrity and ideological sincerity of the other. Sanmugathasan asserts that the pro-Moscow leaders have been seduced by a "bourgeois" style of living and the personal gratifications of playing the parliamentary game, and that they lack concern for or understanding of the working class. He traces the Party split to a strike in 1963 by employees of the Ceylon Transport Board, which, he claims, was undermined by the Party leadership, who were more concerned with parliamentary relations with the SLFP and LSSP than with close liaison with the working class. According to Sanmugathasan, the Central Committee members supporting the strike later formed the pro-Peking Party and those who opposed the strike remained with the regular Party.[56] Keuneman claims that the Peking line and the interjection of the issues of the Sino-Soviet dispute into the Ceylon Party are simply a mask for the personal ambitions of Sanmugathasan and other pro-Peking dissidents, who earlier had displayed no sympathy for China and little interest in ideological questions. Further, Keuneman alleges, money from Chinese sources has been used lavishly by the pro-Peking group to attract and hold supporters.[57]

Differences of personality and perspective may have contributed to the schism and the subsequent hostility. The top leadership of the Party on the eve of the split was composed of the same men who established the Party two decades earlier. The dissidents who formed the pro-Peking Party were from the second level and second generation of Party leaders. They may have felt their own ambitions thwarted by the continuation in office of the veteran leaders, or they may have felt that those leaders were doing little to strengthen the Party. The top Party leaders, who continue to head the regular Party, are generally intellectual, articulate, and urbane. They are fluent speakers and writers, and several have served in Parliament or in local government. The dissidents seem to have been primarily Party bureaucrats, many of them involved in trade union work, who were scarcely known outside the Party. Only one had served in Parliament, more than a decade earlier, and he left the pro-Peking group a short time after the split. The arguments revolving around the "revolutionary" and "peaceful" paths to socialism may reflect the difference in outlook between the trade union or Party functionary and the public figure familiar with parliamentary debate and the public platform.

After some early successes in the trade unions and other Communist-led organizations, the position of the pro-Peking Party appears to have eroded considerably. The pro-Moscow Party retained the popularly known veteran Communist leaders, including the handful of Communist M.P.'s, and held onto the existing Party organization. Soon after the split, disagreements broke out within the leadership of the pro-Peking Party, and one of its more prominent members, Premalal Kumarasiri, who had been named General Secretary at the January Congress, left the Party with a few followers. The 1965 election pointed up the dearth of popular support for the pro-Peking group. A factor of considerable importance to the rivalry is the almost unanimous acceptance outside the Party of the pro-Moscow, Keuneman-Wickremasinghe Party as the true continuation of the Communist Party. At a time when the regular Party was establishing particularly close relations with the LSSP and SLFP, the pro-Peking Party found itself almost totally isolated politically. Sanmugathasan has repeatedly called for cooperation among "progressives" and has in particular sought alliance with the SLFP,[58] but the regular Party has insisted on the complete isolation of the pro-Peking Communists as the price of its cooperation. The pro-Peking Communists and their trade unions were excluded from the May Day rallies organized by the United Left Front and the coalition, and they were not allowed to cooperate with the coalition during the 1965 election campaign.[59] The support of members and sympathizers of other Parties, particularly the LSSP, was credited with being one of the important factors in the regular Party's successful competition within the trade unions.[60]

Despite the pro-Peking Communists' setbacks in the labor movement, the CTUF remains the core of their strength. The CTUF has retained an important part of the Federation's activists, and it has a few pockets of support among certain categories of workers, such as movie theater employees. The one major area in which its strength is considered significant and possibly increasing is among the Indian Tamil workers on tea and rubber estates. The coalition's emphasis on communal and language issues since 1965 has caused many members of both the Ceylon and Indian Tamil minorities to desert the LSSP and regular Communist trade unions, and some of the Indian Tamil estate laborers have moved to the CTUF estate-workers' union.[61] Sanmugathasan has also found some support among the Ceylon Tamils of the "untouchable" castes. The pro-Peking Communists have energetically exploited growing caste restiveness among the Hindu Tamils of the North and, during 1967, long-subdued caste tensions began to reach significant proportions and attract considerable attention. The double frustration of belonging to the Tamil-speaking minority of the Island and, within Tamil society, of belonging to castes of low status, reportedly has prompted many low-caste Tamil youths to turn to the revolutionary line of the pro-Peking Communists. The fact that the leader of the pro-Peking Party is himself a Tamil unquestionably adds to the Party's appeal within the Tamil community. A final area in which some support for the pro-Peking Communists is discernible is among university undergraduates. The long-standing dominance of Marxism among university students has apparently declined considerably in the last decade. As the leaders of the LSSP and the regular Communist Party age, and their rhetoric becomes less revolutionary and more parliamentary, those students who still adhere to Marxism seem to be turning to the "ultra-left" Marxists of the LSSP(R) and the pro-Peking Communist Party.[62]

The pro-Moscow Party appears to have retained the position and most of the support which the Communists held before the split. However, the rupture in the Party and the appearance of a second, violently hostile, Communist Party has undoubtedly been costly to the Communists. The regular Party has lost a number of the young militants who formed the cadres of the Party and its trade unions. Its leaders are subjected to incessant harassment, denunciation, and ridicule by the rival Party, and they have been forced to defend themselves repeatedly against charges of being revisionists and "parlor" Communists. The Party was undoubtedly seriously shaken in the early days of the split and the leaders of the regular Party have continued to devote a substantial proportion of their energies to fighting the pro-Peking Party.[63]

CONCLUSION

Possibly the two most significant developments in the history of the Ceylon Communist Party are the schism of 1963 and the participation in the coalition with the SLFP and LSSP after 1965. Following the schism and the emergence of two Communist Parties, the pro-Moscow Party seems to have established itself as the continuation of the old Party and has held most of the strength and support commanded by the Party before the split. The pro-Peking Party appears to have declined into a vocal but weak splinter group, effectively isolated from other political parties and possessing only small and scattered pockets of support. Nonetheless, the existence of a second Communist Party, which if small seems well financed and aggressive, undoubtedly poses, for the regular Party, a constant and disturbing distraction, a source of embarrassment, and a potential threat of competition for the loyalty of the Party's supporters. The bitter conflict between the two Parties unquestionably drains a major share of the energies and resources of both.

After years of rivalry with the LSSP and hopes for alliance with the SLFP, the admission of the regular Party into the opposition coalition probably represents the pinnacle of Communist achievement. As a coalition partner, it is a member of a highly important political formation which constitutes the alternative to the present government and is a serious contender for power. To the extent that the Communists can influence coalition actions, their political effectiveness is vastly enhanced. Entrance into the coalition, however, has not converted the Communist Party into a powerful political force. The small size and limited electoral successes of the Party undoubtedly reduce its voice in coalition decisions; furthermore, the possibility always exists that the coalition will not survive the trials of opposition. Although it enjoys a position of considerable potential significance, the Party remains only the second Marxist Party of Ceylon, an active and at times adroit participant in Ceylonese politics, but one whose role is restricted by its small size and slight popular support.

NOTES

1. Pieter Keuneman, *Twenty Years of the Ceylon Communist Party* (Colombo: Communist Party [1963]), p. 4. On the history of the LSSP, see Leslie Goonewardene, *A Short History of the Lanka Sama Samaja Party* (Colombo: *Lanka Sama Samaja* Party, 1960).
2. The two Parties have continued to use identical names. As the pro-Moscow Party is considerably stronger and generally recognized by non-Communists as the continuation of the old Communist Party, this Party will be referred to as the regular or pro-Moscow Party, and the other Communist Party as the pro-Peking Party.
3. See Robert N. Kearney, "Militant Public Service Trade Unionism in a New State: The Case of Ceylon," *Journal of Asian Studies*, XXV, No. 3 (May, 1966), pp. 409–10.
4. See Bryce Ryan, *Caste in Modern Ceylon* (New Brunswick, N.J.: Rutgers University Press, 1953), pp. 276–79.
5. On the factional struggle, see Keuneman,*Twenty Years*, pp. 11–12.
6. S. A. Wickremasinghe, "At 13 I was a Communist," *Ceylon Observer* (Colombo daily), November 14, 1961, p. 4.
7. *Forward* (Colombo), July 5, 1967. *Forward* is the English-language weekly of the Communist Party and, since the Party split, of the regular Party.
8. *Laṅkā Komiyunist Pakshayē Vyavasthā Mālāva* [Ceylon Communist Party's Constitution] (Colombo: Communist Party, n.d.), pp. 26–27.
9. Congresses were held in April 1945, January 1948, September 1948, September 1950, May 1955, October 1960, and January (pro-Peking) or April (pro-Moscow) 1964. In addition, a Special National Conference met in March 1952. The pro-Peking Party held an Eighth Congress in July 1965. One of the charges the pro-Peking dissidents leveled at the pro-Moscow leaders at the time of the split was that they had subverted intra-Party democracy by failing to convene a National Congress every two years.
10. *Laṅkā Komiyunist Pakshayē Vyavasthā Mālāva*, pp. 23, 26–27.
11. *Ibid.*, pp. 5–6.
12. *Draft Thesis for the 6th National Congress of the Ceylon Communist Party* (Colombo: Communist Party, 1960), p. 49. This publication is hereafter cited as *Sixth Congress Thesis*.

13. *Ibid.*, p. 58.

14. U.S. Department of State, Bureau of Intelligence and Research, *World Strength of the Communist Party Organizations: 1962* (Washington, D.C.: Government Printing Office, 1962), p. 77; and *World Strength of the Communist Party Organizations: 1967* (Washington, D.C.: Government Printing Office, 1967), p. 96.

15. My own guess in mid-1967 was that the pro-Moscow Party included possibly 2,000 members, while the pro-Peking Party would have had difficulty in substantiating a claim to more than 200–300 genuine members.

16. *Administration Report of the Commissioner of Labour for 1962–63* (Colombo: Government Press, 1964), p. 59.

17. Pieter Keuneman, "Our 24 Years of Struggle," *Forward*, July 5, 1967, p. 3.

18. Colvin R. de Silva, *Left Disunity: A Reply to a Critic* (Colombo: *Lanka Sama Samaja* Party, June, 1950), p. 3. Emphasis in original.

19. Colvin R. de Silva, *The Why and the Wherefore* (Colombo: *Lanka Sama Samaja* Party, June, 1952), p. 7.

20. *Lanka's Way Forward: Political Resolution of the 5th Congress of the Ceylon Communist Party* (Colombo: Communist Party, 1955), p. 28.

21. Pieter Keuneman, "Success for the Policy of Unity," *World Marxist Review*, III, No. 10 (October, 1960), p. 74; author's interview with Pieter Keuneman, January 11, 1962.

22. See, e.g., Leslie Goonewardene, *The Differences Between Trotskyism and Stalinism* (Colombo: *Lanka Sama Samaja* Party, March, 1954), esp. pp. 1–3.

23. *Sixth Congress Thesis*, pp. 56–58. Changes in Communism and in Moscow's control of foreign Parties following Stalin's death have also been cited by LSSP leaders as facilitating cooperation between the two Marxist parties, for example, during the author's interviews with LSSP Secretary Leslie Goonewardene on June 29, 1965, and July 4, 1967. Both Goonewardene and Keuneman have told the author, however, that fusion into a single Party was unlikely in the near future.

24. See Robert N. Kearney, "The Marxists and Coalition Government in Ceylon," *Asian Survey*, (Berkeley, Calif), V, No. 2 (February, 1965), pp. 120–24.

25. *Manifesto of the Communist Party* (Colombo: Communist Party, 1960), p. 2.

26. Keuneman, "Success for the Policy of Unity," p. 73.

27. *Srī Laṅkā Nidahas Pakshayē Vyavasthā* [Sri Lanka Freedom Party's Constitution], (Colombo: *Sri Lanka* Freedom Party, 1958), p. 1.

28. See, e.g., *Sixth Congress Thesis*, pp. 13, 37.

29. See Pieter Keuneman, *The Politics of the Coup* (Colombo: Communist Party, 1962); Pieter Keuneman, "Towards Unity of the Working Class," *World Marxist Review*, VI, No. 12 (December, 1963), pp. 10–14; "O. B.," "Ceylon: Patriotic Call of the Communist Party," *World Marxist Review*, VI, No. 2 (February, 1963), pp. 65–66.

30. E.g., *Srī Laṅkā Nidahas Pakshayē Mäthivarana Prakāsanaya: 1960* [Sri Lanka Freedom Party's Election Manifesto: 1960] (Colombo: *Sri Lanka* Freedom Party, 1960), pp. 10–11; *Srī Laṅkā Nidahas Pakshayē Saṅvathsara Kalāpaya: 1964* [Sri Lanka Freedom Party's Annual Number: 1964] (Colombo: *Sri Lanka* Freedom Party, 1964), p. 49; and *Srī Laṅkā Nidahas Pakshayē Pasalosväni Sāṅvathsarika Kalāpaya* [*Sri Lanka* Freedom Party's Fifteenth Annual Number] (Colombo fortnightly), June 20, 1964.

31. *Forward*, January 12, 1962.

32. *Election Manifesto of the Sri Lanka Freedom Party: 1965* (Colombo: *Sri Lanka* Freedom Party, 1965). The coalition program is contained in *Sri Lanka* (Colombo, fortnightly), June 20, 1964.

33. For a more detailed discussion of the Marxists and the language issue see Robert

N. Kearney, *Communalism and Language in the Politics of Ceylon* (Durham, N.C.: Duke University Press, 1967), pp. 124–28.

34. *Sixth Congress Thesis*, p. 26.

35. *United Left Front Agreement* (Colombo: Lanka Press, 1963), pp. 9–10; *Sri Lanka*, June 20, 1964.

36. A sharp and detailed attack on the post-election shifts of the LSSP and Communist Party, written from the LSSP(R) standpoint, is contained in Sydney Wanasinghe, "From Marxism to Communalism," *Young Socialist* (Colombo), III, No. 3, (June, 1965), pp. 113–25.

37. Author's interviews with Marxist leaders in 1965 and 1967. Also, see editorial comments in the pro-LSSP newspaper *Nation* (Colombo weekly), July 21, 1967, p. 3.

38. Author's interviews with leaders of the coalition Parties in mid-1967.

39. *Ceylon Observer*, October 27 and 28, 1961.

40. *Statement of the Central Committee, Ceylon Communist Party, on the 22nd Congress of the Communist Party of the Soviet Union* (Colombo: Ceylon Communist Party, April 8, 1962).

41. *On Questions of the International Communist Movement: Statement of the Central Committee of the Ceylon Communist Party* (Colombo: Communist Party, September 26, 1963).

45. *Times of Ceylon* (Colombo daily), January 20, 1964.

43. The statement appears in *Peking Review*, No. 48 (November 29, 1963), pp. 9–16. It was subsequently published as a pamphlet by the Ceylonese pro-Peking Party under the title *Reply to the Central Committee of the Ceylon Communist Party* (Colombo: Worker Publication, n.d.).

44. "To All Marxist-Leninists Inside the Ceylon Communist Party," *Peking Review*, No. 50 (December 13, 1963), pp. 16–17.

45. *Times of Ceylon* (Colombo daily), January 20, 1964.

46. "Revolutionary Leadership of the Ceylon Communist Party Established," *Peking Review*, No. 5 (January 31, 1964), pp. 18–19.

47. Pieter Keuneman, *Under the Banner of Unity: Report of Pieter Keuneman, General Secretary, on Behalf of the Central Committee* (Colombo: Communist Party, 1964), p. 6.

48. *Ibid.*, p. 38.

49. M. G. Mendis, "The Communist Party and the Workers," *Forward*, July 2, 1965, pp. 4–5. Also, author's interview with M. G. Mendis, August 15, 1967.

50. For the (pro-Peking) CTUF denials, see N. Sanmugathasan, *17th Congress Session of the CTUF (Colombo, November 1965): Report by General Secretary* (Colombo: Ceylon Trade Union Federation, 1965), pp. 4–5, 21; and *The History of 25 Years of Proud Service to the Working Class by the Ceylon Trade Union Federation* (Colombo: Ceylon Trade Union Federation, 1965), pp. 43–47. However, non-Communist trade unionists, politicians, and other observers of the labor movement interviewed by the author in June to September 1967 were virtually unanimous in confirming the pro-Moscow Federation's success with the former CTUF rank and file, although the officers and activists of the Federation and its constituent unions were reported to have largely remained with the CTUF. Further confirmation appears in Employers' Federation of Ceylon, *Annual Report and Accounts: 1963–1964* (Colombo: Employers' Federation of Ceylon, 1964), pp. 16–17.

51. *Sixth Congress Thesis*, p. 52. In 1967, Dr. Wickremasinghe reportedly denied the necessity for forceful revolution in Ceylon. *Times of Ceylon*, July 7, 1967.

52. *Forward*, September 25, 1967.

53. Keuneman, "Success for the Policy of Unity," p. 74.

54. *Reply to the Central Committee of the Ceylon Communist Party*, p. 23.

55. N. Sanmugathasan, "The Left Movement Must Adopt Revolutionary Perspectives," *Red Flag* (Colombo), June 29, 1967, p. 3. *Red Flag* is the English-language weekly of the pro-Peking Communists, which commenced publication in February 1967.

56. Author's interview with N. Sanmugathasan, July 1, 1967.

57. Author's interview with Pieter Keuneman, August 3, 1967. See also Keuneman, *Under the Banner of Unity*, pp. 40–45.

58. E.g., *Kamkaruvā* (Colombo), July 10, 1965; *Red Flag*, May 1, 1967, and July 21, 1967. *Kamkaruvā* (Worker) is the Sinhalese-language weekly of the CTUF and, since the Party split, of the pro-Peking Communists.

59. Leaders of the LSSP and SLFP reported, in interviews by the author shortly after the 1965 election, that several overtures were made by the pro-Peking Communists for cooperation with the coalition and that neither the LSSP nor the SLFP had any fundamental objection to ties with the pro-Peking Communists but that the overtures were rejected in the interest of harmonious relations with the pro-Moscow Party.

60. See Keuneman, *Under the Banner of Unity*, pp. 46–47. LSSP members and sympathizers belonging to CTUF unions in the absence of LSSP unions in their places of work reportedly were instructed to support the pro-Moscow Party's new Federation because of the political ties between the LSSP and the pro-Moscow Party in the United Left Front.

61. See Sanmugathasan, *17th Congress Session of the CTUF*, p. 9.

62. The discussion of areas of pro-Peking Communist support is derived from the author's interviews with leaders of both Communist Parties and with non-Communist politicians during 1967.

63. Thus, Keuneman conceded to a Communist Party of India Congress at the end of 1964 that his Party had dissipated considerable energy in "the fight against the anti-Party splitters." *Proceedings of the Seventh Congress of the Communist Party of India* (New Delhi: Communist Party of India, 1965), II, p. 89.

SELECTED BIBLIOGRAPHY

Abhayavardhana, Hector, "Categories of Left Thinking in Ceylon," in *A Miscellany* ("Community Pamphlet," No. 4). Colombo: Community Institute, 1963, pp. 31–57.

Draft Thesis for the 6th National Congress of the Ceylon Communist Party. Colombo: Communist Party, 1960.

Goonewardene, Leslie, *A Short History of the Lanka Sama Samaja Party*. Colombo: *Lanka Sama Samaja* Party, 1960.

The History of 25 Years of Proud Service to the Working Class by the Ceylon Trade Union Federation. Colombo: Ceylon Trade Union Federation, 1965.

Jayawardena, V. K., "The Urban Labour Movement in Ceylon with Reference to Political Factors: 1893–1947." Unpublished Ph.D. dissertation, London School of Economics and Political Science, 1964.

Kearney, Robert N., *Communalism and Language in the Politics of Ceylon*. Durham, N.C.: Duke University Press, 1967.

Kearney, Robert N., "Militant Public Service Trade Unionism in a New State: The Case of Ceylon," *Journal of Asian Studies*, XXV, No. 3, (May, 1966), pp. 397–412.

Keuneman, Pieter, *Twenty Years of the Ceylon Communist Party*. Colombo: Communist Party [1963].

Keuneman, Pieter, *Under the Banner of Unity: Report of Pieter Keuneman, General Secretary, on Behalf of the Central Committee*. Colombo: Communist Party, 1964.

On Questions of the International Communist Movement: Statement of the Central Committee of the Ceylon Communist Party. Colombo: Communist Party, September 26, 1963.

Sanmugathasan, N., *How Can the Working Class Achieve Power?* Colombo: Worker Publication [1963].

Wriggins, W. Howard, *Ceylon: Dilemmas of a New Nation*. Princeton, N.J.: Princeton University Press, 1960.

Pak Il-u, 136
Pak Kŭm-chŏl, 126
Pak Sŏng-ch'ŏl, 126
Pak Yŏng-bin, 123, 135
Pak Yong-guk, 126, 127
Pandjaitan, Brig. Gen. D. I., 282
Pang Hak-se, 123
Pardede, Peris, 299
Parman, Maj. Gen. S., 282, 298
Partai Komunis Indonesia. *See*
Indonesian Communist Party
Party Life, 228
Pasokan Guerrilla Rakyot Sarawak, 249
Pathet Lao, 179, 185–208; effect of
Sino-Soviet dispute on, 205–7
Pe Htay, Thakin, 310
Peking Review, 301
Pemuda Rakjat, 279
P'eng Chen, 58
P'eng Te-huai, 76, 77, 145
People's Action Party (Singapore),
239–40, 247, 256, 261
People's Army (North Korea), 135
People's Daily, 66, 68–69, 78, 264, 266,
338, 345
People's Democracy, 301
People's Liberation Army (China), 56,
63–64, 71, 73–74, 75–77
People's Revolutionary Party (Burma),
311
People's Revolutionary Party (South
Vietnam), 165
People's Rights Protection Committee
(Nepal), 367
People's Volunteer Organization
(Burma), 312–13, 314, 321–22, 326
Perkerikatan Kommunist di India, 275
Phai-Dang, 192
Phak Khon Ngan Lao. *See* Laotian Labor
Party
Phak Pasason Lao. *See* Lao People's
Party
Phetsarat, Prince, 189–91, 202
Phoui Sanaikone, 193
Phoumi Nosavan, General, 203, 206
Phoumi Vongvichit, 199–200, 202
PKI. *See* Indonesian Communist Party
Pradigdo, Sujono, 299
Praja Parishad Party (Nepal), 366, 370,
371
Pravda, 110, 140, 143, 334–35
Progressive Students Organization
(Burma), 316, 317
PUTERA-All Malayan Council for Joint
Action, 250
Pyongyang regime. *See* Korean Workers'
Party

Quinim Pholsena, 207
Quoc, Nguyen Ai. *See* Ho Chi Minh
Quotations from Chairman Mao Tse-tung,
75, 226

Ra'ayat (Brunei), 257
Rahman, Tengku Abdul, 238, 256, 257,
259
Raksha Dal, 367
Ramamurthi, P., 348
Rana regime (Nepal), 364–66, 368, 382
Ranadive, B. T., 332, 335, 340, 353
RAND Corporation, 195, 200
Rangoon University Students United
Front (RUSUF), 316–17
Rao, C. Rajeshwar, 333, 334
Rayamajhi, Keshar Jang, 369, 371, 372,
374, 375–77, 380–81, 386–87
Red Army, 56
Red Flag, 68
Red Flag movement (India), 353–54
Red Flags. *See* Burma, Communist
Party of
Red Guards, 71, 75, 111
Red Socialists. *See* Burma Workers and
Peasants Party
Rewang, 299, 303, 304
Roy, M. N., 310
Ryokichi, Minobe, 221
Ryuji, Nishizawa, 220

Saburo, Edo, 226
Sakirman, 299
Sambu, J., 99
Sampa Rengō (Japan), 223
Sanmugathasan, N., 396, 397, 406–10
Sanusi, Anwar, 299
Sanzō, Nosaka, 213–14, 216, 219
Saranankara, U., 396
Sarawak, Communist activity in, 240–
42, 248–50, 262–63, 264
Sarawak Advanced Youths' Association,
240–41
Sarawak Anti-Fascist League, 240
Sarawak Communist Organization
(SCO), 241, 249, 263
Sarawak Liberation League, 240
Sarawak Overseas Chinese Democratic
Youth League, 240
Sarawak United People's Party (SUPP),
242, 252
Sarinah (Sukarno), 280
Sarma, P. V., 250
Satomi, Hakamada, 219, 227
Savang Vatthana, King, 190
Saw, U, 311
Saw Hunter, 323